Eclipse RCP

FOURTH EDITION

vogella

“Because knowledge feels like magic”

Dedication

For Jennifer, Kiran and Liam

Eclipse RCP

Lars Vogel

Fourth edition

Publication date: 15.02.2026

Contents

Part I: Preface

Thank you for your interest in learning Eclipse RCP programming. Eclipse remains a powerful and mature desktop programming platform, and I'm confident you'll benefit from its rich functionality, stability, and the vibrant community that supports it.

My name is Lars Vogel, and for over two decades, I have been writing, teaching, and advancing Eclipse RCP technology as both an educator and a core contributor to the platform itself.

I am an Eclipse Platform and PDE committer with deep involvement in the Eclipse project's architecture and development. For nearly a decade, I served as co-lead of the Eclipse Platform and e4 projects and was a member of the Eclipse Project Management Committee (PMC), where I helped shape the strategic direction of the Eclipse platform and represented the broader user and adopter community. I stepped down from these leadership roles in 2024-2025 but remain actively engaged in Eclipse development and the community.

Among my recognitions are being named a Java Champion in 2012, receiving the Eclipse Top Contributor Award in 2010, and the Eclipse Top Newcomer Evangelist Award in 2012, reflecting my long-standing commitment to the Eclipse ecosystem and the Java community.

I am the founder and CEO of vogella GmbH, a company I co-founded in 2012 with the mission of democratizing knowledge in the open-source world. Knowledge sharing has always been at the heart of what I do, whether through writing books and comprehensive tutorials, presenting at international software conferences, or directly working with developers and organizations to solve real-world challenges.

Since 2012, vogella GmbH has trained hundreds of clients worldwide, from individual developers to

Fortune 100 corporations, in Eclipse plug-in development, Eclipse RCP applications, and modern software engineering practices. We make a significant portion of our training material freely available at https://www.vogella.com, while our premium content and personalized learning experiences are offered through our platform at https://learn.vogella.com.

This book synthesizes both free and commercial material, distilled from more than a decade of teaching, consulting, and hands-on development. It provides a clear, practical guide that takes you from an empty application to a fully functional Eclipse RCP application. By working through this material, you'll master the essential concepts and patterns needed to build your own professional Eclipse applications.

Whether you're new to Eclipse RCP or looking to deepen your expertise, I hope this book serves as both a comprehensive reference and an inspiring starting point for your journey into Eclipse application development.

About this book

This book gives a detailed introduction to the Eclipse platform and covers all relevant aspects of Eclipse RCP (Rich Client Platform) development.

Each topic in this book has a content section explaining the topic, followed by exercises to practice what you've learned. The exercises are detailed, especially in the first half of the book. This enables you to do the exercises first and later read up on the content, or first read through the content and then do the exercises.

You will be guided through all relevant aspects of Eclipse RCP development using a comprehensive example that you will continue to extend in the exercises.

This book assumes no previous experience with Eclipse plug-in and Eclipse RCP development. It requires a working knowledge of the Java programming language and assumes that you know how to create Java artifacts, like classes, packages and the like. It is helpful if you are already familiar with using the Eclipse IDE, but it is not mandatory as most exercises contain detailed screenshots.

Errata

Every book has errors, or the environment may change. If you find an error or an issue that blocks your progress in the exercises, please let us know via an issue at https://github.com/vogellacompany/support.

Here you can also find the errors that have already been reported.

Alternatively, you can report errors via email: erratabooks@vogella.com.

Exercises, optional exercises, and example code

In this book, you will find lots of example code and exercises. To simulate the creation of a larger application, later exercises are based on earlier exercises. Optional exercises are marked and usually not required for later steps.

The source code for the exercises in this book is available via a GitHub repository. All source code in this book is licensed under the Eclipse Public License.

The URL for this repository is https://github.com/vogellacompany/eclipse_rcp_example. To clone this repository, use the following URL:

```
git://github.com/vogellacompany/eclipse_rcp_example.git
```

See Appendix A for a description of how to import the exercise solutions into your Eclipse workspace.

> This book is long. For an efficient learning experience, focus on the non-optional exercises and copy long code snippets from the above Git repository. You may have to adjust the copied code as your solution might be different or in case the solution contains code for exercises you have not yet implemented.

Screenshots, shortcuts and long lines of code

The screenshots used in this book are based on the Ubuntu 24.04 operating system and the Eclipse 2025-12 release. SWT is operating system specific; hence your system may look different, especially the order of the confirmation dialogs is OS-specific.

For simplicity, the shortcuts listed in this book should be valid for Windows and Linux users. Mac users must replace the `Ctrl` key with the `Cmd` key for most shortcuts.

The missing Mac shortcuts are primarily due to lack of access to a Mac system.

Sometimes the code example does not fit into one line, which might especially affect you in rare cases where line position matters. I hope you can solve these issues, if not, see the error handling section for information on contacting us.

Acknowledgments

The creation of this book did not follow the typical book creation process. It is partially based on tutorials available on the vogella.com website, and the material in this book has been used in countless RCP training sessions conducted by vogella GmbH. This edition has been thoroughly revised and updated for the Eclipse 2025-12 release. A special thanks for this edition goes to Kiran Vogel Nerlich for testing the exercises and providing feedback and Jennifer Nerlich for helping with the publication process.

Thanks also go to Matthias Becker, Andreas Buchen, Wilfried Saak, Philip Wenig, Hauke Fuhrmann and Alois Zoitl for working on permissions to add screenshots of their private or company applications to this book.

Also, my thanks go to the reviewers of past editions: Dirk Fauth, René Brandstetter, Aurélien Pupier, Eric Moffatt, Rabea Gransberger, Matthias Mailänder, Paul Webster, Remy Suen, Sopot Çela, Kai Tödter, Brian de Alwis, Matthew Hall, Cole Markham, Phill Perryman, Marcel Bruch, Boris Bokowski, Daniel Stainhauser, Christoph Keimel, Holger Voormann, and Simon Scholz.

I would like to thank the Eclipse platform development team for their shared efforts and support over all these years. The Eclipse team is amazing, and it is great to see the project still vibrant even after more than 24 years of existence.

Part II: Introduction to Eclipse RCP

1. Introduction to Eclipse-based applications

Eclipse RCP (Rich Client Platform) applications leverage the Eclipse framework to build feature-rich, standalone desktop applications.

An Eclipse application consists of individual software components called *plug-ins*, which can use and extend other plug-ins. For instance, a plug-in can add new entries to a menu defined by another plug-in.

The Eclipse IDE can be viewed as a special Eclipse RCP application focused on supporting software development. For example, the Java development tools (JDT) provide functionality for developing Java applications.

An Eclipse RCP application typically uses the same base components as the Eclipse IDE. On top of these, the RCP client developer adds application-specific components. This is depicted in the following diagram.

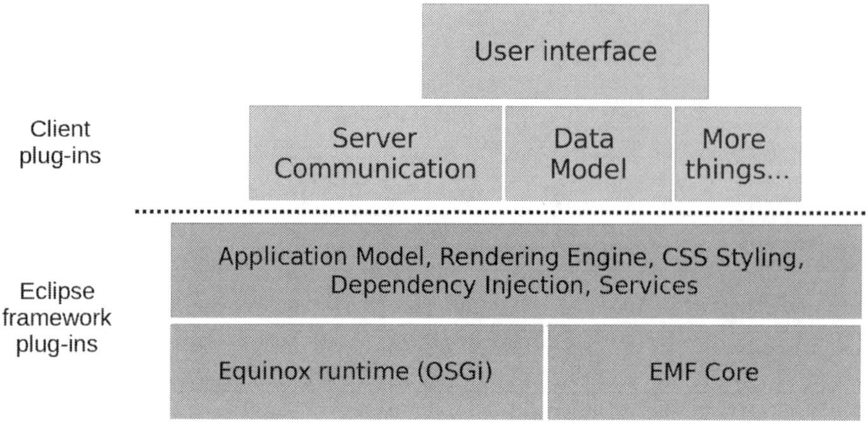

2. Why use Eclipse RCP

Desktop applications are still core tools that drive companies.

Companies frequently use desktop applications to handle their internal processes. Their software often requires a complex user interface and is frequently developed in-house, even if software development is not their primary business. These companies rarely have a large software development team dedicated to maintaining and updating their in-house software.

To develop these in-house applications, companies typically prefer solutions that are easy to use, provide a rich API, and ensure a stable application programming interface (API). They require their selected framework to be easy to maintain, especially if they use the software to support their main line of work.

Eclipse RCP excels in this space.

Customers choose Eclipse RCP because the Eclipse framework:

- forms the foundation of multiple successful IDEs
- is stable and widely used, which is an important indicator that it will be supported for many years to come
- provides native user interface components that are fast and reliable
- has a strong modular approach, allowing developers to design component-based systems
- is the foundation for products of companies such as Red Hat, IBM, Microsoft, and SAP, ensuring that the Eclipse framework remains flexible, fast, and continues to evolve

Additionally, the Eclipse platform fosters a large community of individuals who provide support, information, and extensions to the Eclipse framework. It enables customers to contribute to the framework to meet their specific needs.

The Eclipse development team makes a significant effort to keep its API stable, enabling developers to use, update, and maintain it with minimal effort. Moreover, the Eclipse API is constantly enhanced and improved, which benefits RCP users with every release.

3. Examples of existing Eclipse RCP applications

Eclipse RCP applications are frequently used as feature-rich desktop applications within companies. Therefore, only a few of these applications are publicly available. This section provides examples of RCP applications to illustrate the capabilities of the Eclipse framework.

Portfolio Performance is an open-source RCP application primarily developed by Andreas Buchen. The Portfolio Performance application is an open-source tool designed for tracking, analyzing, and visualizing investment portfolios. It provides detailed insights into portfolio performance, asset allocation, and returns over time through customizable charts and reports.

Visit https://www.portfolio-performance.info/ for more information.

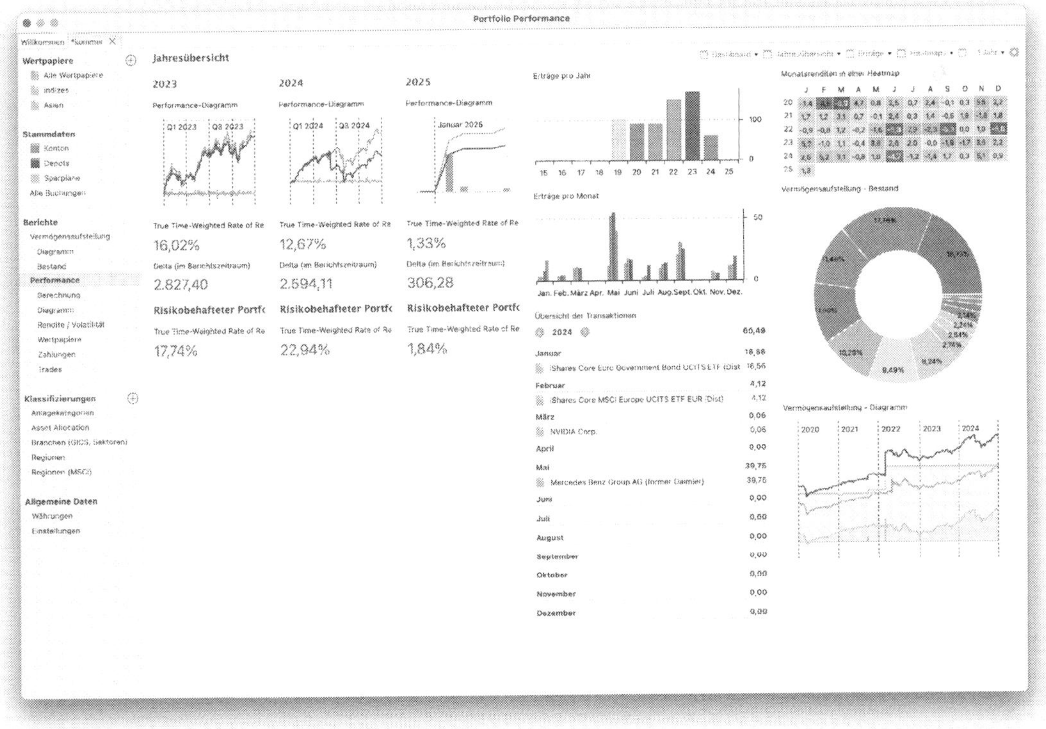

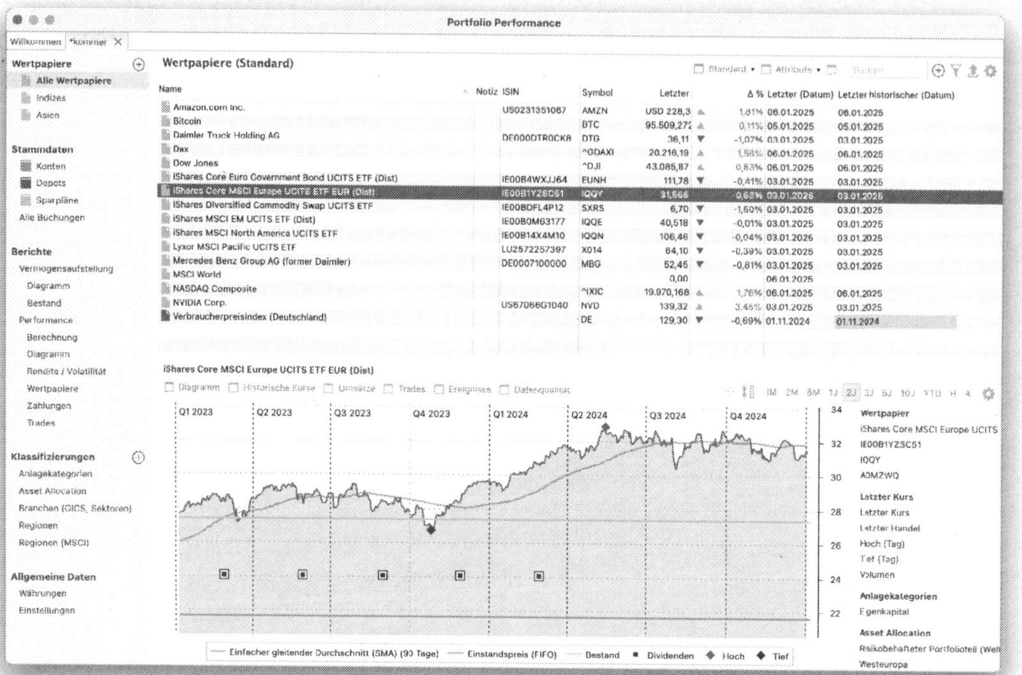

The ***4diac IDE***, part of the *Eclipse 4diac™* project, supports the development of automation systems that comply with the IEC 61499 standard. This software is widely used in the industry and by researchers exploring IEC 61499.

Visit https://github.com/eclipse-4diac/4diac-ide for more information.

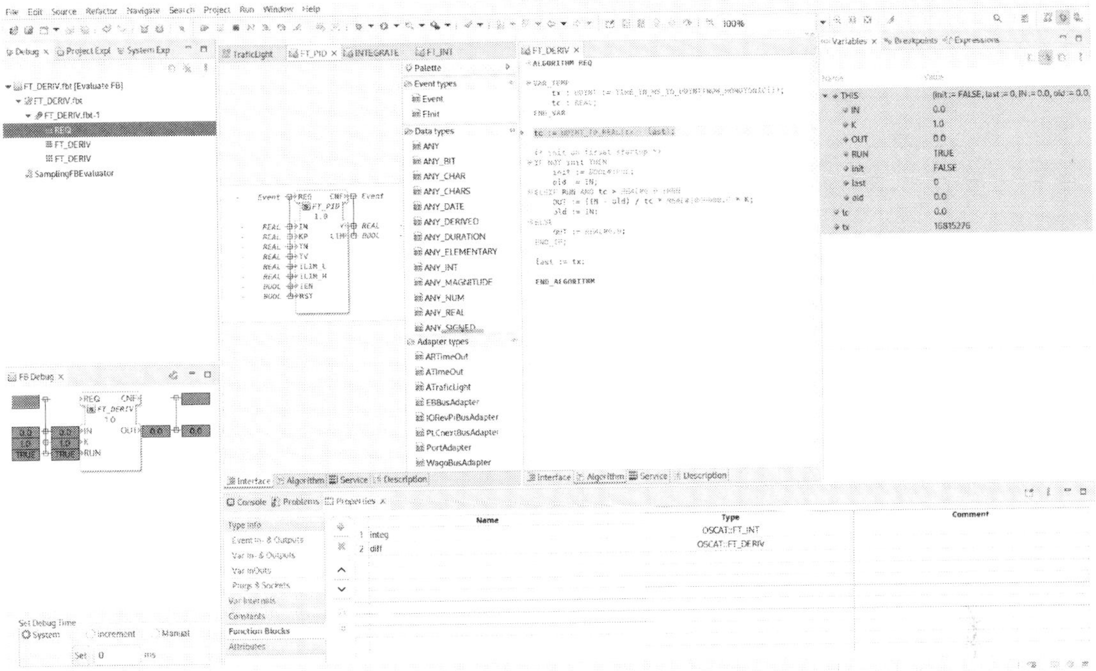

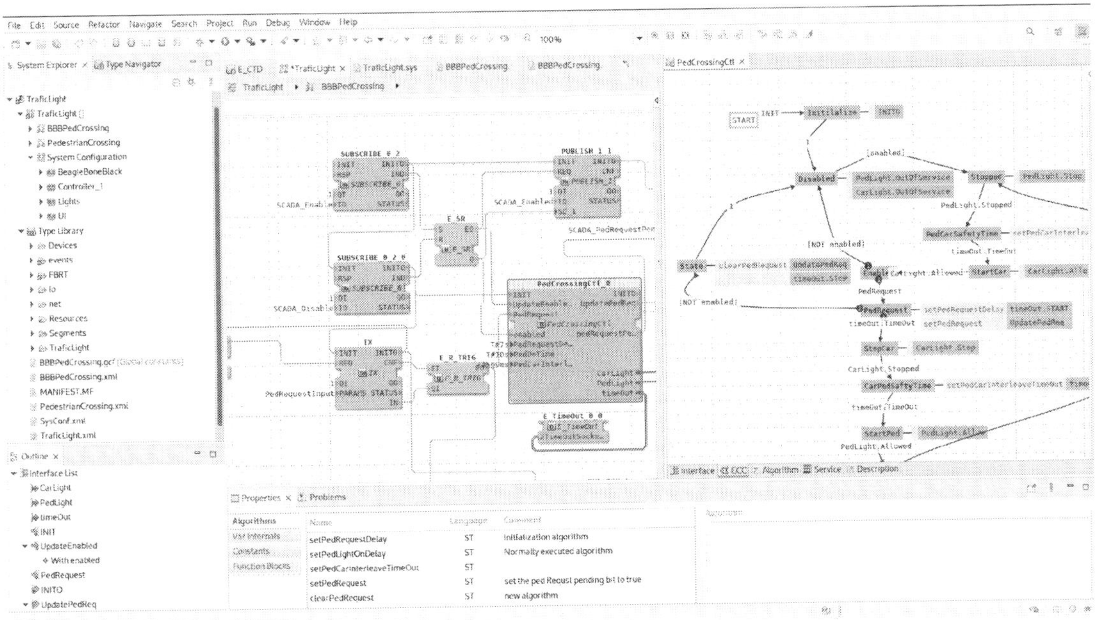

OpenChrom® is an open-source software application for analyzing chromatographic, mass spectrometric, and spectroscopic data in chemical analytics. The software is used in both quality control and research and development. The Lablicate GmbH offers commercial extensions for this product.

Visit https://www.openchrom.net and https://www.lablicate.com for more information.

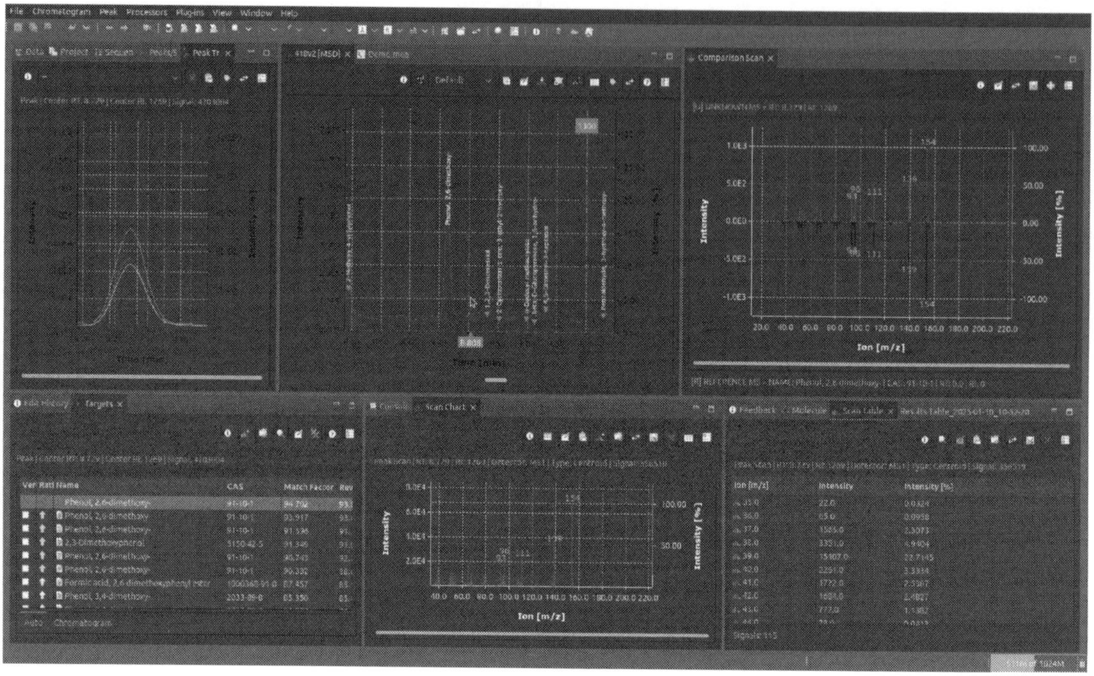

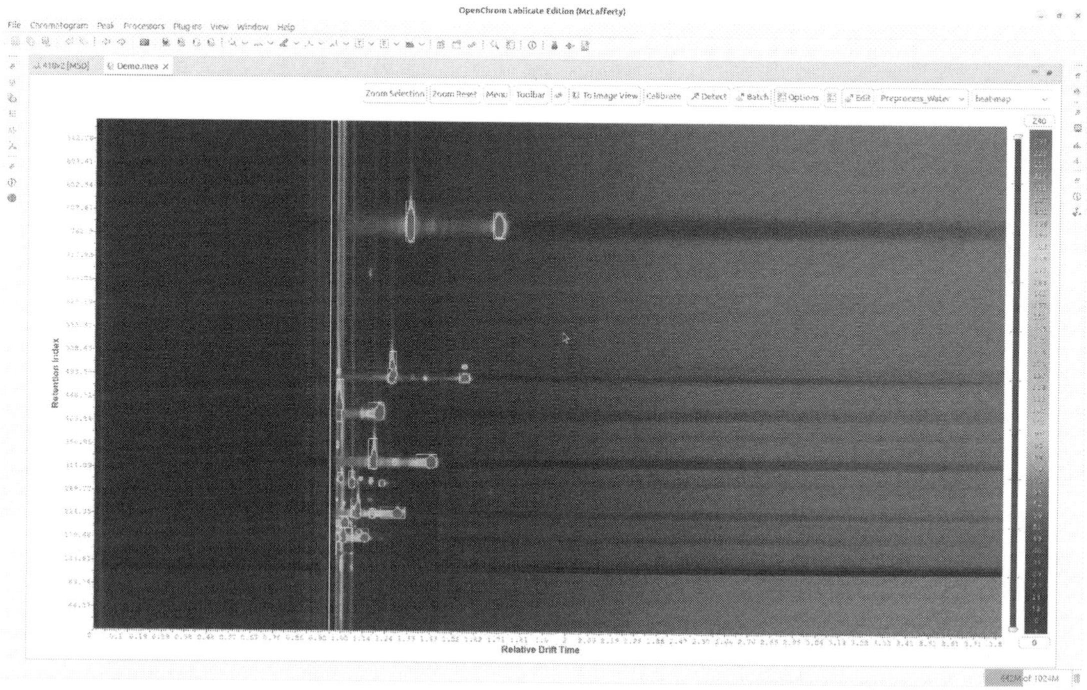

The commercial ***AFIS*** application, developed by **AFIS GmbH**, manages and executes refueling operations on airfields. Delivery notes are validated, archived, and exported on the following day.

Visit https://www.afis.aero/ for more information.

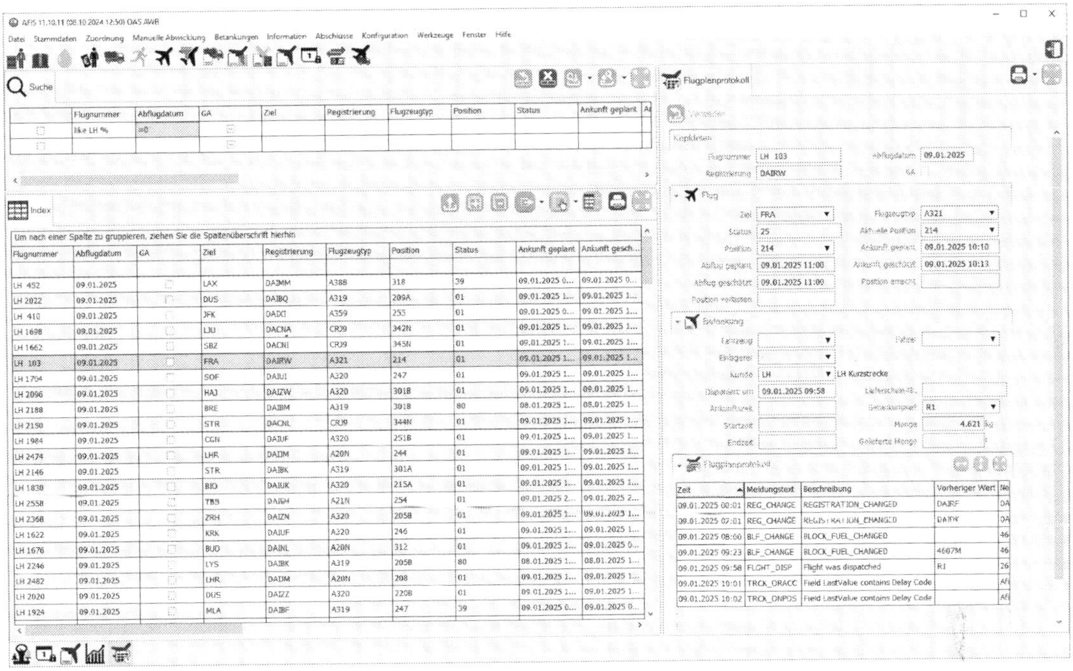

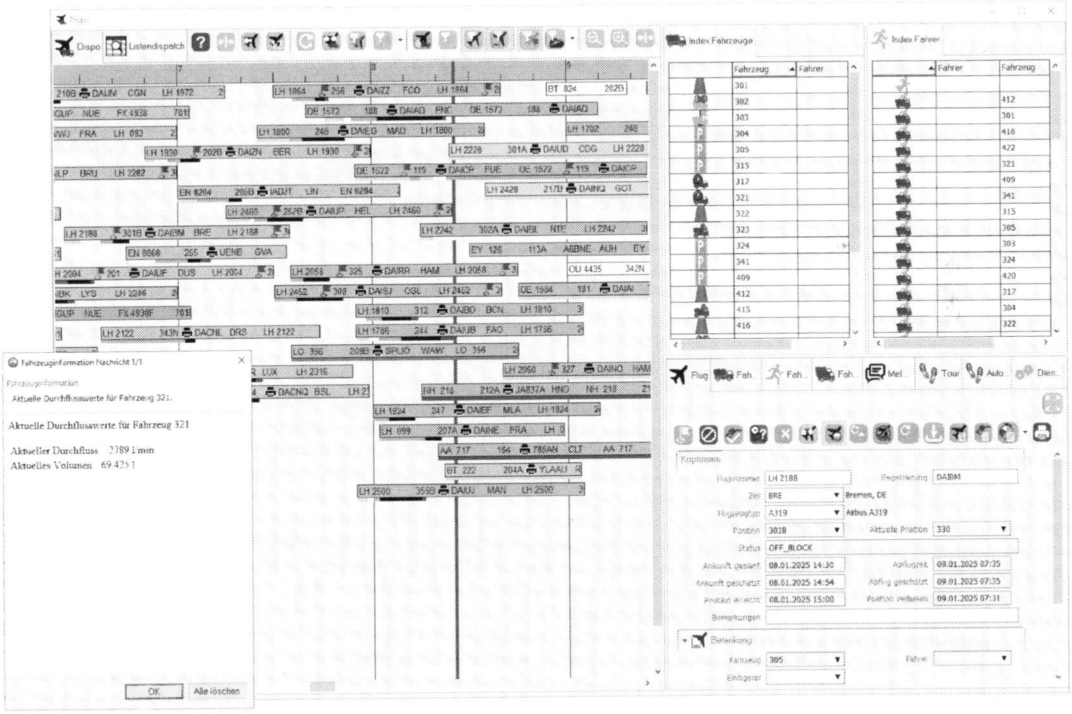

MINOVA Information Services GmbH develops several commercial tools built on the Eclipse platform.

The ***TTA application*** is used to manage and control a tank farm. The application handles inventory management in the storage facility and controls automated loading processes, among other things.

Visit https://www.minova.de/en/tta.html for more information.

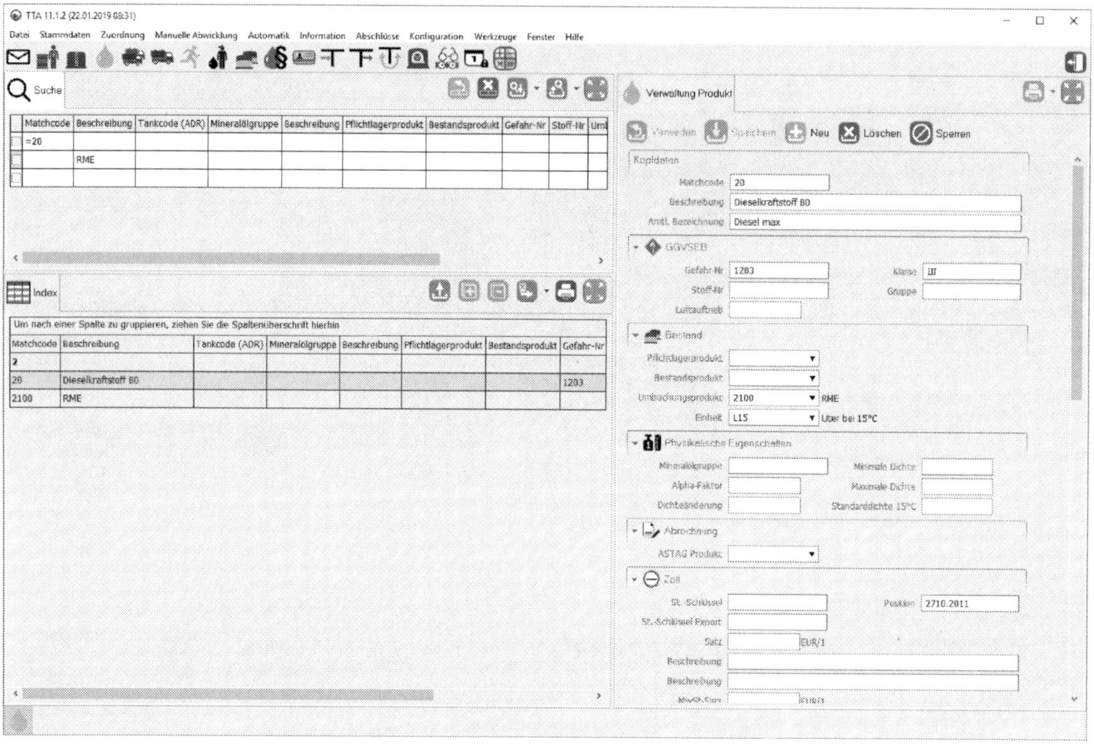

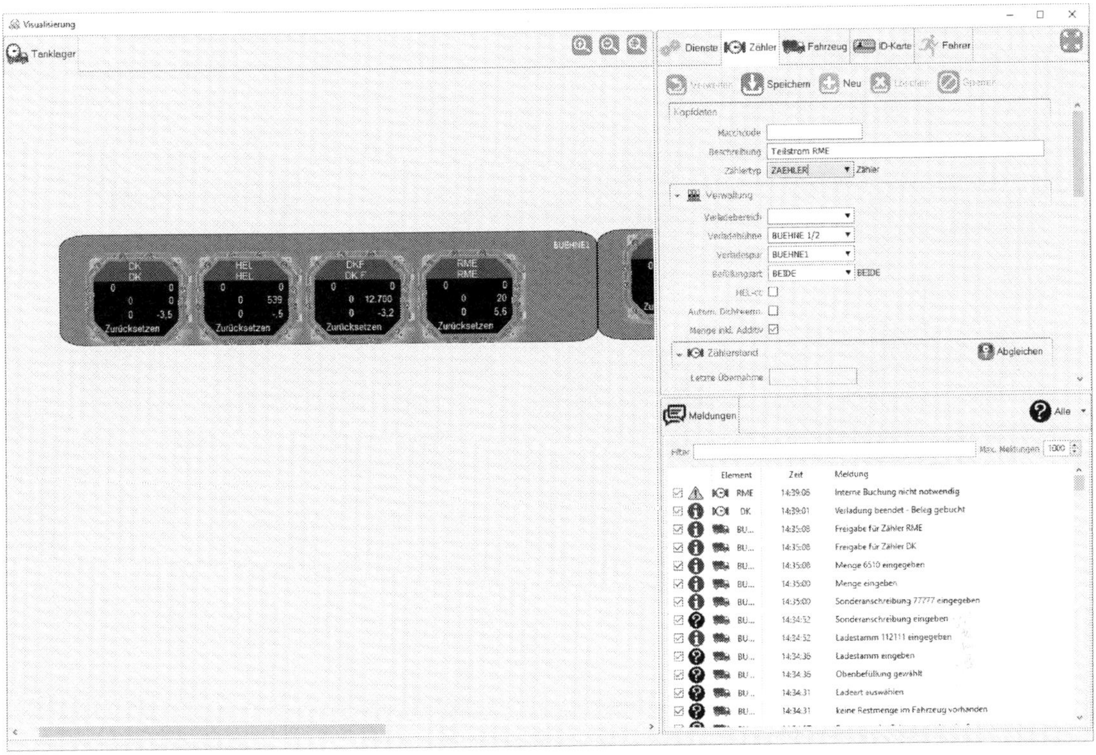

DISPO is a comprehensive support system designed for dispatchers, specifically catering to the needs of the mineral oil industry. The system supports gas station supply management by ensuring optimal delivery timing through visual and textual alerts, with options for connecting tank gauges and cashier systems for efficient single-point deliveries.

Visit https://www.minova.de/en/dispo.html for more information.

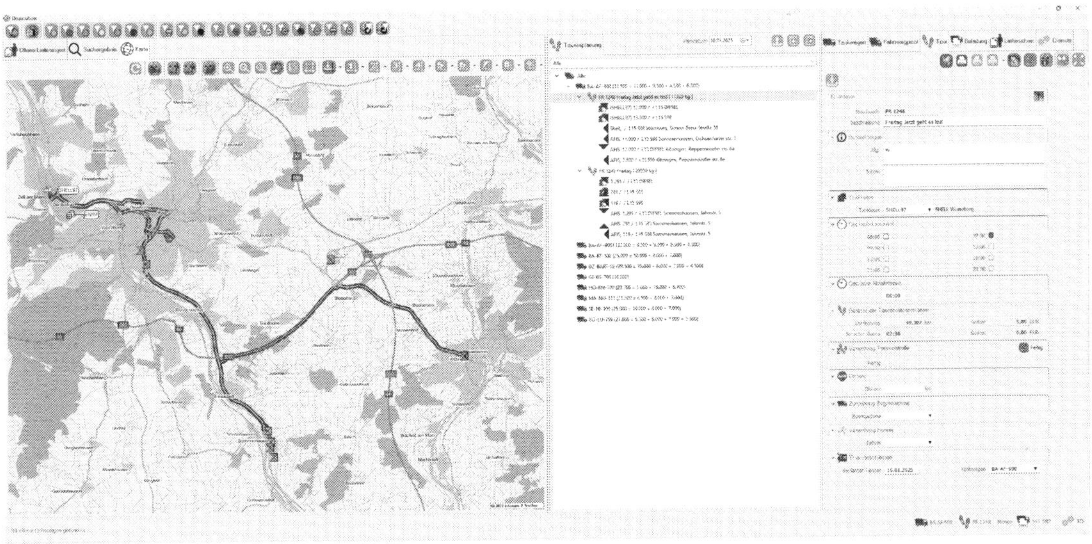

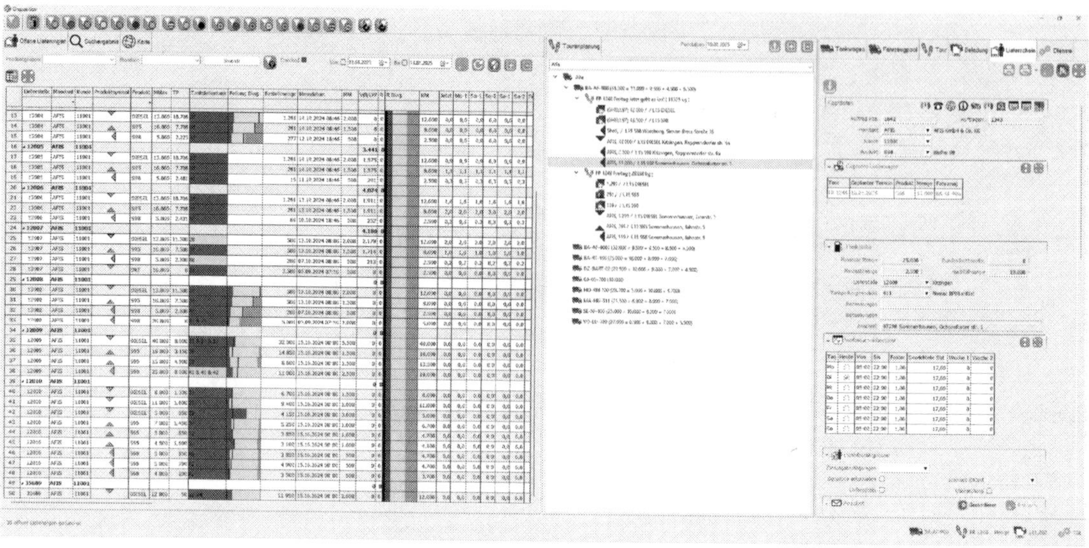

AFIS GmbH and **MINOVA Information Services GmbH** sponsor the **Free Tables** open-source project, which is used in their applications. See https://github.com/minova-afis/aero.minova.freetables for details.

SAP SE develops the **ABAP development tools for Eclipse**, providing a state-of-the-art IDE for ABAP development. It enables ABAP developers who want to build or extend ABAP applications based on SAP products to perform their ABAP development tasks.

Visit https://www.sap.com/ and https://tools.hana.ondemand.com/#abap for more information.

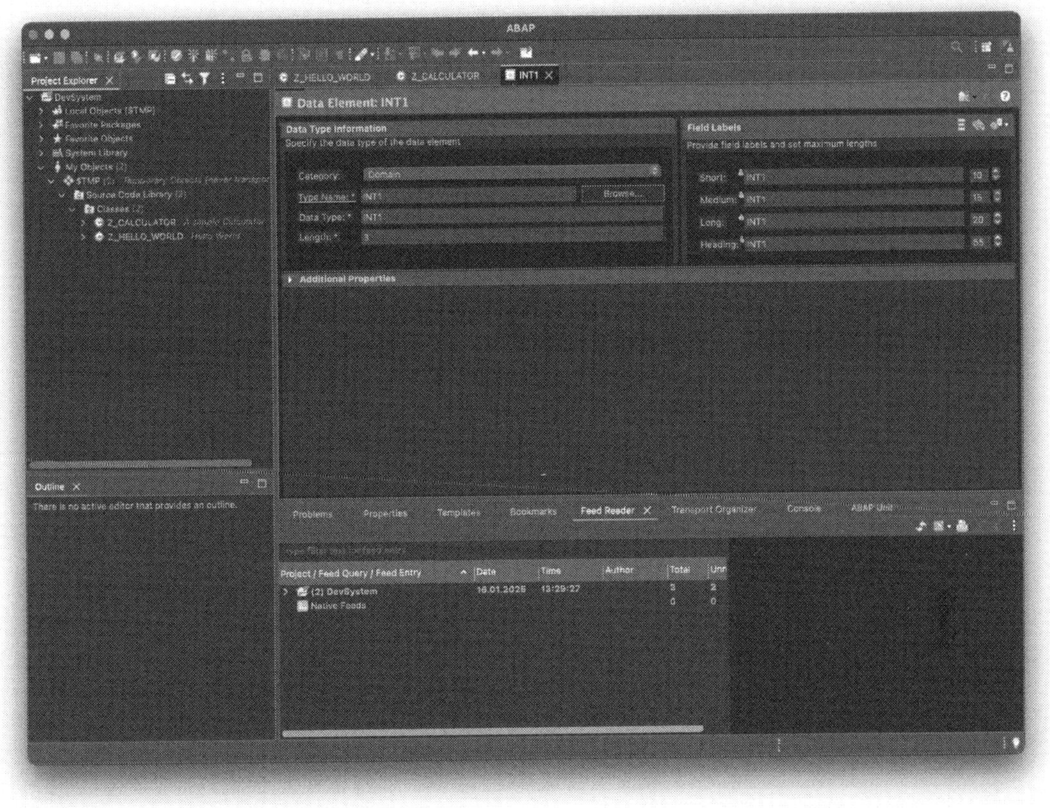
ABAP
Project Explorer
Z_HELLO_WORLD
Z_CALCULATOR
INT1
Data Element: INT1
Data Type Information
Specify the data type of the data element
Category:
Domain
Type Name:*
Browse...
Data Type:*
Length:*
Field Labels
Provide field labels and set maximum lengths
Short:
Medium:
Long:
Heading:
Additional Properties
Outline
There is no active editor that provides an outline.
Problems
Properties
Templates
Bookmarks
Feed Reader
Transport Organizer
Console
ABAP Unit
Project / Feed Query / Feed Entry
Date
Time
Author
Total
(2) DevSystem
Native Feeds

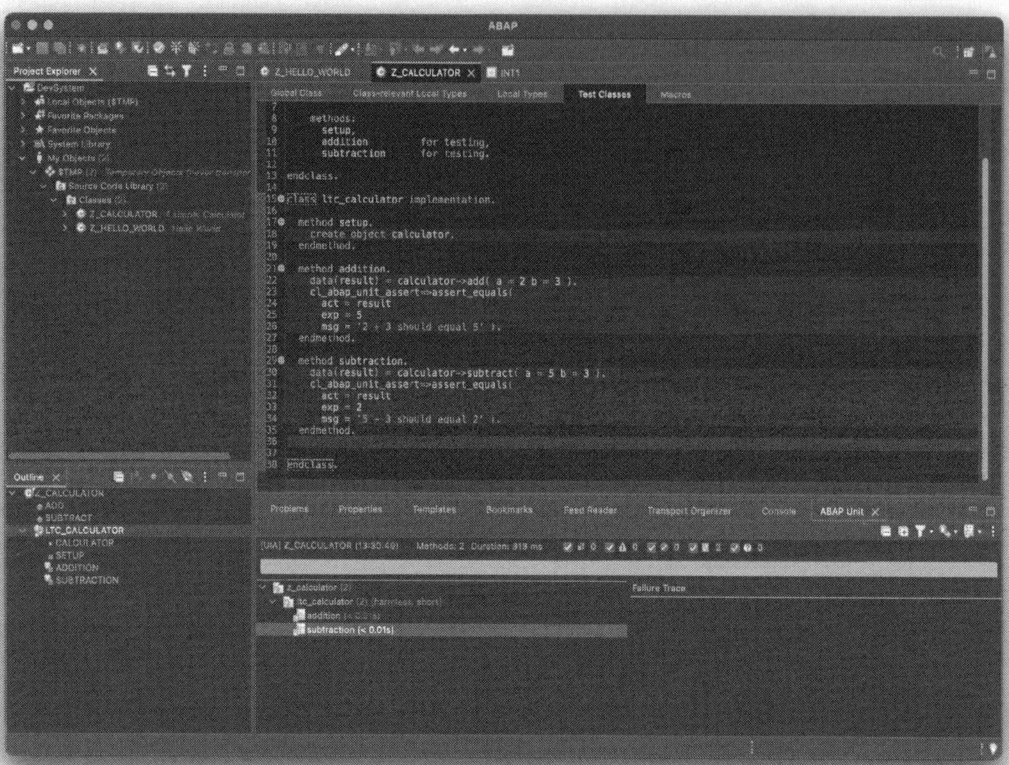

IT.UV Software GmbH develops the commercial **mogena.uv© Modeller NG** application. This is a powerful modeling platform that enables the design and 100% generation of comprehensive business applications. Built on the Eclipse e4 RCP framework with e(fx)clipse and JavaFX for UI, it integrates GEF for modeling complex BPMN processes, supporting precise and flexible application development for statutory accident insurance.

Visit https://www.ituv-software.de/arbeitsbereiche/framework-entwicklung/ for more information.

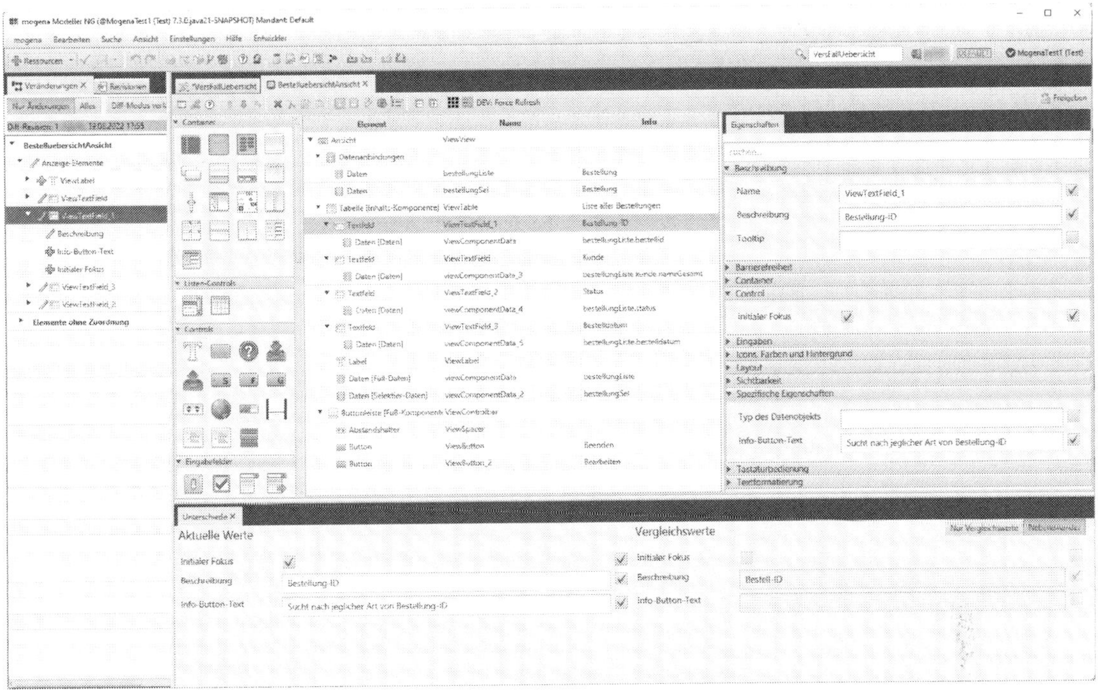

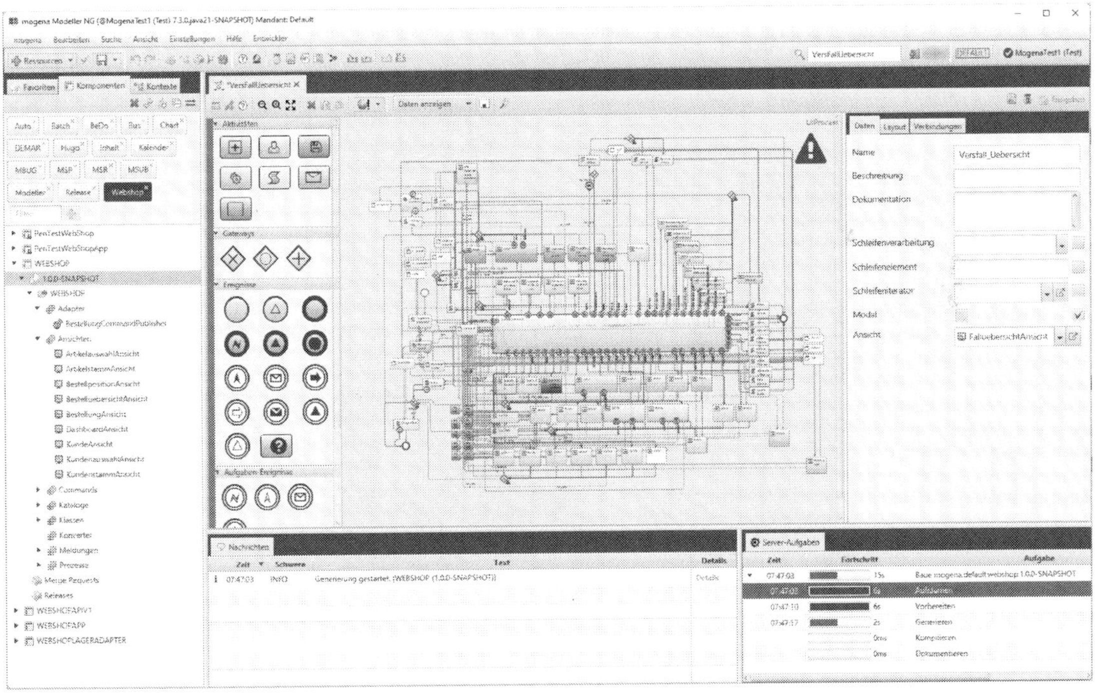

Scheidt & Bachmann Signalling Systems develops and produces innovative solutions for railway signalling technology, including digital interlockings, level crossings and train management and simulation systems. The company ensures safe and efficient control of rail traffic through state-of-the-art hardware and software platforms as well as integrated control and operating systems. With over 150 years of experience, it is a leading partner for infrastructure operators worldwide and offers planning, installation, maintenance, and training.

Website: https://www.scheidt-bachmann.de

Screenshot of the **PlanPro Werkzeugkoffer** (PlanPro Toolbox), an enhanced version of the Eclipse Signalling Engineering Toolbox (https://projects.eclipse.org/projects/technology.set) for use at the Deutsche Bahn. The tool is used for visualizing and validating planning data of interlocking systems. The parts shown are:

- Top left: an infrastructure view on the data with switch 26 highlighted.
- Top right: a table showing the switches, again with switch 26 highlighted.
- Bottom left: a validation report in PDF.
- Bottom right: a text view of the planning data (in XML format).

Developed by Scheidt & Bachmann System Technik GmbH on behalf of Deutsche Bahn InfraGO, which retains all rights, see https://www.dbinfrago.com/planpro

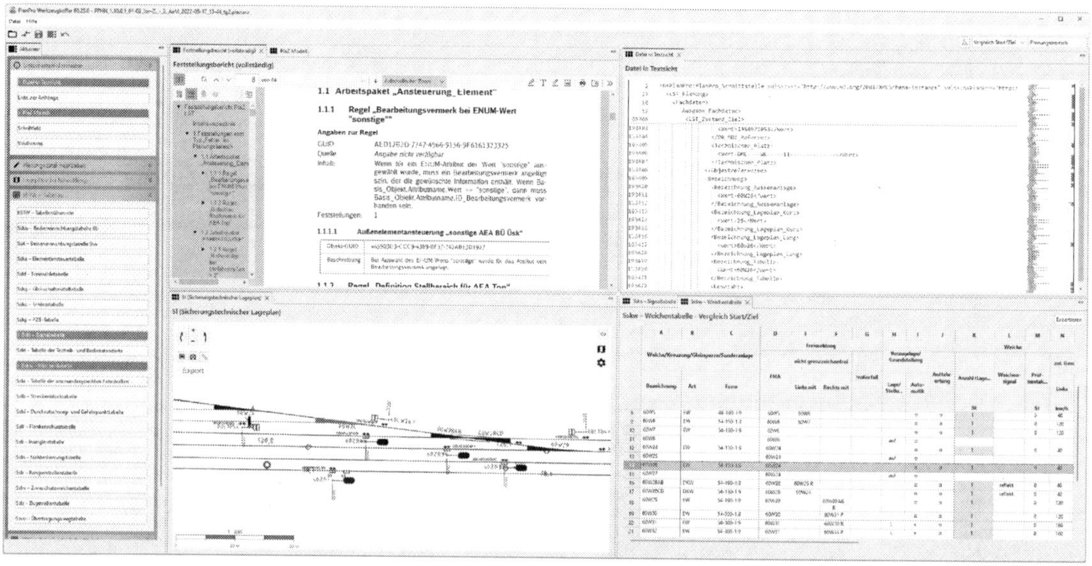

Another tool from Scheidt & Bachmann is **AMBER (Advanced Model Based Environment for Railways)**, an internal configuration tool used by railway engineering teams for configuring their products such as the ZSB2000 interlocking system. It combines numerous views, code generators, and seamless integration with legacy .NET components. The application encompasses more than 1.5 million lines of code and automates complex configuration processes, providing significant efficiency gains in railway system engineering.

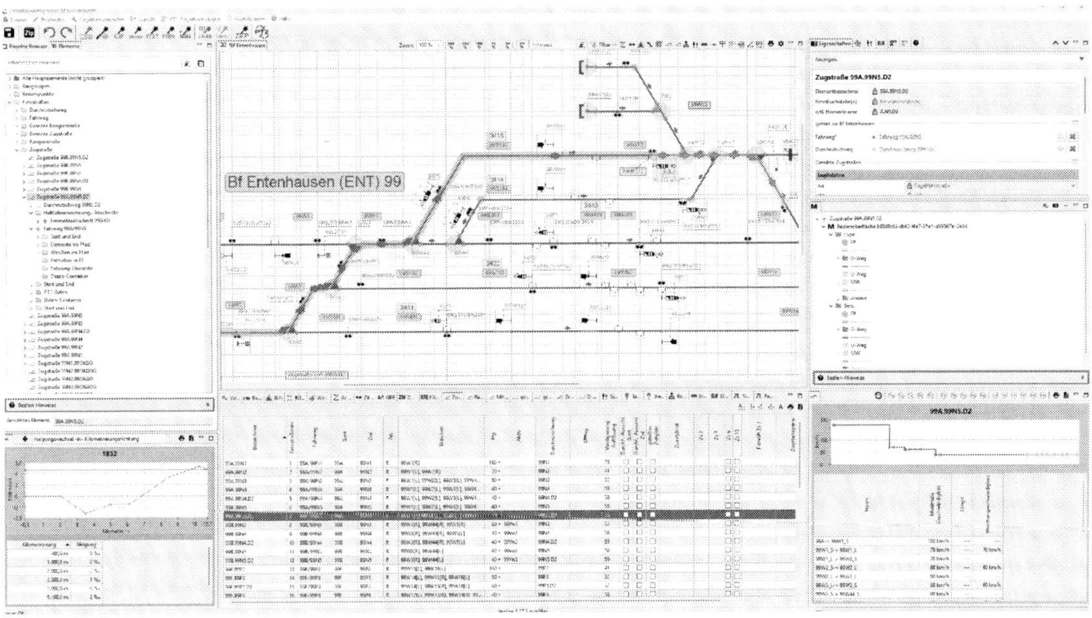
Bf Entenhausen (ENT) 99
Zugstraße 99A.99N5.D2
99A.99N5.D2

Part III: Installation

4. Installation of the Eclipse IDE and its prerequisites

In this chapter, you will ensure that you have installed the Eclipse IDE for Eclipse plug-in and application development.

4.1. Download the Eclipse IDE

To develop Eclipse plug-ins and applications, you need to download an Eclipse IDE suitable for this task. The Eclipse project offers multiple downloads specifically for this purpose. The most commonly used options are:

- The *Eclipse SDK* - minimal functionality needed for Eclipse-based development, SDK stands for Software Development Kit
- The *Eclipse IDE for Eclipse Committers* package provides additional functionality such as Git support

Download one of these. The *Eclipse IDE for Eclipse Committers* package includes a Java runtime; no additional download is needed.

We describe two alternatives:

- the *SDK* download (recommended)
- *Eclipse IDE for Eclipse Committers*

The appearance of the download page may change over time.

4.1.1. Alternative 1: Download the Eclipse SDK

Download the latest version from https://download.eclipse.org/eclipse/downloads/ by clicking the link for the most recent release (the version with the highest number) on the SDK download page. The download section will look similar to the screenshot below.

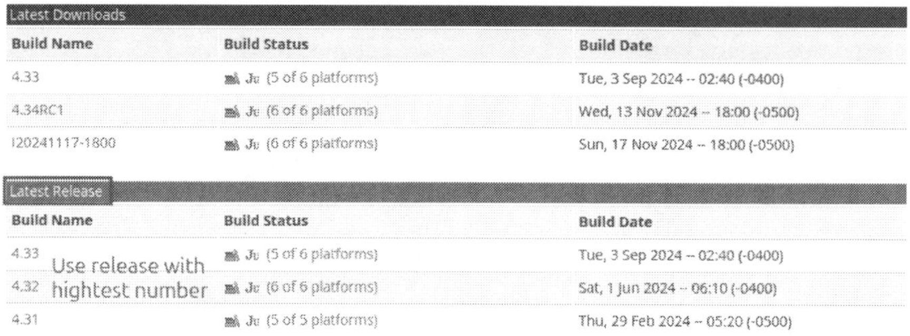

Latest Downloads

Build Name	Build Status	Build Date
4.33	Ju (5 of 6 platforms)	Tue, 3 Sep 2024 -- 02:40 (-0400)
4.34RC1	Ju (6 of 6 platforms)	Wed, 13 Nov 2024 -- 18:00 (-0500)
I20241117-1800	Ju (6 of 6 platforms)	Sun, 17 Nov 2024 -- 18:00 (-0500)

Latest Release

Build Name	Build Status	Build Date
4.33	Ju (5 of 6 platforms)	Tue, 3 Sep 2024 -- 02:40 (-0400)
4.32	Ju (6 of 6 platforms)	Sat, 1 Jun 2024 -- 06:10 (-0400)
4.31	Ju (5 of 5 platforms)	Thu, 29 Feb 2024 -- 05:20 (-0500)

The download is a compressed archive containing multiple files. The format depends on your platform:

- Windows uses the *zip* format
- Linux uses the *tar.gz* format
- macOS uses the DMG (Disk Image) format.

The Eclipse SDK does not include a Java runtime; you need to provide this separately.

4.1.2. Alternative 2: Download the Eclipse IDE for Eclipse Committers package

Eclipse provides pre-built packages that can be used. Download the installer for the `Eclipse IDE for Eclipse Committers` package from the Eclipse packages [https://www.eclipse.org/downloads/packages/] website.

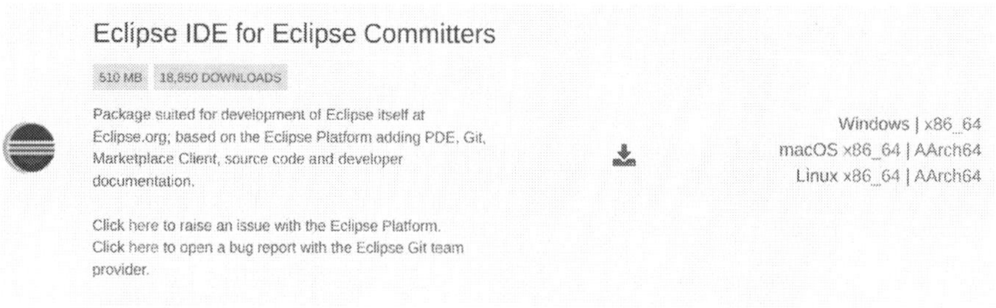

This download includes a Java runtime; you do not need to install one separately.

You can use the Eclipse installer to install this package. The installer is useful if you want to download several versions of Eclipse. It uses a shared installation pool for common plug-ins, which reduces the required space.

4.2. Installing Java

If your installation requires installing the Java runtime, ensure that you install the latest Java long-term release. At the time of this writing, this is Java 21. Later versions of Java are suitable to use as well.

You can test whether the JRE is correctly installed by using the Windows console. To open a console on Windows, press `Win` + `R`, type *cmd*, and press `Enter`. Next, type the following command:

```
java -version
```

If the JRE is correctly installed, this command prints information about your Java installation. If you see that you have the desired JRE version installed, no additional step is necessary.

If the command line indicates that the program could not be found, you need to install Java.

You can get a Java runtime from https://adoptium.net/. It contains instructions on how to install Java for all supported platforms. For the Windows and Mac platform, you also find native installer software.

If you have problems installing Java on your system, search online using a query like "How to install Java runtime on [YOUR OS]." Replace `YOUR OS` with your operating system, e.g., Windows, Ubuntu, macOS, etc. This should result in helpful links.

5. Starting and configuring the Eclipse IDE

In this chapter, you start and configure your IDE so that you are ready to start developing Eclipse plug-ins and applications.

5.1. Starting to use the Eclipse IDE

Double-click the `eclipse.exe` (Microsoft Windows) or `eclipse` (Linux/Mac) file from your installation directory to start the Eclipse IDE.

> *What to do if the Eclipse IDE does not start*
>
> The 2025-06 release of the Eclipse IDE requires Java 21 to run. Ensure that your Java runtime meets the minimum required version.

5.1.1. Picking a workspace

The Eclipse IDE prompts you to select a *workspace* to store its configuration.

If you already use the Eclipse IDE, select a new workspace. This avoids unintended side effects when working with existing projects.

To get started, choose an empty directory and click the Launch button.

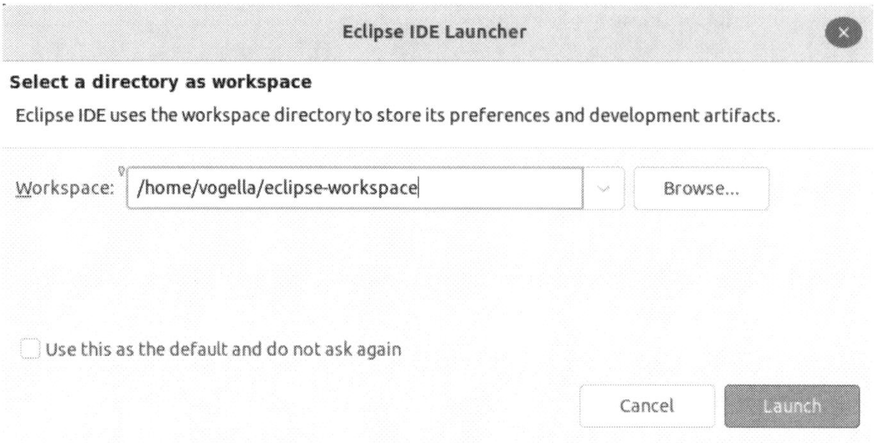

The Eclipse IDE starts and shows the *Welcome* page. Close this page by clicking the *x* next to the *Welcome* tab.

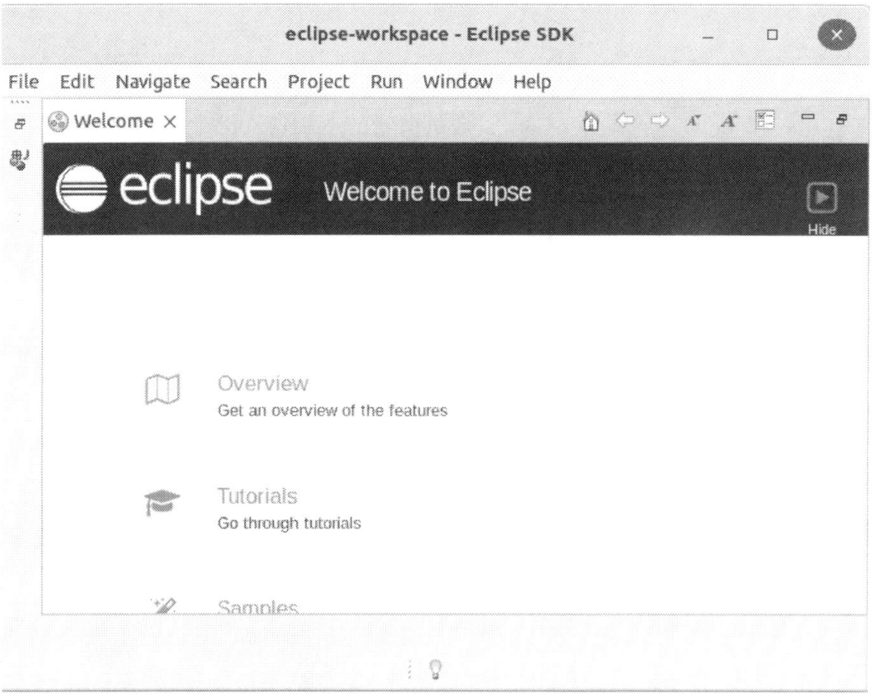

After closing the welcome screen, the IDE should look similar to the following screenshot.

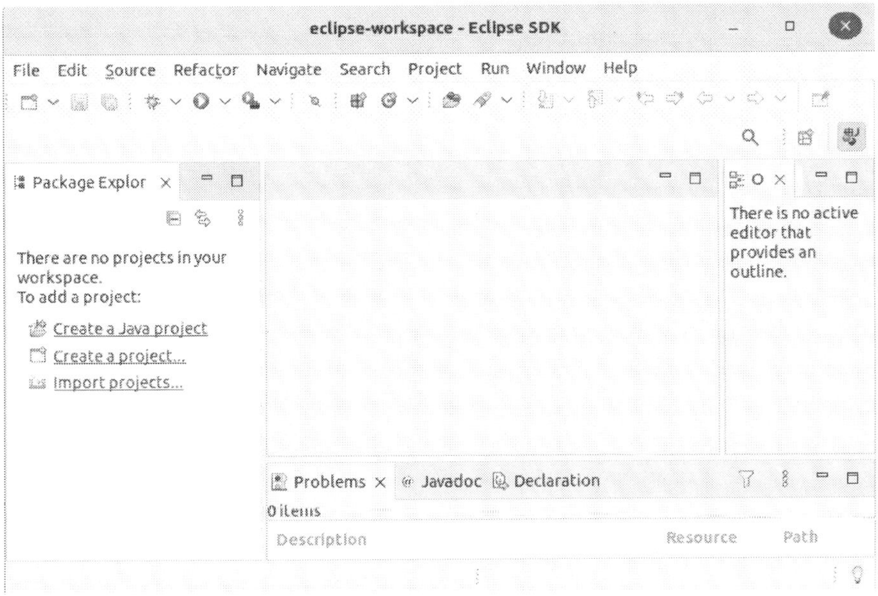

5.1.2. Appearance

By default, Eclipse ships with a light theme. If you prefer, you can switch to a dark theme via the **Window › Preferences › General › Appearance** menu. The *Theme* selection allows you to switch to the *Dark* theme of Eclipse.

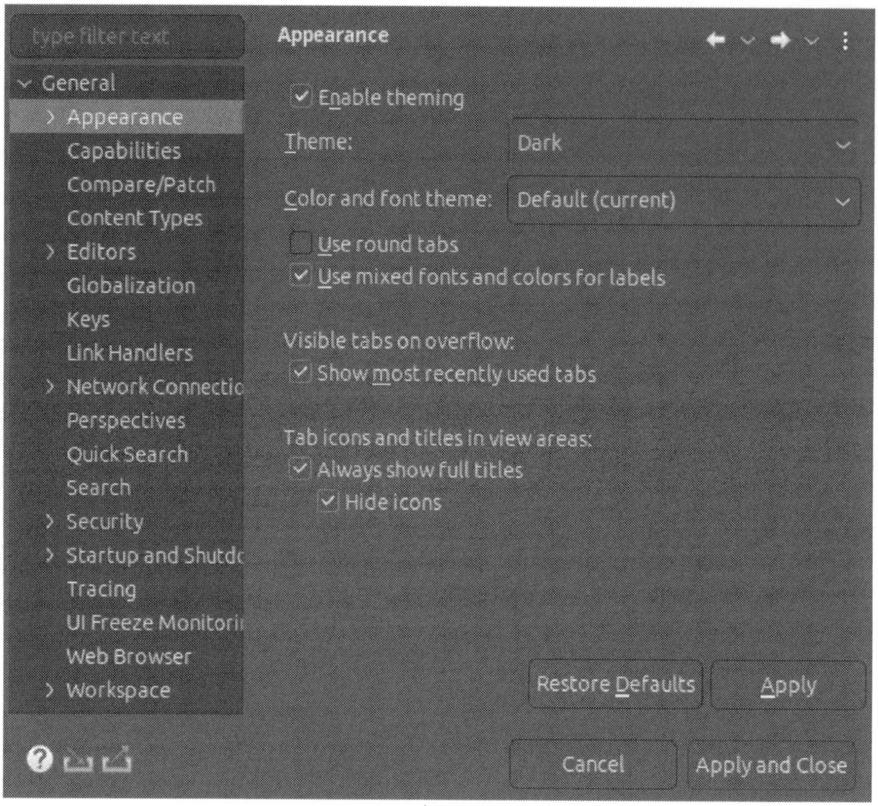

You need to restart your IDE after changing the theme, as some native OS styling features require a restart.

5.2. Enable access to plug-ins

The Java tools limit the scope of search-related activities based on the libraries used in your Java projects. By default, Eclipse includes elements from open projects including their dependencies as well as elements from the standard Java library.

For example, the Open Type dialog `Ctrl` + `Shift` + `T` does not find the `ISources` interface unless it is referenced by a project in your workspace.

As a plug-in developer, you want to have access to all classes in your current *target platform*. The *target platform* is the set of plug-ins against which you develop. By default, the target platform consists of the plug-ins from the Eclipse IDE installation.

You can configure the Eclipse Java tools to include all classes from the current target platform by adjusting the **Window › Preferences › Plug-in Development › Include all plug-ins from target in Java search** setting.

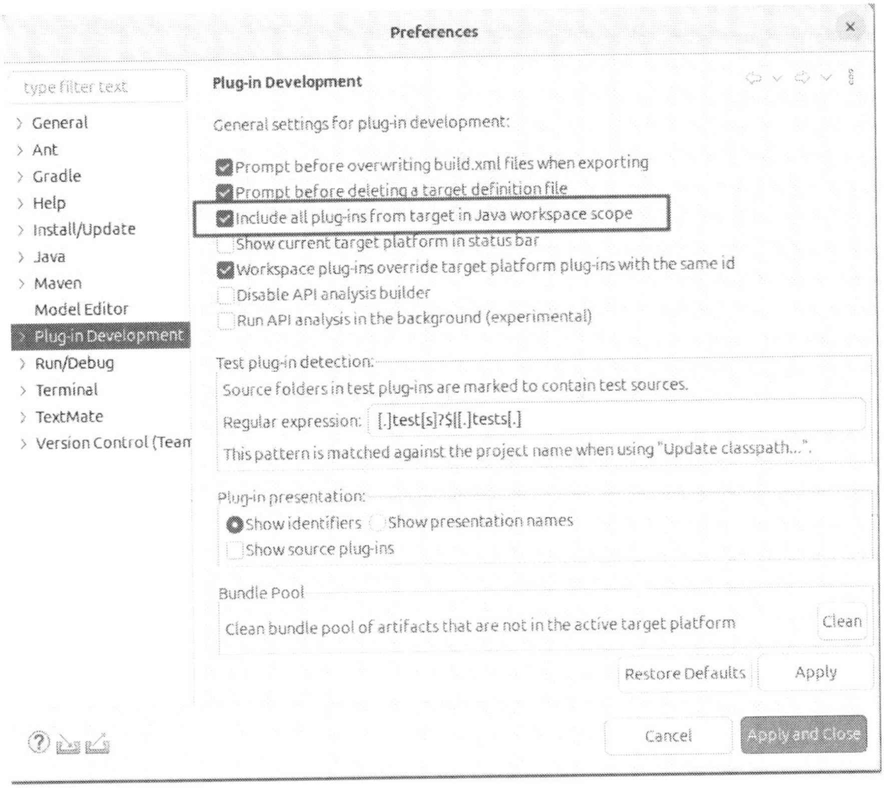

If you skipped the above text, ensure at least that you have configured the setting from the above screenshot in your preferences.

5.3. Auto-save in Eclipse IDE

While Eclipse compiles source code automatically, it does not save your changes by default. You have to save your changes manually via the **File › Save** menu entry or via the keyboard shortcut `Ctrl+S` (`Cmd+S` on macOS).

As a convenience, Eclipse provides an auto-save feature that saves all dirty editors automatically after a certain period of inactivity. You can enable this feature in the Eclipse Preferences via **Window › Preferences › General › Editors › Autosave** menu.

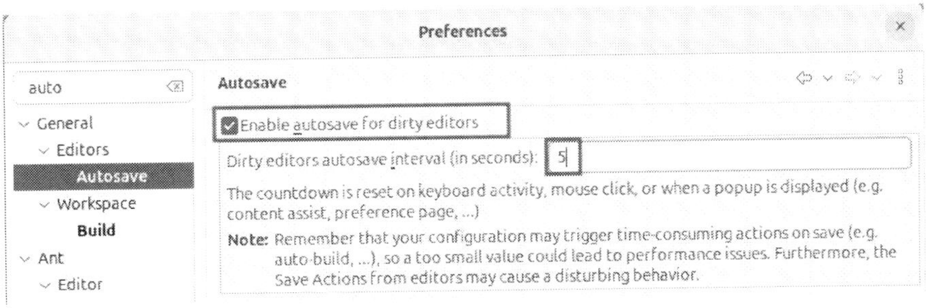

This setting is recommended for beginners as some changes are not applied until you save the corresponding editor.

Part IV: Target platform, products and features

6. Defining available Java libraries with the target platform

6.1. Using the target platform to define the available libraries

Before you can start developing Eclipse components, you need to define libraries to compile against.

Eclipse uses *target files* to define the set of available Java libraries (via JAR files) for Eclipse development. This set is called the *target platform* and can be used by your plug-in projects in your workspace.

Using a target file to control and specify the available libraries and their versions is a good practice. A target definition file is typically shared between developers to ensure that everyone is using the same foundation for development.

If no target file is defined and activated, the Eclipse IDE itself is used as the target platform, providing its JAR files as libraries. This should be avoided as it makes the development dependent on the specific version of the IDE being used.

6.2. Creating a target platform

You can create a target definition file by navigating to **File › New › Other... › Plug-in Development › Target Definition**.

You can add new libraries via the Add... button in the Locations section. Different options are supported, for example:

- Eclipse (p2) update sites
- File locations
- Standard Java libraries from Maven repositories (which require an IDE extension)

The following is an example of a target definition file:

```
<?xml version="1.0" encoding="UTF-8" standalone="no"?>
<?pde version="3.8"?>
<target name="target-platform">
    <locations>
        <location includeAllPlatforms="false" includeConfigurePhase="true"
includeMode="planner" includeSource="true" type="InstallableUnit">
            <repository location="https://download.eclipse.org/releases/latest"/>
            <unit id="org.eclipse.equinox.compendium.sdk.feature.group"/>
            <unit id="org.eclipse.equinox.core.feature.feature.group"/>
        </location>
    </locations>
</target>
```

Entries for Eclipse update sites are defined via the `includeMode` property, which defines how dependencies of Eclipse components are handled:

- planner = includes dependencies automatically in the target platform
- slicer = does not include dependencies automatically in the target platform

> For external libraries prefer the usage of Maven dependencies as described later.

6.3. Setting a target platform as active

Activating a target platform will download the necessary JAR files, convert them into plug-ins if needed, and make them available for development.

You can activate and switch the target platform in the Eclipse Preferences. Select **Window › Preferences › Plug-in Development › Target Platform**.

It is possible to activate a target platform via the target file editor with the *Set as Active Target Platform* link on the first page.

6.4. Update sites for Eclipse components

The Eclipse project offers update sites for different versions.

Use the following URL if you develop against the latest release.

- https://download.eclipse.org/releases/latest

You can develop with a specific release, for example:

- https://download.eclipse.org/releases/2025-12 2025 December release
- https://download.eclipse.org/releases/2025-09 2025 September release
- https://download.eclipse.org/releases/2025-06 2025 June release
- https://download.eclipse.org/releases/2025-03 2025 March release
- https://download.eclipse.org/releases/2024-12 2024 December release
- https://download.eclipse.org/releases/2024-09 2024 September release

7. Versions

It is possible to define the desired version of a library via the version tag, as demonstrated in the following example.

```
<unit id="org.eclipse.platform.feature.group" version="4.34.0.v20241120-1800"/>
```

To see the available versions, you can use code completion via `Ctrl` + `Space` in the version field. As of the 2024-12 release, the version tag is optional and defaults to `0.0.0`. The default of `0.0.0` defines that any version of the library can be used. This allows you to change the URL to another release without having to update the individual versions.

8. Exercise: Create a target platform definition file

In this exercise, you create a target definition file to define the available libraries during development.

8.1. Create a project of the type general

Create a new General-type project named *target-platform* via the **File › New › Other... › General › Project** menu path.

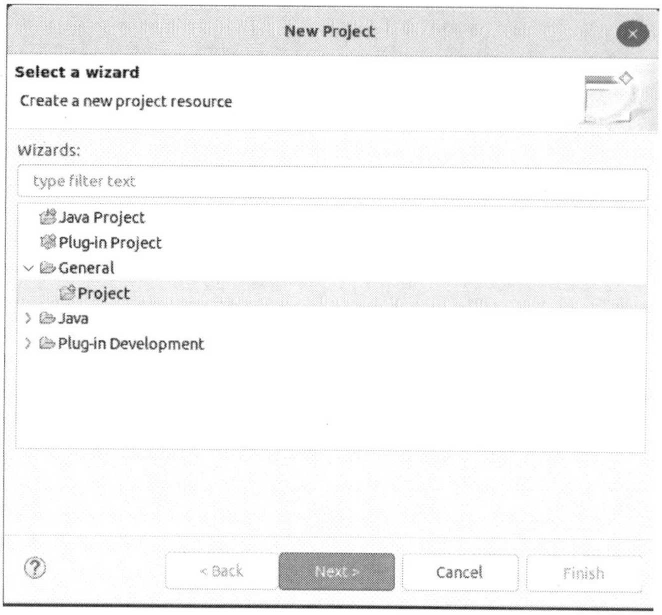

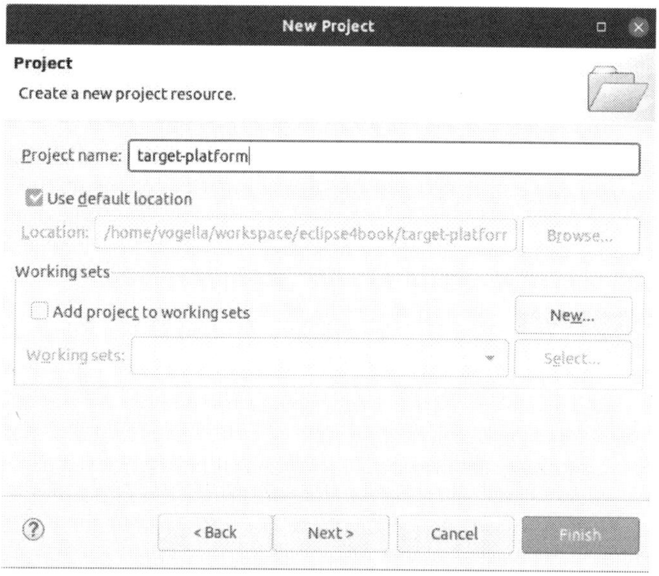

8.2. Create a target definition file

Create a new target definition file via the **File › New › Other... › Plug-in Development › Target Definition** menu path.

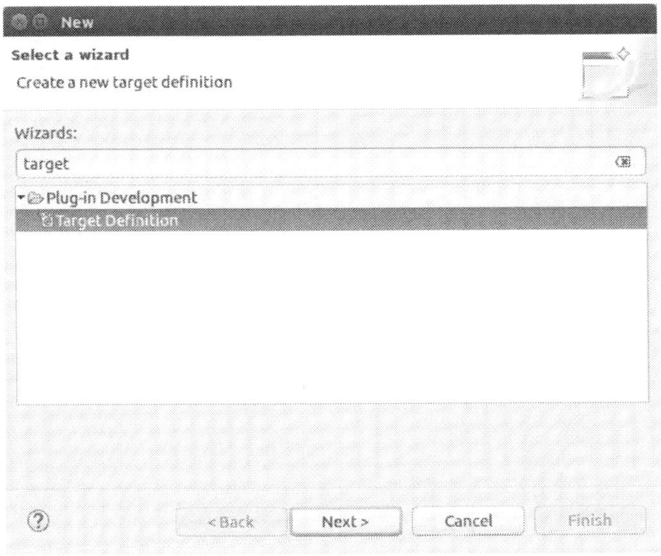

Use `target-platform` as file name and press the Finish button.

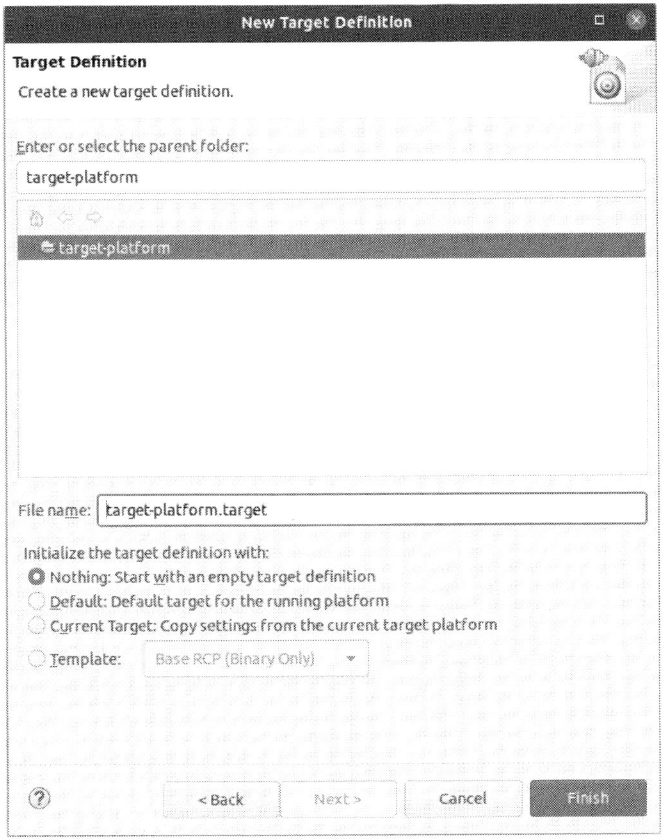

This creates a new file and opens the *Target Definition* editor.

8.3. Defining the target platform content for Eclipse RCP development

In this exercise, you add the Eclipse libraries for developing Eclipse RCP applications to your target definition.

Ensure your target definition file is open in the *Target Definition* editor, then switch to the *Source* tab of the editor. Copy and paste the following text into the file:

```
<?xml version="1.0" encoding="UTF-8" standalone="no"?>
<?pde version="3.8"?>
<target name="target-platform">
 <locations>
  <location includeAllPlatforms="false" includeConfigurePhase="true"
includeMode="planner" includeSource="true" type="InstallableUnit">
   <repository location="https://download.eclipse.org/releases/2025-12"/>
   <unit id="org.eclipse.equinox.sdk.feature.group"/>
   <unit id="org.eclipse.platform.feature.group"/>
  </location>
 </locations>
</target>
```

Save the target definition file.

Your `repository location` points to an *Eclipse update site* containing Java libraries. The *unit* entries define the libraries you want to use. Maven repositories are not used in this example.

8.4. Activating the target definition file

In the target file editor, select the *Definition* tab.

After the target is resolved, press the *Set as Active Target Platform* to activate it.

After activation, this changes to *Reload Target Platform*.

See Section 8.5 if the label does not change.

Avoid using the Eclipse IDE until the target is resolved and activated. Activating a target definition accesses the network. Interrupting this process may result in an inconsistent state of the target platform.

8.5. Known issues with the target platform editor

The target platform editor has some known issues, which are hard to reproduce and therefore not fixed yet.

- Label does not change to *Reload Target Platform* after activation
- You see an error similar to: `An internal error occurred during: "Resolving "target-platform" target definition"`.

In both cases, close the target definition editor and restart your Eclipse IDE. Open the target definition file again and activate it again or verify that the status is correct.

Also, in the past, you sometimes had to restart the Eclipse IDE to use a newly added library from your target platform. This issue should be resolved in the latest Eclipse release, but if you encounter it again, try restarting the IDE.

8.6. Optional: Checking the content of the target platform

Use the **Window › Show View › Other...OSGi › Bundle Repositories** menu to open the *Bundle Repositories* view. Use this view to review the available versions of your plug-ins from your target platform. To see details from the selected plug-in you can use the *OSGi Resolution* view.

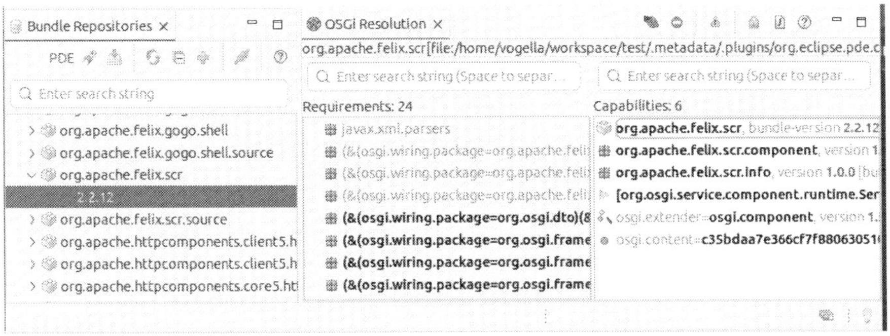

8.7. Solving potential issues with the target definition

Your target platform depends on external update sites and the availability of the network. These update sites might change over time, so you should be able to revert your target platform settings in case you face issues.

If you have problems accessing the network, you can temporarily use the Eclipse IDE as a target platform via **Window › Preferences › Plug-in Development › Target Platform**.

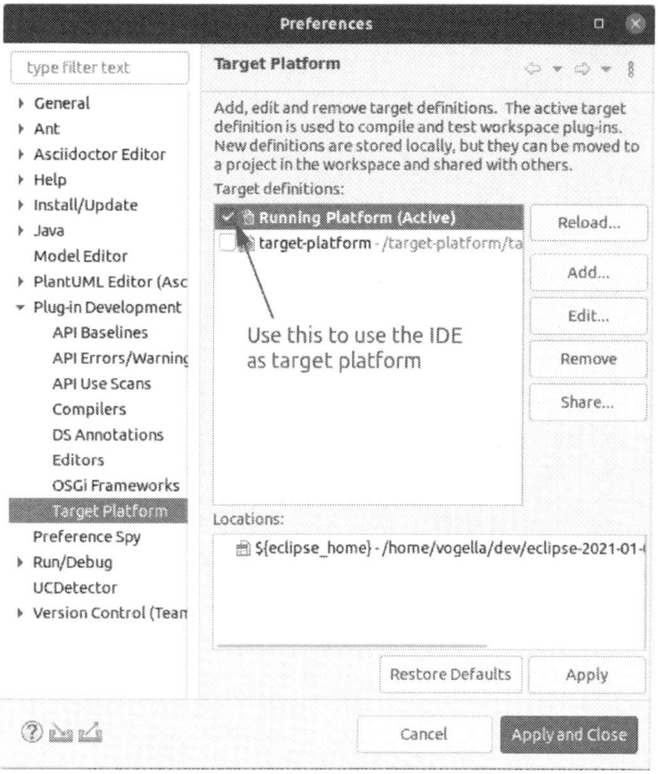

9. Product configuration file

9.1. Using a product configuration file

A *product configuration file* (product) defines the configuration of an Eclipse application. This includes icons, the splash screen, and the necessary plug-ins and features.

The Eclipse IDE allows you to create new product files via the **File › New › Other › Plug-in Development › Product Configuration** wizard and provides an editor to easily change the file.

A product configuration must define the main application class. The default applications for Eclipse applications are:

- `org.eclipse.ui.ide.workbench` for Eclipse IDE-based applications
- `org.eclipse.e4.ui.workbench.swt.E4Application` for Eclipse RCP applications not related to the IDE

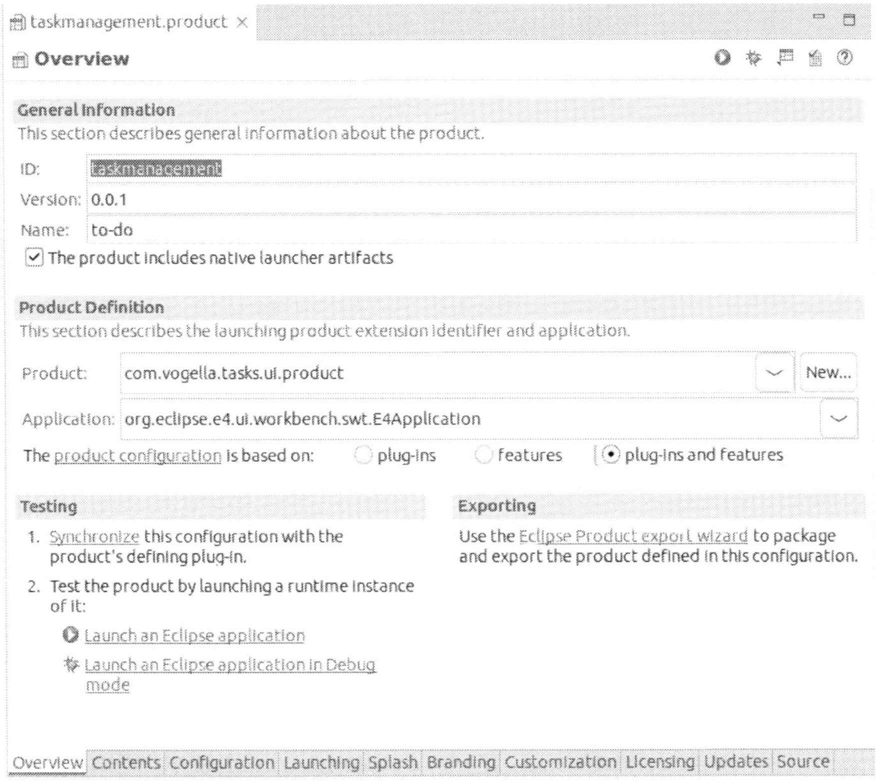

Custom applications implementing the `IApplication` interface can be used.

On the *Overview* tab of this editor, you can start the product. Pressing the *Synchronize* link writes the relevant product configuration information into the *plugin.xml* file.

On the *Contents* tab, you define the set of plug-ins and features that are included in the final application.

9.2. Splash screen

The *Splash* tab allows you to specify the plug-in that contains the splash screen.

The splash screen image can be in any of the following formats: PNG, JPG, GIF, or BMP. Transparency and animation are not supported.

The name is predefined as *splash.EXTENSION* and must be located in the root of the plug-in's directory. Therefore, you need to put one of the following files into the project main directory:

- splash.png
- splash.jpg
- splash.jpeg

- splash.gif
- splash.bmp

The predefined name and location of the splash screen image can be changed via the *osgi.splashPath* parameter, while the file name can be changed with the *-showsplash path_to_file* option.

9.3. Icons, launcher name, and program and VM arguments

You can configure the launcher name and icon for your product. The launcher is the executable program that is created during the deployment of the product. A launcher is platform-specific. For example, the default launcher is called *eclipse.exe* on the *Windows* platform. This launcher has an associated icon. To change the name and the icon, select the *Launching* tab of your product configuration.

Here, you can specify the file name of the launcher and the icon that should be used. Ensure that the icons are in the correct format; otherwise, Eclipse will not use them.

> The icon configuration depends on the platform you are using. Eclipse allows you to export your application for multiple platforms and uses the correct ones based on your product configuration.

In the *Launching Arguments* section, you can specify parameters for your Eclipse application and arguments for the Java runtime environment. *Program Arguments* are parameters passed to the Eclipse application.

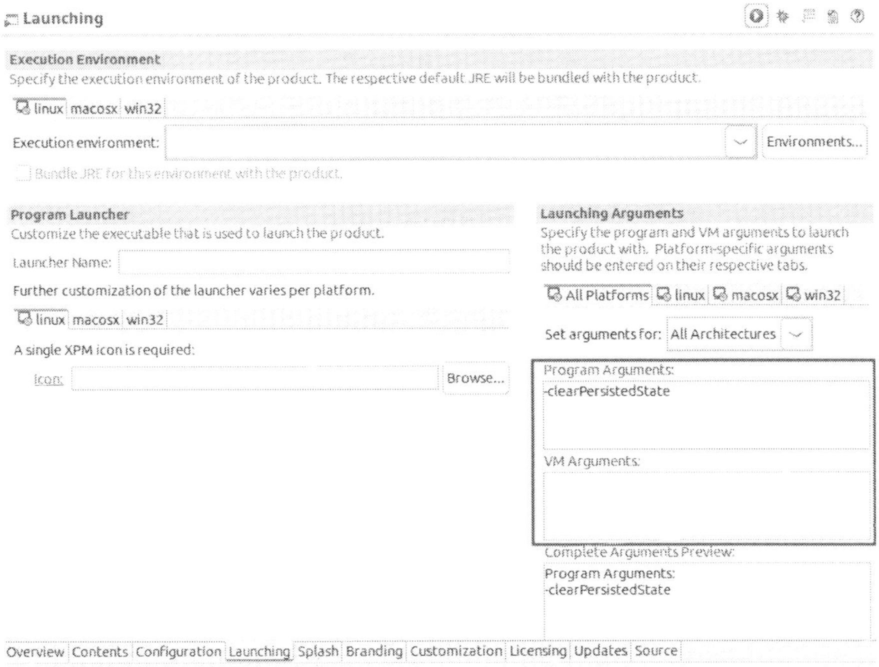

9.4. Product configuration limitations for Eclipse RCP applications

Currently, the definition of the splash handlers that can be registered via the *Customization* part of the *Splash* tab is not used by modern Eclipse RCP applications. Additionally, the configuration in the *About Dialog* and the *Welcome Page* section on the *Branding* tab is not directly supported in Eclipse RCP applications. These only work for Eclipse applications using the 3.x API.

10. Using features

10.1. Definition of feature projects and features

Using the Eclipse wizards, you can create feature projects in a similar way to how you create plug-in projects. An Eclipse feature project defines a *feature*.

A feature describes a list of plug-ins and other features that can be seen as a set of related components. It has a name, a version number, and, in most cases, license information assigned to it.

A feature is described via a *feature.xml* file. The following listing shows an example of such a file.

```
<?xml version="1.0" encoding="UTF-8"?>
<feature
      id="com.vogella.eclipse.featuretest.feature"
      label="Feature"
      version="1.0.0.qualifier"
```

```
        provider-name="vogella GmbH">

    <description url="https://www.example.com/description">
        [Enter Feature Description here.]
    </description>

    <copyright url="https://www.example.com/copyright">
        [Enter Copyright Description here.]
    </copyright>

    <license url="https://www.example.com/license">
        [Enter License Description here.]
    </license>

    <plugin
            id="com.vogella.eclipse.featuretest.feature"
            version="0.0.0"
     />

</feature>
```

The grouping of plug-ins into logical units makes it easier to handle a set of plug-ins. Instead of adding many individual plug-ins to your product configuration file, you can group them using features. This increases the visibility of your application structure.

Features can be used to install them into Eclipse applications and for the definition of Eclipse products. Features can be used as a basis to define a launch configuration.

Eclipse provides several predefined features, e.g., the `org.eclipse.e4.rcp` that contains the most commonly used plug-ins for Eclipse applications.

10.2. Feature or plug-in based products

A product can either be based on plug-ins or on features. This setting is done on the *Overview* tab of the product configuration file.

On the *Contents* tab in the product editor, you enter the plug-ins or features your product consists of.

A product can include dependencies automatically.

10.3. Creating a feature

You can create a new feature project via the **File › New › Other... › Plug-in Development › Feature Project** menu entry.

If you open the *feature.xml* file, you can change the feature properties using a special editor.

The *Information* tab allows you to enter a description and copyright related information for this feature.

The *Included Plug-ins* tab allows you to change the included plug-ins in the feature. If you want to add a plug-in to a feature, use this tab. A frequent error made by new Eclipse developers is to add it to the *Dependencies* tab.

The *Included Features* tab allows you to include other features in this feature. The *Dependencies* tab allows you to define other features that must be present to use this feature.

The *Build* tab is used for the build process and should include the *feature.xml* file. The last two tabs give access to the configuration files in text format.

11. Deployment of the application

11.1. Creating a stand-alone version of the application

An Eclipse application needs to be exported (also called deployed) to run outside the Eclipse IDE. Exporting your product creates a folder with all required artifacts to run your application. This includes a native launcher tailored to the platforms, such as Windows or Linux that you exported it for.

Earlier releases of Eclipse supported a manual export via the product file and these options are still present in the user interface. Unfortunately, this does not work reliably anymore as the Eclipse platform development relies on a *command line build* using Maven to produce its components.

Therefore, it is recommended to set up a Maven Tycho build for building and deploying your application. With the latest Tycho version, setting up a build for Eclipse-based applications and plug-ins can be done efficiently.

See Chapter 191 for setting up a Maven Tycho build for your Eclipse components.

11.2. Checklist for common export problems

If the export encounters a problem, please refer to the following table for a solution:

Table 1. Problems with the product export

Problem	Possible cause
Export fails	Try using an empty target directory, sometimes the export cannot delete the existing files and therefore fails.
No executable file after the export	Check the flag *The product includes native launcher artifacts* in your .product file on the *Overview* tab.

Problem	Possible cause
Product could not be found	Validate that all dependencies are included in the product. Delete an existing launch configuration and restart the product from the IDE to see if everything is configured correctly.
Splash screen or other icons are missing	Check the *build.properties* file to see if all required images and icons are included in the export.
Splash screen is missing	Ensure that you have entered the defining plug-in in the *Splash* tab on the product configuration file. If this is not set, the splash screen is not displayed after the export. Unfortunately, it is displayed if you start the plug-in from the Eclipse IDE.
Issues during the start of the application	Check the log file in the workspace folder of your exported application to see the error messages during the start process. Alternatively, add the "-consoleLog" parameter to the ".ini" file in the folder of the exported application.
applicationXMI argument is missing	Check the *build.properties* file to see if the *Application.e4xmi* and the *plugin.xml* files are included in the export.
Service could not be found or injected	Make sure that the bundle that provides the service has the `Activate this plug-in when one of its classes is loaded` flag set. Also make sure that the `org.apache.felix.scr` bundle is started automatically with a `Start Level` less than 4.
Application ID could not be found	Define a start level of 1 and set auto-start to true for the `org.eclipse.core.runtime` plug-in.
Translations not available in the exported product	Ensure, via the *build.properties* file of the relevant plug-in, that the files containing the translations are included in the export.

12. Exercise: Create an RCP application using the Eclipse wizard

In the following exercise, you will create an Eclipse RCP application using a template and launch it via the IDE. The generated files are not yet explained, but this should enable you to see a running application and review the involved configuration files.

12.1. Create project

Create a project named `com.example.e4.rcp` using the **File › New › Other... › Plug-in Development › Plug-in Project** menu entry.

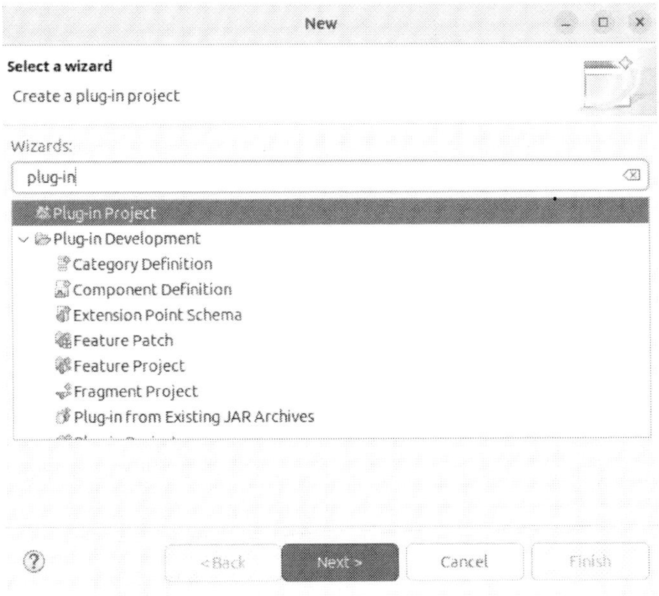

Use the settings similar to the following screenshots.

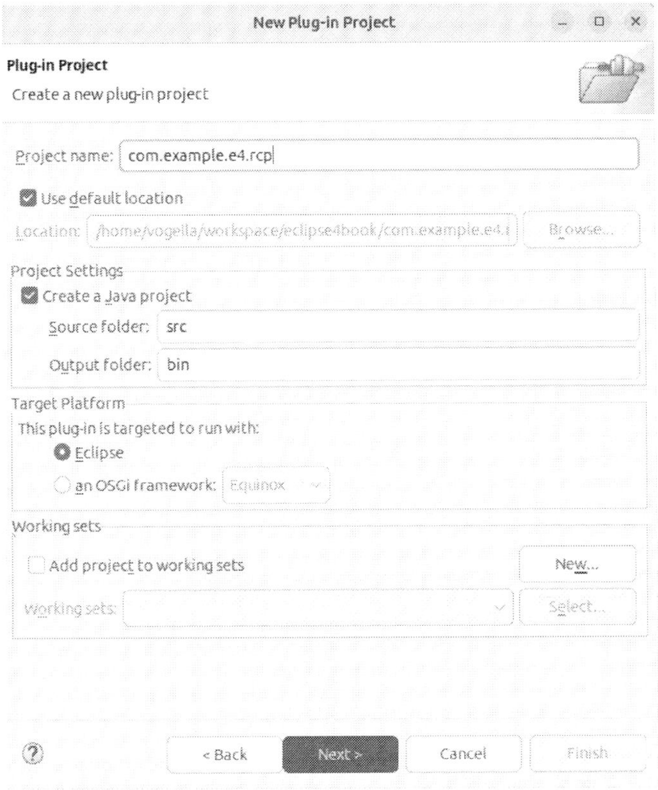

Press Next.

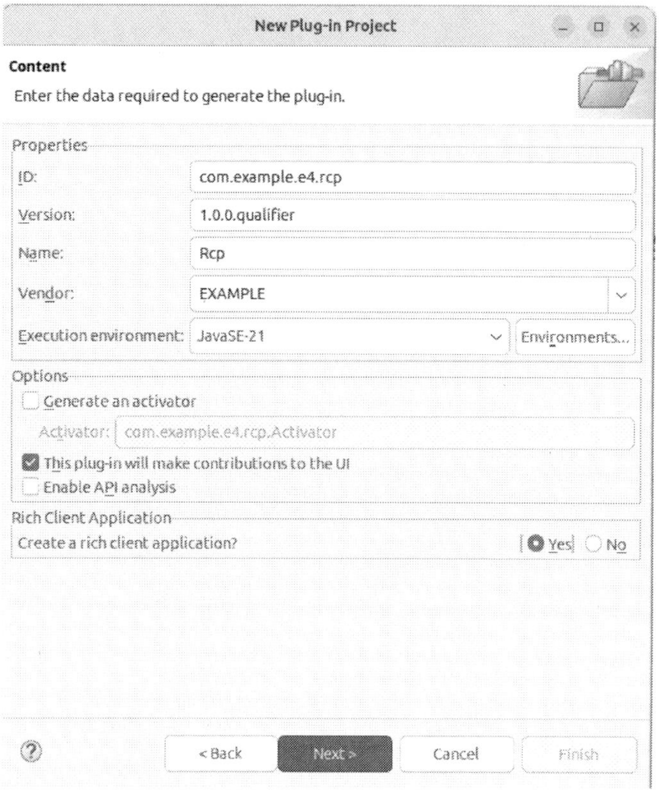
New Plug-in Project
Content
Enter the data required to generate the plug-in.
Properties
ID:
com.example.e4.rcp
Version:
1.0.0.qualifier
Name:
Rcp
Vendor:
EXAMPLE
Execution environment:
JavaSE-21
Environments...
Options
Generate an activator
Activator:
com.example.e4.rcp.Activator
This plug-in will make contributions to the UI
Enable API analysis
Rich Client Application
Create a rich client application?
Yes
No
< Back
Next >
Cancel
Finish

Press Next.

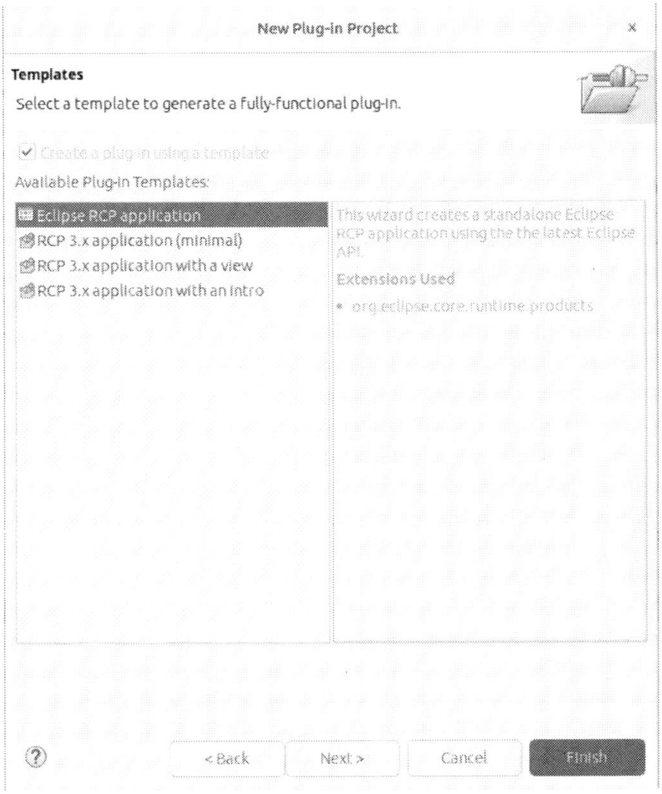

Press Next.

On the last wizard page, select the *Create sample content (parts, menu, etc.)* flag. Via this flag, you configure that the generated application has example content, e.g., a view and some menu and toolbar entries.

The wizard adds the `clearPersistedState` startup option to the product configuration file. This ensures that the latest state of your application model is used when the application is started.

12.2. Launch the application using the product file

Open the generated product file by double-clicking on the product file.

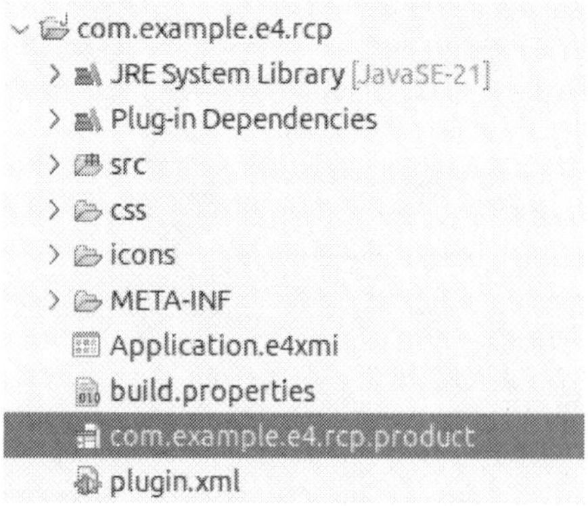

Switch to the *Overview* tab in the editor and press the *Launch an Eclipse application* hyperlink to start your application. This option is highlighted in the screenshot below.

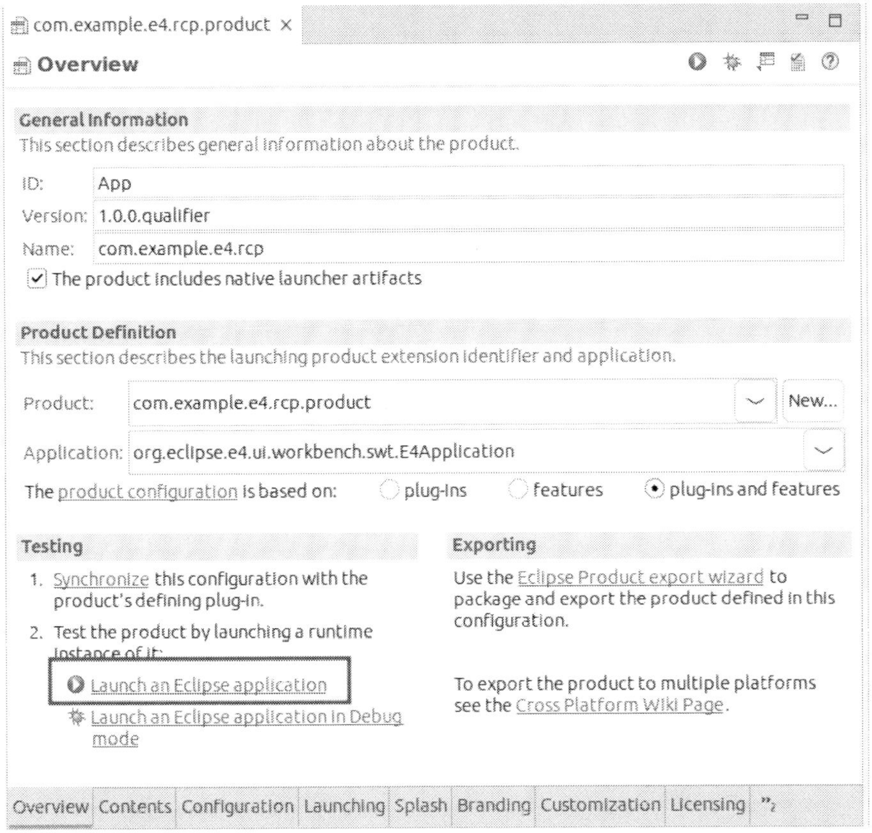

12.3. Validate

As a result, your Eclipse application should start. The application should look similar to the following screenshot.

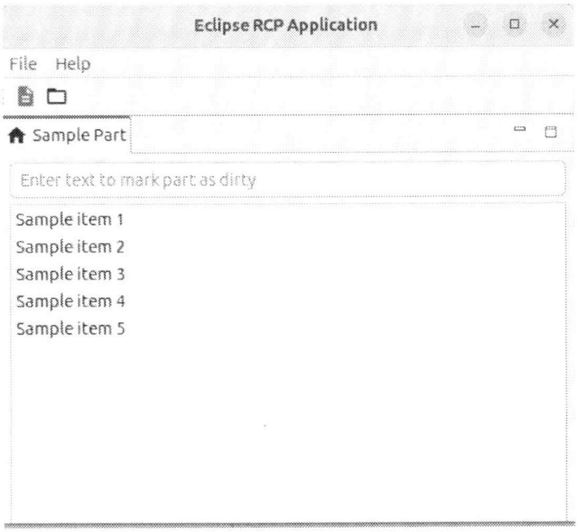

12.4. Error analysis

If you see an empty window, it means you pressed the Finish button prematurely (after selecting the template) or forgot to select the `Create sample content` flag on the last tab.

To fix this, delete the generated plug-in and create it again, making sure to select the correct values as described in Chapter 12.

13. Optional exercise: Use a custom feature in the product

You could group your plug-ins into a custom feature. This is not required and can be unnecessary overhead if you only have one plug-in. It is useful if you have many plug-ins, so that you can group them.

13.1. Create a feature project

Create a new feature project named *com.example.e4.feature* via the **File › New › Other... › Plug-in Development › Feature Project** entry. The following screenshot shows the first wizard page.

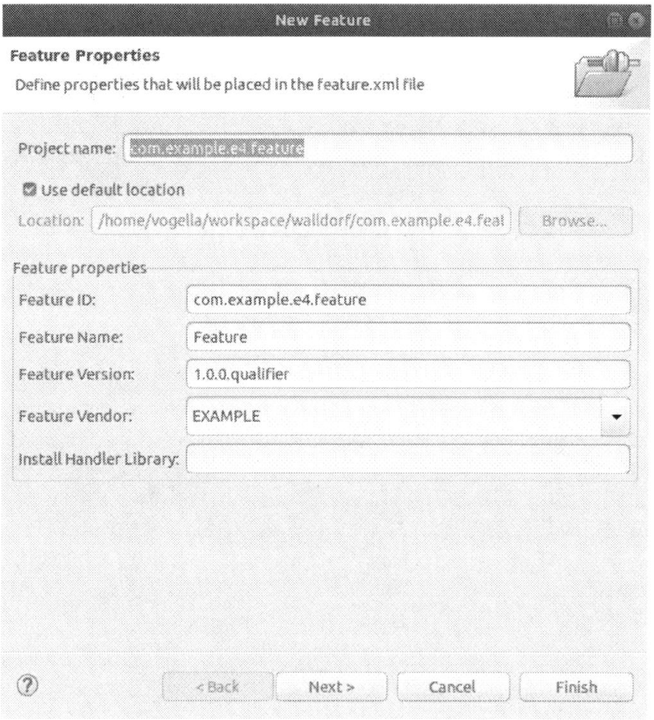

Include the `com.example.e4.rcp` plug-in into the new feature.

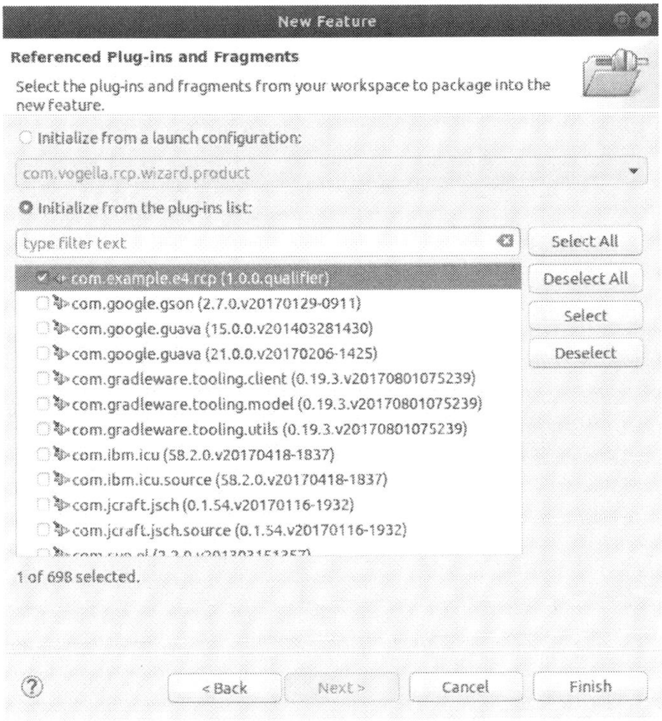

13.2. Create a new project for the product configuration file

Currently, the `com.example.e4.rcp` plug-in contains the `.product` file. While you could leave the `.product` file in its current location, a typical project setup keeps the product in its own project. This is because a product defines settings for the whole application and does not closely relate to only one plug-in.

Therefore, create a new project of type *General* named `com.example.e4.product` and move the product file to this project.

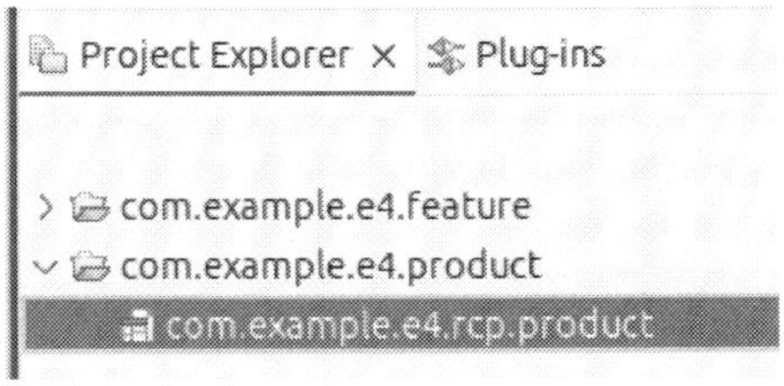

13.3. Ensure that the product configuration file allows the use of plug-ins and features.

Ensure that the `.product` file is open. Select the *Overview* tab and ensure the *plug-ins and features* option is selected.

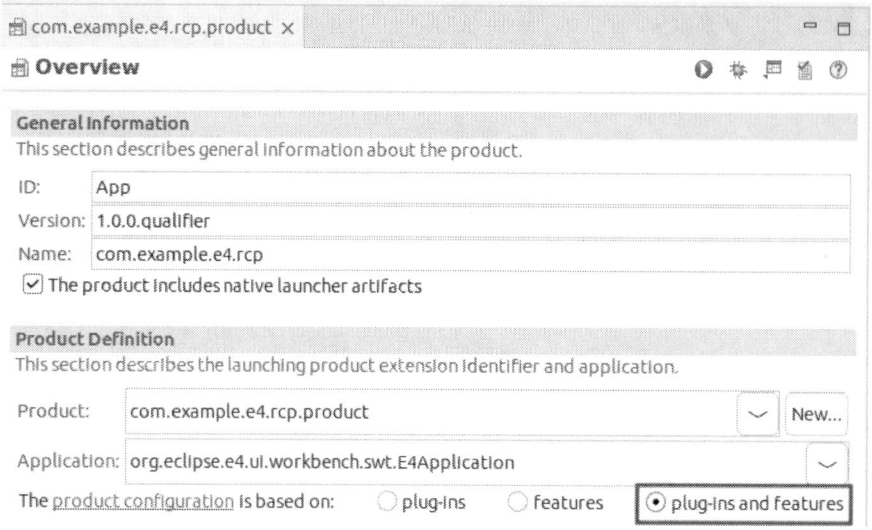

13.4. Add the features as content to the product

Switch to the *Contents* tab in your product editor. The following entries should already be present.

- `org.eclipse.e4.rcp`
- `com.example.e4.rcp`

Remove the `com.example.e4.rcp` entry via the Remove button. We want to add the feature instead of the plug-in.

Add the following feature to your product via the Add Feature... button.

- `com.example.e4.feature`

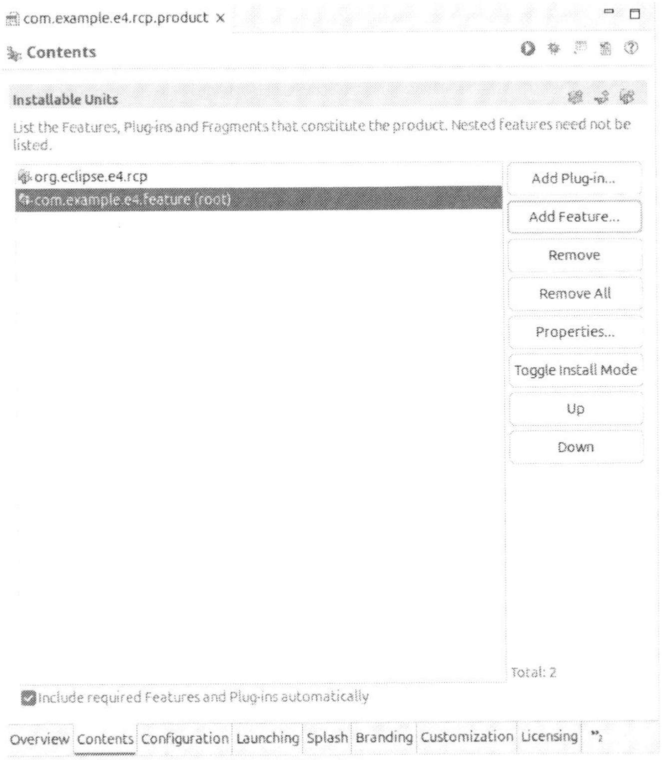

The *Include required Features and Plug-ins automatically* includes required dependencies.

13.5. Start the application via the product

Start your application using the product configuration file and ensure that the application starts correctly. If everything is configured correctly, the application should start as before with no visual difference.

If the application does not start, check that you start your application using the product configuration and **not** with an existing launch configuration. This ensures that your new product configuration is used.

Part V: The Eclipse application model

14. Describing the structure of an Eclipse application

The structure of an Eclipse application is described via an *application model*. At startup, this application model is constructed based on multiple configuration files and adjusted by code logic resulting in a runtime application model. This runtime application model is the basis for the running application and it is kept in sync with the application during runtime by the framework.

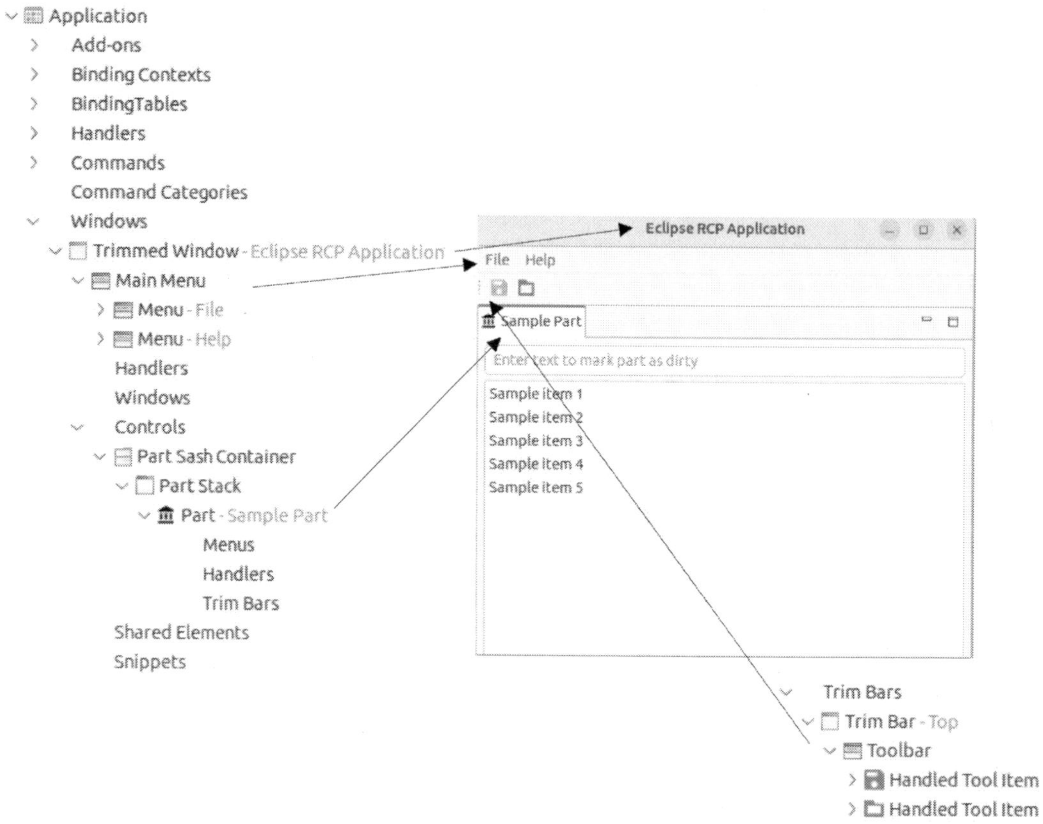

This model contains the parts of the application as individual model elements and their hierarchical relationship. Some of these model elements are visible to the user. For example, windows, parts (views and editors), menus, toolbars. Other elements are not directly visible to the user, for example, handlers, commands, and key bindings.

Each model element has attributes that describe its current state, e.g., the size and the position of a window. The application model expresses the relationship between model elements via a hierarchy. If necessary, a model element can contain links to Java classes or static resources. For example, a part contains a link to the Java classes that are initialized when the part becomes visible.

The base of the application model is typically defined as a static file. For an Eclipse RCP application this file is, by default, called `Application.e4xmi` and located in the main directory of the plug-in that defines the product extension. The Eclipse IDE ships with its own base application file provided by the Eclipse Platform.

This file is read at application startup and is used to construct the initial application model. Changes to the model are persisted, and if a changed model is present, the application is restored from this model the next time it is started.

The application model is extensible, e.g., other plug-ins can contribute to it via *model processors* and *model fragments*.

During startup, the Eclipse framework parses the available information about the application model (Application.e4xmi, persisted user changes and model contributions). It stores the available information and their hierarchy in Java objects at runtime. These objects are called *model objects* and at runtime, they represent the attributes from the model elements.

An Eclipse IDE runtime or an Eclipse RCP application running in compatibility mode adds additional model elements based on other configuration data, like view contributions via plugin.xml.

14.1. Connecting model elements to classes and resources

Model elements can point to a class or to a static resource via a Uniform Resource Identifier (URI). For this purpose, Eclipse supports two URI patterns. In most cases, Eclipse instantiates the referred objects or resources lazily. For example, the classes for a part are instantiated when the part becomes visible.

The following table describes the supported URI patterns. The example assumes that the bundle is called *test* for brevity.

Table 2. URI pattern for class and static file references

Pattern	Description

`bundleclass://Bundle-SymbolicName/package.className`
 	
Example:
 	
`bundleclass://test/test.parts.MySavePart`
	Identifier for a Java class. It consists of the following parts: `bundleclass://` is a fixed prefix. Bundle-SymbolicName is defined in the `MANIFEST.MF` file. The Bundle-SymbolicName is followed by a '/' and the fully qualified class name.

`platform:/plugin/Bundle-SymbolicName/path/filename.extension`
 	
Example:
 	
`platform:/plugin/com.test.plugin/icons/save_edit.png`
	Used to identify resources. Identifier for a resource in a plug-in. `platform:/plugin/` is a fixed prefix, followed by the Bundle-SymbolicName, followed by the path to the file and the filename.

For example, a part has a `Class URI` attribute that points to a Java class via the `bundleclass://` URI. This class provides the specific implementation of the part.

An example for a static resource reference is the `Icon URI` attribute of a part. This attribute can point to an icon that is used for the part.

14.2. Overview of the model objects

The following text provides an overview of the available model elements in the application model.

14.2.1. Application

The application object is represented as an `MApplication` object at runtime and serves as the root of the application.

14.2.2. Windows

Eclipse applications consist of one or more windows, their model representation is an `MWindow` or the `MTrimmedWindow` object. `MTrimmedWindow` can contain trimbars (that can hold toolbars).

14.2.3. Parts

Parts are user interface components that allow you to navigate and modify data. Their model representation is an `MPart`.

Parts can be stacked or positioned next to each other depending on the container into which they are dropped. A part can have a drop-down menu, context menus, and a toolbar.

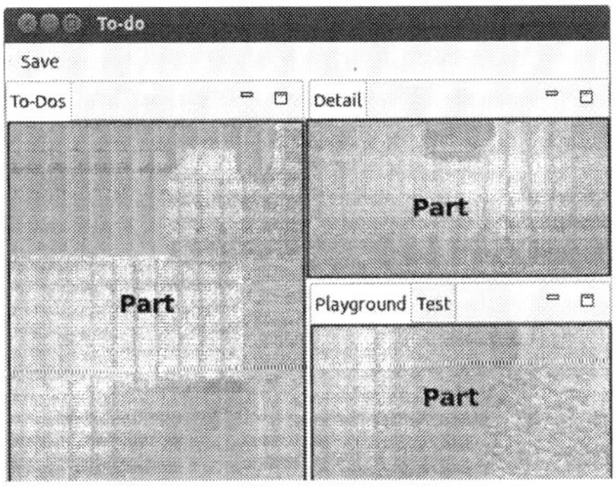

Parts can be classified as *views* and *editors*.

Views are typically used to display and modify a set of data, such as a tree or table of data elements. If the view allows you to change data, this change is typically directly applied to the underlying data structure without the need to save explicitly.

For example, the *Project Explorer* view in the Eclipse IDE allows you to browse a set of files. If you rename a file via the *Project Explorer* view, the file name is directly changed on the file system.

Editors are typically used to modify a single data element. To apply the changes made in an editor to the data structure, the user must explicitly save the editor content.

For example, the *Java* editor is used to modify Java source files. Changes to the source file are applied once the user selects the Save button. A dirty editor tab is marked with an asterisk to the left of the name of the modified file.

14.2.4. Available part containers

Parts can be directly assigned to a window or a perspective. They can be grouped and arranged using stacks (*Part Stack*) or sash containers (*Part Sash Container*).

A part stack arranges its children like a browser. It contains a stack of parts and shows their headers while the content of one part is displayed. The user can switch to another part by selecting the corresponding tab.

A part sash container displays all its children at the same time either horizontally or vertically aligned.

The following screenshot shows a simple Eclipse application layout using two part sash containers and three part stacks.

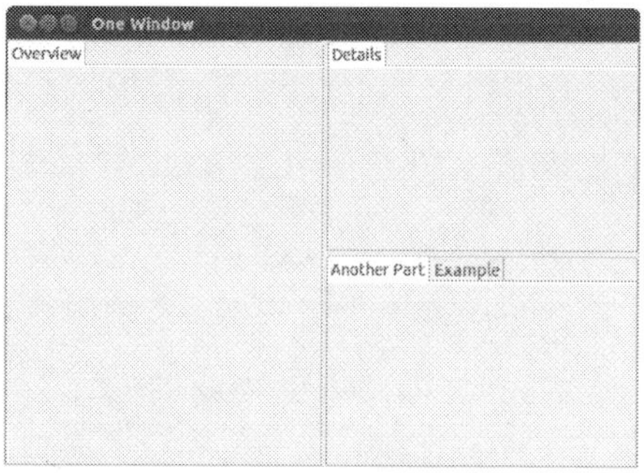

On the top of this layout there is a part sash container that contains another part sash container and one part stack. These two elements are displayed side by side. The part sash container on the next level contains two part stacks. The hierarchy is depicted in the following graphic.

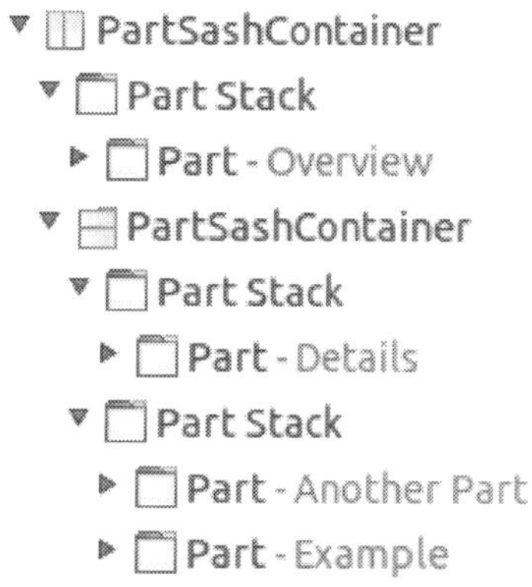

You can use the *Container Data* attribute on a child of a part sash container to assign a layout weight. This layout weight is interpreted as the relative space the corresponding child element should get assigned in the part sash container. The setting is depicted in the following screenshot.

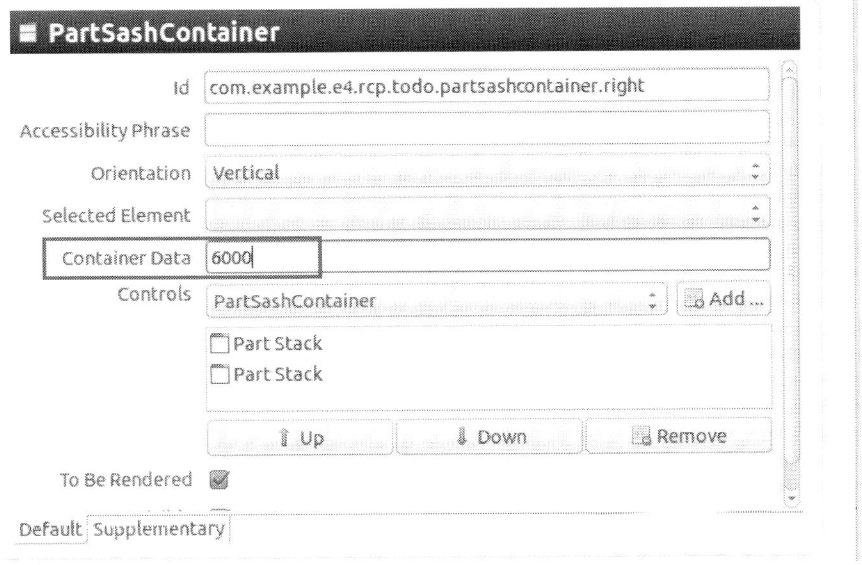

If you set the *Container Data* for one element, you must define it for all the other elements as well. Otherwise, the missing values are interpreted as high, and these elements take up all available space.

The initial total of all the container data values is maintained when elements in the sash are moved. To allow fine-grained dragging, this total must be commensurate with the screen resolution. A value that is too low (i.e., 50 / 50) causes the part to be moved multiple pixels per sash unit, which the user will perceive as a jerky movement. Therefore, use a sufficiently high value, e.g., 10000.

14.2.5. Perspectives

A perspective is an optional container for other part containers and parts. It is represented by `MPerspective` objects that must be placed in an `MPerspectiveStack` object. Only one of the perspectives in a perspective stack can be activated and made visible. It is possible to have shared elements between perspectives.

For example, the Eclipse IDE uses perspectives to provide view arrangements appropriate for different tasks, like development or debugging.

Switching perspectives can be done via the `EPartService` service provided by the Eclipse platform.

14.2.6. Table overview of available model objects

The following table lists the types of the important model objects.

Table 3. Eclipse model elements

Model element	Description
MApplication	Describes the application object. All other model elements are contained in this object.
MAddon	A self-contained component typically without user interface. It can register for events in the application lifecycle and handle these events.
MWindow	Represents a window in your application.
MTrimmedWindow	Similar to MWindow but it allows containing toolbars for the windows (via the TrimBars model elements).
MPerspective	Represents a different layout of parts to be shown inside the window. Should be contained in a MPerspectiveStack.
MPart	Represents the model element part, such as a view or an editor.
MDirtyable	Property of MPart that can be injected. If set to true, this property informs the Eclipse platform that this part contains unsaved data, i.e., it is dirty. In a handler you can query this property to provide a save option.
MPartDescriptor	MPartDescriptor is a template for new parts. A new part based on this part descriptor can be created and shown via the Eclipse framework.
Snippets	Snippets can be used to pre-configure model parts that you want to create during runtime. You can use the Eclipse framework to clone such a snippet and use the resulting object to attach it to the application model at runtime.

15. Extending the application model from other plug-ins

15.1. Contributions

Every plug-in can contribute to the application model via:

- Static contributions - contributed via text files; these extensions are called fragments or *model fragments*.
- Dynamic contributions - contributed via Java classes; these extensions are called *processors* or *model processors*.

These model contributions must be registered via the `org.eclipse.e4.workbench.model` extension point. They are read during startup and are used to build the runtime application model.

This runtime application model reflects your current application. Changes during the application's runtime are written back to the model. For example, if the user positions a part into another stack via drag and drop.

If the Eclipse application is closed, these changes are recorded and saved in the *workbench.xmi* file. This file is located in the *.metadata/.plugins/org.eclipse.e4.workbench* folder. If certain model elements should not be persisted during shutdown, you can add the constant `persistState` defined via `IWorkbench.PERSIST_STATE` to the `persistedState` of the model element.

You can change the application via your code by changing the model elements. The Eclipse platform has listeners registered on most parts of the model, and updates the application if you change the model.

The persisted state of the application model can be deleted at the start of your application using the *clearPersistedState* parameter as a launch parameter. In most cases, this is undesirable behavior for an exported application and is only used during development.

Comparison with Eclipse 3.x

The programming model of Eclipse 3.x primarily uses extension points to define contributions to the application. These extensions define new parts, new menus, etc. In modern Eclipse applications you use fragments and processors.

15.2. Model fragments

A model *fragment* is a file that typically ends with the *.e4xmi* extension. It specifies additional model elements and which model element it extends. For example, a fragment can contribute a new menu containing several new menu entries to the main menu of the application.

In the fragment the *Feature Name* is a link to the model element that you want to extend. The following table lists some *Feature Name* values and their purposes.

Table 4. Contribution, Feature Name and Element id

You want to contribute to a	Feature Name	Element Id
Command to the application	commands	ID of your application
Handler to the application	handlers	ID of your application
New MenuItem / HandledMenuItem to existing menu	children	ID of the menu
New menu to the main menu of the window	children	ID of your main menu
New Part to existing PartStack	children	ID of your PartStack

If you want to contribute to an element of the application model you can:

- specify the ID of the element to which you are contributing

- use an XPath expression to describe the model element that should be extended

The following table gives several examples of how you can use XPath expressions to define the model element you want to extend.

Table 5. Sample XPaths for the Application Model

XPath	Element in Application Model
xpath:/	The slash (/) always addresses the root element of an XML file, which is always the MApplication element.
xpath://mainMenu	Contribute to the main menu.
xpath://mainMenu/children	Contribute to all children of the main menu, e.g., to every menu in it.
xpath://mainMenu/*[1]	Contribute to the first child of the main menu. In most applications this would be the menu:File menu.
xpath://mainMenu/[@[local-name()='type' and .='menu:Menu']]	Contribute to the first menu of the main menu. This XPath is more detailed than the one above since it requires that the main menu child is of type *menu:Menu*. In most applications this would be the menu:File menu.
xpath://trimBars[@side="Bottom"]	Contribute to the bottom trimbar.
xpath://trimBars[not(@side)]	Contribute to the top trimbar. When the `MTrimBar` is on top the side attribute is omitted, therefore `not(@side)` is used.
xpath://children[@*[local-name()='type' and .='basic:Part']]	Contribute to a `MPart`.
xpath://children[@*[local-name()='type' and .='basic:Part']][./tags = 'Editor']	Contribute to a `MPart` that is tagged with the *Editor* tag.

15.3. Position of new model elements

Fragments define the desired position of new model elements via the *Position in List* attribute. The following values are allowed:

Table 6. Position in list

Value	Description
first	Positions the element at the beginning of the list.
index:theIndex	Places the new model elements at position *theIndex*. Example: *index:0*
before:theOtherElementsId	Places the new model elements before the model element with the ID *theOtherElementsId*.
after:theOtherElementsId	Places the new model elements after the model element with the ID *theOtherElementsId*.

Fragments of independent plug-ins are processed in the order of the dependencies in the `MANIFEST.MF` file. Therefore, the use of first and index might not always give the desired result.

15.4. Model processors

With a *processor* you can modify the application model via program code during the start of the application. This enables the dynamic creation, removal or modification of model elements.

15.5. Exercises

You will practice the usage of model fragments in Chapter 157 and processors in Chapter 159.

16. Eclipse spies

16.1. Model spy for the application model

The application model of an Eclipse application is available at runtime. The application can access the model and change it via a defined API.

To analyze and modify the runtime model, you can use the model spy, which allows you to modify the application model interactively. This tool is called *Model Spy* and can be integrated into your RCP application. Most changes are directly applied, e.g., if you change the orientation of a part sash container, your user interface is updated automatically.

In the model spy, you can select a part in the application model, right-click on it and select *Show Control* to get the part highlighted.

> *Model spy and the Eclipse IDE*
>
> If installed, you can use the model spy to see the application model of the running Eclipse IDE itself. You can open it via the `Alt` + `Shift` + `F9` shortcut.

> If you modify the Eclipse IDE model, you should be careful as this might put the running Eclipse IDE into a bad state. To fix such issues, start the Eclipse IDE from the command line with the *-clearPersistedState* parameter.

16.2. Context spy

The context spy allows you to see the key-value pairs that are available for dependency injection. Therefore, you can use it to see the content of the `IEclipseContext`.

16.3. Preference Spy for tracing preference changes

The *Preference Spy* provides a way to trace preference value changes. The Preference Spy is part of the PDE tools.

You can open the Preference Spy with the `Shift` + `Alt` + `F11` shortcut or via **Window › Spies... › Preference Spy...**.

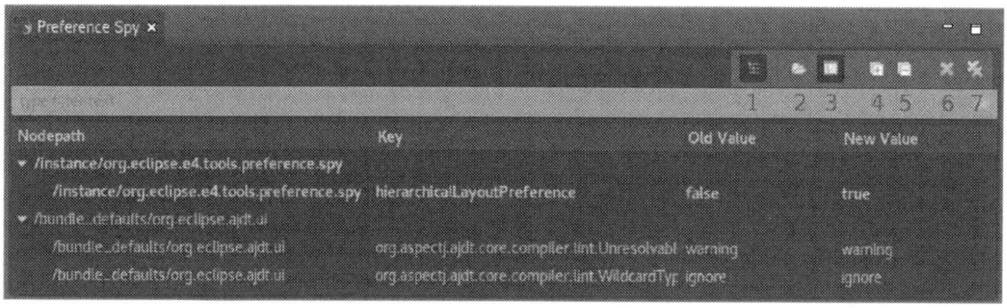

In the upper right corner, you see the controls for the Preference Spy. They can be used to:

1. toggle between flat and hierarchical layout
2. show all preferences
3. toggle tracing preferences changes
4. expand all preferences
5. collapse all preferences
6. remove entry from view
7. remove all entries from view

On the picture you see the hierarchical layout. Furthermore, tracing of preferences changes is enabled. The bold entries depict the recently changed preferences with the old and new value. The non bold entries are any other preferences that can be shown by pressing the button to show all preferences (2).

17. Exercise: Creating the base for a task management application

In this exercise, you create a standard Eclipse plug-in. Afterwards, you convert the generated plug-in into an Eclipse RCP application. This plug-in is used as the basis for your user interface components.

Depending on your previous work, you may see additional or fewer projects compared to the screenshots.

To avoid confusion with earlier generated projects, you may want to close them. Closed projects are ignored during development. To close a project, right-click on it and select *Close Project* from the context menu. To open it again, right-click on it again and select *Open Project*.

Do not close the project that contains your target definition file; otherwise your target platform will become invalid.

17.1. Creating a plug-in project

Create a new plug-in project via the **File › New › Other... › Plug-in Development › Plug-in Project** menu entry with the `com.vogella.tasks.ui` name.

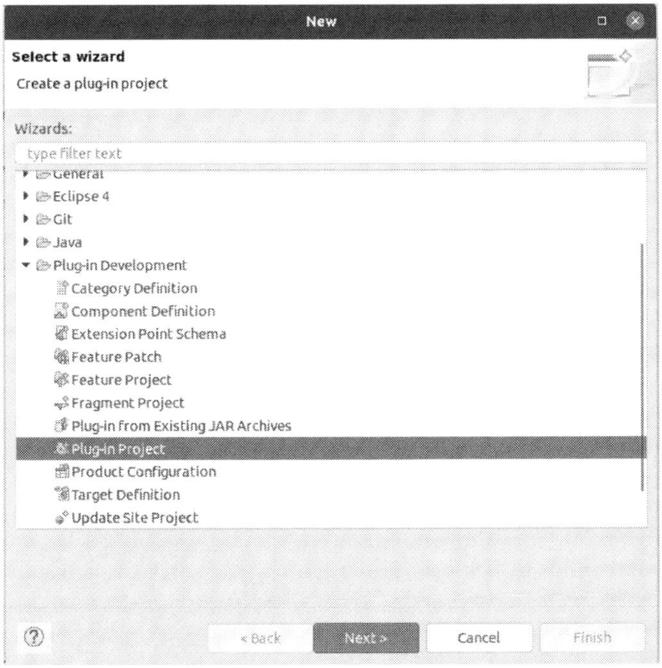

On the first wizard page enter *com.vogella.tasks.ui* as project name and press the Next button.

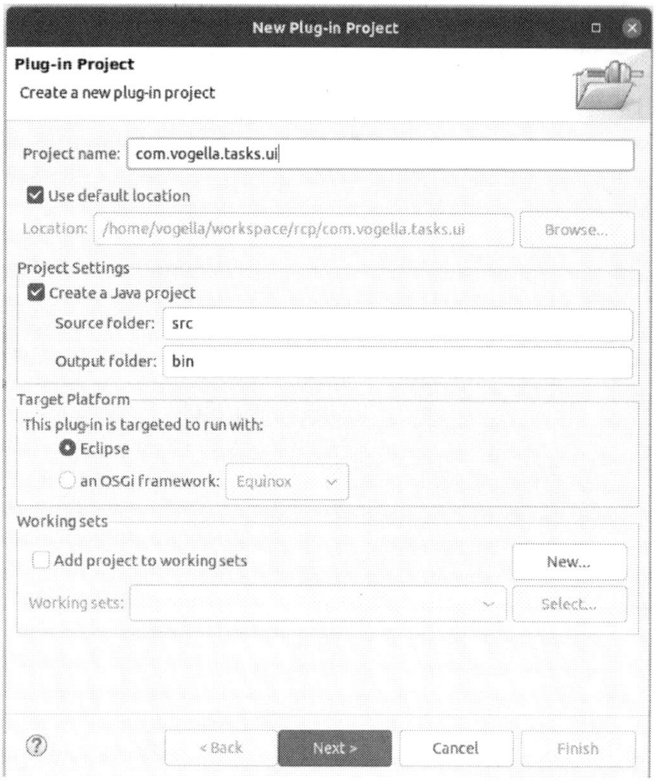

On the next wizard page ensure that the following settings are made:

- Select *No* at the *Would you like to create a rich client application?* option
- Uncheck the *This plug-in will make contributions to the UI* option
- Uncheck the *Generate an activator* option

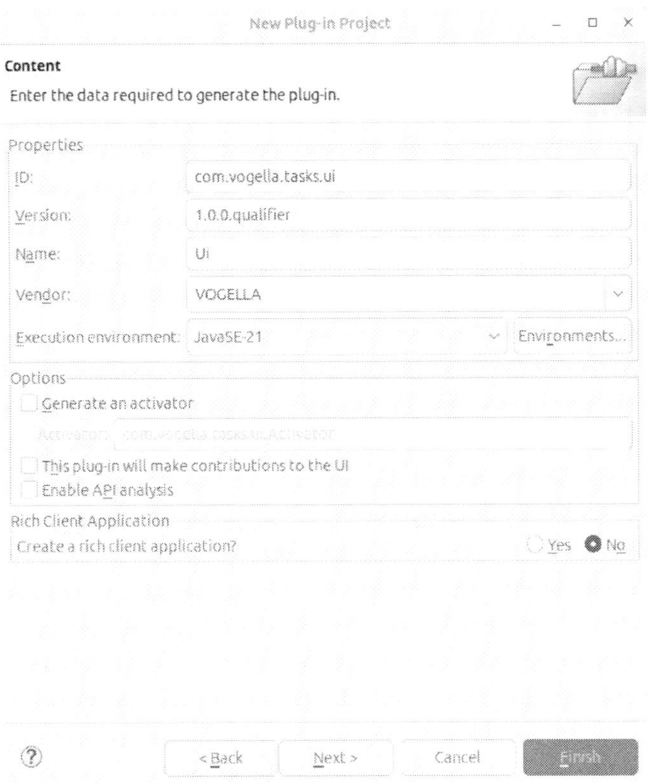

Press the Finish button.

If you click the Next button instead of Finish, the wizard shows you a template selection page. Do NOT select a template and finish the wizard.

17.2. Review the generated project

Open the project and verify that the *src* folder contains no Java classes.

Open the `META-INF\MANIFEST.MF` file. In the manifest editor switch to the *Dependencies* tab and ensure that there are no entries.

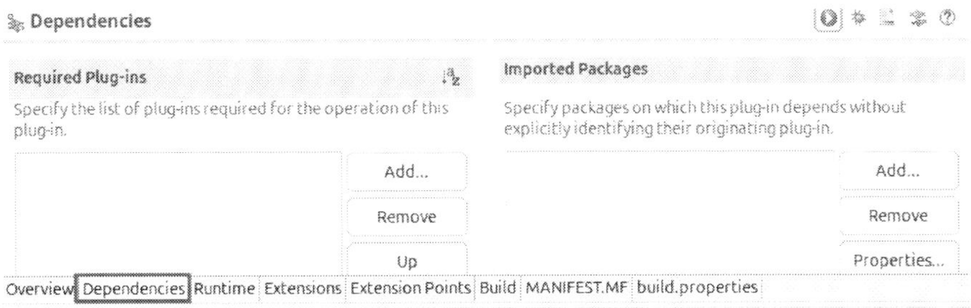

17.3. Create a feature project

Create a new feature project named *com.vogella.tasks.feature* via **File › New › Other... › Plug-in Development › Feature Project**.

You can press the Finish button on the first wizard page.

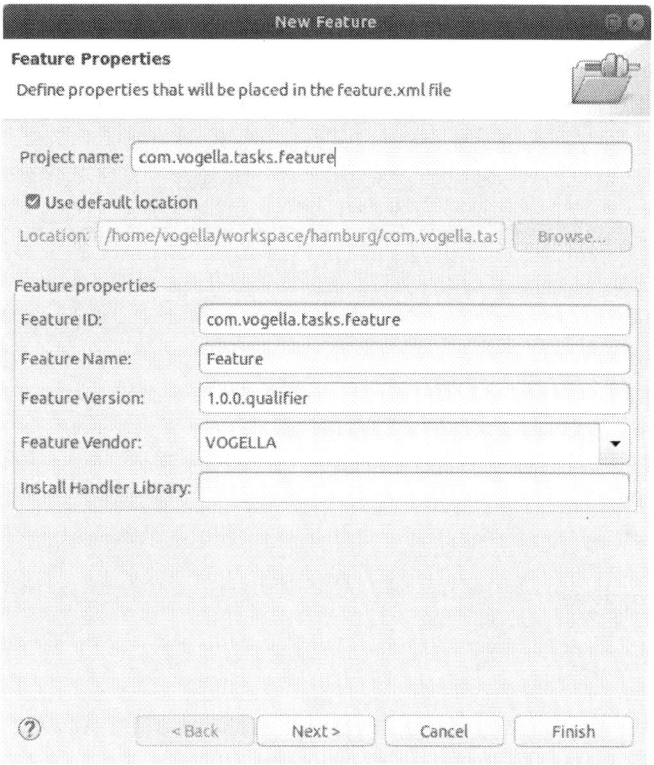

Afterwards, select the *Included Plug-ins* tab in the editor of the *feature.xml* file. Press the Add... button and include the `com.vogella.tasks.ui` plug-in into this feature.

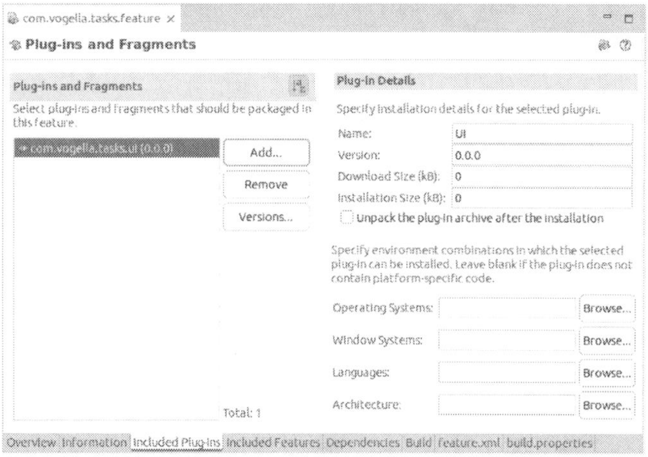

Ensure you have added the plug-in on the *Included Plug-ins* tab to include it in your feature. Using the *Dependencies* tab is incorrect for this exercise.

17.4. Create a project to host the product configuration file

Create a new project named *com.vogella.tasks.product* via the **File › New › Other... › General › Project** menu entry.

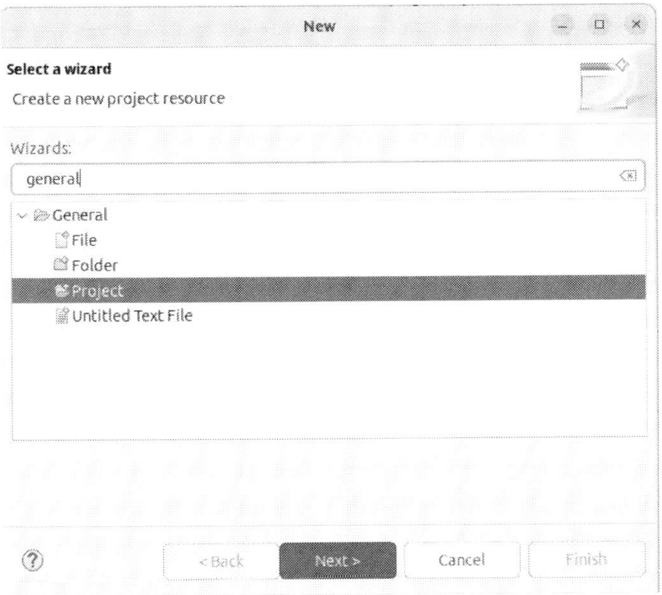

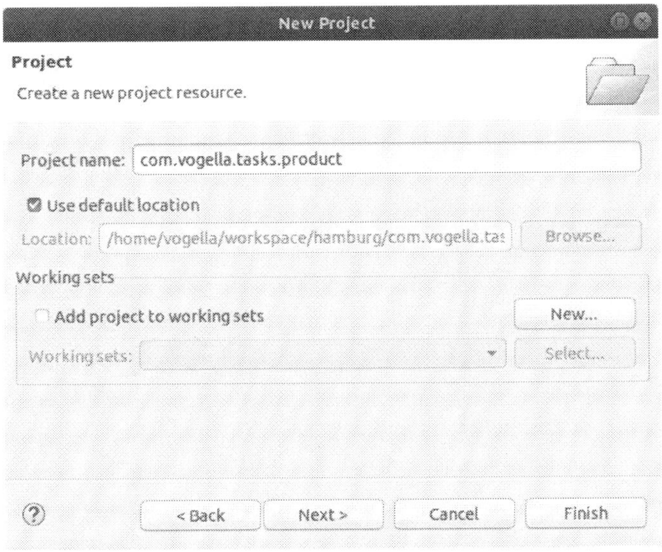

Press Finish.

17.5. Create a product configuration file

Right-click on the *com.vogella.tasks.product* project and select **New › Other... › Plug-in Development › Product Configuration**.

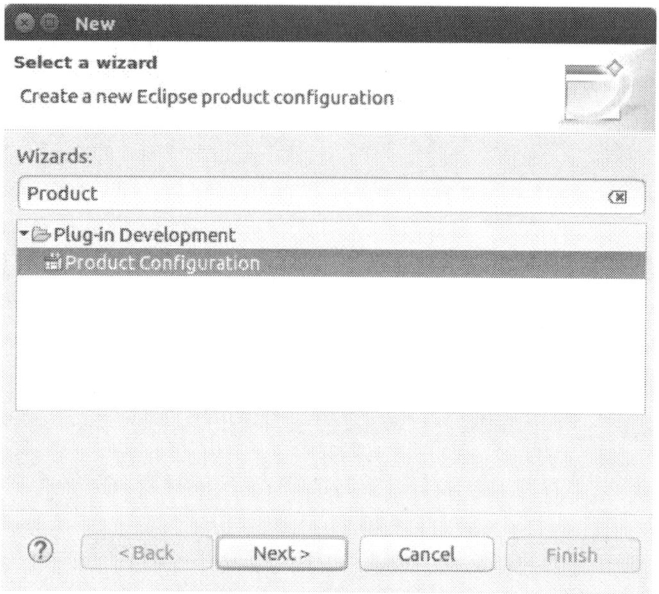

Create a product configuration file named *taskmanagement.product* inside the *com.vogella.tasks.product* folder.

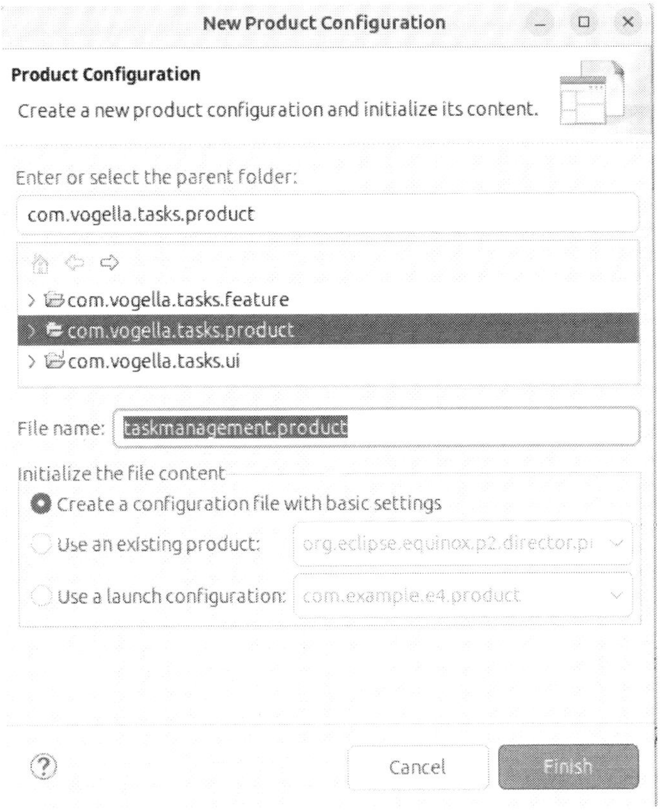

Press the Finish button. The file is created and opened in an editor.

Press the New... button on the *Overview* tab of the product editor.

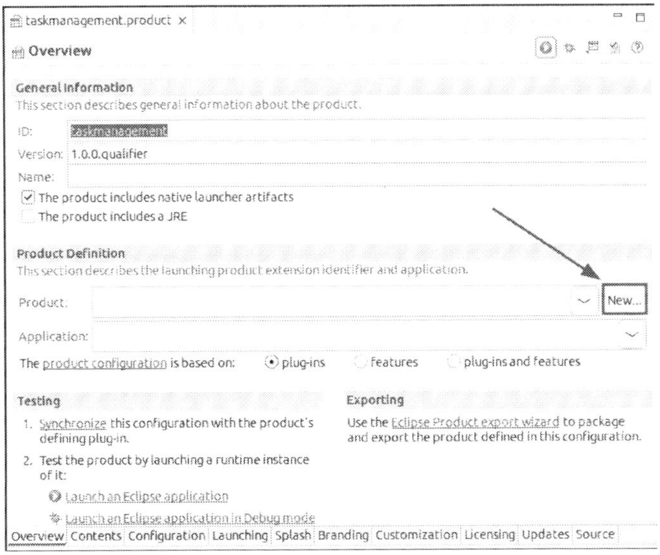

Use the following data:

- `taskmanagement` as the *Product Name*
- `com.vogella.tasks.ui` as the *Defining Plug-in*
- `product` as the *Product ID*
- `org.eclipse.e4.ui.workbench.swt.E4Application` in the *Application* combo box.

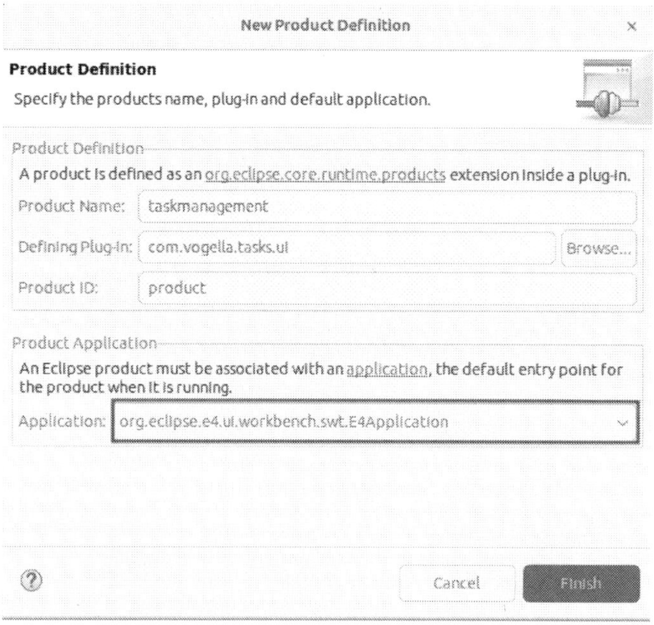

Ensure that an ID, version, and name are set. Version should be set to `1.0.0`. Also ensure that you have selected that the product configuration is based on *plug-ins and features*.

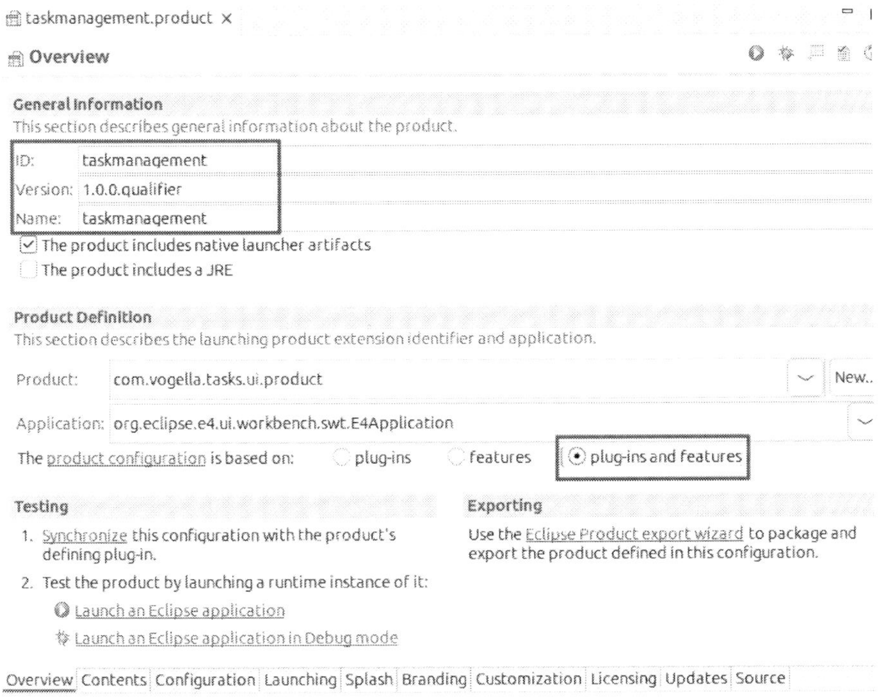

17.6. Enter the feature as content into the product

Select the *Contents* tab and add the following features via the Add Feature... button.

- `org.eclipse.e4.rcp`
- `com.vogella.tasks.feature`

The expected output is shown in the screenshot below.

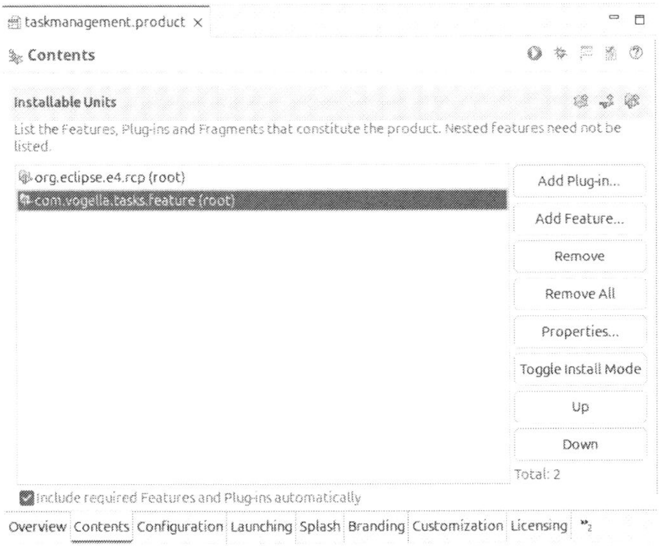

17.7. Configure the start levels

Switch to the *Configuration* tab in the product editor and press the Add Recommended... button. These settings are, for example, used by the Maven/Tycho build system; hence, it is good practice to configure them.

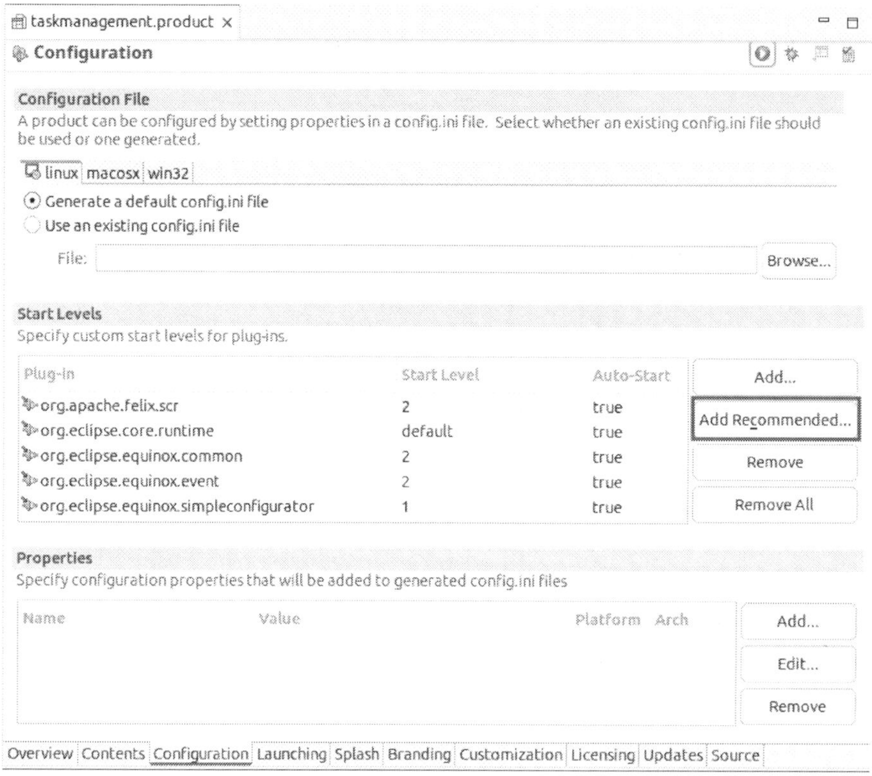

17.8. Create an application model

Create an application model file in your `com.vogella.tasks.ui` plug-in via the **File › New › Other... › Eclipse 4 › Model › New Application Model** menu entry.

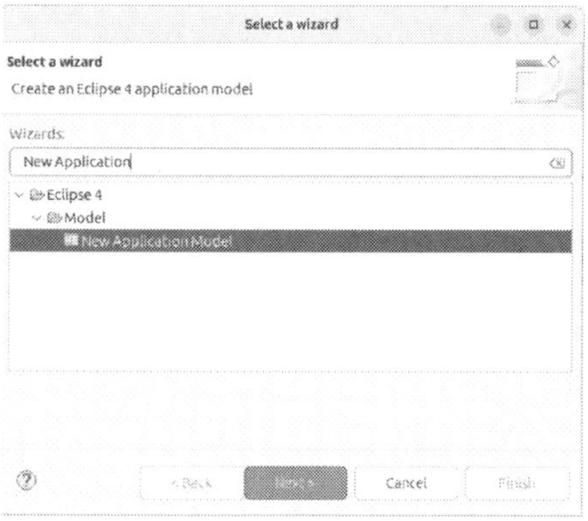

Enter your `com.vogella.tasks.ui` application plug-in as the container and use the file name suggested by the wizard.

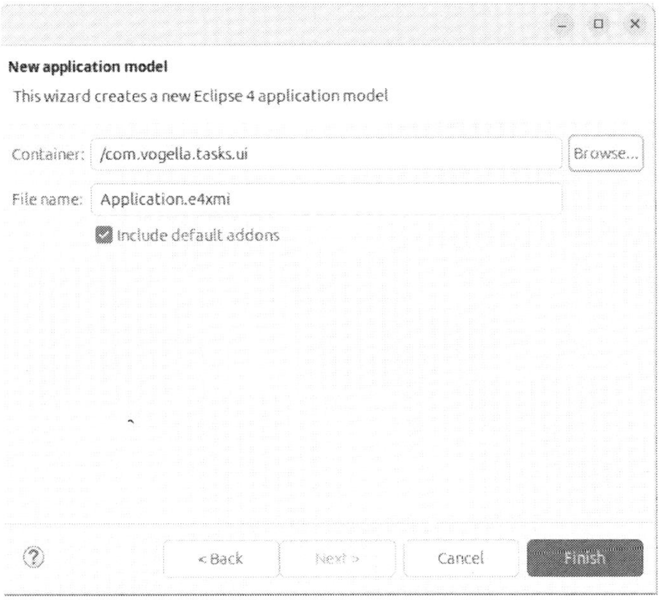

Press the Finish button to create the application model file and to open it in an editor.

17.9. Add a window to the application model

Add one window to your application model.

Right-click on the *Windows* node, and select `Trimmed Window` as depicted in the following screenshot.

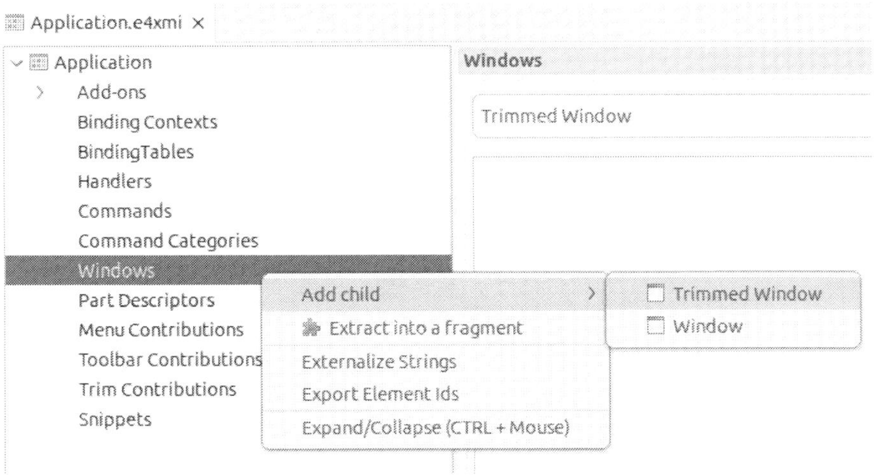

Enter the `com.vogella.tasks.ui.trimmedwindow.taskmanager` ID, the position and size of the window, and a label as shown in the screenshot below.

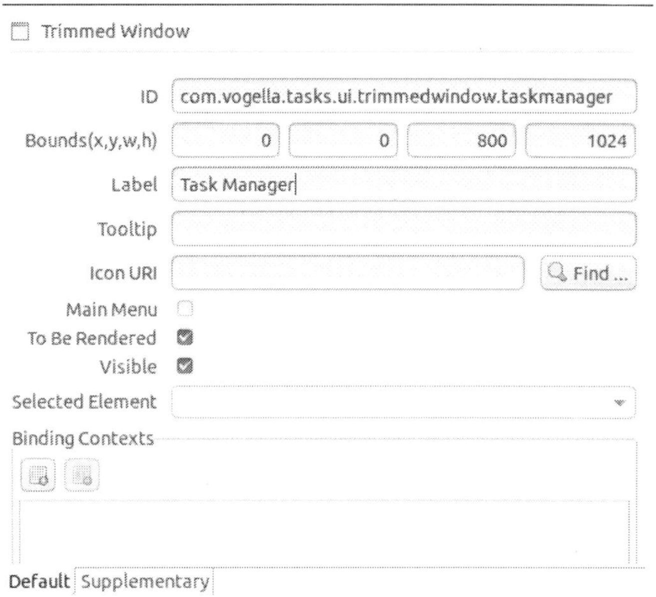

17.10. Delete persisted UI state at startup

If you start and close your application, the last state of the application is persisted by the framework and restored the next time you start this application. This is undesirable during development, as the latest state from the application model file should be used. To ensure that the latest version of your application model is always used, add the following parameter to your product file on the *Launching* tab.

```
-clearPersistedState
```

The following screenshot shows this setting in the product configuration file.

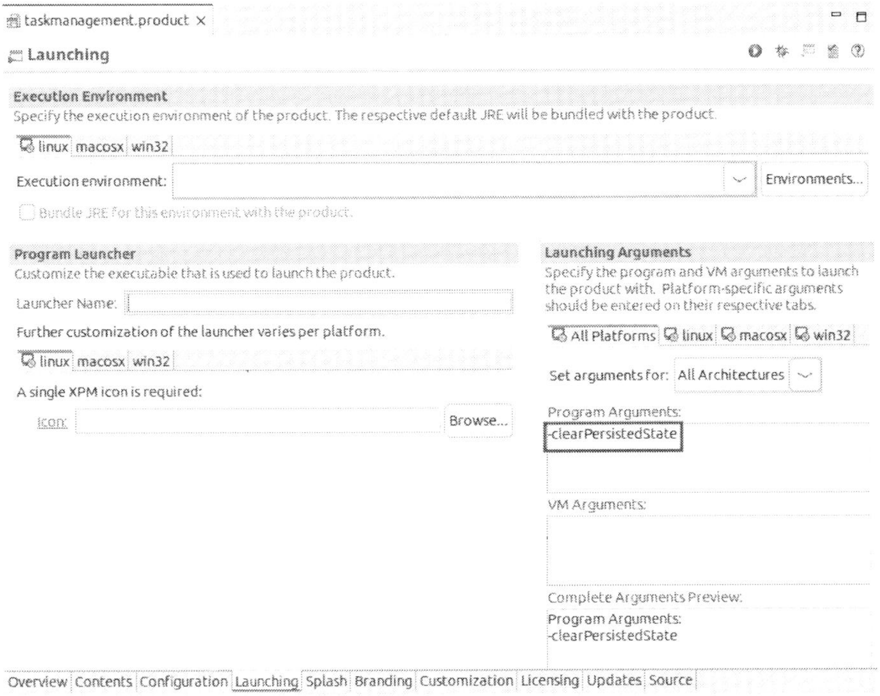

Ensure that you used the - sign and that the parameter is typed correctly. It must be: *-clearPersistedState*

17.11. Set the launcher name

Your command line build, which you will configure later, should create an executable named *Taskman*. On the *Launching* tab of your product file, enter *Taskman* in the *Launcher Name* field.

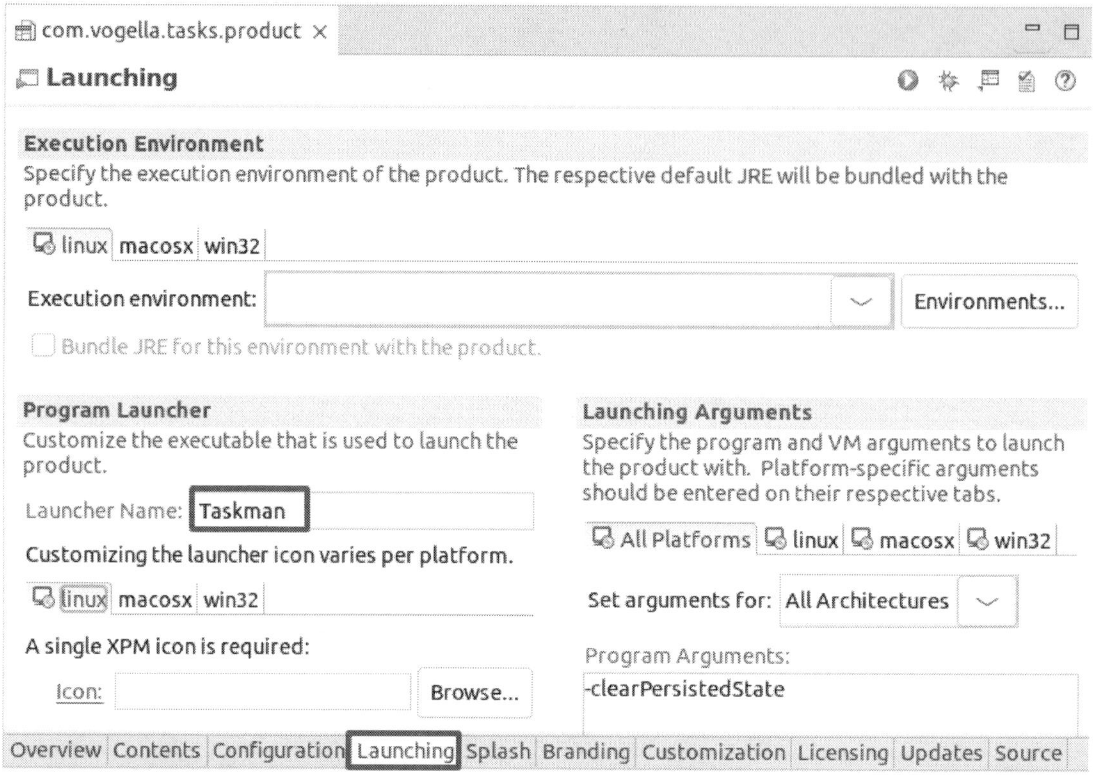

17.12. Start the application and validate the result

Open the product file and select the *Overview* tab. Press the *Launch an Eclipse application* hyperlink in the *Testing* section.

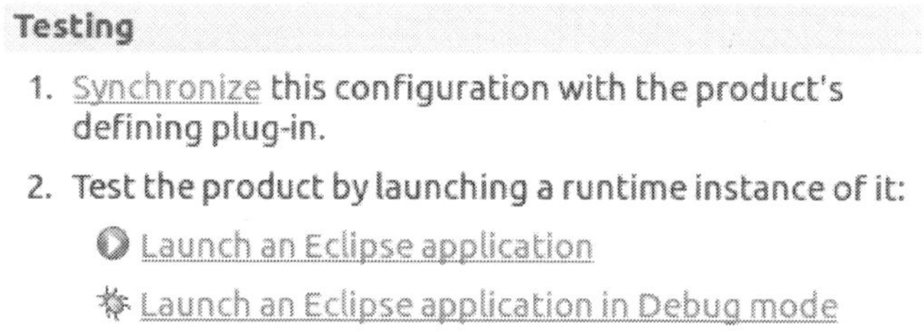

Validate that your application starts. You should see an empty window that can be moved, resized, minimized, maximized, and closed.

18. Exercise: Create the user interface building blocks

18.1. Desired user interface

In this exercise, you create the basis of the application user interface. At the end of this exercise, your user interface should look similar to the following screenshot.

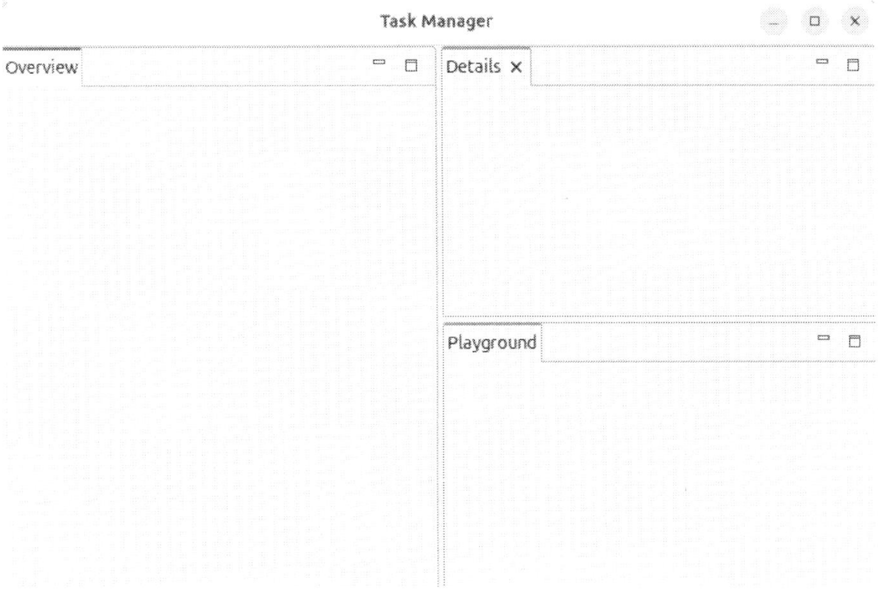

Open the *Application.e4xmi* file in the *Eclipse model editor* via a double-click or right-click on it and select the **Open With** menu.

18.1.1. Add part sash and part stack containers

Select *Controls* below the window and add a part sash container element.

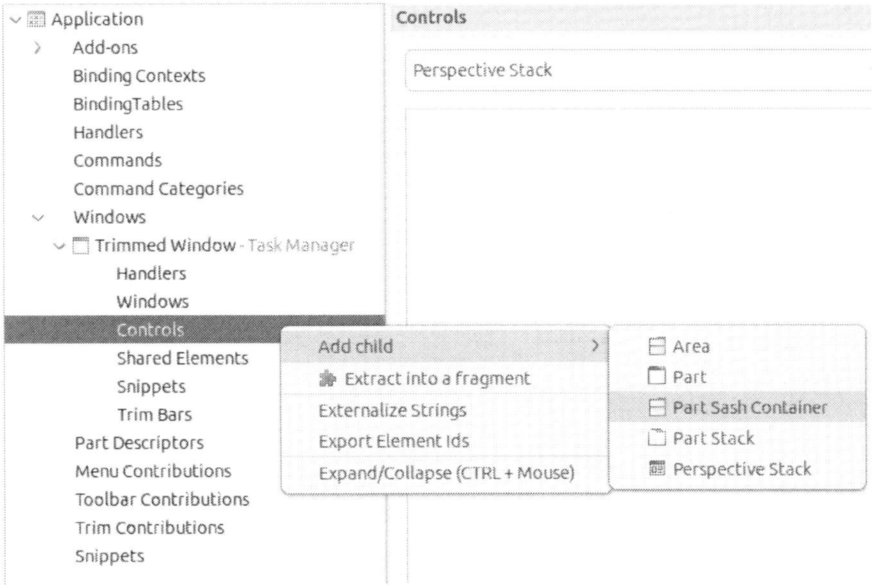

Change its *Orientation* attribute to *Horizontal* and enter the *com.vogella.tasks.ui.partsashcontainer.main* value into the ID field.

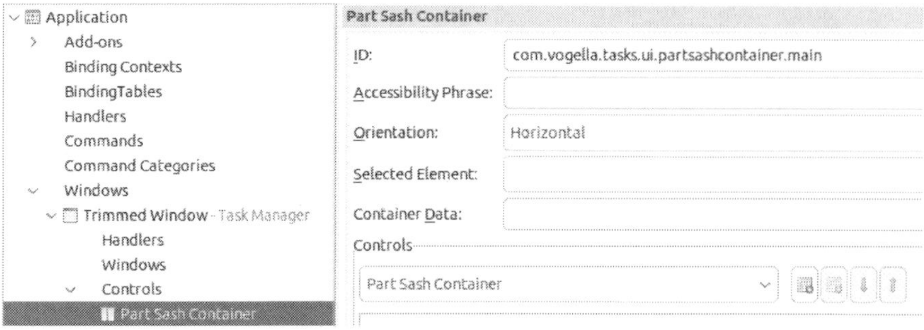

Add a **part stack** as the first child to your part sash container element.

Reselect the parent part sash container and add a **part sash container** element. Add two part stacks to this new element.

After these changes, your application model should look similar to the following screenshot.

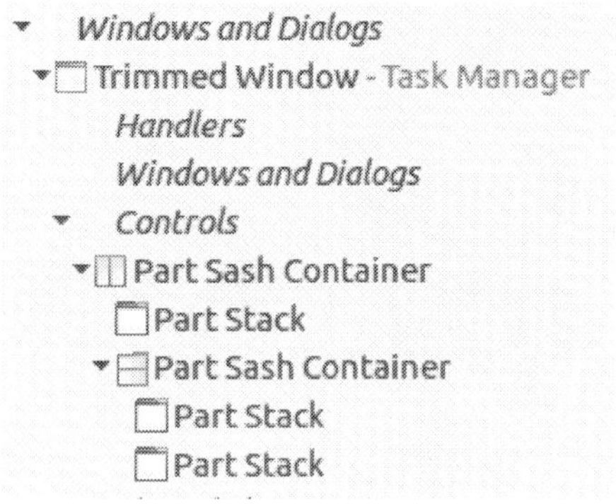

18.1.2. Create the parts

Add one part to each stack, via right-clicking on each part stack and selecting the **Add Child › Part** menu entry. Use the IDs and labels from the following table.

> Enter the name first. The ID should be adjusted based on the name if the label was empty.

Table 7. Label and ID for the parts

Label	ID Suffix
Overview	com.vogella.tasks.ui.part.overview
Details	com.vogella.tasks.ui.part.details
Playground	com.vogella.tasks.ui.part.playground

The final structure of your application model should be similar to the following screenshot. In the screenshot, the overview part is selected in the tree, and hence you see its data.

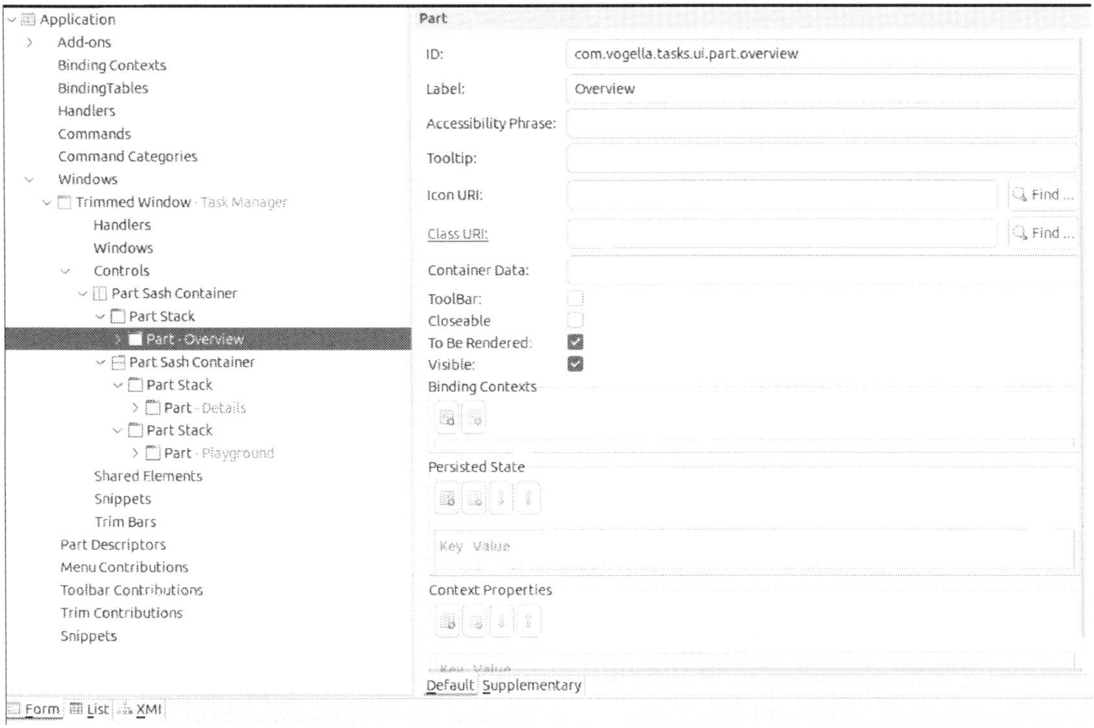

18.1.3. Validate the user interface

Start your product and validate that the user interface looks as planned. See Section 18.1 for the desired result.

Reassign your model elements, if required. The model editor supports drag and drop for reassignment.

Also note that you can already see the structure, even though you have not created any Java classes so far.

18.2. Define the API that can be used

To use classes from other plug-ins in a plug-in, you need to add dependencies to them in the `MANIFEST.MF` file of the plug-in. In this exercise, you will prepare to use classes from another plug-in.

Open the *META-INF/MANIFEST.MF* file in your `com.vogella.tasks.ui` plug-in and select the *Dependencies* tab. Use the Add... button in the *Required Plug-ins* section to add the following plug-ins as dependencies:

- `org.eclipse.core.runtime`
- `org.eclipse.jface`
- `org.eclipse.e4.core.di`
- `org.eclipse.e4.ui.workbench`
- `org.eclipse.e4.ui.di`
- `org.eclipse.e4.core.di.extensions`
- `org.eclipse.e4.core.contexts`

> The `org.eclipse.jface` plug-in also provides access to the `org.eclipse.swt` plug-in (as it re-exports its packages).

Use the Add... button in the *Imported Packages* section to add the following plug-ins as dependencies:

- `jakarta.annotation`
- `jakarta.inject`

The result should be similar to the following screenshot (version may differ).

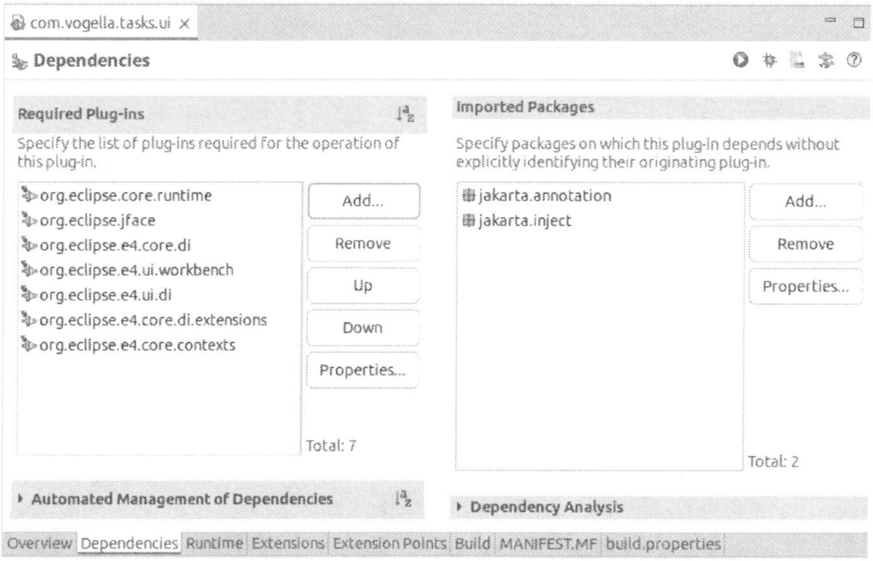

> The added version numbers are minimum versions, allowing you to use a newer version of the plug-in while preventing the use of an older version that may lack the required API.

You can see the resulting changes on the *MANIFEST.MF* tab of the manifest editor. The following is a potential solution (plug-in versions have been removed from the listing)

```
Manifest-Version: 1.0
Bundle-ManifestVersion: 2
Bundle-Name: Ui
Bundle-SymbolicName: com.vogella.tasks.ui;singleton:=true
Bundle-Version: 1.0.0.qualifier
Bundle-Vendor: VOGELLA
Automatic-Module-Name: com.vogella.tasks.ui
Bundle-RequiredExecutionEnvironment: JavaSE-21
Require-Bundle: org.eclipse.core.runtime,
 org.eclipse.jface,
 org.eclipse.e4.core.di,
 org.eclipse.e4.ui.workbench,
 org.eclipse.e4.ui.di,
 org.eclipse.e4.core.di.extensions,
 org.eclipse.e4.core.contexts
Import-Package: jakarta.annotation,
 jakarta.inject
```

18.3. Create Java classes and connect with the parts

18.3.1. Create a new package and some Java classes

Create the `com.vogella.tasks.ui.parts` package in the application plug-in.

Create the following three Java classes in this package:

- *TodoOverviewPart*
- *TodoDetailsPart*
- *PlaygroundPart*

These classes should not extend another class, nor should they implement any interface.

You can create the classes by clicking on the *Class URI* hyperlink in the detail pane of the model editor for the part. This connects the created class to the model object. If you do this, you can skip Section 18.3.2.

Add a constructor to each class that prints the class name to the console. The following code shows the `TodoDetailsPart` class.

```
package com.vogella.tasks.ui.parts;

public class TodoDetailsPart {
    public TodoDetailsPart() {
        System.out.println(this.getClass().getSimpleName());
```

```
    }
}
```

18.3.2. Connect the Java classes with the parts

In your application model connect the class with the corresponding part model element. You can do this via the *Class URI* property of the part model element.

> The model editor allows you to search for an existing class via the Find... button. The initial list of *Contribution Classes* is empty, start typing in the *Class Name* field to see the results.

The following table gives an overview of which elements should be connected.

Table 8. Mapping Java classes with part model element

Class	Part ID suffix
TodoOverviewPart	com.vogella.tasks.ui.part.overview
TodoDetailsPart	com.vogella.tasks.ui.part.details
PlaygroundPart	com.vogella.tasks.ui.part.playground

The following screenshot shows the result for the overview part.

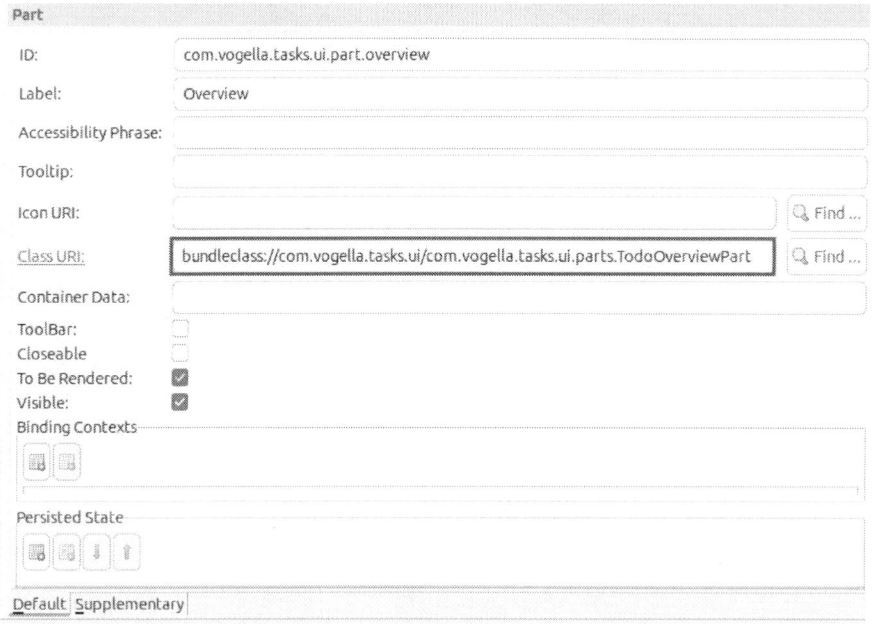

18.3.3. Validate

Start your application. It should start, but you should see no difference in the user interface.

To validate the creation of model objects at runtime, check the *Console* view for `System.out.println()` output.

19. Exercise: Use icons within the application

19.1. Get icons from the Eclipse IDE

You can use the *Plug-in Image Browser* view to get icons from Eclipse. Use `Ctrl` + `3`, type *Plug-in Image Browser*, and press Enter to open the view.

You can search for an icon, and if you select it, use the save button to save it. In the screenshot, we select the save icon and save it to our workspace via the toolbar. Since the 2025-09 release, the view also supports SVG files.

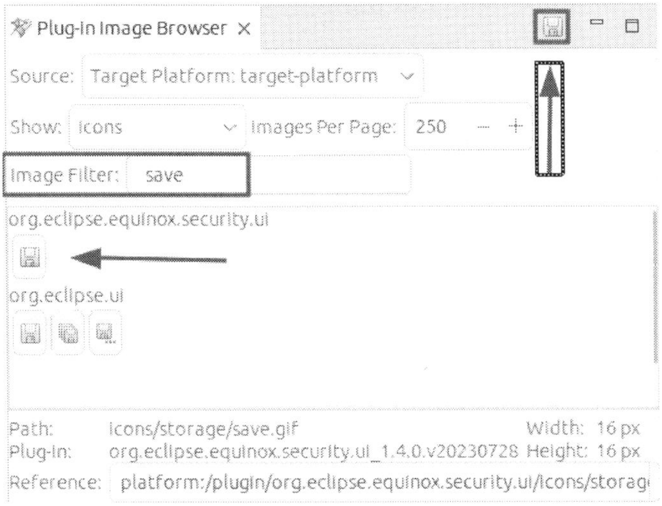

19.2. Use icons from outside Eclipse

Use the Internet to find attractive icons for your parts. For example, at the time of this writing, a great source for modern-looking icons is the Google Fonts [https://fonts.google.com/icons] webpage. As of the Eclipse 2025-06 release, SVG files can be used in Eclipse. Before this release, only PNG and GIF files were supported.

> If you are using a release older than Eclipse 2025-06, you can use your favorite graphical editor to manually create 16×16px and 32×32px PNG versions of this SVG. Use the `@2x.png` suffix for the 32×32px version of the file. This naming convention allows the Eclipse framework to automatically select the appropriate version for HiDPI screens.

Copy the images into a new folder named `img` in the `com.vogella.tasks.ui` project.

Refer to your new icons using the `Icon URI` property in the part.

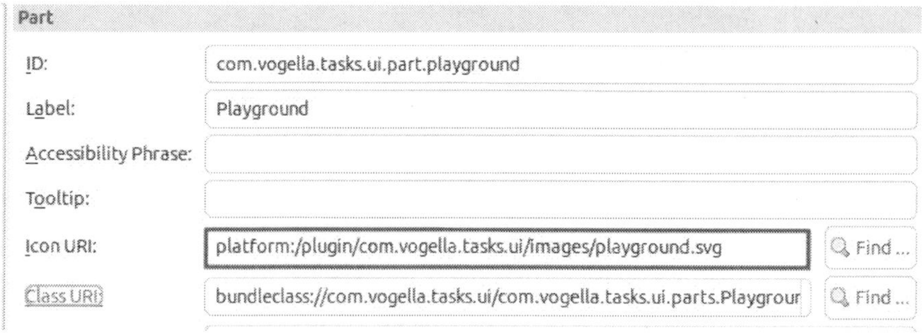

If you restart your application, the parts should use your new icons.

19.3. Ensure that icons are exported

Verify that the icons are included in your export by checking the *build* tab of the `build.properties` file. Add the necessary file paths, if they are missing.

20. Optional exercise: Use the model spy

In this exercise, you will add the model spy to your Eclipse application. The model spy is a development tool to see your current application model and to modify it at runtime.

> The spies are debugging tools and are not intended for use in a production application. As a result, this exercise might not work, or you may see additional exceptions in your log file caused by the tool.

20.1. Add the spies to the target platform

Add the spy feature to your target platform so that you can add this feature to your application. Add new entries to your target platform to make the spies available.

> You may have multiple additional entries in this file, for example if you added the JDT tools to your target file, you would see an entry for `org.eclipse.jdt.feature.group`.

```
<?xml version="1.0" encoding="UTF-8" standalone="no"?>
<?pde version="3.8"?>
<target name="target-platform">
    <locations>
        <!-- all your old entries should stay here -->

        <!-- add these new entries. We use a new location entry but you could add them to
the existing entry-->
        <location includeAllPlatforms="false" includeConfigurePhase="true"
includeMode="planner" includeSource="true" type="InstallableUnit">
            <repository location="https://download.eclipse.org/releases/latest"/>
                <unit id="org.eclipse.pde.spies.feature.group"/>
        </location>
    </locations>
</target>
```

Reload the target platform after this change by clicking the Reload Target Platform button on the *Definition* tab of the target definition editor.

20.2. Add a top level menu entry to the window

Add a main menu to your window. This can be done via the `Main Menu` property on the window application model.

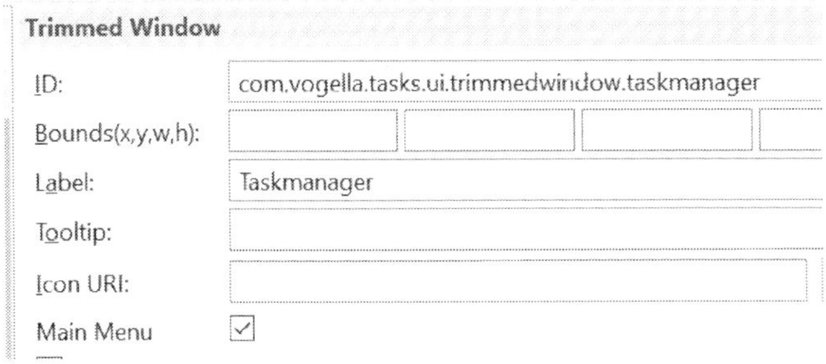

Ensure that the menu ID is set to `org.eclipse.ui.main.menu`.

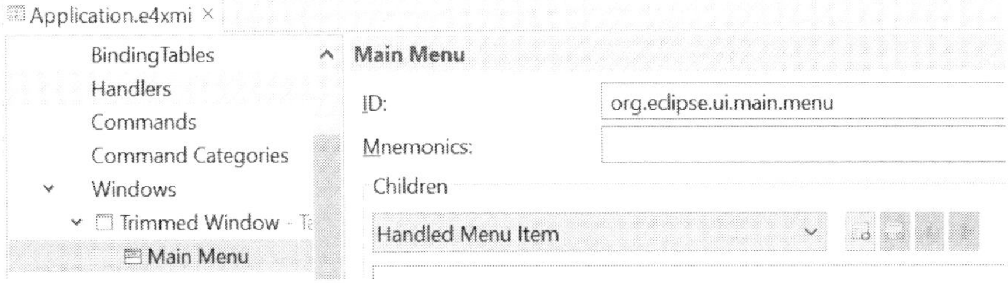

20.3. Add the model spy to the runtime configuration

Open the run configuration of your product via the **Run › Run Configurations...** menu entry.

Switch to the plug-ins tab and select the *Launch with: Plug-ins selected below* option.

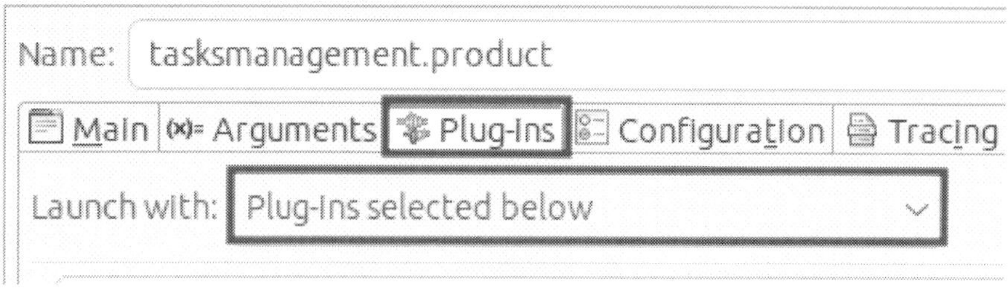

Add the `org.eclipse.pde.spy.model` plug-in.

Press the Validate Plug-ins button to ensure that all dependencies are included. If something is reported as missing, you can add the missing plug-ins via the Select Required button.

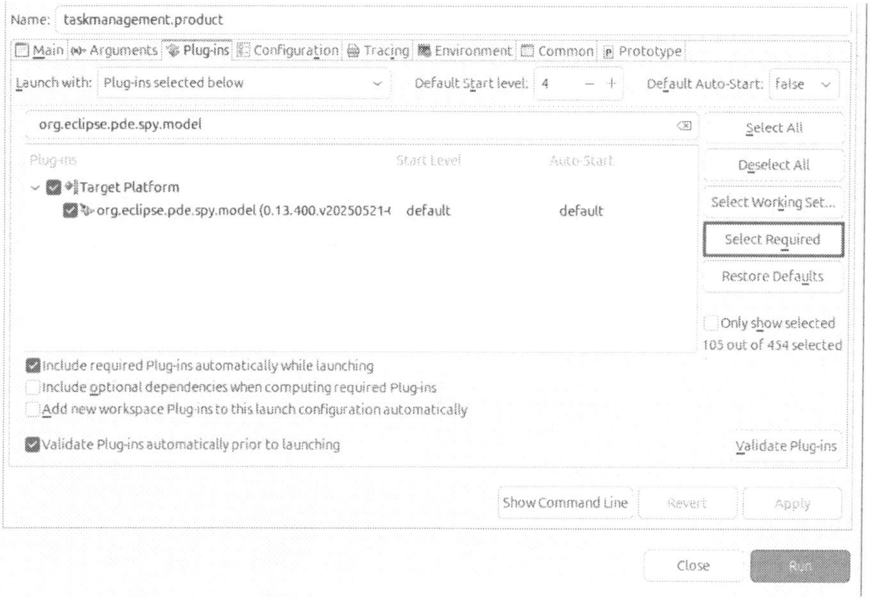

Then, click Apply and Run.

20.4. Opening the model spy in the application

After you have added the new plug-ins to your run configuration press the Run button in the run configuration you just added.

Do not start the application now via the product. Starting via the product resets your changes in the runtime configuration.

INFO: See the next section for possible errors in case you cannot open the model spy in your application.

To display the model spy, use the **Window › Spies › Model Spy** menu entry.

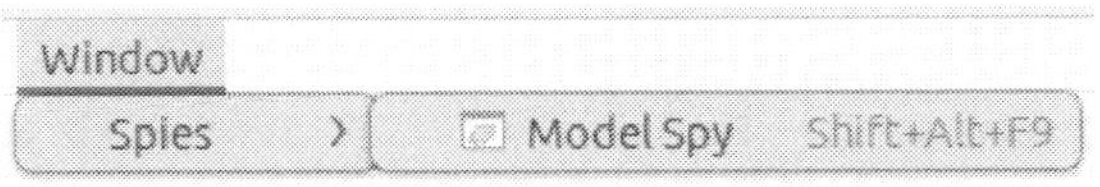

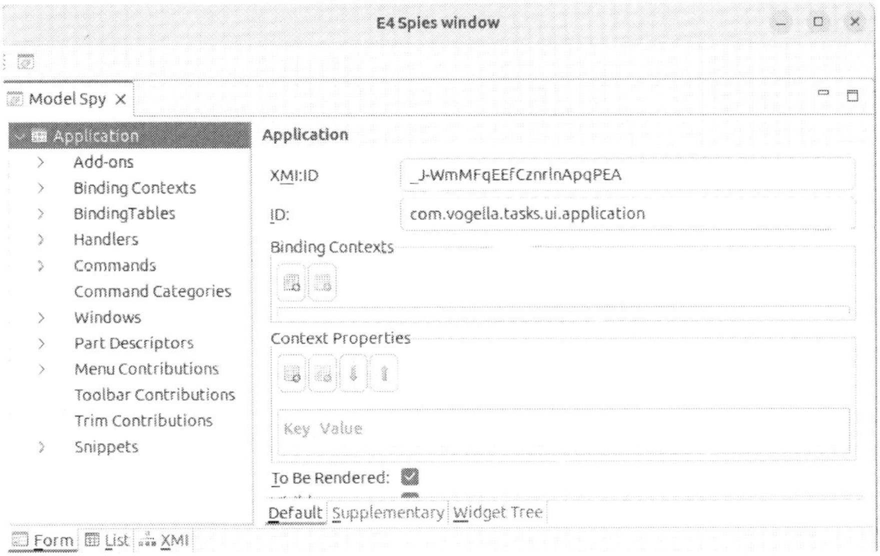

Use the model spy to change the runtime application model.

> Setting the `toBeRendered` element to false destroys the element. If you do this for the application or the last window, the application will shut down. If you do not use the `-clearPersistedState` flag, this state will be restored at the next start, e.g., at restart, your application will shut down again.

For example, add a part (with a label) or change the size of the window. All changes should become immediately visible (except changes for new menu entries, due to a bug).

20.5. Remove model spy from the run configuration

After testing with the tool enabled, start your application again from your product configuration file to remove the model spy plug-in from your run configuration.

> If you leave the model spy included in your run configuration, it might cause side effects. For example, in the past it created exceptions if key bindings were present in the application.

21. Optional exercise: Use the context spy

In this exercise, you add the context spy to your application.

The spies are debugging tools and are not intended to be used in a production application. It might happen that this exercise does not work, or that you see additional exceptions in your log file, caused by the tool.

21.1. Ensure that spies are available in the target platform

If you skipped the previous exercise, you need to add the spies to your target platform. Your target platform file should contain the following entry.

```
<unit id="org.eclipse.pde.spies.feature.group"/>
```

21.2. Add the context spy to the runtime

Add `org.eclipse.pde.spy.context` to your launch configuration via **Run › Run Configurations...** and the *Plug-ins* tab.

Start your application with this launch configuration.

If something is reported as missing, you can add the missing plug-ins via the Select Required button. Press the Validate Plug-ins button to ensure that all dependencies are included.

21.3. Opening the context spy in the application

In your RCP application, you can open the context spy via the **Window › Spies › Context spy** menu entry. Select one of the tree entries in the context spy view to see the key-value pairs provided by the context.

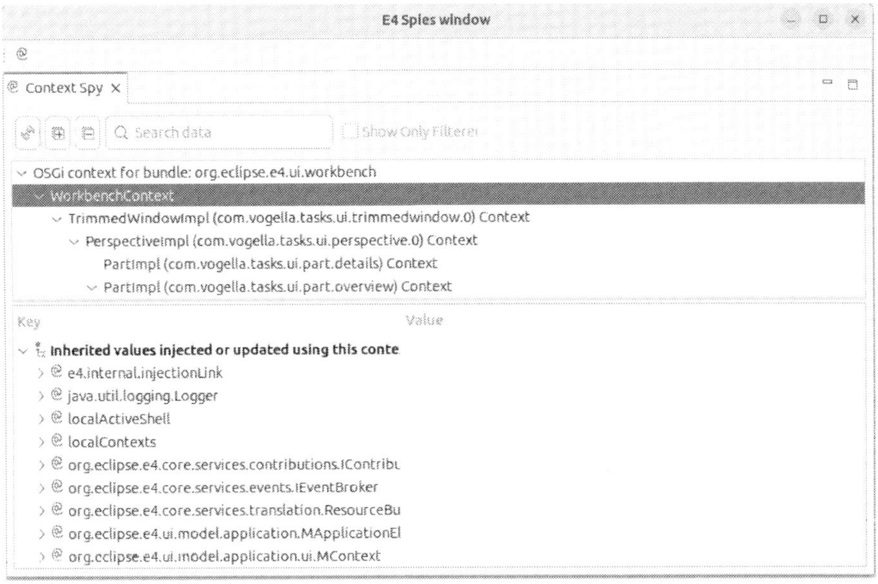

After you finish testing with the context spy, please remove it again from the launch configuration. The spies are debugging tools which may result in strange side effects if you include them in your product.

22. Optional exercise: Review the Eclipse application class

During the development of your RCP application, you will often need to look at the Eclipse source code to understand how the framework works. This exercise will help you to get familiar with the Eclipse source code and how to find the relevant classes.

This exercise requires that you have selected the following option **Window › Preferences › Plug-in Development › Include all plug-ins from target in Java workspace scope**.

22.1. Code review questions:

Type `Ctrl` + `Shift` + `T` to open the `E4Application` class.

Review the code and find out:

1. Which method is responsible for loading the `Application.e4xmi` file?
2. Which parameter allows you to reference a file other than `Application.e4xmi`?
3. What class or interface is responsible for reading the `Application.e4xmi`?
4. In which interface is the `clearPersistedState` flag defined?

Try to answer the questions without looking at the solution below.

22.2. Solution: Review the Eclipse application class

Which method is responsible for loading the `Application.e4xmi` file?

Answer: The `E4Application.loadApplicationModel(…)` method is responsible for loading the application model.

Which parameter allows you to reference a file other than `Application.e4xmi`?

Answer: The `-applicationXMI` parameter allows you to override the default file used for the application model.

What class or interface is responsible for reading the `Application.e4xmi`?

Answer: `IModelResourceHandler` from the `org.eclipse.e4.ui.workbench` package.

In which interface is the `clearPersistedState` flag defined?

Answer: `IWorkbench` defines this flag.

Part VI: Using dependency injection

23. Dependency injection in Java

23.1. An introduction to dependency injection

Dependency injection (DI) is a concept in which objects receive their required dependencies from external sources rather than creating them internally. DI can be implemented in any programming language. The general concept behind dependency injection is called **Inversion of Control** (IoC).

A Java class has a dependency on another class if it uses an instance of that class. This is known as a *class dependency*. For example, a class that accesses a logging service has a dependency on the service class.

Ideally, Java classes should be as independent as possible from other Java classes. This improves their reusability and allows them to be tested independently of other classes.

If a Java class creates an instance of another class using the `new` operator, it cannot be easily tested in isolation, as it has a *hard dependency*. The following example demonstrates a class without hard dependencies:

```
package com.vogella.tasks.ui.parts;
```

```java
import java.util.logging.Logger;

public class MyClass {

    private Logger logger;

    public MyClass(Logger logger) {
        this.logger = logger;
        // Write an info log message
        logger.info("This is a log message.");
    }
}
```

> This is a standard Java class. Its only distinguishing characteristic is that it avoids directly creating objects.

A framework class, often referred to as the *dependency container*, can analyze the dependencies of a class. Using this analysis, it can create an instance of the class and inject the required objects into the class's defined dependencies using Java reflection.

By avoiding hard dependencies, a Java class is decoupled from specific implementations, making it easier to test. For example, such a class can be tested in isolation using *mock* objects.

Mock objects (mocks) are substitutes that mimic the behavior of real objects. Unlike real objects, mocks are not programmed but are configured to behave in specific, predefined ways. The term "mock" means to mimic or imitate.

When dependency injection is used, a Java class can be tested in isolation, enabling better test coverage and maintainability.

23.2. Using annotations to describe class dependencies

There are several ways to describe the dependencies of a class. One of the most common approaches is using Java annotations to define dependencies directly within the class.

The standard Java annotations for defining dependencies were introduced in Java Specification Request 330 (JSR 330). This specification defines the `@Inject` and `@Named` annotations that are now maintained and provided by the **Jakarta** project.

The following example demonstrates a class that uses annotations to define its dependencies:

```java
import jakarta.annotation.PostConstruct;
import jakarta.inject.Inject;

public class MyPart {
```

```
    @Inject private Logger logger;

    // Inject class for database access
    @Inject private DatabaseAccessClass dao;

    @PostConstruct
    public void createControls(Composite parent) {
        logger.info("UI will start to build");
        Label label = new Label(parent, SWT.NONE);
        label.setText("Eclipse 4");
        Text text = new Text(parent, SWT.NONE);
        text.setText(dao.getNumber());
    }
}
```

> This class uses the `new` operator to create user interface components. This indicates that the corresponding user interface toolkit is tightly coupled and not intended to be replaced during testing. In this case, you have intentionally chosen a hard dependency on the UI toolkit.

23.3. Injection points in a class defined by JSR 330

Dependency injection can be performed on:

- the constructor of the class (constructor injection)
- a field (field injection)
- the parameters of a method (method injection)

It is possible to use dependency injection on static and on non-static fields and methods. Avoiding dependency injection on static fields and methods is a good practice. This approach has several restrictions and can be difficult to debug.

- Static fields will be injected after the first object of the class has been created via DI, which means no access to the static field in the constructor
- Static fields cannot be marked as final, otherwise the compiler or the application complains at runtime about them
- Static methods are called only once after the first instance of the class is created

23.4. Order in which dependency injection is performed on a class

According to the specification, the injection is done in the following order:

- constructor injection

- field injection
- method injection

The order in which the methods or fields annotated with `@Inject` are called is not defined. You cannot assume that the methods or fields are called in the order of their declaration in the class.

> As fields and method parameters are injected after the constructor is called, you cannot use injected member variables in the constructor.

24. Dependency injection in Eclipse

24.1. Define class dependencies in Eclipse

The programming model in Eclipse supports constructor, method and field injection. This was originally defined in the Java Specification Request 330 (JSR 330) and has been moved to the `Jakarta` namespace. The most important annotations are covered in Section 24.2, other more specialized annotations are covered in their corresponding chapters.

The Eclipse dependency framework verifies that the key and the type of the injected object are valid. For example, if you specify that you want to have an object of type `Task` for the "xyz" key, as shown in the following field declaration, the framework will only inject an object if it finds one with an assignable type.

```
@Inject @Named("xyz") Todo todo;
```

24.2. Annotations to define class dependencies in Eclipse

The following table gives an overview of dependency injection related annotations based on JSR 330 and the Eclipse specific ones.

Table 9. Basic annotations for dependency injection

Annotation	Description
`@jakarta.inject.Inject`	Defined by JSR 330, can be added to a field, a constructor or a method. The Eclipse framework tries to inject the corresponding objects into the fields or the parameters of the instance.
`@jakarta.inject.Named`	Defined by JSR 330, defines the key for the value which should be injected. By default, the fully qualified class name is used as the key. Several keys for default values are defined as constants in the `IServiceConstants` interface.

Annotation	Description
`@Optional`	Eclipse specific annotation, marks an injected value to be optional. If no valid object can be determined for the given key (and type), the framework does not throw an exception. The specific behavior depends on where the `@Optional` is placed. If the key cannot be resolved the following occurs: • for parameters: a `null` value will be injected • for methods: the method calls will be skipped • for fields: the values will not be injected Note that null is an acceptable value to be set in the context, and it is different from a key being removed from the context. For example, if the following is called `context.set(SOMEKEY, null)`, anybody listening for SOMEKEY will be injected with null.
`@GroupUpdates`	Eclipse specific annotation, indicates that updates for this @Inject should be batched. If you change such objects in the Eclipse context, the update is triggered by the `processWaiting()` method of the `IEclipseContext` object. This annotation is intended to be used by the platform for performance optimization and should rarely be necessary in RCP applications.

The Eclipse platform supports additional annotations for special purposes, e.g., for receiving events (sent by the event service) or working with preferences.

24.3. The objects on which Eclipse performs dependency injection

The Eclipse runtime creates objects for the Java classes referred by the application model. During this instantiation, the Eclipse runtime scans the class definition for annotations. Based on these annotations the Eclipse framework performs the injection.

Eclipse does not automatically inject dependencies into objects that are created with the `new` operator.

24.4. Dynamic dependency injection based on key-value changes

The Eclipse framework tracks which object expressed a dependency on which key and type. If the value associated with a key changes, the Eclipse framework re-injects the new value into any object that depends on the corresponding type. This means applications can be freed from having to install (and remove) listeners.

For example, you can define via `@Inject` that you want to get the current selection injected. If the selection changes, the Eclipse framework will inject the new value.

The reinjection only works on methods and fields that are marked with `@Inject`. It will not work on parameters injected into constructors, and methods that are marked with `@PostConstruct`, as these methods are only executed once.

> This does not mean that Eclipse tracks the fields of the value to which the key points. For example, if the *mykey1* key points to a `Task` object as a value, and the key points to a new object, this triggers the reinjection of the value to all objects that have a relevant class dependency. But if a field inside the existing `Task` object changes, it does not trigger a reinjection.

24.5. OSGi services and Eclipse dependency injection

OSGi services are available for dependency injection in Eclipse applications. If you define your custom OSGi services, you can inject them into your model objects. This removes the need to create singleton or factory implementations in your application to access data.

If a requested key is not found in the Eclipse context hierarchy, the Eclipse framework searches dynamically for a suitable OSGi service in the OSGi registry.

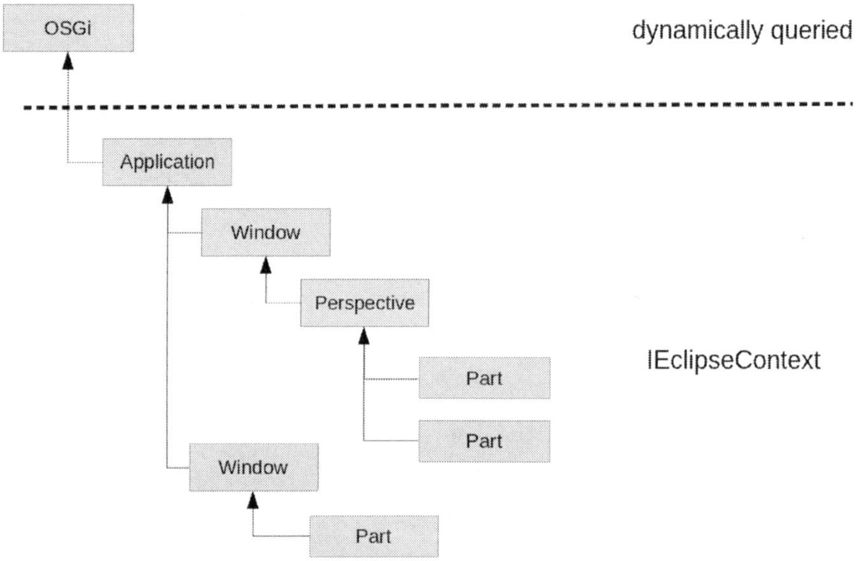

For example, if you have an OSGi service declared for the `TaskService` interface you can inject it via the following code snippet into a field of an Eclipse part.

```
@Inject TaskService service;
```

25. The Eclipse context

25.1. Definition of the Eclipse context

During startup of an Eclipse application, the Eclipse runtime creates an object based on the `IEclipseContext` interface. This object is called the *context*, or the *Eclipse context*.

The context is similar to a `Map` data structure, in which objects can be placed under a certain key. The key is a String, and in several cases the fully qualified class name is used as the key. The value (to which the key points) can be injected into other objects. Unlike a map, the Eclipse context is hierarchical and can dynamically compute values for requested keys.

For certain model objects (see Section 25.2) a local context is created. Such a context is associated with an application model object.

The different context objects are connected to form a hierarchical tree structure based on the structure of your application model. The highest level in this hierarchy is the application context.

A sample context hierarchy is depicted in the following picture.

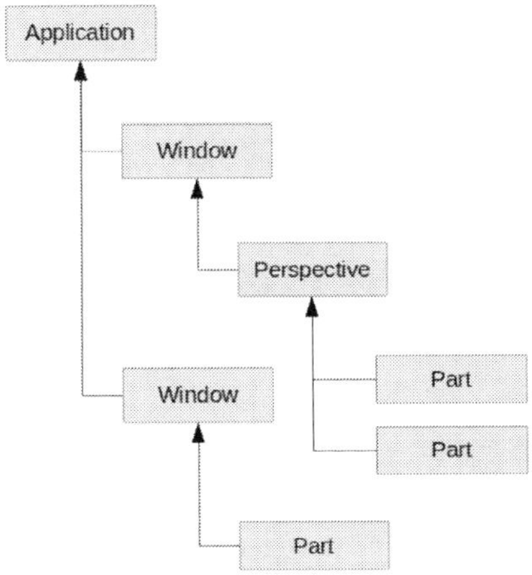

Objects can be placed at different levels in the context hierarchy. This enables the same key to point to different objects in the hierarchy.

For example, a part can express a dependency on a `Composite` object via a field declaration similar to: `@Inject Composite parent;` Since parts have different local contexts they can receive different objects of the type `Composite`.

25.2. Which model elements have a local context?

The following model elements implement the `MContext` interface and therefore have their own context:

- `MApplication`
- `MWindow`
- `MPerspective`
- `MPart`
- `MPopupMenu`

25.3. Life cycle of the Eclipse context

During startup, the Eclipse framework creates the context hierarchy from the application model. By default, it assigns specific objects to predefined keys in the context, such as services that control Eclipse framework functionality.

The Eclipse platform creates both model objects and objects derived from class URI attributes. For each model element with a custom context the Eclipse framework determines which objects should be available in the local context of the model object. If required, it creates the required Java objects referred by the *Class URI* property of the model elements. This is the case if a part is visible to the user.

> The renderer framework is responsible for creating the local context of the UI related model elements. This framework allows you to define classes that are responsible for setting up the UI implementation of the model objects. A class responsible for a model element is called the *renderer* for this model element.
>
> For example, the `ContributedPartRenderer` class is the default renderer for part model objects. This renderer creates a `Composite` for every part and puts this `Composite` into the local context of the part.

After the initial creation of the Eclipse context hierarchy, the framework or the application code can change the key-value pairs stored in the context. In this case, objects which were created with the related Eclipse functionality are updated with the new values.

Objects in the context are persisted in memory (transient), i.e., once the application is stopped the context gets destroyed.

25.4. Object selection for dependency injection

As described in Section 24.3 an object that is created by Eclipse can use annotations to describe its class dependencies.

During dependency injection for an object created by Eclipse, the Eclipse framework searches for a suitable object based on the specified key. The search starts in the local context associated with the application model object. If this key is not available, Eclipse continues to search in the parent context. This process continues until the main context has been reached.

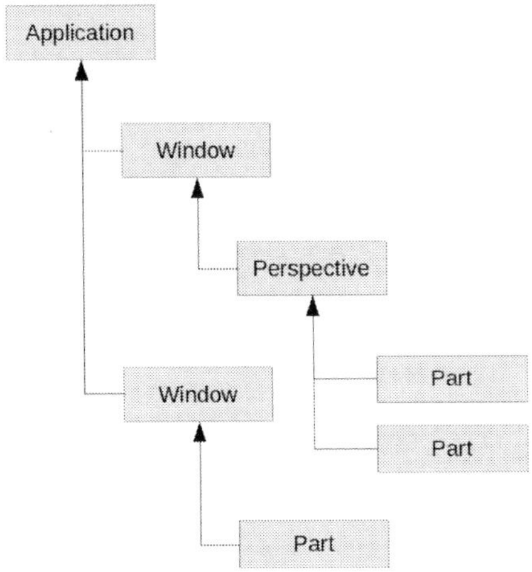

As you learn in later chapters, the Eclipse context is not the only possible source of objects that can be injected. Other examples that are covered later are OSGi services, preferences, events and custom objects. The search happens (mostly) transparently for the caller of the injection.

25.5. Accessing model objects in the code

For the class references in the application model, the Eclipse framework creates the corresponding objects when needed. Such an object has access to its corresponding model object via dependency injection.

For example, in the part's implementation, you can access the model information of a part via: `@Inject MPart part;`

25.6. Default entries in the Eclipse context

The Eclipse framework creates several objects in the context, including:

- model objects - contain the data of the application model
- services - software components that are defined by the Eclipse platform or via the OSGi service registry
- several other objects that have explicitly been added to the context

The context can be modified by the application code and the framework. As the Eclipse framework automatically tracks the dependencies of the objects it creates, it can update them as described in Section 24.4.

25.7. Qualifiers for accessing the active part or shell

The Eclipse platform places the part that is currently selected and the active shell into the `IEclipseContext` of the application object. The related keys are defined in the

`IServiceConstants` interface.

For example, the following method would allow you to track the current active part in another part.

```
// tracks the active part
@Inject
@Optional
public void receiveActivePart(
    @Named(IServiceConstants.ACTIVE_PART) MPart activePart) {
    if (activePart != null) {
        System.out.println("Active part changed "
                + activePart.getLabel());
    }
}
```

To track the active shell use the `IServiceConstants.ACTIVE_SHELL` key.

```
// tracks the active shell
@Inject
@Optional
public void receiveActiveShell(
    @Named(IServiceConstants.ACTIVE_SHELL) Shell shell) {
    if (shell != null) {
        System.out.println("Active shell (Window) changed");
    }
}
```

Eclipse uses handlers to define actions that can be triggered via menu or toolbar entries. For a handler implementation class it is not necessary to use these qualifiers, as a handler is executed in the active context of the application.

25.8. Tracking a child context with @Active

The `@Active` annotation allows you to track values in a child context. The Eclipse framework keeps track of the current active branch in the hierarchy of the `IEclipseContext`. For example, if the user selects a part, the path in the `IEclipseContext` hierarchy from the root to the `IEclipseContext` of the part is the current active branch.

With the `@Active` annotation you can track values in the current active branch of a child element. Whenever the active branch changes and the value of the referred key changes this value is re-injected into the object that uses the `@Active` annotation.

The usage of this annotation is demonstrated by the following code snippet.

```java
public class MyOwnClass {
    @Inject
    void setChildValue(
            @Optional @Named("key_of_child_value") @Active String value) {
        this.childValue = value;
    }
}
```

The `@Active` annotation is currently unused within the Eclipse framework itself and the author of this script has not yet managed to find a good use case for this annotation.

25.9. DI in Eclipse 3.x API code

Eclipse dependency injection functionality was developed for the Eclipse 4.x release. Code that is still based on the 3.x API and runs on a 4.x runtime can access objects available for DI via the `PlatformUI` class.

```java
// get current active context, allows access to objects with the get method
IEclipseContext activeContext = PlatformUI.getWorkbench().getService(IEclipseContext
.class);
// or retrieve object directly
MyOSGiService osgiService = PlatformUI.getWorkbench().getService(MyOSGiService.class);
```

26. Using annotations to define behavior

26.1. API definition in a framework

If you use a framework in your application, you need to have a convention for how your application interacts with the framework. For example, if a Java object is responsible for handling a toolbar button click, the framework needs to know which method of this object needs to be called.

For this purpose, every framework defines an Application Programming Interface (API). This API defines how you can interact with the framework from your code. The API defines the interaction of application objects created or controlled by the framework. Typically, a framework uses inheritance or annotations for this purpose.

26.2. API definition via inheritance

The "traditional" way of defining an API is via inheritance. This approach requires that your classes extend or implement framework classes and interfaces. The Eclipse 3.x platform API used this approach.

The framework defines, for example, an abstract class which defines methods to be implemented.

In the example of the toolbar button the method might be called `execute()` and the framework knows that this method must be called once the button is clicked.

API definition via inheritance is a simple way to define an API, but it couples the classes tightly to the framework. For example, testing the class without the framework is difficult. It makes extending or updating the framework difficult because such an update may affect clients. This is why the Eclipse 4.x does not use this approach anymore.

26.3. API definition via annotations

The Eclipse 4.x platform API is based on annotations, e.g., annotations are used to identify which methods should be called at a certain point in time. These annotations are called *behavior annotations*.

The following table lists the available behavior annotations for parts.

Table 10. Eclipse lifecycle annotations for parts

Annotation	Description
`@PostConstruct`	Is called after the class is constructed and the field and method injection has been performed.
`@PreDestroy`	Is called before the class is destroyed. Can be used to clean up resources.
`@Focus`	Is called whenever the part gets the focus.
`@Persist`	Is called if a save request on the part is triggered by the Eclipse framework.
`@PersistState`	Is called before the model object is disposed, so that the part is able to save its instance state. This method is called before the @PreDestroy method.

The `@PostConstruct`, `@PreDestroy` annotations are included in the `jakarta.annotation` package. `@Persist`, `@PersistState` and `@Focus` are part of the `org.eclipse.e4.ui.di` package.

Eclipse defines additional behavior annotations for commands and for the application lifecycle that are covered in the respective chapters.

Behavior annotations imply that the framework needs to provide the specified parameters to the method, i.e., the framework performs method dependency injection. If you add the `@Inject` annotation, the method is called twice, first during the dependency injection phase and later for the behavior annotation. This is typically undesirable and therefore considered an error.

26.4. Use the @PostConstruct method to build the user interface

It is recommended to construct the user interface of a part in a method annotated with the `@PostConstruct` annotation. It would be possible to create the user interface in the constructor, but this is not recommended as field and method injection have not been done at this point.

Creating the user interface in an `@PostConstruct` method requires that `@Inject` methods are aware that the user interface might not have been created yet.

27. Exercise: Use @PostConstruct

27.1. Implement an @PostConstruct method

Add the following method to your `TodoOverviewPart`, `TodoDetailsPart`, and `PlaygroundPart` classes. In case you created constructors for these classes, you can remove them.

```
import org.eclipse.swt.widgets.Composite;

import jakarta.annotation.PostConstruct;
// more code

@PostConstruct
public void createControls(Composite parent) {
    System.out.println(this.getClass().getSimpleName()
    + " @PostConstruct method called.");
}
```

27.2. Validate

Run your application and validate that the `@PostConstruct` method is called.

Ensure that your import statement is correct if you receive an error message similar to the following: `Unable to process "TodoOverviewPart#createControls()": no actual value was found for the argument "Composite".`

```
import org.eclipse.swt.widgets.Composite;

// MORE code
```

28. Exercise: Using dependency injection in the code

You can create objects using DI and make them available for other objects by placing them in the

IEclipseContext. In case you want to use DI for the creation of your custom objects, you can use the ContextInjectionFactory as demonstrated in this example.

28.1. Implementation

Create the following class.

```
package com.vogella.tasks.ui.parts;

import jakarta.inject.Inject;

public class ACustomClass {
    @Inject
    public String string;

    @Override
    public String toString() {
        return string;
    }
}
```

Change your playground part to the following.

```
package com.vogella.tasks.ui.parts;

import jakarta.inject.Inject;
import jakarta.inject.Named;

import org.eclipse.e4.core.contexts.ContextInjectionFactory;
import org.eclipse.e4.core.contexts.EclipseContextFactory;
import org.eclipse.e4.core.contexts.IEclipseContext;

public class PlaygroundPart {
    @Inject
    public PlaygroundPart(@Named("applicationContext") IEclipseContext ctx) { ❶

        IEclipseContext localCtx = EclipseContextFactory.create();
        localCtx.set(String.class, "My object available for DI");

        // You could connect your new local context with an existing context hierarchy
//      localCtx.setParent(context);

        // Create instance via factory (DI!)
        ACustomClass p = ContextInjectionFactory.make(ACustomClass.class, localCtx);
        // persist the newly created object in the application context
        // this makes the object available via DI for the whole application
```

```
        ctx.set(ACustomClass.class, p);❷
    }
}
```

❶ Retrieves the application context

❷ Make the new object available for dependency injection

28.2. Retrieve the created object via DI

Adjust your `TodoDetailsPart` class to get the new object injected.

```
package com.vogella.tasks.ui.parts;

import org.eclipse.e4.core.di.annotations.Optional;

import jakarta.inject.Inject;

public class TodoDetailsPart {

    @Inject @Optional ❶
    public void createControls(ACustomClass customObject) {
        System.out.println("Received: " + customObject);
    }
}
```

❶ Using `@Optional` at the method level instructs the framework to call this method only if the context key can be found in the relevant `IEclipseContext` hierarchy

28.3. Validate

Start your product and ensure that you see the correct output on the console. Afterwards, remove the `System.out` statement.

Part VII: Modularity based on OSGi

29. Introduction to software modularity with OSGi

OSGi is a set of specifications. Its core specification defines a component and service model for Java applications.

A software component in OSGi is called *bundle* or *plug-in*, both terms are interchangeable. Services are Java implementations that OSGi allows you to start and access.

An application consists of different components and services. A solid and clean software architecture consists of components that can change their internal implementation without affecting other components. OSGi supports creating such an architecture.

The OSGi specification defines a way for plug-ins to define:

- their API
- their dependencies
- provided and required services

A plug-in is therefore a cohesive, self-contained unit that explicitly defines its dependencies on other components and services.

OSGi defines that plug-ins and services can be dynamically installed, activated, deactivated, updated and uninstalled.

The OSGi specification has several implementations, for example Eclipse Equinox, Knopflerfish OSGi or Apache Felix.

Eclipse Equinox is the reference implementation of the base OSGi specification. It is also the runtime environment on which Eclipse applications are based.

Java 9 provides its own module system to describe software component dependencies, but it has not yet been adopted by the Eclipse module system.

30. OSGi configuration files

30.1. The manifest file (MANIFEST.MF)

OSGi uses the *META-INF/MANIFEST.MF* file (called the *manifest* file) from the standard Java specification to define its metadata. The Java specification defines that additional key-value pairs can be added to this file without affecting runtimes which do not understand these key-value combinations. Therefore, OSGi plug-ins can be used without restrictions in other Java environments.

The following listing is an example for a manifest file containing OSGi metadata.

```
Manifest-Version: 1.0
Bundle-ManifestVersion: 2
Bundle-Name: Popup Plug-in
Bundle-SymbolicName: com.example.myosgi; singleton:=true
Bundle-Version: 1.0.0
Bundle-Activator: com.example.myosgi.Activator
Require-Bundle: org.eclipse.ui,
 org.eclipse.core.runtime
Bundle-ActivationPolicy: lazy
Bundle-RequiredExecutionEnvironment: JavaSE-21
```

The following table gives an overview of the OSGi metadata used in the manifest file.

Table 11. OSGi identifiers in the manifest file

Identifier	Description
Bundle-Name	Short description of the plug-in.
Bundle-SymbolicName	The unique technical name of the plug-in. If this plug-in is providing an extension or an extension point it must be marked as Singleton. You do this by adding the following statement after the Bundle-SymbolicName identifier: `; singleton:=true`

Identifier	Description
Bundle-Version	Defines the plug-in version and must be incremented if a new version of the plug-in is published.
Bundle-Activator	Defines an activator class that implements the `BundleActivator` interface. An instance of this class is created when the plug-in gets activated. Its `start()` and `stop()` methods are called whenever the plug-in is started or stopped. An OSGi activator can be used to configure the plug-in during startup. The execution of an activator may increase the startup time of the application, therefore this functionality should be avoided if possible.
Bundle-RequiredExecutionEnvironment (BREE)	Specify which Java version is required to run the plug-in. If this requirement is not fulfilled, then the runtime does not load the plug-in. The OSGi specification deprecates it, but the Eclipse Plug-in development tooling still uses it, hence this is also used in this description.
Bundle-ActivationPolicy	Setting this to *lazy* instructs the OSGi runtime that this plug-in should be activated if one of its classes and interfaces are used by other plug-ins. Must be in Equinox if the plug-in provides services.
Bundle-ClassPath	The Bundle-ClassPath specifies where to load classes from the bundle. The default is `.`, which allows classes to be loaded from the root of the bundle. You can also add JAR files to it, these are called *nested JAR files*.

30.2. Unique identifier for plug-ins

The combination of `Bundle-SymbolicName` and `Bundle-Version` uniquely identifies a plug-in.

Each plug-in has a unique name (id) that is defined via the `Bundle-SymbolicName` property. By convention, this name uses the reverse domain name of the plug-in author. For example, if you own the "example.com" domain then the symbolic name would start with "com.example".

Each plug-in defines its version number in the `Bundle-Version` property. OSGi recommends to use the following schema for versions in the `Bundle-Version` field identifier.

<major>.<minor>.<patch/service>

If you change your plug-in code you increase the version according to the following rule set.

- *<major>* is increased if changes are not backwards compatible.
- *<minor>* is increased if public API has changed but all changes are backwards compatible.
- *<service>* is increased if all changes are backwards compatible.

For more information on this version scheme see the Version Numbering Wiki [https://github.com/

eclipse-platform/eclipse.platform/blob/master/docs/VersionNumbering.md].

31. Specifying the API of a plug-in and its dependencies

An OSGi runtime restricts access to classes from other plug-ins. To access classes from other plug-ins, a plug-in needs to define dependencies to these plug-ins or their packages. In addition, the plug-in must define the used packages as API.

The only exception are packages from the Java runtime environment that can be accessed by default.

All these restrictions are enforced via a specific OSGi `classloader`. Each plug-in has its own classloader. Access to restricted classes is not possible without using reflection.

> Unfortunately, OSGi cannot prevent you from using Java reflection to access these classes. This is because OSGi is based on the Java runtime that does not yet support a modularity layer.

31.1. Defining the API of a plug-in

A plug-in defines its API via the `Export-Package` identifier in its manifest file. All packages that are not explicitly exported are not visible to other plug-ins.

The following screenshot shows one plug-in which exports one package as API in the Eclipse manifest editor.

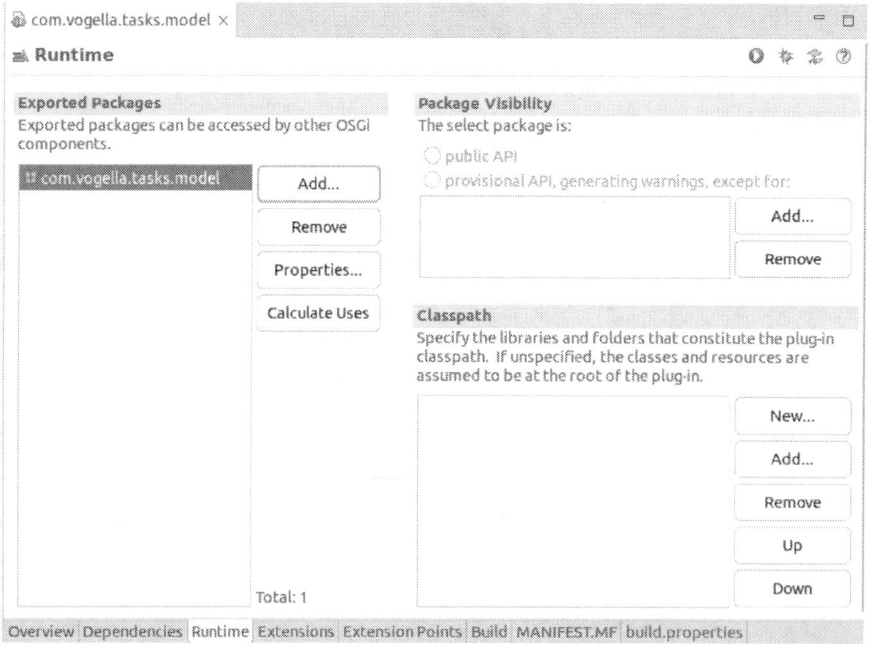

31.2. Defining dependencies of a plug-in

To access classes from another plug-in A in the source code of your plug-in B you need to:

- export the corresponding package in plug-in A
- define a dependency in plug-in B to plug-in A or the package

The following screenshot shows an example dependency definition in the Eclipse manifest editor.

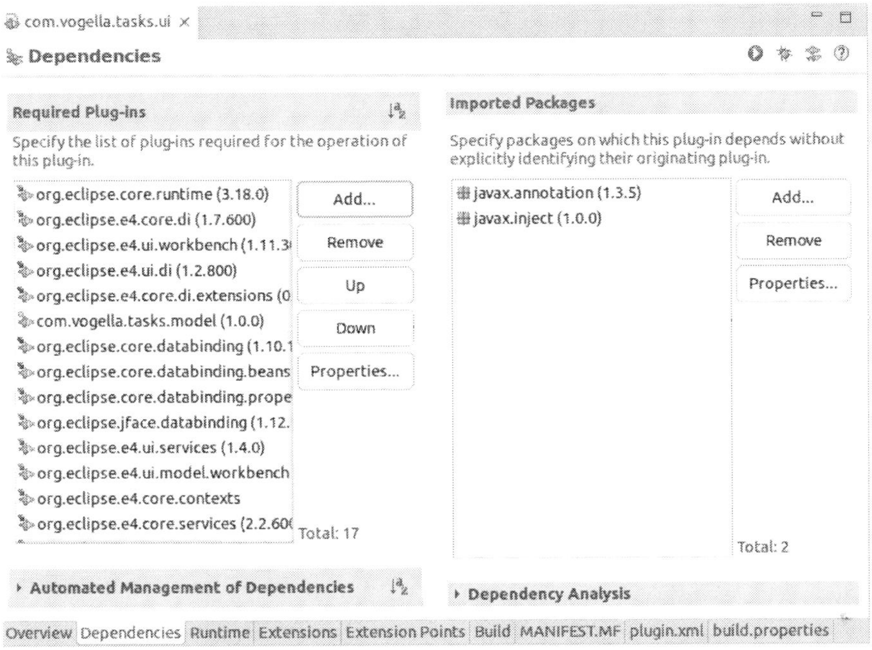

A plug-in dependency allows a plug-in to access all exported packages from this plug-in. A package dependency allows your plug-in to use the classes in this package, independent of which plug-in provides it.

> Using package dependencies allows you to exchange the plug-in that provides this package. The OSGi specification promotes the usage of package dependencies. If you require this flexibility, prefer the usage of package dependencies.

> For legacy reasons, OSGi supports a dynamic import of packages. You should not use this feature, it is a symptom of a non-modular design.

31.3. Dependencies using versions

A plug-in can define that it depends on a certain version (or a range) of another plug-in. For example, plug-in A can define that it depends on plug-in C in version 2.0. Another plug-in B can define that it depends on version 1.0 of plug-in C.

31.4. Life cycle of plug-ins

During startup, the OSGi runtime reads the plug-in's manifest file. The runtime validates if all dependencies are present and can be resolved.

If all required dependencies are resolved, the plug-in is in the *RESOLVED* status; otherwise it stays in the *INSTALLED* status.

In case several plug-ins exist that can satisfy the dependency, the plug-in with the highest valid version is used.

If the versions are the same, the plug-in with the lowest unique identifier (ID) is used. Every plug-in gets this ID assigned by the framework during the installation.

When the plug-in starts, its status is *STARTING*. If a plug-in sets the *lazy* flag to true in its manifest, the Equinox runtime moves that plug-in to the *ACTIVE* state, if one of its classes or interfaces is used. In this state the plug-in can provide OSGi services in Equinox.

> Other OSGi runtimes behave differently, for example Felix always activates all plug-ins.

This lifecycle is depicted in the following graphic.

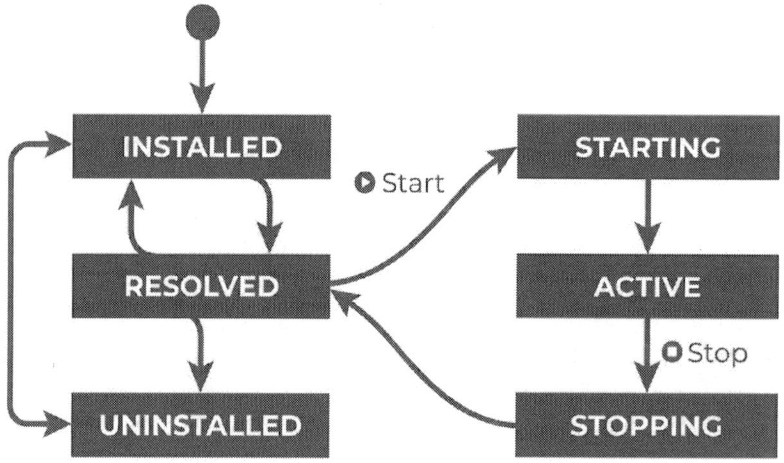

31.5. Defining a Provisional API using x-internal and x-friends

OSGi allows you to define provisional APIs, i.e., packages that can be accessed by other plug-ins, but are not yet considered stable APIs. This can be done via the `x-internal` or the `x-friends` flag.

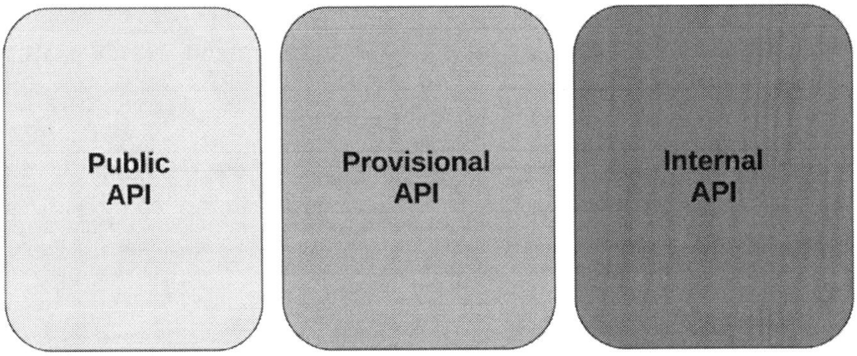

The following screenshot shows how to define a package as provisional API.

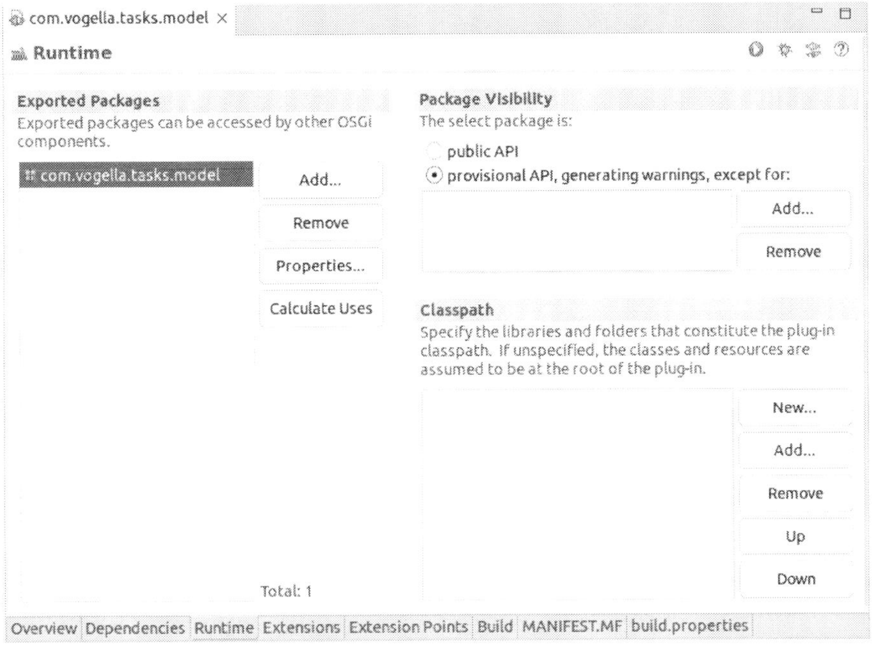

Such a setting would result in the package flagged as x-internal.

```
Manifest-Version: 1.0
Bundle-ManifestVersion: 2
Bundle-Name: Model
Bundle-SymbolicName: com.vogella.tasks.model
Bundle-Version: 1.0.0.qualifier
Bundle-Vendor: VOGELLA
Automatic-Module-Name: com.vogella.tasks.model
Bundle-RequiredExecutionEnvironment: JavaSE-21
Export-Package: com.vogella.tasks.model;x-internal:=true
```

`x-friends` also defines provisional API and allows you to define a set of plug-ins that can access the provisional API without a warning or error message. `x-friends` automatically replaces `x-internal` if you use the Eclipse manifest editor and add a plug-in to the *Package Visibility* section on the *Runtime* tab.

```
Manifest-Version: 1.0
Bundle-ManifestVersion: 2
Bundle-Name: Model
Bundle-SymbolicName: com.vogella.tasks.model
Bundle-Version: 1.0.0.qualifier
Bundle-Vendor: VOGELLA
Automatic-Module-Name: com.vogella.tasks.model
Bundle-RequiredExecutionEnvironment: JavaSE-21
Export-Package: com.vogella.tasks.model;x-friends:="another.bundle"
```

You can configure the Java editor to show an error, warning or to ignore usage of provisional API. The default is to display a warning message. You can adjust this in the Eclipse preferences via the **Window › Preferences › Java › Compiler › Errors/Warnings** preference setting.

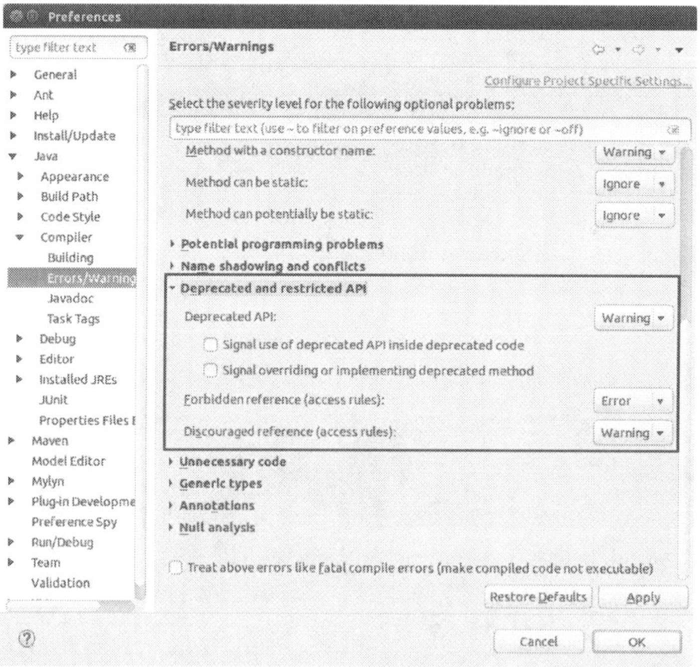

31.6. Eclipse platform API

The Eclipse platform project marks almost all packages either as public API or as provisional API. If the Eclipse platform project releases an API, the platform project plans to keep this API stable for as long as possible.

If an API is marked as provisional, the platform team may change it in future releases. If you use such an API, be prepared to make adjustments to your application when you move to a newer Eclipse release.

If you use an unreleased API, you see a *Discouraged access: The ... is not API (restriction on required project ...)* warning in the Java editor.

You can turn off these warnings for your workspace via **Window › Preferences › Java › Compiler › Errors/Warnings** and by setting the *Discouraged reference (access rules)* flag to *Ignore*.

Alternatively, you can turn off these warnings on a per-project basis. To do so, right-click on the project, select **Properties › Java Compiler**, and then use the same path as for accessing the global settings. You might have to activate the *Enable project specific settings* checkbox at the top of the Error/Warnings preference page.

31.7. Understanding Eclipse-BuddyPolicy: Registered

In OSGi and Eclipse plug-in development, the `Eclipse-BuddyPolicy` header is used to specify how a bundle (plug-in) can request or provide class-loading assistance to other bundles. The `Registered` policy requires explicit registration of "buddies" (other bundles) using the `Eclipse-RegisterBuddy` header.

A bundle that declares `Eclipse-BuddyPolicy: Registered` in its `MANIFEST.MF` allows other bundles (buddies) to assist with its class loading, but only if those buddies explicitly register themselves. Other bundles can register themselves as buddies using the `Eclipse-RegisterBuddy` header in their `MANIFEST.MF`. Example: When the bundle with the `Registered` policy tries to load a class that is not available in its own classpath, it consults its registered buddies. The buddies are then allowed to attempt to load the class.

The process of class loading is the following:

1. Bundle B registers itself as a buddy for Bundle A.
2. When Bundle A encounters a class that it cannot resolve, it consults its registered buddies.
3. If Bundle B can resolve the class, it loads it on behalf of Bundle A.

31.7.1. Example Scenario

The `MANIFEST.MF` of bundle A allows buddy registration via the `Eclipse-BuddyPolicy:` entry.

```
Bundle-SymbolicName: com.example.bundleA
Eclipse-BuddyPolicy: Registered
```

The `MANIFEST.MF` of bundle B registers a buddy via the following `Eclipse-RegisterBuddy:` entry.

```
Bundle-SymbolicName: com.example.bundleB
Eclipse-RegisterBuddy: com.example.bundleA
```

31.7.2. Key Notes

Unlike other policies (e.g., `Global` or `Dependent`), the `Registered` policy requires a more controlled and explicit setup for buddy relationships. This makes it more predictable and avoids the risks of overly permissive class loading. The buddy relationship is resolved at runtime, not at compile time.

The `Registered` policy is often used in scenarios where specific bundles must assist with loading classes (e.g., extension points or modular frameworks with shared responsibilities).

31.7.3. Best Practices

Buddy policies, including `Registered`, should be used sparingly. Relying on OSGi's modular class loading and proper exports/imports is generally preferable.

32. OSGi Services

Services enable functionality for other software components. A *service interface* in OSGi is defined in a plug-in by a standard Java class or an interface. Service implementations for a service interface are published to the OSGi *service registry* so that other plug-ins can access them.

Multiple plug-ins can provide a service implementation for the service interface. Plug-ins can access the service implementation via the service interface.

During the declaration of a service it is possible to specify key-values pairs that can be used to configure the service.

A service can be dynamically started and stopped, and plug-ins that use services must be able to handle this dynamic behavior. The plug-ins can register listeners to be informed if a service is started or stopped.

To provide a service a plug-in needs to be in the `ACTIVE` lifecycle status.

OSGi provides several ways of defining, providing and consuming services. The following description focuses on the usage of declarative services.

32.1. OSGi declarative services (OSGi ds)

The OSGi *declarative services* (DS) allows you to define and consume services via metadata.

Tooling allows you to generate service metadata based on annotations in your source code. This topic is covered in the exercises for the Eclipse IDE.

The following is an example of using an annotation to define an OSGi service. It provides a service implementation for the `TaskService` interface.

```
import org.osgi.service.component.annotations.Component;
// more stuff

@Component
public class TransientTaskServiceImpl implements TaskService {
    // as before ...
}
```

> The preferred way of defining OSGi services is to use the annotations, because this is the simplest way possible. Alternatively, you can also define and register the service component definition manually via an XML file or use the OSGi API for starting, stopping and tracking services. This is covered later.

The annotation is used to generate an XML file, which is read once the plug-in gets activated.

OSGi service definitions can be:

- delayed component - a service that is not activated until requested. This means class and implementation loading is delayed until that time. This type must define an OSGi service.
- immediate component - service is activated as soon as its dependencies are satisfied, does not need to specify a service
- factory component - creates and activates a new service on request, service is not reused if it becomes unsatisfied or unregistered

The following table gives a brief overview of the OSGi ds terminology, you can skip this table and return to it, in case you want to look up a definition.

Table 12. OSGi ds terminology

Term	Definition
Service component	A Java class inside a bundle that is declared via Component Description and managed by a service component runtime.
Component Description	The declaration of a Service Component, contained in an XML document or defined via annotations that are used to generate the XML document.

Term	Definition
Component Configuration	A Component Description that is parameterized with component properties. It is used to track the component dependencies and manages the Component Instance.
Component Instance	The instance of the component implementation class. It is created when a Component Configuration is activated and discarded if the Component Configuration is deactivated.

32.2. Accessing the BundleContext

Sometimes you need to access information about the bundle, e.g., the bundle version or the bundle name. Access to the bundle and its bundleContext is performed via the `Bundle` and `BundleContext` classes.

You can use the `FrameworkUtil` class from the OSGi framework to access the `BundleContext` for a class.

```
Bundle bundle = FrameworkUtil.getBundle(this.getClass());
BundleContext bundleContext = FrameworkUtil.getBundle(this.getClass()).
getBundleContext();
```

32.3. Immediately activate service

If you want to activate a service immediately after its dependencies are satisfied, the `immediate` parameter to the `@Component` annotation can be used.

32.4. Setting the start level for declarative services

You need to ensure that the `org.apache.felix.scr` plug-in is started before any application plug-in that wants to consume a service.

You can ensure this in your run configuration by setting the *auto-start* field to `true` and the start level to a value lower than 4 (4 is the default) for the `org.apache.felix.scr` plug-in.

The Eclipse RCP framework automatically starts the required plug-ins for using declarative OSGi services. It is not required to manually set a start level in your product configuration file.

32.5. Good practice for defining services

It is a good practice to define a service via a plug-in which only contains the interface definition. Another plug-in would provide the implementation for this service. This allows you to change the implementation of the service via a different plug-in.

32.6. Life cycle

A plug-in that provides a service must be in its `ACTIVE` lifecycle status. Therefore, ensure that the *Activate this plug-in when one of its classes is loaded* flag is set in the `MANIFEST.MF` file. The DS annotation support in Eclipse sets this flag automatically, if you use the default settings

> The above will set the Lazy Activation Policy [https://www.osgi.org/developer/design/lazy-start/] setting via the Bundle-ActivationPolicy key in the manifest. This is necessary for the Eclipse runtime (Equinox), other OSGi runtimes will always activate bundles if their dependencies are fulfilled. This flag ensures that the bundle is activated (auto-started) as soon as one of its classes is accessed.

OSGi Services have their own lifecycle, the following states are possible:

State	Definition
Enabled/Disabled	The initial enabled state of a component is specified via a component description. All components are disabled when the bundle is stopped. It is possible to change the enabled state programmatically at runtime via ComponentContext.
UNSATISFIED	The component is not ready to be started. See satisfied for the necessary criteria. This status can also be reached again if a component becomes unsatisfied.
SATISFIED	A component is in this state when it is enabled and the required referenced services are available. If the `ConfigurationAdmin` is used and configuration-policy=required is specified, a configuration object also needs to be available to bring a component to a satisfied state.
REGISTERED	A component is in REGISTERED state if it is SATISFIED and not yet requested. Only applies for delayed components.
ACTIVE	The component was activated due to immediate activation or, in case of a Delayed Component, it was requested.

If the bundle is started, an OSGi component called SCR checks if the bundle contains component descriptions. It accomplishes this by reading the MANIFEST.MF and searching for Service-Components. If it finds one, it will start to process the component description and create a component configuration. If the configuration is enabled, it checks for required references and configurations if necessary. If all of these conditions are met, the component can be activated.

An Immediate Component will activate as soon as its requirements are fulfilled.

In contrast, a Delayed Component moves to the REGISTERED state and waits for the first request to its provided service. If a Component Configuration contains dynamic references, the references can rebind in ACTIVE state, otherwise it will be re-activated. If a Component Configuration becomes unsatisfied (e.g., a bound service becomes unavailable), the Component Configuration will be deactivated. A Delayed Component will also be deactivated and return to the REGISTERED state if no other bundle references it anymore.

33. Using the OSGi console

33.1. Access to the OSGi console for the Eclipse application

If you specify the *-console* parameter in your run configuration, you can use a console or terminal to interact with the OSGi console.

The OSGi console is like a command-line shell. In this console you can type a command to perform an OSGi action. This can be useful to analyze problems on the OSGi layer of your application.

Use, for example, the command `ss` to get an overview of all bundles, their status and bundle-id. The following table is a reference of the most important OSGi commands.

Table 13. OSGi commands

Command	Description
help	Lists the available commands.
ss	Lists the installed bundles and their status.
ss *vogella*	Lists bundles and their status that have *vogella* within their name.
start *<bundle-id>*	Starts the bundle with the *<bundle-id>* ID.
stop *<bundle-id>*	Stops the bundle with the *<bundle-id>* ID.
diag *<bundle-id>*	Diagnoses a particular bundle. It lists all missing dependencies.
install *URL*	Installs a bundle from a URL.
uninstall *<bundle-id>*	Uninstalls the bundle with the *<bundle-id>* ID.
bundle *<bundle-id>*	Shows information about the bundle with the *<bundle-id>* ID, including the registered and used services.
headers *<bundle-id>*	Shows the MANIFEST.MF information for a bundle.
services *filter*	Shows all available services and their consumers. Filter is an optional LDAP filter, e.g., to see all services that provide a ManagedService implementation use the "services (objectclass=*ManagedService)" command.
scr:list	lists all DS components
scr:info <id>	dump detailed information for a selected DS component

Add the `-noExit` to keep the OSGi console running, even if the application fails to start. This is useful for error analysis.

33.2. Required bundles

The following plug-ins are necessary to use the OSGi console. The easiest way to add them to your Eclipse application is to add them directly via the runtime configuration.

- `org.eclipse.equinox.console`
- `org.apache.felix.gogo.command`
- `org.apache.felix.gogo.runtime`
- `org.apache.felix.gogo.shell`

33.3. Accessing the OSGi console via a telnet client

If you want to access your application using a Telnet client, you can add another parameter to the `-console` parameter. This specifies the port to which you can connect via the telnet protocol.

-console 5555

To access such an application, use a Telnet client. For instance, on Linux, use the command: `telnet localhost 5555`. In an OSGi console accessed via telnet, you can use tab completion and a command history similar to the *Bash* shell on Linux.

The port must be specified if you want to access the OSGi console via the *Console* view of the Eclipse IDE. Use only `-console` for this.

33.4. Access to the Eclipse OSGi console

You can also access the OSGi console of your running Eclipse IDE. In the *Console* view, you find a menu entry with the tooltip *Open Console*. If you select *Host OSGi Console*, you will have access to your running OSGi instance.

Please note that interfering with your running Eclipse IDE via the OSGi console, may put the Eclipse IDE into a bad state.

The plug-in development tooling (PDE) must be installed in Eclipse. If you can create plug-ins using the wizard, PDE is installed.

34. Using the OSGi service API

While the preferred way of defining and providing OSGi services is based on OSGi ds, you can also use OSGi API for this. This chapter describes this API, in case you need it.

34.1. Registering services via the BundleContext

A bundle can also register itself for the events(`ServiceEvents`) of the `BundleContext`. These are, for example, triggered if a new bundle is installed or uninstalled or if a new service is registered.

To publish a service in your bundle use:

```
BundleContext bundleContext = FrameworkUtil.getBundle(this.getClass()).
getBundleContext();
bundleContext.registerService(IMyService.class.getName(), new MzServiceImpl(), null);
```

Once the service is no longer used, you must deregister it with OSGi. OSGi counts the usage of services to enable the dynamic replacement of services. So once the service is no longer used by your implementation, unregister it. This is demonstrated by the following code:

```
context.ungetService(serviceReference);
```

In the `registerService()` method from the `BundleContext` class you can specify arbitrary properties in the dictionary parameter.

You can use the `getProperty()` method of the `ServiceReference` class from the `org.osgi.framework` package, to access a specific property.

34.2. Accessing a service via API

A bundle can acquire a service via the `BundleContext` class. The following code demonstrates this.

```
BundleContext bundleContext = FrameworkUtil.getBundle(this.getClass()).
getBundleContext();
ServiceReference<?> serviceReference = bundleContext.getServiceReference(IMyService.
class.getName());
IMyService service = (IMyService) bundleContext.getService(serviceReference);
```

34.3. Using an activator for service registration

Avoid using activators as they can slow down the startup of your application.

A bundle can define a `Bundle-Activator` (Activator) in its declaration. This class must implement the `BundleActivator` interface.

If defined, OSGi injects the `BundleContext` into the `start()` and `stop()` methods of the implementing `Activator` class.

```java
import org.osgi.framework.BundleActivator;
import org.osgi.framework.BundleContext;


public class Activator implements BundleActivator {

    public void start(BundleContext context) throws Exception {
        System.out.println("Starting bundle");
        // do something with the context, e.g.,
        // register services
    }

    public void stop(BundleContext context) throws Exception {
        System.out.println("Stopping bundle");
        // do something with the context, e.g.,
        // unregister service
    }
}
```

35. Using fragment projects

35.1. Definition of OSGi fragments

A *fragment* is an optional attachment to another plug-in. This plug-in is called the *host plug-in*. At runtime, the fragment is merged with its host plug-in. Therefore, for the Equinox runtime, the host plug-in and fragment are treated as a single plug-in.

Fragments are optional; the host plug-in is unaware of their presence at runtime.

The Eclipse IDE supports the creation of fragments via *fragment projects*. To create a fragment project select **File › New › Other... › Plug-in Development › Fragment Project**.

35.2. Typical use cases for fragments

Fragments can be used to contain test classes. This way, the tests can access and test the internal API of the plug-in classes. Alternatively, tests can be contained in their own plug-in. In this case, they can only test the external API of other plug-ins.

Fragments can contribute property files for additional translations. This allows you to contribute translations for a new language without adjusting other parts of the code.

In addition, fragments can provide native code that is specific to certain operating systems. A platform filter can be used to define that the fragment is only valid for a certain operating system.

For example, the SWT user interface implementation of Eclipse uses this approach.

Fragments can also be used to contain resources like icon sets or other images. This allows you to customize your application icons via the provided fragment.

35.3. Example manifest for a fragment

The following listing shows a manifest file for a fragment that is only valid for the Windows OS. The OS is specified via the `Eclipse-PlatformFilter` property and the `Fragment-Host` makes this a fragment. If you remove `Fragment-Host`, the component is a regular plug-in again.

```
Manifest-Version: 1.0
Bundle-ManifestVersion: 2
Bundle-Name: %fragmentName
Bundle-SymbolicName: org.eclipse.ui.win32
Bundle-Version: 3.4.300.qualifier
Bundle-ClassPath: .
Bundle-Vendor: %providerName
Fragment-Host: org.eclipse.ui.ide;bundle-version="[3.2.0,4.0.0)"
Bundle-Localization: fragment-win32
Export-Package: org.eclipse.ui.internal.editorsupport.win32;x-internal:=true
Eclipse-PlatformFilter: (osgi.ws=win32)
Bundle-RequiredExecutionEnvironment: JavaSE-21
Automatic-Module-Name: org.eclipse.ui.win32
```

The available platform filters are:

- Eclipse-PlatformFilter: (osgi.ws=win32)
- Eclipse-PlatformFilter: (osgi.ws=gtk)
- Eclipse-PlatformFilter: (osgi.ws=cocoa)

36. Creating (Simple) Plug-ins

The Eclipse IDE provides multiple templates and options for creating plug-ins. These templates and options add code or configuration elements to the generated code and often help you complete tasks more quickly. In this script, we typically want to maintain control and understand what we are doing, so we often avoid these additional options.

If you are asked to create a *simple plug-in* via the **File › New › Other... › Plug-in Development › Plug-in Project** menu entry, use the following options:

- No activator
- No contributions to the user interface
- Not a rich client application

- Generated without a template

37. Exercise: Create a plug-in for the task data model

In this exercise, you create a plug-in that contains the definition of a data model. You also make this data model available to other plug-ins to provide certain packages as API.

37.1. Create the plug-in for the data model

Create a simple plug-in project via the **File › New › Other... › Plug-in Development › Plug-in Project** menu entry. See Chapter 36 for more information.

Name the plug-in `com.vogella.tasks.model`.

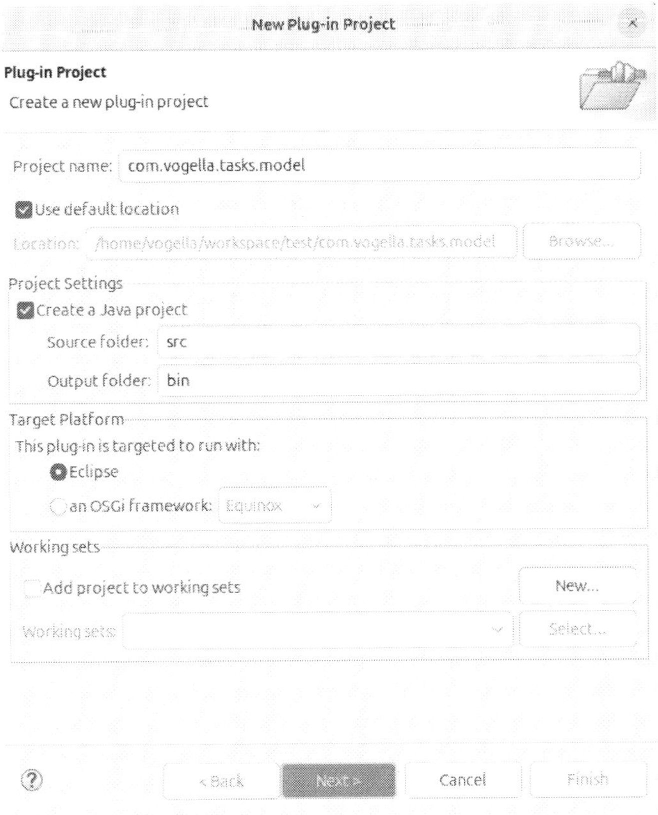

The following screenshot depicts the second page of the plug-in project wizard and its corresponding settings.

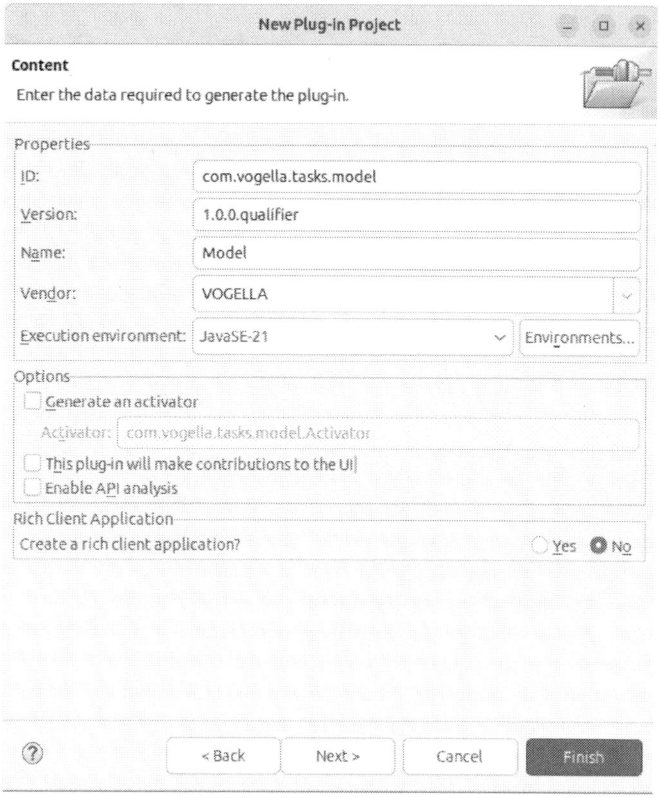

Press the Finish button on this page to avoid the usage of templates.

37.2. Create the base class

Create the `com.vogella.tasks.model` package and the following model class.

```
package com.vogella.tasks.model;

import java.time.LocalDate;

public class Task {

    private final long id;
    private String summary = "";
    private String description = "";
    private boolean done = false;
    private LocalDate dueDate = LocalDate.now();

}
```

You see an error for your final id field. This error is solved in the next section.

37.3. Generate two constructors

Generate **two** constructors:

- a constructor using only the *id* field
- a constructor using all fields

You can do this via the Select **Source › Generate Constructor using Fields...** menu entry.

Ensure that you have created both constructors, because they are required in the following exercises.

37.4. Generate getter and setter methods

Use the **Source › Generate Getter and Setter...** menu to create getters and setters for your fields.

Why is the id field marked as final?

The *id* field is final; therefore, Eclipse generates only a getter method for it. This behavior is correct and intentional. Since this field will be used to generate the `equals()` and `hashCode()` methods, it should remain immutable. Changing a field that is used in the `equals()` and `hashCode()` methods can create bugs that are hard to identify, i.e., an object is contained in a `HashMap` but not found.

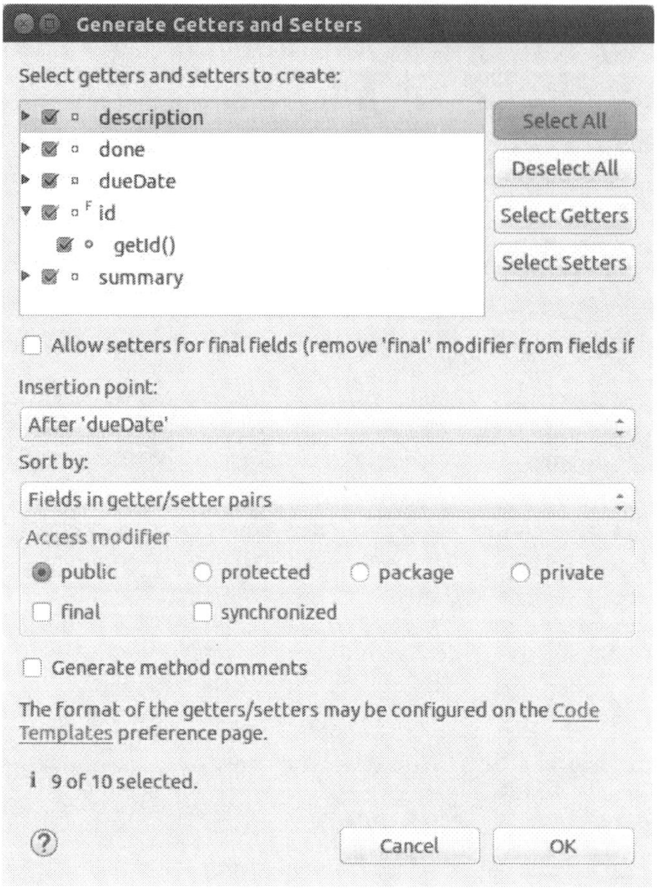

At this point the resulting class should look like the following listing.

```
package com.vogella.tasks.model;

import java.time.LocalDate;

public class Task {

    private final long id;
    private String summary = "";
    private String description = "";
    private boolean done = false;
    private LocalDate dueDate = LocalDate.now();

    public String getSummary() {
        return summary;
    }
    public void setSummary(String summary) {
        this.summary = summary;
    }
```

```
    public String getDescription() {
        return description;
    }
    public void setDescription(String description) {
        this.description = description;
    }
    public boolean isDone() {
        return done;
    }
    public void setDone(boolean done) {
        this.done = done;
    }
    public LocalDate getDueDate() {
        return dueDate;
    }
    public void setDueDate(LocalDate dueDate) {
        this.dueDate = dueDate;
    }
    public long getId() {
        return id;
    }
    public Task(long id, String summary, String description, boolean done, LocalDate
dueDate) {
        this.id = id;
        this.summary = summary;
        this.description = description;
        this.done = done;
        this.dueDate = dueDate;
    }
    public Task(long id) {
        this.id = id;
    }
}
```

37.5. Generate the toString() method

Use the **Source › Generate toString()...** menu entry to generate a `toString()` method for the `Task` class based on the *id* and *summary* field.

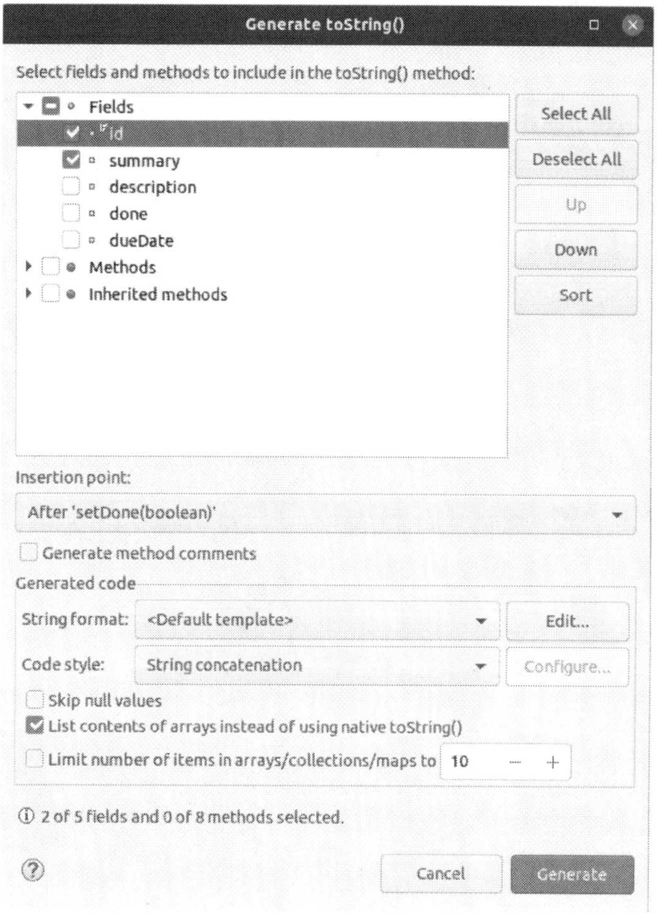

37.6. Generate the hashCode() and equals() methods

Use the **Source › Generate hashCode() and equals()...** menu entry to generate the `hashCode()` and `equals()` methods based on the *id* field. Generate the 1.7 or higher version.

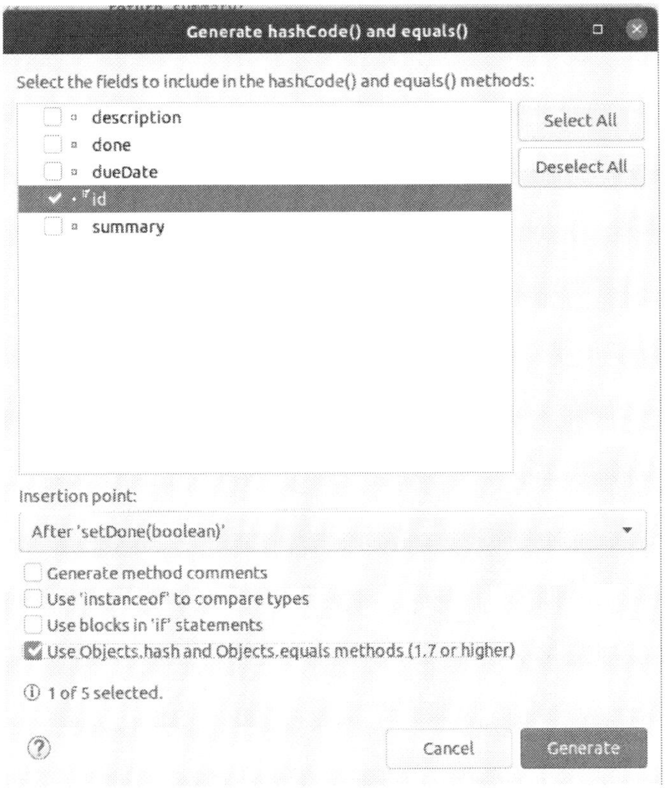

37.7. Write a copy() method

Add the following `copy()` method to the class.

```
public Task copy() {
    return new Task(
            this.id,
            this.summary,
            this.description,
            this.done,
            this.dueDate);
}
```

37.8. Add constants for its fields

To access the fields on `Task` later, create the following constants in the class.

```
    public static final String FIELD_ID = "id";
    public static final String FIELD_SUMMARY = "summary";
    public static final String FIELD_DESCRIPTION = "description";
    public static final String FIELD_DONE = "done";
```

```
    public static final String FIELD_DUEDATE = "dueDate";
```

37.9. Validate

The resulting `Task` class should now look similar to the following.

```
package com.vogella.tasks.model;

import java.time.LocalDate;
import java.util.Objects;

public class Task {

    public static final String FIELD_ID = "id";
    public static final String FIELD_SUMMARY = "summary";
    public static final String FIELD_DESCRIPTION = "description";
    public static final String FIELD_DONE = "done";
    public static final String FIELD_DUEDATE = "dueDate";

    private final long id;
    private String summary = "";
    private String description = "";
    private boolean done = false;
    private LocalDate dueDate = LocalDate.now();

    public Task(long id, String summary, String description, boolean done, LocalDate
dueDate) {
        this.id = id;
        this.summary = summary;
        this.description = description;
        this.done = done;
        this.dueDate = dueDate;
    }

    public Task(long id) {
        this.id = id;
    }

    public String getSummary() {
        return summary;
    }

    public void setSummary(String summary) {
        this.summary = summary;
    }

    public String getDescription() {
```

```
        return description;
    }

    public void setDescription(String description) {
        this.description = description;
    }

    public boolean isDone() {
        return done;
    }

    public void setDone(boolean done) {
        this.done = done;
    }

    public LocalDate getDueDate() {
        return dueDate;
    }

    public void setDueDate(LocalDate dueDate) {
        this.dueDate = dueDate;
    }

    public long getId() {
        return id;
    }

    @Override
    public String toString() {
        return "Task [id=" + id + ", summary=" + summary + "]";
    }

    public Task copy() {
        return new Task(this.id, this.summary, this.description, this.done, this.
dueDate);
    }

    @Override
    public int hashCode() {
        return Objects.hash(id);
    }

    @Override
    public boolean equals(Object obj) {
        if (this == obj)
            return true;
        if (obj == null)
            return false;
        if (getClass() != obj.getClass())
```

```
            return false;
        Task other = (Task) obj;
        return id == other.id;
    }
}
```

37.10. Define a service interface to access tasks

Create the following `TaskService` interface.

```
package com.vogella.tasks.model;

import java.util.List;
import java.util.Optional;
import java.util.function.Consumer;

public interface TaskService {

    /**
     * Get all tasks
     */
    List<Task> getAll();

    /**
     * Updates existing task or create new task
     *
     * @param task
     * @return
     */
    boolean update(Task task);

    /**
     * Returns an Optional wrapping a task or an empty Optional if no task exists for the
given id
     *
     * @param task
     * @return empty optional if not found, otherwise Optional holding the task
     */

    Optional<Task> get(long id);

    /**
     *  Deletes the task with the id
     * @param id task id to delete
     * @return true if task existed and was deleted, false otherwise
     */
    boolean delete(long id);
```

```
    /**
     * Allows specifying a consumer that retrieves all tasks
     *
     * @param tasksConsumer
     */

    void consume(Consumer<List<Task>> tasksConsumer);

}
```

37.11. Define the API of the model plug-in

Export the `com.vogella.tasks.model` package to define it as API.

For this, open the `MANIFEST.MF` file and select the *Runtime* tab. Add `com.vogella.tasks.model` to the exported packages.

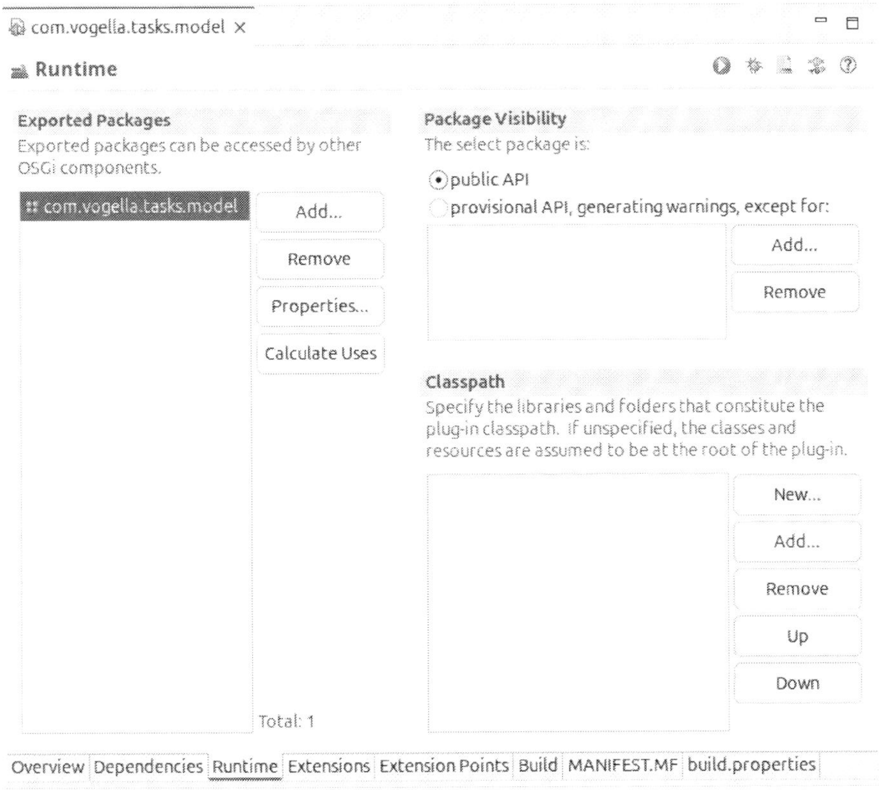

37.12. Next Steps

In the following exercises, you will implement and use an OSGi service that uses this data model.

38. Exercise: Implementing and providing an OSGi service

In this exercise, you create a plug-in for a service implementation. This implementation provides access to the task data.

> This service implementation uses transient data storage, i.e., the data is not persisted between application restarts. A later exercise will persist the data as JSON on the file system.

38.1. Create a new plug-in for the OSGi service

Create a new simple plug-in project called `com.vogella.tasks.services`.

> The macOS operating system treats folders ending with *.service* as special, therefore we use the *.services* ending.

38.2. Define the dependencies in the service plug-in

To use classes from other plug-ins in a plug-in, you need to add a dependency to them.

To achieve this, open the `MANIFEST.MF` file of the `com.vogella.tasks.services` plug-in. Select the *Dependencies* tab and add the following to the *Imported Packages* selection:

- `com.vogella.tasks.model`

The expected output is shown in the screenshot below.

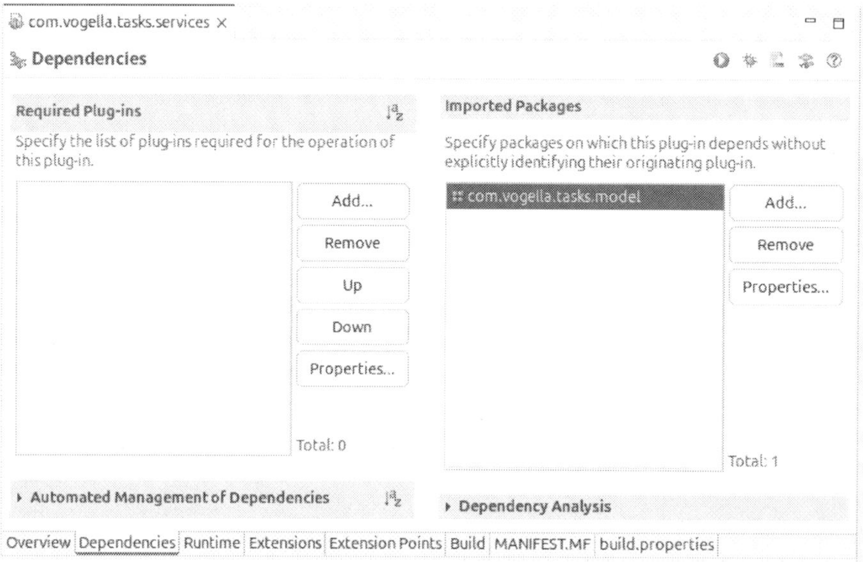

The text file should look similar to the following listing.

```
Manifest-Version: 1.0
Bundle-ManifestVersion: 2
Bundle-Name: Services
Bundle-SymbolicName: com.vogella.tasks.services
Bundle-Version: 1.0.0.qualifier
Import-Package: com.vogella.tasks.model
Bundle-Vendor: VOGELLA
Automatic-Module-Name: com.vogella.tasks.services
Bundle-RequiredExecutionEnvironment: JavaSE-21
```

38.3. Enable annotation processing and plug-in activation

You want to generate OSGi service metadata based on annotations in classes. For this, enable the option under **Window › Preferences › Plug-in Development › DS annotations**.

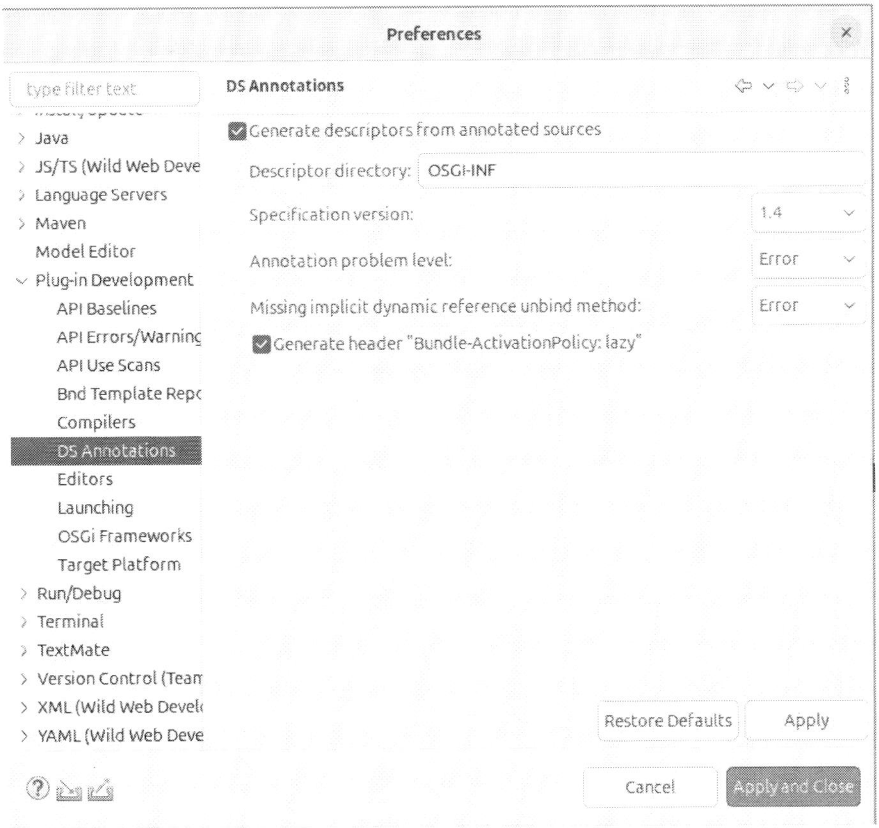

38.4. Provide an implementation of the TaskService interface

Create the `com.vogella.tasks.services.internal` package in your service plug-in and add the following class.

```
package com.vogella.tasks.services.internal;

import java.time.LocalDate;
import java.util.ArrayList;
import java.util.List;
import java.util.Optional;
import java.util.concurrent.atomic.AtomicInteger;
import java.util.function.Consumer;
import java.util.stream.Collectors;

import org.osgi.service.component.annotations.Component;

import com.vogella.tasks.model.Task;
import com.vogella.tasks.model.TaskService;

@Component ❶
public class TransientTaskServiceImpl implements TaskService {

    private static AtomicInteger current = new AtomicInteger(1);
    private List<Task> tasks;

    public TransientTaskServiceImpl() {
        tasks = createTestData();
    }

    @Override
    public List<Task> getAll() {
        return tasks.stream().map(Task::copy).collect(Collectors.toList());
    }

    @Override
    public void consume(Consumer<List<Task>> taskConsumer) {
        // always pass a new copy of the data
        taskConsumer.accept(tasks.stream().map(Task::copy).collect(Collectors.toList()));
    }

    // create or update an existing instance of a task object
    @Override
    public synchronized boolean update(Task newTask) {
        // hold the Optional object as a reference to determine if the object is
        // newly created or not
        Optional<Task> taskOptional = findById(newTask.getId());

        // get the actual object or create a new one
        Task task = taskOptional.orElse(new Task(current.getAndIncrement()));
        task.setSummary(newTask.getSummary());
        task.setDescription(newTask.getDescription());
        task.setDone(newTask.isDone());
```

```
        task.setDueDate(newTask.getDueDate());

        if (!taskOptional.isPresent()) {
            tasks.add(task);
        }
        return true;
    }

    @Override
    public Optional<Task> get(long id) {
        return findById(id).map(Task::copy);
    }

    @Override
    public boolean delete(long id) {
        Optional<Task> deletedTask = findById(id);
        deletedTask.ifPresent(t -> tasks.remove(t));
        return deletedTask.isPresent();
    }

    // Example data, change if you like
    private List<Task> createTestData() {
        List<Task> list = List.of(
                create("Application model", "Dynamics"), create("Application model",
"Flexible and extensible"),
                create("DI", "@Inject as programming mode"), create("OSGi", "Services"),
                create("SWT", "Widgets"), create("JFace", "Especially Viewers!"),
                create("CSS Styling", "Style your application"),
                create("Eclipse services", "Selection, model, Part"),
                create("Renderer", "Different UI toolkit"), create("Compatibility Layer",
"Run Eclipse 3.x"));
        return new ArrayList<>(list);
    }

    private Task create(String summary, String description) {
        return new Task(current.getAndIncrement(), summary, description, false,
            LocalDate.now().plusDays(current.longValue()));
    }

    private Optional<Task> findById(long id) {
        return tasks.stream().filter(t -> t.getId() == id).findAny();
    }
}
```

❶ The `@Component` annotation triggers the generation of OSGi metadata to the class available as OSGi services for the `TaskService` interface.

38.5. Optional: Make due date different

Currently, all tasks have the same due date. You can change this by modifying the `create()` method in the `TransientTaskServiceImpl.

```
private Task create(String summary, String description) {
    int id = current.getAndIncrement();
    // Use the id to deterministically vary the due date
    LocalDate baseDate = LocalDate.now();
    // Create a consistent offset between -3 and +3 days based on the id
    int offset = (id % 7) - 3;
    LocalDate dueDate = baseDate.plusDays(offset);
    return new Task(id, summary, description, false, dueDate);
}
```

38.6. Check manifest

The full manifest looks similar to the following listing:

```
Manifest-Version: 1.0
Bundle-ManifestVersion: 2
Bundle-Name: Services
Bundle-SymbolicName: com.vogella.tasks.services
Bundle-Version: 1.0.0.qualifier
Import-Package: com.vogella.tasks.model
Service-Component: OSGI-INF/com.vogella.tasks.services.TransientTaskServiceImpl.xml
Bundle-Vendor: VOGELLA
Automatic-Module-Name: com.vogella.tasks.services
Bundle-ActivationPolicy: lazy
Bundle-RequiredExecutionEnvironment: JavaSE-21
```

38.7. Add the new plug-in to the product

Add your new plug-ins to your feature:

- `com.vogella.tasks.services`
- `com.vogella.tasks.model`

Ensure that you use the *Plug-ins* tab on the `feature.xml` file. Start your application via your product configuration to ensure that the plug-ins added to the feature are correctly included in the runtime.

> Every time you create a new plug-in and refer to it in your `MANIFEST.MF` file, you have to add it to your feature (`feature.xml`) to include it in your product.

38.8. Further steps

By default, the OSGi runtime initializes and provides services on demand. Therefore, you must explicitly consume an OSGi service for it to start. This is done in the next exercises.

39. Exercise: Consume the OSGi service

In this exercise, you consume the `TaskService` OSGi services you declared earlier.

39.1. Update the plug-in dependencies

In the `MANIFEST.MF` file of your `com.vogella.tasks.ui` plug-in, define a dependency to:

- `com.vogella.tasks.model`

39.2. Get the TaskService injected

Change your `TodoOverviewPart` class so that the `TaskService` implementation is injected into it using your `@PostConstruct` method. Print the number of tasks on the console as demonstrated in the following example.

```
package com.vogella.tasks.ui.parts;

import jakarta.annotation.PostConstruct;

import org.eclipse.swt.widgets.Composite;

import com.vogella.tasks.model.TaskService;

public class TodoOverviewPart {
    @PostConstruct
    public void createControls(Composite parent, TaskService taskService) {
        taskService.consume(tasks -> {
            System.out.println("Number of task objects " + tasks.size());
        });
    }
}
```

39.3. Validate the implementation

Start your application using the product and ensure that you see the number of tasks printed to the console. This number should match the number of tasks created by the `createTestData()` method in the `TransientTaskServiceImpl` class.

See the next section for potential problem areas if this does not work.

39.4. Remove the System.out statement

Remove the test output in `TodoOverviewPart`.

```
package com.vogella.tasks.ui.parts;

import jakarta.annotation.PostConstruct;

import org.eclipse.swt.widgets.Composite;

import com.vogella.tasks.model.TaskService;

public class TodoOverviewPart {
    @PostConstruct
    public void createControls(Composite parent, TaskService taskService) {
        // TODO implement user interface once you learned SWT
    }
}
```

39.5. Error analysis in case the injection did not work

Ensure that you have saved everything (check that the Save All button is inactive).

If you get compilation errors trying to access your classes, ensure that you have exported the required packages as API.

If startup errors occur, verify that `com.vogella.tasks.services` and `com.vogella.tasks.model` are included in your feature. Also, ensure that you used the product to start your application.

If the `TaskService` object cannot be injected, ensure that the *Activate this plug-in when one of its classes is loaded* flag for the plug-in has been set in the `MANIFEST.MF` file of your service plug-in. This should be done automatically by the DS annotation processor.

Based on your annotations, Eclipse creates the necessary OSGi DS files at build time. Review the generated files. The generated component file should look like the following example.

```
<?xml version="1.0" encoding="UTF-8"?>
<scr:component xmlns:scr="http://www.osgi.org/xmlns/scr/v1.1.0"
name="com.vogella.tasks.services.internal.TransientTaskServiceImpl">
   <service>
      <provide interface="com.vogella.tasks.model.TaskService"/>
   </service>
   <implementation class="com.vogella.tasks.services.internal.TransientTaskServiceImpl"/>
</scr:component>
```

This file should also be included in your `build.properties`; this is done automatically by the DS processor.

Eclipse adds a reference to the component file in the `MANIFEST.MF` file under the `Service-Component` reference.

39.6. Reflect on the current service usage design

With this setup, you have completely hidden the specific implementation of the service from the usage. This design is depicted in the following screenshot.

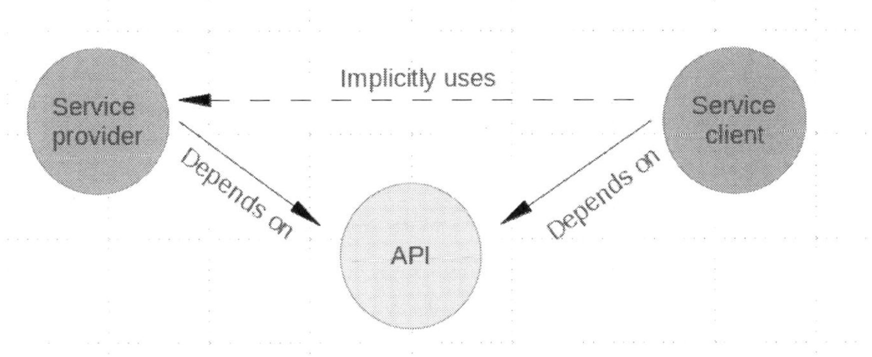

The current service implementation does not persist the data, as it is just a test service. You could replace it with another service implementation. This would not require any changes to your source code or in the dependencies of the consuming plug-ins. You would only have to replace the corresponding service plug-in in your product configuration file (via your feature).

40. Optional exercise: OSGi service capabilities

With capabilities, you can ensure that a bundle providing a service is available when your consumer bundle is resolved. NOTE: Adding `Provide-Capability` and `Require-Capability` is optional, but this ensures that your plug-in does not resolve if no service implementation is present.

40.1. Add the provided capability to the service manifest

The service implementation should define that it provides the `TaskService` service. For this, add the following entry in the manifest.

```
Provide-Capability: osgi.service;
objectClass=com.vogella.tasks.model.TaskService
```

The full manifest looks similar to the following listing:

```
Manifest-Version: 1.0
```

```
Bundle-ManifestVersion: 2
Bundle-Name: Services
Bundle-SymbolicName: com.vogella.tasks.services
Bundle-Version: 1.0.0.qualifier
Import-Package: com.vogella.tasks.model
Bundle-Vendor: VOGELLA
Automatic-Module-Name: com.vogella.tasks.services
Bundle-RequiredExecutionEnvironment: JavaSE-21
Provide-Capability: osgi.service; objectClass=com.vogella.tasks.model.TaskService
```

40.2. Add the required capability to the consumer manifest

In the `MANIFEST.MF` file of your `com.vogella.tasks.ui` plug-in define a dependency to:

Add to the MANIFEST.MF that this plug-in requires an implementation of the `TaskService` interface by adding the following line to the manifest.

```
Require-Capability:
osgi.service;filter:="(objectClass=com.vogella.tasks.model.TaskService)"
```

The full manifest looks similar to the following listing:

```
Manifest-Version: 1.0
Bundle-ManifestVersion: 2
Bundle-Name: Ui
Bundle-SymbolicName: com.vogella.tasks.ui;singleton:=true
Bundle-Version: 1.0.0.qualifier
Bundle-Vendor: VOGELLA
Automatic-Module-Name: com.vogella.tasks.ui
Bundle-RequiredExecutionEnvironment: JavaSE-21
Require-Bundle: org.eclipse.core.runtime,
 org.eclipse.jface,
 org.eclipse.e4.core.di,
 org.eclipse.e4.ui.workbench,
 org.eclipse.e4.ui.di,
 org.eclipse.e4.core.di.extensions,
 org.eclipse.e4.core.contexts
Import-Package: com.vogella.tasks.model,
 jakarta.annotation,
 jakarta.inject
Require-Capability:
osgi.service;filter:="(objectClass=com.vogella.tasks.model.TaskService)"
```

40.3. Explanation

If the service is not available, the consumer plug-in will not resolve and you will see an error message.

41. Optional exercise: Create an image loader service

In this exercise, you create a service for your application that allows you to load images. We use the same plug-in for the interface definition and the service definition. This is a valid setup if you plan to have only one service implementation.

41.1. Creating a new plug-in

Create a new simple plug-in named *com.vogella.imageloader.services*. See Chapter 36 for more information.

Add the following entries as plug-in dependencies to your new plug-in.

- `org.eclipse.core.runtime`
- `org.eclipse.jface`

> The `org.eclipse.jface` plug-in re-exports the `org.eclipse.swt` plug-in. Therefore, if you define a dependency on `org.eclipse.jface`, you can use the classes from `org.eclipse.swt`.

41.2. Creating the service interface

Create the following interface named `IBundleResourceLoader`.

```
package com.vogella.imageloader.services;

import org.eclipse.jface.resource.ImageDescriptor;
import org.eclipse.swt.graphics.Image;

public interface IBundleResourceLoader {

    /**
     * Retrieves an image descriptor for the specified resource.
     * <p><b>Note:</b> The service does NOT dispose the provided image.
     * The consumer of the image is responsible for calling the {@code dispose()} method
     * on the created Image object once the Image is not required anymore.
     * This can be automated with the usage of LocalResourceManager.
     *
     * @param clazz the class used to locate the resource
     * @param path the path to the image resource
     * @return the image descriptor for the specified resource
     */
    public ImageDescriptor getImageDescriptor(Class<?> clazz, String path);
```

```
    /**
     * Resizes an image.
     * <p><b>Note:</b> The caller must dispose both the original and the returned image.
     * @param image the image to resize
     * @param width the new width
     * @param height the new height
     * @return a new resized image
     */
    public Image resize(Image image, int width, int height);
}
```

41.3. Creating a service implementation

> Ensure that the OSGi DS annotation *Generate descriptors from annotated sources* setting is active via **Window › Preferences › Plug-in Development › DS Annotations**.

Create the following class. It allows you, via its `getImageDescriptor()` method, to load an ImageDescriptor from a plug-in.

```
package com.vogella.imageloader.services.internal;

import java.net.URL;

import org.eclipse.core.runtime.FileLocator;
import org.eclipse.core.runtime.Path;
import org.eclipse.jface.resource.ImageDescriptor;
import org.eclipse.swt.SWT;
import org.eclipse.swt.graphics.GC;
import org.eclipse.swt.graphics.Image;
import org.eclipse.swt.widgets.Display;
import org.osgi.framework.Bundle;
import org.osgi.framework.FrameworkUtil;
import org.osgi.service.component.annotations.Component;

import com.vogella.imageloader.services.IBundleResourceLoader;

@Component
public class BundleResourceLoaderImpl implements IBundleResourceLoader {

    @Override
    public ImageDescriptor getImageDescriptor(Class<?> clazz, String path) {
        Bundle bundle = FrameworkUtil.getBundle(clazz);
        URL url = FileLocator.find(bundle,
```

```
            new Path(path), null);
        return ImageDescriptor.createFromURL(url);
    }

    @Override
    public Image resize(Image image, int width, int height) {
        Image scaled = new Image(Display.getDefault(), width, height);
        GC gc = new GC(scaled);
        gc.setAntialias(SWT.ON);
        gc.setInterpolation(SWT.HIGH);
        gc.drawImage(image, 0, 0, image.getBounds().width, image.getBounds().height, 0,
0, width, height);
        gc.dispose();
//      image.dispose(); // caller needs to do this
        return scaled;
    }
}
```

41.4. Adding the new plug-in to the feature project

Add the new plug-in to your product configuration file via your feature project.

41.5. Exporting the API

Export the package that contains the interface via the corresponding `MANIFEST.MF` file. This allows you to consume the service in another plug-in.

For this, open the `MANIFEST.MF` editor, switch to the *Runtime* tab and use the *Add* button to add the new package.

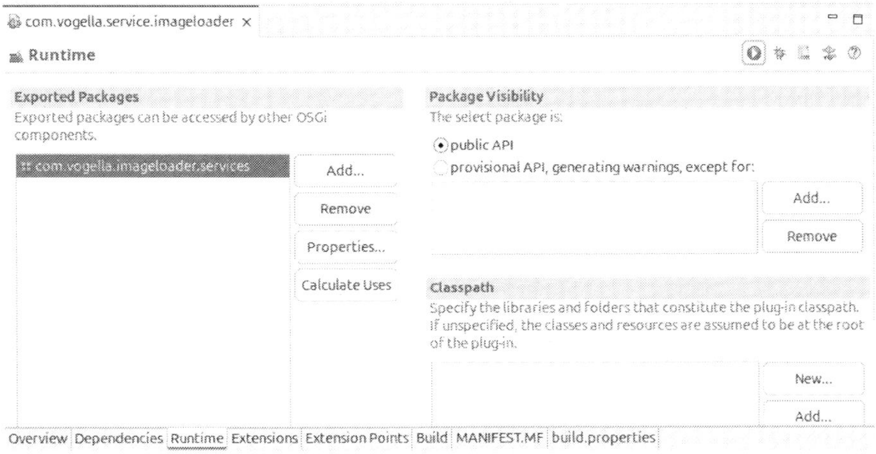

41.6. Adding the dependencies to the new plug-in

Define a dependency on the new package (or the whole plug-in) in the `MANIFEST.MF` file of your `com.vogella.tasks.ui` plug-in.

Also ensure you have a dependency on `org.eclipse.jface` in your `com.vogella.tasks.ui` manifest.

41.7. Using the new service

In your `com.vogella.tasks.ui` plug-in, create a folder named *`images`*. Add an image file named `vogella.png` to this folder. You can find such an image via a Google search for **vogella.png**, or use any **.png** file of your choice.

Your project should now contain the following structure:

```
com.vogella.tasks.ui
├── META-INF/
├── OSGI-INF/
├── icons/
├── src/
└── images/
    └── vogella.png
```

The vogella.png should be placed directly in the *com.vogella.tasks.ui/images* folder, not in a subfolder or the *src* folder.

Use the image loader service in your `PlaygroundPart` class. The following code demonstrates the usage of your service based on the path name from above.

```
package com.vogella.tasks.ui.parts;

import jakarta.annotation.PostConstruct;

import org.eclipse.jface.resource.JFaceResources;
import org.eclipse.jface.resource.LocalResourceManager;
import org.eclipse.jface.resource.ResourceManager;
import org.eclipse.swt.SWT;
import org.eclipse.swt.graphics.Image;
import org.eclipse.swt.widgets.Composite;
import org.eclipse.swt.widgets.Label;

import com.vogella.imageloader.services.IBundleResourceLoader;

public class PlaygroundPart {
    @PostConstruct
```

```
    public void createControls(Composite parent, IBundleResourceLoader loader) {
        Label label = new Label(parent, SWT.NONE);

        // the following code assumes that you have a vogella.png file
        // in a folder named "images" in this plug-in
        ResourceManager resourceManager =
                new LocalResourceManager(JFaceResources.getResources(), label);
        Image image = resourceManager.
                create(
                        loader.getImageDescriptor(this.getClass(),
"images/vogella.png"));
        label.setImage(image);
    }
}
```

The result might look like the following.

Since you added plug-ins, start your application via the product configuration file to pick up all changes.

Add the new folder to your **build.properties** file to ensure that the image is included in the build.

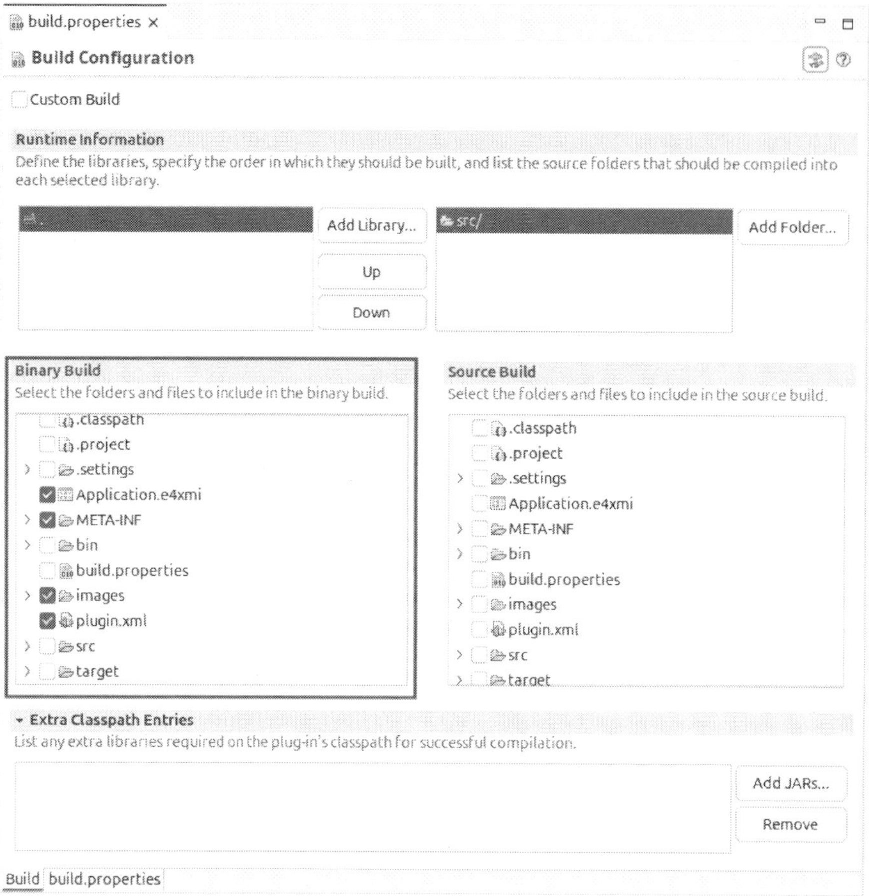

41.8. Optional exercise: Display a SVG image

Search the internet for a SVG image of your choice and add it to your project. Adjust the `PlaygroundPart` class to load this image.

```
Image image = resourceManager.
          create(loader.getImageDescriptor(this.getClass(), "images/sbahn.svg"));
```

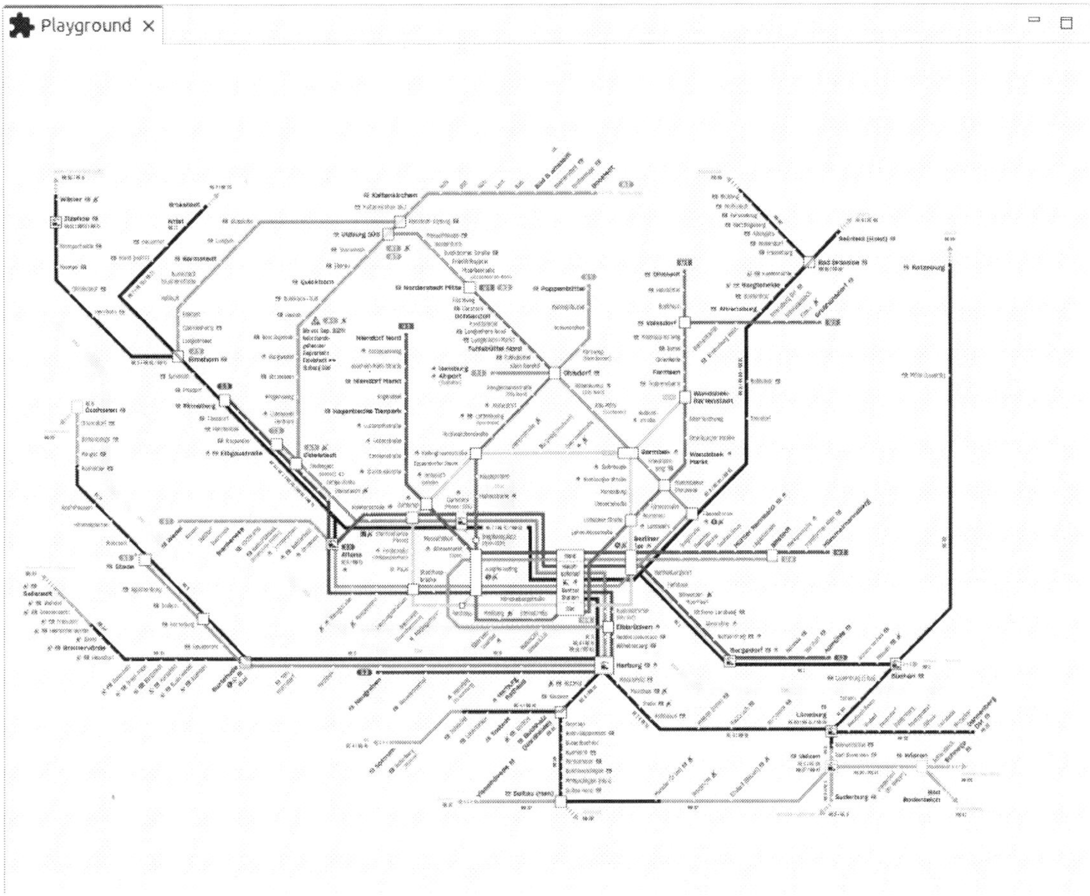

Ensure that this image is also included in the `build.properties` file.

41.9. Reflection on the implementation

In this example, the service interface and the implementation class are contained in the same plug-in. Therefore, this plug-in needs to export the interface and consuming plug-ins must define a dependency on the package or plug-in. In the first OSGi service exercise, we separated the implementation and the service interface. This allows you to replace the service implementation with another plug-in.

Both approaches are valid. You typically put the interface and implementation in one plug-in if you do not expect an alternative service implementation.

42. Optional exercise: Use the OSGi console

In this exercise, you learn how to use the OSGi console to analyze the state of your plug-ins at runtime.

Ensure that the `-console` parameter is set in your run configuration as runtime parameter.

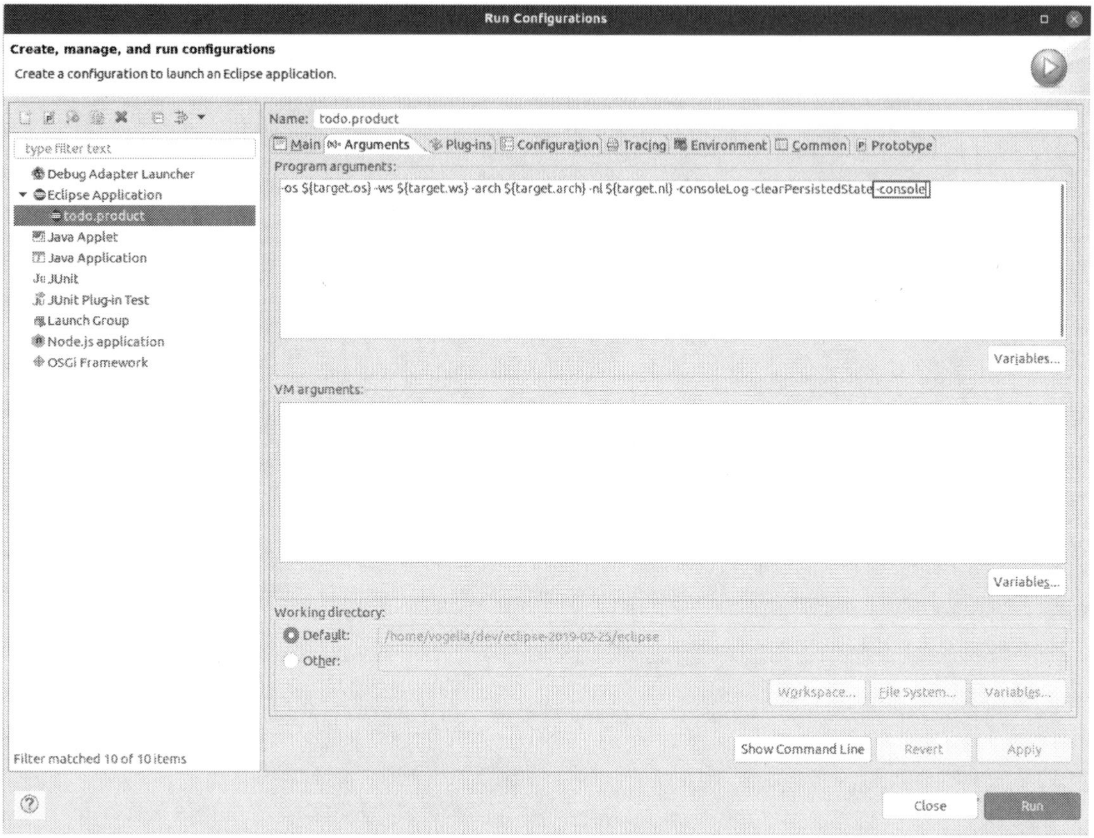

To use the console, you need to have the following components included in your runtime:

- org.eclipse.equinox.console
- org.apache.felix.gogo.command
- org.apache.felix.gogo.runtime
- org.apache.felix.gogo.shell

If you followed this description, this should already be the case.

Click the `Validate` button to ensure all dependencies are included. If something is missing, use the Select Required button to add it.

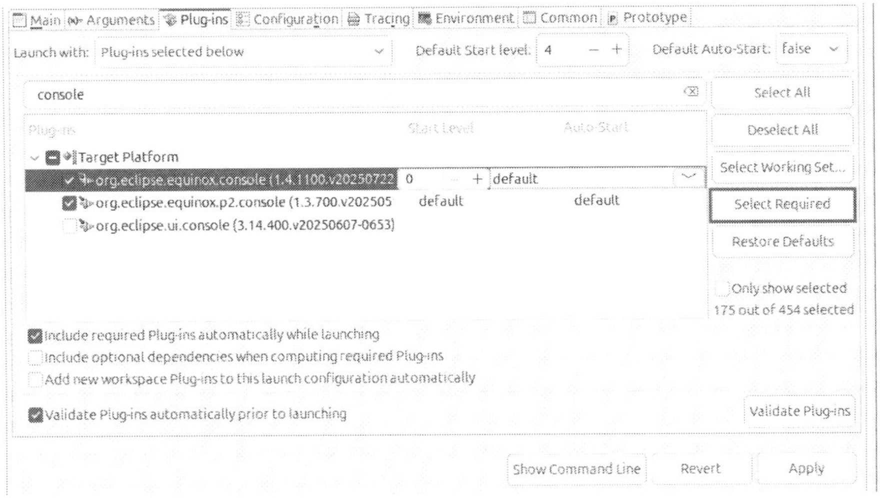

Start your application. In the *Console* view of Eclipse, use the following commands:

- `ss` - see short status of your plug-ins, also shows the IDs of the plug-ins
- `bundle <id-of-the-plug-in>` - get an overview of the bundle
- `diag <id-of-the-plug-in>` - get information about the bundle
- `scr:list` - show all the OSGi components
- `scr:list <id-of-the-plug-in>` - show the OSGi components of that plug-in

Part VIII: User interface development with SWT and JFace

43. SWT overview

43.1. Using SWT and JFace

The Standard Widget Toolkit (*SWT*) is a Java-based user interface library for developing desktop applications. SWT supports Windows, Linux, and macOS.

It provides many standard widgets, such as buttons and text fields, as well as the option to create custom widgets.

SWT uses the native widgets of the platform whenever possible. The native widgets of the operating system are accessed by the SWT framework via the *Java Native Interface* (JNI). If a widget is not natively available on a platform, SWT emulates this widget on that platform.

JFace adds additional functionality on top of SWT, making it easier to use. In this description, we use the JFace builder API on top of the SWT API to simplify the creation of SWT-based user interfaces.

43.2. Display and Shell

The `Display` and `Shell` classes are key components of SWT applications.

An `org.eclipse.swt.widgets.Shell` class represents a window.

The `org.eclipse.swt.widgets.Display` class is responsible for managing event loops, fonts, and colors. It also controls communication between the user interface thread and other threads. `Display` is therefore the basis for all SWT functionality.

Every SWT application requires at least one `Display` and one or more `Shell` instances.

43.3. Event loop

An event loop transfers user input events from the underlying native operating system widgets to the SWT event system.

The programmer explicitly starts and checks the event loop to update the user interface. The loop calls the `readAndDispatch()` method, which retrieves events from the native operating system event queue and dispatches them to the SWT event system. Without this loop, the application will terminate immediately. The loop is executed until the main shell is closed.

For example, the following creates an SWT application that sets up and executes the event loop.

```
Display display = new Display();
Shell shell = new Shell(display);
shell.open();

while (!shell.isDisposed()) { ❶
    if (!display.readAndDispatch()) { ❷
        display.sleep(); ❸
    }
}

// disposes all associated windows and their components
display.dispose();
```

❶ run the event loop as long as the window is open

❷ read the next OS event queue and transfer it to an SWT event

❸ if there are currently no other OS events to process, sleep until the next OS event is available

If SWT is used for an Eclipse IDE plug-in or an Eclipse RCP application, the event loop is provided by the Eclipse framework.

44. SWT Widgets

44.1. Available widgets in the SWT library

SWT widgets are located in the packages `org.eclipse.swt.widgets` and `org.eclipse.swt.custom`. Widgets extend either the `Widget` or the `Control` class. Several of these widgets are depicted in the following screenshot of the SWT widget homepage [https://eclipse.dev/eclipse/swt/widgets/index.html].

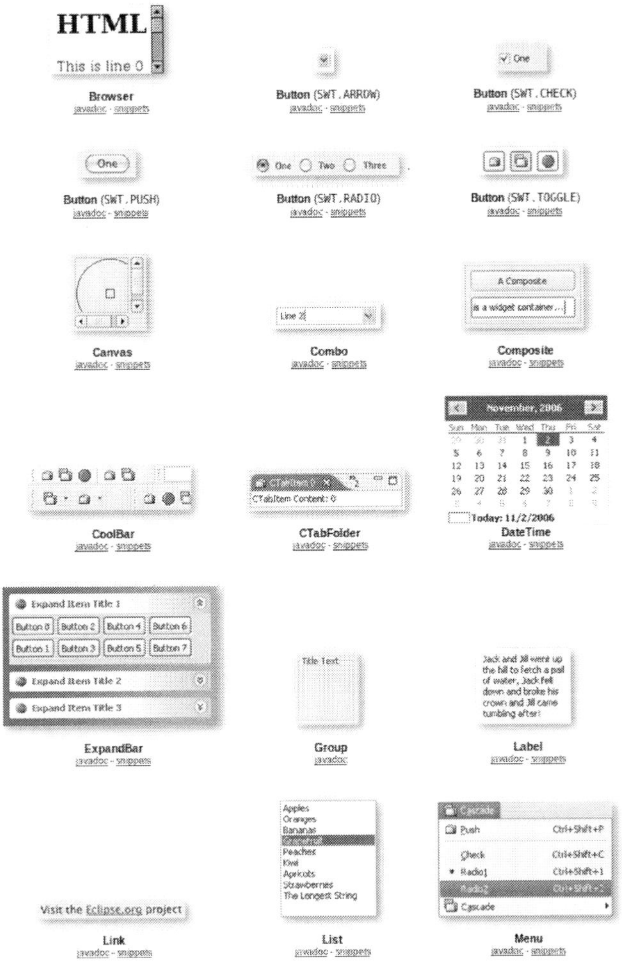

The `Composite` class is a container for other widgets.

The `Group` class is another container that can contain other widgets. It also draws a border around itself and allows you to set a header for the grouped widgets.

44.2. Constructing and configuring widgets

SWT widgets, except for the `Shell` object, are always constructed with a parent widget that contains them.

The second parameter of the widget constructor contains the *style bits*. Depending on the provided style bits, the widget adjusts its look and feel as well as its behavior. Each widget documents the supported style bits in its Javadoc.

The possible style bits are predefined in the `SWT` class. If no special style is required, you can pass `SWT.NONE`.

For example, the following code snippet creates a push button or a checkbox, depending on the passed style flags.

```
Button b1 = new Button(shell, SWT.PUSH);

Button b2 = new Button(shell, SWT.CHECK);
```

After construction, the widget offers methods to configure its behavior.

```
Button b1 = new Button(parent, SWT.PUSH);
b1.setText("Press me");
b1.addSelectionListener(SelectionListener.widgetSelectedAdapter(e-> System.out.println
("Pressed")));
```

JFace offers a builder API for multiple SWT widgets that simplifies the creation of widgets. The above example can be rewritten as follows:

```
WidgetFactory.button(SWT.PUSH).text("Press me").onSelect(e-> System.out.println(
"Pressed")).create(parent);
```

Or in case you use a static import for `WidgetFactory`.

```
import static org.eclipse.jface.widgets.WidgetFactory.button;
// more code
button(SWT.PUSH).text("Press me").onSelect(e-> System.out.println("Pressed")).create
(parent);
```

44.3. Custom widgets and native widgets

SWT provides custom-drawn widgets in `org.eclipse.swt.custom` package for cases in which the native widgets are not sufficient for the needs of SWT. For example, the `CCombo` class allows you to set the height of the widget, which the `Combo` class does not support. Custom-drawn widgets usually start with the additional prefix `C` to indicate that they are custom widgets, e.g., `CCombo`.

Another example is `StyledText`, a class that provides advanced features for displaying text, e.g., drawing a background.

Widgets in `org.eclipse.swt.widgets` are implemented with platform-specific code. On the other hand, widgets from the package `org.eclipse.swt.custom` are implemented in pure Java. Custom widgets are not supposed to use the internal classes of SWT as these classes may be different on the various platforms. Every custom widget should extend the `Composite` or `Canvas` class. API compliance is guaranteed only for these base classes.

If the new custom widget is supposed to contain other widgets, it should extend `Composite`. Otherwise, it should extend the `Canvas` class.

44.4. Memory management

SWT widgets retain a reference to the native widget. Such references are not automatically released by the system.

When a container, such as a `Shell`, is disposed of, it automatically releases all its children.

For certain widgets, you must explicitly call their `dispose()` method when they are no longer needed. These are the following widgets:

- `Cursor`
- `Display`
- `Font`
- `GC`
- `Image`
- `Printer`
- `Region`.

> JFace provides a way to dispose of such objects based on another widget, via the `LocalResourceManager` class.

44.5. Event Listener

You can register listeners for specific events on SWT controls. For example, a `ModifyListener` to listen to changes in a `Text` widget or a `SelectionListener` for selection (click) events on a `Button` widget. The pure SWT implementation uses `add` followed by the type of event. For example:

```
Button button =  new Button(shell, SWT.PUSH);
button.setText("Press me");

//register listener for the selection event
button.addSelectionListener(SelectionListener.widgetSelectedAdapter(e -> System.out
.println("Called!")));
```

`FocusListener` is another example for such a listener interface.

The `Listener` interfaces contain several methods, and therefore, Eclipse provides empty default implementations for these interfaces. This allows you to implement only the methods you are interested in. These implementations follow the naming convention:

Name*Listener › Name*Adapter

For example, the `SelectionListener` interface has an abstract class, `SelectionAdapter`, that provides default implementations of its methods.

The JFace builder API simplifies event registration by providing methods that accept a lambda for certain events.

```
import static org.eclipse.jface.widgets.WidgetFactory.button;
// more code
button(SWT.PUSH).text("Press me").onSelect(e-> System.out.println("Pressed")).create
(parent);
```

If you want to add a listener to the whole application, you can use the `Display` class. For example, to add a global mouse listener use `Display.addFilter(SWT.MouseMove, listener)`. If you add filters to the `Display` you may interfere with existing listeners. Ensure that you test your code accordingly.

44.6. Colors in SWT

Colors can be defined in SWT or system colors can be reused.

```
Device device = Display.getCurrent();
Color red = new Color (device, 255, 0, 0);

// Using system colors

Display display = Display.getCurrent();
Color blue = display.getSystemColor(SWT.COLOR_BLUE);
Color listBackground = display.getSystemColor(SWT.COLOR_LIST_BACKGROUND);
```

If you create colors, you do NOT need to call `dispose()` since the Eclipse 2020-06 release.

45. Positioning widgets

45.1. Manually placing widgets on a Composite

Controls must be placed inside their container. You can manually define their position and size using the `setBounds` method. This method allows you to specify the starting position, width, and height. The coordinates start at the top-left corner of the containing `Composite`.

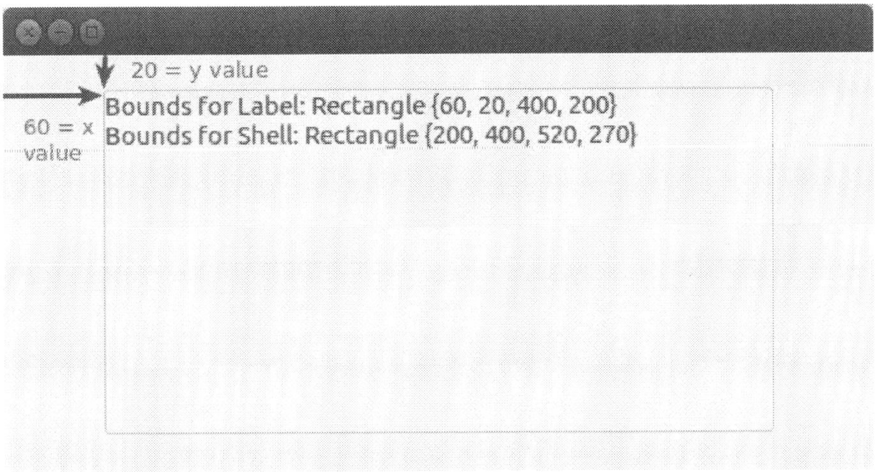


```
package com.vogella.swt.widgets.layout;

import org.eclipse.swt.SWT;
import org.eclipse.swt.events.MouseEvent;
import org.eclipse.swt.events.MouseListener;
import org.eclipse.swt.widgets.Display;
import org.eclipse.swt.widgets.Label;
import org.eclipse.swt.widgets.Shell;

public class SWTLayoutPositionTracker {

    static String newLine = System.getProperty("line.separator");
    private static Label positionLabel;
    private static Shell shell;
    public static void main(String[] args) {
        Display display = new Display();
        shell = new Shell(display);
        positionLabel = new Label(shell, SWT.BORDER);
        int x= 60;
        int y=20;
        int width =400;
```

```
        int height=200;

        positionLabel.setBounds(x, y, width, height);
        int toolbarSize = 30;

        shell.setBounds(200, 400, width+2*x , height + 2*y +toolbarSize);
        shell.open();

        shell.addMouseMoveListener(e -> showSize(e));
        positionLabel.addMouseMoveListener(e -> showSize(e));

        while (!shell.isDisposed()) {
            if (!display.readAndDispatch())
                display.sleep();
        }
        display.dispose();
    }

    public static void showSize(MouseEvent e) {
        int x = e.x;
        int y = e.y;
        String s = "Bounds for Label: " + positionLabel.getBounds() + newLine;
        s+= "Bounds for Shell: " + shell.getBounds()  + newLine;
        s+= "Mouse pointer: " + x + " " + y;
        positionLabel.setText(s);
    }
}
```

`setBounds` defines both the position and size. You can also use `setLocation` and `setSize` to define the position and size separately.

45.2. The role of a layout manager

A layout manager is responsible for arranging the widgets within a container, such as a `Composite`. SWT offers several standard layout managers. The following table provides an overview of them.

Table 14. Layout Manager

Layout Manager	Description
AbsoluteLayout	Allows you to specify the exact position, width, and height of components. As user interfaces may be used on screens with different sizes, this layout manager should generally be avoided.
FillLayout	Arranges equal-sized widgets in a single row or column.

Layout Manager	Description
RowLayout	Arranges the widgets in rows or columns and allows you to control the layout with options such as wrap, spacing, and fill.
GridLayout	Arranges widgets in a grid.
BorderLayout	Allows you to arrange the widgets in different regions, SWT.TOP, SWT.CENTER, SWT.LEFT, SWT.RIGHT, SWT.BOTTOM.
FormLayout	Arranges the widgets with the help of the associated attachments.
StackLayout	This layout stacks all the controls on top of each other and resizes all controls to have the same size and location. The control specified in `topControl` is visible and all other controls are not visible.

If you assign a layout manager to a control, you no longer need to call `pack()`. You can call the `pack()` method if a control has no layout. You typically call `pack()` on a container to make it resize to fit its contents, regardless of whether layout managers are used.

45.3. Layout Data

Each SWT widget can have a layout specific settings class assigned to it, e.g., `GridData` for a `GridLayout`. This allows the developer to control the arrangement of the widgets within the layout.

In the following example, you specify that a widget should span two columns in a `GridLayout`.

```
button = new Button(parent, SWT.PUSH);
GridData gridData = new GridData();
gridData.horizontalSpan = 2;
button.setLayoutData(gridData);
```

> The layout data used must match the layout manager; otherwise, an exception is thrown at runtime.

The layout will be automatically calculated when the container is displayed. You can tell a `Composite` to recalculate its layout with the `composite.requestLayout()` method.

> Layout data objects should not be reused as the layout manager expects that every user interface element has a unique layout data object.

45.4. FillLayout

`FillLayout` divides the available space provided by the container equally to all widgets. It can arrange the widgets either horizontally (`SWT.HORIZONTAL`) or vertically (`SWT.VERTICAL`). It also allows you to set the space between the widgets (attribute `spacing`) and the margins of the widgets to the container via the `marginWidth` and `marginHeight` attributes.

45.5. RowLayout

`RowLayout` orders UI components in a row (`SWT.HORIZONTAL`) or in a column (`SWT.VERTICAL`). `RowLayout` supports wrapping of widgets (property `wrap`) by default. Via the `pack` property, you can define if widgets have their preferred size (default) or if they grab the available space. It is also possible to set margins at the top, bottom, left, and right. If you set `justify`, the widgets will be spread throughout the available space.

Each element can specify its height and width using a `RowData` element.

45.6. GridLayout

`GridLayout` allows you to arrange the user interface components in a Grid with a certain number of columns. It is also possible to specify column and row spanning.

You can use `new GridData()` and assign properties to the new object. Alternatively, you can use one of its richer constructors to define certain attributes during construction. For example, via the following constructor:

```
new GridData(horizontalAlignment,
    verticalAlignment,
    grabExcessHorizontalSpace,
    grabExcessVerticalSpace,
    horizontalSpan,
    verticalSpan)
```

The most important attributes are defined in the following table.

Table 15. GridData

Parameter	Description
horizontalAlignment	Defines how the control is positioned horizontally within a cell (one of: `SWT.LEFT`, `SWT.CENTER`, `SWT.RIGHT`, or `SWT.FILL`).
verticalAlignment	Defines how the control is positioned vertically within a cell (one of: `SWT.TOP`, `SWT.CENTER`, `SWT.END`, `SWT.BOTTOM` (treated the same as SWT.END), or `SWT.FILL`).
grabExcessHorizontalSpace	Defines whether the control is extended by the layout manager to take all the remaining horizontal space.
grabExcessVerticalSpace	Defines whether the control grabs any remaining vertical space.

Parameter	Description
horizontalSpan	Defines the number of column cells that the control takes.
verticalSpan	Defines the number of row cells that the control will take up.
heightHint	Defines the preferred height in pixels.
widthHint	Defines the preferred width in pixels.

If the widget has the `grabExcessHorizontalSpace` attribute set to true, it will grab available space in its container. `SWT.FILL` tells the widget to fill the available space. Therefore, `grabExcessHorizontalSpace` and `SWT.FILL` are often used together.

45.7. Using GridDataFactory

The `GridDataFactory` class can be used to create `GridData` objects. This class provides a convenient shorthand for creating and initializing these objects. The following listing demonstrates its usage and compares it with the direct usage of `GridData`.

```
// listBox is an SWT widget

// GridDataFactory version
GridDataFactory.fillDefaults().grab(true, true).hint(150, 150).applyTo(listBox);

// Equivalent SWT version
GridData listBoxData = new GridData(GridData.FILL_BOTH);
listBoxData.widthHint = 150;
listBoxData.heightHint = 150;
listBoxData.minimumWidth = 1;
listBoxData.minimumHeight = 1;
listBox.setLayoutData(listBoxData);
```

The Javadoc of this class contains several examples for it.

45.8. BorderLayout

`BorderLayout` allows you to place widgets in different regions via the `BorderData#region`.

- SWT.TOP
- SWT.CENTER
- SWT.LEFT
- SWT.RIGHT
- SWT.BOTTOM

The top, left, right, and bottom widgets get their necessary space; the rest is available for the widgets placed in the center.

The usage is demonstrated here, in which a given `Composite` uses this layout.

```
var layoutManager = new BorderLayout();
var display = Display.getDefault();
parent.setLayout(layoutManager);
// TOP
var topLabel = new Label(parent, SWT.NONE);
topLabel.setBackground(display.getSystemColor(SWT.COLOR_RED));
topLabel.setLayoutData(new BorderData(SWT.TOP));

// CENTER
var centerLabel = new Label(parent, SWT.NONE);
centerLabel.setBackground(display.getSystemColor(SWT.COLOR_GREEN));
centerLabel.setLayoutData(new BorderData(SWT.CENTER));

// BOTTOM
var bottomLabel = new Label(parent, SWT.NONE);
bottomLabel.setBackground(display.getSystemColor(SWT.COLOR_BLUE));
bottomLabel.setLayoutData(new BorderData(SWT.BOTTOM));

// LEFT
var leftLabel = new Label(parent, SWT.NONE);
leftLabel.setText("LEFT");
leftLabel.setBackground(display.getSystemColor(SWT.COLOR_YELLOW));
leftLabel.setLayoutData(new BorderData(SWT.LEFT));

// RIGHT we have two widgets
var rightLabel1 = new Label(parent, SWT.NONE);
rightLabel1.setText("RIGHT");
rightLabel1.setBackground(display.getSystemColor(SWT.COLOR_DARK_CYAN));
rightLabel1.setLayoutData(new BorderData(SWT.RIGHT));

var rightLabel2 = new Label(parent, SWT.NONE);

rightLabel2.setBackground(display.getSystemColor(SWT.COLOR_GRAY));
rightLabel2.setLayoutData(new BorderData(SWT.RIGHT));
```

The result looks similar to the following screenshot.

45.9. FormLayout

`FormLayout` works by creating `FormAttachments` for each side of the widget, and storing them in the layout data. The specific side of the widget is attached either to a position in the parent `Composite` or to another widget within the layout. This allows you to control on a detailed level the placement of individual widgets within the layout.

45.10. Adding and removing children from a Composite

You can add children at runtime to a `Composite`. By default, they are placed after the existing controls, but you can reposition them via the `moveAbove` and `moveBelow` method calls.

To remove a child from a layout, call its `dispose` method. To update the parent composite after you have removed or added children, call its `requestLayout` method.

The following is an example of how to dynamically create new rows in an existing layout and how to remove these rows.

```
package com.vogella.swt.widgets.layout;

import java.util.ArrayList;
import java.util.List;

import org.eclipse.swt.SWT;
import org.eclipse.swt.events.MouseAdapter;
import org.eclipse.swt.events.MouseEvent;
import org.eclipse.swt.events.SelectionAdapter;
import org.eclipse.swt.events.SelectionEvent;
import org.eclipse.swt.graphics.Color;
import org.eclipse.swt.layout.FillLayout;
import org.eclipse.swt.layout.GridData;
import org.eclipse.swt.layout.GridLayout;
import org.eclipse.swt.widgets.Button;
import org.eclipse.swt.widgets.Composite;
import org.eclipse.swt.widgets.Display;
import org.eclipse.swt.widgets.Label;
import org.eclipse.swt.widgets.MessageBox;
```

```
import org.eclipse.swt.widgets.Shell;

public class SWTDynamicLayoutChanges {

    static int number = 0;
    private static List<Color> colors;
    private static int colorIndex;

    public static void main(String[] args) {

        Display display = new Display();
        Shell shell = new Shell(display);
        colorIndex = 0;
        colors = new ArrayList<>();
        colors.add(Display.getDefault().getSystemColor(SWT.COLOR_RED));
        colors.add(Display.getDefault().getSystemColor(SWT.COLOR_GREEN));
        colors.add(Display.getDefault().getSystemColor(SWT.COLOR_YELLOW));
        colors.add(Display.getDefault().getSystemColor(SWT.COLOR_CYAN));
        colors.add(new Color (Display.getDefault(), 122, 122, 122));
        colors.add(new Color (Display.getDefault(), 255, 51, 227));
        colors.add(new Color (Display.getDefault(), 27, 82, 255));
        colors.add(new Color (Display.getDefault(), 240, 201, 27));
        colors.add(new Color (Display.getDefault(), 188, 188, 188));
        colors.add(Display.getDefault().getSystemColor(SWT.COLOR_DARK_MAGENTA));

        GridLayout gridLayout = new GridLayout(1, false);
        gridLayout.marginWidth = 0;
        gridLayout.marginHeight = 0;
        gridLayout.verticalSpacing = 0;
        gridLayout.horizontalSpacing = 0;
        shell.setLayout(gridLayout);

        Composite top = new Composite(shell, SWT.NONE);
        GridData d1 = new GridData(SWT.FILL, SWT.FILL, true, true);
        top.setLayoutData(d1);
        top.setBackground(Display.getDefault().getSystemColor(SWT.COLOR_GREEN));

        createLayer(shell);
        createLayer(shell);
        createLayer(shell);

        shell.setBounds(100, 100, 800, 600);
        shell.open();

        while (!shell.isDisposed()) {
            if (!display.readAndDispatch())
                display.sleep();
        }
        display.dispose();
```

```
    }

    private static Composite createLayer(Composite parent) {

        Composite layer = new Composite(parent, SWT.NONE);
        layer.setLayout(new FillLayout());
        for (int i = 0; i < 10; i++) {
            Label label = new Label(layer, SWT.NONE);
            label.setText("I go \u26F7");
            label.addMouseListener(new MouseAdapter() {

                @Override
                public void mouseDown(MouseEvent e) {
                    Shell shell =Display.getDefault().getActiveShell();
                    MessageBox dialog =
                            new MessageBox(shell, SWT.ICON_QUESTION | SWT.OK| SWT.
CANCEL);
                    dialog.setText("My info");
                    dialog.setMessage("Do you want to do this?");
                    dialog.open();
                }
            });
        }
        Button removeButton = new Button(layer, SWT.PUSH);
        removeButton.setText("Remove");
        removeButton.addSelectionListener(new SelectionAdapter() {
            @Override
            public void widgetSelected(SelectionEvent e) {
                layer.dispose();
                parent.requestLayout();
            }
        });

        Button addButton = new Button(layer, SWT.PUSH);
        addButton.setText("Add");
        addButton.addSelectionListener(new SelectionAdapter() {
            @Override
            public void widgetSelected(SelectionEvent e) {
                Composite composite = createLayer(parent);
                composite.moveAbove(addButton.getParent());
                parent.requestLayout();
            }
        });

        GridData d2 = new GridData(SWT.FILL, SWT.TOP, true, false);
        layer.setLayoutData(d2);
        if (colorIndex > colors.size()-1 ) {
            colorIndex = 0;
        }
```

```
        layer.setBackground(colors.get(colorIndex++));
        return layer;
    }
}
```

45.11. Triggering a re-layout of a Composite

As of Eclipse 4.7 you should use the `requestLayout()` method call on the `Composite` class, as this triggers an asynchronous layout call.

The `Composite` widget also defines the `layout()` method which triggers a synchronous layout. The `layout()` method will recursively call `layout()` on child composites as well. Prefer using `requestLayout()` on the individual composites if necessary, as this is faster. The `layout()` method also accepts child widgets and flags.

Table 16. Layout flags

Flag	Description
SWT.ALL	Flag forces all descendants to be marked for layout. The usage of this flag is generally discouraged. If it is actually doing something, it could be replaced by a series of calls to `requestLayout`.
SWT.CHANGED	The flag causes subsequent calls to `Layout.layout(…)` to receive `true` for the second argument, which forces the layout to recursively flush all caches. Avoid doing this, as this is performance-intensive. If something has changed, the layout should be notified via `Layout.flushCache(control)`, which is automatically done when you invoke `requestLayout`. This is either a brute-force workaround for a stale layout bug or was just unnecessary. The usage of `SWT.CHANGED` should not be necessary in client code if the rest of the layout is correctly defined.

45.12. Example: Using GridLayout manager

The following example demonstrates the usage of the `GridLayout` class in the `com.example.swt.widgets` project.

```
package com.example.swt.widgets.layouts;

import org.eclipse.swt.SWT;
import org.eclipse.swt.layout.GridData;
import org.eclipse.swt.layout.GridLayout;
import org.eclipse.swt.layout.RowLayout;
import org.eclipse.swt.widgets.Button;
import org.eclipse.swt.widgets.Composite;
```

```
import org.eclipse.swt.widgets.Display;
import org.eclipse.swt.widgets.Group;
import org.eclipse.swt.widgets.Label;
import org.eclipse.swt.widgets.Shell;
import org.eclipse.swt.widgets.Spinner;
import org.eclipse.swt.widgets.Text;

public class GridLayoutSWT {
    public static void main(String[] args) {
        Display display = new Display();
        Shell shell = new Shell(display);
        GridLayout layout = new GridLayout(2, false);

        // set the layout to the shell
        shell.setLayout(layout);

        // create a label and a button
        Label label = new Label(shell, SWT.NONE);
        label.setText("A label");
        Button button = new Button(shell, SWT.PUSH);
        button.setText("Press Me");

        // create a new label that will span two columns
        label = new Label(shell, SWT.BORDER);
        label.setText("This is a label");
        // create new layout data
        GridData data = new GridData(SWT.FILL, SWT.TOP, true, false, 2, 1);
        label.setLayoutData(data);

        // create a new label which is used as a separator
        label = new Label(shell, SWT.SEPARATOR | SWT.HORIZONTAL);

        // create new layout data
        data = new GridData(SWT.FILL, SWT.TOP, true, false);
        data.horizontalSpan = 2;
        label.setLayoutData(data);

        // creates a push button
        Button b = new Button(shell, SWT.PUSH);
        b.setText("New Button");

        data = new GridData(SWT.LEFT, SWT.TOP, false, false, 2, 1);
        b.setLayoutData(data);

         // create a spinner with min value 0 and max value 1000
        Spinner spinner = new Spinner(shell, SWT.READ_ONLY);
        spinner.setMinimum(0);
        spinner.setMaximum(1000);
        spinner.setSelection(500);
```

```
spinner.setIncrement(1);
spinner.setPageIncrement(100);
GridData gridData = new GridData(SWT.FILL, SWT.FILL, true, false);
gridData.widthHint = SWT.DEFAULT;
gridData.heightHint = SWT.DEFAULT;
gridData.horizontalSpan = 2;
spinner.setLayoutData(gridData);

Composite composite = new Composite(shell, SWT.BORDER);
gridData = new GridData(SWT.FILL, SWT.FILL, true, false);
gridData.horizontalSpan = 2;
composite.setLayoutData(gridData);
composite.setLayout(new GridLayout(1, false));

Text txtTest = new Text(composite, SWT.NONE);
txtTest.setText("Testing");
gridData = new GridData(SWT.FILL, SWT.FILL, true, false);
txtTest.setLayoutData(gridData);

Text txtMoreTests = new Text(composite, SWT.NONE);
txtMoreTests.setText("Another test");

Group group = new Group(shell, SWT.NONE);
group.setText("This is my group");
gridData = new GridData(SWT.FILL, SWT.FILL, true, false);
gridData.horizontalSpan = 2;
group.setLayoutData(gridData);
group.setLayout(new RowLayout(SWT.VERTICAL));
Text txtAnotherTest = new Text(group, SWT.NONE);
txtAnotherTest.setText("Another test");

// Children of this widget should get a fixed size
Composite fixedElements = new Composite(shell, SWT.BORDER);
gridData = new GridData(SWT.FILL, SWT.FILL, true, false);
gridData.horizontalSpan = 2;
fixedElements.setLayoutData(gridData);
fixedElements.setLayout(new GridLayout(2, false));
Label label2 = new Label(fixedElements, SWT.BORDER);
GridData layoutData = new GridData(SWT.BEGINNING, SWT.CENTER, false, false);
layoutData.widthHint=200;
label2.setLayoutData(layoutData);
label2.setText("Fixed");
Label label3 = new Label(fixedElements, SWT.BORDER);
GridData layoutData2 = new GridData(SWT.BEGINNING, SWT.CENTER, false, false);
layoutData2.widthHint=20;
label3.setLayoutData(layoutData2);
label3.setText("Small but still fixed");

shell.pack();
```

```
        shell.open();
        while (!shell.isDisposed()) {
            if (!display.readAndDispatch()) {
                display.sleep();
            }
        }
        display.dispose();
    }
}
```

Start your application. The expected output is shown in the screenshot below.

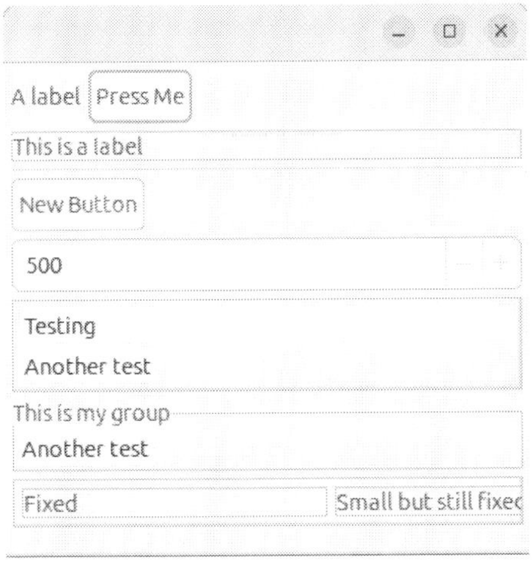

Resize the window and observe how the arrangement of the widgets changes.

45.13. Example: Using GridLayout to assign a fixed ratio to its children

The following example shows how the first child of the grid layout receives 25% of the available space, while the other receives 75%. Since GridLayout only supports fixed sizes, you must register a resize listener on its container.

```
package com.example.swt.widgets.layouts;

import org.eclipse.swt.SWT;
import org.eclipse.swt.graphics.Point;
import org.eclipse.swt.layout.GridData;
import org.eclipse.swt.layout.GridLayout;
import org.eclipse.swt.widgets.Composite;
import org.eclipse.swt.widgets.Display;
import org.eclipse.swt.widgets.Shell;

public class GridLayoutWithFixedColumnDistribution {
    public static void main(String[] args)
```

```
    {
        Display display = Display.getDefault();
        Shell shell = new Shell(display);
        shell.setLayout(new GridLayout(2, false));

        Composite left = new Composite(shell, SWT.BORDER);
        Composite right = new Composite(shell, SWT.BORDER);

        GridData leftData = new GridData(SWT.FILL, SWT.FILL, true, true);
        GridData rightData = new GridData(SWT.FILL, SWT.FILL, true, true);

        left.setLayoutData(leftData);
        right.setLayoutData(rightData);

        shell.addListener(SWT.Resize, arg0 -> {
            Point size = shell.getSize();

            leftData.widthHint = (int) (size.x * 0.75);
            rightData.widthHint = size.x - leftData.widthHint;

            System.out.println(leftData.widthHint + " + " + rightData.widthHint + " = " +
size.x);
        });

        shell.open();
        shell.requestLayout();

        while (!shell.isDisposed())
        {
            if (!display.readAndDispatch())
                display.sleep();
        }
        display.dispose();
    }
}
```

46. Other SWT examples

The following code snippets provide examples of how to use SWT. You are not expected to read through all of them; they are provided as reference in case you need a code example while coding.

46.1. Tab order of elements

The tab order is the order in which elements are selected when switching between them with the Tab key. You can specify the tab order of controls via the `setTabList()` method of a `Composite`. For this, you provide an array of the controls, where the order of the controls in the array specifies the tab order.

```
package com.example.swt.widgets


import org.eclipse.swt.SWT;
import org.eclipse.swt.layout.RowLayout;
import org.eclipse.swt.widgets.Button;
import org.eclipse.swt.widgets.Control;
import org.eclipse.swt.widgets.Display;
import org.eclipse.swt.widgets.Shell;

public class TabExample {
    public static void main(String[] args) {
        Display display = Display.getDefault();
        Shell shell = new Shell(display);
        shell.setLayout(new RowLayout());
        Button b1 = new Button(shell, SWT.PUSH);
        b1.setText("Button1");
        Button b2 = new Button(shell, SWT.PUSH);
        b2.setText("Button2");
        Button b3 = new Button(shell, SWT.PUSH);
        b3.setText("Button3");

        Control[] controls = new Control[] { b2, b1, b3 };
        shell.setTabList(controls);
        shell.pack();
        shell.open();
        while (!shell.isDisposed()) {
            if (!display.readAndDispatch()) {
                display.sleep();
            }
        }
        display.dispose();
    }
}
```

Defining a tab order for your controls is important to increase accessibility and to allow advanced users quick navigation.

46.2. DateTime widget

The following code demonstrates how to use the `DateTime` widget.

```
package com.vogella.swt.widgets;

import org.eclipse.swt.SWT;
import org.eclipse.swt.layout.GridLayout;
```

```java
import org.eclipse.swt.layout.RowLayout;
import org.eclipse.swt.widgets.Composite;
import org.eclipse.swt.widgets.DateTime;
import org.eclipse.swt.widgets.Display;
import org.eclipse.swt.widgets.Shell;

public class DateTimeExample {

    public static void main(String[] args) {

        // setup the SWT window
        Display display = new Display();
        final Shell shell = new Shell(display);
        shell.setLayout(new RowLayout());

        // initialize a parent composite with a grid layout manager
        Composite parent = new Composite(shell, SWT.NONE);
        GridLayout gridLayout = new GridLayout();
        gridLayout.numColumns = 1;
        parent.setLayout(gridLayout);
        DateTime calendar = new DateTime(parent, SWT.CALENDAR);
        DateTime date = new DateTime(parent, SWT.DATE);
        DateTime time = new DateTime(parent, SWT.TIME);
        // Date Selection as a drop-down
        DateTime dateD = new DateTime(parent, SWT.DATE | SWT.DROP_DOWN);

        shell.pack();
        shell.open();
        while (!shell.isDisposed()) {
            if (!display.readAndDispatch())
                display.sleep();
        }
        // tear down the SWT window
        display.dispose();
    }
}
```

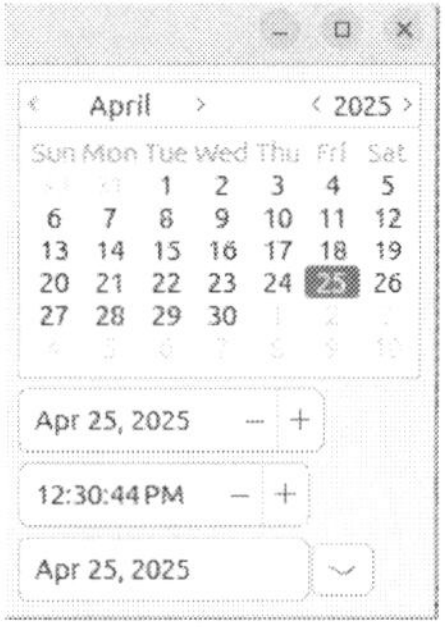

46.3. Image

Images can be displayed using labels. The following class demonstrates this using some system images.

```
package com.vogella.swt.widgets;

import java.util.ArrayList;
import java.util.List;

import org.eclipse.swt.SWT;
import org.eclipse.swt.graphics.Image;
import org.eclipse.swt.layout.GridLayout;
import org.eclipse.swt.layout.RowLayout;
import org.eclipse.swt.widgets.Composite;
import org.eclipse.swt.widgets.Display;
import org.eclipse.swt.widgets.Label;
import org.eclipse.swt.widgets.Shell;

public class Photo {

    public static void main(String[] args) {

        // setup the SWT window
        Display display = new Display();
        final Shell shell = new Shell(display);
        shell.setLayout(new RowLayout());
        shell.setText("Photo Application");

        // initialize a parent composite with a grid layout manager
        // with 5 columns
        Composite parent = new Composite(shell, SWT.NONE);
        GridLayout gridLayout = new GridLayout();
        gridLayout.numColumns = 5;
        parent.setLayout(gridLayout);

        // Get the Display default icons
        List<Image> imageList = new ArrayList<Image>();

        imageList.add(display.getSystemImage(SWT.ICON_WARNING));
        imageList.add(display.getSystemImage(SWT.ICON_WORKING));
        imageList.add(display.getSystemImage(SWT.ICON_QUESTION));
        imageList.add(display.getSystemImage(SWT.ICON_INFORMATION));
        imageList.add(display.getSystemImage(SWT.ICON_ERROR));

        for (Image image : imageList) {
            Label label = new Label(parent, SWT.NONE);
            label.setImage(image);
```

```
        }
        // show the SWT window

        shell.pack();
        shell.open();

        while (!shell.isDisposed()) {
            if (!display.readAndDispatch())
                display.sleep();
        }
        // tear down the SWT window
        display.dispose();
        // if you do not use system images you would have to release them
        // not necessary in this example
        // for (Image image : imageList) {
        //     if (image != null) {
        //      image.dispose();
        //     }
        //     }
    }
}
```

The expected output is shown in the screenshot below.

You can also load your own images from disk; just remember to dispose of them later. The code assumes that you have a file named `my_image.png` in a subfolder of your current package called `images`.

```
new Image(getDisplay(), getClass().getResourceAsStream("images/my_image.png"));
```

46.4. Table

Create the following class.

```
package de.vogella.swt.table;

import org.eclipse.swt.SWT;
import org.eclipse.swt.layout.GridData;
import org.eclipse.swt.layout.GridLayout;
import org.eclipse.swt.widgets.Display;
```

```
import org.eclipse.swt.widgets.Shell;
import org.eclipse.swt.widgets.Table;
import org.eclipse.swt.widgets.TableColumn;
import org.eclipse.swt.widgets.TableItem;

public class SWTTable {
    public static void main(String[] args) {
        Display display = new Display();
        Shell shell = new Shell(display);
        shell.setLayout(new GridLayout());

        Table table = new Table(shell, SWT.MULTI | SWT.BORDER | SWT.FULL_SELECTION);
        table.setLinesVisible(true);
        table.setHeaderVisible(true);
        GridData data = new GridData(SWT.FILL, SWT.FILL, true, true);
        data.heightHint = 200;
        table.setLayoutData(data);

        String[] titles = { "First Name", "Last Name", "Age" };
        for (int i = 0; i < titles.length; i++) {
            TableColumn column = new TableColumn(table, SWT.NONE);
            column.setText(titles[i]);
            table.getColumn(i).pack();
        }

        for (int i = 0 ; i<= 50 ; i++){
            TableItem item = new TableItem(table, SWT.NONE);
            item.setText (0, "Person " +i );
            item.setText (1, "LastName " +i );
            item.setText (2, String.valueOf(i));
        }

        for (int i=0; i<titles.length; i++) {
            table.getColumn (i).pack ();
        }
        shell.pack();
        shell.open();
        while (!shell.isDisposed()) {
            if (!display.readAndDispatch()) {
                display.sleep();
            }
        }
    }
}
```

If you run this application, it displays a table.

46.5. Tree and Menu

Create the following class.

```
package com.vogella.swt.widgets;

import static org.eclipse.swt.events.SelectionListener.widgetSelectedAdapter;

import org.eclipse.swt.SWT;
import org.eclipse.swt.layout.FillLayout;
import org.eclipse.swt.widgets.Display;
import org.eclipse.swt.widgets.Menu;
import org.eclipse.swt.widgets.MenuItem;
import org.eclipse.swt.widgets.Shell;
import org.eclipse.swt.widgets.Tree;
import org.eclipse.swt.widgets.TreeItem;

public class TreeMenuTest {
    public static void main(String[] args) {
        Display display = Display.getDefault();
        Shell shell = new Shell(display);
        shell.setLayout(new FillLayout());
        final Tree tree = new Tree(shell, SWT.V_SCROLL);
        for (int i = 0; i < 5; i++) {
            TreeItem item = new TreeItem(tree, SWT.NONE);
            item.setText(String.valueOf(i));
            for (int j = 0; j < 3; j++) {
                TreeItem subItem = new TreeItem(item, SWT.NONE);
                subItem.setText(String.valueOf(i) + " " + String.valueOf(j));
            }
        }
        tree.pack();
        Menu menu = new Menu(tree);
        MenuItem menuItem = new MenuItem(menu, SWT.NONE);
        menuItem.setText("Print Element");

        menuItem.addSelectionListener(widgetSelectedAdapter( e->  System.out.println(
tree.getSelection()[0].getText())));

        tree.setMenu(menu);
        shell.setSize(400, 200);
        shell.open();
        while (!shell.isDisposed()) {
            if (!display.readAndDispatch()) {
                display.sleep();
            }
        }
    }
```

```
}
```

If you run this application, it displays a tree. Right-click any item to display the context menu.

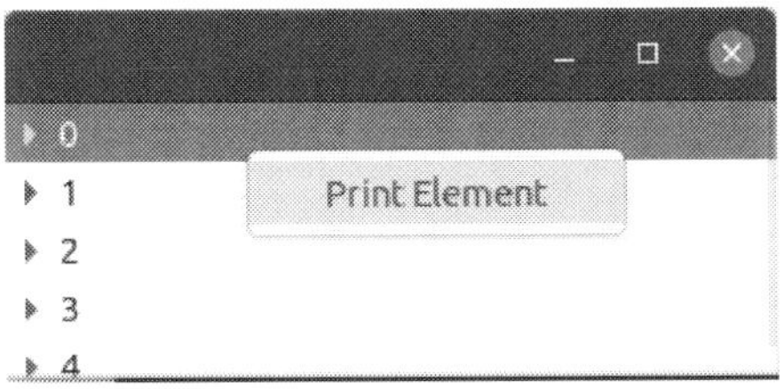

If you select the menu, the text of the selected item will be printed to the console.

46.6. CTabFolder

`CTabFolder` and `CTabItem` let you create a tabbed container where each page is accessible through a tab. This widget supports background colors, which the `TabFolder` and `TabItem` widget do not support.

```
package com.vogella.swt.widgets.ctabfolder;

import org.eclipse.swt.SWT;
import org.eclipse.swt.custom.CTabFolder;
import org.eclipse.swt.custom.CTabItem;
import org.eclipse.swt.layout.GridData;
import org.eclipse.swt.layout.GridLayout;
import org.eclipse.swt.widgets.Display;
import org.eclipse.swt.widgets.Shell;
import org.eclipse.swt.widgets.Text;

public class CTabFolderExample {
    public static void main(String[] args) {
        Display display = new Display();
        Shell shell = new Shell(display);
        shell.setLayout(new GridLayout());
        // SWT.BOTTOM to show at the bottom
        CTabFolder folder = new CTabFolder(shell, SWT.BOTTOM);
        GridData data = new GridData(SWT.FILL,
                SWT.FILL, true, true,
                2, 1);
        folder.setLayoutData(data);
        folder.setSelectionForeground(display.getSystemColor(SWT.COLOR_RED));
        CTabItem cTabItem1 = new CTabItem(folder, SWT.NONE);
        cTabItem1.setText("Tab1");
        CTabItem cTabItem2 = new CTabItem(folder, SWT.NONE);
        cTabItem2.setText("Tab2");
        CTabItem cTabItem3 = new CTabItem(folder, SWT.NONE);
```

```
        cTabItem3.setText("Tab3");

        Text text = new Text(folder, SWT.BORDER);
        text.setText("Hello");
        cTabItem1.setControl(text);

        shell.pack();
        shell.open();
        while (!shell.isDisposed()) {
            if (!display.readAndDispatch()) {
                display.sleep();
            }
        }
    }
}
```

If you run this application, you will see several tabbed cards. The SWT.BOTTOM style bit on the folder widget makes the tab appear at the bottom.

46.7. Key bindings for SWT widgets

You can add `KeyListener` to an SWT widget via the `addKeyListener` method. This method receives a `KeyEvent` object. The `e` object provides, for example:

- `e.character`: which char was pressed
- `e.stateMask`: which modifier keys were pressed (CTRL, ALT, SHIFT, COMMAND, ALT_GR)
- `keyCode`: integer representation of the key based on constants defined in the SWT class.

The following source code demonstrates how to register a `KeyListener` with an SWT widget and how to evaluate the event.

```
package com.vogella.swt.widgets;
```

```
import org.eclipse.swt.SWT;
import org.eclipse.swt.events.KeyEvent;
import org.eclipse.swt.events.KeyListener;
import org.eclipse.swt.layout.GridLayout;
import org.eclipse.swt.widgets.Button;
import org.eclipse.swt.widgets.Display;
import org.eclipse.swt.widgets.Shell;

public class SWTKeyEvent {
    public static void main(String[] args) {
        Display display = new Display();
        Shell shell = new Shell(display);
        shell.setText("KeyListener Example");
        shell.setLayout(new GridLayout());

        Button button = new Button(shell, SWT.CENTER);
        button.setText("Type here and optionally use meta keys");
        button.addKeyListener(KeyListener.keyPressedAdapter(e-> handleKeyEvent(e)));

        shell.pack();
        shell.open();

        while (!shell.isDisposed()) {
            if (!display.readAndDispatch())
                display.sleep();
        }
        display.dispose();
    }

    private static void handleKeyEvent(KeyEvent e) {
        String string = "";

        // check click together?
        if ((e.stateMask & SWT.ALT) != 0)
            string += "ALT ";
        if ((e.stateMask & SWT.CTRL) != 0)
            string += "CTRL ";
        if ((e.stateMask & SWT.SHIFT) != 0)
            string += "SHIFT ";

        if (e.keyCode == SWT.BS) {
            string += "BACKSPACE ";
        }

        if (e.keyCode == SWT.ESC) {
            string += "ESCAPE ";
        }
```

```
        // check characters (digits are from 48 to 57)
        if ((e.keyCode >= 97 && e.keyCode <= 122) || (e.keyCode >= 48 && e.keyCode <=
57)) {
            string += " " + e.character + " - keyCode = " + e.keyCode;
        }

        if (!string.equals("")) {
            System.out.println(string);
        }
    }
}
```

If you run this application and move the cursor over the button widget and type, you should see the output in the *Console* view.

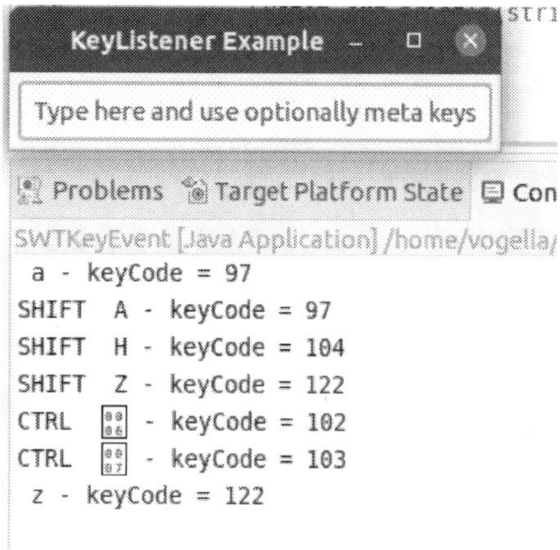

46.8. Global filtering of user interface events

You can use the `addFilter` method from the `Display` class to filter globally for events as long as your application has focus. The following code demonstrates this.

```
package de.vogella.swt.listener;

import org.eclipse.swt.SWT;
import org.eclipse.swt.widgets.Display;
import org.eclipse.swt.widgets.Event;
import org.eclipse.swt.widgets.Listener;
import org.eclipse.swt.widgets.Shell;

public class GlobalListener {

    public static void main(String[] args) {
        Display display = new Display();
        Shell shell = new Shell(display);
```

```
        shell.open();
        display.addFilter(SWT.KeyDown, new Listener() {
            @Override
            public void handleEvent(Event event) {
                char c = event.character;
                System.out.println(c);
            }
        });

        while (!shell.isDisposed()) {
            if (!display.readAndDispatch())
                display.sleep();
        }
    }
}
```

46.9. Fonts in SWT

You can change the font of text in SWT. You do this by creating a `Font` and applying it to the desired control.

```
Label label = new Label(parent, SWT.NONE);
Font font = new Font(label.getDisplay(), new FontData("Mono", 10, SWT.ITALIC));
label.setFont(font);
label.setText("Some text");
```

To modify the current font you can retrieve the `FontData`, change it, and create a new `Font` from it.

```
Label label = new Label(parent, SWT.NONE);
FontData fontData = label.getFont().getFontData()[0];
// we can change this since getFontData() creates a new FontData instance
fontData.setStyle(SWT.ITALIC);
label.setFont(new Font(label.getDisplay(), fontData));
```

You can deploy and use custom fonts for your application. To use a custom font, you have to load it with the Display.

```
boolean fontLoaded = Display.getDefault().loadFont("fonts/CustomFont.ttf");
if (fontLoaded) {
    Font font = new Font(Display.getDefault(), "Custom Font", 12, SWT.NORMAL);
    label.setFont(font);
}
```

Please remember that fonts do not get automatically disposed with the widget that uses them.

46.10. Unicode in SWT

SWT supports the display of `Unicode` characters. Depending on your OS and default font, you might have to change the font of your control to a font that supports Unicode characters.

```
Label label = new Label(parent, SWT.NONE);
label.setFont(new Font(Display.getCurrent(), "Arial Unicode MS", 12, SWT.NORMAL));
label.setText("Follow your \u2764!");
```

47. SWT builder API via JFace

The JFace library adds a builder API to SWT widgets, providing a concise and modern way to build SWT-based user interfaces.

The following example shows how to use the `ButtonFactory` to create a new button.

```
import static org.eclipse.jface.widgets.ButtonFactory.newButton;
....

newButton(SWT.PUSH).text("Press me").onSelect(e-> System.out.print("Testing")).create
(shell);
```

48. SWT snippets and examples

The SWT Snippets [https://github.com/eclipse-platform/eclipse.platform.swt/blob/master/examples/org.eclipse.swt.snippets/Snippets.md] are examples of stand-alone SWT applications using various SWT widgets.

You can copy these snippets and paste them directly into a project with an SWT dependency inside the Eclipse IDE. Each snippet contains a main method, allowing it to be started directly.

You can paste classes from the clipboard onto a project or package. Eclipse automatically creates the Java class based on the content of the clipboard.

The SWT Examples [https://github.com/eclipse-platform/eclipse.platform.swt/blob/master/examples/org.eclipse.swt.examples/Readme.md] page provides test programs for widgets and custom-drawn SWT widgets.

49. The Nebula widgets

The Eclipse Nebula [https://eclipse.org/nebula/] project provides additional widgets for SWT. For example, it offers several visualization widgets, as shown in the following screenshot.

Visualization :

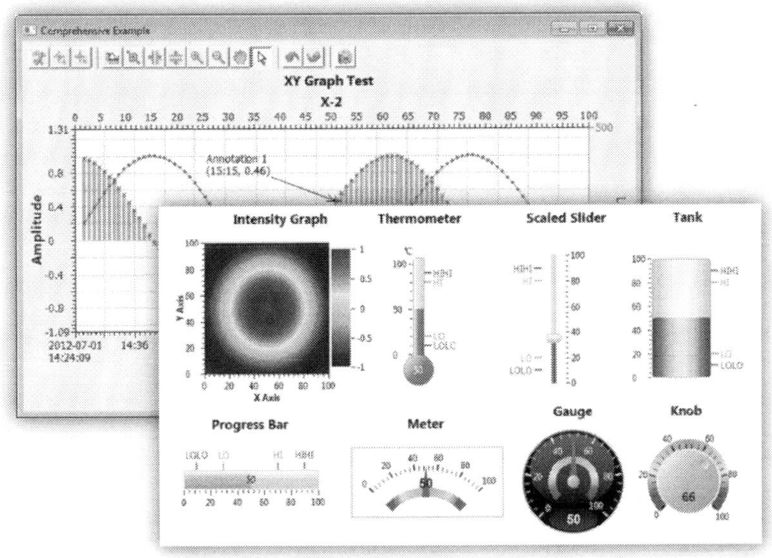

See https://github.com/EclipseNebula/nebula/blob/master/docs/Widgets.md for an overview of the available widgets.

To use these widgets in your application, add their update site to your target platform.

50. Using the SWT Designer for visual UI design

50.1. Overview of the SWT Designer

SWT Designer is a visual editor used to create graphical user interfaces. It is a two-way parser; for example, you can edit the source code or use a graphical editor to modify the user interface. *SWT Designer* synchronizes between the two representations.

SWT Designer is part of the WindowBuilder project. WindowBuilder provides the foundation and SWT Designer adds the support for working with SWT-based applications.

50.2. Using SWT Designer

SWT Designer provides a special editor. This editor can work with Eclipse 4 parts, SWT and JFace dialogs, JFace wizards, etc.

The following screenshot demonstrates what the editor looks like.

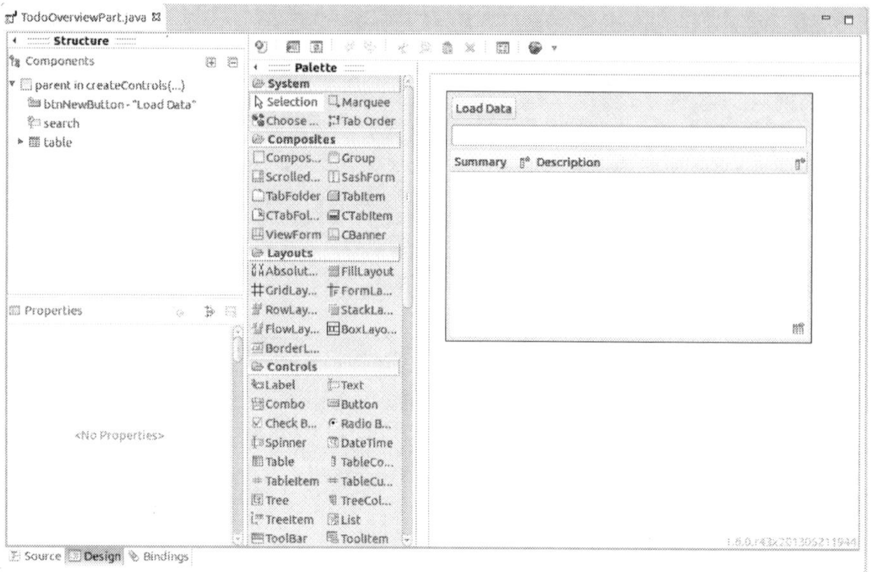

SWT Designer allows you to drag and drop SWT components into an existing layout. You can configure layout settings and create event handlers for your widgets.

SWT Designer contributes additional SWT and JFace templates to the Eclipse IDE. For example, you can use it to create `Composites` and add these to the Eclipse user interface. To create a new `Composite` select **File › New › Other... › WindowBuilder › SWT Designer › SWT › Composite**.

SWT Designer supports establishing data binding via the JFace Data Binding framework.

51. Exercise: Implementing a user interface with SWT and JFace

51.1. Implementing a view for displaying task objects

Change the `TodoOverviewPart` in the `com.vogella.tasks.ui` plug-in.

Use the static method `org.eclipse.jface.widgets.WidgetFactory.button` to create a button. Use the `WidgetFactory.label` method to create a label with the default text set to: "Data not available."

If the button is pressed, read the number of tasks from your `TaskService` service. Assign this number to the text of the label.

The resulting user interface should look similar to the following screenshot.

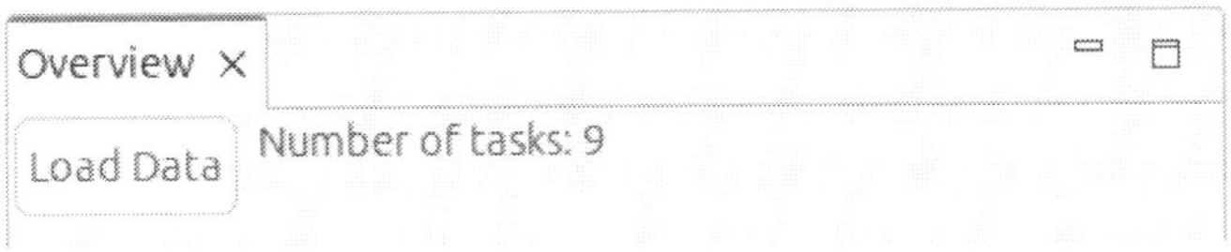

The following code may serve as an entry point.

```
import static org.eclipse.jface.layout.GridLayoutFactory.fillDefaults;
import static org.eclipse.jface.widgets.WidgetFactory.button;
import static org.eclipse.jface.widgets.WidgetFactory.label;

// to build your widgets
fillDefaults().numColumns(2).applyTo(parent);
button(SWT.PUSH).text("Load Data").onSelect(e -> update()).create(parent);
label = label(SWT.NONE).text("Number of tasks: ")
    .layoutData(GridDataFactory.fillDefaults().grab(true, false).create()).create(
parent);
}

private void update() {
    label.setText("This should use the service, get it injected");

}
```

The following listing contains a possible implementation of this exercise as a reference for the reader.

```
package com.vogella.tasks.ui.parts;

import static org.eclipse.jface.layout.GridLayoutFactory.fillDefaults;
import static org.eclipse.jface.widgets.ButtonFactory.newButton;
import static org.eclipse.jface.widgets.LabelFactory.newLabel;

import jakarta.annotation.PostConstruct;
import jakarta.inject.Inject;

import org.eclipse.jface.layout.GridDataFactory;
import org.eclipse.swt.SWT;
import org.eclipse.swt.widgets.Composite;
import org.eclipse.swt.widgets.Label;

import com.vogella.tasks.model.TaskService;

public class TodoOverviewPart {

    @Inject
    TaskService taskService;

    private Label label;

    @PostConstruct
    public void createControls(Composite parent) {
        fillDefaults().numColumns(2).applyTo(parent);
        newButton(SWT.PUSH).text("Load Data").onSelect(e -> updateLabel()).create(
parent);
        label = newLabel(SWT.NONE).text("Number of tasks: ")
                .layoutData(GridDataFactory.fillDefaults().grab(true, false).create
()).create(parent);
    }

    private void updateLabel() {
        label.setText("Number of tasks: " + taskService.getAll().size());

    }
}
```

51.2. Implement a part to display task details

Change the `TodoDetailsPart` class so that you create a user interface similar to the following.

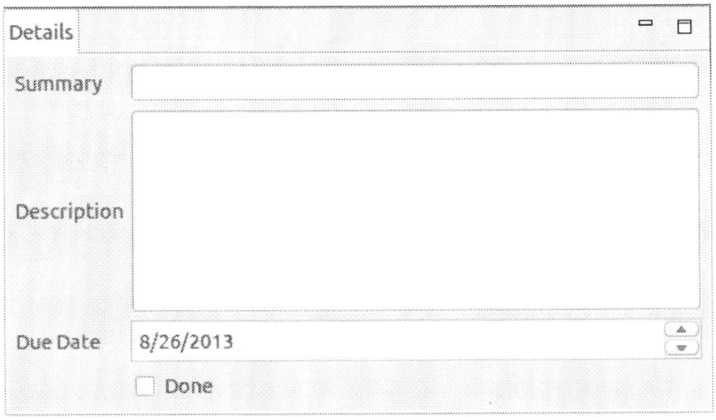

Use a `DateTime` widget for the *Due Date* selection. Use a `@Focus` method to set the focus to your first text field.

The following code shows an example implementation of this method.

```
@Focus
public void onFocus() {
    // The following assumes that you have a Text field named txtSummary
    txtSummary.setFocus();
}
```

> If you do not focus on an SWT widget in your method annotated with `@Focus`, the framework may call this method twice. This is done by the Eclipse framework to ensure consistency within the application. If you correctly place the focus on one SWT widget, the method is called every time the part is activated by the user.

Ensure that you also set the focus to an SWT widget in your `TodoOverviewPart` class.

The following listing contains a possible implementation of this exercise as a reference for the reader.

```
package com.vogella.tasks.ui.parts;


import jakarta.annotation.PostConstruct;

import org.eclipse.e4.ui.di.Focus;
import org.eclipse.jface.layout.GridDataFactory;
import org.eclipse.jface.widgets.LabelFactory;
import org.eclipse.jface.widgets.WidgetFactory;
import org.eclipse.swt.SWT;
import org.eclipse.swt.layout.GridLayout;
```

```
import org.eclipse.swt.widgets.Button;
import org.eclipse.swt.widgets.Composite;
import org.eclipse.swt.widgets.DateTime;
import org.eclipse.swt.widgets.Text;

public class TodoDetailsPart {
    private Text txtSummary;
    private Text txtDescription;
    private DateTime dateTime;
    private Button btnDone;

    @PostConstruct
    public void createControls(Composite parent) {
        parent.setLayout(new GridLayout(2, false));

        GridDataFactory gdFactory = GridDataFactory.fillDefaults();
        LabelFactory labelFactory = LabelFactory.newLabel(SWT.NONE);

        labelFactory.text("Summary").create(parent);

        txtSummary = WidgetFactory.text(SWT.BORDER).layoutData(gdFactory.grab(true,
false).create())//
                .create(parent);

        labelFactory.text("Description").create(parent);
        txtDescription = WidgetFactory.text(SWT.BORDER | SWT.MULTI | SWT.V_SCROLL)
                .layoutData(gdFactory.align(SWT.FILL, SWT.FILL).grab(true, true).
create()).create(parent);

        labelFactory.text("Due Date").create(parent);

        dateTime = WidgetFactory.dateTime(SWT.BORDER)
                .layoutData(gdFactory.align(SWT.FILL, SWT.CENTER).grab(false, false
).create()).create(parent);

        labelFactory.text("").create(parent);

        btnDone = WidgetFactory.button(SWT.CHECK).text("Done").create(parent);
    }

    @Focus
    public void setFocus() {
        txtSummary.setFocus();
    }
}
```

52. Exercise: Prepare TodoDetailsPart for data

The `TodoDetailsPart` class will be used to modify the data of our task objects. In this exercise, we prepare the class for its future usage.

52.1. Add dependency

Add the `org.eclipse.e4.ui.services` plug-in as a dependency to your `com.vogella.tasks.ui` plug-in via the `MANIFEST.MF` file. This is required to use the `IServiceConstants` interface in the next section.

52.2. Prepare for dependency injection

Create the following new code in the `TodoDetailsPart` class.

```
package com.vogella.tasks.ui.parts;

// imports listed to help you importing the correct statement

import java.util.List;

import jakarta.annotation.PostConstruct;
import jakarta.inject.Inject;
import jakarta.inject.Named;

import org.eclipse.e4.core.di.annotations.Optional;
import org.eclipse.e4.ui.di.Focus;
import org.eclipse.e4.ui.services.IServiceConstants;
import org.eclipse.jface.layout.GridDataFactory;
import org.eclipse.jface.widgets.LabelFactory;
import org.eclipse.jface.widgets.WidgetFactory;
import org.eclipse.swt.SWT;
import org.eclipse.swt.layout.GridLayout;
import org.eclipse.swt.widgets.Button;
import org.eclipse.swt.widgets.Composite;
import org.eclipse.swt.widgets.DateTime;
import org.eclipse.swt.widgets.Text;

import com.vogella.tasks.model.Task;

// more code
// ....
// ....

// define a new field
private java.util.Optional<Task> task = java.util.Optional.empty();
```

```
// more code
// ....
// ....

@PostConstruct
public void createControls(Composite parent) {
    // ... existing code for creating user interface
    updateUserInterface(task); // ❶
}

// Add the following new methods to your code

@Inject
public void setTasks(@Optional @Named(IServiceConstants.ACTIVE_SELECTION) List<Task>
tasks) { ❶
    if (tasks == null || tasks.isEmpty() || tasks.get(0) == null) {
        this.task = java.util.Optional.empty();
    } else {
        this.task = java.util.Optional.of(tasks.get(0));
    }
    // Remember the task as a field and update the user interface
    updateUserInterface(this.task);
}

// allows you to disable or enable the user interface fields
// if no task is set
private void enableUserInterface(boolean enabled) {
    if (txtSummary != null && !txtSummary.isDisposed()) {
        txtSummary.setEnabled(enabled);
        txtDescription.setEnabled(enabled);
        dateTime.setEnabled(enabled);
        btnDone.setEnabled(enabled);
    }
}

private void updateUserInterface(java.util.Optional<Task> task) { ❷
    if (!task.isPresent()) {
        enableUserInterface(false);
        return; // nothing left to do
    }

    enableUserInterface(true);
    // the following check ensures that the user interface is available,
    // it assumes that you have a text widget named "txtSummary"
    if (txtSummary != null && !txtSummary.isDisposed()) {
        enableUserInterface(true);
        txtSummary.setText(task.get().getSummary());
        txtDescription.setText(task.get().getDescription());
        // more code to fill the widgets with data from your task object
```

```
        // more code
        // ....
        // ....
    }
}
```

❶ The currently active selected list of tasks is injected into it. It uses a special String key defined by the `IServiceConstants.ACTIVE_SELECTION` constant.

❷ This method disables the widgets if no data object is available, otherwise, it shows the data.

In this method, you have to check the availability of the SWT widgets. Methods annotated with `@Inject` are invoked before the method annotated with `@PostConstruct`.

At the moment the new `setTasks()` method is not called, neither by the Eclipse framework nor by your code. It will be used later in your wizard and once you have implemented the usage of the selection service.

53. Optional exercise: Use the SWT browser widget

53.1. Use the SWT browser widget to display Google maps

In this exercise, you learn how to use the SWT browser widget.

Change the `PlaygroundPart` class so the part looks like the following screenshot.

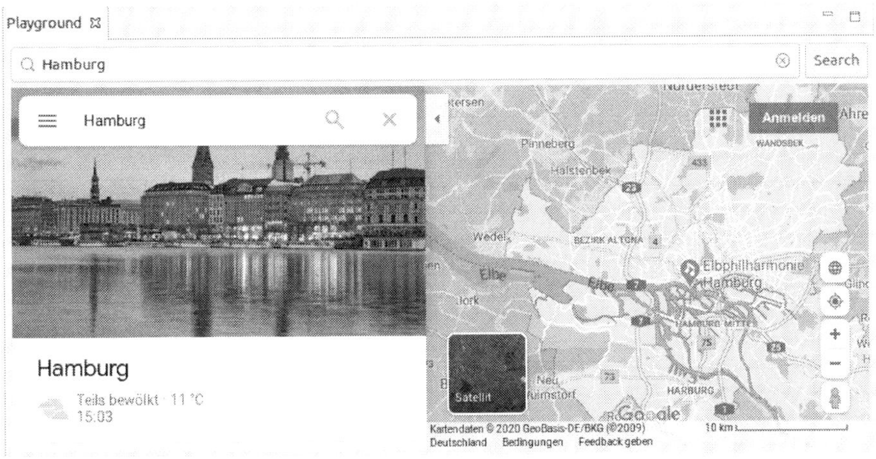

This example might not work if Google changes its API.

If you enter some text in the text field and press the button, the map should be centered based on the input in the text field. This input should be interpreted as a city name.

53.2. Solution

Your `PlaygroundPart` class should look similar to the following code.

```
package com.vogella.tasks.ui.parts;

import static org.eclipse.jface.layout.GridDataFactory.fillDefaults;
import static org.eclipse.jface.widgets.WidgetFactory.button;
import static org.eclipse.jface.widgets.WidgetFactory.text;

import java.io.UnsupportedEncodingException;
import java.net.URLEncoder;

import jakarta.annotation.PostConstruct;

import org.eclipse.e4.ui.di.Focus;
import org.eclipse.swt.SWT;
import org.eclipse.swt.browser.Browser;
import org.eclipse.swt.layout.GridLayout;
import org.eclipse.swt.widgets.Composite;
import org.eclipse.swt.widgets.Text;

public class PlaygroundPart {
    private Text text;
    private Browser browser;

    @PostConstruct
    public void createControls(Composite parent) {
        parent.setLayout(new GridLayout(2, false));

        text = text(SWT.BORDER).message("Enter City").layoutData(fillDefaults().grab(
true, false).create())
                .create(parent);
        button(SWT.PUSH).text("Search").onSelect(e -> updateBrowser()).create(parent);

        browser = new Browser(parent, SWT.NONE);
        browser.setLayoutData(fillDefaults().grab(true, true).span(2, 1).create());

    }

    private void updateBrowser() {
        String city = text.getText();
        if (city.isEmpty()) {
            return;
        }
        try {
```

```
            browser.setUrl("https://www.google.com/maps/place/" + URLEncoder.encode(city,
"UTF-8") + "/&output=embed");

        } catch (UnsupportedEncodingException e1) {
            e1.printStackTrace();
        }
    }

    @Focus
    public void onFocus() {
        text.setFocus();
    }
}
```

54. Optional exercise: Using SWT Canvas for animated particles

In this exercise, you create a new part that demonstrates the usage of the SWT Canvas by creating an animated particle system with connecting lines and gradient backgrounds.

54.1. Create a new part class

Create a new class `ParticleCanvas` in the package `com.vogella.tasks.ui.parts`.

Add the following code to create an animated particle system:

```
package com.vogella.tasks.ui.parts;
import java.util.ArrayList;
import java.util.List;

import org.eclipse.swt.SWT;
import org.eclipse.swt.graphics.Color;
import org.eclipse.swt.graphics.GC;
import org.eclipse.swt.graphics.Rectangle;
import org.eclipse.swt.widgets.Canvas;
import org.eclipse.swt.widgets.Composite;
import org.eclipse.swt.widgets.Display;

import jakarta.annotation.PostConstruct;

public class ParticleCanvas {

    private static class Particle {
        double x, y, vx, vy;
        int size;
        Color color;
```

```
    Particle(int w, int h, Display d) {
        x = Math.random() * w;
        y = Math.random() * h;
        vx = (Math.random() - 0.5) * 3;
        vy = (Math.random() - 0.5) * 3;
        size = (int)(Math.random() * 8 + 3);
        int r = (int)(Math.random() * 100 + 155);
        int g = (int)(Math.random() * 100 + 100);
        int b = (int)(Math.random() * 155 + 100);
        color = new Color(d, r, g, b);
    }

    void update(int w, int h) {
        x += vx;
        y += vy;
        if (x < 0 || x > w) {
            vx *= -1;
        }
        if (y < 0 || y > h) {
            vy *= -1;
        }
        x = Math.max(0, Math.min(w, x));
        y = Math.max(0, Math.min(h, y));
    }
}
@PostConstruct
public void createUserInterface(Composite parent) {

    Canvas canvas = new Canvas(parent, SWT.DOUBLE_BUFFERED);
    List<Particle> particles = new ArrayList<>();

    canvas.addListener(SWT.Resize, e -> {
        particles.clear();
        Rectangle r = canvas.getBounds();
        for (int i = 0; i < 80; i++) {
            particles.add(new Particle(r.width, r.height, parent.getDisplay()));
        }
    });

    canvas.addPaintListener(e -> {
        GC gc = e.gc;
        gc.setAntialias(SWT.ON);
        Rectangle r = canvas.getBounds();

        // Gradient background
        gc.setForeground(parent.getDisplay().getSystemColor(SWT.COLOR_BLACK));
        gc.setBackground(new Color(parent.getDisplay(), 20, 20, 40));
        gc.fillGradientRectangle(0, 0, r.width, r.height, true);
```

```
            // Draw connections
            gc.setAlpha(30);
            gc.setForeground(new Color(parent.getDisplay(), 100, 150, 255));
            for (int i = 0; i < particles.size(); i++) {
                for (int j = i + 1; j < particles.size(); j++) {
                    Particle p1 = particles.get(i);
                    Particle p2 = particles.get(j);
                    double dist = Math.hypot(p1.x - p2.x, p1.y - p2.y);
                    if (dist < 100) {
                        gc.drawLine((int)p1.x, (int)p1.y, (int)p2.x, (int)p2.y);
                    }
                }
            }

            // Draw particles
            gc.setAlpha(200);
            for (Particle p : particles) {
                gc.setBackground(p.color);
                gc.fillOval((int)p.x - p.size/2, (int)p.y - p.size/2, p.size, p.size);
            }
        });

        // Animation loop
        parent.getDisplay().timerExec(30, new Runnable() {
            @Override
            public void run() {
                if (!canvas.isDisposed()) {
                    Rectangle r = canvas.getBounds();
                    for (Particle p : particles) {
                        p.update(r.width, r.height);
                    }
                    canvas.redraw();
                    parent.getDisplay().timerExec(30, this);
                }
            }
        });
    }
}
```

54.2. Add the part to the application model

Add this new part to your application model to the last stack (where the playground part is also located).

54.3. Test the application

Start your Eclipse RCP application. You should see a new part in the bottom-right area, if you select it, it displays an animated particle system with connecting lines and a gradient background.

55. Install SWT Designer

To install SWT Designer use the **Help › Install New Software** menu entry and enter the following update site to use it. https://download.eclipse.org/windowbuilder/latest/

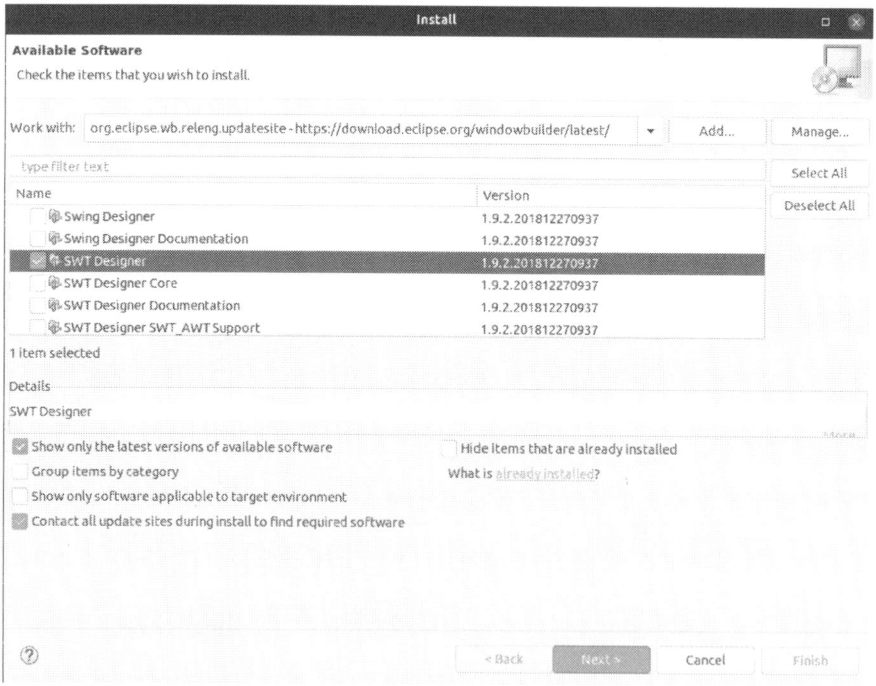

The WindowBuilder downloads [https://eclipse.dev/windowbuilder/downloads/] page lists the available SWT designer releases. Typically, the latest release is the best to use.

56. Optional exercise: Getting started with SWT Designer

Most exercises in this book use the latest platform API, which SWT Designer does not yet support. Therefore, it is recommended not to use SWT Designer for the rest of the exercises after you finish this one.

56.1. Building a user interface

Add a new part to your application. The implementation class of this view should be `WindowBuilderPlaygroundPart`.

The following exercise assumes that you have SWT Designer already installed.

Right-click on your `WindowBuilderPlaygroundPart` class and select **Open With › WindowBuilder Editor**.

WindowBuilder uses the `@PostConstruct` method to identify that a class is an Eclipse part. This method needs to specify at least a `Composite` as parameter.

```
package com.vogella.tasks.ui.parts;

import jakarta.annotation.PostConstruct;

import org.eclipse.swt.widgets.Composite;

public class WindowBuilderPlaygroundPart {

    // the WindowBuilder / SWTDesigner tooling
    // uses the @PostConstruct method to figure out
    // that the class is an Eclipse 4 part

    // one method must be annotated with @PostConstruct and
    // must receive at least an SWT Composite

    @PostConstruct
    public void createControls(Composite parent) {
        System.out.println(this.getClass().getSimpleName()
        + " @PostConstruct method called.");
    }
}
```

Switch to the *Design* tab in the WindowBuilder editor. This selection is highlighted in the following screenshot.

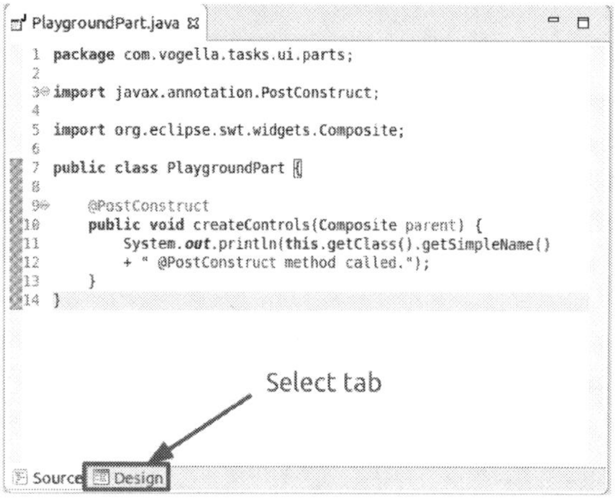

Use the SWT Designer to change the layout of the `Composite` of the part to a `GridLayout`.

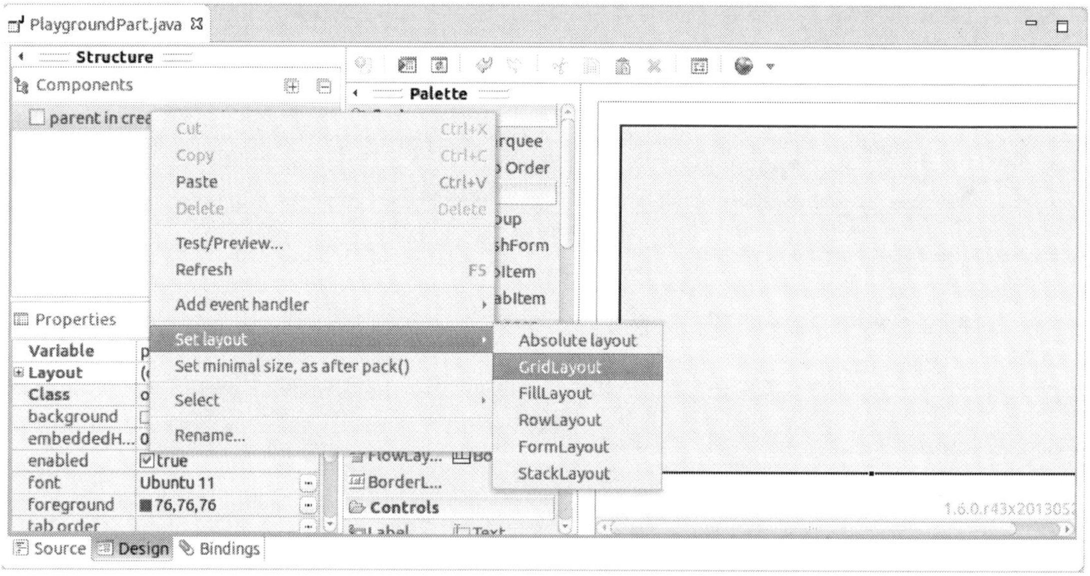

Click in the Palette on *Button* and add a few buttons to your user interface.

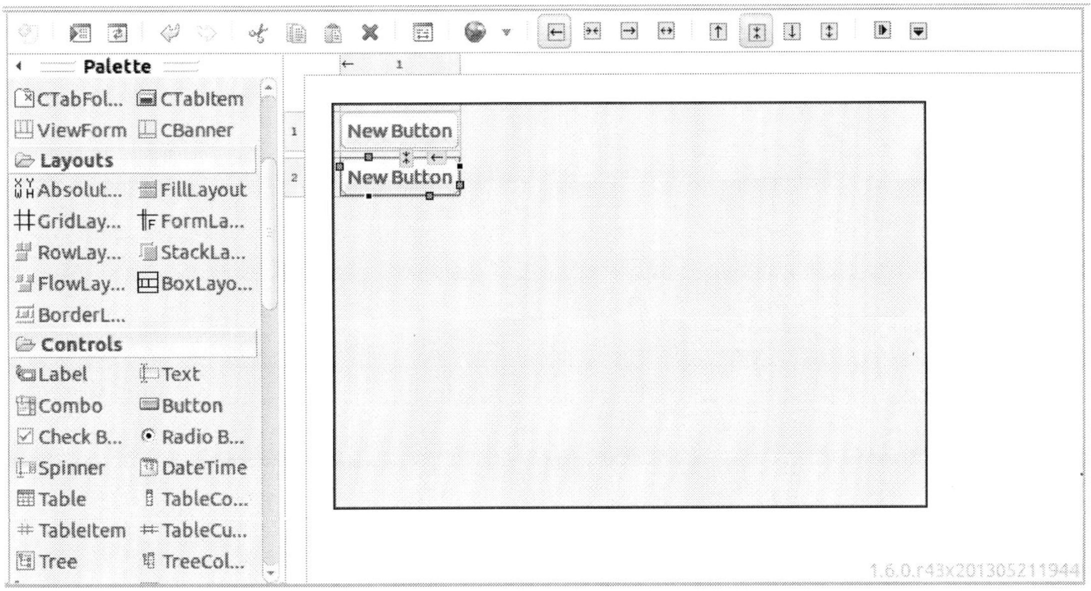

Add a `Label` and a `Text` field.

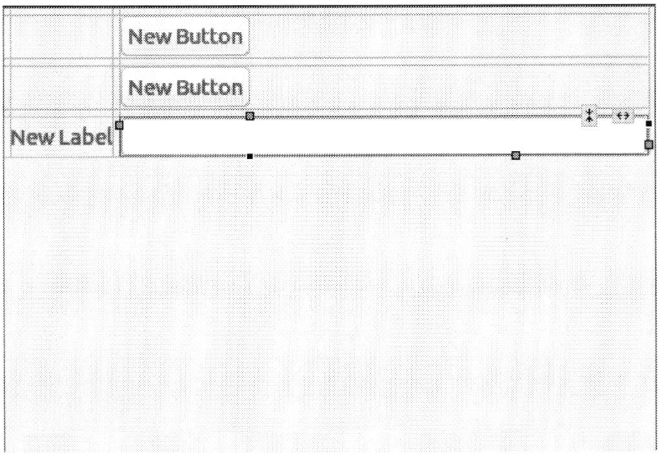

56.2. Add a SelectionListener to the button

Assign a `SelectionListener` (event handler) to one of your buttons for the `widgetSelected`. You can do this via a right-click on the button. Select **Add event handler › selection › widgetSelected**.

56.3. Review the generated code

Switch to the *Source* tab and review the code generated by the SWT Designer.

57. Definition of Eclipse JFace

Eclipse *JFace* is a set of plug-ins based on the user interface toolkit SWT. JFace provides classes and frameworks that simplify common SWT use cases. JFace does not hide the SWT API; therefore, SWT knowledge is still required.

JFace provides the *viewers* framework, which simplifies the mapping of a data model to a visual representation. For example, viewers are available for combo boxes, lists, tables, and trees.

JFace provides helper classes to effectively manage your system resources, like colors, images, and fonts.

In addition, JFace provides support for handling preferences, preference pages, wizards, and dialogs. It contains functionality to support icon decorations and user-input help for SWT controls.

JFace Data Binding is a framework that connects properties of objects. It is typically used to synchronize fields of the user interface with properties of model objects and allows you to include validation and conversion in this synchronization process.

58. JFace resource manager for colors, fonts and images

SWT is based on the native widgets of the OS. Whenever an SWT widget is allocated, a corresponding OS-specific widget is created. The Java garbage collector cannot automatically clean up these OS-specific widget references.

Fortunately, all widgets that are created based on a parent widget are automatically disposed of when the parent `Composite` is disposed of. If you develop Eclipse plug-ins, the `Composite` of a part is automatically disposed of once the part is closed. Therefore, these SWT widgets are handled automatically in Eclipse plug-in projects.

This rule does not apply to fonts and images, as these may be reused in other places. For this reason, they need to be explicitly disposed of. JFace provides the `ResourceManager` and its derived classes for managing such resources automatically.

An instance of the `LocalResourceManager` class is created with a reference to a `Control`. If this `Control` is disposed of, the resources created by the `LocalResourceManager` are disposed of.

```
// create the manager and bind to a widget
ResourceManager resManager =
    new LocalResourceManager(JFaceResources.getResources(), composite);

// create resources
Font font = resManager.
    createFont(FontDescriptor.createFrom("Arial", 10, SWT.BOLD));
// get an imageDescriptor and create an Image object
Image image = resManager.create(imageDescriptor);
```

The `createImage()` method expects an `ImageDescriptor` class.

To get an `ImageDescriptor` from an image file stored in your current plug-in, use the following:

```
Bundle bundle = FrameworkUtil.getBundle(this.getClass());
// use the org.eclipse.core.runtime.Path as an import
URL url = FileLocator.find(bundle,  new Path("icons/alt_window_32.svg"), null);
ImageDescriptor imageDescriptor = ImageDescriptor.createFromURL(url);
```

If you do not have an instance of `Control`, the `LocalResourceManager` provides another constructor.

A popular example is a `LabelProvider`, where you would not want to pass a `Control` to it to properly dispose of system resources afterward:

```java
public class ResourceUsingLabelProvider extends LabelProvider {

    private ResourceManager resourceManager = new LocalResourceManager(JFaceResources
.getResources());

    @Override
    public Image getImage(Object element) {
        if (element instanceof Task) {
            Bundle bundle = FrameworkUtil.getBundle(this.getClass());
            // use the org.eclipse.core.runtime.Path as an import
            URL url = FileLocator.find(bundle, new Path("icons/task.png"), null);
            ImageDescriptor imageDescriptor = ImageDescriptor.createFromURL(url);

            // return the image being created by the resourceManager
            return resourceManager.createImage(imageDescriptor);
        }

        return super.getImage(element);
    }

    @Override
    public void dispose() {
        super.dispose();

        // dispose the ResourceManager yourself
        resourceManager.dispose();
    }
}
```

In case you do not pass a Control to the `LocalResourceManager`, you have to dispose of the `ResourceManager` yourself.

Prefer using `ResourceManager` to create resources. This avoids issues with system resources and can prevent an `SWTException` with the message `No more handles`.

To create disabled images, you can create an `ImageDescriptor` with the `createWithFlags(ImageDescriptor, SWT.IMAGE_DISABLE)` method. Afterward, use the `LocalResourceManager` to create the `Image` from this new descriptor.

59. ControlDecoration

The `ControlDecoration` class allows you to place image decorations on SWT controls. These decorations can have a description text that is displayed once the user places the mouse over them.

During the layout of your screen, you need to make sure that enough space is available to display these decorations.

The following code snippet demonstrates their usage.

```
// create here a text widget

Text text= ...

// create the decoration for the text UI component
ControlDecoration deco =  new ControlDecoration(text, SWT.TOP | SWT.RIGHT);

// reuse an existing image
Image image = FieldDecorationRegistry.
    getDefault().
    getFieldDecoration(FieldDecorationRegistry.DEC_INFORMATION).
    getImage();
// set description and image
deco.setDescriptionText("This is a tooltip text");
deco.setImage(image);
// hide deco if not in focus
deco.setShowOnlyOnFocus(true);

//hide the decoration if the text widget has content
text.addModifyListener(e -> {
    Text source = (Text) e.getSource();
    if (!source.getText().isEmpty()) {
        deco.hide();
    } else {
        deco.show();
    }
});
```

You can hide and show the decoration via the corresponding methods, as demonstrated in the following code snippet.

```
deco.hide();
deco.show();
```

60. User input help with field assistance

Eclipse allows you to define assistance for user input for widgets. The `org.eclipse.jface.fieldassist` package provides this functionality.

For example, you can define input help for a text field or a combo box so that the user gets possible input values presented.

The `ContentProposalAdapter` is responsible for providing the possible input values. Its constructor takes:

- `Control`: The widget for which suggestions are supplied.
- `IControlContentAdapter`: Maps the value from the `IContentProposal` to the widget and maps data back from the widget.
- `IContentProposalProvider`: Provides an array of `IContentProposal` objects.
- `KeyStroke`: Defines the keys that activate this content proposal.
- `char[]`: Characters that auto-activate this code completion.

In the following example, the content proposal should get activated via certain keys ("." and "#") as well as the `Ctrl` + `Space` key combination.

The following code demonstrates the usage of the field assistance functionality.

```
import static org.eclipse.jface.layout.GridDataFactory.fillDefaults;
import static org.eclipse.jface.widgets.WidgetFactory.text;

parent.setLayout(new GridLayout(2, false));

text = text(SWT.BORDER).message("Enter City")
        .layoutData(fillDefaults()
        .grab(true, false).create())
        .create(parent);

// Define field assists for the text widget
// use "." and " " activate the content proposals
char[] autoActivationCharacters = new char[] { '.', ' ' };
KeyStroke keyStroke;
try {
    keyStroke = KeyStroke.getInstance("Ctrl+Space");
    new ContentProposalAdapter(text, new TextContentAdapter(),
    new SimpleContentProposalProvider("ProposalOne", "ProposalTwo", "ProposalThree"),
    keyStroke, autoActivationCharacters);
} catch (ParseException e1) {
    e1.printStackTrace();
}
```

Trigger the content assists in your editor. The expected output is shown in the screenshot below.

60.1. Field assistance without filtering

The `AutoCompleteField` can be used to dynamically calculate proposals. You find an example in the exercises.

The `AutoCompleteField` class that we are using comes with default settings that cannot be changed. This includes filtering, which is activated by default. `AutoCompleteField` does not provide a way to change this, but since it is only doing some initial wiring, we can implement it ourselves without too much unnecessary duplication.

```
public class AutoCompleteFieldPart {

    private static class AutoComplete {
        private SimpleContentProposalProvider proposalProvider;
        private ContentProposalAdapter adapter;

        public AutoComplete(Control control, IControlContentAdapter
controlContentAdapter, String... proposals) {
            proposalProvider = new SimpleContentProposalProvider(proposals);
            adapter = new ContentProposalAdapter(control, controlContentAdapter,
proposalProvider, null, null);
            adapter.setPropagateKeys(true);
            adapter.setProposalAcceptanceStyle(ContentProposalAdapter.PROPOSAL_REPLACE);
        }

        public void setProposals(String... proposals) {
            proposalProvider.setProposals(proposals);
        }
    }
    // more code..
}
```

60.2. Field assist with custom filtering

The correct place to change the filter behavior is in the `IContentProposalProvider#getProposals()` method. The following code shows an implementation of `IContentProposalProvider` that takes the caret position into consideration when applying the filter.

The input "/b|in" ("|" marks the caret position) should show proposals for all folders starting with a "b".

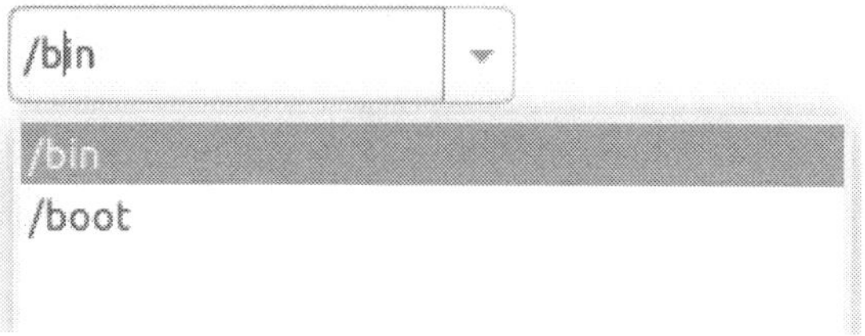


```
import java.util.regex.Pattern;
import org.eclipse.swt.widgets.Control;

// more imports

public class AutoCompleteFieldPart {

    private static class SubstringMatchContentProposalProvider implements
IContentProposalProvider {

        private List<String> proposals = Collections.emptyList();

        @Override
        public IContentProposal[] getProposals(String contents, int position) {
            if (position == 0) {
                return null;
            }
            String substring = contents.substring(0, position);
            Pattern pattern = Pattern.compile(substring,
                    Pattern.LITERAL | Pattern.CASE_INSENSITIVE | Pattern.UNICODE_CASE);
            IContentProposal[] filteredProposals = proposals.stream()
                    .filter(proposal -> proposal.length() >= substring.length() &&
pattern.matcher(proposal).find())
                    .map(ContentProposal::new).toArray(IContentProposal[]::new);
            // callers expect us to return null if we do not find any matching proposal
            return filteredProposals.length == 0 ? null : filteredProposals;
        }

        public void setProposals(List<String> proposals) {
            this.proposals = proposals;
```

```
        }
    }

    private static class AutoComplete {
        private SubstringMatchContentProposalProvider proposalProvider;
        private ContentProposalAdapter adapter;

        public AutoComplete(Control control, IControlContentAdapter
controlContentAdapter, List<String> proposals) {
            proposalProvider = new SubstringMatchContentProposalProvider();
            proposalProvider.setProposals(proposals);
            adapter = new ContentProposalAdapter(control, controlContentAdapter,
proposalProvider, null, null);
            adapter.setPropagateKeys(true);
            adapter.setProposalAcceptanceStyle(ContentProposalAdapter.PROPOSAL_REPLACE);
        }

        public void setProposals(List<String> proposals) {
            proposalProvider.setProposals(proposals);
        }
    }
    // more code..
}
```

61. Eclipse JFace viewers

61.1. Purpose of the JFace viewer framework

The JFace viewer framework allows you to display a domain model in a standard SWT widget, like a list, combo, tree, or table, without converting the domain model beforehand.

A viewer allows you to set a *content provider* that provides the data for the viewer. The content provider makes no assumption about the presentation of the data model.

You can assign at least one *label provider* to a viewer. The label provider defines how the data from the model is displayed in the viewer.

61.2. Standard JFace viewer

JFace provides several standard viewer implementations. These viewers are part of the `org.eclipse.jface.viewers` package. The following list contains the most important ones.

- `ComboViewer`
- `ListViewer`
- `TreeViewer`

- `TableViewer`

61.3. Standard content and label provider

The related interfaces for defining a content provider are described in the following table.

Table 17. Content providers

Interface	Default implementation	Description
IStructuredContentProvider	ArrayContentProvider	Used for the `List-`, `Combo-`, and `TableViewer` classes. JFace provides a default implementation for collections and arrays with the `ArrayContentProvider` class. Because the `ArrayContentProvider` class does not store any data, it is possible to share an instance with several viewers. To get a shared instance, use the `ArrayContentProvider.getInstance()` method.
ITreeContentProvider	Not available	Used for the `TreeViewer` class. It has additional methods to determine the children and the parents of the elements.

Important standard label providers are listed in the following table.

Table 18. Label providers

Required class	Standard label providers	Description
ILabelProvider	LabelProvider	Used for lists and trees, can return an icon and a label per element.
CellLabelProvider	ColumnLabelProvider	Used for tables. Defines a label provider per column.

62. JFace combo viewer

The `ComboViewer` class simplifies the implementation of an SWT combo (drop-down box).

Assume the following data model.

```
package com.vogella.eclipse.viewer;
```

```java
public class Person {
    private String firstName;
    private String lastName;
    private boolean married;

    public Person(String firstName, String lastName) {
        this.firstName = firstName;
        this.lastName = lastName;
    }

    public String getFirstName() {
        return firstName;
    }

    public void setFirstName(String firstName) {
        this.firstName = firstName;
    }

    public String getLastName() {
        return lastName;
    }

    public void setLastName(String lastName) {
        this.lastName = lastName;
    }

    public boolean isMarried() {
        return married;
     }

    public void setMarried(boolean married) {
        this.married = married;
    }
}
```

The following example snippet shows you how you could use this given data model in a `ComboViewer`. The listener is notified whenever the selection of the viewer changes.

```java
// the following code is executed by the method which
// creates the user interface
// assumes parent is an SWT Composite

GridLayout layout = new GridLayout(2, false);
parent.setLayout(layout);

Label label = new Label(parent, SWT.NONE);
label.setText("Select a person:");
```

```java
final ComboViewer viewer = new ComboViewer(parent, SWT.READ_ONLY);

// the ArrayContentProvider object does not store any state;
// therefore, you can reuse instances

viewer.setContentProvider(ArrayContentProvider.getInstance());
viewer.setLabelProvider(new LabelProvider() {
    @Override
    public String getText(Object element) {
        if (element instanceof Person) {
            Person person = (Person) element;
            return person.getFirstName();
        }
        return super.getText(element);
    }
});

List<Person> persons = Arrays.asList(new Person("Lars", "Vogel"),
        new Person("Tim", "Taler"), new Person("Jim", "Knopf"));

// set the input of the Viewer,
// this input is sent to the content provider
// must be called after setContentProvider

viewer.setInput(persons);

//react to the selection change of the viewer
//note that the viewer returns the actual object

viewer.addSelectionChangedListener(new ISelectionChangedListener() {
    @Override
    public void selectionChanged(SelectionChangedEvent event) {
        IStructuredSelection selection = (IStructuredSelection) event
            .getSelection();
        if (selection.size() > 0){
            System.out.println(((Person) selection.getFirstElement())
                    .getLastName());
        }
    }
});
```

You can get and set selections using Java objects based on your domain model.

```java
// you can select an object directly via the domain object
Person person = persons.get(0);
viewer.setSelection(new StructuredSelection(person));

// retrieves the selection, returns the data model object
```

```
IStructuredSelection selection = viewer.getStructuredSelection();
Person p = (Person) selection.getFirstElement();
```

63. JFace table viewer

63.1. Using tables with JFace

You can use the `TableViewer` class to create tables using the JFace framework. This class wraps the `Table` widget and makes it simpler to use with a custom data model. The table widget can still be accessed to set its properties.

```
// define the TableViewer
viewer = new TableViewer(parent, SWT.MULTI | SWT.H_SCROLL
            | SWT.V_SCROLL | SWT.FULL_SELECTION | SWT.BORDER);

// create the columns
// not yet implemented
createColumns(viewer);

// make lines and header visible
final Table table = viewer.getTable();
table.setHeaderVisible(true);
table.setLinesVisible(true);
```

63.2. Content provider for JFace tables

A content provider supplies the data that should be displayed in a viewer like `TableViewer`.

Eclipse provides an implementation of this interface via the `ArrayContentProvider` class. The `ArrayContentProvider` class supports Arrays or Collections as input, containing the domain data. You can implement your own content provider for a table by implementing the interface `IStructuredContentProvider` from the `org.eclipse.jface.viewers` package.

The `getElements()` method converts the viewer's input into an array of elements. Once the `setInput()` method on the viewer is called, it uses the content provider to convert it. This is the reason why the content provider must be set before the `setInput()` method is called.

Each object in the Array returned by the content provider is displayed as an individual element by the viewer. In the case of the table viewer, each object is displayed as an individual row.

The usage of the content provider is demonstrated with the following code snippet.

```
// this code is placed after the definition of
// the viewer
```

```
// set the content provider
viewer.setContentProvider(ArrayContentProvider.getInstance());

// provide the input to the viewer
// setInput() calls getElements() on the
// content provider instance
viewer.setInput(someData...);
```

63.3. Columns and label providers

Columns for a JFace `TableViewer` object are defined by creating instances of the `TableViewerColumn` class.

Each `TableViewerColumn` object needs to have a label provider assigned to it via the `setLabelProvider()` method. The label provider defines what data is displayed in the column. The label provider for a table viewer column is called per row and gets the corresponding object as its input. It uses this input to determine which data is displayed in the column for this row.

Typically, the label provider returns a String, but more complex implementations are possible.

The `setLabelProvider()` method on the `TableViewerColumn` expects an instance of the abstract `CellLabelProvider` class. A default implementation of this class is provided by the `ColumnLabelProvider` class. Its usage is demonstrated in the following code snippet.

```
// create a column for the first name
TableViewerColumn colFirstName = new TableViewerColumn(viewer, SWT.NONE);
colFirstName.getColumn().setWidth(200);
colFirstName.getColumn().setText("Firstname");
colFirstName.setLabelProvider(new ColumnLabelProvider() {
    @Override
    public String getText(Object element) {
        Person p = (Person) element;
        return p.getFirstName();
    }
});

// create more text columns if required...

// create column for married property of Person
// uses getImage() method instead of getText()
// CHECKED and UNCHECK are fields of type ImageDescriptor

TableViewerColumn colMarried = new TableViewerColumn(viewer, SWT.NONE);
colMarried.getColumn().setWidth(200);
colMarried.getColumn().setText("Married");
```

```java
colMarried.setLabelProvider(new ColumnLabelProvider() {

    private ResourceManager resourceManager = new LocalResourceManager(JFaceResources
.getResources());

    @Override
    public String getText(Object element) {
        return null;  // no string representation, we only want to display the image
    }

    @Override
    public Image getImage(Object element) {
        if (((Person) element).isMarried()) {
            return resourceManager.create(CHECKED);
        }
        return resourceManager.create(UNCHECKED);
    }

    @Override
    public void dispose() {
        super.dispose();
        resourceManager.dispose();
    }
});
```

The above code uses two fields that contain `Image` instances. These fields could for example be initialized via the following code. Using the classes in this code requires a dependency on the `org.eclipse.core.runtime` plug-in.

```java
// fields for your class
// assumes that you have these two icons
// in the "icons" folder
private final ImageDescriptor CHECKED = getImageDescriptor("checked.svg");
private final ImageDescriptor UNCHECKED = getImageDescriptor("unchecked.svg");

// more code...

private static ImageDescriptor getImageDescriptor(String file) {
    Bundle bundle = FrameworkUtil.getBundle(this.getClass());
    URL url = FileLocator.find(bundle, new Path("icons/" + file), null);
    return ImageDescriptor.createFromURL(url);
}
```

63.4. Reflect data changes in the viewer

To reflect data changes in the data model that is displayed by the viewer, you can call the `viewer.refresh()` method. This method updates the viewer based on the data that is assigned to it.

To change the data use the `viewer.setInput()` method.

63.5. Selection change listener

Via the `addSelectionChangedListener` method you can add a listener to a viewer. This listener is an implementation of the `ISelectionChangedListener` interface. The following code shows an example that gets the selected element of the viewer.

```
viewer.addSelectionChangedListener(new ISelectionChangedListener() {
    @Override
    public void selectionChanged(SelectionChangedEvent event) {
        IStructuredSelection selection = viewer.getStructuredSelection();
        Object firstElement = selection.getFirstElement();
        // do something with it
    }
});
```

63.6. Selecting elements of the Table

There are many different ways to select an element in a table.

Either the low-level SWT `Table` API can be used:

```
viewer.getTable().select(int index);
viewer.getTable().select(int[] indices);
viewer.getTable().select(int start, int end);
viewer.getTable().selectAll();
```

Or the JFace `TableViewer` API:

```
StructuredSelection structuredSelection = new StructuredSelection(listOfPersons);
viewer.setSelection(structuredSelection);
// or
// Second param is used to reveal (make visible) the selection in the viewer
viewer.setSelection(structuredSelection, true);
```

In typical cases, it is desirable to select certain objects; therefore, the JFace API is more commonly used. But if the indices are known or all items should be selected the low-level SWT API is sufficient.

64. JFace table features

64.1. Column editing support

To make a column in a table editable, you need an object of type `EditingSupport`.

The following code shows an example of an `EditingSupport` implementation.

```
package de.vogella.jface.tableviewer.edit;

import org.eclipse.jface.viewers.CellEditor;
import org.eclipse.jface.viewers.EditingSupport;
import org.eclipse.jface.viewers.TableViewer;
import org.eclipse.jface.viewers.TextCellEditor;

import com.vogella.eclipse.viewer.Person;

public class FirstNameEditingSupport extends EditingSupport {

    private final TableViewer viewer;
    private final CellEditor editor;

    public FirstNameEditingSupport(TableViewer viewer) {
        super(viewer);
        this.viewer = viewer;
        this.editor = new TextCellEditor(viewer.getTable());
    }

    @Override
    protected CellEditor getCellEditor(Object element) {
        return editor;
    }

    @Override
    protected boolean canEdit(Object element) {
        return true;
    }

    @Override
    protected Object getValue(Object element) {
        return ((Person) element).getFirstName();
    }

    @Override
    protected void setValue(Object element, Object userInputValue) {
        ((Person) element).setFirstName(String.valueOf(userInputValue));
        viewer.update(element, null);
    }
```

```
}
```

The `EditingSupport` implementation defines how the content can be changed. The `getCellEditor()` method returns an object of type `CellEditor`. This object creates the controls to change the data.

The `canEdit()` method defines whether the cell can be edited. The `getValue()` method receives the current object and returns the value that should be edited.

The method `setValue()` in `EditingSupport` receives the value modified by the user. In this method, you assign the value to your data object.

JFace provides the following default implementations for cell editors:

- `TextCellEditor`
- `ColorCellEditor`
- `CheckboxCellEditor`
- `DialogCellEditor`
- `ComboBoxViewerCellEditor`

The `TableViewerColumn` class provides the `setEditingSupport()` method to set the editor for the table column.

```
colFirstName.setEditingSupport(new FirstNameEditingSupport(viewer));
```

From an application design perspective, editing within a table can be cumbersome for the user. If the end user has to edit a large amount of data, you should offer a dialog, wizard, or part to edit the data.

64.2. Filtering data

A JFace viewer supports filtering of data via the `setFilters()` or `addFilter()` methods. These methods expect `ViewerFilter` objects as arguments.

For each registered `ViewerFilter` object the `select()` method is called. The method returns `true` if the data should be shown and `false` if it should be filtered.

```
package de.vogella.jface.tableviewer.filter;

import org.eclipse.jface.viewers.Viewer;
import org.eclipse.jface.viewers.ViewerFilter;

import de.vogella.jface.tableviewer.model.Person;
```

```java
public class PersonFilter extends ViewerFilter {

    private String searchString;

    public void setSearchText(String s) {
        // ensure that the value can be used for matching
        this.searchString = ".*" + s + ".*";
    }

    @Override
    public boolean select(Viewer viewer,
            Object parentElement,
            Object element) {
        if (searchString == null || searchString.length() == 0) {
            return true;
        }
        Person p = (Person) element;
        if (p.getFirstName().matches(searchString)) {
            return true;
        }
        if (p.getLastName().matches(searchString)) {
            return true;
        }
        return false;
    }
}
```

All filters are checked whenever the input of the viewer changes, or whenever its `refresh()` method is called.

If more than one filter is defined for a viewer, all filters must return `true` to display the data.

64.3. Sorting data with ViewerComparator

JFace supports sorting of the viewer content via the `setComparator()` method on the viewer object. This method expects a `ViewerComparator` object. By default, it will sort based on the `toString()` method of the objects in the viewer.

```java
// sort according to due date
viewer.setComparator(new ViewerComparator() {
    public int compare(Viewer viewer, Object e1, Object e2) {
        Todo t1 = (Todo) e1;
        Todo t2 = (Todo) e2;
        return t1.getDueDate().compareTo(t2.getDueDate());
    };
```

```
});
```

64.4. TableColumnLayout

With the `TableColumnLayout` class you can define the width of the columns in the table. This can be done based on a fixed or percentage value.

Using `TableColumnLayout` requires a `Composite` which only contains the table widget. This `Composite` gets the `TableColumnLayout` assigned.

```
Composite tableComposite = new Composite(parent, SWT.NONE);
TableColumnLayout tableColumnLayout = new TableColumnLayout();
tableComposite.setLayout(tableColumnLayout);
TableViewer viewer =
    new TableViewer(tableComposite,
            SWT.MULTI |
            SWT.H_SCROLL |
            SWT.V_SCROLL |
            SWT.FULL_SELECTION |
            SWT.BORDER);
```

The `TableColumnLayout` requires that you define a fixed or relative size for all columns.

```
// fixed size
tableColumnLayout.
    setColumnData(colFirstName.getColumn(),
            new ColumnPixelData(50));

// alternatively use relative size
// last parameter defines if the column is allowed
// to be resized
tableColumnLayout.
    setColumnData(colFirstName.getColumn(),
            new ColumnWeightData(20, 200, true));
```

64.5. Changing the selection highlight color

It is possible to change the selection color of the line in a JFace table via a listener.

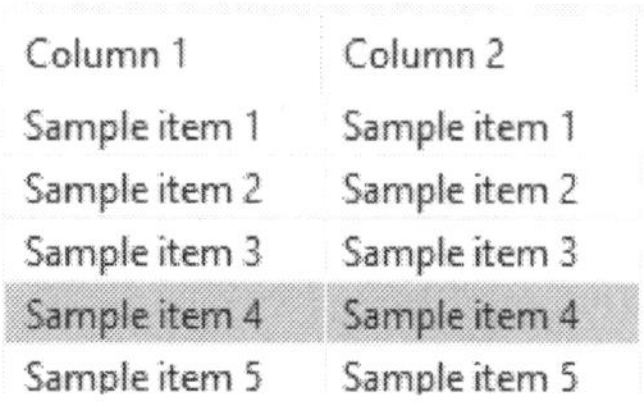

The following code is an example implementation for this.

```
package e4.parts;

import org.eclipse.jface.viewers.TableViewer;
import org.eclipse.swt.SWT;
import org.eclipse.swt.graphics.Color;
import org.eclipse.swt.graphics.GC;
import org.eclipse.swt.graphics.RGB;
import org.eclipse.swt.widgets.Composite;
import org.eclipse.swt.widgets.Event;
import org.eclipse.swt.widgets.Listener;
import org.eclipse.swt.widgets.Table;
import org.eclipse.swt.widgets.TableColumn;

public class CustomTableViewer {

    static Color goldColor = new Color(new RGB(255, 215, 0));

    public static TableViewer createTableViewer(Composite parent) {
        TableViewer tableViewer = new TableViewer(parent, SWT.FULL_SELECTION);
        Table table = tableViewer.getTable();
        table.setHeaderVisible(true);
        table.setLinesVisible(true);

        // Define columns
        String[] titles = { "Column 1", "Column 2" };
        for (String title : titles) {
            TableColumn column = new TableColumn(table, SWT.NONE);
            column.setText(title);
            column.setWidth(100);
        }
        table.addListener(SWT.EraseItem, new Listener() {
            public void handleEvent(Event event) {
                event.detail &= ~SWT.HOT;
                if ((event.detail & SWT.SELECTED) == 0)
                    return; /// item not selected

                Table table = (Table) event.widget;
                int clientWidth = table.getClientArea().width;

                GC gc = event.gc;
                Color oldBackground = gc.getBackground();

                gc.setBackground(goldColor);
                gc.fillRectangle(0, event.y, clientWidth, event.height);

                gc.setBackground(oldBackground);
```

```
                event.detail &= ~SWT.SELECTED;
            }
        });

        return tableViewer;
    }
}
```

64.6. Flexible styling or drawing the content of a column

A `StyledCellLabelProvider` supports flexible styling of the content in a column. `StyledCellLabelProvider` extends `CellLabelProvider` and allows you to style the text which is displayed in the cell.

The following example shows how to use a `StyledCellLabelProvider`. In this example, a portion of a predefined text is highlighted.

```
// define column
TableViewerColumn colTesting = new TableViewerColumn(viewer, SWT.NONE);
colTesting.getColumn().setText("Testing");
colTesting.getColumn().setWidth(200);

// set label provider
colTesting.setLabelProvider(new StyledCellLabelProvider() {
    @Override
    public void update(ViewerCell cell) {
        cell.setText("This is a test (15)");
        StyleRange myStyledRange =
                new StyleRange(16, 2, null,
                        Display.getCurrent().getSystemColor(SWT.COLOR_YELLOW));
        StyleRange[] range = { myStyledRange };
        cell.setStyleRanges(range);
        super.update(cell);
    }
});
```

As a result, the number "15" will be highlighted as depicted in the following screenshot.

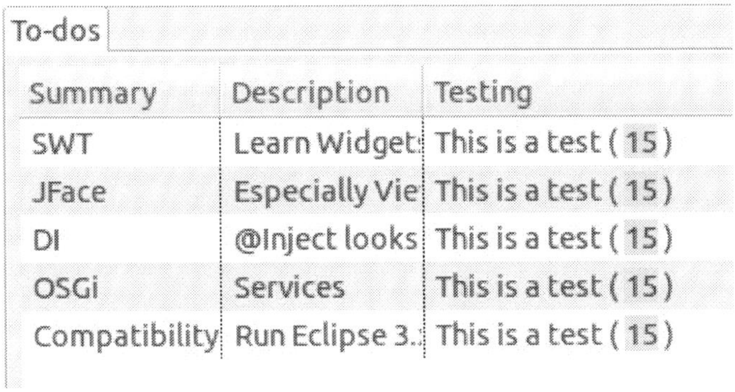

The `OwnerDrawLabelProvider` class is a label provider that handles custom drawing.

The following example draws a text and an image into the cell.

```
TableViewerColumn colHelloAndIcon = new TableViewerColumn(viewer, SWT.NONE);
colHelloAndIcon.getColumn().setText("Column 1");
colHelloAndIcon.getColumn().setWidth(200);

// ICON is an Image
colHelloAndIcon.setLabelProvider(new OwnerDrawLabelProvider() {
    @Override
    protected void measure(Event event, Object element) {
        Rectangle rectangle = ICON.getBounds();
        event.setBounds(new Rectangle(
            event.x,
            event.y,
            rectangle.width + 200 ,
            rectangle.height));
    }

    @Override
    protected void paint(Event event, Object element) {
        Rectangle bounds = event.getBounds();
        event.gc.drawText("Hello", bounds.x, bounds.y);
        Point point = event.gc.stringExtent("Hello");
        event.gc.drawImage(ICON, bounds.x + 5 + point.x, bounds.y);
    }
});
```

64.7. Table column menu and hiding columns

You can add a menu to your table. This menu can include a menu entry for each column. This allows you to add arbitrary popup actions to your columns.

You can use it, for example, to hide and show columns based on the width setting as demonstrated in the following code snippet.

```
// define the menu and assign to the table
contextMenu = new Menu(viewer.getTable());
viewer.getTable().setMenu(contextMenu);

// create your columns as usual...

// afterwards add a MenuItem for each column to the table menu
for (TableColumn tableColumn : viewer.getTable().getColumns() ){
    createMenuItem(contextMenu, tableColumn);
}

// the createMenuItem() method adds a MenuItem
// per column to the menu

private void createMenuItem(Menu parent, final TableColumn column) {
    final MenuItem itemName = new MenuItem(parent, SWT.CHECK);
    itemName.setText(column.getText());
    itemName.setSelection(column.getResizable());
    itemName.addSelectionListener(new SelectionAdapter() {
          @Override
          public void widgetSelected(SelectionEvent e) {
            if (itemName.getSelection()) {
                column.setWidth(150);
                column.setResizable(true);
            } else {
                column.setWidth(0);
                column.setResizable(false);
            }
        }
    });
```

```
}
```

64.8. Tooltips for viewers

You can use tooltips for the cells of the viewer. To achieve this, you have to activate the tooltips for a viewer.

```
// activate the tooltip support for the viewer
ColumnViewerToolTipSupport.enableFor(viewer, ToolTip.NO_RECREATE);
```

In your `CellLabelProvider` you specify the related methods for displaying the tooltip.

```
colFirstName.setLabelProvider(new ColumnLabelProvider() {
  @Override
  public String getText(Object element) {
    Person p = (Person) element;
    return p.getFirstName();
  }

  @Override
  public String getToolTipText(Object element) {
    return "Tooltip (" + ((Person)element).getLastName() + ")";
  }

  @Override
  public Point getToolTipShift(Object object) {
    return new Point(5, 5);
  }

  @Override
  public int getToolTipDisplayDelayTime(Object object) {
    return 100; // msec
  }

  @Override
  public int getToolTipTimeDisplayed(Object object) {
    return 5000; // msec
  }
});
```

64.9. Virtual tables with LazyContentProvider

If you have a huge number of lines that you want to display in the table, you can use a `LazyContentProvider`. This provider allows you to fetch the data when it is needed instead of loading everything into memory. As a result of the lazy loading, you gain a better memory footprint and improve performance for a large set of data. The following code demonstrates its usage.

```
private class MyLazyContentProvider implements ILazyContentProvider {
  private TableViewer viewer;
  private Person[] elements;

  public MyLazyContentProvider(TableViewer viewer) {
    this.viewer = viewer;
  }

  public void dispose() {
  }

  public void inputChanged(Viewer viewer, Object oldInput, Object newInput) {
    this.elements = (Person[]) newInput;
  }

  public void updateElement(int index) {
    viewer.replace(elements[index], index);
  }
}
```

```
// create your table with the virtual flag
final TableViewer v = new TableViewer(shell, SWT.VIRTUAL);

// create TableColumns with label providers as before...
// ...

v.setContentProvider(new MyLazyContentProvider(v));

// special settings for the lazy content provider
v.setUseHashlookup(true);

// create the model and set it as input
Person[] model = createModel();
v.setInput(model);
// you must explicitly set the items count
v.setItemCount(model.length);
```

64.10. Alternative table implementations

It is possible to use other table implementations. Most notable is the NatTable [https://www.eclipse.org/nattable/] implementation. It provides a flexible and powerful framework for creating tables, grids and trees that show great performance for a huge number of rows and columns.

65. JFace TreeViewer

65.1. Using viewers to display a tree

The `TreeViewer` class provides viewer support for displaying trees. The usage of this class is similar to the `TableViewer` class. The main difference is that the `TreeViewer` class requires a structured content provider. Typically, your content provider has to implement the `ITreeContentProvider` interface to be used with your `TreeViewer` class.

A `TreeViewer` can be used similarly to a `TableViewer`, which shows a list of elements by using the following content provider:

```
public class TreeContentProvider implements ITreeContentProvider {
    @Override
    public boolean hasChildren(Object element) {
        return false;
    }

    @Override
    public Object getParent(Object element) {
        return null;
    }

    @Override
    public Object[] getElements(Object inputElement) {
        return ArrayContentProvider.getInstance().getElements(inputElement);
    }

    @Override
    public Object[] getChildren(Object parentElement) {
        return null;
    }
}
```

This `ITreeContentProvider` just delegates to the `ArrayContentProvider` in its `getElements` method and the elements have no children.

```
    @PostConstruct
    public void postConstruct(Composite parent) {
        TreeViewer viewer = new TreeViewer(parent);
        viewer.setContentProvider(new TreeContentProvider());
        viewer.getTree().setHeaderVisible(true);
        viewer.getTree().setLinesVisible(true);

        TreeViewerColumn viewerColumn = new TreeViewerColumn(viewer, SWT.NONE);
        viewerColumn.getColumn().setWidth(300);
```

```
        viewerColumn.getColumn().setText("Names");
        viewerColumn.setLabelProvider(new ColumnLabelProvider());

        viewer.setInput(new String[] { "Simon Scholz", "Lars Vogel", "Dirk Fauth", "Wim
Jongman", "Tom Schindl" });

        GridLayoutFactory.fillDefaults().generateLayout(parent);
    }
```

65.2. Selection and double-click listener

JFace allows you to access the SWT controls to define listeners on your viewer. For example, you can add a `SelectionListener` implementation to the SWT control which is wrapped in the JFace object. The following code snippet demonstrates how to expand a tree with a mouse click.

```
// the viewer field is an already configured TreeViewer
Tree tree = (Tree) viewer.getControl();
tree.addSelectionListener(new SelectionAdapter() {
  @Override
  public void widgetSelected(SelectionEvent e) {
      TreeItem item = (TreeItem) e.item;
        if (item.getItemCount() > 0) {
            item.setExpanded(!item.getExpanded());
            // update the viewer
            viewer.refresh();
        }
    }
});
```

Viewers allow you to attach specific listeners directly. The following example shows how to expand an instance of a `TreeViewer` with a double-click.

```
viewer.addDoubleClickListener(new IDoubleClickListener() {
    @Override
    public void doubleClick(DoubleClickEvent event) {
        TreeViewer viewer = (TreeViewer) event.getViewer();
        IStructuredSelection thisSelection = (IStructuredSelection) event.getSelection();

        Object selectedNode = thisSelection.getFirstElement();
        viewer.setExpandedState(selectedNode,
                !viewer.getExpandedState(selectedNode));
    }
});
```

65.3. Adjusting tree columns when expanded

If a `TreeViewer` has multiple columns, clipping the first column (containing expandable items) looks unprofessional.

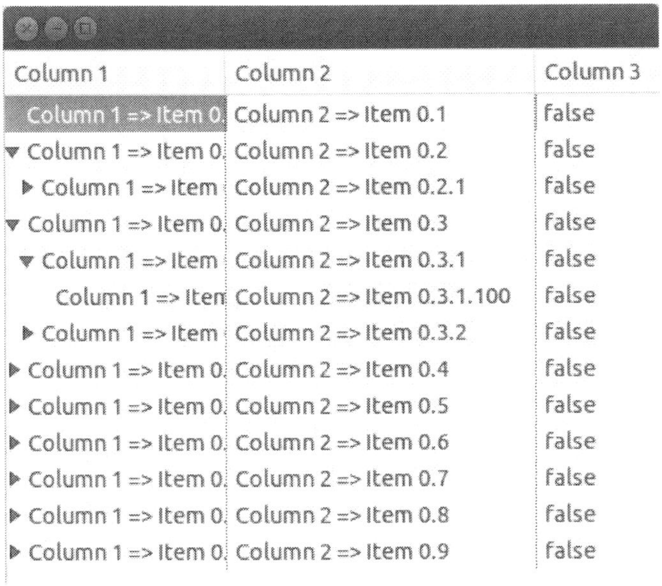

To make a column fit its content, you can call the column's `pack()` method as follows:

```
// the viewer field is an already configured TreeViewer
Tree tree = (Tree) viewer.getControl();

Listener listener = new Listener() {

   @Override
   public void handleEvent(Event event) {
      TreeItem treeItem = (TreeItem) event.item;
      final TreeColumn[] treeColumns = treeItem.getParent().getColumns();
      display.asyncExec(new Runnable() {

         @Override
         public void run() {
            for (TreeColumn treeColumn : treeColumns)
                 treeColumn.pack();
         }
      });
   }
};

tree.addListener(SWT.Expand, listener);
```

With this code every column of the `Tree` will have the appropriate width, when a `TreeItem` is expanded, so that the contents of the column are not clipped.

65.4. Increasing the font size

The font size can be increased by setting a `Font` for the underlying SWT `Tree`.

```
    @PostConstruct
    public void postConstruct(Composite parent) {

        ResourceManager resourceManager = new LocalResourceManager(JFaceResources
.getResources(), parent);

        TreeViewer viewer = new TreeViewer(parent);
        viewer.setContentProvider(new TreeContentProvider());
        viewer.getTree().setHeaderVisible(true);
        viewer.getTree().setLinesVisible(true);
        viewer.getTree().setFont(resourceManager.createFont(FontDescriptor.createFrom
("Arial", 32, SWT.ITALIC)));

        TreeViewerColumn viewerColumn = new TreeViewerColumn(viewer, SWT.NONE);
        viewerColumn.getColumn().setWidth(300);
        viewerColumn.getColumn().setText("Names");
        viewerColumn.setLabelProvider(new ColumnLabelProvider());

        viewer.setInput(new String[] { "Simon Scholz", "Lars Vogel", "Dirk Fauth", "Wim
Jongman", "Tom Schindl" });

        GridLayoutFactory.fillDefaults().generateLayout(parent);
    }
```

66. Exercise: Providing a table for the tasks

In this exercise, you implement a table to display your tasks objects. The `TodoOverviewPart` class is used for this.

66.1. Check dependencies

Ensure via the `MANIFEST.MF` file that the `org.eclipse.jface` plug-in is available as a dependency to the `com.vogella.tasks.ui` plug-in. You should have added this dependency already in another exercise.

66.2. Create implementation

Create a JFace table implementation with the `summary` and `description` fields as table columns.

Your part should still have the *Load Data* button. Load the data into the viewer once this button is pressed.

You can use the following example code as a base for this exercise.

```
package com.vogella.tasks.ui.parts;

import static org.eclipse.jface.layout.GridLayoutFactory.fillDefaults;
import static org.eclipse.jface.widgets.ButtonFactory.newButton;

import jakarta.annotation.PostConstruct;
import jakarta.inject.Inject;

import org.eclipse.e4.ui.di.Focus;
import org.eclipse.jface.viewers.ArrayContentProvider;
import org.eclipse.jface.viewers.ColumnLabelProvider;
import org.eclipse.jface.viewers.TableViewer;
import org.eclipse.jface.viewers.TableViewerColumn;
import org.eclipse.swt.SWT;
import org.eclipse.swt.layout.GridData;
import org.eclipse.swt.widgets.Composite;
import org.eclipse.swt.widgets.Table;

import com.vogella.tasks.model.Task;
import com.vogella.tasks.model.TaskService;

public class TodoOverviewPart {
    @Inject
    TaskService taskService;

    private TableViewer viewer;

    @PostConstruct
    public void createControls(Composite parent) {
        fillDefaults().numColumns(1).applyTo(parent);

        newButton(SWT.PUSH).text("Load Data").onSelect(e -> update()).create(parent);

        viewer = new TableViewer(parent, SWT.MULTI | SWT.FULL_SELECTION);
        Table table = viewer.getTable();
        table.setHeaderVisible(true);
        table.setLinesVisible(true);
        table.setLayoutData(new GridData(SWT.FILL, SWT.FILL, true, true));
        viewer.setContentProvider(ArrayContentProvider.getInstance());

        // create column for the summary property
        TableViewerColumn colSummary = new TableViewerColumn(viewer, SWT.NONE);
        colSummary.setLabelProvider(new ColumnLabelProvider() {
```

```
            @Override
            public String getText(Object element) {
                Task todo = (Task) element;
                return todo.getSummary();
            }
        });
        colSummary.getColumn().setWidth(100);
        colSummary.getColumn().setText("Summary");

        // create column for description property
        TableViewerColumn colDescription = new TableViewerColumn(viewer, SWT.NONE);
        colDescription.setLabelProvider(new ColumnLabelProvider() {
            @Override
            public String getText(Object element) {
                Task todo = (Task) element;
                return todo.getDescription();
            }
        });
        colDescription.getColumn().setWidth(200);
        colDescription.getColumn().setText("Description");

        // initially the table is also filled
        // the btnLoadData is used to update the data if the model changes
        taskService.consume(viewer::setInput);
    }

    @Focus
    public void setFocus() {
        viewer.getControl().setFocus();
    }

    private void update() {
        taskService.consume(viewer::setInput);
    }
}
```

The expected output is shown in the screenshot below.

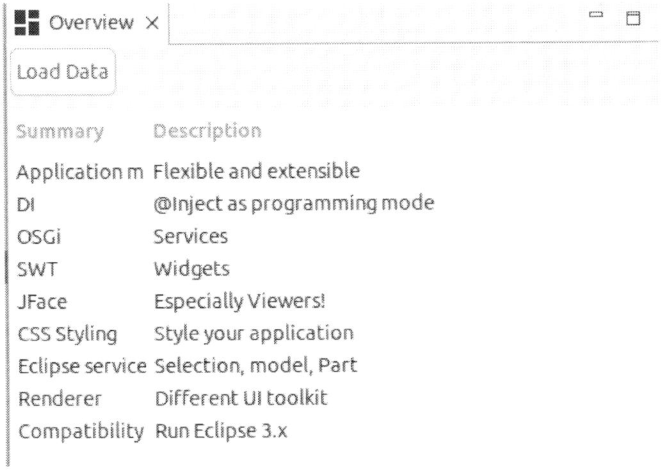

The *Load Data* button is required for later exercises.

The SWT table widgets show an additional column on Windows containing empty space. This is how the native Windows widget handles this. To avoid this, you can use a table layout with column weights.

67. Optional exercise: Extending the table

67.1. Create a Button to select all elements

Allow all elements in the table to be selected via a button. One way of achieving this is to use the `Table selectAll()` method.

```
Button selectAllButton = new Button(parent, SWT.PUSH);
selectAllButton.setLayoutData(new GridData(SWT.BEGINNING, SWT.CENTER, false, false));
selectAllButton.setText("Select All");
selectAllButton.addSelectionListener(new SelectionAdapter() {
    @Override
    public void widgetSelected(SelectionEvent e) {
        viewer.setSelection(new StructuredSelection((java.util.List)viewer.getInput()));
    }
});
```

Place the button beside or underneath the *Load data* button.

67.2. Add a keyboard shortcut to the table

Also, add a shortcut to your viewer to perform an action.

```
viewer.getTable().addKeyListener(KeyListener.keyPressedAdapter(e -> {
    if (e.stateMask == SWT.CTRL && e.keyCode == 'z') {
        System.out.println("Pressed z");
    }
}));
```

67.3. Add a filter to the table

Also, add a filter text box to the part. Use the text in the filter text box as a filter for the displayed items in the table. Ensure that you only show the table entries that contain the text of the filter box in their summary or description field.

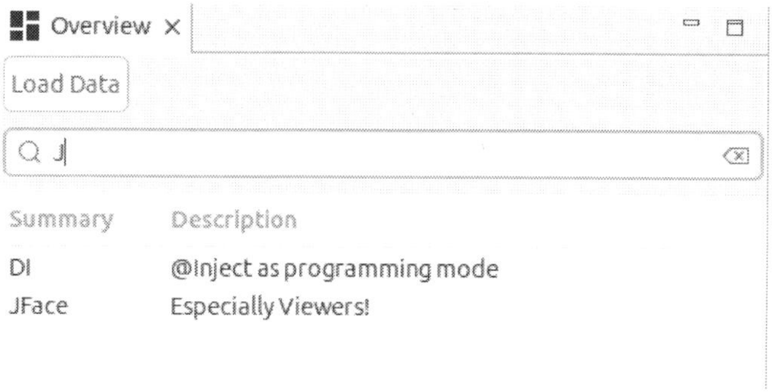

The following code snippet can be used as a starting point.

```
// TableViewer must be a field
private TableViewer viewer;

// define this new field
protected String searchString="";

@PostConstruct
public void createControls(Composite parent) {

// EXISTING CODE TO BUILD THE UPDATE BUTTON
// ...
// ...

Text search = new Text(parent, SWT.SEARCH | SWT.CANCEL
        | SWT.ICON_SEARCH );

// assuming that GridLayout is used
search.setLayoutData(new GridData(SWT.FILL, SWT.CENTER, false, false,
        1, 1));
search.setMessage("Filter");
```

```
// filter at every keystroke
search.addModifyListener(new ModifyListener() {
    @Override
    public void modifyText(ModifyEvent e) {
        Text source = (Text) e.getSource();
        searchString = source.getText();
        // trigger update in the viewer
        viewer.refresh();
    }
});

// SWT.SEARCH | SWT.CANCEL is not supported under Windows 7 and
// so the following SelectionListener will not work under Windows 7
search.addSelectionListener(new SelectionAdapter() {
    public void widgetDefaultSelected(SelectionEvent e) {
        if (e.detail == SWT.CANCEL) {
            Text text = (Text) e.getSource();
            text.setText("");
            //
        }
    }
});

// EXISTING CODE WHICH DEFINES THE VIEWER.....
// ...
// ...
// ...

// add a filter that will search in the summary and description field
viewer.addFilter(new ViewerFilter() {
    @Override
    public boolean select(Viewer viewer, Object parentElement,
        Object element) {
        Task task = (Task) element;
        return task.getSummary().contains(searchString)
                || task.getDescription().contains(searchString);
        }
});
```

67.4. Sort the table based on summary

Ensure that the table is sorted by the `summary` column.

Use the following example code for this.

```
// sort according to due date, needs to be adjusted for the exercise
viewer.setComparator(new ViewerComparator() {
```

```
    public int compare(Viewer viewer, Object e1, Object e2) {
        Task t1 = (Task) e1;
        Task t2 = (Task) e2;
        return t1.getDueDate().compareTo(t2.getDueDate());
    };
});
```

68. Optional exercise: Use ComboViewer

In this exercise, you create a new part that allows you to delete a task object from your model based on the selection in your `ComboViewer`. The expected output is shown in the screenshot below.

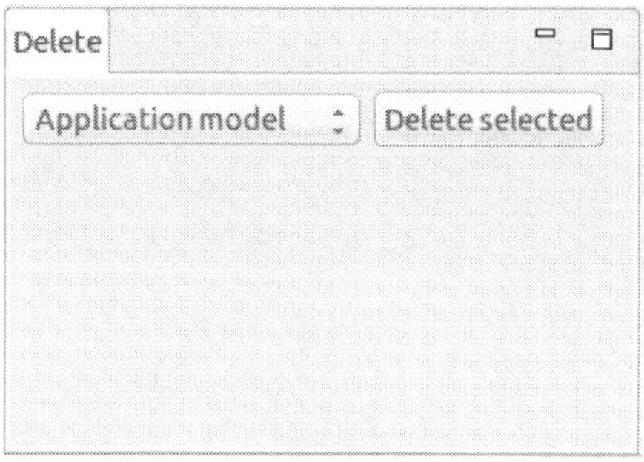

68.1. Implementation

Ensure that the `org.eclipse.jface` plug-in is available as a dependency to your `com.vogella.tasks.ui` plug-in. If you followed the previous exercises, this should already be the case.

Create a new class named `TodoDeletionPart`.

Implement a `ComboViewer` that contains your task items. Add a button to the part. If this button is pressed, the `delete()` method of your `TaskService` should be called.

You can use the following example code as a reference.

```
package com.vogella.tasks.ui.parts;

import java.util.List;

import jakarta.annotation.PostConstruct;
import jakarta.inject.Inject;

import org.eclipse.e4.ui.di.Focus;
import org.eclipse.jface.viewers.ArrayContentProvider;
import org.eclipse.jface.viewers.ComboViewer;
```

```java
import org.eclipse.jface.viewers.IStructuredSelection;
import org.eclipse.jface.viewers.LabelProvider;
import org.eclipse.jface.viewers.StructuredSelection;
import org.eclipse.swt.SWT;
import org.eclipse.swt.events.SelectionAdapter;
import org.eclipse.swt.events.SelectionEvent;
import org.eclipse.swt.layout.GridLayout;
import org.eclipse.swt.widgets.Button;
import org.eclipse.swt.widgets.Composite;

import com.vogella.tasks.model.Task;
import com.vogella.tasks.model.TaskService;


public class TodoDeletionPart {

    @Inject
    private TaskService taskService;

    private ComboViewer viewer;

    @PostConstruct
    public void createControls(Composite parent) {
        parent.setLayout(new GridLayout(2, false));
        viewer = new ComboViewer(parent, SWT.READ_ONLY);
        viewer.setLabelProvider(new LabelProvider() {
            @Override
            public String getText(Object element) {
                Task todo = (Task) element;
                return todo.getSummary();
            }
        });
        viewer.setContentProvider(ArrayContentProvider.getInstance());

        taskService.consume(this::updateViewer);

        Button button = new Button(parent, SWT.PUSH);
        button.addSelectionListener(new SelectionAdapter() {
            @Override
            public void widgetSelected(SelectionEvent e) {
                IStructuredSelection selection = viewer.getStructuredSelection();
                if (!selection.isEmpty()) {
                    Task firstElement = (Task) selection.getFirstElement();
                    taskService.delete(firstElement.getId());
                    taskService.consume(TodoDeletionPart.this::updateViewer);
                }
            }
        });
        button.setText("Delete selected");
```

```
    }

    private void updateViewer(List<Task> todos) {
        viewer.setInput(todos);
        if (!todos.isEmpty()) {
            viewer.setSelection(new StructuredSelection(todos.get(0)));
        }
    }

    @Focus
    public void focus() {
        viewer.getControl().setFocus();
    }
}
```

If you face issues with the selection in the viewer or the deletion, ensure that the `equals()` and `hashCode()` methods in the `Task` class are correct (they should be based on the `id` field).

68.2. Add the new part to the application model

Add a new part in your application model that refers to this new class.

68.3. Validation

Delete entries in your data model. The `ComboViewer` should be updated automatically.

Validate that the number of entries in your data model has been reduced. You can reload the data by pressing the Load Data button in the `TodoOverviewPart` part.

69. Optional exercise: Providing input help for the user

In this exercise, you will learn how to add field assistance to input boxes.

69.1. Using field assistance together with a text field

Add field assistance functionality to a `Text` widget. This allows the user to select predefined cities.

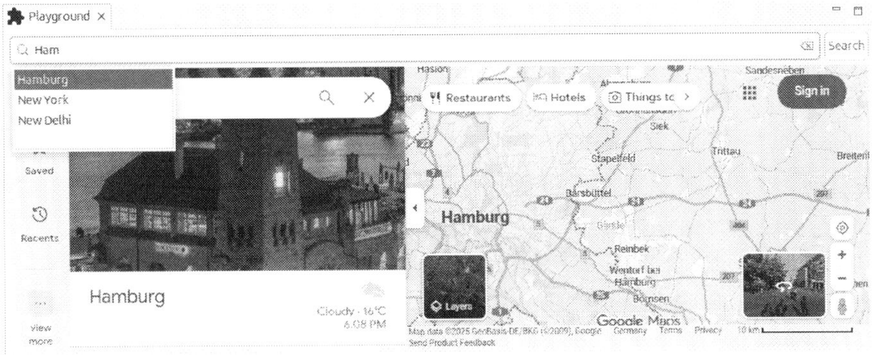

The following code snippet should be sufficient to implement this.

```
ContentProposalAdapter contentProposal = new ContentProposalAdapter(text, new
TextContentAdapter(),
                new SimpleContentProposalProvider("Hamburg", "New York", "New Delhi"),
null, null);
contentProposal.setPopupSize(new Point(200, 100));
contentProposal.setProposalAcceptanceStyle(ContentProposalAdapter.PROPOSAL_REPLACE);
```

Find below a full solution.

```
package com.vogella.tasks.ui.parts;

import static org.eclipse.jface.layout.GridDataFactory.fillDefaults;
import static org.eclipse.jface.widgets.WidgetFactory.button;
import static org.eclipse.jface.widgets.WidgetFactory.text;

import java.io.UnsupportedEncodingException;
import java.net.URLEncoder;

import org.eclipse.e4.ui.di.Focus;
import org.eclipse.jface.fieldassist.ContentProposalAdapter;
import org.eclipse.jface.fieldassist.SimpleContentProposalProvider;
import org.eclipse.jface.fieldassist.TextContentAdapter;
import org.eclipse.swt.SWT;
import org.eclipse.swt.browser.Browser;
import org.eclipse.swt.events.SelectionListener;
import org.eclipse.swt.graphics.Point;
import org.eclipse.swt.layout.GridLayout;
import org.eclipse.swt.widgets.Composite;
import org.eclipse.swt.widgets.Text;

import jakarta.annotation.PostConstruct;

public class PlaygroundPart {
```

```
    private Text text;
    private Browser browser;

    @PostConstruct
    public void createControls(Composite parent) {
        parent.setLayout(new GridLayout(2, false));

        text = text(SWT.BORDER | SWT.SEARCH | SWT.ICON_SEARCH | SWT.ICON_CANCEL).message
("Enter City")
                .layoutData(fillDefaults().grab(true, false).create()).create(parent);
        text.addSelectionListener(SelectionListener.widgetDefaultSelectedAdapter(e ->
updateBrowser()));

        ContentProposalAdapter contentProposal = new ContentProposalAdapter(text, new
TextContentAdapter(),
                new SimpleContentProposalProvider("Hamburg", "New York", "New Delhi"),
null, null);

        contentProposal.setPopupSize(new Point(200, 100));
        contentProposal.setProposalAcceptanceStyle(ContentProposalAdapter
.PROPOSAL_REPLACE);
        button(SWT.PUSH).text("Search").onSelect(e -> updateBrowser()).create(parent);

        browser = new Browser(parent, SWT.NONE);
        browser.setLayoutData(fillDefaults().grab(true, true).span(2, 1).create());
    }

    private void updateBrowser() {
        String city = text.getText();
        if (city.isEmpty()) {
            return;
        }
        try {
            browser.setUrl("https://www.google.com/maps/place/" + URLEncoder.encode(city,
"UTF-8") + "/&output=embed");

        } catch (UnsupportedEncodingException e1) {
            e1.printStackTrace();
        }
    }

    @Focus
    public void onFocus() {
        text.setFocus();
    }
}
```

69.2. Add control decoration

Currently, the user sees no indication that input help is available. Add a control decoration to the text field to show the user that input help is available.

The following should be sufficient to implement this. Find below a full solution.

```
private void addControlDecoration() {
    // create the decoration for the text component
    // using a predefined image
    ControlDecoration deco = new ControlDecoration(text, SWT.TOP | SWT.LEFT);
    Image image = FieldDecorationRegistry.getDefault().getFieldDecoration
(FieldDecorationRegistry.DEC_INFORMATION)
            .getImage();
    // set description and image
    deco.setDescriptionText("Use Ctrl + SPACE to see possible values");
    deco.setImage(image);
    // always show decoration
    deco.setShowOnlyOnFocus(false);

    // hide the decoration if the text widget has content
    text.addModifyListener(e -> {
        Text source = (Text) e.getSource();
        if (!source.getText().isEmpty()) {
            deco.hide();
        } else {
            deco.show();
        }
    });
}
```

```
package com.vogella.tasks.ui.parts;

import static org.eclipse.jface.layout.GridDataFactory.fillDefaults;
import static org.eclipse.jface.widgets.WidgetFactory.button;
import static org.eclipse.jface.widgets.WidgetFactory.text;

import java.io.UnsupportedEncodingException;
import java.net.URLEncoder;

import jakarta.annotation.PostConstruct;

import org.eclipse.e4.ui.di.Focus;
import org.eclipse.jface.fieldassist.ContentProposalAdapter;
import org.eclipse.jface.fieldassist.ControlDecoration;
import org.eclipse.jface.fieldassist.FieldDecorationRegistry;
import org.eclipse.jface.fieldassist.SimpleContentProposalProvider;
```

```
import org.eclipse.jface.fieldassist.TextContentAdapter;
import org.eclipse.swt.SWT;
import org.eclipse.swt.browser.Browser;
import org.eclipse.swt.events.SelectionListener;
import org.eclipse.swt.graphics.Image;
import org.eclipse.swt.layout.GridLayout;
import org.eclipse.swt.widgets.Composite;
import org.eclipse.swt.widgets.Text;

public class PlaygroundPart {
    private Text text;
    private Browser browser;

    @PostConstruct
    public void createControls(Composite parent) {
        parent.setLayout(new GridLayout(2, false));

        text = text(SWT.BORDER | SWT.SEARCH | SWT.ICON_SEARCH | SWT.ICON_CANCEL).message
("Enter City")
                .layoutData(fillDefaults().grab(true, false).create()).create(parent);
        text.addSelectionListener(SelectionListener.widgetDefaultSelectedAdapter(e ->
updateBrowser()));

        ContentProposalAdapter contentProposal = new ContentProposalAdapter(text, new
TextContentAdapter(),
                new SimpleContentProposalProvider("Hamburg", "New York", "New Delhi"),
null, null);
        addControlDecoration();
        contentProposal.setProposalAcceptanceStyle(ContentProposalAdapter
.PROPOSAL_REPLACE);
        button(SWT.PUSH).text("Search").onSelect(e -> updateBrowser()).create(parent);

        browser = new Browser(parent, SWT.NONE);
        browser.setLayoutData(fillDefaults().grab(true, true).span(2, 1).create());
    }

    private void addControlDecoration() {
        // Create a decoration for the text component using a predefined image
        ControlDecoration deco = new ControlDecoration(text, SWT.TOP | SWT.LEFT);
        Image image = FieldDecorationRegistry.getDefault().getFieldDecoration
(FieldDecorationRegistry.DEC_INFORMATION)
                .getImage();
        // Set description and image
        deco.setDescriptionText("Use Ctrl + SPACE to see possible values");
        deco.setImage(image);
        // Always show decoration
        deco.setShowOnlyOnFocus(false);

        // Hide the decoration if the text widget has content
```

```
        text.addModifyListener(e -> {
            Text source = (Text) e.getSource();
            if (!source.getText().isEmpty()) {
                deco.hide();
            } else {
                deco.show();
            }
        });
    }

    private void updateBrowser() {
        String city = text.getText();
        if (city.isEmpty()) {
            return;
        }
        try {
            browser.setUrl("https://www.google.com/maps/place/" + URLEncoder.encode(city,
"UTF-8") + "/&output=embed");

        } catch (UnsupportedEncodingException e1) {
            e1.printStackTrace();
        }
    }

    @Focus
    public void onFocus() {
        text.setFocus();
    }
}
```

69.3. Using field assists together with combo boxes

In this exercise, you will implement user input help (via field assists) for a combo box. It lets the user enter a system path and fills the proposals with the directories contained in the given path.

Add a new part to your application. Implement the following class for this part and link it in the application model.

```
package com.vogella.tasks.ui.parts;

import java.io.File;
import java.io.IOException;
import java.nio.file.Files;
import java.nio.file.InvalidPathException;
import java.nio.file.Path;
import java.nio.file.Paths;
import java.util.List;
```

```
import java.util.stream.Collectors;
import java.util.stream.Stream;

import jakarta.annotation.PostConstruct;

import org.eclipse.jface.fieldassist.AutoCompleteField;
import org.eclipse.jface.fieldassist.ComboContentAdapter;
import org.eclipse.jface.layout.GridLayoutFactory;
import org.eclipse.swt.SWT;
import org.eclipse.swt.widgets.Combo;
import org.eclipse.swt.widgets.Composite;

public class AutoCompleteFieldPart {

    private Path lastDir;

    @PostConstruct
    public void createControls(Composite parent) {
        GridLayoutFactory.fillDefaults().applyTo(parent);

        Combo combo = new Combo(parent, SWT.NONE);
        AutoCompleteField autoCompleteField = new AutoCompleteField(combo, new
ComboContentAdapter());

        combo.addModifyListener(e -> {
            Path dir = getPathWithoutFileName(combo.getText());
            if (dir == null || dir.equals(lastDir) || !isDirectory(dir)) {
                return;
            }
            lastDir = dir;
            try (Stream<Path> paths = Files.list(dir)) {
                List<String> directories = filterPaths(paths);
                autoCompleteField.setProposals(directories.toArray(new String[
directories.size()]));
            } catch (IOException ex) {
                // ignore
            }
        });
    }

    private Path getPathWithoutFileName(String inputPath) {
        int lastIndex = inputPath.lastIndexOf(File.separatorChar);
        if (separatorNotFound(lastIndex)) {
            return null;
        } else if (endsWithSeparator(inputPath, lastIndex)) {
            return getPath(inputPath);
        } else {
            return getPath(removeFileName(inputPath, lastIndex));
        }
```

```
    }

    private boolean separatorNotFound(int lastIndex) {
        return lastIndex < 0;
    }

    private boolean endsWithSeparator(String inputPath, int lastIndex) {
        return lastIndex == inputPath.length();
    }

    private String removeFileName(String text, int lastIndex) {
        if (lastIndex == 0) {
            return File.separator;
        } else {
            return text.substring(0, lastIndex);
        }
    }

    private Path getPath(String text) {
        try {
            return Paths.get(text);
        } catch (InvalidPathException ex) {
            return null;
        }
    }

    private boolean isDirectory(Path dir) {
        try {
            return Files.isDirectory(dir);
        } catch (SecurityException ex) {
            return false;
        }
    }

    private List<String> filterPaths(Stream<Path> paths) {
        return paths.filter(path -> {
            String[] directoriesInPath = path.toString().split(File.separator);
            String fileName = directoriesInPath[directoriesInPath.length - 1];
            String lastDirectory = directoriesInPath[directoriesInPath.length - 2];
            return !lastDirectory.equals(".") && !fileName.startsWith(".") && Files
.isDirectory(path);
        }).map(Path::toString).collect(Collectors.toList());
    }
}
```

The result should allow you to select a path whenever you type the directory separator.

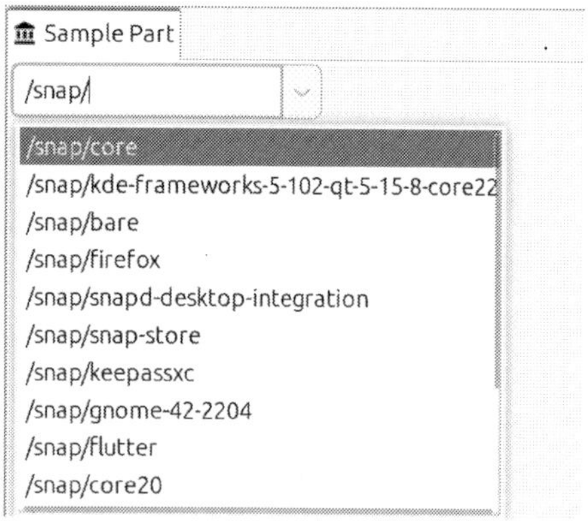

69.4. Using field assists with task service input

To use your task service as content proposals, you have to wrap your objects into your custom `ContentProposal`.

```
package com.vogella.tasks.ui.parts.contentassists;

import org.eclipse.jface.fieldassist.ContentProposal;

import com.vogella.tasks.model.Task;

public class TaskContentProposal extends ContentProposal {
    private Task task;

    public TaskContentProposal(String content, Task task) {
        super(content);
        this.task = task;
    }

    public Task getTask() {
        return task;
    }
}
```

Write your custom content provider.

```
package com.vogella.tasks.ui.parts.contentassists;

import java.util.List;
import java.util.regex.Pattern;

import org.eclipse.jface.fieldassist.IContentProposal;
import org.eclipse.jface.fieldassist.IContentProposalProvider;
```

```
import com.vogella.tasks.model.Task;

public class TaskContentProposalProvider implements IContentProposalProvider {

    private List<Task> tasks;
    public TaskContentProposalProvider(List<Task> tasks) {
        this.tasks = tasks;
    }


    @Override
    public IContentProposal[] getProposals(String contents, int position) {
        String substring = contents.substring(0, position);
        Pattern pattern = Pattern.compile(substring, Pattern.LITERAL | Pattern
.CASE_INSENSITIVE | Pattern.UNICODE_CASE);
        IContentProposal[] filteredProposals = tasks.stream()
                .filter(task -> task.getSummary().length() >= substring.length()
                        && pattern.matcher(task.getSummary()).find())
                .map(task -> new TaskContentProposal(task.getSummary() + " --- " + task
.getDescription(), task))
                .toArray(TaskContentProposal[]::new);
        return filteredProposals.length == 0 ? null : filteredProposals;
    }

    // This is a simpler version of the above implementation
//  @Override
//  public IContentProposal[] getProposals(String contents, int position) {
//
//      for (Task task : tasks) {
//          if (task.getSummary().toLowerCase().startsWith(contents.toLowerCase())) {
//              proposals.add(new TaskContentProposal(task.getSummary(), task));
//          }
//      }
//      return proposals.toArray(new TaskContentProposal[0]);
//  }

    public void setProposals(List<Task> tasks) {
        this.tasks = tasks;
    }
}
```

Now you can use these objects to define input help. You can register a listener to get notified whenever the user selects your proposal.

```
Text text = WidgetFactory.text(SWT.BORDER)
                .layoutData(GridDataFactory.fillDefaults().grab(true, false).create())
                .create(parent);
        TaskContentProposalProvider taskContentProposalProvider = new
```

```
TaskContentProposalProvider(new ArrayList<>());
        ContentProposalAdapter contentProposal = new ContentProposalAdapter(text,
                new TextContentAdapter(), taskContentProposalProvider, null, null);

        contentProposal.addContentProposalListener(proposal -> {
            TaskContentProposal p = (TaskContentProposal) proposal;
            System.out.println(p.getTask().getSummary());
        });
        contentProposal.setProposalAcceptanceStyle(ContentProposalAdapter
.PROPOSAL_REPLACE);

        WidgetFactory.button(SWT.PUSH).onSelect(e -> {
            taskContentProposalProvider.setProposals(taskService.getAll());
            contentProposal.refresh();

            // This will work as of the 2020-12 release
            contentProposal.openProposalPopup();
        }).text("Press to add the content proposals from the service").create(parent);
```

69.5. Using field assists in a table editor

Review the snippet [https://github.com/vogella/eclipse.platform.ui/blob/master/examples/org.eclipse.jface.snippets/Eclipse%20JFace%20Snippets/org/eclipse/jface/snippets/viewers/Snippet060TextCellEditorWithContentProposal.java] and integrate table editing with content proposals into a new view.

70. Optional exercise: Implementing a File browser

Now you will create a file browser for your file system using a `TreeViewer`. This exercise is standalone and can be used to practice the steps for creating an Eclipse RCP application.

70.1. Create a new application

Use the **File › New › Other... › Plug-in Project** menu entry and create a new Eclipse RCP application named `com.example.e4.filebrowser` without sample data. Make sure to uncheck *Create sample content* on the last page of the wizard.

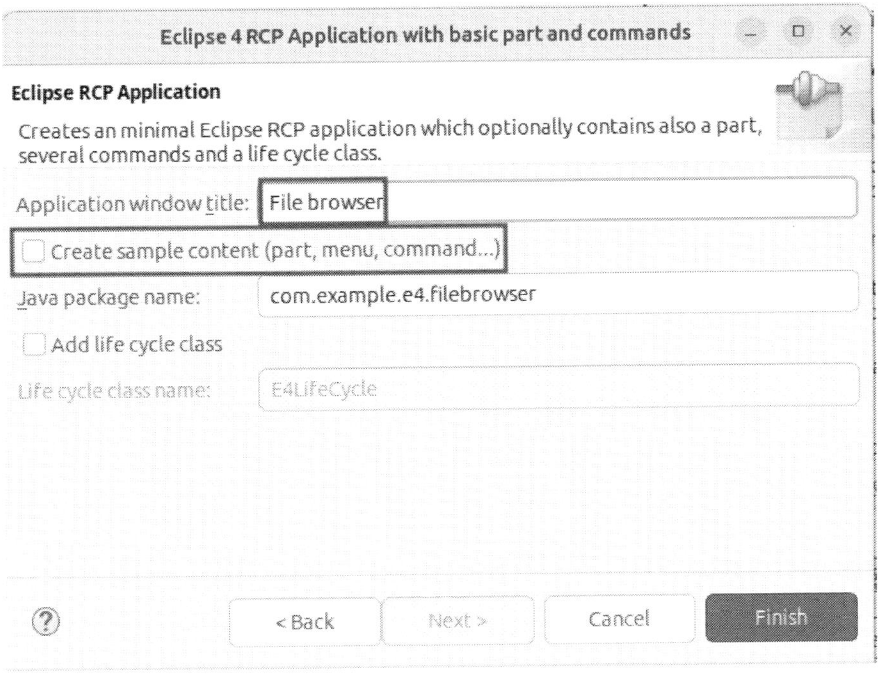

70.2. Update the manifest dependencies

Ensure that you have correct dependencies.

```
Manifest-Version: 1.0
Bundle-ManifestVersion: 2
Bundle-Name: Filebrowser
Bundle-SymbolicName: com.example.e4.filebrowser;singleton:=true
Bundle-Version: 1.0.0.qualifier
Bundle-Vendor: EXAMPLE
Require-Bundle: org.eclipse.jface,
 org.eclipse.e4.ui.di,
 org.eclipse.core.runtime
Bundle-RequiredExecutionEnvironment: JavaSE-21
Automatic-Module-Name: com.example.e4.filebrowser
Import-Package: jakarta.annotation;version="[2.1.0,3.0.0)"
Require-Capability: eclipse.swt;filter:="(image.format=svg)"
```

70.3. Add an image file

If the new project does not have an `icons` folder, create one.

Download or create an icon named `folder.svg`. For example, https://fonts.google.com/icons allows you to download SVG or PNG files for a folder. Place this image into a new folder named `icons` in the `com.example.e4.filebrowser` plug-in.

70.4. Create the view implementation

Use Ctrl+Shift+T to open the `ITreeContentProvider` interface. Review the Javadoc of this class to understand the methods of this interface.

Afterwards, implement the following class. It assumes that you added the `folder.svg` icon to the `icons` folder. It demonstrates the usage of a `ViewLabelProvider`.

```
package com.example.e4.filebrowser;

import java.io.File;
import java.net.URL;

import org.eclipse.core.runtime.FileLocator;
import org.eclipse.core.runtime.Path;
import org.eclipse.e4.ui.di.Focus;
import org.eclipse.jface.resource.ImageDescriptor;
import org.eclipse.jface.resource.JFaceResources;
import org.eclipse.jface.resource.LocalResourceManager;
import org.eclipse.jface.resource.ResourceManager;
import org.eclipse.jface.viewers.DelegatingStyledCellLabelProvider;
import org.eclipse.jface.viewers.DelegatingStyledCellLabelProvider.IStyledLabelProvider;
import org.eclipse.jface.viewers.ITreeContentProvider;
import org.eclipse.jface.viewers.LabelProvider;
import org.eclipse.jface.viewers.StyledString;
import org.eclipse.jface.viewers.TreeViewer;
import org.eclipse.jface.viewers.Viewer;
import org.eclipse.swt.SWT;
import org.eclipse.swt.graphics.Image;
import org.eclipse.swt.widgets.Composite;
import org.osgi.framework.Bundle;
import org.osgi.framework.FrameworkUtil;

import jakarta.annotation.PostConstruct;

public class FileBrowserPart {
    private TreeViewer viewer;

    @PostConstruct
    public void createControls(Composite parent) {
        viewer = new TreeViewer(parent, SWT.MULTI | SWT.H_SCROLL | SWT.V_SCROLL);
        viewer.setContentProvider(new ViewContentProvider());
        viewer.setLabelProvider(new DelegatingStyledCellLabelProvider(
                new ViewLabelProvider(createImageDescriptor())));
        viewer.setInput(File.listRoots());
    }

    private ImageDescriptor createImageDescriptor() {
```

```java
        Bundle bundle = FrameworkUtil.getBundle(ViewLabelProvider.class);
        URL url = FileLocator.find(bundle, new Path("icons/folder.svg"), null);
        return ImageDescriptor.createFromURL(url);
    }

    class ViewContentProvider implements ITreeContentProvider {
        @Override
        public Object[] getElements(Object inputElement) {
            return (File[]) inputElement;
        }

        @Override
        public Object[] getChildren(Object parentElement) {
            File file = (File) parentElement;
            return file.listFiles();
        }

        @Override
        public Object getParent(Object element) {
            File file = (File) element;
            return file.getParentFile();
        }

        @Override
        public boolean hasChildren(Object element) {
            File file = (File) element;
            if (file.isDirectory()) {
                return true;
            }
            return false;
        }
    }

    class ViewLabelProvider extends LabelProvider implements IStyledLabelProvider {

        private ImageDescriptor directoryImage;
        private ResourceManager resourceManager;

        public ViewLabelProvider(ImageDescriptor directoryImage) {
            this.directoryImage = directoryImage;
        }

        @Override
        public StyledString getStyledText(Object element) {
            if(element instanceof File) {
                File file = (File) element;
                StyledString styledString = new StyledString(getFileName(file));
                String[] files = file.list();
                if (files != null) {
```

```
                    styledString.append(" ( " + files.length + " ) ",
                            StyledString.COUNTER_STYLER);
                }
                return styledString;
            }
            return null;
        }

        @Override
        public Image getImage(Object element) {
            if(element instanceof File) {
                if(((File) element).isDirectory()) {
                    return getResourceManager().create(directoryImage);
                }
            }

            return super.getImage(element);
        }

        @Override
        public void dispose() {
            if(resourceManager != null) {
                resourceManager.dispose();
                resourceManager = null;
            }
        }

        protected ResourceManager getResourceManager() {
            if(resourceManager == null) {
                resourceManager = new LocalResourceManager(JFaceResources.
getResources());
            }
            return resourceManager;
        }

        private String getFileName(File file) {
            String name = file.getName();
            return name.isEmpty() ? file.getPath() : name;
        }
    }

    @Focus
    public void setFocus() {
        viewer.getControl().setFocus();
    }
}
```

70.5. Update the application model

The application window should be named `File Browser`.

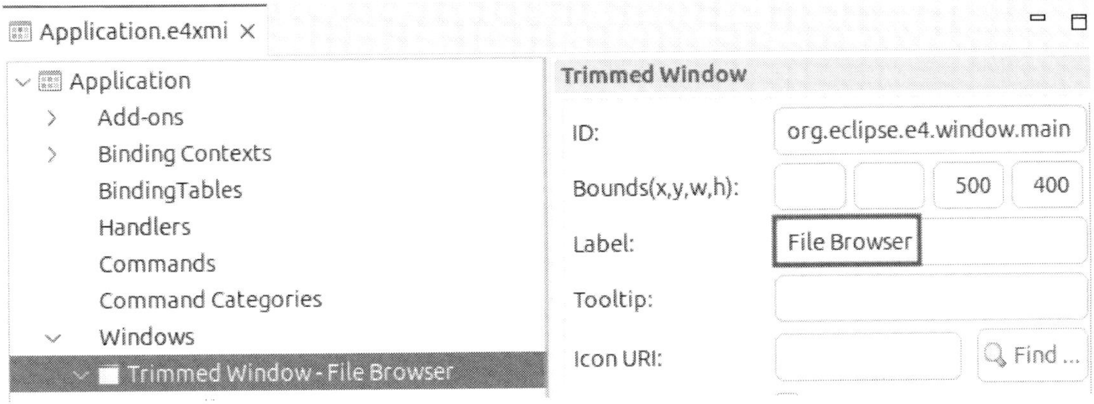

Create a new model for the part. Link from your part in the application model to your new class. We do not need a perspective stack. Therefore, directly add a part stack with a part to your application model.

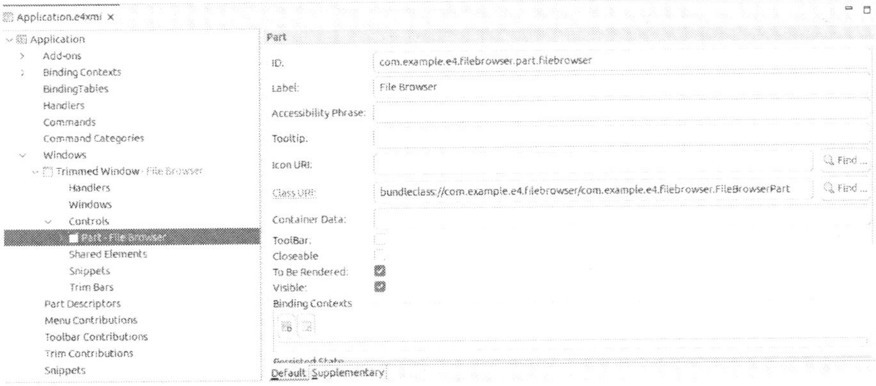

70.6. Validate

Start your new application and ensure that you see the content of your file system in your tree.

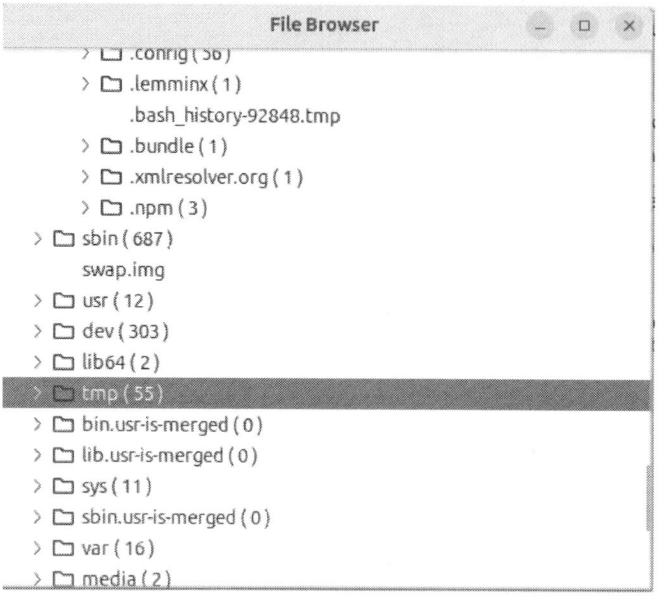

71. Optional exercise: Add multiple columns to a tree viewer

> This exercise extends the work from the Optional exercise: Implementing a File browser exercise.

71.1. Using TreeViewerColumns in the file browser

To add multiple columns to a `TreeViewer`, the `TreeViewerColumn` class is used. A `TreeViewerColumn` itself is a wrapper around the `TreeColumn` widget from SWT.

```
// make the table header visible to see the column's text
viewer.getTree().setHeaderVisible(true);

TreeViewerColumn viewerColumn = new TreeViewerColumn(viewer, SWT.NONE);
TreeColumn column = viewerColumn.getColumn();
column.setText("Name");
column.setWidth(300);
```

Instead of applying a single `CellLabelProvider` to the entire viewer, each `TreeViewerColumn` can have its own `CellLabelProvider`. This allows you to define the label for each column separately. To do so, assign a label provider to the column using the `TreeViewerColumn#setLabelProvider` method.

```
package com.example.e4.filebrowser;
```

```
import java.io.File;
import java.net.URL;
import java.text.DateFormat;
import java.util.Date;

import jakarta.annotation.PostConstruct;

import org.eclipse.core.runtime.FileLocator;
import org.eclipse.core.runtime.Path;
import org.eclipse.e4.ui.di.Focus;
import org.eclipse.jface.resource.ImageDescriptor;
import org.eclipse.jface.resource.JFaceResources;
import org.eclipse.jface.resource.LocalResourceManager;
import org.eclipse.jface.resource.ResourceManager;
import org.eclipse.jface.viewers.DelegatingStyledCellLabelProvider;
import org.eclipse.jface.viewers.DelegatingStyledCellLabelProvider.IStyledLabelProvider;
import org.eclipse.jface.viewers.ITreeContentProvider;
import org.eclipse.jface.viewers.LabelProvider;
import org.eclipse.jface.viewers.StyledString;
import org.eclipse.jface.viewers.TreeViewer;
import org.eclipse.jface.viewers.TreeViewerColumn;
import org.eclipse.jface.viewers.Viewer;
import org.eclipse.swt.SWT;
import org.eclipse.swt.graphics.Image;
import org.eclipse.swt.widgets.Composite;
import org.osgi.framework.Bundle;
import org.osgi.framework.FrameworkUtil;

public class FileBrowserPart {
    private TreeViewer viewer;

    private static final DateFormat dateFormat = DateFormat.getDateInstance();

    @PostConstruct
    public void createControls(Composite parent) {
        viewer = new TreeViewer(parent, SWT.MULTI | SWT.H_SCROLL | SWT.V_SCROLL);
        viewer.setContentProvider(new ViewContentProvider());
        viewer.getTree().setHeaderVisible(true);

        TreeViewerColumn mainColumn = new TreeViewerColumn(viewer, SWT.NONE);
        mainColumn.getColumn().setText("Name");
        mainColumn.getColumn().setWidth(300);
        mainColumn.setLabelProvider(
                new DelegatingStyledCellLabelProvider(
                        new ViewLabelProvider(createImageDescriptor())));

        TreeViewerColumn modifiedColumn = new TreeViewerColumn(viewer, SWT.NONE);
        modifiedColumn.getColumn().setText("Last Modified");
        modifiedColumn.getColumn().setWidth(100);
```

```
        modifiedColumn.getColumn().setAlignment(SWT.RIGHT);
        modifiedColumn
                .setLabelProvider(new DelegatingStyledCellLabelProvider(
                        new FileModifiedLabelProvider(dateFormat)));

        TreeViewerColumn fileSizeColumn = new TreeViewerColumn(viewer, SWT.NONE);
        fileSizeColumn.getColumn().setText("Size");
        fileSizeColumn.getColumn().setWidth(100);
        fileSizeColumn.getColumn().setAlignment(SWT.RIGHT);
        fileSizeColumn.setLabelProvider(new DelegatingStyledCellLabelProvider(
                new FileSizeLabelProvider()));

        viewer.setInput(File.listRoots());
    }

    private ImageDescriptor createImageDescriptor() {
        Bundle bundle = FrameworkUtil.getBundle(ViewLabelProvider.class);
        URL url = FileLocator.find(bundle, new Path("icons/folder.svg"), null);
        return ImageDescriptor.createFromURL(url);
    }

    class ViewContentProvider implements ITreeContentProvider {
        @Override
        public Object[] getElements(Object inputElement) {
            return (File[]) inputElement;
        }

        @Override
        public Object[] getChildren(Object parentElement) {
            File file = (File) parentElement;
            return file.listFiles();
        }

        @Override
        public Object getParent(Object element) {
            File file = (File) element;
            return file.getParentFile();
        }

        @Override
        public boolean hasChildren(Object element) {
            File file = (File) element;
            if (file.isDirectory()) {
                return true;
            }
            return false;
        }
    }
```

```
class ViewLabelProvider extends LabelProvider implements IStyledLabelProvider {

    private ImageDescriptor directoryImage;
    private ResourceManager resourceManager;

    public ViewLabelProvider(ImageDescriptor directoryImage) {
        this.directoryImage = directoryImage;
    }

    @Override
    public StyledString getStyledText(Object element) {
        if (element instanceof File) {
            File file = (File) element;
            StyledString styledString = new StyledString(getFileName(file));
            String[] files = file.list();
            if (files != null) {
                styledString.append(" ( " + files.length + " ) ", StyledString
.COUNTER_STYLER);
            }
            return styledString;
        }
        return null;
    }

    @Override
    public Image getImage(Object element) {
        if (element instanceof File) {
            if (((File) element).isDirectory()) {
                return getResourceManager().create(directoryImage);
            }
        }

        return super.getImage(element);
    }

    @Override
    public void dispose() {
        if (resourceManager != null) {
            resourceManager.dispose();
            resourceManager = null;
        }
    }

    protected ResourceManager getResourceManager() {
        if (resourceManager == null) {
            resourceManager = new LocalResourceManager(JFaceResources.
getResources());
        }
        return resourceManager;
```

```
        }

        private String getFileName(File file) {
            String name = file.getName();
            return name.isEmpty() ? file.getPath() : name;
        }
    }

    class FileModifiedLabelProvider extends LabelProvider implements IStyledLabelProvider
{

        private DateFormat dateLabelFormat;

        public FileModifiedLabelProvider(DateFormat dateFormat) {
            dateLabelFormat = dateFormat;
        }

        @Override
        public StyledString getStyledText(Object element) {
            if (element instanceof File) {
                File file = (File) element;
                long lastModified = file.lastModified();
                return new StyledString(dateLabelFormat.format(new Date(lastModified)));
            }
            return null;
        }
    }

    class FileSizeLabelProvider extends LabelProvider implements IStyledLabelProvider {

        @Override
        public StyledString getStyledText(Object element) {
            if (element instanceof File) {
                File file = (File) element;
                if (file.isDirectory()) {
                    // a directory is just a container and has no size
                    return new StyledString("0");
                }
                return new StyledString(String.valueOf(file.length()));
            }
            return null;
        }
    }

    @Focus
    public void setFocus() {
        viewer.getControl().setFocus();
    }
```

```
}
```

71.2. Validate

Start your new application and verify that you see the content of your file system in your tree.

72. Searchable TreeViewer

This example shows how to make a JFace TreeViewer searchable. Pressing `Ctrl-F` opens a search dialog. If a tree item is found it gets selected.

```
public class SearchDialog extends Dialog {

    public SearchDialog(Shell parent) {
        super(parent);
    }

    private Tree tree;
    private SearchableTreeViewer searchableTreeViewer;
    private Button searchButton;
    private Text searchField;
    private TreeSearchAlgorithm algorithm;

    public SearchDialog(Shell parent, SearchableTreeViewer searchableTreeViewer,
TreeSearchAlgorithm algorithm) {
        super(parent);
        this.searchableTreeViewer = searchableTreeViewer;
        this.algorithm = algorithm;
        tree = searchableTreeViewer.getTree();
    }

    @Override
    protected Control createDialogArea(Composite parent) {
```

```
        Composite container = (Composite) super.createDialogArea(parent);
        container.setLayout(new FillLayout());
        searchField = new Text(container, SWT.NONE);
        return container;
    }

    @Override
    protected void createButtonsForButtonBar(Composite parent) {
        searchButton = createButton(parent, IDialogConstants.PROCEED_ID, "Search",
false);
        searchButton.addSelectionListener(SelectionListener.widgetSelectedAdapter(this
::search));
    }

    private void search(SelectionEvent event) {
        TreeItem found = algorithm.search(tree.getItems(), searchField.getText());
        if (found != null) {
            searchableTreeViewer.setSelection(new StructuredSelection(found.getData()),
true);
            close();
        } else {
            System.out.println("Nothing Found");
        }
    }
}
```

```
public interface TreeSearchAlgorithm {

    public TreeItem search(TreeItem[] treeItems, String searchTerm);
}
```

```
public class TreeContentProvider implements ITreeContentProvider {
    @Override
    public boolean hasChildren(Object element) {
        return false;
    }

    @Override
    public Object getParent(Object element) {
        return null;
    }

    @Override
    public Object[] getElements(Object inputElement) {
        return ArrayContentProvider.getInstance().getElements(inputElement);
    }
```

```
    @Override
    public Object[] getChildren(Object parentElement) {
        return null;
    }
}
```

```
public class SearchableTreeViewer extends TreeViewer {

    private Composite parent;

    public SearchableTreeViewer(Composite parent, TreeSearchAlgorithm algorithm) {
        super(parent);
        this.parent = parent;
        parent.addKeyListener(KeyListener.keyPressedAdapter(event -> {
            if (event.stateMask == SWT.CTRL && event.keyCode == 'f') {
                startSearchDialog(algorithm);
            }
        }));
    }

    private void startSearchDialog(TreeSearchAlgorithm algorithm) {
        SearchDialog searchDialog = new SearchDialog(parent.getShell(), this, algorithm);
        searchDialog.open();
    }
}
```

```
public class TreeWindow extends ApplicationWindow {


    public TreeWindow() {
        super(null);
        // Don't return from open() until window closes
        setBlockOnOpen(true);

        // Open the main window
        open();

        // Dispose the display
        Display.getCurrent().dispose();
    }

    @Override
    protected void configureShell(Shell shell) {
        super.configureShell(shell);

        // Set the title bar text and the size
```

```
        shell.setText("Searchable Tree");
        shell.setSize(400, 400);
    }

    @Override
    protected Control createContents(Composite parent) {
        Composite composite = new Composite(parent, SWT.NONE);
        composite.setLayout(new FillLayout());
        SearchableTreeViewer treeViewer = new SearchableTreeViewer(composite,
                (treeItems, searchText) -> {
                    final String upperSearchText = searchText.toUpperCase();
                    for (TreeItem item : treeItems) {
                        if (item.getText().toUpperCase().contains(upperSearchText)) {
                            return item;
                        }
                    }
                    return null;
                });
        treeViewer.setContentProvider(new TreeContentProvider());
        TreeViewerColumn viewerColumn = new TreeViewerColumn(treeViewer, SWT.NONE);
        treeViewer.getTree().setHeaderVisible(true);
        treeViewer.getTree().setLinesVisible(true);
        viewerColumn.getColumn().setWidth(300);
        viewerColumn.getColumn().setText("Names");
        viewerColumn.setLabelProvider(new ColumnLabelProvider());
        treeViewer.setInput(new String[] { "Simon Scholz", "Lars Vogel", "Dirk Fauth",
"Wim Jongman", "Tom Schindl" });
        return composite;
    }

    public static void main(String[] args) {
        new TreeWindow();
    }
}
```

Part IX: Usage of custom widgets in SWT

73. Custom widgets in SWT

A custom widget is a UI element that is typically created because the existing native widgets cannot support a certain requirement. Custom SWT widgets are typically developed in pure Java.

SWT provides custom widgets in the `org.eclipse.swt.custom` package, such as `CLabel`, `CCombo`, `StyledText` and others. In addition, the Eclipse Nebula [https://eclipse.org/nebula] project provides multiple custom widgets.

There are three common approaches to create a custom SWT widget:

- Compound custom widgets that contain other existing widgets (`Composite`)
- Custom-drawn widgets that have no children and we simply draw on (`Canvas`)
- Mixing both (`Composite` and `Canvas`)

Here is an example of a compound composite. This snippet uses the `JFace` factory API.

```
package com.vogella.rcp.custom.widgets.widget;

import org.eclipse.jface.layout.GridDataFactory;
```

```
import org.eclipse.jface.layout.GridLayoutFactory;
import org.eclipse.swt.SWT;
import org.eclipse.swt.widgets.Composite;
import org.eclipse.swt.widgets.Label;
import org.eclipse.swt.widgets.Text;

public class LabeledTextWidget extends Composite {

    private Label label;
    private Text text;

    public LabeledTextWidget(Composite parent, int style) {
        this(parent, style, SWT.NONE, SWT.BORDER);
    }

    public LabeledTextWidget(Composite parent, int style, int labelStyle, int textStyle)
{
        super(parent, style);
        GridLayoutFactory.fillDefaults().numColumns(2).applyTo(this);

        label = new Label(this, labelStyle); ❶
        GridDataFactory.fillDefaults().applyTo(label);

        text = new Text(this, textStyle); ❷
        GridDataFactory.fillDefaults().grab(true, false).applyTo(getText());
    }

    public void setLabelText(String text) {
        checkWidget();
        label.setText(text);
    }

    public Text getText() {
        checkWidget();
        return text;
    }
}
```

❶ Pass `this` to the child widgets of your compound custom widget, do not use the parent `Composite`

❷ Pass `this` to the child widgets of your compound custom widget, do not use the parent `Composite`

74. General guidelines for custom widgets

If you develop custom widgets, you should follow the following guidelines.

74.1. Disposing the system resources

If you allocate system resources, like fonts or images, you must dispose of them once you no longer use them.

To achieve this, attach a `DisposeListener` to your widget with the `addDisposeListener()` method of `Canvas` or `Composite`. Alternatively, use the JFace `LocalResourceManager` to create system resources and have them automatically disposed when the widget they are registered with is disposed.

```
package com.vogella.rcp.custom.widgets.widget;

import org.eclipse.jface.resource.FontDescriptor;
import org.eclipse.jface.resource.JFaceResources;
import org.eclipse.jface.resource.LocalResourceManager;
import org.eclipse.jface.resource.ResourceManager;
import org.eclipse.swt.SWT;
import org.eclipse.swt.graphics.Color;
import org.eclipse.swt.graphics.Font;
import org.eclipse.swt.graphics.RGB;
import org.eclipse.swt.widgets.Canvas;
import org.eclipse.swt.widgets.Composite;

public class ResourceManagerCanvas extends Canvas {

    private ResourceManager resourceManager;

    public ResourceManagerCanvas(Composite parent, int style) {
        super(parent, style);
        // The LocalResourceManager attaches the DisposeHandler to the Canvas for you
        resourceManager = new LocalResourceManager(JFaceResources.getResources(), this);

        // Always create colors, fonts and images with the ResourceManager instance
        Color orange = resourceManager.createColor(new RGB(255, 191, 0));
        Font boldArialFont = resourceManager.createFont(FontDescriptor.createFrom(
"Arial", 12, SWT.BOLD));
        // Draw your widget.....
    }
}
```

You should not override the `dispose()` method of the `Canvas` or `Composite` to dispose of your system resources. Always add a `DisposeListener` instead, so that the actual disposal can be handled by the framework itself.

It is not necessary to dispose `Color` objects since the 4.17 release.

74.2. Fail fast

At the beginning of each method, you should invoke the `checkWidget` method, before any other call to functionality of the custom widget. The `checkWidget` method of the `Widget` class checks preconditions for the proper use of a `Widget`. This involves checking whether the widget is not disposed and is not accessed from a thread other than the SWT one.

```
package com.vogella.rcp.custom.widgets.widget;

import org.eclipse.swt.widgets.Composite;

public class CustomWidget extends Composite {

    public CustomWidget(Composite parent, int style) {
        super(parent, style);
    }

    public void callFunctionalityOfCustomWidget() {
        checkWidget();

        // do custom things with the CustomWidget
    }

}
```

74.3. Implement the computeSize method

By implementing the `computeSize` method, you give `Layout` classes or other widgets the option to determine the size of your custom widget. In this case the `Layout` of the parent `Composite` is able to align its child widgets properly.

```
package com.vogella.rcp.custom.widgets.widget;

import org.eclipse.swt.SWT;
import org.eclipse.swt.graphics.Point;
import org.eclipse.swt.widgets.Composite;

public class ComputeSizeWidget extends Composite {

    private static final int LINE_WIDTH = 30;
    private static final int LINE_HEIGHT = 2;

    public ComputeSizeWidget(Composite parent, int style) {
        super(parent, style);

        // draw a line with a width of 30 and a height of 2.
```

```
    }

    @Override
    public Point computeSize(int wHint, int hHint, boolean changed) {

        // try to consider the given hints. Here we decided to use the smallest
        // value so that the line would not be bigger than 30x2.
        // In case the SWT.DEFAULT flag for the hints is used, we simply stick to
        // the LINE_WIDTH and LINE_HEIGHT.
        int width = wHint != SWT.DEFAULT ? Math.min(wHint, LINE_WIDTH) : LINE_WIDTH;
        int height = hHint != SWT.DEFAULT ? Math.min(hHint, LINE_HEIGHT) : LINE_HEIGHT;

        return new Point(width, height);
    }
}
```

74.4. Use SWT errors

If errors occur in your custom widget, use one of the three static error methods of the SWT class.

- `public static void error (int code)`
- `public static void error (int code, Throwable throwable)`
- `public static void error (int code, Throwable throwable, String detail)`

The *code* parameter of each `error` method must be one of the `SWT.ERROR_*` constants. If a parameter of a method must not be null, call `SWT.error(SWT.ERROR_NULL_ARGUMENT)` if it is `null`.

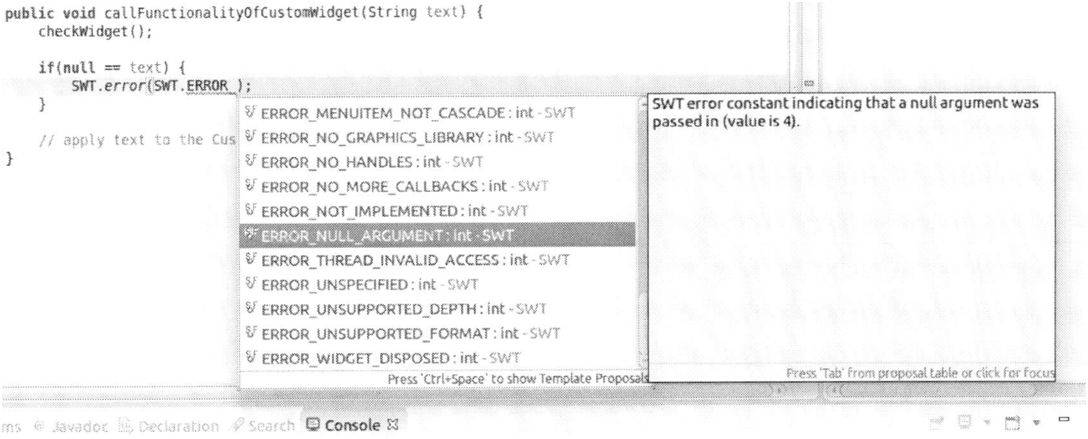

Also have a look at the other `SWT.ERROR_*` constants, which can be used. They are all described in detail in the JavaDoc.

74.5. Support bidirectional behavior

The `SWT` class contains two style flags that can be passed to a widget's constructor, where you can define the bidirectional behavior of a widget. `SWT.RIGHT_TO_LEFT` is used to write the widget's text and other included elements from right to left. `SWT.LEFT_TO_RIGHT` is the default for most widgets.

75. Custom-drawn widgets

As noted, `Canvas` should be used for self-drawn widgets that do not have children. To draw on a widget use the `addPaintListener` method to draw on a `Canvas` or `Composite`. Use the `redraw()` method instead of directly calling your internal paint methods, so that the framework may queue all redraw requests and do them all at once.

```
package aaa.parts;

import org.eclipse.jface.resource.FontDescriptor;
import org.eclipse.jface.resource.JFaceResources;
import org.eclipse.jface.resource.LocalResourceManager;
import org.eclipse.jface.resource.ResourceManager;
import org.eclipse.swt.SWT;
import org.eclipse.swt.graphics.Color;
import org.eclipse.swt.graphics.Font;
import org.eclipse.swt.graphics.GC;
import org.eclipse.swt.graphics.Point;
import org.eclipse.swt.graphics.RGB;
import org.eclipse.swt.widgets.Canvas;
import org.eclipse.swt.widgets.Composite;

public class CustomCanvasWithPaintListener extends Canvas {

    private final int BORDER_MARGIN = 4;

    private ResourceManager resourceManager;

    private String text = "";

    public CustomCanvasWithPaintListener(Composite parent, int style) {
        super(parent, style);
        // The LocalResourceManager attaches the DisposeHandler to the Canvas
        // for you
        resourceManager = new LocalResourceManager(
                JFaceResources.getResources(), this);

        // Draw your widget.....
        addPaintListener(paintEvent -> {
            GC gc = paintEvent.gc;
```

```
            paintBorderAndText(gc);
        });
    }

    protected void paintBorderAndText(GC gc) {

        Font boldArialFont = resourceManager.createFont(FontDescriptor.createFrom(
"Arial", 14, SWT.BOLD));
        gc.setFont(boldArialFont);
        // Use setFont before textExtent, so that the size of the text is calculated
correctly
        Point textExtent = gc.textExtent(getText());
        // System colors may be used without the resourceManager, because those
        // System colors are maintained by the OS itself
        gc.setBackground(getDisplay().getSystemColor(SWT.COLOR_BLACK));
        // Always begin with the background so that everything is drawn upon it
        gc.fillRoundRectangle(3, 3, textExtent.x + BORDER_MARGIN, textExtent.y +
BORDER_MARGIN, 8, 8);
        // Draw the orange border
        Color orange = resourceManager.createColor(new RGB(255, 191, 0));
        gc.setBackground(orange);
        gc.setForeground(orange);

        gc.drawRoundRectangle(3, 3, textExtent.x + BORDER_MARGIN, textExtent.y
                + BORDER_MARGIN, 8, 8);
        // And finally draw the given text
        gc.drawString(getText(), 5, 4, true);
    }

    public String getText() {
        checkWidget();
        return text;
    }

    public void setText(String text) {
        checkWidget();
        this.text = text;
        // Use redraw() instead of directly calling the paintBorderAndText(GC gc) method.
        getParent().layout();
        redraw();
    }
}
```

This widget can be used via the following code:

```
parent.setLayout(new GridLayout(1, false));

CustomCanvasWithPaintListener paintListenerCanvas = new CustomCanvasWithPaintListener
```

```
(parent, SWT.NONE);
paintListenerCanvas.setText("This is a custom-drawn widget");
paintListenerCanvas.setLayoutData(GridDataFactory.fillDefaults().create());
```

The widget should look similar to the following screenshot.

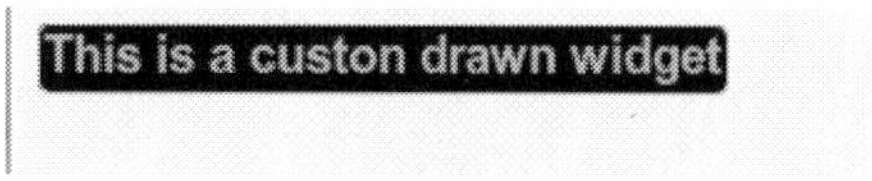

75.1. SWT events and listener

The widget should also handle user interactions. Therefore, it should fire events like other widgets do, i.e., a Button that fires a `widgetSelected` event to its attached `SelectionListener`. While you can add custom events and listeners for specific needs, in most cases the existing SWT events are sufficient. Imagine a custom-drawn button that obviously should reuse a default `SelectionListener`. In case you reuse such an existing SWT event, you should either support `TypedListener` or use SWT's low-level `Listener` API, which can be applied to every widget by using the `addListener(int, Listener)` method. For custom-drawn widgets, you will likely want to add custom event listeners that suit the widget's special purposes.

Suppose we have a custom Gameboy widget, where we want to be able to listen to the clicks on the Gameboy's buttons. The first thing to do is to define a custom event that is derived from `java.util.EventObject`.

```
package com.vogella.rcp.custom.widgets.widget.gameboy;

import java.util.EventObject;

public class GameboySelectionEvent extends EventObject {

    private static final long serialVersionUID = 1059740358205812736L;

    public static final int BUTTON_POWER = 0;
    public static final int BUTTON_A = 1;
    public static final int BUTTON_B = 2;
    public static final int BUTTON_START = 3;
    public static final int BUTTON_SELECT = 4;
    public static final int BUTTON_UP = 5;
    public static final int BUTTON_DOWN = 6;
    public static final int BUTTON_LEFT = 7;
    public static final int BUTTON_RIGHT = 8;

    private int gameboyButton;

    public GameboySelectionEvent(Object source, int gameboyButton) {
        super(source);
```

```
        assert (gameboyButton < 9 && gameboyButton > -1);
        this.gameboyButton = gameboyButton;
    }

    public int getButton() {
        return gameboyButton;
    }
}
```

This event implementation provides information about which button was selected. Normally you just define a getter for specific event information and pass the values to the constructor of the custom event. The next thing to do is to provide a listener interface to which the event is passed in case a certain event occurs.

```
package com.vogella.rcp.custom.widgets.widget.gameboy;

import java.util.EventListener;

/**
 * This listener is used to be registered for the {@link GameboyWidget} and will
 * be invoked every time a button on the {@link GameboyWidget} is selected.
 *
 */
public interface GameboySelectionListener extends EventListener {

    public void gameboyButtonSelected(GameboySelectionEvent gameboySelectionEvent);
}
```

The last step is to provide an API to add and remove your custom listener and to fire your custom events to the listener.

75.2. Positions in custom drawings

In custom drawings, the positions of the elements inside it should be stored. The positions of certain elements inside the custom widget can be found after they are drawn. This is especially important, if elements of the drawing should trigger certain events. Now that we know how to draw a custom widget with a `PaintListener` and defined our listener interfaces and events, we need to figure out when those events should be fired. Therefore, we need to track the positions of our custom drawings on the widget. To do such a tracking we implement a `HoverCheck` class that enables us to recognize whenever a certain part of a widget is hovered.

```
package com.vogella.rcp.custom.widgets.widget.listener;

import java.beans.PropertyChangeListener;
import java.beans.PropertyChangeSupport;
```

```
import org.eclipse.swt.SWT;
import org.eclipse.swt.events.DisposeEvent;
import org.eclipse.swt.events.DisposeListener;
import org.eclipse.swt.graphics.Point;
import org.eclipse.swt.graphics.Rectangle;
import org.eclipse.swt.widgets.Control;
import org.eclipse.swt.widgets.Event;
import org.eclipse.swt.widgets.Listener;

public class HoverCheck implements Listener, DisposeListener {

    private PropertyChangeSupport changeSupport = new PropertyChangeSupport(this);

    private Control containerWidget;
    private Point widgetCoords;
    private Point widgetSize;

    private boolean hovering;

    public HoverCheck(Control containerWidget, Point widgetCoords,
            Point widgetSize) {
        assert (containerWidget != null);
        this.containerWidget = containerWidget;
        this.widgetCoords = widgetCoords;
        this.widgetSize = widgetSize;
        containerWidget.addDisposeListener(this);
        containerWidget.addListener(SWT.MouseMove, this);
    }

    @Override
    public void handleEvent(Event event) {
        switch (event.type) {
        case SWT.MouseMove:
            Rectangle targetBounds = containerWidget.getBounds();

            // just override the original size of the Rectangle, because the
            // getBounds() method always creates a new Rectangle instance every
            // time it gets called.
            targetBounds.x += widgetCoords.x;
            targetBounds.y += widgetCoords.y;
            targetBounds.width = widgetSize.x;
            targetBounds.height = widgetSize.y;

            if (targetBounds.contains(event.x, event.y)) {
                if (!isHovering()) {
                    setHovering(true);
                }
            } else {
```

```
                if (isHovering()) {
                    setHovering(false);
                }
            }
            break;
        default:
            break;
        }
    }

    @Override
    public void widgetDisposed(DisposeEvent e) {
        if (containerWidget != null && !containerWidget.isDisposed()) {
            containerWidget.removeListener(SWT.MouseMove, this);
        }
    }

    public void addHoverListener(PropertyChangeListener hoverChangeListener) {
        changeSupport
                .addPropertyChangeListener("hovering", hoverChangeListener);
    }

    public void removeHoverListener(PropertyChangeListener hoverChangeListener) {
        changeSupport.removePropertyChangeListener("hovering",
                hoverChangeListener);
    }

    public boolean isHovering() {
        return hovering;
    }

    protected void setHovering(boolean hovering) {
        changeSupport.firePropertyChange("hovering", isHovering(),
                this.hovering = hovering);
    }
}
```

Inside this class we pass the widget itself, the x, y coordinates and the size of the part, where hovering should be checked. With this information we are able to create a `Rectangle` that represents the position and size of this special part (i.e. a Gameboy button) and can use the Rectangle's `contains` method to check if the current mouse position is within this Rectangle. In the GameboyWidget itself, we can use this HoverCheck class to figure out, if a certain button on the Gameboy was selected.

```
package com.vogella.rcp.custom.widgets.widget.gameboy;

import java.beans.PropertyChangeEvent;
```

```
import java.beans.PropertyChangeListener;
import java.net.URL;
import java.util.ArrayList;
import java.util.Collection;

import org.eclipse.core.runtime.FileLocator;
import org.eclipse.core.runtime.Path;
import org.eclipse.jface.resource.ImageDescriptor;
import org.eclipse.jface.resource.JFaceResources;
import org.eclipse.jface.resource.LocalResourceManager;
import org.eclipse.jface.resource.ResourceManager;
import org.eclipse.swt.SWT;
import org.eclipse.swt.events.PaintEvent;
import org.eclipse.swt.events.PaintListener;
import org.eclipse.swt.graphics.GC;
import org.eclipse.swt.graphics.Image;
import org.eclipse.swt.graphics.Point;
import org.eclipse.swt.graphics.Rectangle;
import org.eclipse.swt.widgets.Canvas;
import org.eclipse.swt.widgets.Composite;
import org.eclipse.swt.widgets.Event;
import org.eclipse.swt.widgets.Listener;
import org.osgi.framework.Bundle;
import org.osgi.framework.FrameworkUtil;

import com.vogella.rcp.custom.widgets.widget.listener.HoverCheck;

public class GameboyWidget extends Canvas {

    private static final int Y_OFFSET = 10;
    private static final int X_OFFSET = 10;

    private ResourceManager resourceManager;

    private Collection<GameboySelectionListener> gameboySelectionListeners = new
ArrayList<GameboySelectionListener>();

    private HoverCheck buttonAHoverCheck;
    private HoverCheck buttonBHoverCheck;

    private Image gameBoyImage;

    public GameboyWidget(Composite parent, int style) {
        super(parent, style);
        resourceManager = new LocalResourceManager(
                JFaceResources.getResources(), this);
        gameBoyImage = loadGameboyImage();

        setupButtonHoverChecks();
```

```java
    addPaintListener(this::paint);

    addListener(SWT.MouseDown, event -> {
        if (buttonAHoverCheck.isHovering()) {
            System.out.println("Button A was clicked");
            fireGameboySelectionChanged(new GameboySelectionEvent(this,
                    GameboySelectionEvent.BUTTON_A));
        } else if (buttonBHoverCheck.isHovering()) {
            System.out.println("Button B was clicked");
            fireGameboySelectionChanged(new GameboySelectionEvent(this,
                    GameboySelectionEvent.BUTTON_B));
        }
    });
}

private void setupButtonHoverChecks() {
    Point buttonsSize = new Point(40, 40);
    buttonAHoverCheck = new HoverCheck(this, new Point(266, 330), buttonsSize);
    buttonAHoverCheck.addHoverListener(event ->  {
        if (Boolean.TRUE.equals(event.getNewValue())) {
            setCursor(getDisplay().getSystemCursor(SWT.CURSOR_HAND));
        } else {
            setCursor(null);
        }
    });

    buttonBHoverCheck = new HoverCheck(this, new Point(211, 353), buttonsSize);
    buttonBHoverCheck.addHoverListener(event -> {
        if (Boolean.TRUE.equals(event.getNewValue())) {
            setCursor(getDisplay().getSystemCursor(SWT.CURSOR_HAND));
        } else {
            setCursor(null);
        }
    });
}

protected void paint(PaintEvent event) {
    event.gc.drawImage(gameBoyImage, X_OFFSET, Y_OFFSET);
}

@Override
public Point computeSize(int wHint, int hHint, boolean changed) {
    Rectangle bounds = gameBoyImage.getBounds();

    // Just return the size of the Gameboy image
    return new Point(bounds.width, bounds.height);
}
```

```
    public void addGameboySelectionListener(
            GameboySelectionListener selectionListener) {
        gameboySelectionListeners.add(selectionListener);
    }

    public void removeGameboySelectionListener(
            GameboySelectionListener selectionListener) {
        gameboySelectionListeners.remove(selectionListener);
    }

    protected void fireGameboySelectionChanged(
            GameboySelectionEvent selectionEvent) {
        for (GameboySelectionListener gameboySelectionListener :
gameboySelectionListeners) {
            gameboySelectionListener.gameboyButtonSelected(selectionEvent);
        }
    }

    private Image loadGameboyImage() {
        Bundle bundle = FrameworkUtil.getBundle(getClass());
        URL imgUrl = FileLocator.find(bundle, new Path("images/gameboy.jpg"),
                null);
        ImageDescriptor imgDescriptor = ImageDescriptor.createFromURL(imgUrl);
        return resourceManager.createImage(imgDescriptor);
    }
}
```

76. Custom composite with highlights

Next, you develop a custom composite that highlights itself when the mouse enters. This composite automatically changes color when the mouse enters or leaves its area.

```
package com.vogella.swt.widgets;

import org.eclipse.swt.SWT;
import org.eclipse.swt.events.MouseEvent;
import org.eclipse.swt.events.MouseTrackAdapter;
import org.eclipse.swt.graphics.Color;
import org.eclipse.swt.layout.GridData;
import org.eclipse.swt.layout.GridLayout;
import org.eclipse.swt.widgets.Composite;
import org.eclipse.swt.widgets.Control;
import org.eclipse.swt.widgets.Display;

public class HighlightComposite extends Composite {

    private static Color regularColor;
    private static Color selectionColor;

    private final class MouseTrackAdapterExtension extends MouseTrackAdapter {

        @Override
        public void mouseEnter(MouseEvent e) {
            HighlightComposite.this.setBackground(selectionColor);
        }

        @Override
        public void mouseExit(MouseEvent e) {

            HighlightComposite.this.setBackground(regularColor);
        }
    }

    MouseTrackAdapter mouseTracker = new MouseTrackAdapterExtension();

    public HighlightComposite(final Composite parent, int style) {
        super(parent, style);
        regularColor = parent.getBackground();
        selectionColor = Display.getCurrent().getSystemColor(SWT.COLOR_RED);

        GridData gdHigh = new GridData(GridData.FILL);
        this.setLayoutData(gdHigh);

        setBackground(Display.getCurrent().getSystemColor(SWT.COLOR_GREEN));
        GridLayout layHigh = new GridLayout(2, false);
```

```
        layHigh.marginHeight = 0;
        layHigh.marginWidth = 0;
        layHigh.horizontalSpacing = 0;
        HighlightComposite.this.setLayout(layHigh);

        addMouseTrackListener(mouseTracker);
    }

    public void addMouseTrackListener() {
        for (Control c : super.getChildren()) {
            c.addMouseTrackListener(mouseTracker);
        }
    }
}
```

The usage of this new composite is demonstrated by the following code.

```
@PostConstruct
public void createControls(Composite parent) {
    HighlightComposite highlightComposite = new HighlightComposite(parent, SWT.NONE);

    Text modelWidget = new Text(highlightComposite, SWT.SINGLE | SWT.LEAD | SWT.BORDER);
    modelWidget.setLayoutData(new GridData(SWT.FILL, SWT.CENTER, true, false));
    modelWidget.setText("Hello");
    modelWidget.addModifyListener(e -> {
        part.setDirty(true);
        System.out.println("This must be saved by the user!!!");
    });
}
```

In this example, the color of the `Composite` changes when the mouse enters.

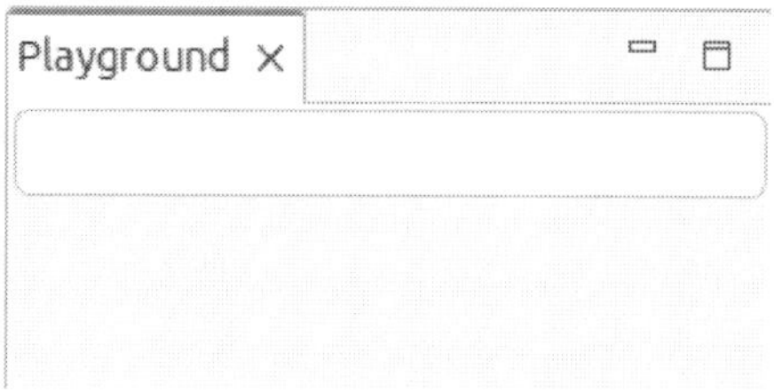

77. Optional exercise: Create a custom widget based on canvas

In this section, you create a custom `Checkbox` widget that visually represents a custom-drawn checkbox.

77.1. Create a new plug-in

Create a new simple plug-in named `com.vogella.swt.widgets`. See Chapter 36 for more information.

77.2. Add dependencies

Add the following dependencies to the `com.vogella.swt.widgets` plug-in:

- org.eclipse.core.runtime
- org.eclipse.jface

The manifest file should look similar to the following afterward (version constraints have been removed):

```
Manifest-Version: 1.0
Bundle-ManifestVersion: 2
Bundle-Name: Widgets
Bundle-SymbolicName: com.vogella.swt.widgets
Bundle-Version: 1.0.0.qualifier
Bundle-Vendor: VOGELLA
Automatic-Module-Name: com.vogella.swt.widgets
Bundle-RequiredExecutionEnvironment: JavaSE-21
Require-Bundle: org.eclipse.jface,
 org.eclipse.core.runtime
```

77.3. Create custom widget

Create the following `Checkbox` class.

```
package com.vogella.swt.widgets;

import java.util.ArrayList;
import java.util.List;

import org.eclipse.swt.SWT;
import org.eclipse.swt.events.SelectionEvent;
import org.eclipse.swt.events.SelectionListener;
```

```
import org.eclipse.swt.graphics.Color;
import org.eclipse.swt.graphics.GC;
import org.eclipse.swt.graphics.Point;
import org.eclipse.swt.widgets.Canvas;
import org.eclipse.swt.widgets.Composite;

public class Checkbox extends Canvas {

    private List<SelectionListener> selectionListener = new ArrayList<>();

    private boolean isSelected;
    private String text = "";
    private Point textExtent;
    private Color checkColor;
    private Color centerColor;

    public Checkbox(Composite parent, int style) {
        super(parent, style);
        addListeners();
    }

    private void addListeners() {
        addPaintListener(e -> {
            GC gc = e.gc;
            gc.setAntialias(SWT.ON);
            gc.setBackground(getCenterColor() != null && !getCenterColor().isDisposed() ?
getCenterColor()
                    : getDisplay().getSystemColor(SWT.COLOR_WIDGET_BACKGROUND));
            gc.setForeground(getForeground());
            gc.fillRoundRectangle(4, 4, 16, 16, 6, 6);
            gc.drawRoundRectangle(4, 4, 16, 16, 6, 6);
            if (getSelection()) {
                gc.setLineWidth(4);
                gc.setForeground(getCheckColor() != null && !getCheckColor().isDisposed()
? getCheckColor()
                        : getDisplay().getSystemColor(SWT.COLOR_WIDGET_FOREGROUND));

                gc.drawLine(6, 7, 13, 16);
                gc.drawLine(11, 16, 21, 0);
            }

            textExtent = gc.textExtent(text);

            gc.setForeground(getForeground());
            gc.setBackground(getBackground());
            gc.drawText(text, 24, 4);
        });

        addListener(SWT.MouseDown, e -> {
```

```
            setSelection(!getSelection());
            selectionListener.forEach(l -> l.widgetSelected(new SelectionEvent(e)));
            redraw();
        });
    }

    @Override
    public Point computeSize(int wHint, int hHint, boolean changed) {
        checkWidget();
        int textWidth = textExtent != null ? textExtent.x : 0;
        return super.computeSize(Math.max(26 + textWidth, wHint), Math.max(26, hHint),
changed);
    }

    public boolean getSelection() {
        checkWidget();
        return isSelected;
    }

    public void setSelection(boolean isSelected) {
        checkWidget();
        this.isSelected = isSelected;
    }

    public void setText(String string) {
        checkWidget();
        if (string == null) {
            SWT.error(SWT.ERROR_NULL_ARGUMENT);
        }
        text = string;

        redraw();
    }

    public String getText() {
        checkWidget();
        return text;
    }

    public void addSelectionListener(SelectionListener listener) {
        checkWidget();
        if (null == listener) {
            SWT.error(SWT.ERROR_NULL_ARGUMENT);
        }
        selectionListener.add(listener);
    }

    public void removeSelectionListener(SelectionListener listener) {
        checkWidget();
```

```
        if (null == listener) {
            SWT.error(SWT.ERROR_NULL_ARGUMENT);
        }
        selectionListener.remove(listener);
    }

    public Color getCheckColor() {
        checkWidget();
        return checkColor;
    }

    public void setCheckColor(Color checkColor) {
        checkWidget();
        this.checkColor = checkColor;
    }

    public Color getCenterColor() {
        checkWidget();
        return centerColor;
    }

    public void setCenterColor(Color centerColor) {
        checkWidget();
        this.centerColor = centerColor;
    }
}
```

77.4. Allow usage of the new custom widget

To use the widget elsewhere, export its package by adding the appropriate entry to the `MANIFEST.MF` file of `com.vogella.swt.widgets`.

```
Manifest-Version: 1.0
Bundle-ManifestVersion: 2
Bundle-Name: Widgets
Bundle-SymbolicName: com.vogella.swt.widgets
Bundle-Version: 1.0.0.qualifier
Bundle-Vendor: VOGELLA
Automatic-Module-Name: com.vogella.swt.widgets
Bundle-RequiredExecutionEnvironment: JavaSE-21
Require-Bundle: org.eclipse.jface,
 org.eclipse.core.runtime
Export-Package: com.vogella.swt.widgets
```

77.5. Update the feature and product

Add `com.vogella.swt.widgets` to your feature and ensure you start it via the product.

77.6. Use the new widget in the Playground part

Add a dependency to `com.vogella.swt.widgets` in the `MANIFEST.MF` file of `com.vogella.tasks.ui`.

Use the `Checkbox` class inside your playground part of the Eclipse application.

The result looks similar to the following. A normal `Button` with the `CHECK` style is added to the screenshot for comparison.

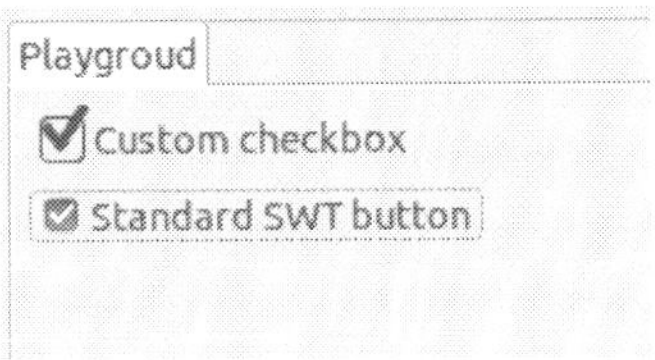

78. Optional exercise: Create additional custom widgets

In this optional exercise, you build additional widgets.

78.1. Build a compound widget

A compound widget is a general term for a widget that combines several other widgets.

Assume that you frequently need to use a `Label` together with a `Text` widget. Create a `LabelWithText` custom widget extending `Composite` that contains a `Label` and a `Text` widget.

Define the `setLabel()` / `getLabel()` and `setText()` / `getText()` methods as the API for this widget.

Use this widget in your `PlaygroundPart` part.

78.2. Canvas with an image and text on it

Create an *image* folder in the *com.vogella.swt.widgets* plug-in and save a file named *vogella.svg* in this folder.

Create a class named `ImageWithText` that extends `Canvas`. Draw the words *Advanced Trainings* on an image of your choosing.

```
package com.vogella.swt.widgets;
```

```java
import org.eclipse.swt.SWT;
import org.eclipse.swt.events.PaintEvent;
import org.eclipse.swt.events.PaintListener;
import org.eclipse.swt.graphics.Image;
import org.eclipse.swt.graphics.Point;
import org.eclipse.swt.graphics.Rectangle;
import org.eclipse.swt.widgets.Canvas;
import org.eclipse.swt.widgets.Composite;
import org.eclipse.swt.widgets.Display;

public class ImageWithText extends Canvas {

    private Image image;

    public ImageWithText(Composite parent, int style) {
        super(parent, style);
        Display display = parent.getDisplay();
        image = new Image(parent.getDisplay(), ImageWithText.class.getResourceAsStream
("/image/vogella.svg"));

        this.addPaintListener(new PaintListener() {
            @Override
            public void paintControl(PaintEvent e) {
                Rectangle bounds = image.getBounds();
                e.gc.drawImage(image, 0, 0);

                e.gc.setForeground(display.getSystemColor(SWT.COLOR_RED));
                e.gc.setFont(display.getSystemFont());

                String text = "Advanced Trainings";
                Point textSize = e.gc.textExtent(text);

                // position the text
                int x = (bounds.width - textSize.x) / 2 + 20;
                int y = 0;

                e.gc.drawText(text, x, y, true);
            }
        });
    }

    @Override
    public void dispose() {
        image.dispose();
        super.dispose();
    }
}
```

Use the `ImageWithText` widget in the `PlaygroundPart`.

The expected output is shown in the screenshot below.

> Resources, like `Image` objects that have been drawn with the `GC`, must be disposed of afterward.

79. Optional exercise: Use Nebula widgets

Nebula widgets are custom-drawn widgets that you can use in your plug-ins. In this exercise, you will add the Nebula update site to your target platform and start using a few of them.

79.1. Start using some Nebula widgets in the application

Add Nebula to your target platform. For this, look up the latest update site on https://download.eclipse.org/nebula/updates/. Details on the release can be found at https://github.com/eclipse/nebula/releases.

> You need to open this URL in a browser to see the actual update site URL.

For example, an additional entry in your target platform could look like this:

```
<location includeAllPlatforms="false" includeConfigurePhase="true" includeMode="planner"
includeSource="true" type="InstallableUnit">
    <repository location="https://download.eclipse.org/nebula/updates/release"/>
    <unit id="org.eclipse.nebula.widgets.chips.feature.feature.group"/>
</location>
```

After this addition, reload the target platform via the *Overview* tab and the Reload Target Platform button.

Use at least one of the widgets in your application.

For example, to use the Chips widget, add the following as dependencies to your `com.vogella.tasks.ui` MANIFEST.MF.

- org.eclipse.nebula.widgets.chips

Also, add these plug-ins to your feature.

```
Chips chip1 = new Chips(parent, SWT.CLOSE);
chip1.setText("Example");
chip1.setChipsBackground(Display.getDefault().getSystemColor(SWT.COLOR_RED));
```

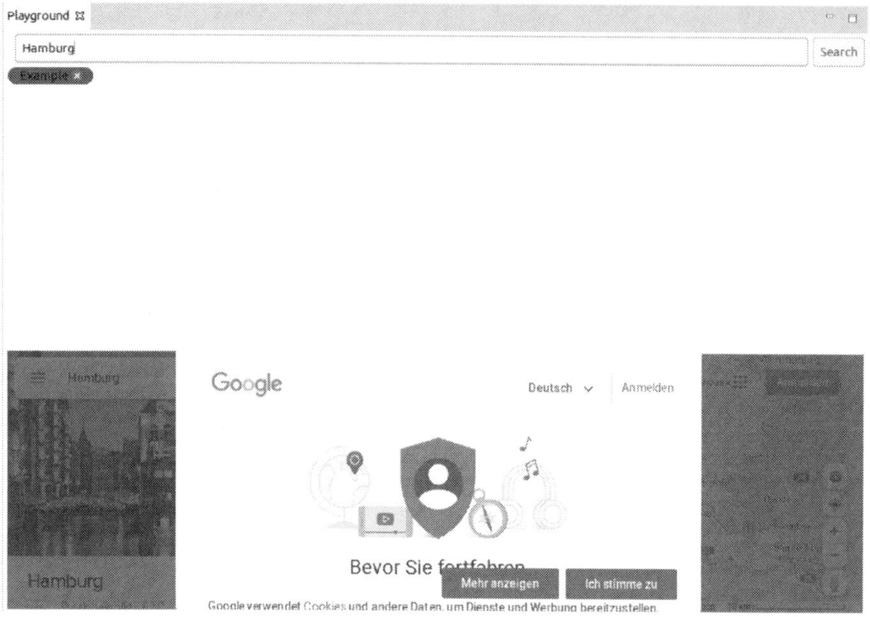

More examples of Chips usage can be found in the following snippet: https://github.com/eclipse/nebula/blob/master/widgets/chips/org.eclipse.nebula.widgets.chips.snippets/src/org/eclipse/nebula/widgets/chips/ChipsSnippet.java

79.2. Review the Nebula widgets code

This exercise requires some base knowledge of Git. If you are not familiar with the usage of Git, please skip it. Open Eclipse with a new workspace.

For this, clone the source code. The valid clone URL can be found here: https://github.com/eclipse/nebula

Part X: Defining menus, toolbars and key bindings

80. Menu and toolbar application objects

80.1. Adding menu and toolbar entries

You can add menus and toolbars to your Eclipse application using the application model and position these entries at various locations. You can, for example, add a menu to a window or a part. Each element defines, directly or indirectly, one or more links to a class that is responsible for the execution. These classes are responsible for the behavior once the menu or toolbar entry is selected. Such a class is called *handler class*.

80.2. Using commands and handlers

The Eclipse application model allows you to specify *commands* and *handlers.*

You can use the *Direct MenuItem* or *Direct ToolItem* model elements. These entries define a reference to a class (handler class). An instance of this handler class is created by the framework and its annotated methods are called by the framework if necessary. Menus and toolbars support separators.

A command is a declarative description of an abstract action that can be performed, for example, *Save*, *Edit*, or *Copy*.

A command is independent of its implementation details. The Eclipse framework does not provide standard commands, e.g., you have to create all required commands in your application model.

The behavior of a command is defined via a handler. A handler model element points to a class (handler class) via the `contributionURI` property of the handler. This attribute is displayed as *Class URI* in the model editor.

Commands are used by the *Handled MenuItem* and *Handled ToolItem* model elements.

Prefer using commands over the usage of direct (menu or tool) items. Using commands together with handlers allows you to define different handlers for different scopes (applications or part) and you can define key bindings for the handler's associated commands.

80.3. Behavior annotations and dependency injection for handler classes

In a handler class exactly one method must be annotated with the `@Execute` annotation. In addition, you can annotate one method with the `@CanExecute` annotation. If multiple methods in a handler class are annotated with the same annotation, only one of them will be executed by the framework. The Eclipse runtime uses dependency injection to provide the parameters of the method. The purpose of these annotations is described in the following table.

Table 19. Behavior annotations for handler classes

Annotation	Description
`@Execute`	Marks the method which is responsible for the action of the handler class. The framework executes this method once the related user interface element, e.g., the menu entry, is selected.
`@CanExecute`	Marks a method to be visited by the Eclipse framework to check if the handler class can be executed. If a handler class returns `false` in this method, Eclipse disables the corresponding user interface element. For example, the save button is active if the handler class returns true in the `@CanExecute` method. The default for this method is true, which means, if the handler class can always be executed, it does not need to implement a `@CanExecute` method.

The following example demonstrates the implementation of a handler class.

```
package com.vogella.tasks.ui.handlers;

// import statements cut out
// ..

public class ExitHandler {
    @Execute
    public void execute(IWorkbench workbench) {
        workbench.close();
```

```
    }

    // NOT REQUIRED IN THIS EXAMPLE
    // just to demonstrate the usage of the annotation
    @CanExecute
    public boolean canExecute() {
        return true;
    }
}
```

A handler instance does not have its own `IEclipseContext`. It is executed with the Eclipse context of the active model element that has an Eclipse context. In most common cases this is the context of the active part.

All required parameters should be injected into the method annotated with `@Execute`, as you want the handler class to retrieve its runtime information during execution.

> To ensure that you get the expected values from the active context, always inject the required values as parameters into your methods annotated with `@Execute` or `@CanExecute`.

80.4. Determining the relevant handler for a command

If a command is selected, the runtime determines the relevant handler for the command. The application model allows you to create a handler for the application, a window and a part.

Each command can have only one valid handler for a given scope. The Eclipse framework selects the handler most specific to the currently selected model element.

For example, if you have two handlers for the "Copy" command, one for the window and another one for the part, then the runtime selects the handler closest to the model element that is currently selected by the user.

80.5. Trigger the evaluation of the can execute method

A method annotated with `@CanExecute` is called by the framework if a change in the Eclipse context happens. For example, if you select a new part. If the method returns `false`, the framework disables any menu and tool items that point to that command.

You can request the re-evaluation of the `@CanExecute` methods by sending out an event via the event broker.

```
// evaluate all @CanExecute methods
eventBroker.post(UIEvents.REQUEST_ENABLEMENT_UPDATE_TOPIC, UIEvents.ALL_ELEMENT_ID);
```

```
// evaluate a context via a selector
Selector s = (a selector that has an MApplicationElement or an ID);
eventBroker.post(UIEvents.REQUEST_ENABLEMENT_UPDATE_TOPIC, s);

// See  https://bugs.eclipse.org/bugs/show_bug.cgi?id=427465 for discussion on the
implementation details
```

80.6. Mnemonics

The application model allows you to define *mnemonics*. A mnemonic appears as an underlined letter in the menu when the user presses and holds the `ALT` key and allows the user to quickly access menu entries by keyboard.

You specify mnemonics by prefixing the letter intended as the mnemonic with an ampersand (&) in the label definition. For example, if you use the label *&Save*, the S will be underlined if the `Alt` key is pressed.

80.7. Naming scheme for command and handler IDs

A good convention is to start IDs with the *top-level package name* of your project and to use only lowercase letters.

The IDs of commands and handlers should reflect their relationship. For example, if you implement a command with the `com.example.contacts.commands.show` ID, you should use `com.example.contacts.handler.show` as the ID for the handler. If you have more than one handler for one command, add another suffix to it, describing its purpose, e.g., `com.example.contacts.handler.show.details`.

In case you implement commonly used functions in your RCP application, e.g., save, copy, you should use the existing platform IDs, as some Eclipse contributions expect these IDs to better integrate with the OS (e.g., on macOS, preferences are normally placed under the first menu). A list of command IDs is available in `org.eclipse.ui.IWorkbenchCommandConstants`.

.Default IDs for commonly used commands

Command	ID
Save	org.eclipse.ui.file.save
Save All	org.eclipse.ui.file.saveAll
Undo	org.eclipse.ui.edit.undo
Redo	org.eclipse.ui.edit.redo
Cut	org.eclipse.ui.edit.cut

Command	ID
Copy	org.eclipse.ui.edit.copy
Paste	org.eclipse.ui.edit.paste
Delete	org.eclipse.ui.edit.delete
Import	org.eclipse.ui.file.import
Export	org.eclipse.ui.file.export
Select All	org.eclipse.ui.edit.selectAll
About	org.eclipse.ui.help.aboutAction
Preferences	org.eclipse.ui.window.preferences
Exit	org.eclipse.ui.file.exit

81. View, popup and dynamic menus

81.1. View menus

You can define one menu in a part as a *view menu*, it renders as a *Kebab* menu as highlighted in the image below.

To add a view menu entry, select the *Menus* entry under the part and append a *ViewMenu* model entry to it.

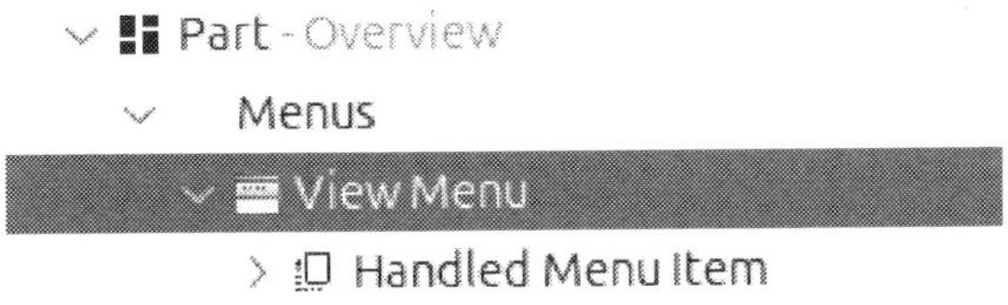

> The application model allows you to define more than one menu. But the default Eclipse implementation supports only one menu for a part.

81.2. Popup menu (context menu)

You can define a popup menu for SWT controls via the application model. See the exercise for detailed steps on how to achieve this.

81.3. Dynamic menu and toolbar entries

You can create menu and toolbar entries at runtime with the *DynamicMenuContribution* model element.

This model element points to a class in which you annotate a method with the `@AboutToShow` annotation. The annotated method is called if the user selects the user interface element. The `@AboutToHide` annotation can be used to annotate a method that is called before the menu is hidden.

In these methods, you can dynamically create menu entries.

82. Toolbars, ToolControls and drop-down tool items

82.1. Adding toolbars to parts

Toolbars in the application model are defined within the *Trimbars* model element. A trimbar can be defined for *TrimmedWindow* model elements. Via its *Side* attribute, you define whether the trim bar should be placed on the top, left, right, or bottom of the resulting window.

To add a toolbar to a view, set the *Toolbar* flag on the model element for the part and create the entries in the application model.

Such an example setup is displayed in the following screenshot.

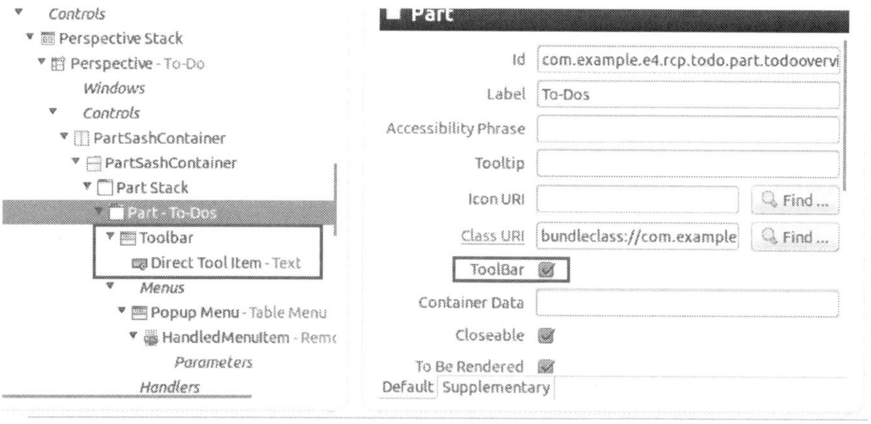

82.2. ToolControls

ToolControl model element points to a Java class that creates controls that are displayed in the toolbar.

For example, the following code creates a `Text` field in the toolbar which looks like a search field.

```java
package com.vogella.tasks.ui.toolcontrols;

import org.eclipse.jface.layout.GridDataFactory;
import org.eclipse.swt.SWT;
import org.eclipse.swt.layout.GridLayout;
import org.eclipse.swt.widgets.Composite;
import org.eclipse.swt.widgets.Text;

import jakarta.annotation.PostConstruct;

public class SearchToolControl {

    @PostConstruct
    public void createGui(Composite parent) {
        final Composite comp = new Composite(parent, SWT.NONE);
        comp.setLayout(new GridLayout());
        Text text = new Text(comp, SWT.SEARCH | SWT.CANCEL | SWT.ICON_SEARCH | SWT.
BORDER);
        text.setMessage("Search");
        GridDataFactory.fillDefaults().hint(130, SWT.DEFAULT).applyTo(text);
    }
}
```

You can add such a `ToolControl`, for example, to your windows trimbar as depicted in the following screenshot.

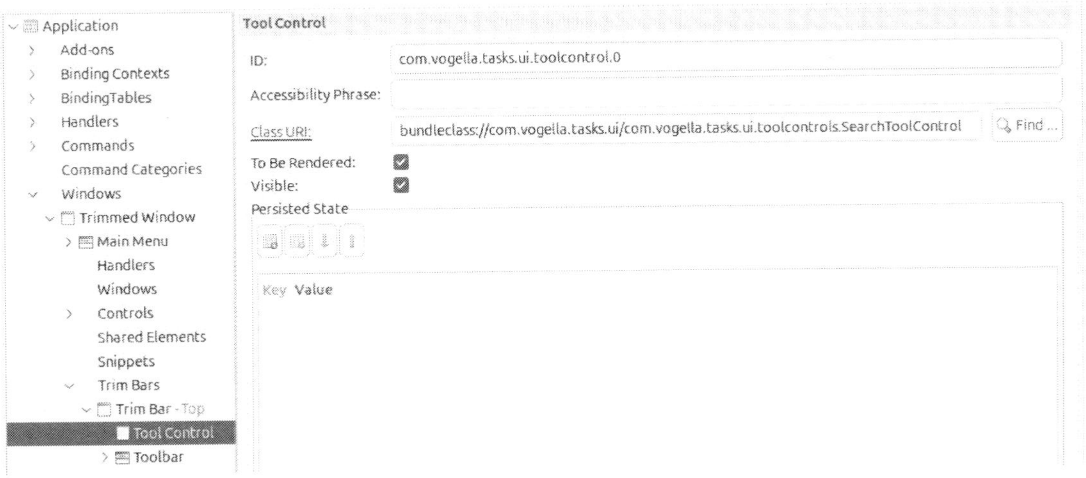

The following screenshot shows this `ToolControl` used in an example RCP application.

82.3. Drop-down tool items

Set the *Menu* attribute on a tool item to be able to define a menu similar to the Run As... button in the Eclipse IDE. This button is depicted in the following screenshot.

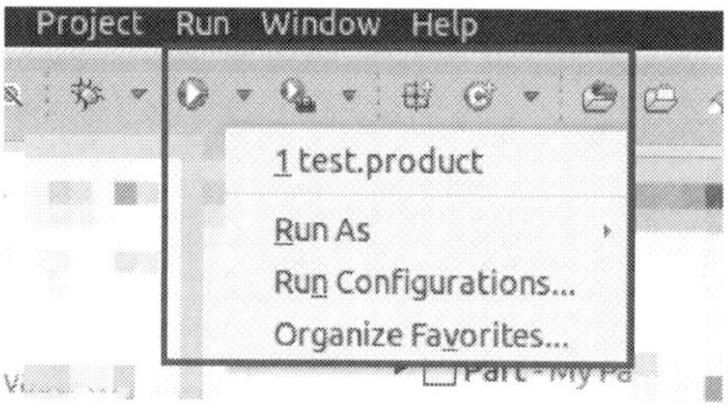

83. More on commands and handlers

83.1. Passing parameters to commands

You can pass parameters to commands. To achieve this, select a command and press the Add button in the *Parameters* section.

The ID is the identifier that you can use to get the parameter value injected via the `@Named` annotation.

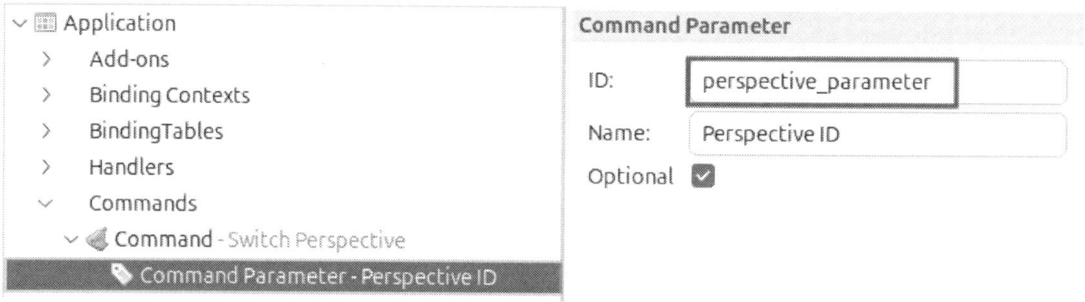

In your HandledMenuItem or HandledToolItem, add a parameter and put the ID from the command parameter definition into the *Name* field. The entry from the *Value* field is passed to the handler of the command.

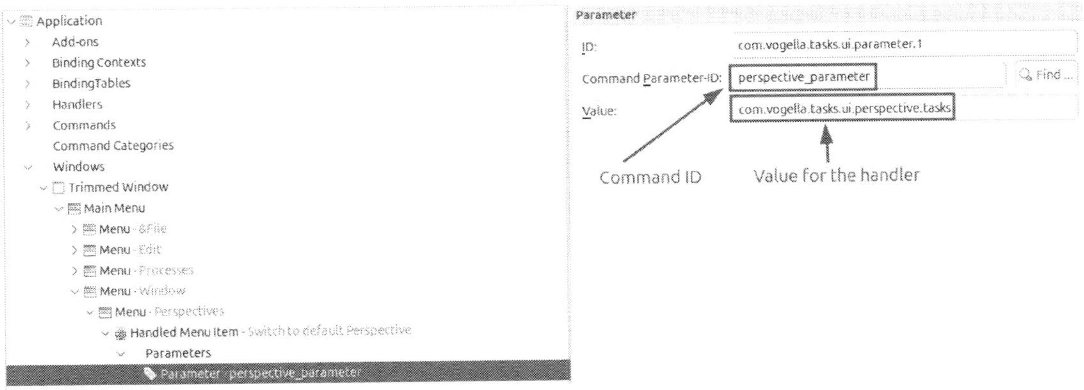

The ID of the parameter is the important one. This ID must be injected via the `@Named` annotation and used as *Name* (second field) during the definition of the menu or toolbar. This is highlighted in the following screenshot.

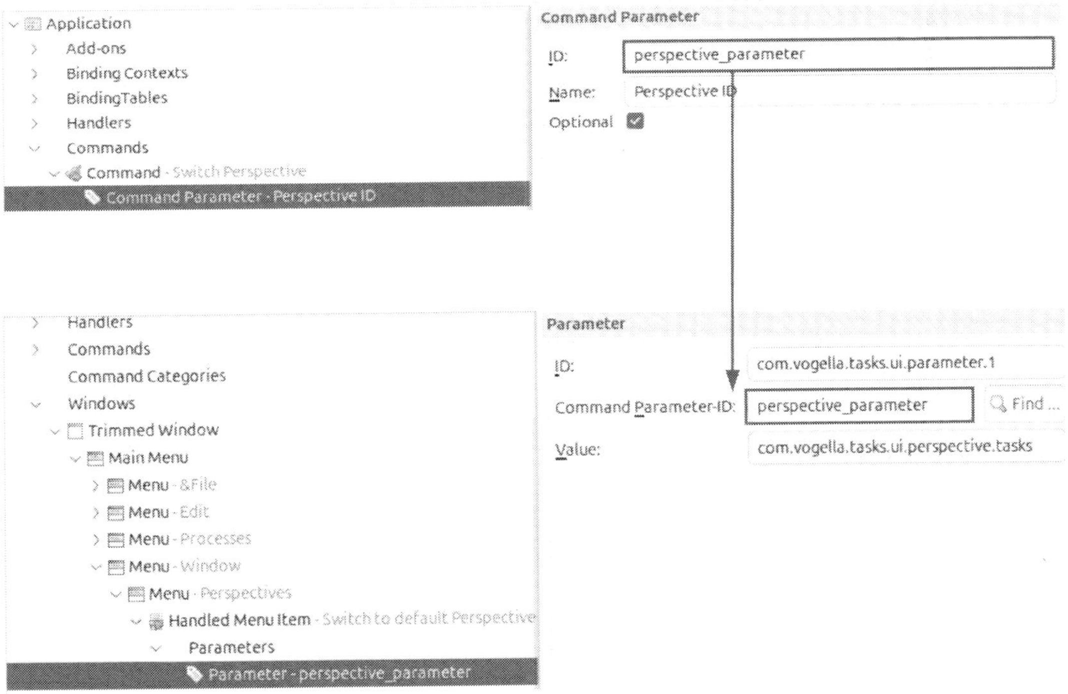

To get the parameter injected into your handler class, you specify the ID of the parameter via the `@Named` annotation. This is demonstrated in the following code example.

```
package com.vogella.tasks.ui.handlers;

import java.util.List;
```

```java
import jakarta.inject.Named;

import org.eclipse.e4.core.di.annotations.Execute;
import org.eclipse.e4.ui.model.application.MApplication;
import org.eclipse.e4.ui.model.application.ui.advanced.MPerspective;
import org.eclipse.e4.ui.model.application.ui.basic.MWindow;
import org.eclipse.e4.ui.workbench.modeling.EModelService;
import org.eclipse.e4.ui.workbench.modeling.EPartService;

// switcher perspectives based on a command parameter
public class PerspectiveSwitchHandler {

    @Execute
    public void switchPerspective(
            MWindow window,
            EPartService partService,
            EModelService modelService,
            @Named("perspective_parameter") String perspectiveId) {
        // use parameter to find perspectives
        List<MPerspective> perspectives = modelService.findElements(window,
                perspectiveId, MPerspective.class, null);

        // switch to perspective with the ID if found
        if (!perspectives.isEmpty()) {
            partService.switchPerspective(perspectives.get(0));
        }
    }
}
```

Instead of injecting each parameter individually, you can inject the `ParameterizedCommand` and access its parameters through the API.

```java
package com.vogella.tasks.ui.handlers;

import jakarta.inject.Named;

import org.eclipse.e4.core.di.annotations.Execute;

public class TestHandlerWithCommandInjected {
    private String parametername = "com.vogella.tasks.ui" +
            ".commandparameter.input";
    @Execute
    public void execute(ParameterizedCommand command) {
      Object queryId = command.getParameterMap().get(parametername);
      // more...
    }
}
```

83.2. Imperative and core expressions

The visibility of menus, toolbars, and their entries can be controlled using *core expressions* and *imperative expressions*. These expressions allow the application to show or hide elements dynamically based on a defined condition.

The *imperative expressions* are Java classes. The *core expressions* are defined in the plugin.xml file. Both types of expressions can be used in the application model and are evaluated at runtime.

The visibility of a top-level menu entry cannot currently be controlled by the *visibleWhen* attribute.

83.2.1. Using imperative expressions

Imperative expressions are Java classes that can use dependency injection to access the application context. The method annotated with `@Evaluate` is called to evaluate the expression. For example, the following code checks if the current selection is of type `Task` or a collection containing this type.

```
package com.vogella.tasks.ui.expressions;

import org.eclipse.e4.core.di.annotations.Evaluate;
import org.eclipse.e4.core.di.annotations.Optional;

import com.vogella.tasks.model.Task;

import jakarta.inject.Named;

import java.util.Collection;

public class CheckSelection {
    @Evaluate
    public boolean evaluate(@Optional @Named("org.eclipse.ui.selection") Object o) {
        if (o instanceof Task) {
            return true;
        }
        if (o instanceof Collection<?>) {
            for (Object item : (Collection<?>) o) {
                if (item instanceof Task) {
                    return true;
                }
            }
        }
        return false;
    }
}
```

This expression can be used in the application model to control the visibility of a menu or toolbar entry.

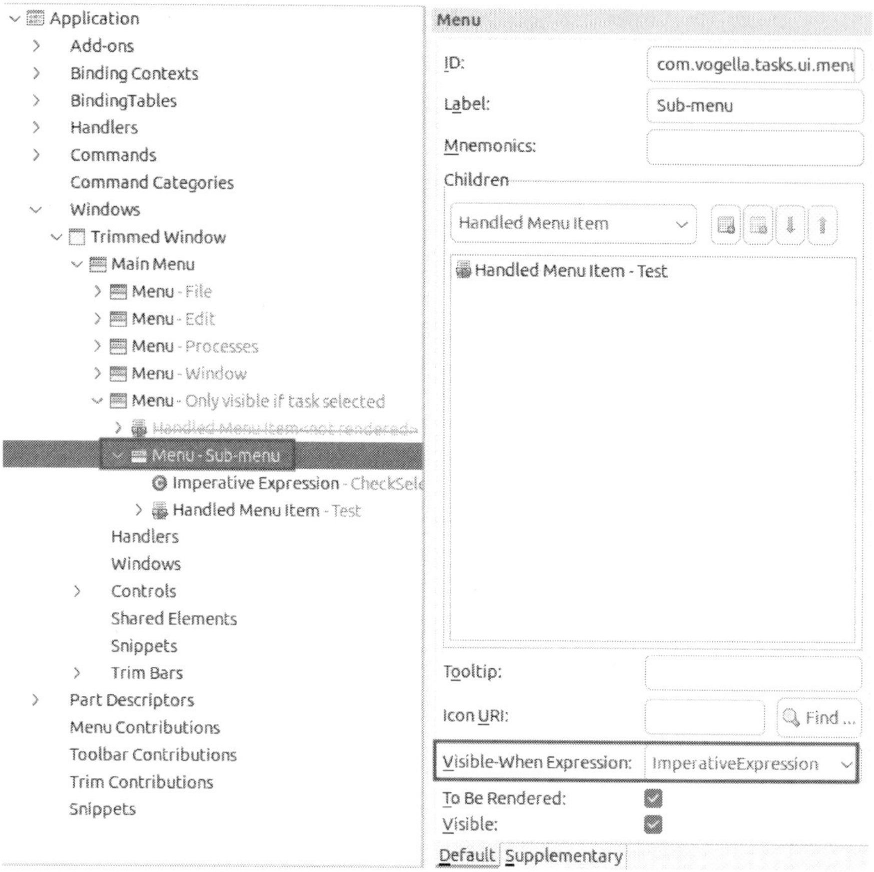

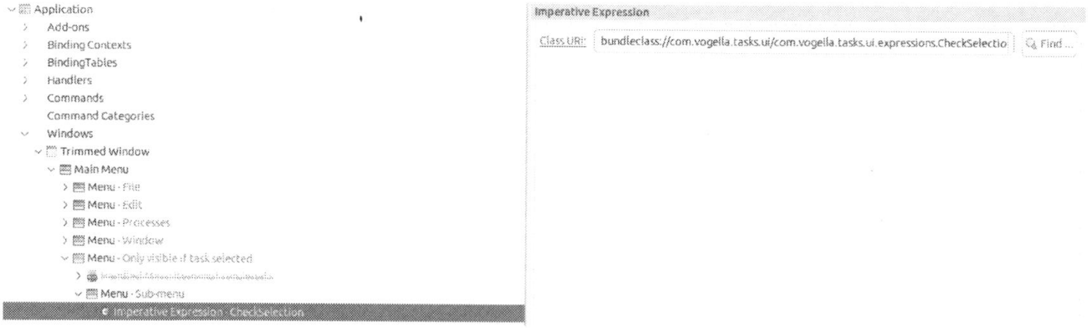

The related UI entry is only visible if the expression evaluates to `true`.

83.2.2. Using core expressions

To use core expressions, you add an extension to the `org.eclipse.core.expressions.definitions` extension point. To add this extension point to your application, open the *plugin.xml* file and select the *Dependencies* tab in the editor. Add the `org.eclipse.core.expressions` plug-in in the *Required Plug-ins* section.

Next, select the *Extensions* tab, click the Add button, and add the `org.eclipse.core.expressions.definitions` extension. You define an ID under which the core expression can be referred to in the application model.

Via a right-click on the extension, you can start building your expression.

The following example can be used to restrict the visibility of a menu entry based on the type of the current selection. You will later learn how to set the current selection. Please note that the variable for the selection is currently called `org.eclipse.ui.selection`.

```
<extension
         point="org.eclipse.core.expressions.definitions">
      <definition
            id="com.vogella.tasks.ui.task.selection">
         <with
               variable="org.eclipse.ui.selection">
            <iterate
                  ifEmpty="false"
                  operator="or">
               <instanceof
                     value="com.vogella.tasks.model.Task">
               </instanceof>
            </iterate>
         </with>
      </definition>
   </extension>
```

This core expression can be assigned to a menu entry in the application model to control the visibility of model elements.

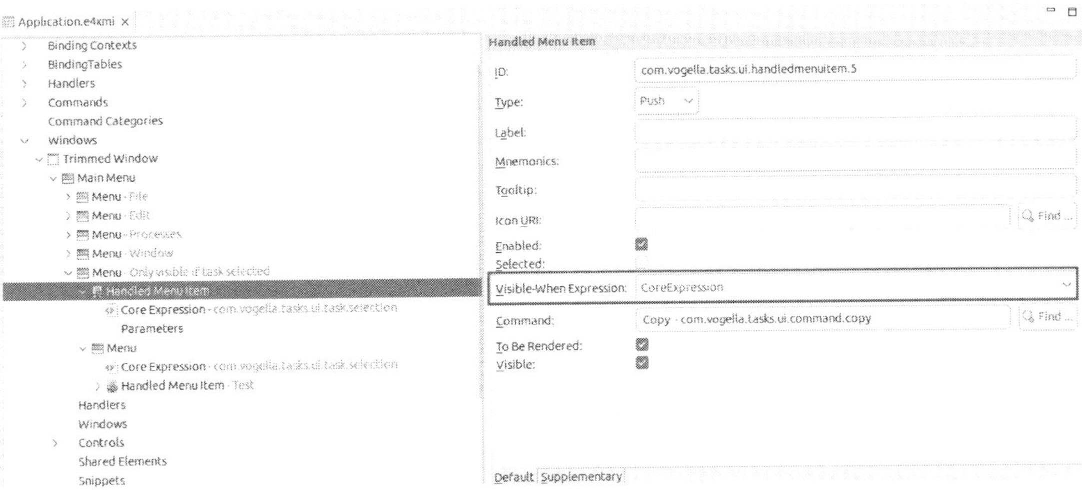

Ensure to also assign the expression ID.

See Chapter 180 for details on using and adding extension points to your application.

This approach is similar to the definition of core expressions in Eclipse 3.x.

The values available for Eclipse are contained in the `ISources` interface and documented in the Eclipse core expressions documentation [https://github.com/eclipse-platform/eclipse.platform.ui/blob/master/docs/Command_Core_Expressions.md]. Eclipse does not always support the same variables, but the documentation page might still be helpful.

83.3. Evaluate own values in core expressions

You can place values in the `IEclipseContext` of your application and use these for your visible-when evaluation.

The following code demonstrates an example handler class that places a value for the *myactivePartId* key in the context (you will learn more about modifying the `IEclipseContext` later).

```
@Execute
public void execute(IEclipseContext context) {
  // put an example value in the context
  context.set("myactivePartId",
  "com.example.e4.rcp.todo.part.todooverview");
}
```

The following code shows an example core expression that evaluates to `true` if a *myactivePartId* key with the value `com.example.e4.rcp.ui.parts.todooverview` is found in the context.

```
<extension
         point="org.eclipse.core.expressions.definitions">
      <definition
```

```
            id="com.example.e4.rcp.todo.todooverviewselected">
        <with
              variable="myactivePartId">
            <equals
                  value="com.example.e4.rcp.todo.part.todooverview">
            </equals>
        </with>
      </definition>
</extension>
```

This core expression can be assigned to a menu entry to control its visibility.

84. Key bindings

84.1. Using key bindings in the application

It is possible to define key bindings (shortcuts) for your Eclipse application. This requires two steps: first, you need to enter values for the *Binding Context* node of your application model.

Afterwards, you need to enter the key bindings for the relevant binding context in the *BindingTable* node of your application model. A binding table is always assigned to a specific binding context. A binding context can have several binding tables assigned to it.

Binding contexts are defined hierarchically, so that key bindings in a child override the matching key binding in the parent.

> Even though they sound similar, a binding context is used for key bindings, while the Eclipse context (`IEclipseContext`) is used as a source for dependency injection.

84.2. JFace default values for binding contexts

The binding context is identified via its ID. They can be assigned to a window or a part in the application model. This defines which keyboard shortcuts are valid for the window and which are valid for the part.

Eclipse JFace uses predefined IDs to identify binding contexts. These IDs are based on the `org.eclipse.jface.contexts.IContextIds` class. JFace distinguishes between shortcuts for dialogs, windows, or both.

The following table gives an overview of the supported IDs and their validity.

Table 20. Default BindingContext values

Context ID	Description
org.eclipse.ui.contexts.dialogAndWindow	Key bindings valid for dialogs and windows
org.eclipse.ui.contexts.dialog	Key bindings valid for dialogs
org.eclipse.ui.contexts.window	Key bindings valid for windows

As an example, `Ctrl` + `C` (Copy) would be defined in *dialogAndWindows* as it is valid everywhere, but `F5` (Refresh) might only be defined for a Window and not for a Dialog.

84.3. Define shortcuts

The *BindingTable* node in the application model allows you to create key bindings based on a binding context. For this, you create a new *BindingTable* model element and define a reference to the binding context via its ID.

In your key binding entry, you specify the key sequence and the command associated with this shortcut.

The control keys differ between platforms, for example, on macOS and Linux. You can use Ctrl, but this would be hardcoded. It is better to use the M1 - M4 meta keys.

Table 21. Key mapping

Control Key	Mapping for Windows and Linux	Mapping for Mac
M1	Ctrl	Command
M2	Shift	Shift
M3	Alt	Alt
M4	Undefined	Ctrl

These values are defined in the `SWTKeyLookup` class.

84.4. Activation of key bindings

When multiple key bindings are defined, the `ContextSet` class determines which one to activate by default. It follows a hierarchy, where the most specific binding context is considered first, and the root context is evaluated last.

You can use the `EContextService` service that allows you to explicitly activate and deactivate a binding context via the `activateContext()` and `deactivateContext()` methods.

84.5. Key bindings for a part

You can assign a specific binding context to be active while a part is active.

Key bindings assigned to a part are active in addition to those from the currently active binding context, meaning global key bindings remain active alongside part-specific ones.

85. Exercise: Adding menus

In this exercise, you create commands and handlers for your application. Afterwards, you will create menu entries using these commands.

85.1. Create command model elements

Open the *Application.e4xmi* file of your `com.vogella.tasks.ui` plug-in and select the *Commands* entry.

Via the Add... button you can create new commands. This selection is highlighted in the following screenshot.

The name and the ID are the important fields. Create the following commands.

Table 22. Commands

ID	Name
org.eclipse.ui.file.saveAll	Save
org.eclipse.ui.file.exit	Exit
com.vogella.tasks.ui.command.createtask	Create task
com.vogella.tasks.ui.command.removetask	Remove task
com.vogella.tasks.ui.command.fortesting	For testing

85.2. Creating the handler classes

Create the `com.vogella.tasks.ui.handlers` package for your handler classes.

All handler classes implement an `execute()` method annotated with `@Execute`.

```
package com.vogella.tasks.ui.handlers;

import org.eclipse.e4.core.di.annotations.Execute;

public class SaveAllHandler {
    @Execute
    public void execute() {
      System.out.println((this.getClass().getSimpleName() + " called"));
    }
```

```
}
```

Now, create the following classes by copying the above class.

- SaveAllHandler
- ExitHandler
- NewTaskHandler
- RemoveTaskHandler
- TestHandler

85.3. Creating handler model elements

Select the application-scoped *Handlers* entry in your application model and create the handlers from the following table for your commands. For the definition of handlers the ID, command and class are the relevant information.

Use the `com.vogella.tasks.ui.handler` prefix for all IDs of the handlers.

Table 23. Handlers

Handler ID	Command	Class
.saveall	Save	SaveAllHandler
.exit	Exit	ExitHandler
.newtask	Create task	NewTaskHandler
.removetask	Remove task	RemoveTaskHandler
.fortesting	For testing	TestHandler

The application model editor shows both the name and the ID of the command. The class URI follows the `bundleclass://` schema, the table only defines the class name to make the table more readable. For example, for the handler with the `com.vogella.tasks.ui.handler.saveall` ID uses the following entry to point to its handler class.

```
bundleclass://com.vogella.tasks.ui/com.vogella.tasks.ui.handlers.SaveAllHandler
```

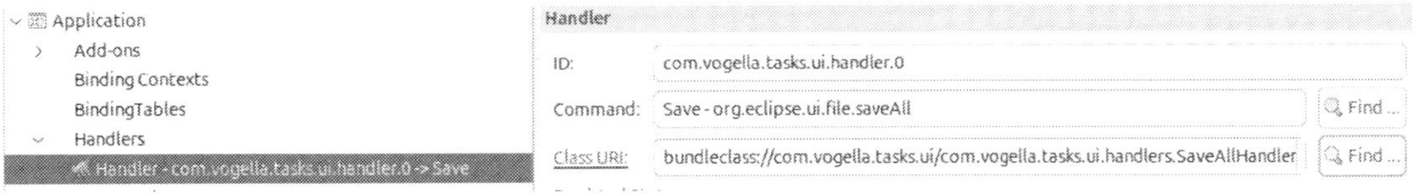

85.4. Adding a menu

In your *Application.e4xmi* file select your *TrimmedWindow* entry in the model and flag the *Main Menu* attribute.

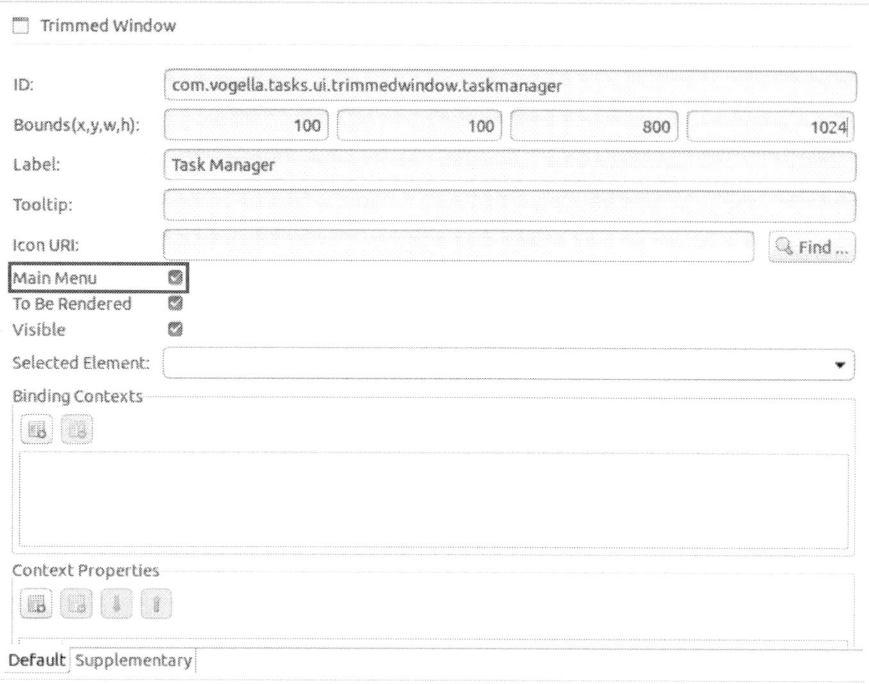

Assign the `org.eclipse.ui.main.menu` ID to your main menu.

> Ensure that the ID of the main menu is correct. You use it later to contribute another menu entry via another plug-in.

Add two menus: one with the label **File** and another with the label **Edit**.

Also set the *org.eclipse.ui.file.menu* ID for the File menu. Use *com.vogella.tasks.ui.menu.edit* as ID for the Edit menu.

Add a *Handled MenuItem* model element to the **File** menu. This item should reference the *Save* command via the *Command* attribute.

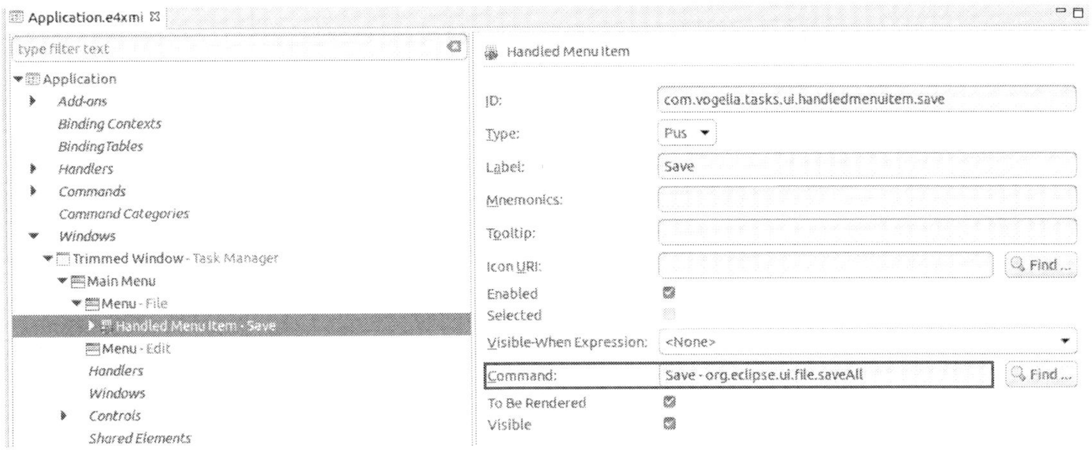

Add a *Separator* after the *Save* menu item in your **File** menu. Also add a *Handled MenuItem* model element pointing to the *Exit* via the *Command* attribute.

Add all other commands you created to the *Edit* menu.

Afterwards, the menu structure should be like the following:

File and Edit Menus

```
File
├── Save
└── Exit
Edit
├── Create task
├── Remove task
└── For testing
```

85.5. Implement a handler class for exit

To test if your handler is working, change your `ExitHandler` class, so that it closes your application, once selected.

```
package com.vogella.tasks.ui.handlers;

import org.eclipse.e4.core.di.annotations.Execute;
import org.eclipse.e4.ui.workbench.IWorkbench;

public class ExitHandler {
    @Execute
    public void execute(IWorkbench workbench) {
        workbench.close();
    }
```

```
}
```

85.6. Validate

Validate that your save handlers are called if you select them in the menu.

85.7. Possible issue: Exit menu entry on macOS

If you use the `org.eclipse.ui.file.exit` ID for your exit command, the Eclipse framework maps the menu entry to its default menu location on the macOS. If the exit menu is not visible in its defined position, check its default location for macOS.

86. Exercise: Add a context menu to a table

In this exercise, you will implement a context menu for a table in your `TodoOverviewPart` and link it to the delete command.

86.1. Adding dependencies

Add the following entries as plug-in dependencies to the `MANIFEST.MF` file of your application plug-in.

- `org.eclipse.e4.ui.workbench.swt`
- `org.eclipse.e4.ui.model.workbench`
- `org.eclipse.e4.ui.services`

86.2. Implementation

Create a *Popup Menu* with the `com.vogella.tasks.ui.popupmenu.table` ID in the application model for the part that contains the SWT control.

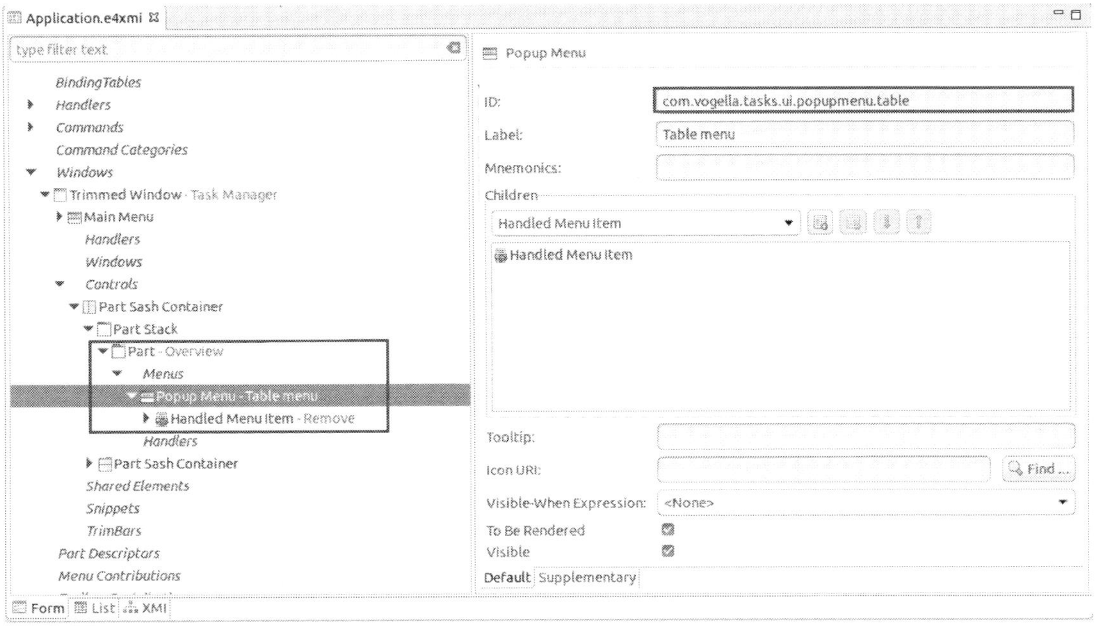

The popup menu can contain entries such as `HandledMenuItem` elements.

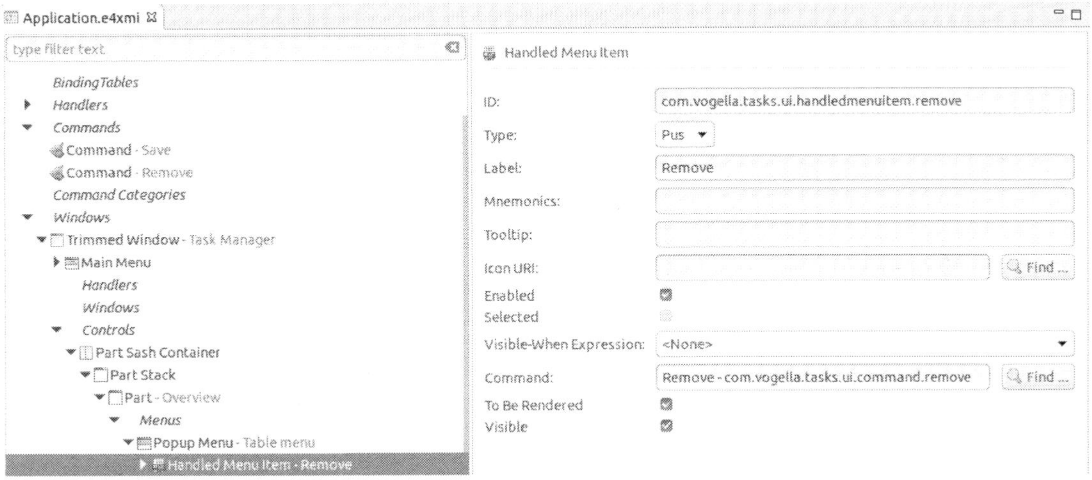

The popup menu can be assigned to an SWT control with the `EMenuService` service. This class provides the `registerContextMenu(control, id)` method for this purpose. The *id* parameter of the `registerContextMenu` method must be the ID attribute of your *Popup Menu* model element.

The following pseudo-code shows an example for the registration. The popup menu must be registered on the SWT control. The following example demonstrates how to access this control.

```
package com.vogella.tasks.ui.parts;
```

```java
import jakarta.annotation.PostConstruct;

import org.eclipse.e4.ui.services.EMenuService;
import org.eclipse.swt.SWT;
import org.eclipse.swt.widgets.Composite;
import org.eclipse.swt.widgets.Text;

public class TodoOverviewPart {

    @PostConstruct
    public void createControls(Composite parent, EMenuService menuService) {
        // more code...
        TableViewer viewer = new TableViewer(parent, SWT.FULL_SELECTION | SWT.MULTI);

        // more code

        // register context menu on the table
        menuService.registerContextMenu(
                viewer.getControl(),
                "com.vogella.tasks.ui.popupmenu.table");
    }
}
```

Change the `RemoveTaskHandler` so that it writes: "Soon, I will delete your task."

> You will modify the `RemoveTaskHandler` to delete the selected task once you have learned about the selection service.

87. Exercise: Adding a toolbar

In this exercise, you add a toolbar to your application.

87.1. Adding a toolbar

Select the *TrimBars* node under your *TrimmedWindow* entry and press the Add... button. The *Side* attribute should be set to *Top*, so that all toolbars assigned to that trimbar appear on the top of the application.

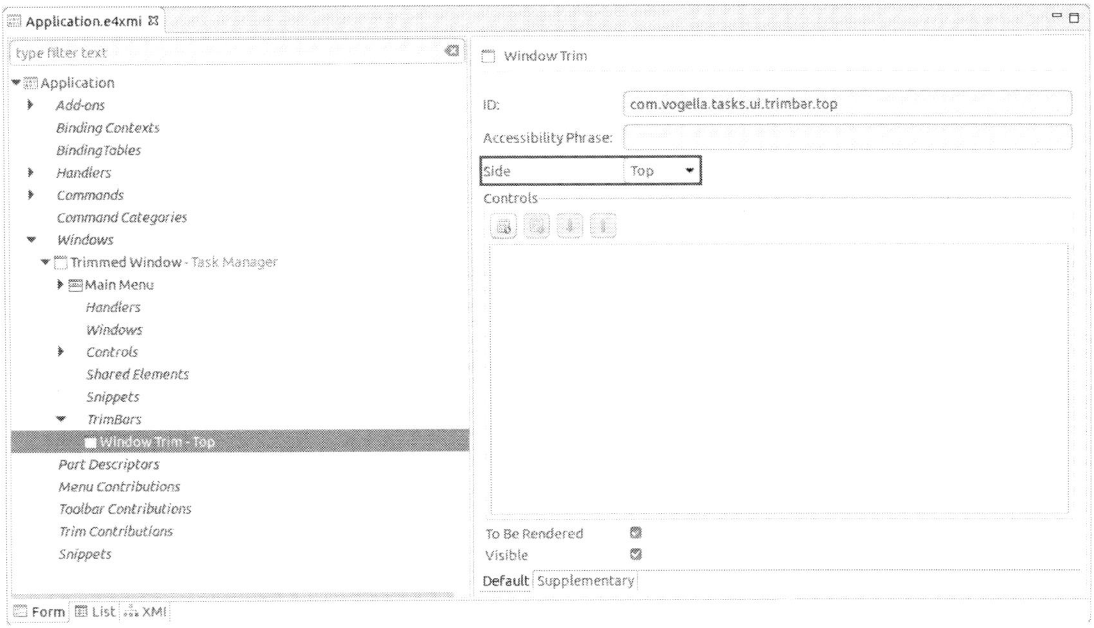

Add a *ToolBar* model element to your TrimBar. Add a *Handled ToolItem* to this toolbar that points to the `org.eclipse.ui.file.saveAll` command.

Set the label for this entry to *Save*.

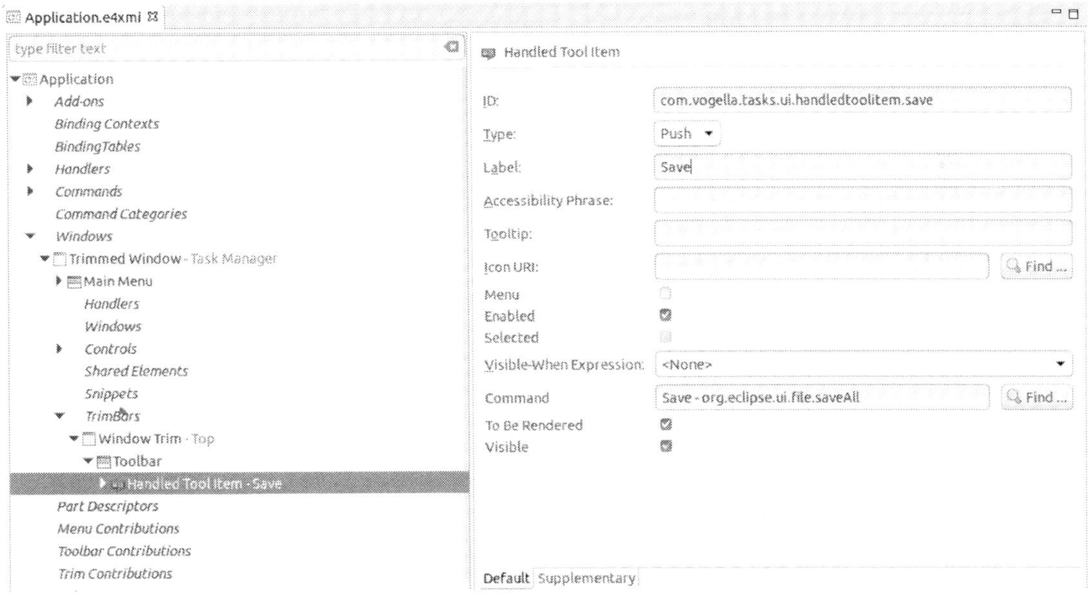

87.2. Validate

Validate that your save handler is called if you select Save from the menu or the toolbar.

88. Exercise: Define key bindings

88.1. Create binding context entries

Select the *Binding Contexts* entry in your application model. Define a new entry with the `org.eclipse.ui.contexts.dialogAndWindow` ID. Set the name to *Windows and Dialogs*.

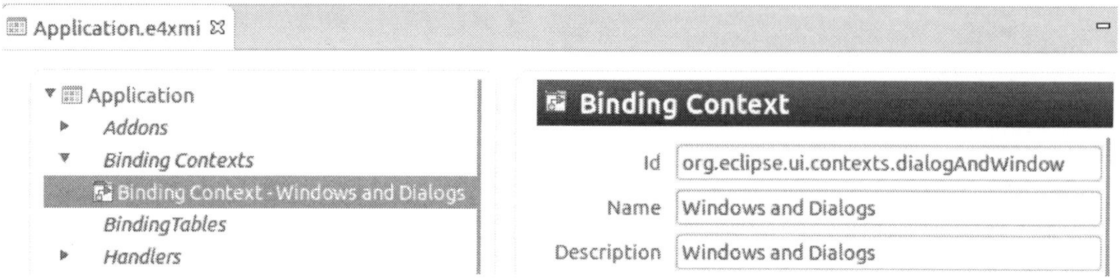

Afterwards, add the following sub-entries:

Table 24. Binding context entries

ID	Name
org.eclipse.ui.contexts.dialog	Dialogs
org.eclipse.ui.contexts.window	Windows

The resulting entry is depicted in the following screenshot.

The name attribute of a binding context entry cannot be empty.

88.2. Create a binding table

Key bindings are defined via a binding table which is defined for a certain binding context. Create a new binding table for the `org.eclipse.ui.contexts.dialogAndWindow` binding context similar to the following screenshot.

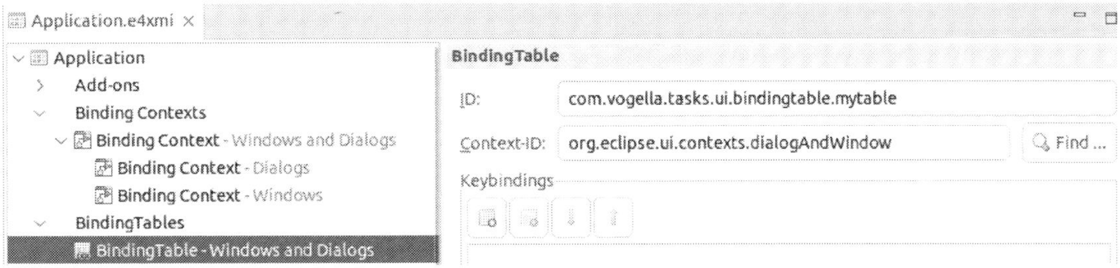

88.3. Create key bindings for a BindingContext

Create a key binding for your Save command using the `M1` + `S` shortcut.

The required entries are depicted in the following screenshots.

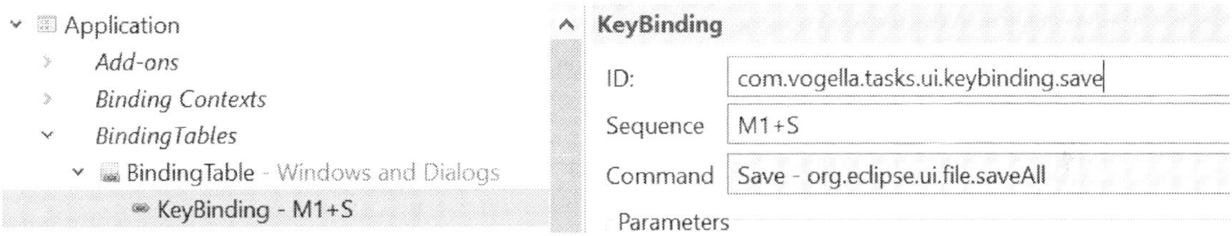

Afterwards, create a key binding for your Exit command with the `M1` + `X` shortcut.

Run your program and test it.

89. Optional exercise: Extend the usage of commands

Extend your application with the following steps:

89.1. Add icons for the toolbar

Find beautiful icons for your app and use them in your toolbar. A possible source is the Google Fonts [https://fonts.google.com/icons] webpage.

For example, a toolbar with the remove command could look like this:

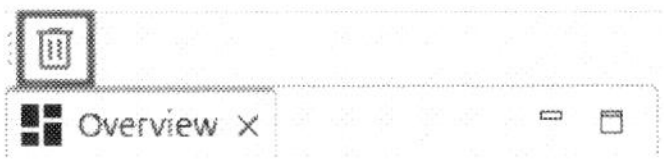

89.2. Add a copy command and a handler specific to a view

Add a new command to your application with the name *Copy* and the ID *com.vogella.tasks.ui.command.copy*. Add it to the *Edit* menu and a new handled menu item.

Create the following class:

```java
package com.vogella.tasks.ui.handlers;

import org.eclipse.e4.core.di.annotations.Execute;

public class TasksCopyHandler {
    @Execute
    public void execute() {
        System.out.println("Copy triggered from the overview part");
    }
}
```

Now create a handler specific to the *Overview* part.

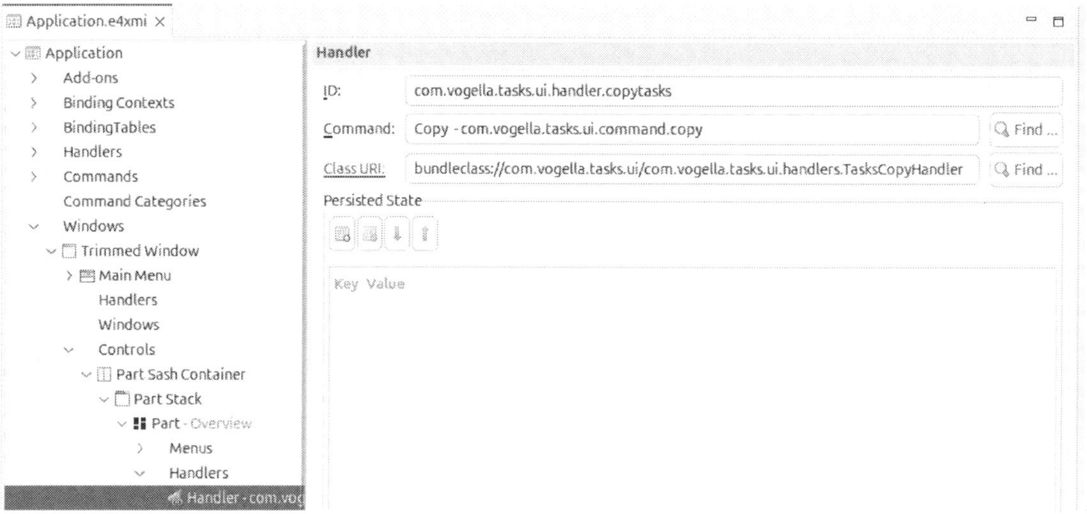

The *Copy* menu entry should now only be active if the *Overview* part is selected.

89.3. Using the view toolbar

Add a toolbar to your *Overview* part and add at least one handled tool item to it. If possible, link to a fitting icon, as toolbar entries without an icon look strange.

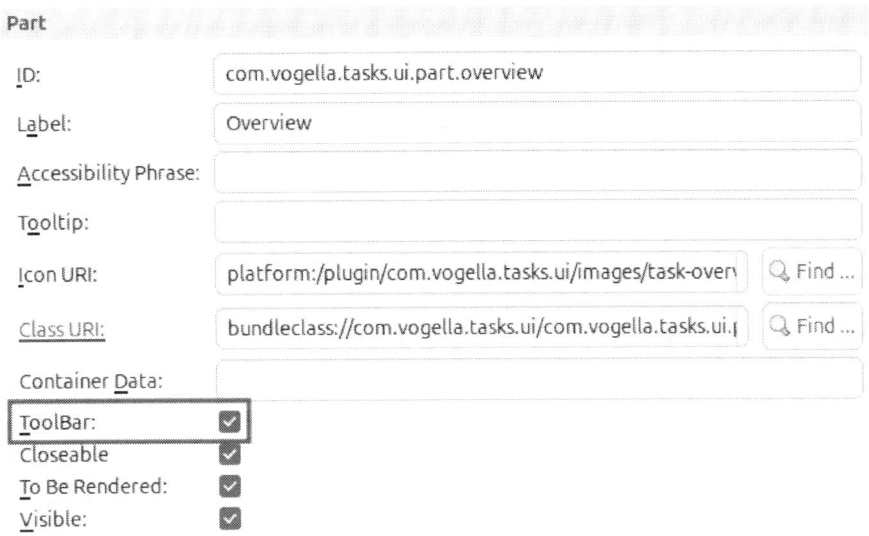

You can now add entries to the view toolbar.

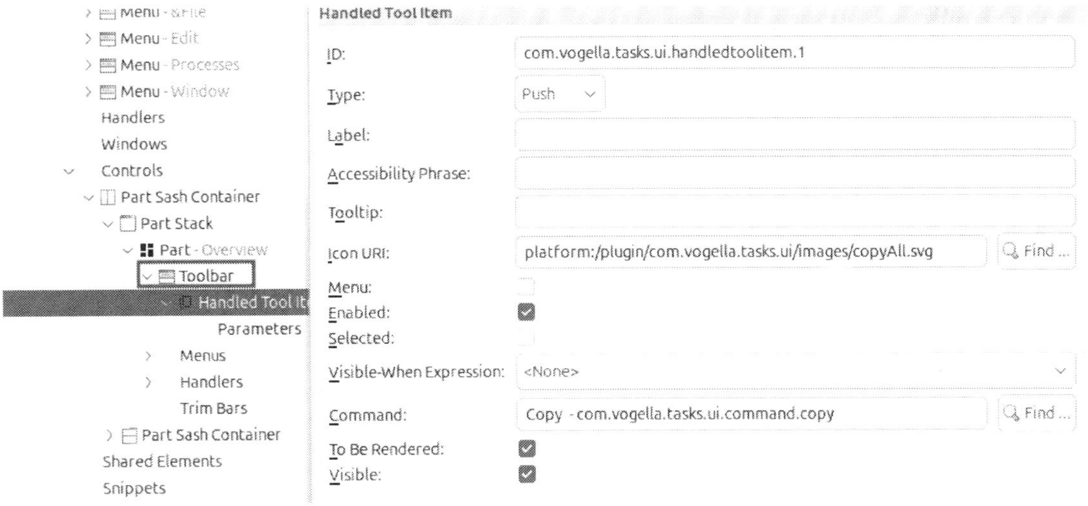

You should see them in the view toolbar, the icon if you added one, otherwise the label.

89.4. Add a view menu to the part

Add a view menu to your `TodoOverviewPart` part. The view menu is displayed as part of the view toolbar via the *Kebab* icon.

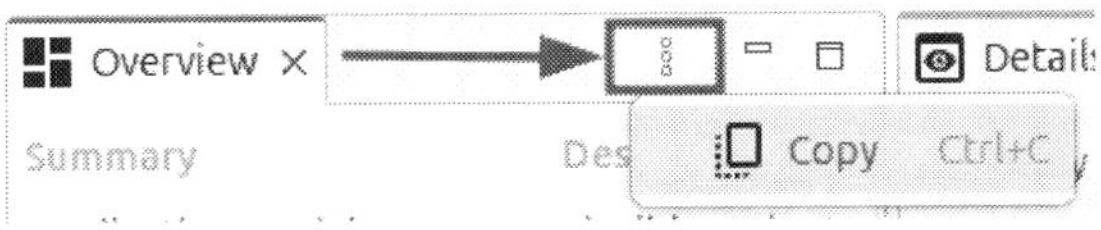

For this, you need to set the *Toolbar* flag in the part metadata as you did in Section 89.3. Add at least one entry to it, for example the `com.vogella.tasks.ui.command.createtask` command.

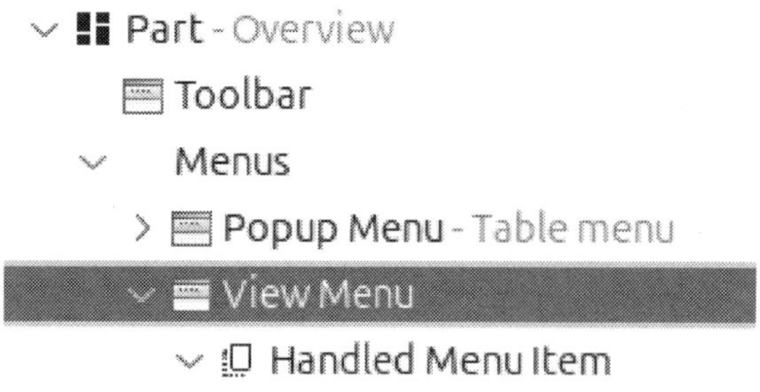

89.5. What are the trimbar entries for in the part?

> The trimbar entries for the view are unused in the default Eclipse implementation. Clients could use them in combination with custom renderers.

Part XI: Styling the Eclipse application with CSS

90. Eclipse and declarative styling

The visual appearance of your Eclipse application can be styled using external files based on the CSS 2.1 standard. CSS selectors used in Eclipse are identifiers, which relate to widgets or other elements, for example predefined pseudo classes. Non-standard properties are prefixed with either `swt-` or `eclipse-`.

The following example shows a CSS file that defines the styling for an Eclipse application.

```
Label, Button {
    font: Verdana 10px;
    background-color: #e0e0e0;
    color: black;
}

Text {
    font: Verdana 10px;
}

Table, Tree {
    background-color: #f2f2f2;
```

```
    swt-header-background-color: #d0d0d0;
    swt-header-color: black;
    color: black;
}

Composite Text {
    background-color: white;
    color: black;
}

SashForm {
    background-color: #c1d5ef;
}

.MTrimBar {
    color: white;
    font: Verdana 8px;
}

Shell, Composite, .MTrimBar {
    background-color: #e0e0e0;
}

CTabItem:selected {
    background-color: #d0d0d0;
    color: black;
}
```

SWT has certain limitations concerning component styling. These limitations are based on the restrictions of the underlying operating system or limitations in SWT itself. For example, it is not possible to style menus because this is not supported by SWT. In every Eclipse release, these limitations are reduced, as full styling for SWT widgets is an important feature.

> In most cases it is possible to overcome the styling restrictions of SWT in RCP applications. For example, you can use `NatTable` to display your tables. NatTable is a flexible table and tree implementation that allows full styling. For other components you can use custom widgets or use a `PaintListener` to draw on top of the widget.

NOTE: To turn off styling completely, you can provide the `cssTheme none` parameter as a launch argument.

91. Styling using themes

Styling can be defined via two means:

* Using themes - allows dynamic theme switching
* Using applicationCSS - allows defining fixed styling

You can define *themes* for styling your application. This can be done via extensions in the *plugin.xml* file. To create new themes you define extensions for the `org.eclipse.e4.ui.css.swt.theme` extension point. Such an extension defines an ID for the style and a pointer to the CSS file.

You can define the default theme via the `cssTheme` property in your `org.eclipse.core.runtime.products` extension. This can be used to define a fixed styling.

> You need to set `cssTheme`, otherwise the theming service is not available at runtime.

The Eclipse platform provides the theme service with an instance of the `IThemeEngine` interface. Via this instance you can change the active theme at runtime. The switching of themes is demonstrated in the following handler code.

```
package com.vogella.tasks.ui.handlers;

import org.eclipse.e4.core.di.annotations.Execute;
import org.eclipse.e4.ui.css.swt.theme.IThemeEngine;

public class ThemeSwitchHandler {
    private static final String DEFAULT_THEME = "com.vogella.eclipse.css.default";
    private static final String RAINBOW_THEME = "com.vogella.eclipse.css.rainbow";

    @Execute
    public void switchTheme(IThemeEngine engine) {
        if (!engine.getActiveTheme().getId().equals(DEFAULT_THEME)){
            // second argument defines that change is
            // persisted and restored on restart
            engine.setTheme(DEFAULT_THEME, true);
        } else {
            engine.setTheme(RAINBOW_THEME, true);
        }
    }
}
```

You can specify a fixed styling of your application. This is done via a property for the `org.eclipse.core.runtime.products` extension point in the *plugin.xml* file.

The value of the `applicationCSS` property points to your CSS file via a URI. The URI follows the `platform:/plugin/BundleSymbolicName/path/file` convention. The following example demonstrates such a URI:

```
platform:/plugin/com.vogella.tasks.ui/css/default.css
```

The screenshot shows an example of the *plugin.xml* file with a defined `applicationCSS` property.

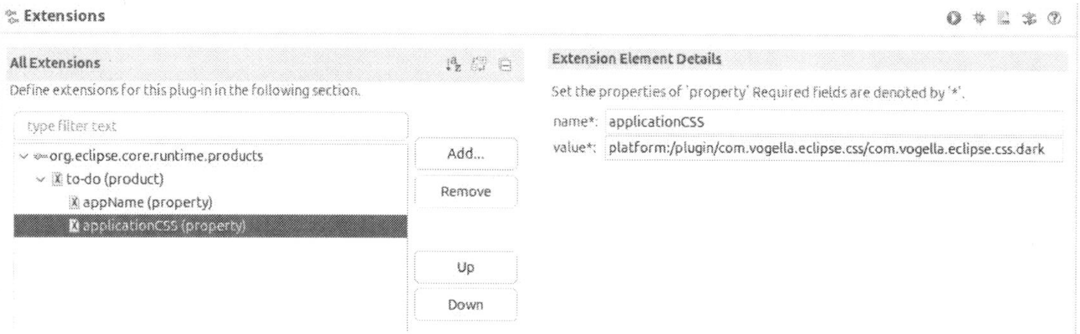

The corresponding file is shown below.

```
<?eclipse version="3.4"?>
<plugin>

 <extension
   id="product"
   point="org.eclipse.core.runtime.products">
  <product
    application="org.eclipse.e4.ui.workbench.swt.E4Application"
    name="to-do">
   <property
       name="appName"
       value="to-do">
   <property
     name="applicationCSS"
     value="platform:/plugin/com.example.e4.rcp.todo/css/default.css">
  </product>
 </extension>

</plugin>
```

92. CSS support for standard Eclipse elements

92.1. CSS attributes and selectors

CSS selectors used in Eclipse are identifiers that relate to widgets or other elements, for example, predefined pseudo classes. Non-standard properties are prefixed with either swt- or eclipse-.

You can use the swt-data-class attribute to query the class hierarchy of an object. For example, the following selector will identify all `Shells` elements from a JFace dialog:

```
Shell[swt-data-class ~= 'org.eclipse.jface.dialogs.Dialog'] {

    background-color: rgb(236, 245, 250);
    swt-background-mode: force;
}
```

The CSS attributes for SWT widgets that can be styled are listed under the following link: https://github.com/eclipse-platform/eclipse.platform.ui/blob/master/docs/CSS.md

Model elements of your Eclipse application, e.g., *MPartStack* or *MPart* can be used as selectors for styling. The CSS selectors are based on the Java classes for the model elements. Some examples are given in the following table.

Table 25. Model elements and CSS selectors

Model Element	CSS Selector
MPart	.MPart
MPartStack	.MPartStack
MPartSashContainer	.MPartSashContainer

For example, you could hide the minimize and maximize button of a *MPartStack* via the following CSS rule.

```
.MPartStack {
    swt-maximize-visible: false;
    swt-minimize-visible: false;
}
```

92.2. CSS pseudo classes in Eclipse

Eclipse supports *CSS pseudo classes*, but these are disabled by default. You can enable them via the Java property `org.eclipse.e4.ui.css.dynamic=true`.

The following table lists several of the available pseudo classes.

Table 26. CSS pseudo classes in Eclipse

CSS pseudo classes	Description
Button:checked	Selects checked buttons
:active	For example, shell:active selects the active shell

CSS pseudo classes	Description
:selected	Allows you to style a selected element, e.g., a part in a PartStack.

```
Button {
    background: yellow;
}

Button:checked {
    background: blue;
}

Button:disabled {
    background: green;
}
```

You can test the effect of this CSS with the following coding.

```
Button pushButton = ButtonFactory.newButton(SWT.PUSH).text("Press me").create(parent);
Button checkButton= ButtonFactory.newButton(SWT.CHECK).onSelect(t -> pushButton
.setEnabled(!pushButton.getEnabled())).text("Press me").create(parent);
checkButton.setSelection(true);
```

Currently, only the `selected` property of the button (checked) is evaluated dynamically. This could be enhanced in the framework, but would require a code contribution.

See Pseudo classes in SWT [https://github.com/eclipse-platform/eclipse.platform.ui/blob/master/docs/CSS.md#Pseudo-classes-which-can-be-used-in-CSS-to-style-SWT-widgets] for the project documentation.

92.3. Styling based on a CSS class or ID

You can assign a CSS ID or class to widgets in your source code and use them as selectors for styling. An identifier is supposed to be unique while a class can be assigned to several elements.

The following example demonstrates how to set an identifier and a class on SWT widgets.

```
// IStylingEngine is injected
@Inject IStylingEngine engine;

// more code....

Label label = new Label(parent, SWT.NONE);
```

```
Text text = new Text(parent, SWT.BORDER);

// set the ID, should be unique in the same window
engine.setID(label, "MyCSSTagForLabel");

// set the class, can be used several times
engine.setClassname(text, "error");
```

The `setID` and `setClassname` methods use the `setData` method on the widget. You could use the SWT `setData` method directly, as demonstrated in the following example.

```
// more code....

Label label = new Label(parent, SWT.NONE);
Text text = new Text(parent, SWT.BORDER);

// set the ID, must be unique in the same window
text.setData("org.eclipse.e4.ui.css.id", "MyCSSTagForLabel");

// set the class, can be used several times
label.setData("org.eclipse.e4.ui.css.CssClassName", "MyCSSTagForLabel")
```

These IDs or classes can be addressed in the CSS file via the **#** or the `.` selector.

```
#MyCSSTagForLabel{
    color: blue;
}

.error {
    border: 1px red;
}
```

Another example would be the assignment of an image to a label via CSS.

```
#logo {
    background-image:
url('platform:/plugin/com.vogella.rcp.customization/icons/img_login.png');
}
```

On the label you must set the CSS id or the class.

```
imgLabel.setData("org.eclipse.e4.ui.css.id", "logo");
```

92.4. Ignore certain widgets during styling

The `org.eclipse.e4.ui.css.disabled` key can be used to instruct the CSS engine to ignore certain widgets.

```
// more code....
yourWidget.setData("org.eclipse.e4.ui.css.disabled", Boolean.TRUE);
```

92.5. Colors and gradients

Colors can be defined in different ways. For example, the color white can be described as `white`, `rgb(255,255,255)` or `#ffffff`.

Since Eclipse 4.3 color constants from SWT can be used, e.g., `SWT.COLOR_BLACK` or `SWT.COLOR_WIDGET_BACKGROUND`.

```
Text {
    color: COLOR-CYAN;
    background-color: COLOR-WIDGET-BACKGROUND;
}

.MPart .InfoPane {
    color: COLOR-INFO-FOREGROUND;
    background-color: COLOR-INFO-BACKGROUND;
}
```

Note that the CSS value uses a "-" whereas the SWT constants use an "_".

Styling supports gradients for the background color of user interface widgets. Linear and radial gradients are supported. The definition of gradients is demonstrated in the following listing.

```
/* linear gradient */
/* background-color: gradient linear color_1 [color_2]* [percentage]* */

/* for example */
background-color: gradient linear white black
background-color: gradient linear white black blue
background-color: gradient linear white black 50%
background-color: gradient linear white black 50% 20%

/* radial gradient */
/* background-color: gradient radial color_1 [color_2]* [percentage]* */

/* for example */
```

```
background-color: gradient radial white black
background-color: gradient radial white black 50%
```

If you use the optional percentage in the definition, then the color change will be done after the defined percentage. The following picture shows the result of different settings.

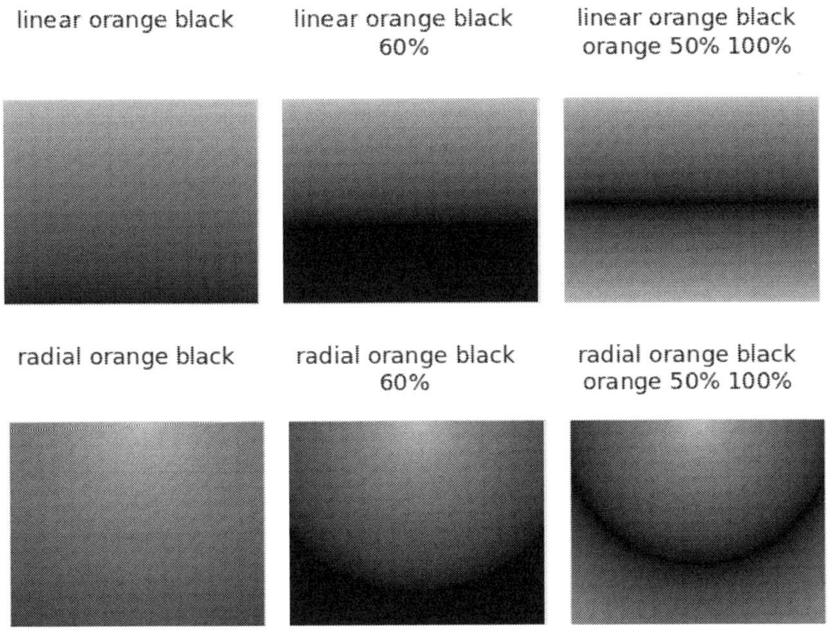

> The current gradient specification is not compliant with the CSS specification and it might change in the future.

92.6. CSS imports

Eclipse supports the import of existing stylesheets via the `@import` directive using the platform URI notation.

For example, the following stylesheet would import an existing dark theme of the `org.vogella.ui.themes` plug-in.

```
@import url("platform:/plugin/org.vogella.ui.themes/css/e4-dark.css");

/* add new CSS rules here. You can also override settings defined in the imported CSS
by using the same selector-property combination */
```

> If you import CSS files from another plug-in, it requires that the plug-in that

contains the imported CSS file is included in your runtime.

92.7. Extending an existing theme

You can add additional styling to an existing theme. For example, if you defined additional settings for the default dark theme of the Eclipse IDE in a file called `css\additional.css`, you can register it with the following extension.

```
<extension
        point="org.eclipse.e4.ui.css.swt.theme">
    <stylesheet
          uri="css/additional.css">
        <themeid
              refid="org.eclipse.e4.ui.css.theme.e4_dark">
        </themeid>
    </stylesheet>
  </extension>
```

92.8. Example: Hide the close button

You can hide the close button of your parts with the following CSS.

```
CTabItem {
    swt-show-close: false !important;
}
```

93. CSS Tools

93.1. CSS Spy

The *CSS spy* tool helps you see the possible styling options for selected elements. *CSS spy* is part of the *e4 tooling* project and can be installed from its update site.

You can open the *CSS spy* via the `Shift` + `Alt` + `F5` shortcut.

CSS spy allows you to see the available properties and the current style settings.

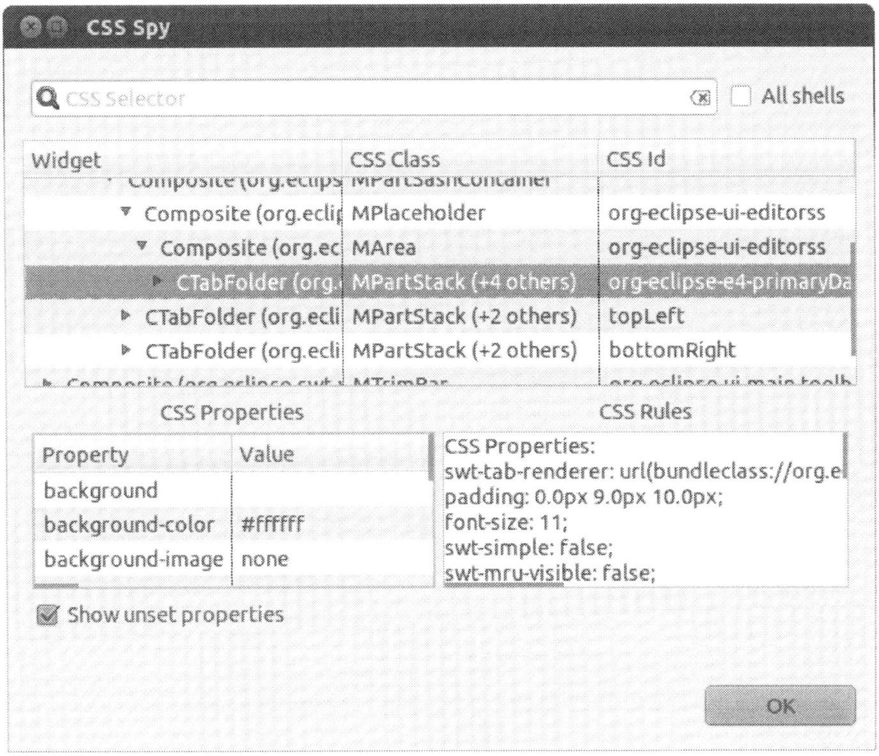

93.2. CSS Scratchpad

The *CSS Scratchpad* allows you to change CSS rules interactively. It is part of the *e4 tooling* project.

You open it via the `Ctrl` + `Shift` + `Alt` + `F6` shortcut.

If you click the Apply button, the entered CSS is applied at runtime to your application.

94. Exercise: Use CSS styling

In this exercise, you style your application. The user can switch the styling at runtime.

94.1. Create a new plug-in and add dependencies

Create a new simple plug-in named `com.vogella.eclipse.css`. See Chapter 36 for more information.

Add the `org.eclipse.e4.ui.css.swt.theme` plug-in as a plug-in dependency to the manifest file of your new plug-in.

94.2. Create the CSS files

Create a folder named `css` in the root of your `com.vogella.eclipse.css` plug-in. Create the following *css/default.css* file.

```
Label, Button {
    font: Verdana 10px;
    background-color: #e0e0e0;
    color: black;
}

Text {
    font: Verdana 10px;
}

Table, Tree {
    background-color: #f2f2f2;
    swt-header-background-color: #d0d0d0;
    swt-header-color: black;
    color: black;
}

Composite Text {
    background-color: white;
    color: black;
}

SashForm {
    background-color: #c1d5ef;
}

.MTrimBar {
    color: white;
    font: Verdana 8px;
}

Shell, Composite, .MTrimBar {
    background-color: #e0e0e0;
}

CTabItem:selected {
    background-color: #d0d0d0;
    color: black;
}
```

In addition, create the following *css/rainbow.css* file.

```
Shell {
    swt-background-mode: default;
    background-color: red orange yellow green orange 30% 60% 75% 95%
}

.MPartStack {
    font-size: 22px;
    color: orange;
}
```

94.3. Create the theme extensions

Select the *Extensions* tab in the `MANIFEST.MF` editor.

> If the *Extensions* tab does not exist, click on the *Extensions* link in the *Overview* tab.

Create two extensions for the `org.eclipse.e4.ui.css.swt.theme` extension point. For this, press the Add... button in the *Extensions* tab.

Select the `org.eclipse.e4.ui.css.swt.theme` extension point and press the Finish button.

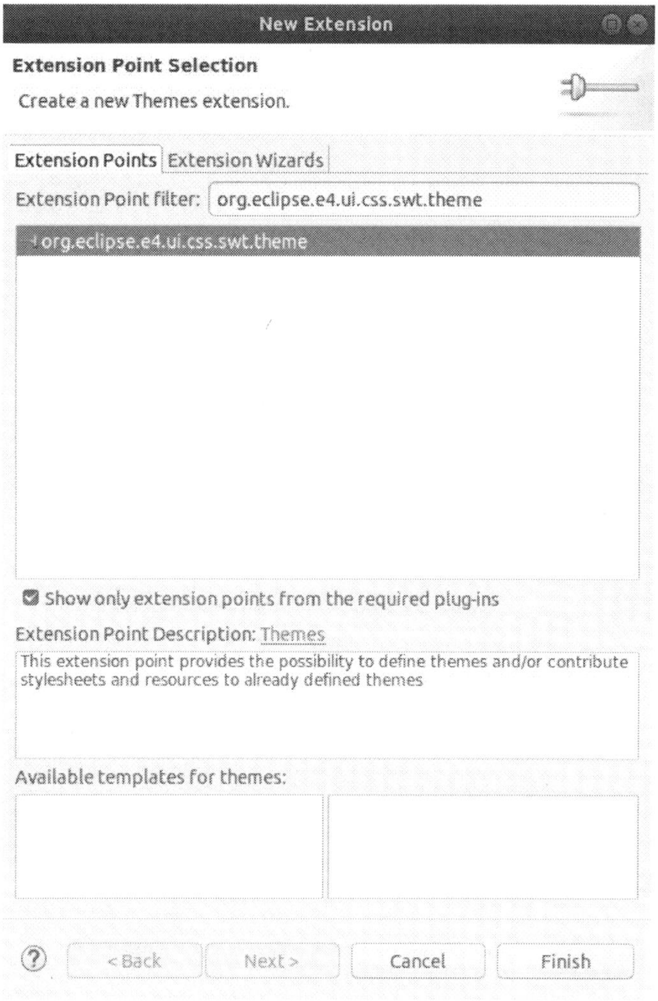

Right-click on the `org.eclipse.e4.ui.css.swt.theme` extension and select the **New › theme** menu entry to create a new theme.

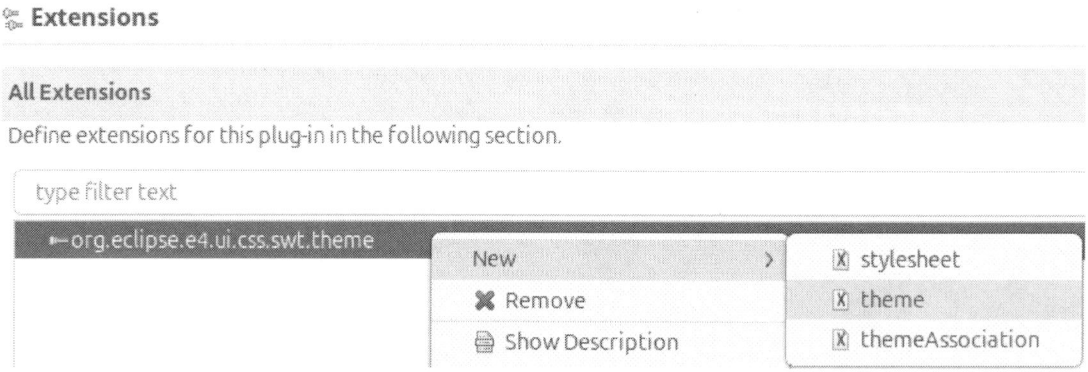

The following screenshots show the extensions you should create.

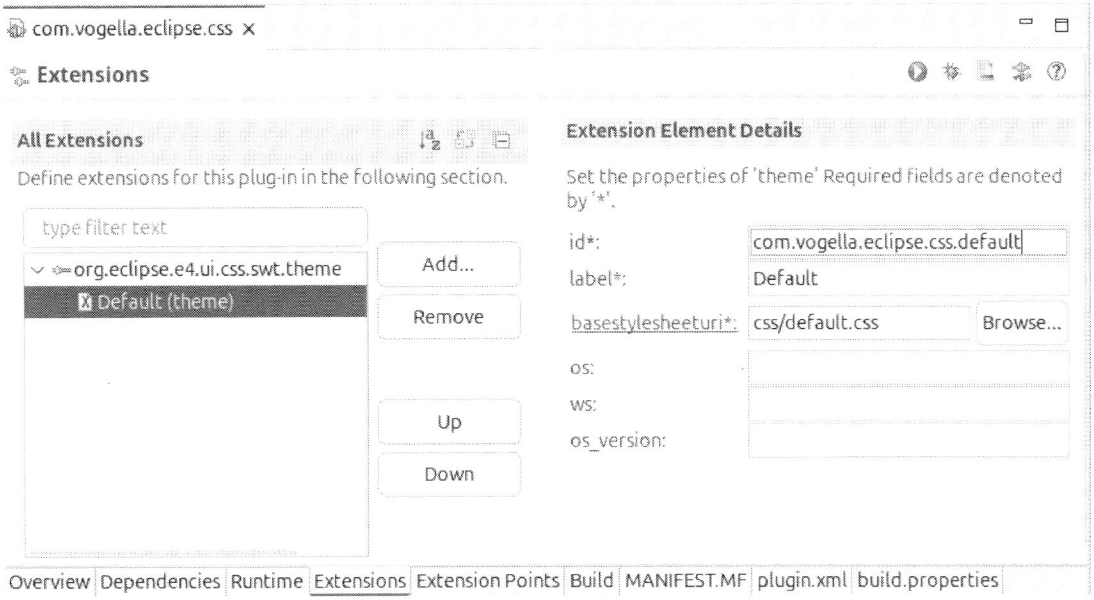

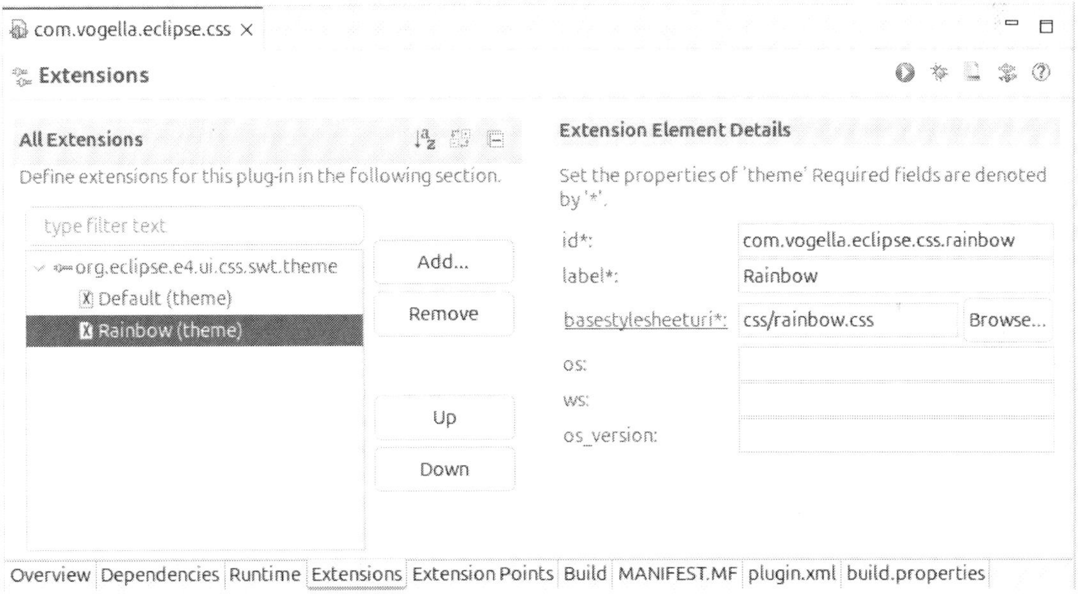

If you open the *plugin.xml* tab in the `MANIFEST.MF` editor or if you open the *plugin.xml* file in a text editor, it should look similar to the following listing.

```
<?xml version="1.0" encoding="UTF-8"?>
<?eclipse version="3.4"?>
<plugin>
   <extension
         point="org.eclipse.e4.ui.css.swt.theme">
      <theme
            basestylesheeturi="css/default.css"
```

```
            id="com.vogella.eclipse.css.default"
            label="Default">
      </theme>
      <theme
            basestylesheeturi="css/rainbow.css"
            id="com.vogella.eclipse.css.rainbow"
            label="Rainbow">
      </theme>
   </extension>

</plugin>
```

94.4. Adjust the build.properties file

Make sure all CSS files are included in your build through the *build.properties* file of your plug-in. This makes them available in the exported application.

The `build.properties` file should look similar to the following listing:

```
source.. = src/
output.. = bin/
bin.includes = META-INF/,\
               .,\
               plugin.xml,\
               css/
```

94.5. Setting the default theme in the application

Now you need to configure the default theme via a property on your product extension.

For this, open the `plugin.xml` file in your `com.vogella.tasks.ui` plug-in and select the *Extensions* tab. Add the `cssTheme` property to your product and point to the `com.vogella.eclipse.css.default` theme.

To add a new property, right-click on the product and click on *property* to add a new property. Do NOT press the Add... button.

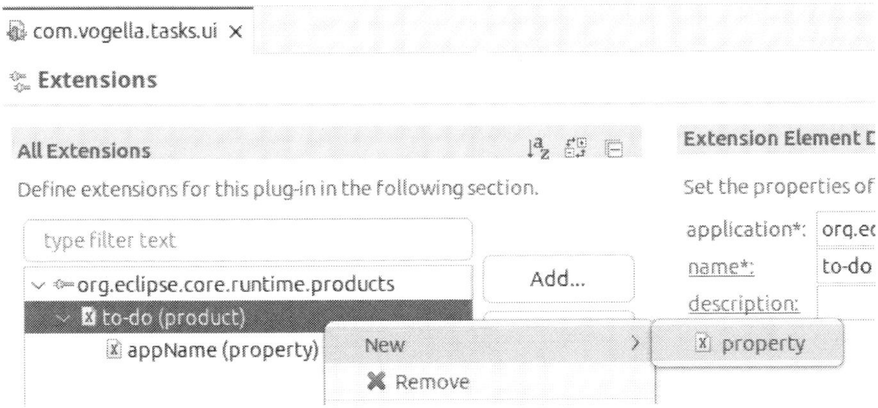

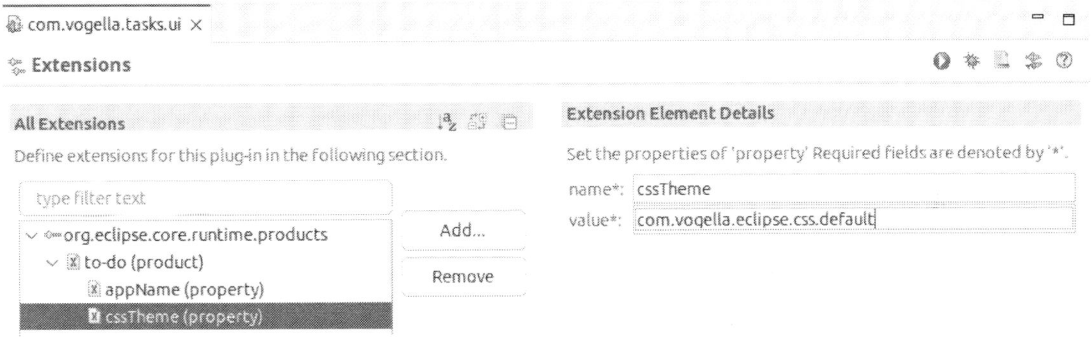

This must be done in the `com.vogella.tasks.ui` plug-in and NOT the `com.vogella.eclipse.css` plug-in.

If present, remove an existing entry for `applicationCSS`. `applicationCSS` is an alternative way to define fixed styling for the application, but it is not used in this exercise.

Ensure that the `cssTheme` property is correctly set. Without it, the `IThemeEngine` does not work.

The entry in the `plugin.xml` of `com.vogella.tasks.ui` should look similar to the following:

```
<?xml version="1.0" encoding="UTF-8"?>
<?eclipse version="3.4"?>
<plugin>

   <extension
         id="product"
         point="org.eclipse.core.runtime.products">
      <product
            name="to-do"
            application="org.eclipse.e4.ui.workbench.swt.E4Application">
         <property
```

```
                name="appName"
                value="Task Management">
            </property>
            <property>
                name="cssTheme"
                value="com.vogella.eclipse.css.default">
            </property>
        </product>
    </extension>

</plugin>
```

94.6. Add the new plug-in to the product (via the feature)

Add your `com.vogella.eclipse.css` plug-in to your feature. Afterward, start the application via the product configuration file.

94.7. Validate

Start your application and ensure that the application is styled according to the `cssTheme` property setting. Your application might look similar to the following (screenshot from Linux):

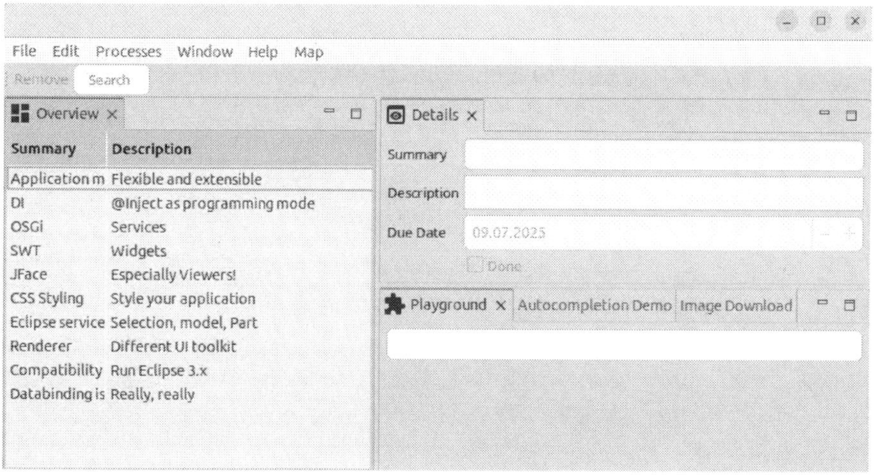

94.8. Improve the styling

Try adjusting the colors and styling of your application to achieve a visually appealing design.

95. Exercise: Implementing dynamic theme switching

In this exercise, you use the `IThemeEngine` service to change the theme at runtime.

> `IThemeEngine` has not yet been released as an official API. If you use it, you

will see the message `The type 'IThemeEngine' is not API`. Since there is no official API for theme switching yet, you need to rely on this provisional one.

95.1. Ensure you have a plug-in or package dependency on the theme engine

Ensure you have a plug-in or package dependency on the theme engine `org.eclipse.e4.ui.css.swt.theme` in your manifest file of `com.vogella.tasks.ui`.

If you have it already, it will be filtered from the available additions if you press the Add button. Do NOT add a dependency to the source plug-in.

95.2. Implement a new menu entry

Create a new Java class that allows you to switch between the themes.

```
package com.vogella.tasks.ui.handlers;

import org.eclipse.e4.core.di.annotations.Execute;
import org.eclipse.e4.ui.css.swt.theme.IThemeEngine;

public class ThemeSwitchHandler {
    private static final String DEFAULT_THEME = "com.vogella.eclipse.css.default";
    private static final String RAINBOW_THEME = "com.vogella.eclipse.css.rainbow";

    @Execute
    public void switchTheme(IThemeEngine engine) {
        if (!engine.getActiveTheme().getId().equals(DEFAULT_THEME)){
            // second argument defines that change is
            // persisted and restored on restart
            engine.setTheme(DEFAULT_THEME, true);
        } else {
            engine.setTheme(RAINBOW_THEME, true);
        }
    }
}
```

Define a new command and a handler in your application model for switching the style. Assign the above class to the handler.

Add a menu entry to the application model to use your handler for style switching.

95.3. Validate theme switching

Start the application and select your new menu entry. Afterwards, the styling of your application should use the *rainbow* theme.

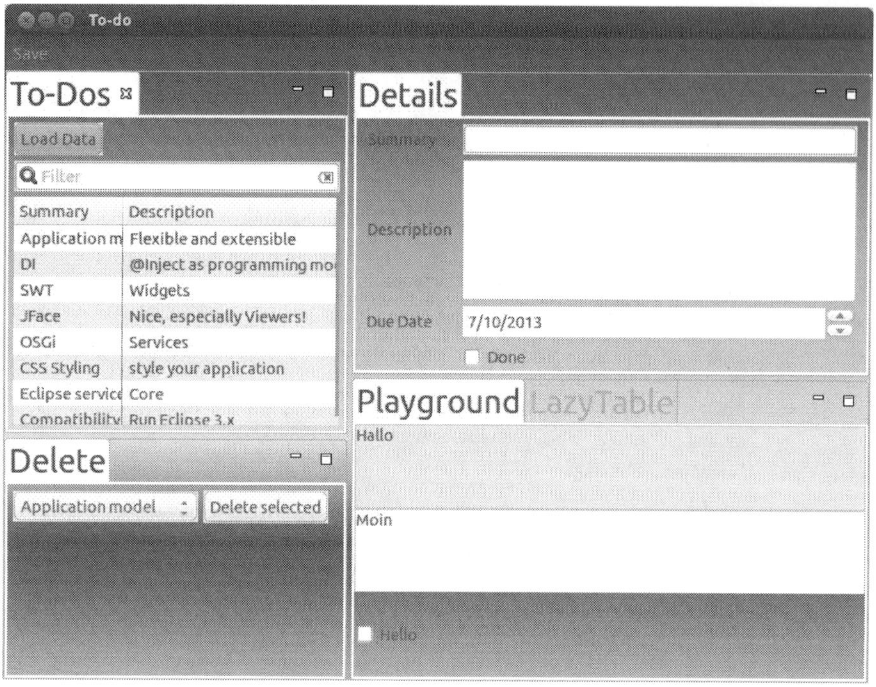

Changes in styling may require a restart of your application. The CSS engine resets the majority of the SWT properties, but not all widgets respond to this reset.

96. Optional exercise: Implement a dark theme

Define a new theme, this time a dark theme, in the `plugin.xml` file. Here is an example for a CSS file that defines a dark theme.

```
CTabFolder {
    color: #bbbbbb; /* Inactive tab text */
    swt-tab-outline: #2a2a2a; /* Border color for selected tab */
    swt-outer-keyline-color: #3a3a3a; /* Border color for the tabs container */
    swt-unselected-tabs-color: #2e2e2e #252525 100% 100%; /* Background for unselected
tabs */
    swt-selected-tab-fill: #3d3d3d; /* Background for selected tab */
    swt-unselected-hot-tab-color-background: #161616; /* Hovered tab background */
    swt-selected-tab-highlight: none;
}

CTabFolder.active {
    swt-selected-tab-highlight: #316c9b;
    swt-selected-highlight-top: false;
```

```
}

CTabItem,
CTabItem CLabel {
    background-color: #3d3d3d;
    color: #999999; /* Inactive, unselected tab text */
}

CTabItem.busy {
    color: #888888;
}

Text, Composite, Button, Shell, Composite {
    background-color: #3d3d3d;
    color: #bbbbbb; /* Light grey text color */
}

Label {
    color: #3d3d3d /* Light grey text color */
}

Shell {
    background-color: #3d3d3d;
    color: #e0e0e0;
}

Shell Label {
    background-color: #3d3d3d;
    color: #e0e0e0;
}

.MTrimBar {
    background-color: #3d3d3d;
    color:           #e0e0e0;
}

/* Base table & tree background and text */
Table, Tree {
    swt-header-background-color: #333333;
    swt-header-color: #d0d0d0;
    background-color: #2b2b2b;
    color:           #e0e0e0;
    font-size:       12px;
}
```

Add another menu entry to your application model to switch to the *dark* theme.

The result may look similar to the following screenshot (taken under Linux).

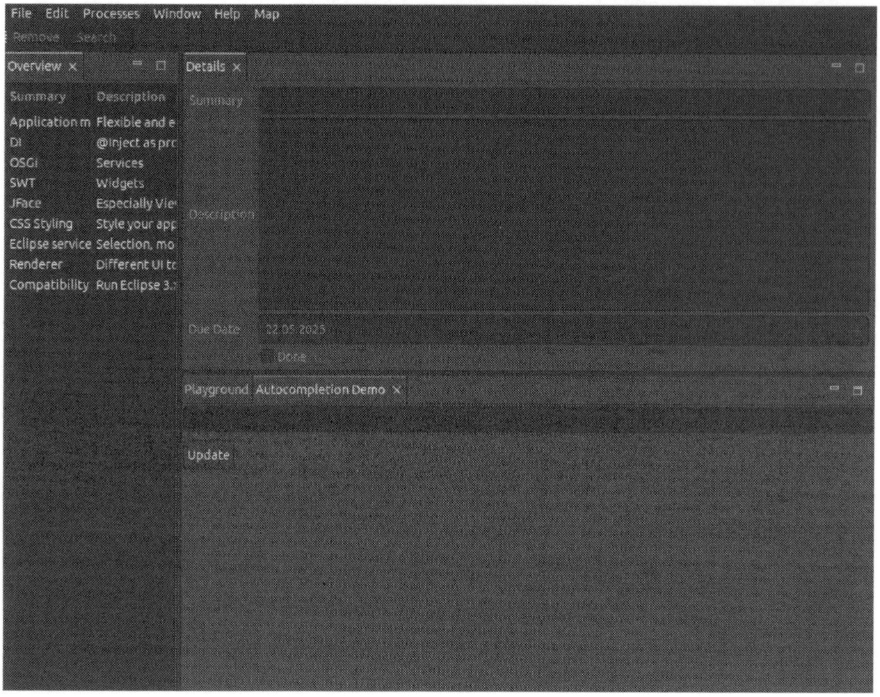

The `DateTime` widget can currently not be styled via CSS under Windows. This is a limitation in the Windows API.

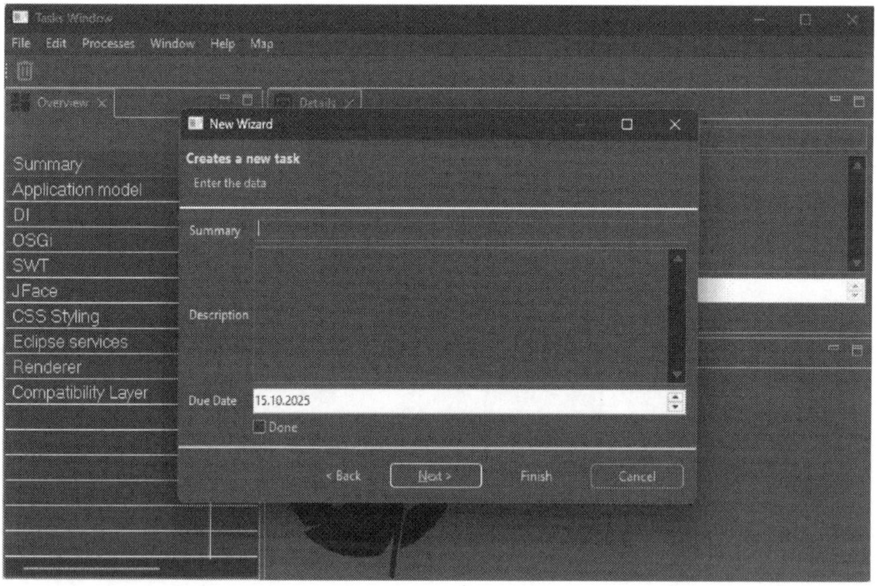

97. Optional exercise: Use the CSS spy

Start the CSS spy in your Eclipse IDE via **Windows › Spies › CSS Spy**.

Add the CSS Spy temporarily to your runtime application using the same way you integrated the model spy.

Use the CSS spy to analyze the widgets and their CSS properties.

Only a few CSS attributes can be changed via the CSS spy at runtime, as the developers of the spies wanted to have a fast way to change these attributes. As the CSS spy is Open Source, others could add the functionality to modify more CSS attributes at runtime.

98. Optional exercise: Create a custom CTabFolderRenderer

The target of this exercise is to create custom tabs for an Eclipse application.

98.1. Ensure that certain dependencies are present

In the `com.vogella.eclipse.css` plug-in, ensure you have at least the following plug-ins available in your `MANIFEST.MF`.

- org.eclipse.jface

98.2. Create a custom CTabFolderRenderer

Continue to use the `com.vogella.eclipse.css` plug-in for this part of the exercise. Create a package named *com.vogella.eclipse.css.renderer* and a class named `CustomTabFolderRenderer`, which extends `org.eclipse.swt.custom.CTabFolderRenderer`.

The implementation looks like this:

```
package com.vogella.eclipse.css.renderer;

import org.eclipse.jface.resource.JFaceResources;
import org.eclipse.jface.resource.LocalResourceManager;
import org.eclipse.jface.resource.ResourceManager;
import org.eclipse.swt.SWT;
import org.eclipse.swt.custom.CTabFolder;
import org.eclipse.swt.custom.CTabFolderRenderer;
import org.eclipse.swt.graphics.Color;
import org.eclipse.swt.graphics.GC;
import org.eclipse.swt.graphics.Point;
```

```java
import org.eclipse.swt.graphics.RGB;
import org.eclipse.swt.graphics.Rectangle;

public class CustomTabFolderRenderer extends CTabFolderRenderer {

    private static final int TAB_WIDTH_ADJUSTMENT = 20;
    private static final int TAB_HEIGHT = 50;
    private static final int UNDERLINE_TRIM_HEIGHT = 5;
    private ResourceManager resourceManager;

    public CustomTabFolderRenderer(CTabFolder parent) {
        super(parent);
        // resource manager for proper resource handling
        resourceManager = new LocalResourceManager(JFaceResources.getResources(),
parent);
    }

    @Override
    protected Point computeSize(int part, int state, GC gc, int wHint, int hHint) {
        // get the sizes for other parts of the CTabFolder
        Point computeSize = super.computeSize(part, state, gc, wHint, hHint);

        // handle the size of the tabs
        if (0 <= part && part < parent.getItemCount()) {
            // make parts bigger
            computeSize.x += TAB_WIDTH_ADJUSTMENT;
            // return the computed x size and a fixed tab height
            return new Point(computeSize.x, TAB_HEIGHT);
        }

        return computeSize;
    }

    @Override
    protected void draw(int part, int state, Rectangle bounds, GC gc) {
        // default drawing is done in the super class
        super.draw(part, state, bounds, gc);

        // draw on the selected tab
        adjustSelectedTab(part, state, bounds, gc);
    }

    private void adjustSelectedTab(int part, int state, Rectangle bounds, GC gc) {
        if (0 <= part && part < parent.getItemCount()) {
            if (bounds.width == 0 || bounds.height == 0)
                return;
            if ((state & SWT.SELECTED) != 0) {
                drawHeaderTrim(bounds, gc);
            }
```

```
        }
    }

    private void drawHeaderTrim(Rectangle bounds, GC gc) {
        Color origBg = gc.getBackground();
        Color bgColor = resourceManager.createColor(new RGB(0, 132, 180));
        gc.setBackground(bgColor);
        // draw line at the bottom
        gc.fillRectangle(bounds.x, bounds.y + bounds.height - UNDERLINE_TRIM_HEIGHT,
bounds.width,
                UNDERLINE_TRIM_HEIGHT);
        gc.setBackground(origBg);
    }
}
```

98.3. Apply the custom renderer via CSS

Add the following lines to the `default.css` file in the `com.vogella.eclipse.css` plug-in.

```
.MPartStack, CTabFolder {
    /* Point to the CustomTabFolderRenderer implementation */
    swt-tab-renderer:
url('bundleclass://com.vogella.eclipse.css/com.vogella.eclipse.css.renderer.CustomTabFold
erRenderer');
    background-color: white;
}

.MPart {
    background-color: white;
}

CTabItem {
    background-color: white;
}

CTabItem:selected {
    color: rgb(0, 132, 180);
}
```

98.4. Verify

Start your application and verify that the new tab renderer is applied.

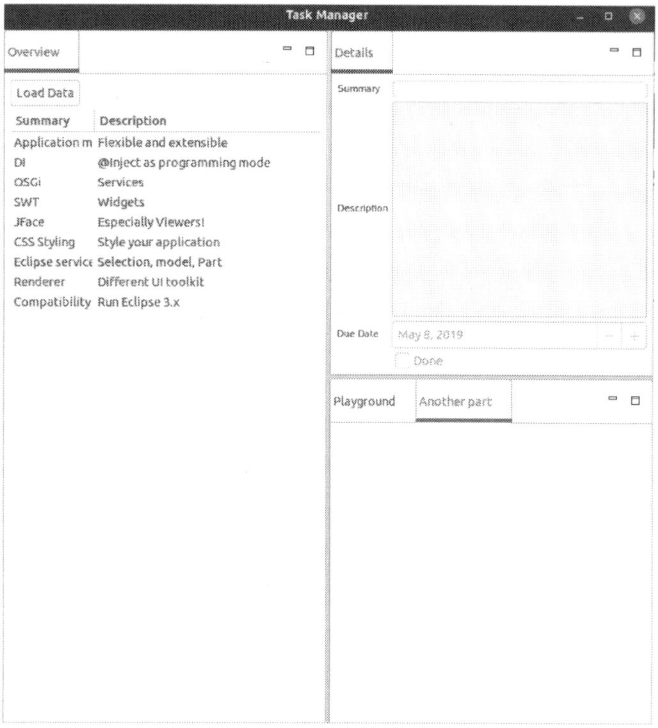

99. Optional exercise: CSS styling for custom widgets

The target of this exercise is to style the custom checkbox widget. This requires the registration of a custom CSS element provider and a property handler.

99.1. Add dependencies

Ensure that the following dependencies are present in the MANIFEST.MF of the *com.vogella.eclipse.css* project:

- org.eclipse.e4.ui.css.swt.theme
- org.eclipse.e4.ui.css.core
- org.eclipse.e4.ui.css.swt
- com.vogella.swt.widgets
- org.eclipse.jface

99.2. Create a custom CSS element provider and a property handler

CSS element provider and property handler can be contributed by the *org.eclipse.e4.ui.css.core.elementProvider* and *org.eclipse.e4.ui.css.core.propertyHandler* extension points.

Add the *org.eclipse.e4.ui.css.core.propertyHandler* to the *plugin.xml* of the *com.vogella.eclipse.css* project.

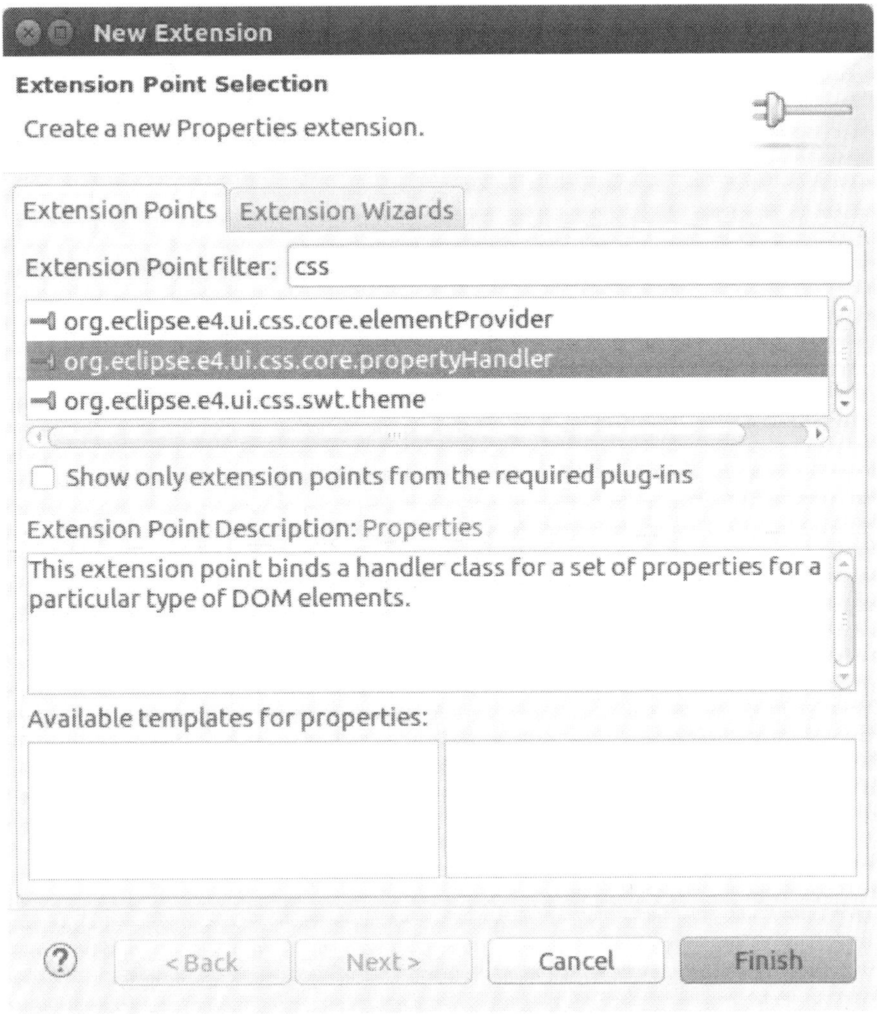

A property handler needs an adapter, the handler, and properties that are handled by the property handler.

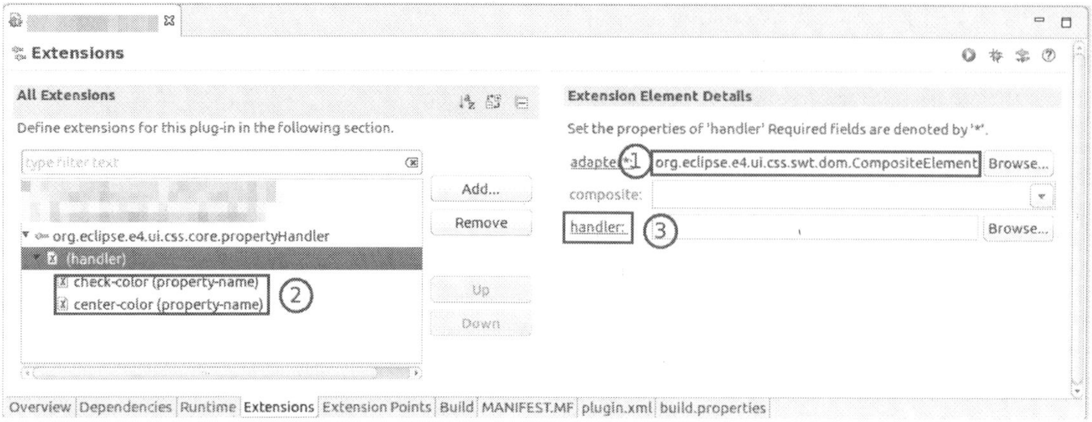

1. Add the `org.eclipse.e4.ui.css.swt.dom.CompositeElement` class as an adapter.
2. Add the *check-color* and *center-color* properties as property names.
3. Press the handler link to create a property handler.

The property handler class should be named `CheckboxPropertyHandler` and extend `org.eclipse.e4.ui.css.swt.properties.AbstractCSSPropertySWTHandler`.

The implementation of the `CheckboxPropertyHandler` should look like this:

```
import org.eclipse.e4.ui.css.core.dom.properties.ICSSPropertyHandler;
import org.eclipse.e4.ui.css.core.dom.properties.converters.ICSSValueConverter;
import org.eclipse.e4.ui.css.core.engine.CSSEngine;
import org.eclipse.e4.ui.css.swt.properties.AbstractCSSPropertySWTHandler;
import org.eclipse.swt.graphics.Color;
import org.eclipse.swt.widgets.Control;
import org.w3c.dom.css.CSSValue;

import com.vogella.swt.widgets.Checkbox;

@SuppressWarnings("restriction")
public class CheckboxPropertyHandler extends AbstractCSSPropertySWTHandler implements
ICSSPropertyHandler {

    private static final String CHECK_COLOR = "check-color";
    private static final String CENTER_COLOR = "center-color";

    @Override
    protected void applyCSSProperty(Control control, String property, CSSValue value,
String pseudo, CSSEngine engine)
            throws Exception {
        if (control instanceof Checkbox) {
            Checkbox checkboxWidget = (Checkbox) control;
            if (CHECK_COLOR.equalsIgnoreCase(property) && (value.getCssValueType() ==
```

```
CSSValue.CSS_PRIMITIVE_VALUE)) {
                Color newColor = (Color) engine.convert(value, Color.class, control
.getDisplay());
                checkboxWidget.setCheckColor(newColor);
            } else if (CENTER_COLOR.equalsIgnoreCase(property)
                    && (value.getCssValueType() == CSSValue.CSS_PRIMITIVE_VALUE)) {
                Color newColor = (Color) engine.convert(value, Color.class, control
.getDisplay());
                checkboxWidget.setCenterColor(newColor);
            }
        }
    }

    @Override
    protected String retrieveCSSProperty(Control control, String property, String pseudo,
CSSEngine engine)
            throws Exception {
        if (control instanceof Checkbox) {
            Checkbox checkboxWidget = (Checkbox) control;
            if (CHECK_COLOR.equalsIgnoreCase(property)) {
                ICSSValueConverter cssValueConverter = engine.getCSSValueConverter(
String.class);
                return cssValueConverter.convert(checkboxWidget.getCheckColor(), engine,
null);
            } else if (CENTER_COLOR.equalsIgnoreCase(property)) {
                ICSSValueConverter cssValueConverter = engine.getCSSValueConverter(
String.class);
                return cssValueConverter.convert(checkboxWidget.getCenterColor(), engine,
null);
            }
        }
        return null;
    }
}
```

The CSS implementation is currently not an API, so without `@SuppressWarnings("restriction")` you will see warnings.

99.3. Adjust CSS file

Add the following contents to the default CSS file:

```
Checkbox {
    check-color: yellow;
    center-color: gray;
    color: yellow;
    background-color: black;
```

```
}
```

99.4. Validate

Start your product via the product configuration file. Ensure you are using the default CSS theme and validate that the checkbox inner colors are according to your CSS configuration.

Part XII: Dialogs and wizards

100. Dialogs in Eclipse

Eclipse allows you to use *dialogs* to prompt the user for additional information or provide the user with feedback. The Eclipse platform offers several standard dialogs via SWT and JFace.

101. SWT dialogs

SWT provides an API to use the native dialogs from the OS platform.

The default SWT dialogs are listed below.

- `ColorDialog` - for selecting a color
- `DirectoryDialog` - for selecting a directory
- `FileDialog` - for selecting a file
- `FontDialog` - for selecting a font
- `MessageBox` - for opening a message dialog

The following code demonstrates the usage of the `MessageBox` class to open a message dialog.

```
// create a dialog with ok and cancel buttons and a question icon
MessageBox dialog = new MessageBox(shell, SWT.ICON_QUESTION | SWT.OK| SWT.CANCEL);
```

```
dialog.setText("My info");
dialog.setMessage("Do you really want to do this?");

// open dialog and await user selection
returnCode = dialog.open();
```

102. JFace Dialogs

102.1. Dialogs from JFace

JFace contains several frequently used dialogs that are not based on the native dialogs as well as a framework for building custom dialogs.

> Even though JFace dialogs are not native, they follow the native platform semantics for things like the button order.

102.2. Using the builder API for creating message dialogs

It is possible to use a builder API to create a message dialog.

```
PlainMessageDialog.getBuilder(shell, "Copied to clipboard").message("Selected task copied
to clipboard. Paste in any editor")
            .buttonLabels(List.of("Close")).build().open();
```

102.3. Using the static helper methods of the JFace MessageDialog class

The `MessageDialog` class provides static methods to open commonly used dialogs, for example an information or a warning dialog. The following code demonstrates the usage of these static methods.

```
// standard message dialogs
MessageDialog.openConfirm(shell, "Confirm", "Please confirm");
MessageDialog.openError(shell, "Error", "Error occurred");
MessageDialog.openInformation(shell, "Info", "Info for you");
MessageDialog.openQuestion(shell, "Question", "Really, really?");
MessageDialog.openWarning(shell, "Warning", "I am warning you!");
```

The resulting dialogs are depicted in the following screenshots.

102.4. Using the JFace MessageDialog class directly

The `MessageDialog` class allows the customization of the buttons in the dialog.

The following code demonstrates its usage.

```
// customized MessageDialog with configured buttons
MessageDialog dialog = new MessageDialog(shell, "My Title", null,
    "My message", MessageDialog.ERROR, new String[] { "First",
    "Second", "Third" }, 0);
int result = dialog.open();
System.out.println(result);
```

If you open this dialog, it looks similar to the following screenshot.

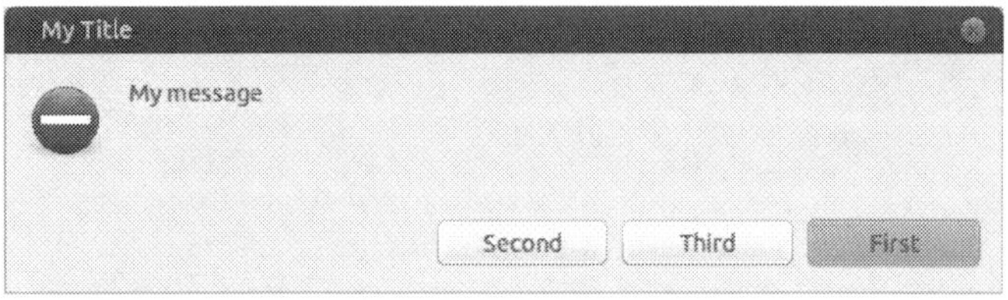

The display of the default button is platform-dependent; the above screenshot shows it on Linux.

Several of these dialogs return the user selection, e.g., the `openConfirm()` method returns true if the user selected the OK button. The following example code prompts the user for confirmation and handles the result.

```
boolean result =
    MessageDialog.openConfirm(shell, "Confirm", "Please confirm");

if (result){
 // OK Button selected do something
} else {
 // Cancel Button selected do something
}
```

102.5. ErrorDialog

The `ErrorDialog` class can be used to display one or more errors to the user. If an error contains additional detailed information then a button is automatically added, which shows or hides this information when pressed by the user.

The following snippet shows a handler class that uses this dialog.

```
package com.vogella.tasks.ui.handlers;

import java.util.ArrayList;
import java.util.List;

import org.eclipse.core.runtime.IStatus;
import org.eclipse.core.runtime.MultiStatus;
import org.eclipse.core.runtime.Status;
import org.eclipse.e4.core.di.annotations.Execute;
import org.eclipse.e4.ui.model.application.ui.basic.MWindow;
import org.eclipse.jface.dialogs.ErrorDialog;
import org.eclipse.swt.widgets.Shell;

public class ShowErrorDialogHandler {
    @Execute
```

```
    public void execute(final Shell shell, MWindow window) {
        // create exception on purpose to demonstrate ErrorDialog
        try {
            String s = null;
            System.out.println(s.length());
        } catch (NullPointerException e) {
            // build the error message and include the current stack trace
            MultiStatus status = createMultiStatus(e.getLocalizedMessage(), e);
            // show error dialog
            ErrorDialog.openError(shell, "Error", "This is an error", status);
        }
    }

    private static MultiStatus createMultiStatus(String msg, Throwable t) {

        List<Status> childStatuses = new ArrayList<>();
        StackTraceElement[] stackTraces = Thread.currentThread().getStackTrace();

        for (StackTraceElement stackTrace: stackTraces) {
            Status status = new Status(IStatus.ERROR,
                    "com.vogella.tasks.ui", stackTrace.toString());
            childStatuses.add(status);
        }

        MultiStatus ms = new MultiStatus("com.vogella.tasks.ui",
                IStatus.ERROR, childStatuses.toArray(new Status[] {}),
                t.toString(), t);
        return ms;
    }
}
```

If you trigger this handler, the dialog shows the exception messages and allows access to details. The detail page contains the stack trace, as depicted in the following screenshot.

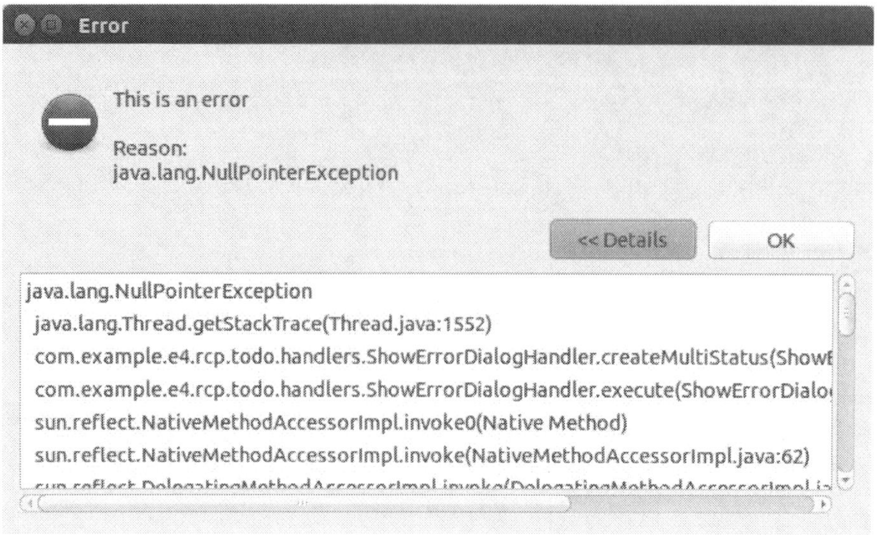

102.6. Creating a custom dialog

The `org.eclipse.jface.dialogs.Dialog` class can be extended to create your own dialog implementation. This class creates an area in which you can place controls and it adds a OK and a Cancel button by default. The method to create these buttons can be overridden if you want to display custom buttons.

Your class needs to implement the `createDialogArea()` method. This method receives a `Composite` that expects to have a `GridData` object assigned as its layout data. Via the `super.createDialogArea(parent)` method call, you can create a `Composite` to which you can add your controls. This is demonstrated by the following example code.

```
package com.vogella.plugin.dialogs.custom;

import org.eclipse.jface.dialogs.Dialog;
import org.eclipse.swt.SWT;
import org.eclipse.swt.events.SelectionAdapter;
import org.eclipse.swt.events.SelectionEvent;
import org.eclipse.swt.graphics.Point;
import org.eclipse.swt.layout.GridData;
import org.eclipse.swt.widgets.Button;
import org.eclipse.swt.widgets.Composite;
import org.eclipse.swt.widgets.Control;
import org.eclipse.swt.widgets.Shell;

public class MyDialog extends Dialog {

    public MyDialog(Shell parentShell) {
        super(parentShell);
    }
```

```
    @Override
    protected Control createDialogArea(Composite parent) {
        Composite container = (Composite) super.createDialogArea(parent);
        Button button = new Button(container, SWT.PUSH);
        button.setLayoutData(new GridData(SWT.BEGINNING, SWT.CENTER, false,
                false));
        button.setText("Press me");
        button.addSelectionListener(new SelectionAdapter() {
            @Override
            public void widgetSelected(SelectionEvent e) {
                System.out.println("Pressed");
            }
        });

        return container;
    }

    // overriding this methods allows you to set the
    // title of the custom dialog
    @Override
    protected void configureShell(Shell newShell) {
        super.configureShell(newShell);
        newShell.setText("Selection dialog");
    }

    @Override
    protected Point getInitialSize() {
        return new Point(450, 300);
    }
}
```

TIP: The example code demonstrates how to set the title of your custom dialog via the `configureShell()` method.

If you open this dialog it looks similar to the following screenshot.

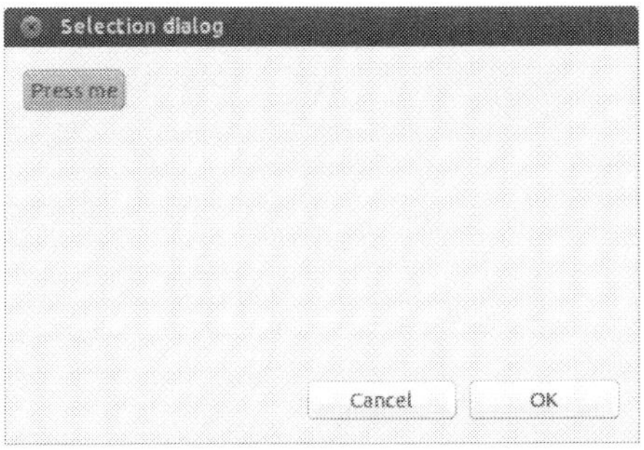

102.7. TitleAreaDialog

You can implement your custom dialog based on the `TitleAreaDialog` class.

`TitleAreaDialog` reserves space for providing user feedback. You can set the text in this space via the `setMessage()` and `setErrorMessage()` methods.

The following example shows a custom defined `TitleAreaDialog`.

```
package com.vogella.plugin.dialogs.custom;

import org.eclipse.jface.dialogs.IMessageProvider;
import org.eclipse.jface.dialogs.TitleAreaDialog;
import org.eclipse.swt.SWT;
import org.eclipse.swt.layout.GridData;
import org.eclipse.swt.layout.GridLayout;
import org.eclipse.swt.widgets.Composite;
import org.eclipse.swt.widgets.Control;
import org.eclipse.swt.widgets.Label;
import org.eclipse.swt.widgets.Shell;
import org.eclipse.swt.widgets.Text;

public class MyTitleAreaDialog extends TitleAreaDialog {

    private Text txtFirstName;
    private Text lastNameText;

    private String firstName;
    private String lastName;

    public MyTitleAreaDialog(Shell parentShell) {
        super(parentShell);
    }

    @Override
    public void create() {
        super.create();
        setTitle("This is my first custom dialog");
        setMessage("This is a TitleAreaDialog", IMessageProvider.INFORMATION);
    }

    @Override
    protected Control createDialogArea(Composite parent) {
        Composite area = (Composite) super.createDialogArea(parent);
        Composite container = new Composite(area, SWT.NONE);
        container.setLayoutData(new GridData(SWT.FILL, SWT.FILL, true, true));
        GridLayout layout = new GridLayout(2, false);
        container.setLayout(layout);
```

```java
        createFirstName(container);
        createLastName(container);

        return area;
    }

    private void createFirstName(Composite container) {
        Label lbtFirstName = new Label(container, SWT.NONE);
        lbtFirstName.setText("First Name");

        GridData dataFirstName = new GridData();
        dataFirstName.grabExcessHorizontalSpace = true;
        dataFirstName.horizontalAlignment = GridData.FILL;

        txtFirstName = new Text(container, SWT.BORDER);
        txtFirstName.setLayoutData(dataFirstName);
    }

    private void createLastName(Composite container) {
        Label lbtLastName = new Label(container, SWT.NONE);
        lbtLastName.setText("Last Name");

        GridData dataLastName = new GridData();
        dataLastName.grabExcessHorizontalSpace = true;
        dataLastName.horizontalAlignment = GridData.FILL;
        lastNameText = new Text(container, SWT.BORDER);
        lastNameText.setLayoutData(dataLastName);
    }

    @Override
    protected boolean isResizable() {
        return true;
    }

    // save content of the Text fields because they get disposed
    // as soon as the Dialog closes
    private void saveInput() {
        firstName = txtFirstName.getText();
        lastName = lastNameText.getText();
    }

    @Override
    protected void okPressed() {
        saveInput();
        super.okPressed();
    }

    public String getFirstName() {
```

```
        return firstName;
    }

    public String getLastName() {
        return lastName;
    }
}
```

This dialog is depicted in the following screenshot.

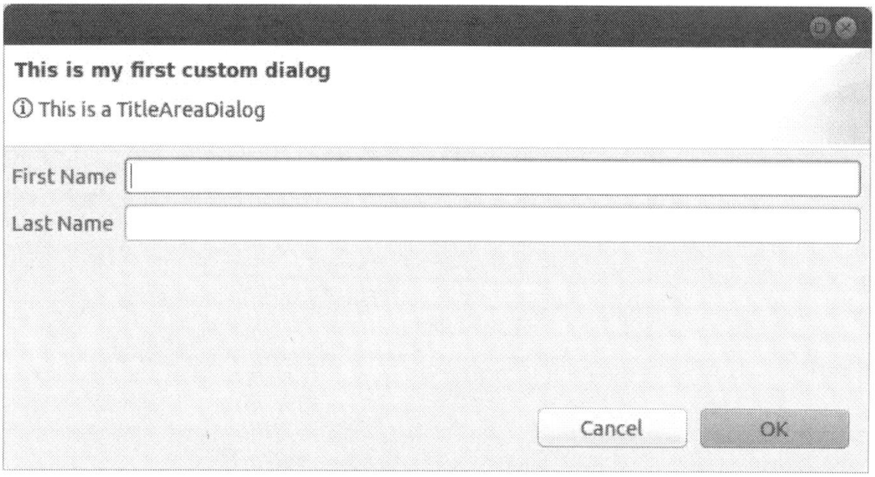

The usage of this dialog is demonstrated in the following code snippet. This code might, for example, be used in a handler.

```
// more imports
import org.eclipse.jface.window.Window;
import org.eclipse.swt.widgets.Shell;


var dialog = new MyTitleAreaDialog(shell);
// just to demonstrate how to set the title background color
dialog.setTitleAreaColor(Display.getDefault().getSystemColor(SWT.COLOR_DARK_GRAY).getRGB(
));

// now open the dialog
dialog.create();
if (dialog.open() == Window.OK) {
    System.out.println(dialog.getFirstName());
    System.out.println(dialog.getLastName());
}
```

NOTE: The title area image and color can be set via the `setTitleImage()` and `setTitleAreaColor()` methods, respectively.

102.8. Creating a non-modal / non-blocking dialog

Use the `setShellStyle` method to create a non-modal dialog.

```
package com.vogella.tasks.ui.handlers;

import org.eclipse.jface.dialogs.Dialog;
import org.eclipse.swt.SWT;
import org.eclipse.swt.graphics.Point;
import org.eclipse.swt.layout.GridData;
import org.eclipse.swt.widgets.Button;
import org.eclipse.swt.widgets.Composite;
import org.eclipse.swt.widgets.Control;
import org.eclipse.swt.widgets.Shell;

public class MyNonModalDialog extends Dialog {

    public MyNonModalDialog(Shell parentShell) {
        super(parentShell);
        setShellStyle(SWT.CLOSE | SWT.MODELESS | SWT.BORDER | SWT.TITLE);
        setBlockOnOpen(false);
    }

    @Override
    protected Control createDialogArea(Composite parent) {
        Composite container = (Composite) super.createDialogArea(parent);
        Button button = new Button(container, SWT.PUSH);
        button.setLayoutData(new GridData(SWT.BEGINNING, SWT.CENTER, false, false));
        button.setText("Press");
        return container;
    }

    @Override
    protected Point getInitialSize() {
        return new Point(450, 300);
    }
}
```

103. Exercise: Create a password dialog

Create a new class called *PasswordDialog* which extends the *Dialog* in your `com.vogella.tasks.ui` plug-in. This dialog allows users to enter a username and a password.

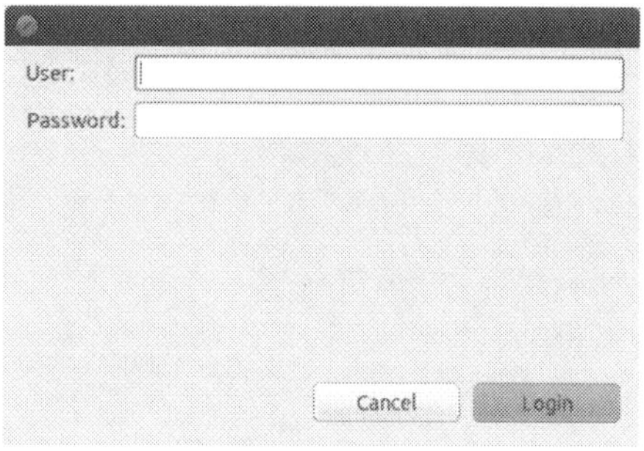


```
package com.vogella.tasks.ui.dialogs;

import org.eclipse.jface.dialogs.Dialog;
import org.eclipse.jface.dialogs.IDialogConstants;
import org.eclipse.swt.SWT;
import org.eclipse.swt.graphics.Point;
import org.eclipse.swt.layout.GridData;
import org.eclipse.swt.layout.GridLayout;
import org.eclipse.swt.widgets.Composite;
import org.eclipse.swt.widgets.Control;
import org.eclipse.swt.widgets.Label;
import org.eclipse.swt.widgets.Shell;
import org.eclipse.swt.widgets.Text;

public class PasswordDialog extends Dialog {
    private Text txtUser;
    private Text txtPassword;
    private String user = "";
    private String password = "";

    public PasswordDialog(Shell parentShell) {
        super(parentShell);
    }

    @Override
    protected Control createDialogArea(Composite parent) {
        Composite container = (Composite) super.createDialogArea(parent);
        GridLayout layout = new GridLayout(2, false);
        layout.marginRight = 5;
        layout.marginLeft = 10;
        container.setLayout(layout);

        Label lblUser = new Label(container, SWT.NONE);
        lblUser.setText("User:");

        txtUser = new Text(container, SWT.BORDER);
        txtUser.setLayoutData(new GridData(SWT.FILL, SWT.CENTER, true, false,
                1, 1));
```

```
        txtUser.setText(user);
        txtUser.addModifyListener(e -> {
            Text textWidget = (Text) e.getSource();
            String userText = textWidget.getText();
            user = userText;
        });

        Label lblPassword = new Label(container, SWT.NONE);
        GridData gridDataPasswordLabel = new GridData(SWT.LEFT, SWT.CENTER, false,false);
        gridDataPasswordLabel.horizontalIndent = 1;
        lblPassword.setLayoutData(gridDataPasswordLabel);
        lblPassword.setText("Password:");

        txtPassword = new Text(container, SWT.BORDER| SWT.PASSWORD);
        txtPassword.setLayoutData(new GridData(SWT.FILL, SWT.CENTER, true, false));
        txtPassword.setText(password);
        txtPassword.addModifyListener(e -> {
            Text textWidget = (Text) e.getSource();
            String passwordText = textWidget.getText();
            password = passwordText;
        });
        return container;
    }

    // override method to use "Login" as label for the OK button
    @Override
    protected void createButtonsForButtonBar(Composite parent) {
        createButton(parent, IDialogConstants.OK_ID, "Login", true);
        createButton(parent, IDialogConstants.CANCEL_ID, IDialogConstants.CANCEL_LABEL,
false);
    }

    @Override
    protected Point getInitialSize() {
        return new Point(450, 300);
    }

    @Override
    protected void okPressed() {
        user = txtUser.getText();
        password = txtPassword.getText();
        super.okPressed();
    }

    public String getUser() {
        return user;
    }

    public void setUser(String user) {
```

```
        this.user = user;
    }

    public String getPassword() {
        return password;
    }

    public void setPassword(String password) {
        this.password = password;
    }
}
```

To use the dialog in your application, create a new menu entry (and a command with a handler) that allows you to open this dialog. The class associated with the handler should be called *EnterCredentialsHandler*.

```
package com.vogella.tasks.ui.handlers;

import org.eclipse.e4.core.di.annotations.Execute;
import org.eclipse.jface.window.Window;
import org.eclipse.swt.widgets.Shell;

import com.vogella.tasks.ui.dialogs.PasswordDialog;

public class EnterCredentialsHandler {

    @Execute
    public void execute(
            Shell shell) {
        PasswordDialog dialog = new PasswordDialog(shell);

        // get the new values from the dialog
        if (dialog.open() == Window.OK) {
            String user = dialog.getUser();
            String pw = dialog.getPassword();
        }
    }
}
```

Ensure that your handler links to the `EnterCredentialsHandler` class and not to the `PasswordDialog`.

104. Exercise: Implementing dialogs

104.1. Confirmation dialog at exit

Ensure that the `org.eclipse.jface` plug-in is defined as a dependency in your `com.vogella.tasks.ui` plug-in.

In your `ExitHandler` class, ensure that the user wants to exit the application via a confirmation dialog. This is done in the following code.

```
package com.vogella.tasks.ui.handlers;

import org.eclipse.e4.core.di.annotations.Execute;
import org.eclipse.e4.ui.workbench.IWorkbench;
import org.eclipse.jface.dialogs.MessageDialog;
import org.eclipse.swt.widgets.Shell;

public class ExitHandler {
    @Execute
    public void execute(IWorkbench workbench, Shell shell) {
        boolean result = MessageDialog.openConfirm(shell, "Close",
                "Close application?");
        if (result) {
            workbench.close();
        }
    }
}
```

A handler is executed within the context from which it is called. It should receive all its input via its `@Execute` method. Field or constructor injection in a handler only works for special cases, i.e., objects provided by an `ExtendedObjectSupplier`.

Test your implementation. If you select the Cancel button on the confirmation dialog, the application should not terminate.

104.2. Optional exercise: Use the custom exit dialog

Review (shortly) the Microsoft user interface guidance for creating dialogs [https://msdn.microsoft.com/en-us/library/windows/desktop/dn742499(v=vs.85).aspx].

Maybe you want to provide your custom dialog with additional elements.

Create the following class.

```
package com.vogella.tasks.ui.dialogs;

import org.eclipse.jface.dialogs.Dialog;
import org.eclipse.jface.dialogs.IDialogConstants;
import org.eclipse.swt.widgets.Composite;
import org.eclipse.swt.widgets.Shell;

public class ExitDialog extends Dialog {

    public ExitDialog(Shell parentShell) {
        super(parentShell);
    }

    @Override
    protected void createButtonsForButtonBar(Composite parent) {
        createButton(parent, IDialogConstants.OK_ID, "Exit", true);
        createButton(parent, IDialogConstants.CANCEL_ID, "Don't exit", false);

    }

    protected void configureShell(Shell shell) {
        super.configureShell(shell);
        shell.setText("Exit your application?");
    }
}
```

Use your new dialog in your handler:

```
package com.vogella.tasks.ui.handlers;

import org.eclipse.e4.core.di.annotations.Execute;
import org.eclipse.e4.ui.workbench.IWorkbench;
import org.eclipse.jface.dialogs.IDialogConstants;
import org.eclipse.jface.dialogs.MessageDialog;
import org.eclipse.swt.widgets.Shell;

import com.vogella.tasks.ui.dialogs.ExitDialog;

public class ExitHandler {
    @Execute
    public void execute(IWorkbench workbench, Shell shell) {
```

```
        ExitDialog exitDialog = new ExitDialog(shell);
        int open = exitDialog.open();
        if (open == IDialogConstants.OK_ID) {
            workbench.close();
        }
    }
}
```

105. Exercise: Create a wizard to create new tasks

This exercise demonstrates reusing your part implementation in a wizard. In this exercise, you create a wizard that allows you to create a new `Task` object and add it to the data managed by the `TaskService` service.

105.1. Create classes for the wizard

Create the `com.vogella.tasks.ui.wizards` package in the `com.vogella.tasks.ui` plug-in.

Create a `CreateTaskPage1` class extending `WizardPage` for your first wizard page.

In your `createControl` method of the wizard page, reuse the `TodoDetailsPart` class for defining the user interface.

```
package com.vogella.tasks.ui.wizards;

import java.util.Collections;

import org.eclipse.jface.wizard.WizardPage;
import org.eclipse.swt.SWT;
import org.eclipse.swt.widgets.Composite;

import com.vogella.tasks.model.Task;
import com.vogella.tasks.ui.parts.TodoDetailsPart;

public class CreateTaskPage1 extends WizardPage {

    private Task task;

    public CreateTaskPage1(Task todo) {
        super("page1");
        this.task = todo;
        setTitle("Creates a new task");
        setDescription("Enter the data");
    }

    @Override
```

```
    public void createControl(Composite parent) {
        Composite container = new Composite(parent, SWT.NONE);
        // usage of the new operator
        // no automatic dependency injection
        TodoDetailsPart part = new TodoDetailsPart(); ❶
        part.createControls(container); ❷
        part.setTasks(Collections.singletonList(task)); ❸
        setPageComplete(true);
        setControl(container);
    }
}
```

❶ You create the `TodoDetailsPart` instance with the `new` operator, so the framework does not perform dependency injection.

❷ sets the parent Composite

❸ sets the task managed by this wizard

Create the following class for the second page of the wizard. It contains only a *Confirm* checkbox.

```
package com.vogella.tasks.ui.wizards;

import org.eclipse.jface.widgets.WidgetFactory;
import org.eclipse.jface.wizard.WizardPage;
import org.eclipse.swt.SWT;
import org.eclipse.swt.events.SelectionAdapter;
import org.eclipse.swt.events.SelectionEvent;
import org.eclipse.swt.layout.GridLayout;
import org.eclipse.swt.widgets.Button;
import org.eclipse.swt.widgets.Composite;

public class CreateTaskPage2 extends WizardPage {

    public CreateTaskPage2() {
        super("wizardPage");
        setTitle("Validate");
        setDescription("Check to create the task item");
    }

    @Override
    public void createControl(Composite parent) {
        Composite container = new Composite(parent, SWT.NONE);
        GridLayout layout = new GridLayout(1, true);
        container.setLayout(layout);
        Button button = WidgetFactory.button(SWT.CHECK).text("Data has been validated"
).create(container);
        button.addSelectionListener(new SelectionAdapter() {
            @Override
```

```
            public void widgetSelected(SelectionEvent e) {
                setPageComplete(button.getSelection());
            }
        });
        setPageComplete(false);
        setControl(container);
    }
}
```

Create the `TaskWizard` class that extends the `Wizard` class and add `CreateTaskPage1` and `CreateTaskPage2` as pages to it.

```
package com.vogella.tasks.ui.wizards;

import org.eclipse.jface.wizard.Wizard;

import com.vogella.tasks.model.Task;

public class TaskWizard extends Wizard {

    private Task task;

    public TaskWizard(Task todo) {
        this.task = todo;
        setWindowTitle("New Wizard");
    }

    @Override
    public void addPages() {
        addPage(new CreateTaskPage1(task));
        addPage(new CreateTaskPage2());
    }

    @Override
    public boolean performFinish() {
        return true;
    }
}
```

105.2. Adjust part to update the data model via the user interface

To capture the changes in the user interface in your `Task` object, you need to extend your `TodoDetailsPart` class.

Add a `ModifyListener` to your text fields in your `TodoDetailsPart` class. In these listeners, write the `text` attribute of the `Text` widgets back to the `Task` object.

```
// find this code in your @PostConstruct method
// NOTE: your variable names may be different!!!

txtSummary = WidgetFactory.text(SWT.BORDER).layoutData(gdFactory.grab(true, false).
create())//
                .create(parent);

//NEW
txtSummary.addModifyListener(e -> { // ❶
    if (task.isPresent()) {
            task.get().setSummary(txtSummary.getText());
    }
});

// this is already in your @PostConstruct method
labelFactory.text("Description").create(parent);
txtDescription = WidgetFactory.text(SWT.BORDER | SWT.MULTI | SWT.V_SCROLL)
        .layoutData(gdFactory.align(SWT.FILL, SWT.FILL).grab(true, true).create()).
create(parent);

//NEW
txtDescription.addModifyListener(e -> { // ❷
    if (task.isPresent()){
        task.get().setDescription(txtDescription.getText());
    }
});

// more code
```

❶ Adds a listener to the `txtSummary` field after its initialization

❷ Adds a listener to your `txtDescription` field after its initialization

> You could also add listeners to your check button and `DateTime` widget to write changes back to the data model. However, we are skipping this step here because you will soon learn about the Eclipse data binding framework that simplifies this process.

105.3. Adjust handler implementation

Call the wizard from your `NewTaskHandler` class, which you added to the menu in an earlier exercise.

```
package com.vogella.tasks.ui.handlers;

import java.time.LocalDate;
```

```java
import org.eclipse.e4.core.di.annotations.Execute;
import org.eclipse.jface.window.Window;
import org.eclipse.jface.wizard.WizardDialog;
import org.eclipse.swt.widgets.Shell;

import com.vogella.tasks.model.Task;
import com.vogella.tasks.model.TaskService;
import com.vogella.tasks.ui.wizards.TaskWizard;

public class NewTaskHandler {
    @Execute
    public void execute(Shell shell, TaskService taskService) {
        // use -1 to indicate a not existing id
        Task task = new Task(-1);
        task.setDueDate(LocalDate.now());
        WizardDialog dialog = new WizardDialog(shell, new TaskWizard(task));
        if (dialog.open() == Window.OK) {
            // call service to save task object
            taskService.update(task);
        }
    }
}
```

105.4. Validate

Verify that new tasks can be created. Start your application and validate that you can create new task objects via your wizard.

After using your wizard, refresh your table in the `TodoOverviewPart` via the *Load Data* button to see the entry.

If the modification listeners are not implemented correctly, an empty line may appear in the table.

In a later exercise, you learn how to update your table (and other relevant components of your application) immediately after a change in the data model.

106. Optional exercise: Add a notification to the application

Use the JFace snippets from https://github.com/eclipse-platform/eclipse.platform.ui/blob/master/docs/JFaceSnippets.md#notification to learn how to add a notification to your application.

For example, add a notification after a new task has been created with the `NewTaskHandler`.

For this, add `org.eclipse.jface.notifications` as plug-in dependency to the manifest of the `com.vogella.tasks.ui` plug-in.

Add the following code to the `NewTaskHandler` class.

```
// new import
import org.eclipse.jface.notifications.NotificationPopup;

// more code

// add this code to your execute method at the end
 NotificationPopup.forShell(shell)
                .title("Created a new task", true)
                .delay(2000)
                .text("Task created: " + task.getSummary())
                .build()
                .open();
```

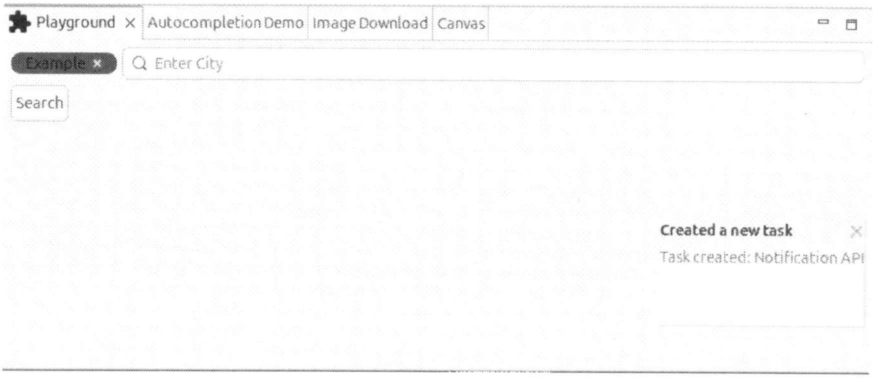

Part XIII: Using data binding

107. Data binding with JFace

107.1. Using JFace Data Binding

The *JFace data binding* framework allows you to synchronize changes in object properties. Validation and conversion during the synchronization process is supported.

For example, you could bind the String property called `firstName` of a `Person` object to a `text` property of the SWT `Text` widget. If you change the text in the user interface, the corresponding property in the `Person` object will be updated.

To observe changes in an attribute of a Java object, the data binding framework registers itself as a listener to this attribute. JFace data binding provides API to register to changes in SWT widgets and JFace UI elements. Other Java objects must implement this support. For example, you can implement `PropertyChangeSupport` according to the Java Bean specification in these Java elements. Or you can use the `WritableValue` interface from JFace inside the model.

The following plug-ins implement data binding.

- org.eclipse.core.databinding
- org.eclipse.core.databinding.beans
- org.eclipse.core.databinding.property

* org.eclipse.jface.databinding

The `IObservableValue` interface is the basis for observing properties in JFace. The data binding framework provides factory classes to create `IObservableValue` objects. The following table gives an overview of available classes to create instances of `IObservableValue`.

Table 27. Factories for the creation of an IObservableValue object

Factory	Description
`PojoProperties`	Used to create `IObservableValue` for Java objects. The term POJO (Plain Old Java Object) refers to a Java object that does not implement a specific framework API.
`BeanProperties`	Used for Java Beans. A Java Bean is a Java object that follows the Java Bean specification. This specification requires that the class implements `getter` and `setter` methods for all its attributes. It must also implement property change support via the `PropertyChangeSupport` class and propagate changes to registered listeners.
`WidgetProperties`	Used for properties of SWT widgets.
`ViewerProperties`	Used for properties of JFace viewer.
`Properties`	Used for properties of non specialized types, like Objects, Collections or Maps.
`Observables`	Used for properties of special Objects, Collections, Maps and Entries of an IObservableMap.

The following code demonstrates how to create an `IObservableValue` object for the `firstName` property of a Java object called `person`.

```
import org.eclipse.core.databinding.beans.typed.BeanProperties;
import org.eclipse.core.databinding.beans.typed.PojoProperties;
// more code

// if person is a pojo
var  pojomodel = PojoProperties.value(Person.class, "firstName", String.class).observe
(person);
var  pojomodel2 = PojoProperties.value(Person.class, "firstName", String.class).observe
(person);


// prefer using beans if your data model provides property change support
var beansModel = BeanProperties.value("firstName").observe(person);
var beansModel2 = BeanProperties.value(Person.class, "firstName", String.class).observe
(person);
```

The next example demonstrates how to create an `IObservableValue` for the `text` property of an SWT `Text` widget called `firstNameText`.

```
import org.eclipse.jface.databinding.swt.typed.WidgetProperties;
// more code

var observe = WidgetProperties.text(SWT.Modify).observe(text);
```

107.2. Example of a Java bean implementation

A Java class that provides `PropertyChangeSupport` looks like the following example.

```
package com.vogella.databinding.example;

import java.beans.PropertyChangeListener;
import java.beans.PropertyChangeSupport;

public class ModelObject {
    private final PropertyChangeSupport changeSupport =
            new PropertyChangeSupport(this);

    public void addPropertyChangeListener(PropertyChangeListener
            listener) {
        changeSupport.addPropertyChangeListener(listener);
    }

    public void removePropertyChangeListener(PropertyChangeListener
            listener) {
        changeSupport.removePropertyChangeListener(listener);
    }

    protected void firePropertyChange(String propertyName, Object oldValue,
            Object newValue) {
        changeSupport.firePropertyChange(propertyName, oldValue, newValue);
    }
}
```

Other domain classes could extend this class. The following example demonstrates that.

```
package com.vogella.databinding.example;

public class Person extends ModelObject {
    private String name;

    public String getName() {
```

```java
        return name;
    }

    public void setName(String name) {
        firePropertyChange("name", this.name, this.name = name);
    }
}
```

107.3. Using the WritableValue class to track changes

If your domain model supports the JFace API, you can use `WritableValue` to provide the option to track values.

```java
import org.eclipse.core.databinding.observable.value.WritableValue;

public class Person {

    private WritableValue<String> firstName = new WritableValue<>();

    private WritableValue<String> lastName = new WritableValue<>();

    /**
     * @return the person's first name
     * @TrackedGetter
     */
    public String getFirstName() {
        return firstName.getValue();
    }

    /**
     * @param firstName
     *            The summary to set.
     */
    public void setFirstName(String firstName) {
        this.firstName.setValue(firstName);
    }

    /**
     * @return Returns the description.
     * @TrackedGetter
     */
    public String getLastName() {
        return lastName.getValue();
    }

    /**
     * @param lastName
```

```
     *            The last name to set.
     */
    public void setLastName(String lastName) {
        this.lastName.setValue(lastName);
    }
}
```

107.4. Data binding and Java objects without change notification

If you connect two properties and one of them cannot be observed, you can still use data binding for a unidirectional binding. For example, you can connect the *text* property of an SWT `Text` field to the *summary* field of a `Task` object, even if a task cannot be observed. In this case, updates in the summary of the `Task` object will not update the `Text` widget. A relevant change in the `Text` widget user interface will update the property in the task object.

108. Create bindings

108.1. Using the ISideEffect API

The `ISideEffect` data binding API allows you to run code whenever an observable changes. An `ISideEffect` is similar to a listener, but it does not need to be attached to any component. Instead, it automatically reacts to changes in the tracked properties.

For example, the following code updates the label with the value of the user name every time the user name changes.

```
IObservableValue<String> username = ...
Label yourUsername = ...

ISideEffect sideEffect =
  ISideEffect.create(
        () -> {return "Your username is: " + username.getValue();},
        yourUsername::setText);
```

ISideEffects can react to changes in multiple observables, and will avoid performing excessive updates, if the observables fire many change events in a short period of time.

You can use the ISideEffectFactory to create several ISideEffect instances that share the same lifecycle. For example, all ISideEffect instances that are created by the ISideEffectFactory obtained from the WidgetSideEffects#createFactory(Widget disposableWidget) method are automatically disposed once the corresponding widget is disposed.

```
ISWTObservableValue personFirstNameTextObservable = WidgetProperties.text(SWT.Modify)
    .observe(personFirstNameText);
```

```java
ISWTObservableValue personLastNameTextObservable = WidgetProperties.text(SWT.Modify)
    .observe(personLastNameText);

ISideEffectFactory sideEffectFactory = WidgetSideEffects.createFactory
(personFirstNameText);

sideEffectFactory.create(person::getFirstName, personFirstNameText::setText);
sideEffectFactory.create(personFirstNameTextObservable::getValue, person::setFirstName);
sideEffectFactory.create(person::getLastName, personLastNameText::setText);
sideEffectFactory.create(personLastNameTextObservable::getValue, person::setLastName);
```

108.2. Connecting properties with the DataBindingContext

The `DataBindingContext` class provides the functionality to connect `IObservableValue` objects.

Via the `DataBindingContext.bindValue()` method two `IObservableValue` objects are connected. The first parameter is the target and the second is the model. During the initial binding the value from the model is copied to the target. The initial copying from model to target is useful for the initial synchronization. For example, if you have an attribute of a `Person` p object and the text attribute of a `Text` txtName widget, you typically want to copy the value from p to txtName at the beginning.

```java
// create new Context
DataBindingContext ctx = new DataBindingContext();

// define the IObservables
IObservableValue target = WidgetProperties.text(SWT.Modify).
    observe(firstName);
IObservableValue model= BeanProperties.
    value(Person.class,"firstName").observe(person);

// connect them
ctx.bindValue(target, model);
```

You can observe nested model properties, e.g., attributes of classes that are contained in another class. The following code demonstrates how to access the `country` property in the `address` field of the object `person`.

```java
IObservable model = PojoProperties.value(Person.class, "address.country").observe(
person);
```

108.3. Observing map properties

You can observe entries of a map via an `IObservableMap` using the `Observables.observeMapEntry()` method. This allows you to control the point in time when you want to update or use the values from the map.

```
import jakarta.annotation.PostConstruct;
import jakarta.inject.Inject;
import jakarta.inject.Named;

import org.eclipse.core.databinding.DataBindingContext;
import org.eclipse.core.databinding.observable.Observables;
import org.eclipse.core.databinding.observable.map.IObservableMap;
import org.eclipse.core.databinding.observable.map.WritableMap;
import org.eclipse.core.databinding.observable.value.IObservableValue;
import org.eclipse.e4.core.di.annotations.Optional;
import org.eclipse.e4.ui.di.Persist;
import org.eclipse.e4.ui.services.IServiceConstants;
import org.eclipse.jface.databinding.swt.ISWTObservableValue;
import org.eclipse.jface.databinding.swt.WidgetProperties;
import org.eclipse.swt.SWT;
import org.eclipse.swt.widgets.Composite;
import org.eclipse.swt.widgets.Text;

import com.vogella.tasks.model.Task;

public class ObservableMapEntry {

    private static final String SECOND_ATTRIBUTE = "secondAttribute";
    private static final String FIRST_ATTRIBUTE = "firstAttribute";

    private IObservableMap attributesMap = new WritableMap();
    private DataBindingContext dbc;
    private Task task;

    @PostConstruct
    public void createUI(Composite parent) {
        dbc = new DataBindingContext();

        Text txtFirstAttribute = new Text(parent, SWT.BORDER);
        Text txtSecondAttribute = new Text(parent, SWT.BORDER);

        // create observables for the Text controls
        ISWTObservableValue txtFirstAttributeObservable =
                WidgetProperties.text(SWT.Modify).observe(txtFirstAttribute);
        ISWTObservableValue txtSecondAttributeObservable = WidgetProperties.text(SWT
.Modify)
                .observe(txtSecondAttribute);
```

```
        // create observables for the Map entries
        IObservableValue firstAttributeObservable =
                Observables.observeMapEntry(attributesMap, FIRST_ATTRIBUTE);
        IObservableValue secondAttributeObservable =
                Observables.observeMapEntry(attributesMap, SECOND_ATTRIBUTE);

        dbc.bindValue(txtFirstAttributeObservable, firstAttributeObservable);
        dbc.bindValue(txtSecondAttributeObservable, secondAttributeObservable);
    }

    @Inject
    @Optional
    public void setModel(@Named(IServiceConstants.ACTIVE_SELECTION) Task task) {
        if (task != null) {
            this.task = task;
            // set new values for the map entries from a model object
            attributesMap.put(FIRST_ATTRIBUTE, task.getSummary());
            attributesMap.put(SECOND_ATTRIBUTE, task.getDescription());
        }
    }

    @Persist
    public void save() {
        if (task != null) {
            // only store the actual values on save and not directly
            task.setSummary((String) attributesMap.get(FIRST_ATTRIBUTE));
            task.setDescription((String) attributesMap.get(SECOND_ATTRIBUTE));
        }
    }
}
```

109. Update strategy, converters and validators

109.1. UpdateValueStrategy

The `bindValue()` method from `DataBindingContext` allows you to specify `UpdateValueStrategy` objects as third and fourth parameters. These objects allow you to control the update of the values. The following values are permitted:

Table 28. UpdateValueStrategy

Value	Description
`UpdateValueStrategy.POLICY_NEVER`	The source observable's state is not tracked and the destination observable's value is never updated.

Value	Description
UpdateValueStrategy.POLICY_ON_REQUEST	The source observable's state is not tracked. Validation, conversion and the update of the destination observable's value are performed only when explicitly requested. Use DataBindingContext.updateModels() or DataBindingContext.updateTargets() to update all bindings at once. Use Binding.updateTargetToModel() or Binding.updateModelToTarget() to update a single binding.
UpdateValueStrategy.POLICY_CONVERT	The source observable's state is tracked, including validation of changes (except for validateBeforeSet(Object)), but the destination observable's value is updated only on request.
UpdateValueStrategy.POLICY_UPDATE	The source observable's state is tracked. Validation, conversion and updating the destination observable's value are performed automatically on each change of the source observable.

If no `UpdateValueStrategy` is specified, the `UpdateValueStrategy.POLICY_UPDATE` is used by default. You can register converters and validators in the `UpdateValueStrategy` object.

109.2. Converter

Converters allow converting the values between the observed properties. Converters are defined based on the `IConverter` interface.

`UpdateValueStrategy.setConverter()` allows setting the converter. The `IConverter.create(Object, Object, Function)` allows creating a converter using a lambda expression. The static `UpdateValueStrategy.create(IConverter)` method allows creating an update strategy with a converter.

For example, you can convert a String to another object and vice versa.

For example, assume you have a `Person` object with a `programmingSkills` property.

```
package com.vogella.rcp.databinding.parts;

import com.vogella.rcp.databinding.parts.ModelObject;

public class Person extends ModelObject {
```

```
    private String name;
    private String[] programmingSkills;

    public String getName() {
        return name;
    }

    public void setName(String name) {
        firePropertyChange("name", this.name, this.name = name);
    }

    public String[] getProgrammingSkills() {
        return programmingSkills;
    }

    public void setProgrammingSkills(String[] programmingSkills) {
        firePropertyChange("programmingSkills", this.programmingSkills,
                this.programmingSkills = programmingSkills);
    }
}
```

The entries of `programmingSkills` should be shown in the `Text` widget as text separated by a comma. Therefore, a conversion is necessary.

To apply these converters an `UpdateValueStrategy` for the binding needs to be defined and applied.

```
package com.vogella.rcp.databinding.parts;

import jakarta.annotation.PostConstruct;

import org.eclipse.core.databinding.DataBindingContext;
import org.eclipse.core.databinding.UpdateValueStrategy;
import org.eclipse.core.databinding.beans.BeanProperties;
import org.eclipse.core.databinding.conversion.IConverter;
import org.eclipse.core.databinding.observable.value.IObservableValue;
import org.eclipse.jface.databinding.swt.WidgetProperties;
import org.eclipse.jface.layout.GridDataFactory;
import org.eclipse.jface.layout.GridLayoutFactory;
import org.eclipse.swt.SWT;
import org.eclipse.swt.events.SelectionAdapter;
import org.eclipse.swt.events.SelectionEvent;
import org.eclipse.swt.layout.GridData;
import org.eclipse.swt.widgets.Button;
import org.eclipse.swt.widgets.Composite;
import org.eclipse.swt.widgets.Label;
import org.eclipse.swt.widgets.Text;
```

```java
public class SamplePart {

    @PostConstruct
    @SuppressWarnings("unchecked")
    public void createPartControl(Composite parent) {
        // create the Person model with programming skills
        Person person = new Person();
        person.setName("John");
        person.setProgrammingSkills(new String[] { "Java", "JavaScript", "Groovy" });
        GridLayoutFactory.swtDefaults().numColumns(2).applyTo(parent);
        Label programmingSkillsLabel = new Label(parent, SWT.NONE);
        programmingSkillsLabel.setText("Programming Skills");
        GridDataFactory.swtDefaults().applyTo(programmingSkillsLabel);
        Text programmingSkillsText = new Text(parent, SWT.BORDER);
        GridDataFactory.fillDefaults().grab(true, false).applyTo(programmingSkillsText);
        // Do the actual binding and conversion
        DataBindingContext dbc = new DataBindingContext();

        // define converters
        IConverter convertToStringArray =
                IConverter.create(String.class, String[].class, (o1) -> ((String) o1
).split(","));
        IConverter convertToString =
                IConverter.create(String[].class, String.class, (o1) -> convert((
String[])o1));;

        // create the observables, which should be bound
        IObservableValue<Text> programmingSkillsTarget = WidgetProperties.text(SWT.
Modify).observe(programmingSkillsText);
        IObservableValue<Person> programmingSkillsModel = BeanProperties.value
("programmingSkills").observe(person);

        // bind observables together with the appropriate UpdateValueStrategies
        dbc.bindValue(programmingSkillsTarget, programmingSkillsModel,
                UpdateValueStrategy.create(convertToStringArray),
                UpdateValueStrategy.create(convertToString));

        // button to check the data model
        Button button = new Button(parent, SWT.PUSH);
        button.setLayoutData(new GridData(SWT.BEGINNING, SWT.CENTER, false, false));
        button.setText("Show data model");
        button.addSelectionListener(new SelectionAdapter() {
            @Override
            public void widgetSelected(SelectionEvent e) {
                for (String string : person.getProgrammingSkills()) {
                    System.out.println(string);
                }
            }
        });
```

```
    }

    private static String convert(String[] fromObject) {
        String[] stringArray = fromObject;
        StringBuilder sb = new StringBuilder();
        int length = stringArray.length;
        for (int i = 0; i < length; i++) {
            String string = stringArray[i];
            sb.append(string);
            if (i + 1 < length) {
                sb.append(",");
            }
        }
        return sb.toString();
    }
}
```

109.3. Validator

A *validator* allows you to implement validation of the data before it is propagated to the other connected property. A class which wants to provide this functionality must implement the `org.eclipse.core.databinding.validation.IValidator` interface.

```
import org.eclipse.core.databinding.DataBindingContext;
import org.eclipse.core.databinding.UpdateValueStrategy;
import org.eclipse.core.databinding.beans.BeanProperties;
import org.eclipse.core.databinding.conversion.IConverter;
import org.eclipse.core.databinding.observable.value.IObservableValue;
import org.eclipse.core.databinding.validation.ValidationStatus;

// converter as before
IConverter convertToStringArray = IConverter.create(String.class, String[].class,
        (o1) -> ((String) o1).split(","));

// ensure perl is not accepted as programming language
UpdateValueStrategy updateStrategy = UpdateValueStrategy.create(convertToStringArray);
updateStrategy.setAfterGetValidator((o1) -> {
    String s = (String) o1;
    if (!s.contains("Perl")) {
        return ValidationStatus.ok();
    }
    return ValidationStatus.error("Perl is not a programming language");

});

Binding bindValue =
    ctx.bindValue(widgetValue, modelValue, updateStrategy, null);
```

The `WizardPageSupport` class allows connecting the result from the data binding context to the given wizard page. This updates the wizard page's completion state and its error message.

110. More on bindings

110.1. ControlDecorators

Data binding allows you to use icon decorators in the user interface that reflect the status of the field validation. This allows you to provide immediate feedback to the user. For the creation of the control decoration you use the return object from the `bindvalue()` method of `DataBindingContext` object.

```
// The following code assumes that a Validator is already defined
Binding bindValue =
  ctx.bindValue(widgetValue, modelValue, strategy, null);

// add some decorations to the control
ControlDecorationSupport.create(bindValue, SWT.TOP | SWT.LEFT);
```

The result might look like the following screenshot.

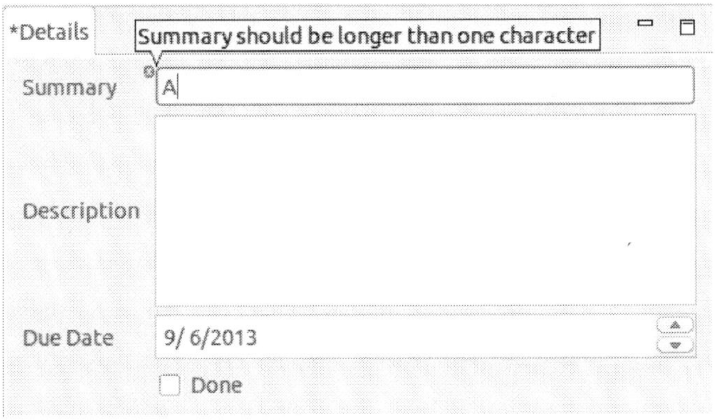

110.2. Binding values of a radio button group

When using radio buttons each button usually represents a certain value. To bind the value according to the selected state in a radio button group, the `SelectObservableValue` class is used.

The following example shows how to bind the currently selected radio value to a `Label`.

```
Group group = new Group(shell, SWT.NONE);
```

```
group.setText("Radio Group with Names");
GridLayoutFactory.fillDefaults().applyTo(group);
GridDataFactory.fillDefaults().grab(true, true).applyTo(group);

// Options for the radio buttons
String[] names = new String[] { "Matthew Hall", "Dirk Fauth", "Lars Vogel",
        "Simon Scholz" };

SelectObservableValue selectedRadioButtonObservable = new SelectObservableValue();
for (String name : names) {
    Button button = new Button(group, SWT.RADIO);
    button.setText(name);
    // Add name as option value in case the appropriate button is selected
    selectedRadioButtonObservable.addOption("Selected: " + name, WidgetProperties
.selection().observe(button));
}

Label label = new Label(shell, SWT.NONE);
GridDataFactory.fillDefaults().applyTo(label);
ISWTObservableValue labelTextObservable = WidgetProperties.text().observe(label);

DataBindingContext dbc = new DataBindingContext();
// bind label text to currently selected option
dbc.bindValue(selectedRadioButtonObservable, labelTextObservable);
```

The result of this snippet, should look like this:

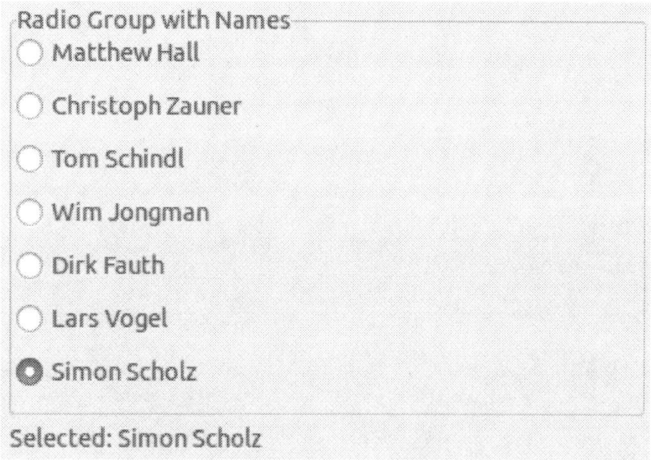

110.3. Listening to all changes in the binding

You can register a listener to all bindings of the `DataBindingContext` class. Your listener will be called when something has changed.

For example, this can be used to determine the status of a part that behaves like an editor. If its data model changes, this editor marks itself as dirty.

```
// define your change listener
// dirty holds the state for the changed status of the editor
IChangeListener listener = new IChangeListener() {
    @Override
    public void handleChange(ChangeEvent event) {
        // Ensure dirty is not null
        if (part!=null){
            part.setDirty(true);
        }
};


private void updateUserInterface(Todo todo) {

    // check that the user interface is available
    if (txtSummary != null && !txtSummary.isDisposed()) {

        // Deregister change listener to the old binding
        IObservableList providers = ctx.getValidationStatusProviders();
        for (Object o : providers) {
            Binding b = (Binding) o;
            b.getTarget().removeChangeListener(listener);
        }

        // dispose the binding
        ctx.dispose();

        // NOTE
        // HERE WOULD BE THE DATABINDING CODE
        // INTENTIONALLY LEFT OUT FOR BREVITY

        // get the validation status provides
        IObservableList bindings =
            ctx.getValidationStatusProviders();

        // not all validation status providers
        // are bindings, e.g., MultiValidator
        // otherwise you could use
        // context.getBindings()

        // register the listener to all bindings
        for (Object o : bindings) {
            Binding b = (Binding) o;
            b.getTarget().addChangeListener(listener);
        }
    }
```

```
}
```

110.4. Placeholder binding with WritableValue

You can create bindings to a `WritableValue` object. A `WritableValue` object can hold a reference to another object.

You can exchange this reference in `WritableValue` and the data binding uses the new (reference) object for its binding. This way you can create the binding once and still exchange the object which is bound by data binding.

To bind to a `WritableValue` you use the `observeDetail()` method, to inform the framework that you would like to observe the contained object.

```
WritableValue value = new WritableValue();

// create the binding
DataBindingContext ctx = new DataBindingContext();
IObservableValue target = WidgetProperties.
    text(SWT.Modify).observe(text);
IObservableValue model = BeanProperties.value("firstName").
        observeDetail(value);

ctx.bindValue(target, model);

// create a Person object named p
Person p = new Person();

// make the binding valid for this new object
value.setValue(p);
```

110.5. ComputedValue and observable trackers

A `ComputedValue` provides an abstract `calculate` method, which is able to compute a value from observable trackers that are referenced in its `calculate` method.

```
public class FormattedName extends ComputedValue {
    private IObservableValue<String> firstName;

    private IObservableValue<String> lastName;

    FormattedName(IObservableValue<String> firstName, IObservableValue<String> lastName)
{
        this.firstName = firstName;
        this.lastName = lastName;
```

```
    }

    @Override
    protected Object calculate() {
        // since lastName and firstName are tracked getter (see JavaDoc of
        // getValue() method) the value of this ComputedValue gets recomputed once
        // lastName or firstName are changed
        String lastName = this.lastName.getValue();
        String firstName = this.firstName.getValue();
        lastName = (lastName != null && lastName.isEmpty()) ? "[Last Name]" : lastName;
        firstName = (firstName != null && firstName.isEmpty()) ? "[First Name]" :
firstName;

        return lastName + "," + firstName;
    }
}
```

The `create` method accepts a Supplier that contains the actual implementation of the calculate method.

```
IObservableValue<String> lastName = // ...
IObservableValue<String> firstName = // ...

IObservableValue<String> formattedName = ComputedValue.create(() -> {
    // since lastName and firstName are tracked getter (see JavaDoc of
    // getValue() method) the value of this ComputedValue gets recomputed once
    // lastName or firstName are changed
    String lastNameValue = lastName.getValue();
    String firstNameValue = firstName.getValue();
    lastNameValue = (lastNameValue != null && lastNameValue.isEmpty()) ? "[Last Name]" :
lastNameValue;
    firstNameValue = (firstNameValue != null && firstNameValue.isEmpty()) ? "[First
Name]" : firstNameValue;

    return lastNameValue + "," + firstNameValue;
});
```

A `ComputedValue` can combine different observables and is recomputed every time one of the tracked getters are touched.

An example of a `ComputedValue` implementation is the `AggregateValidationStatus`. It keeps track of all validation statuses that have been passed to it and aggregates them to one `MultiStatus` or returns the one with maximum severity.

It is a great alternative to converter implementations. For instance, the previously described `AggregateValidationStatus` returns an `IStatus` as a value. If this should be bound to the enable state of a Finish button, having a boolean value would be necessary.

```
// Track the validation status from all binding in the DataBindingContext
AggregateValidationStatus aggregateValidationStatus = new AggregateValidationStatus(dbc
.getBindings(),
        AggregateValidationStatus.MAX_SEVERITY);

// Create a boolean observable, which depends on the ok status
IObservableValue<Boolean> isValidationOk = ComputedValue
        .create(() -> aggregateValidationStatus.getValue().isOK());

ISWTObservableValue buttonEnabledObservable = WidgetProperties.enabled().observe
(finishButton);

// bind the enablement of the finish button to the validation
dbc.bindValue(buttonEnabledObservable, isValidationOk);
```

Applying an `IConverter` to convert from `IStatus` to boolean would be far more overhead.

111. Data Binding for JFace viewers

111.1. Binding viewers

JFace data binding provides functionality to bind the data of JFace viewers. Data binding for these viewers distinguish between changes in the collection and changes in the individual object.

In the case that data binding observes a collection, it requires a content provider which notifies the viewer, once the data in the collection changes.

The `ObservableListContentProvider` class is a content provider that requires a list implementing the `IObservableList` interface. The `Properties` class allows you to wrap another list with its `selfList()` method into an `IObservableList`.

The following snippet demonstrates the usage:

```
// use ObservableListContentProvider
viewer.setContentProvider(new ObservableListContentProvider());

// create sample data
List<Person> persons = createExampleData();

// wrap the input into a writable list
IObservableList input =
   Properties.selfList(Person.class).observe(persons);

// set the IObservableList as input for the viewer
viewer.setInput(input);
```

111.2. Observing list details

You can use the `ObservableMapLabelProvider` class to observe changes of the list elements.

```
ObservableListContentProvider contentProvider =
    new ObservableListContentProvider();

// create the label provider which includes monitoring
// of changes to update the labels

IObservableSet knownElements = contentProvider.getKnownElements();

final IObservableMap firstNames = BeanProperties.value(Person.class,
    "firstName").observeDetail(knownElements);
final IObservableMap lastNames = BeanProperties.value(Person.class,
    "lastName").observeDetail(knownElements);

IObservableMap[] labelMaps = { firstNames, lastNames };

ILabelProvider labelProvider =
    new ObservableMapLabelProvider(labelMaps) {
    public String getText(Object element) {
        return firstNames.get(element) + " " + lastNames.get(element);
    }
};
```

111.3. ViewerSupport

`ViewerSupport` simplifies the setup for JFace viewers in cases where selected columns should be displayed. It registers change listeners on the collection as well as on the individual elements.

`ViewerSupport` creates via the `bind()` method the `LabelProvider` and `ContentProvider` for a viewer automatically.

```
// the MyModel.getPersons() method call returns a List<Person> object
// the WritableList object wraps this object in an IObservableList

input = new WritableList(MyModel.getPersons(), Person.class);

// The following  creates and binds the data
// for the Table based on the provided input
// no additional label provider /
// content provider / setInput required

ViewerSupport.bind(viewer, input,
        BeanProperties.
```

```
        values(new String[] { "firstName", "lastName", "married" }));
```

111.4. Master-Detail binding

The `ViewerProperties` class allows you to create `IObservableValue` for properties of the viewer. For example, you can track the current selection, e.g., which data object is currently selected. This binding is called *Master-Detail* binding as you track the selection of a master.

To access fields in the selection you can use the `PojoProperties` or the `BeanProperties` class. Both provide the `value().observeDetail()` method chain that allows you to observe a detailed value of an `IObservableValue` object.

For example, the following code synchronizes the `summary` property of the `Task` domain object to a `Label` based on the selection of a `ComboViewer`.

```
// assume we have Task domain objects
// tasks is of type: List<Task>
final ComboViewer viewer = new ComboViewer(parent, SWT.DROP_DOWN);
viewer.setContentProvider(ArrayContentProvider.getInstance());
viewer.setLabelProvider(new LabelProvider() {
    public String getText(Object element) {
        Task task = (Task) element;
        return task.getSummary();
    };
});
viewer.setInput(tasks);

// create a Label to map to
Label label = new Label(parent, SWT.BORDER);
// parent has a GridLayout assigned
label.setLayoutData(new GridData(SWT.FILL, SWT.CENTER, true, false));


DataBindingContext dbc = new DataBindingContext();

// for binding to the label
IObservableValue target = WidgetProperties.text().observe(label);

// observe the selection
IViewerObservableValue selectedTask = ViewerProperties
        .singleSelection().observe(viewer);
// observe the summary attribute of the selection
IObservableValue detailValue =
    PojoProperties
        .value("summary", String.class)
        .observeDetail(selectedTask)
```

```
dbc.bindValue(target, detailValue);
```

111.5. Chaining properties

You can chain properties together to simplify observing nested properties. The following examples demonstrate this usage.

```
IObservableValue viewerSelectionSummaryObservable =
    ViewerProperties.singleSelection()
    .value(BeanProperties.value("summary", String.class))
    .observe(viewer);
```

```
IListProperty siblingNames = BeanProperties.
    value("parent").list("children").values("name");
IObservableList siblingNamesObservable =
    siblingNames.observe(node);
```

112. Extending data binding with custom observables

112.1. Developing custom observables

You can implement observables for your own classes.

This implementation can extend the `AbstractObservable` class or one of its subclasses, like the `AbstractObservableValue` class.

For example, assume you have the following custom widget that draws a text on a canvas

```
public class CustomWidget extends Canvas {

    private String text;
    private Point textExtent;

    public CustomWidget(Composite parent) {
        super(parent, SWT.NONE);
        addPaintListener(new PaintListener() {

            @Override
            public void paintControl(PaintEvent e) {
                GC gc = e.gc;

                // draw the text, which can be set
                String textValue = getText() != null ? getText() : "Good Default";
                gc.drawText(textValue, 5, 5);
```

```
                textExtent = gc.textExtent(textValue);
            }
        });
    }

    @Override
    public Point computeSize(int wHint, int hHint, boolean changed) {
        checkWidget();
        return textExtent != null ? textExtent : new Point(30, 12);
    }

    public String getText() {
        checkWidget();
        return text;
    }

    public void setText(String text) {
        checkWidget();
        this.text = text;
        redraw();
    }
}
```

Since there is no predefined `IObservable` for custom widgets, you must implement your own.

While it is possible to use the `PojoProperties` class to create an `IObservableValue` (for example, `PojoProperties.value("text").observe(customWidget)`), this does not produce an `ISWTObservableValue`. As a result, classes such as `ControlDecorationSupport` will not work out of the box with your custom widget.

112.2. Directly implement IObservable

The `CustomWidgetObservableValue` extends `AbstractObservableValue` and implements the `ISWTObservableValue` interface.

```
public class CustomWidgetObservableValue extends AbstractObservableValue
                                                implements ISWTObservableValue {

    private CustomWidget customWidget;

    public CustomWidgetObservableValue(CustomWidget customWidget) {
        this(customWidget, Realm.getDefault());
    }

    public CustomWidgetObservableValue(CustomWidget customWidget, Realm realm) {
```

```
        super(realm);
        this.customWidget = customWidget;
    }

    @Override
    public Object getValueType() {
        return String.class;
    }

    @Override
    protected Object doGetValue() {
        return customWidget.getText();
    }

    @Override
    protected void doSetValue(Object value) {
        customWidget.setText(value.toString());
    }

    @Override
    public Widget getWidget() {
        // implement the ISWTObservableValue interface to enable ControlDecorationSupport
        return customWidget;
    }
}
```

This observable can then be used like this:

```
@PostConstruct
public void createComposite(Composite parent) {
    parent.setLayout(new GridLayout(1, false));

    DataBindingContext dbc = new DataBindingContext();

    CustomWidget widget = new CustomWidget(parent);
    CustomWidgetObservableValue customWidgetObservableValue = new
CustomWidgetObservableValue(widget);

    Task task = //...
    IObservableValue todoSummaryObservable = PojoProperties.value("summary").observe(
task);

    dbc.bindValue(customWidgetObservableValue, todoSummaryObservable);
}
```

112.3. Implement an IProperty rather than IObservable directly

A better approach is to implement the `IProperty` interface, like `IValueProperty`, `IWidgetValueProperty` and others.

Let us implement the solution of the previous section with an `IProperty` implementation.

```
public class CustomWidgetProperty extends WidgetValueProperty {

    @Override
    public Object getValueType() {
        return String.class;
    }

    @Override
    protected Object doGetValue(Object source) {
        if(source instanceof CustomWidget) {
            return ((CustomWidget) source).getText();
        }
        return "";
    }

    @Override
    protected void doSetValue(Object source, Object value) {
        if(source instanceof CustomWidget && value instanceof String) {
            ((CustomWidget) source).setText((String) value);
        }
    }
}
```

This `WidgetValueProperty` can be used like this:

```
@PostConstruct
public void createComposite(Composite parent) {
    parent.setLayout(new GridLayout(1, false));

    DataBindingContext dbc = new DataBindingContext();

    CustomWidget widget = new CustomWidget(parent);

    // Create the property and then observe the widget afterwards
    CustomWidgetProperty customWidgetProperty = new CustomWidgetProperty();
    ISWTObservableValue customWidgetObservableValue = customWidgetProperty.observe(
widget);

    Task task = //...
    IObservableValue todoSummaryObservable = PojoProperties.value("summary").observe(
```

```
task);

    dbc.bindValue(customWidgetObservableValue, todoSummaryObservable);
}
```

112.4. Delegates for common properties of different objects

Delegating properties act a bit like a factory for `IProperty` objects, where the `IProperty` is not created directly, but at the moment, when the `observe` method is called. For instance, a `DelegatingValueProperty` creates a `IValueProperty` according to the object that should be observed.

The decision of which `IValueProperty` to use is made when the observe method is called.

Imagine, we want such a factory for the `IValueProperty` classes we created in the former sections. Therefore, we can derive from `DelegatingValueProperty`.

```
public class VogellaDelegatingValueProperty extends DelegatingValueProperty {

    public VogellaDelegatingValueProperty() {
        this(null);
    }

    public VogellaDelegatingValueProperty(Object valueType) {
        super(valueType);
    }

    @Override
    protected IValueProperty doGetDelegate(Object source) {
        // return appropriate IValueProperty according to the given source,
        // which is passed, when the observe method is called
        if(source instanceof CustomWidget) {
            return new CustomWidgetProperty();
        }else if (source instanceof DateTime) {
            return new DateTimeSelectionProperty();
        }
        return null;
    }
}
```

To have a factory like the `WidgetProperties` class, we could create a `VogellaProperties` class.

```
package com.vogella.operationhistory.databinding;

```

```
import org.eclipse.core.databinding.property.value.IValueProperty;

public class VogellaProperties {

    private VogellaProperties() {
    }

    public static IValueProperty vogellaProperty() {
        // return a vogella property, which can handle different vogella
        // properties
        return new VogellaDelegatingValueProperty();
    }
}
```

You might want to have a look at the `WidgetProperties` that contains several methods with more sense for those delegates.

Here is the code how to use the factory for "vogella" properties and some samples, which fit to the intention of the delegates.

```
public class VogellaPropertiesPart {

    @PostConstruct
    public void createPartControl(Composite parent) {
        CustomWidget customWidget = new CustomWidget(parent);

        // Observable for the CustomWidget by using the delegate
        IObservableValue customWidgetObservable = VogellaProperties.vogellaProperty
().observe(customWidget);

        DateTime dateTime = new DateTime(parent, SWT.DROP_DOWN);
        // Observable for the DateTime by using the delegate
        IObservableValue dateTimeJava8Observable = VogellaProperties.vogellaProperty
().observe(dateTime);

        // ### Real common properties for different kinds of objects ###

        Button button = new Button(parent, SWT.CHECK);
        CCombo combo = new CCombo(parent, SWT.READ_ONLY);

        // see WidgetSelectionProperty for more details
        ISWTObservableValue oldDateTimeObservable = WidgetProperties.selection().observe
(dateTime);
        ISWTObservableValue buttonSelectionObservable = WidgetProperties.selection
().observe(button);
        ISWTObservableValue comboSelectionObservable = WidgetProperties.selection
().observe(combo);
```

```
        // and much more
    }
}
```

113. Example: Custom observable for the DateTime

Java provides a Date and Time API. While JFace data binding provides a standard way to bind to it, we use this as an example of how to write your own custom binding. This should demonstrate how to create your own binding, even though for this particular example you should use the official binding.

Implement the following class.

```
import java.time.LocalDate;
import java.time.LocalDateTime;
import java.time.LocalTime;
import java.time.temporal.ChronoField;
import java.time.temporal.TemporalAccessor;
import java.util.Calendar;
import java.util.Date;

import org.eclipse.jface.databinding.swt.WidgetValueProperty;
import org.eclipse.swt.SWT;
import org.eclipse.swt.widgets.DateTime;

public class DateTimeSelectionProperty extends WidgetValueProperty {

    // this constant is used to correct the differences concerning the month counting
    private static final int MONTH_MAPPING_VALUE = 1;

    public DateTimeSelectionProperty() {
        super(SWT.Selection);
    }

    @Override
    public Object getValueType() {
        // use TemporalAccessor here, because it is the common interface for
        // LocalDate, LocalTime and LocalDateTime.
        return TemporalAccessor.class;
    }

    @Override
    protected Object doGetValue(Object source) {
        DateTime dateTime = (DateTime) source;

        // create LocalTime instance, if SWT.TIME is used,...
        if ((dateTime.getStyle() & SWT.TIME) != 0) {
```

```java
            return LocalTime.of(dateTime.getHours(), dateTime.getMinutes(),
                    dateTime.getSeconds());
        }
        // ... otherwise LocalDate
        return LocalDate.of(dateTime.getYear(), dateTime.getMonth()
                + MONTH_MAPPING_VALUE, dateTime.getDay());
    }

    @Override
    protected void doSetValue(Object source, Object value) {
        DateTime dateTime = (DateTime) source;

        if (value == null)
            throw new IllegalArgumentException(
                    "Cannot set null selection on DateTime");

        TemporalAccessor temporalAccessor = getTemporalAccessor(value);

        if (temporalAccessor == null)
            throw new IllegalArgumentException(
                    "Cannot find TemporalAccessor for the given value");

        // set only hours, minutes and seconds in case the SWT.TIME flag is
        // set,...
        if ((dateTime.getStyle() & SWT.TIME) != 0) {
            dateTime.setTime(temporalAccessor.get(ChronoField.HOUR_OF_DAY),
                    temporalAccessor.get(ChronoField.MINUTE_OF_HOUR),
                    temporalAccessor.get(ChronoField.SECOND_OF_MINUTE));
        } else {
            // ... otherwise set year, month and day.
            dateTime.setDate(temporalAccessor.get(ChronoField.YEAR),
                    temporalAccessor.get(ChronoField.MONTH_OF_YEAR)
                            - MONTH_MAPPING_VALUE,
                    temporalAccessor.get(ChronoField.DAY_OF_MONTH));
        }
    }

    // get TemporalAccessor from a Date, Calendar or TemporalAccessor object
    private TemporalAccessor getTemporalAccessor(Object value) {
        TemporalAccessor temporalAccessor = null;

        if (value instanceof Date) {
            temporalAccessor = LocalDateTime.from(((Date) value).toInstant());
        } else if (value instanceof TemporalAccessor) {
            temporalAccessor = (TemporalAccessor) value;
        } else if (value instanceof Calendar) {
            temporalAccessor = LocalDateTime.from(((Calendar) value)
                    .toInstant());
        }
```

```
        return temporalAccessor;
    }
}
```

Here, we implement a binding between the `DateTime` SWT widget and a `TemporalAccessor`. This can be, for instance, a `java.time.LocalDate` or `java.time.LocalTime`.

The usage of the `DateTimeSelectionProperty` is demonstrated by the following listing.

```
@PostConstruct
public void createComposite(Composite parent) {
    parent.setLayout(new GridLayout(1, false));

    DataBindingContext dbc = new DataBindingContext();

    DateTime dateTime = new DateTime(parent, SWT.DROP_DOWN);

    // use the previously created DateTimeSelectionProperty
    DateTimeSelectionProperty dateTimeSelectionProperty = new
DateTimeSelectionProperty();
    dateTimeObservableValue = dateTimeSelectionProperty.observe(dateTime);

    // create and initialize a placeholder observable
    writableDateTimeModel = new WritableValue();
    writableDateTimeModel.setValue(LocalDate.now());

    // bind DateTime widget to the writable value using our observables
    dbc.bindValue(dateTimeObservableValue, writableDateTimeModel);

    Label label = new Label(parent, SWT.BORDER);
    GridDataFactory.fillDefaults().grab(true, false).applyTo(label);

    ISWTObservableValue dateTimeLabelObservable = WidgetProperties.text().observe(label);

    // bind a Label to the DateTime Widget, to see the changes,
    // which are made in the DateTime widget
    dbc.bindValue(dateTimeLabelObservable, dateTimeObservableValue);

    tableViewer = new TableViewer(parent);
    tableViewer.getTable().setLayoutData(new GridData(GridData.FILL_BOTH));

    tableViewer.add("27.04.1986 00:30:20");
    tableViewer.add("23.06.1976 03:15:30");
    tableViewer.add("27.06.1980 12:05:40");
    tableViewer.add("26.03.2015 22:25:50");
    tableViewer.add("06.12.2015 20:00:10");

    final DateTimeFormatter dateTimeFormatter = DateTimeFormatter.ofPattern("dd.MM.yyyy
```

```
HH:mm:ss");

    // databinding could be used here similar to the following code:
    // dbc.bindValue(ViewerProperties.singleSelection().
    // observe(tableViewer),
    // writableDateTimeModel,
    // stringToLocalDateTimeUpdateStrategy,
    // LocalDateTimeToStringUpdateStrategy)

    // the following uses an ISelectionChangedListener instead of data binding as this
    // results in shorter code
    tableViewer.addSelectionChangedListener(new ISelectionChangedListener() {

        @Override
        public void selectionChanged(SelectionChangedEvent event) {
            ISelection selection = event.getSelection();
            if (selection instanceof IStructuredSelection) {
                String string = (String) ((IStructuredSelection) selection
).getFirstElement();

                // parse string from table with the DateTimeFormatter from above
                LocalDateTime localDateTime = LocalDateTime.parse(string,
dateTimeFormatter);
                // set the selected localDateTime to the WritableValue,
                // which is bound to the DateTime widget
                writableDateTimeModel.setValue(localDateTime);
            }
        }
    });
}
```

In this sample we bind the `DateTime` widget to a `WritableValue` that contains a `TemporalAccessor` instance. Selecting a date in the `TableViewer` updates this `WritableValue`. The `dateTimeObservableValue` is bound to a label, to see the changes by manually manipulating to the `DateTime` widget.

The result looks similar to the following screenshot.

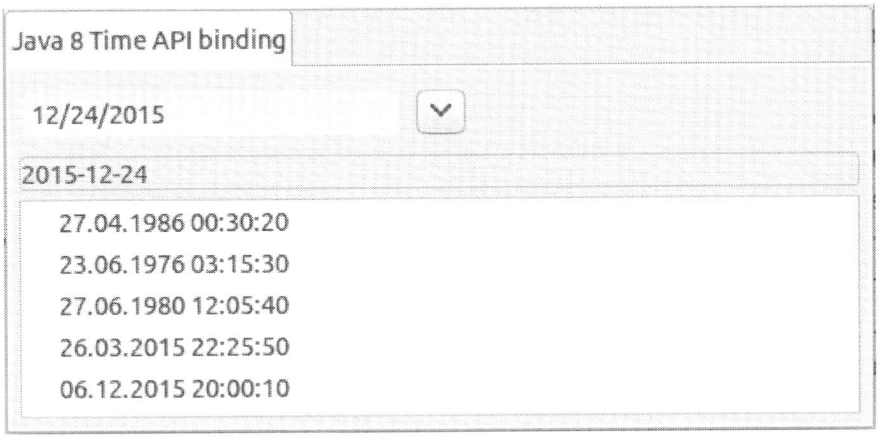

If you select a date in the `TableViewer`, this updates the `WritableValue`. Therefore, the `DateTime` widget and the `Label` are updated, because all these are bound together.

114. Exercise: Data binding for SWT widgets

114.1. Add the new plug-in dependencies to the application plug-in

In the `MANIFEST.MF` file, add the following entries as plug-in dependencies to your `com.vogella.tasks.ui` plug-in.

- org.eclipse.core.databinding
- org.eclipse.core.databinding.beans
- org.eclipse.core.databinding.property
- org.eclipse.jface.databinding

114.2. Update the data model to be observable

Your `Task` class should already contain constants which we can use to facilitate data binding. The constants must reflect the bean property names in the class, otherwise, the data binding will not find the right property to bind to.

Your class now needs to implement the `PropertyChangeSupport` mechanism to make it observable. This is done by adding a `PropertyChangeSupport` field to your class, allowing registration via corresponding methods and firing property change events in the setter methods of your bean properties. See the next listing for the correct implementation.

```
package com.vogella.tasks.model;

import java.beans.PropertyChangeListener;
import java.beans.PropertyChangeSupport;
```

```java
import java.time.LocalDate;

public class Task {

    private PropertyChangeSupport changes = new PropertyChangeSupport(this);

    public static final String FIELD_ID = "id";
    public static final String FIELD_SUMMARY = "summary";
    public static final String FIELD_DESCRIPTION = "description";
    public static final String FIELD_DONE = "done";
    public static final String FIELD_DUEDATE = "dueDate";

    private final long id;
    private String summary = "";
    private String description = "";
    private boolean done = false;
    private LocalDate dueDate = LocalDate.now();

    public Task(long id, String summary, String description, boolean done, LocalDate
dueDate) {
        this.id = id;
        this.summary = summary;
        this.description = description;
        this.done = done;
        this.dueDate = dueDate;
    }

    public Task(long id) {
        this.id = id;
    }

    public String getSummary() {
        return summary;
    }

    public void setSummary(String summary) {
        changes.firePropertyChange(FIELD_SUMMARY, this.summary, this.summary = summary);
    }

    public String getDescription() {
        return description;
    }

    public void setDescription(String description) {
        changes.firePropertyChange(FIELD_DESCRIPTION, this.description, this.description
= description);
    }
    public boolean isDone() {
        return done;
```

```
    }


    public void setDone(boolean isDone) {
        changes.firePropertyChange(FIELD_DONE, this.done, this.done = isDone);
    }

    public LocalDate getDueDate() {
        return dueDate;
    }

    public void setDueDate(LocalDate dueDate) {
        changes.firePropertyChange(FIELD_DUEDATE, this.dueDate, this.dueDate = dueDate);
    }

    public long getId() {
        return id;
    }

    @Override
    public String toString() {
        return "Task [id=" + id + ", summary=" + summary + "]";
    }

    public Task copy() {
        return new Task(this.id, this.summary, this.description, this.done, this.
dueDate);
    }

    public void addPropertyChangeListener(PropertyChangeListener l) {
        changes.addPropertyChangeListener(l);
    }

    public void removePropertyChangeListener(PropertyChangeListener l) {
        changes.removePropertyChangeListener(l);
    }
}
```

114.3. Remove the modification listeners

The synchronization between the task object and the user interface will be handled by the data binding framework. Therefore, delete the modification listeners for the widgets that are used to change the task data in `TodoDetailsPart`. For example, `addModifyListener()` methods in the `TodoDetailsPart` class.

> ⚠ If these listeners are not removed, you will see "strange" side effects like jumping cursors. Ensure that you have removed them. Verify the removal via a

text search for the `ModifyListener` term in your `TodoDetailsPart` class. This search should not find any code after your removal.

114.4. Implement data binding in TodoDetailsPart

Change your implementation of the `TodoDetailsPart` class to use data binding based on the following example code.

```
package com.vogella.tasks.ui.parts;

import java.util.HashMap;
import java.util.List;
import java.util.Map;

import jakarta.annotation.PostConstruct;
import jakarta.annotation.PreDestroy;
import jakarta.inject.Inject;
import jakarta.inject.Named;

import org.eclipse.core.databinding.DataBindingContext;
import org.eclipse.core.databinding.beans.typed.BeanProperties;
import org.eclipse.core.databinding.observable.value.IObservableValue;
import org.eclipse.core.databinding.observable.value.WritableValue;
import org.eclipse.e4.core.di.annotations.Optional;
import org.eclipse.e4.ui.di.Focus;
import org.eclipse.e4.ui.services.IServiceConstants;
import org.eclipse.jface.databinding.swt.typed.WidgetProperties;
import org.eclipse.jface.layout.GridDataFactory;
import org.eclipse.jface.widgets.LabelFactory;
import org.eclipse.jface.widgets.WidgetFactory;
import org.eclipse.swt.SWT;
import org.eclipse.swt.layout.GridLayout;
import org.eclipse.swt.widgets.Button;
import org.eclipse.swt.widgets.Composite;
import org.eclipse.swt.widgets.DateTime;
import org.eclipse.swt.widgets.Text;

import com.vogella.tasks.model.Task;

public class TodoDetailsPart {
    private Text txtSummary;
    private Text txtDescription;
    private DateTime dateTime;
    private Button btnDone;

    // define a new field
    private java.util.Optional<Task> task = java.util.Optional.empty();
```

```
    // observable placeholder for a task
    private WritableValue<Task> observableTodo = new WritableValue<>(); ❶
    private DataBindingContext dbc; ❷

    @PostConstruct
    public void createControls(Composite parent) {
        parent.setLayout(new GridLayout(2, false));

        GridDataFactory gdFactory = GridDataFactory.fillDefaults();
        LabelFactory labelFactory = LabelFactory.newLabel(SWT.NONE);

        labelFactory.text("Summary").create(parent);

        txtSummary = WidgetFactory.text(SWT.BORDER).layoutData(gdFactory.grab(true,
false).create())//
                .create(parent);



        labelFactory.text("Description").create(parent);
        txtDescription = WidgetFactory.text(SWT.BORDER | SWT.MULTI | SWT.V_SCROLL)
                .layoutData(gdFactory.align(SWT.FILL, SWT.FILL).grab(true, true).
create()).create(parent);

        labelFactory.text("Due Date").create(parent);

        // Factory planned for 2020-12 release
        // https://bugs.eclipse.org/bugs/show_bug.cgi?id=567110

        dateTime = new DateTime(parent, SWT.BORDER);
        dateTime.setLayoutData(gdFactory.align(SWT.FILL, SWT.CENTER).grab(false, false
).create());

        labelFactory.text("").create(parent);

        btnDone = WidgetFactory.button(SWT.CHECK).text("Done").create(parent);

        bindData();
        updateUserInterface(task);
    }

    private void bindData() { ❸
        // this assumes that widget field is named "summary"
        if (txtSummary != null && !txtSummary.isDisposed()) {

            dbc = new DataBindingContext();

            Map<String, IObservableValue<?>> fields = new HashMap<>();
            fields.put(Task.FIELD_SUMMARY, WidgetProperties.text(SWT.Modify).observe
```

```
(txtSummary));
            fields.put(Task.FIELD_DESCRIPTION, WidgetProperties.text(SWT.Modify).observe
(txtDescription));
            fields.put(Task.FIELD_DUEDATE, WidgetProperties.localDateSelection().observe
(dateTime));
            fields.put(Task.FIELD_DONE, WidgetProperties.buttonSelection().observe
(btnDone));
            fields.forEach((k, v) -> dbc.bindValue(v, BeanProperties.value(k
).observeDetail(observableTodo)));
        }
    }

    // Add the following new methods to your code

    @Inject
    public void setTasks(@Optional @Named(IServiceConstants.ACTIVE_SELECTION) List<Task>
tasks) {
        if (tasks == null || tasks.isEmpty() || tasks.get(0) == null) {
            this.task = java.util.Optional.empty();
        } else {
            this.task = java.util.Optional.of(tasks.get(0));
        }
        // Remember the task as a field and update the user interface
        updateUserInterface(this.task);
    }
    // allows you to disable or enable the user interface fields
    // if no task is set
    private void enableUserInterface(boolean enabled) {
        if (txtSummary != null && !txtSummary.isDisposed()) {
            txtSummary.setEnabled(enabled);
            txtDescription.setEnabled(enabled);
            dateTime.setEnabled(enabled);
            btnDone.setEnabled(enabled);
        }
    }

    private void updateUserInterface(java.util.Optional<Task> task) {
        if (!task.isPresent()) {
            enableUserInterface(false);
            return; // nothing left to do
        }

        enableUserInterface(true);
        // the following check ensures that the user interface is available,
        // it assumes that you have a text widget named "txtSummary"
        if (txtSummary != null && !txtSummary.isDisposed()) {
            this.observableTodo.setValue(task.get()); ❹
        }
    }
```

```
    @Focus
    public void setFocus() {
        txtSummary.setFocus();
    }

    @PreDestroy ❺
    public void dispose() {
        dbc.dispose();
    }
}
```

❶ New code

❷ New code

❸ New code

❹ Changed code

❺ New code

114.5. Validate

> The details part in your application is currently not supplied with a task; only the wizard can be used to test the data binding. This will be changed in the `ESelectionService` exercise.

To test your data binding, use your task wizard to create new task objects. The following screenshot shows the first page of the wizard.

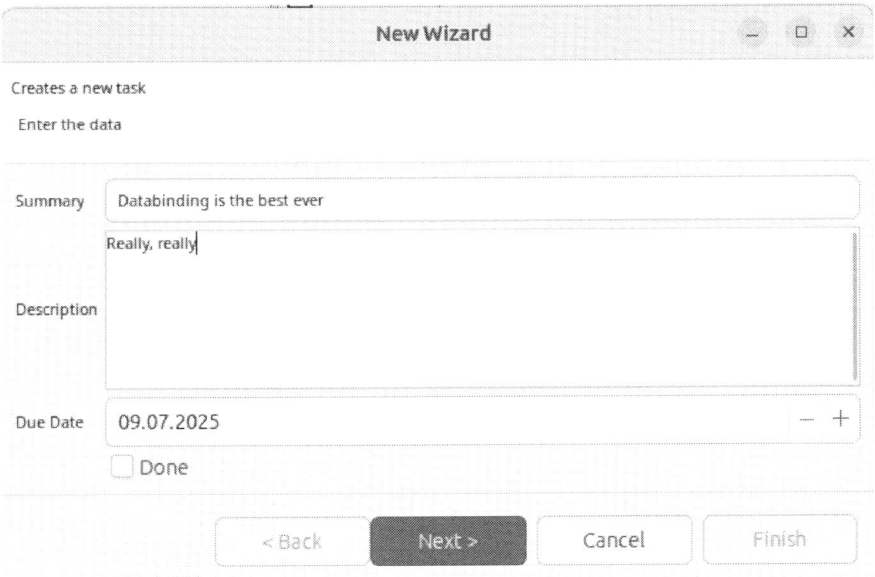

Test if your implementation behaves correctly. Ensure that new task objects are shown in the table after pressing the Load data button.

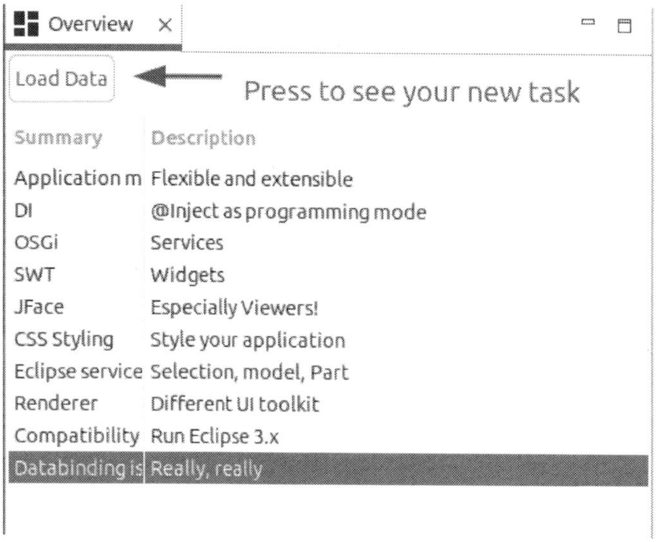

REMEMBER to use the load button to load the data into the table. We will update the table content automatically via the event service in a later exercise.

115. Exercise: Data binding for table viewers

115.1. Implement data binding for the table viewer

Change your implementation of `TodoOverviewPart` to use data binding.

For this, you can delete the `LabelProvider` of your `TableViewerColumn` objects. Also, remove the `viewer.setInput()` and the `ContentProvider`.

The following code demonstrates this implementation.

The following code snippet only contains the data binding relevant part of the code. If you did any of the optional exercises, your implementation may also include a search box, the registration of the popup menu, a filter, or more.

```
package com.vogella.tasks.ui.parts;

import static org.eclipse.jface.layout.GridLayoutFactory.fillDefaults;
import static org.eclipse.jface.widgets.ButtonFactory.newButton;

import java.util.List;
```

```java
import jakarta.annotation.PostConstruct;
import jakarta.inject.Inject;

import org.eclipse.core.databinding.beans.typed.BeanProperties;
import org.eclipse.core.databinding.observable.list.WritableList;
import org.eclipse.e4.ui.di.Focus;
import org.eclipse.jface.databinding.viewers.ViewerSupport;
import org.eclipse.jface.viewers.TableViewer;
import org.eclipse.jface.viewers.TableViewerColumn;
import org.eclipse.swt.SWT;
import org.eclipse.swt.layout.GridData;
import org.eclipse.swt.widgets.Composite;
import org.eclipse.swt.widgets.Table;

import com.vogella.tasks.model.Task;
import com.vogella.tasks.model.TaskService;

public class TodoOverviewPart {

    @Inject
    TaskService taskService;

    private WritableList<Task> writableList;

    private TableViewer viewer;

    @PostConstruct
    public void createControls(Composite parent) {
        fillDefaults().numColumns(1).applyTo(parent);

        newButton(SWT.PUSH).text("Load Data").onSelect(e -> update()).create(parent);

        viewer = new TableViewer(parent, SWT.MULTI | SWT.FULL_SELECTION);
        Table table = viewer.getTable();
        table.setHeaderVisible(true);
        table.setLinesVisible(true);
        table.setLayoutData(new GridData(SWT.FILL, SWT.FILL, true, true));

        // create column for the summary property
        TableViewerColumn colSummary = new TableViewerColumn(viewer, SWT.NONE);
        colSummary.getColumn().setWidth(100);
        colSummary.getColumn().setText("Summary");

        // create column for description property
        TableViewerColumn colDescription = new TableViewerColumn(viewer, SWT.NONE);

        colDescription.getColumn().setWidth(200);
        colDescription.getColumn().setText("Description");
```

```
        // use data binding to bind the viewer
        writableList = new WritableList<>();
        // fill the writable list, when Consumer callback is called. Databinding
        // will do the rest once the list is filled
        taskService.consume(writableList::addAll);
        ViewerSupport.bind(viewer, writableList,
                BeanProperties.values(Task.FIELD_SUMMARY, Task.FIELD_DESCRIPTION));
    }

    public void updateViewer(List<Task> list) {
        if (viewer != null) {
            writableList.clear();
            writableList.addAll(list);
        }
    }
    @Focus
    public void setFocus() {
        viewer.getControl().setFocus();
    }

    private void update() {
        updateViewer(taskService.getAll());
    }
}
```

115.2. Clean up old code

You should have removed calls to the `setInput`, `setContentProvider` and `setLabelProvider` methods. Use the text search in your IDE for these methods to validate this, in case you are having problems.

115.3. Validate

Start your application and load the data into the table via the Load data button. Verify that the table displays data correctly.

Currently, the selection of the table is not sent to the TodoDetailsPart. This will be implemented in a later exercise.

Create a new task via the wizard and verify that the new task is shown in the table.

REMEMBER to use the load button to load the data into the table. We will update the table content automatically via the event service in a later exercise.

116. Optional exercise: Review the data binding snippets

This exercise requires knowledge of using Git, in case you are not familiar with Git, just skip it (or learn to use Git before, e.g., by reading Using Git with the Eclipse IDE [https://www.vogella.com/tutorials/EclipseGit/article.html]).

The data binding snippets are part of the https://github.com/eclipse-platform/eclipse.platform.ui Git repository.

Fork it on GitHub and clone it on your local machine or clone it directly.

> Forking the repo on GitHub is preferred as this gives you the option to contribute enhancements back to the project with pull requests.

> You may want to use a new workspace for importing the data binding snippets into it to avoid confusion with your own code.

Import the `org.eclipse.jface.examples.databinding` project and review the data binding examples. They are provided by the `org.eclipse.jface.examples.databinding.snippets` package.

117. Optional exercise: Data binding for viewer data filtering

Use the information from the snippets to update your implementation of the filter for the viewer to use data binding.

Part XIV: Using Eclipse platform services

118. Eclipse platform services

The services provided by the Eclipse platform simplify the implementation of common tasks. These services can be accessed via dependency injection. The following table gives an overview of the available platform services.

Table 29. Platform services

Service	Description
`EModelService`	Used to search for elements in the model, create new model elements, clone existing snippets and insert new elements into the runtime application model.
`ESelectionService`	Used to retrieve and set the current active selection in the user interface.
`ECommandService`	Gives access to existing commands and allows you to create and modify commands.
`EHandlerService`	Allows you to access, change and trigger handlers.

Service	Description
EPartService	Provides API to access and modify parts. It allows you to switch perspectives and can be used to trigger that a method annotated with @Persist in dirty parts, i.e. if the corresponding part behaves like an editor.
IEventBroker	Provides functionality to send event data and to register for specified events and event topics.
EContextService	Activate and deactivate key bindings defined as BindingContext in the application model. The content referred to in this service is the BindingContext and not the IEclipseContext.
IThemeEngine	Allows switching the styling of the application at runtime.
EMenuService	Registers a popup menu (MPopupMenu) for a control.

Other available services are:

- `org.eclipse.e4.core.services.Adapter` - An adapter can adapt an object to the specified type, allowing clients to request domain-specific behavior for an object. It integrates `IAdaptable` and `IAdapterManager`.
- `org.eclipse.e4.core.services.Logger` - Provides logging functionality
- `org.eclipse.jface.window.IShellProvider` - allows access to a `Shell`, depends on SWT.

119. Selection service

119.1. Using the selection service

The `ESelectionService` service allows you to retrieve and set the user interface selection in each top-level window and part. This selection is stored under the `IServiceConstants.ACTIVE_SELECTION` context key.

119.2. Retrieving the selection service and setting the current selection

A client can get the selection service via dependency injection.

You can change the current selection with the `setSelection()` method of the `ESelectionService` class. This is demonstrated in the following code.

```
@Inject ESelectionService selectionService; ❶

// more code
```

```
viewer.addSelectionChangedListener(event -> { ❷
    IStructuredSelection selection = viewer.getStructuredSelection();
    selectionService.setSelection(selection.getFirstElement()); ❸
});
```

❶ In this example, you use field injection to retrieve the service

❷ viewer is a JFace table viewer in this example

❸ Sets the first selected element of the viewer as UI selection

119.3. Getting the selection

A client can retrieve the current selection from the `ESelectionService` via the `getSelection()` method. The `getSelection(partId)` method allows you to retrieve the selection of a specific part.

The selection can be retrieved via dependency injection. For this, use the `@Named` annotation to specify the `IServiceConstants.ACTIVE_SELECTION` constant. The Eclipse framework ensures that selections are only injected if the request type matches the selection.

The usage of dependency injection to retrieve the selection is demonstrated in the following code.

```
@Inject
public void setTasks(@Optional
        @Named(IServiceConstants.ACTIVE_SELECTION) List<Task> tasks) { ❶
        // do something with the list of todos
}

@Inject
public void setTask(@Optional
        @Named(IServiceConstants.ACTIVE_SELECTION) Task task) { ❷
        // do something with the task
}
```

❶ This method is called if the current selection is a `List`

❷ This method is called if the current selection is a `Task`

120. Model Service

120.1. Definition of the model service

The *model service* gives you access to the application model and allows you to modify it at runtime. It allows you to search for, delete, or create model elements.

This service can be accessed via dependency injection, as demonstrated via the following snippet.

```
@Inject EModelService modelService;
```

120.2. Searching model elements

The `findElements()` method allows you to search for specific model elements. The following code shows an example for using the `findElements()` method.

```
package com.vogella.tasks.ui.handlers;

import java.util.ArrayList;
import java.util.List;

import org.eclipse.e4.core.di.annotations.Execute;
import org.eclipse.e4.ui.model.application.MApplication;
import org.eclipse.e4.ui.model.application.ui.MUIElement;
import org.eclipse.e4.ui.model.application.ui.basic.MPart;
import org.eclipse.e4.ui.workbench.modeling.EModelService;

public class ModelServiceExampleHandler {

    @Execute
    public void execute(MApplication application, EModelService service) {

        // find objects by ID
        findPartsById(application, service);

        // find objects by type
        findParts(application, service);

        // find objects by tags
        findObjectsByTag(application, service);

    }

    // example for search by ID
    private void findPartsById(MApplication application, EModelService service) {
        List<MPart> parts = service.findElements(application, "mypart",
                MPart.class, null);
        System.out.println("Found part(s) : " + parts.size());
    }

    // example for search by type
    private void findParts(MApplication application,
            EModelService service) {
        List<MPart> parts = service.findElements(application, null,
                MPart.class, null);
        System.out.println("Found parts : " + parts.size());
```

```
    }

    // example for search by tag
    private void findObjectsByTag(MApplication application,
            EModelService service) {
        List<String> tags = new ArrayList<>();
        tags.add("justatag");
        List<MUIElement> elementsWithTags = service.findElements(application,
                null, null, tags);
        System.out.println("Found parts(s) : " + elementsWithTags.size());
    }
}
```

The following code demonstrates how you can access the current perspective for a part.

```
package com.vogella.tasks.ui.handlers;

import org.eclipse.e4.core.di.annotations.Execute;
import org.eclipse.e4.ui.model.application.MApplication;
import org.eclipse.e4.ui.model.application.ui.MUIElement;
import org.eclipse.e4.ui.model.application.ui.advanced.MPerspective;
import org.eclipse.e4.ui.workbench.modeling.EModelService;

public class FindPerspectiveHandler {
    @Execute
    public void execute(MApplication application, EModelService service) {
        // search for a part with the following ID
        String ID = "com.example.e4.rcp.parts.tododetail";
        MUIElement element = service.find(ID, application);
        MPerspective perspective = service.getPerspectiveFor(element);
        System.out.println(perspective);
        // TODO do something useful with the perspective
    }
}
```

You can use the `findElements` method with a fifth parameter that allows you to specify additional search flags, e.g., IN_ACTIVE_PERSPECTIVE, OUTSIDE_PERSPECTIVE, IN_ANY_PERSPECTIVE. See the Javadoc of the `findElements` method for further details.

120.3. Creating model elements

As the application model is interactive, you can dynamically create new model elements and add them to your application. For example, you can add new parts to your application. This will be demonstrated in the exercises.

120.4. Cloning elements or snippets

In the application model you can create `Snippet` model elements that can be used to instantiate model objects at runtime. It is possible to copy existing application model elements via the model service.

You can use the `cloneElement()` and `cloneSnippet()` methods of the model service to copy an existing element or snippet. The resulting object can be assigned to another model element.

120.5. Modifying existing model elements

You can access existing model elements, via the model service or via dependency injection and adjust their attributes.

The Eclipse framework automatically keeps track of the application model and changes to the model are reflected immediately in your application.

For example, if you add a new window to your application, it becomes visible instantly. Or if you inject an MPart object and call its `setLabel()` method, the text of the part in a `PartStack` changes immediately.

120.6. Removing a model element

The `deleteModelElement()` method of `EModelService` allows you to remove a model element from your application. It calls `setToBeRendered(false)` on the model element and removes it from its parent container.

121. Example of changing the application model

The following gives example for search model element and changing the application model at runtime.

121.1. Example: Search for a perspective and change its attributes

The following code shows how to access a `PartSashContainer` with the `mypartsashcontainer` ID. It demonstrates how to modify model attributes.

In this example, it changes the *container data* parameter for its children. This will arrange (layout) the parts in the container.

```
@Execute
public void execute(EModelService service, MWindow window) {
    MPartSashContainer find = (MPartSashContainer) service.
        find("mypartsashcontainer", window);
    List<MPartSashContainerElement> list = find.getChildren();
```

```
    int i = 0;
    // make the first part in the container larger
    for (MPartSashContainerElement element : list) {

        if (i > 0) {
            element.setContainerData("20");
        } else {
            element.setContainerData("80");
        }
        i++;
    }
}
```

121.2. Example: Dynamically create a new window

To create new model objects you can use the `createModelElement()` of the model service. After you created such an object you can add it to your application model at runtime.

For example, the creation of a new window for a running application is demonstrated by the following code snippet.

```
// create a new window and set its size
MWindow window = modelService.createModelElement(MWindow.class);
window.setWidth(200);
window.setHeight(300);

// add the new window to the application
application.getChildren().add(window);
```

121.3. Example: Dynamically create a new part

The following code demonstrates how to create and add a new part to the currently active window.

```
package com.vogella.tasks.ui.handlers;

import org.eclipse.e4.core.di.annotations.Execute;
import org.eclipse.e4.ui.model.application.MApplication;
import org.eclipse.e4.ui.model.application.ui.basic.MPart;
import org.eclipse.e4.ui.workbench.modeling.EModelService;
import org.eclipse.e4.ui.workbench.modeling.EPartService;
import org.eclipse.e4.ui.workbench.modeling.EPartService.PartState;

public class DynamicPartHandlerCode {
    // used as reference
    @Execute
```

```
    public void execute(MApplication application, EPartService partService,
            EModelService modelService) {

        // create new part
        MPart mPart = modelService.createModelElement(MPart.class);
        mPart.setLabel("Testing");
        mPart.setElementId("newid");
        mPart.setContributionURI("bundleclass://com.vogella.tasks.ui/"
                + "com.vogella.tasks.ui.parts.DynamicPart");
        partService.showPart(mPart, PartState.ACTIVATE);
    }
}
```

> Typically you would add the part to a predefined `PartStack`. Use the model service to search for the correct one.

122. Part service and editor-like behavior

122.1. Definition of the part service

The *part service* allows you to find and perform actions on parts in the application model.

It allows you to switch perspectives and to create and activate new parts based on part descriptors in the application model.

122.2. Accessing the part service

Use dependency injection to get access to the part service. For example, via the `@Inject EPartService partService;` statement.

122.3. Example: Showing and hiding parts

The following example shows how you can find parts, hide or show them. If the *Visible* attribute of the part was initially set to `false` (not visible), you need to call the `setVisible(true)` method of the model element to ensure that the part gets displayed.

```
@Inject private EPartService partService;

// search part with ID "com.example.todo.rcp.parts.tododetails"
// assume that a part with this ID exists
detailsTodoPart = partService.findPart("com.example.todo.rcp.parts.tododetails");

// hide the part
partService.hidePart(detailsTodoPart);
```

```
//show the part
detailsTodoPart.setVisible(true); // required if initially not visible
partService.showPart(detailsTodoPart, PartState.VISIBLE);
```

122.4. Example: Switching perspectives

The following example demonstrates switching to another perspective using the part service.

```
package com.vogella.tasks.ui.handlers;

import java.util.List;

import org.eclipse.e4.core.di.annotations.Execute;
import org.eclipse.e4.ui.model.application.MApplication;
import org.eclipse.e4.ui.model.application.ui.MUIElement;
import org.eclipse.e4.ui.model.application.ui.advanced.MPerspective;
import org.eclipse.e4.ui.model.application.ui.basic.MPart;
import org.eclipse.e4.ui.workbench.modeling.EModelService;
import org.eclipse.e4.ui.workbench.modeling.EPartService;
import org.eclipse.e4.ui.workbench.modeling.EPartService.PartState;

public class SwitchPerspectiveHandler {
    @Execute
    public void execute(MApplication app, EPartService partService,
            EModelService modelService) {
        MPerspective element =
                (MPerspective) modelService.find("secondperspective", app);
        // now switch perspective
        partService.switchPerspective(element);
    }
}
```

122.5. Using part descriptors

The *part descriptor* model element is a template for the creation of a part. By defining a common set of attributes via such a blueprint it is possible to create concrete instances of it via the part service.

Via the `Multiple` attribute of the part descriptor you configure if multiple instances of this part can be created. An example of such a model element is shown in the following screenshot.

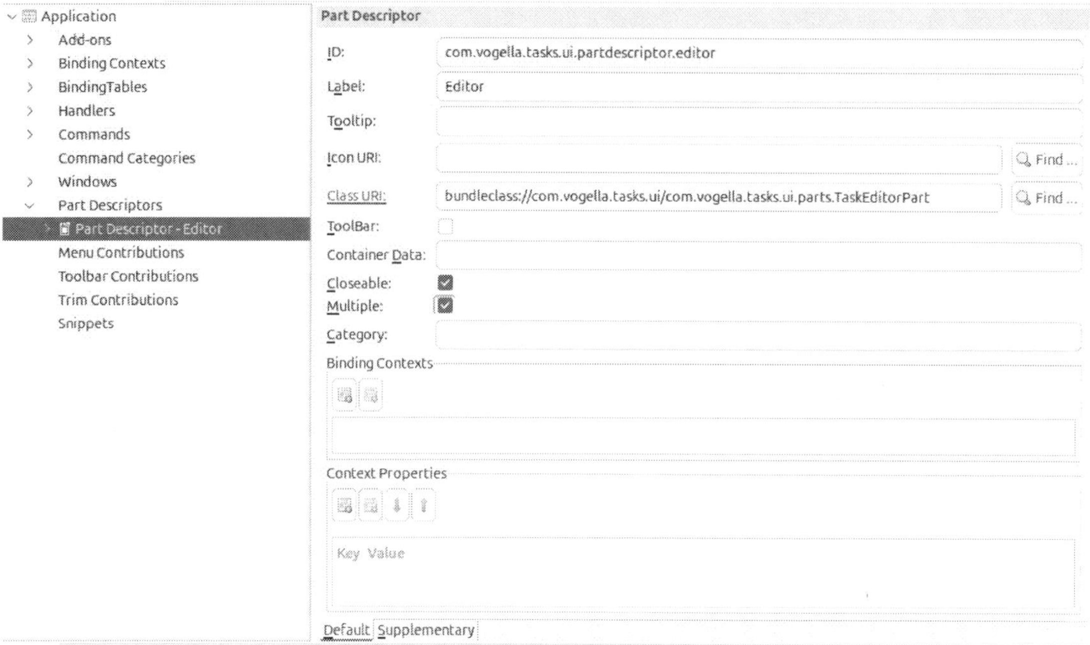

122.6. Example: Part descriptors and creating parts dynamically

The `EPartService` service allows you to create a new part based on a part descriptor. This is demonstrated by the following example code.

```
package com.vogella.tasks.ui.handlers;

import org.eclipse.e4.core.di.annotations.Execute;
import org.eclipse.e4.ui.model.application.ui.basic.MPart;
import org.eclipse.e4.ui.workbench.modeling.EPartService;
import org.eclipse.e4.ui.workbench.modeling.EPartService.PartState;

public class OpenPartHandler {

    // the following code assumes that
    // the "com.vogella.tasks.ui.partdescriptor.fileeditor" ID
    // is used for the part descriptor
    @Execute
    public void execute(EPartService partService) {

        // create a new part based on a part descriptor
        // if multiple parts of this type are allowed a new part
        // is always generated

        MPart part = partService.createPart
("com.vogella.tasks.ui.partdescriptor.fileeditor");
        part.setLabel("New Dynamic Part");
```

```
        // optional you could use the model service to find a certain container and add
the new part to its children

         // now show the new part
        // as it is in this coding not added to a container it is shown in default
container of the application (which is the last container)
        partService.showPart(part, PartState.ACTIVATE);
    }
}
```

122.7. Showing parts

To open and show a part in the application, you can use the `EPartService.showPart(…, PartState.ACTIVATE)` method. If the part is already contained in a container like a stack, it is shown and granted focus.

If it is not yet contained in a container, it is added to one. By default, this is the last container, i.e. in most cases the last stack.

You can use the category field in the part descriptor and a tag in the container to open the new part in the specified container.

A category for a `MPartDescriptor` can be defined like this:

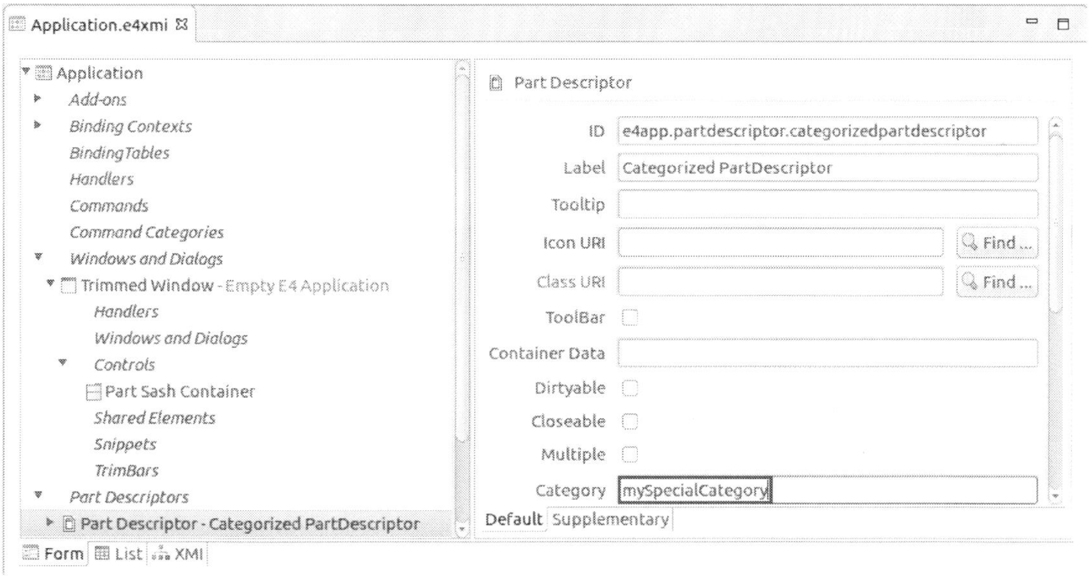

You can add a tag to your container, as depicted in the following screenshot.

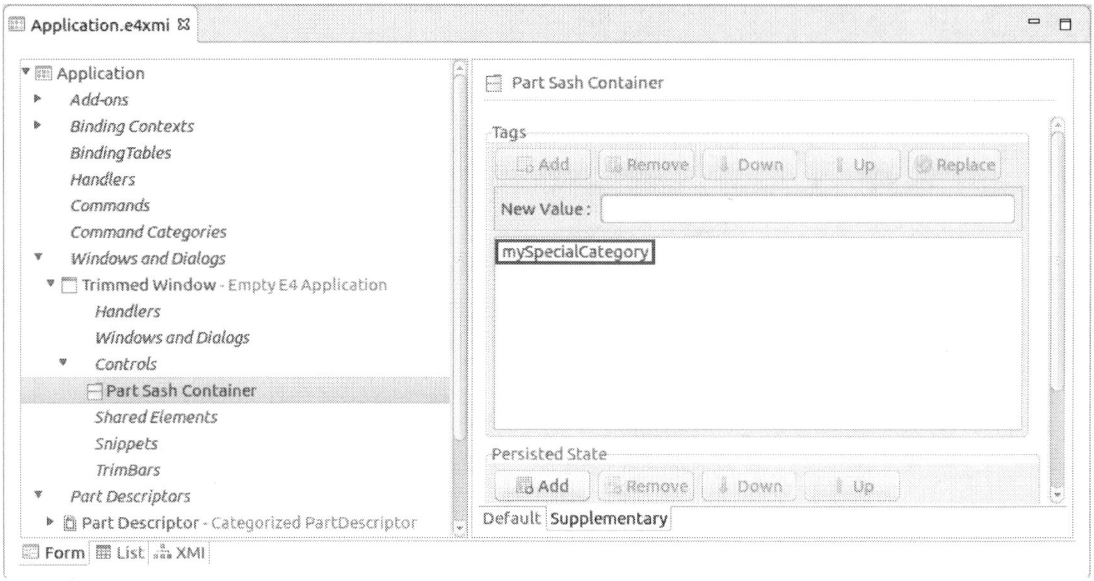

If the tag is the same as the category, the following code opens the new part in the specified container.

```
EPartService partService = getPartService();
partService.showPart("e4app.partdescriptor.categorizedpartdescriptor", PartState.
ACTIVATE);
```

123. Implementing editor-like behavior

123.1. Parts that behave similar to editors

An editor is a part that requires the user to trigger a save operation to persist data changes. Editors that contain data, which can be saved, are typically called *dirty*.

The part service allows you to save dirty parts. Every part can mark itself as dirty, hence behave like an editor.

123.2. `MDirtyable` and `@Persist`

A part has a `MDirtyable` attribute that indicates that it can be marked as dirty. A dirty state indicates that the part contains unsaved changes. The `MDirtyable` object can be injected into a part.

You can use the `setDirty(boolean)` method to mark the part as dirty.

The following snippet demonstrates how to use the `MDirtyable` model property in a part to flag it as dirty after a button was pressed.

```java
import jakarta.annotation.PostConstruct;
import jakarta.inject.Inject;

import org.eclipse.e4.ui.di.Persist;
import org.eclipse.e4.ui.model.application.ui.basic.MPart;
import org.eclipse.swt.SWT;
import org.eclipse.swt.events.SelectionAdapter;
import org.eclipse.swt.events.SelectionEvent;
import org.eclipse.swt.widgets.Button;
import org.eclipse.swt.widgets.Composite;

public class MySavePart {

    @Inject
    MPart part;

    @PostConstruct
    public void createControls(Composite parent) {
        Button button = new Button(parent, SWT.PUSH);
        button.addSelectionListener(new SelectionAdapter() {
            @Override
            public void widgetSelected(SelectionEvent e) {
                part.setDirty(true);
            }
        });
    }
}
```

The part service allows you to query the dirty parts and to call a method annotated with `@Persist` on the dirty parts. This method saves the data of the part and sets the dirty flag back to false if the save operation was successful.

```java
@Persist
public void save(MPart part, TaskService todoService) {
    // save changes via TaskService for example
    todoService.saveTodo(todo);
    // save was successful
    part.setDirty(false);
}
```

Every part is responsible for saving itself. Hence every part that behaves like an editor must have a method annotated with `@Persist`.

123.3. Use part service to trigger save in editors

The part service allows you to trigger the `@Persist` method on the dirty parts via the `saveAll()` method.

The `EPartService` searches in each part which is marked as dirty for a method annotated with `@Persist`. This method is called by the framework and has to save the data which the editor holds. If saving the data was successful it should call the `setDirty(false)` method on the `MDirtyable` object.

The following example demonstrates that.

```
package com.vogella.tasks.ui.handlers;

import org.eclipse.e4.core.di.annotations.Execute;
import org.eclipse.e4.ui.workbench.modeling.EPartService;

public class SaveHandler {

    @Execute
    void execute(EPartService partService) {
        partService.saveAll(false);
    }
}
```

123.4. MPart and multiple editors

You can use the *MPart* model element to create multiple editors. Every model element can have persisted data assigned to it that can be accessed via the `getPersistedState()` method.

In its @PostConstruct method the implementation class can get the `MPart` injected and access its persisted state. This information can be used to configure the editor.

124. Command and Handler service

124.1. Purpose of the command and handler service

The command and handler services provide the functionality to work with commands and handlers.

Via the handler service you can create, activate and trigger handlers based on commands. The command service allows you to access, and configure commands, i.e. by setting the parameters.

124.2. Access to command and handler service

You can use dependency injection to access the services. The relevant interfaces are `ECommandService` and `EHandlerService`.

124.3. Example of executing a command

The following example shows how to execute a handler for an existing command.

```
// create parameter for the command
// optional, can be null
Map<String, String> parameters = new HashMap<String, String>();
parameters.put(Constants.SEARCH_QUERY_ID, id);

ParameterizedCommand cmd =
    commandService.createCommand("com.example.mycommand", parameters);

// execute the registered handler for the command
handlerService.executeHandler(cmd);
```

124.4. Example of assigning a handler to a command

The following example shows how to add a new handler to an existing command. It assumes that the `AboutHandler` class already exists.

```
Command command = commandService.getCommand("com.example.mycommand");

// check if the command is defined
System.out.println(command.isDefined());

// activate handler, assumption: the AboutHandler() class exists already
handlerService.activateHandler("com.example.mycommand",
        new AboutHandler());

// prepare execution of command
ParameterizedCommand cmd =
    commandService.createCommand("com.example.mycommand", null);

// check if the command can be executed
if (handlerService.canExecute(cmd)){
    // execute the command
    handlerService.executeHandler(cmd);
}
```

125. Eclipse Logging

The Eclipse `ILog` class provides a simple set of APIs for logging exceptions, warnings, or other information useful in debugging or servicing a deployed Eclipse product. The intent of the log is to record information that can be used later to diagnose problems in the field. Because this information is not directed at users, you do not need to worry about translating messages or simplifying explanations into a form that users will understand. The idea is that when things go wrong in the field, your users can send you the log file to help you figure out what happened.

Each plug-in has its own log associated with it, but all logged information eventually makes its way into the platform log file (see the `getLogFileLocation` method on `Platform`).

```
 import org.eclipse.core.runtime.ILog;

ILog.get().info("Starting");
ILog.get().error("Generating template failed!", e);
ILog.get().warn("Creating a warning..");
```

During development, you can browse and manipulate the platform log file using the Error Log view (**Window > Show View > General > Error Log**). You can have the log file mirrored in the Java console by starting Eclipse with the `-consoleLog` command-line argument.

More complex logging is available through the `org.eclipse.core.runtime.ILog` interface. You can write `IStatus` objects to the log file, including a `MultiStatus`. `MultiStatus` is used if you have hierarchies of information to display. If you create your own subclass of the utility class Status, you can override the getMessage method to return extra information to be displayed in the log file.

The log level can be configured in the *config.ini* file of your application using the *eclipse.log.level* parameter. The value can be set to *INFO*, *WARNING* and *ERROR*. *INFO* will, for example, show all log messages. By default, Eclipse logs all messages.

126. Exercise: Selection service

In this section, you propagate the selection of the table in the `TodoOverviewPart` to your `TodoDetailsPart`.

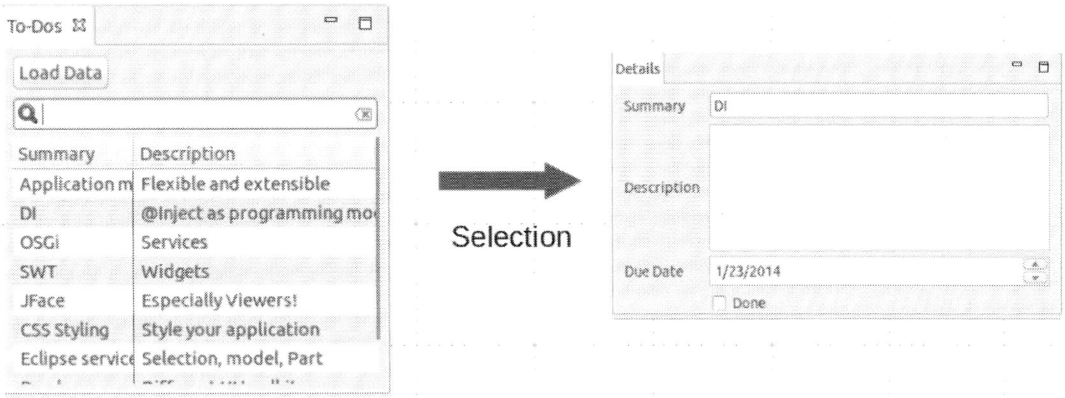

The `org.eclipse.e4.ui.services` plug-in must be defined as a dependency in the `MANIFEST.MF` file of your `com.vogella.tasks.ui` plug-in. Validate that this is the case.

126.1. Retrieving the selection service

In your `TodoOverviewPart` class, acquire the `ESelectionService` service via dependency injection.

```
@Inject
ESelectionService selectionService;
```

126.2. Setting the selection in TodoOverviewPart

Use the selection service to set the selection, once the user selects an entry in the list.

```
// in the import statements
import org.eclipse.jface.viewers.IStructuredSelection;
// more code



// after the viewer is instantiated
    viewer.addSelectionChangedListener(event -> {
            IStructuredSelection selection = viewer.getStructuredSelection();

            @SuppressWarnings("unchecked")
            List<Task> selectedElements= selection.toList();
            // Make a copy and send out only the copy
            List<Task> copiedElements = selectedElements.stream().map(t -> t.copy
()).collect(Collectors.toList()); ❶
            selectionService.setSelection(copiedElements);
        });
```

❶ instead of sending out the selected object, we made a copy of it, so that changes outside this view will not affect this view directly

126.3. Review TodoDetailsPart

In an earlier exercise, you already implemented the logic in `TodoDetailsPart`, no change should be required here. The relevant part of `TodoDetailsPart` is repeated in the following snippet.

```
@Inject
public void setTasks(@Optional @Named(IServiceConstants.ACTIVE_SELECTION) List<Task>
tasks) {
    if (tasks == null || tasks.isEmpty() || tasks.get(0) == null) {
        this.task = java.util.Optional.empty();
    } else {
        this.task = java.util.Optional.of(tasks.get(0));
    }
    // Remember the todo as a field and update the user interface
    updateUserInterface(this.task);
}
```

126.4. Validate selection propagation

Start your application. If you select a row in the JFace table, the selected task objects are propagated via the selection service. The `TodoDetailsPart` extracts the first one and displays it.

> Please keep in mind that `@Inject` based injections run before the `@PostConstruct` method. Hence the `updateUserInterface()` method needs to check if your user interface is already available.
>
> It might also happen that @Inject annotated methods are called before the `@PostConstruct` method. For example, your part may be in a stack but is not selected. Eclipse does not construct the object for the part before it becomes selected by the user. If the selection is set before the part is constructed, its @Inject method is called before the `@PostConstruct` method is called.
>
> The `updateUserInterface()` method call at the end of your `@PostConstruct` method covers this case.

127. Optional exercise: Selection service for deleting data

In this exercise, you allow the user to delete selected tasks.

127.1. Implement the RemoveTaskHandler handler

Change the `RemoveTaskHandler` so that the selected tasks can be deleted.

▼ *Solution example*

```
package com.vogella.tasks.ui.handlers;

import java.util.List;

import jakarta.inject.Named;

import org.eclipse.e4.core.di.annotations.Execute;
import org.eclipse.e4.core.di.annotations.Optional;
import org.eclipse.e4.ui.services.IServiceConstants;
import org.eclipse.jface.dialogs.MessageDialog;
import org.eclipse.swt.widgets.Shell;

import com.vogella.tasks.model.Task;
import com.vogella.tasks.model.TaskService;

public class RemoveTaskHandler {
    @Execute
    public void execute(TaskService taskService,
            @Optional @Named(IServiceConstants.ACTIVE_SELECTION) List<Task> tasks,
            @Named(IServiceConstants.ACTIVE_SHELL) Shell shell) {
        if (tasks != null) {
            tasks.forEach(t -> taskService.delete(t.getId()));
        } else {
            MessageDialog.openInformation(shell, "Deletion not possible", "No todo
selected");
        }
    }
}
```

127.2. Validate that the deletion works

Run your application and select at least one entry in your table. Select your **Edit › Remove** menu entry.

Press the *Load Data* button to update it. Validate that the selected task is not available anymore.

> Currently, your parts are not reacting automatically to new data entries. You have to press the Load Data button in your `TodoOverviewPart` part. You will implement automatic updates of the table in a later exercise.

127.3. Validate that the context menu for deletion works

In an earlier exercise, you defined a context (popup) menu for your table. As the `RemoveTaskHandler` class is now correctly implemented, you should be able to delete selected items with the *Delete* context menu. This should not require additional changes in the `RemoveTaskHandler` class.

To validate that, delete one to-do item via the context menu. Use the Load Data button and verify that the deleted item has been removed from the data model.

127.4. Optional: Enable the deletion handler only if necessary

Enable the deletion handler for tasks only if a `Task` is selected.

```
@CanExecute
public boolean execute(@Optional @Named(IServiceConstants.ACTIVE_SELECTION) List<Task>
tasks) {
    if (tasks == null || tasks.isEmpty()) {
        return false;
    }
    return true;
}
```

128. Exercise: Implement an editor

128.1. Ensure that the required dependencies are available

You should already have the required dependencies in your `com.vogella.tasks.ui` plugin.

Add the following plug-ins as a dependency to the `MANIFEST.MF` file of the `com.vogella.tasks.ui` plug-in.

- `org.eclipse.e4.ui.model.workbench`
- `org.eclipse.e4.ui.workbench.swt`

128.2. Convert TodoDetailsPart to an editor

Use the `setDirty` method of the `MPart` class to tell the Eclipse framework that the part contains unsaved data.

The following example code demonstrates that.

```
package com.vogella.tasks.ui.parts;

import java.util.HashMap;
import java.util.List;
import java.util.Map;

import jakarta.annotation.PostConstruct;
import jakarta.annotation.PreDestroy;
import jakarta.inject.Inject;
import jakarta.inject.Named;

import org.eclipse.core.databinding.Binding;
import org.eclipse.core.databinding.DataBindingContext;
import org.eclipse.core.databinding.beans.typed.BeanProperties;
import org.eclipse.core.databinding.observable.value.IObservableValue;
import org.eclipse.core.databinding.observable.value.WritableValue;
import org.eclipse.e4.core.di.annotations.Optional;
import org.eclipse.e4.ui.di.Focus;
import org.eclipse.e4.ui.di.Persist;
import org.eclipse.e4.ui.model.application.ui.basic.MPart;
import org.eclipse.e4.ui.services.IServiceConstants;
import org.eclipse.jface.databinding.swt.typed.WidgetProperties;
import org.eclipse.jface.layout.GridDataFactory;
import org.eclipse.jface.widgets.LabelFactory;
import org.eclipse.jface.widgets.WidgetFactory;
import org.eclipse.swt.SWT;
import org.eclipse.swt.layout.GridLayout;
import org.eclipse.swt.widgets.Button;
import org.eclipse.swt.widgets.Composite;
import org.eclipse.swt.widgets.DateTime;
import org.eclipse.swt.widgets.Text;

import com.vogella.tasks.model.Task;
import com.vogella.tasks.model.TaskService;

public class TodoDetailsPart {
    private Text txtSummary;
    private Text txtDescription;
    private DateTime dateTime;
    private Button btnDone;

    // define a new field
    private java.util.Optional<Task> task = java.util.Optional.empty();

    // observable placeholder for a task
    private WritableValue<Task> observableTodo = new WritableValue<>();
    private DataBindingContext dbc;
    @Inject
```

```
    private MPart part; ❶

    // pause dirty listener when new selection is set
    private boolean pauseDirtyListener; ❷

    @PostConstruct
    public void createControls(Composite parent) {
        parent.setLayout(new GridLayout(2, false));

        GridDataFactory gdFactory = GridDataFactory.fillDefaults();
        LabelFactory labelFactory = LabelFactory.newLabel(SWT.NONE);

        labelFactory.text("Summary").create(parent);

        txtSummary = WidgetFactory.text(SWT.BORDER).layoutData(gdFactory.grab(true,
false).create())//
                .create(parent);

        labelFactory.text("Description").create(parent);
        txtDescription = WidgetFactory.text(SWT.BORDER | SWT.MULTI | SWT.V_SCROLL)
                .layoutData(gdFactory.align(SWT.FILL, SWT.FILL).grab(true, true).
create()).create(parent);

        labelFactory.text("Due Date").create(parent);

        // Factory planned for 2020-12 release
        // https://bugs.eclipse.org/bugs/show_bug.cgi?id=567110

        dateTime = new DateTime(parent, SWT.BORDER);
        dateTime.setLayoutData(gdFactory.align(SWT.FILL, SWT.CENTER).grab(false, false
).create());

        labelFactory.text("").create(parent);

        btnDone = WidgetFactory.button(SWT.CHECK).text("Done").create(parent);

        bindData();
        updateUserInterface(task);
    }

    private void bindData() {
        // this assumes that widget field is named "summary"
        if (txtSummary != null && !txtSummary.isDisposed()) {

            dbc = new DataBindingContext();

            Map<String, IObservableValue<?>> fields = new HashMap<>();
            fields.put(Task.FIELD_SUMMARY, WidgetProperties.text(SWT.Modify).observe
(txtSummary));
```

```
            fields.put(Task.FIELD_DESCRIPTION, WidgetProperties.text(SWT.Modify).observe
(txtDescription));
            fields.put(Task.FIELD_DUEDATE, WidgetProperties.localDateSelection().observe
(dateTime));
            fields.put(Task.FIELD_DONE, WidgetProperties.buttonSelection().observe
(btnDone));
            fields.forEach((k, v) -> dbc.bindValue(v, BeanProperties.value(k
).observeDetail(observableTodo)));

❸
            dbc.getBindings().forEach(item -> {
                Binding binding = item;
                binding.getTarget().addChangeListener(e -> {
                    if (!pauseDirtyListener && part != null) {
                        part.setDirty(true);
                    }
                });
            });
        }
    }

    // Add the following new methods to your code

    @Inject
    public void setTasks(@Optional @Named(IServiceConstants.ACTIVE_SELECTION) List<Task>
tasks) {
        if (tasks == null || tasks.isEmpty() || tasks.get(0) == null) {
            this.task = java.util.Optional.empty();
        } else {
            this.task = java.util.Optional.of(tasks.get(0));
        }
        // Remember the task as a field and update the user interface
        updateUserInterface(this.task);
    }

    // allows you to disable or enable the user interface fields
    // if no task is set
    private void enableUserInterface(boolean enabled) {
        if (txtSummary != null && !txtSummary.isDisposed()) {
            txtSummary.setEnabled(enabled);
            txtDescription.setEnabled(enabled);
            dateTime.setEnabled(enabled);
            btnDone.setEnabled(enabled);
        }
    }

    private void updateUserInterface(java.util.Optional<Task> task) {
        if (!task.isPresent()) {
            enableUserInterface(false);
```

```
            return; // nothing left to do
        }

        enableUserInterface(true);
        // the following check ensures that the user interface is available,
        // it assumes that you have a text widget named "txtSummary"
        if (txtSummary != null && !txtSummary.isDisposed()) {
            pauseDirtyListener = true; ❹
            this.observableTodo.setValue(task.get());
            pauseDirtyListener = false; //
        }
    }

    @Persist ❺
    public void save(TaskService todoService) {
        task.ifPresent(todoService::update);
        if (part != null) {
            part.setDirty(false);
        }
    }

    @Focus
    public void setFocus() {
        txtSummary.setFocus();
    }

    @PreDestroy
    public void dispose() {
        dbc.dispose();
    }
}
```

❶ Inject the MPart to set its dirty value

❷ boolean to pause the data binding while the task is updated

❸ set a dirty state if one of the bindings is changed

❹ If a new task is set, we pause the data binding for updating the dirty state

❺ method to save

The code is almost the same, but you get `MPart` injected and use its `setDirty` method to indicate whether the part needs a save operation.

> ⚠ You need to check if the part is null because the `TodoDetailsPart` is also used in the wizard to create new to-dos. In this wizard, the part variable is not set, hence it is null.

128.3. Implement the save handler

Change your `SaveAllHandler` handler class, so that the part service is used to call the `@Persist` method of all parts that are marked as dirty.

```
package com.vogella.tasks.ui.handlers;

import org.eclipse.e4.core.di.annotations.Execute;
import org.eclipse.e4.ui.workbench.modeling.EPartService;

public class SaveAllHandler {

    @Execute
    void execute(EPartService partService) {
        partService.saveAll(false);
    }
}
```

In a later exercise, you will implement that the save handler can only be executed if a dirty editor exists.

128.4. Validate

Start your application and select an entry in the table of your *TodoOverviewPart* element. Modify the selected task in the *Details* part. Ensure that the part is marked as dirty.

Select **File › Save** and validate that the editor is not marked as dirty anymore.

Reload the data in the table to ensure that the data was correctly saved.

Create a new task item, with the wizard and ensure that the wizard still works.

128.5. Optional exercise: Enable save only if there is something to save

Also, implement the `@CanExecute` method of the `SaveAllHandler` so that this handler is only active if something is to save.

128.6. Optional exercise: Confirmation dialog for modified data

In case the user has changed data in the `TodoDetailsPart` part and changes the selection in the `TodoOverviewPart` part, allow the user to ignore this update in the details part. Use the `openConfirmation()` method from the `MessageDialog` class for the confirmation dialog.

129. Exercise: Enable handlers and avoiding data loss

129.1. Enable the save handler only if necessary

Change your `SaveAllHandler` class so that the *save* handler is only active if there is something to save.

```
@CanExecute
boolean canExecute(EPartService partService) {
    return !partService.getDirtyParts().isEmpty();
}
```

129.2. Optional exercise: Avoid data loss in the ExitHandler

If the user modified the current task and exits the application via the file menu, they should be prompted if they want to save the data. Change your `ExitHandler` class accordingly.

▼ *Solution example*

```
package com.vogella.tasks.ui.handlers;

import java.util.Arrays;

import org.eclipse.e4.core.di.annotations.Execute;
import org.eclipse.e4.ui.workbench.IWorkbench;
import org.eclipse.e4.ui.workbench.modeling.EPartService;
import org.eclipse.jface.dialogs.PlainMessageDialog;
import org.eclipse.swt.widgets.Shell;

public class ExitHandler {
    @Execute
    public void execute(EPartService partService, IWorkbench workbench, Shell shell) {
        if (!partService.getDirtyParts().isEmpty()) {
            int selectedButton = PlainMessageDialog.getBuilder(shell, "Unsaved data
present").message("Before leaving, you should save or discard your changes."
).buttonLabels(Arrays.asList("Save and exit", "Cancel exit")).build().open();
            boolean confirm = selectedButton == 0;

            if (confirm) {
                partService.saveAll(false);
            } else {
                return;
            }
        }
        // nothing to save, just leave
        workbench.close();
```

```
    }
}
```

130. Optional exercise: Allow to copy to the clipboard

In this exercise, you implement a more realistic implementation of the handler for the copy command. This copy command has been defined in an earlier optional exercise.

This handler allows you to copy the selected task elements to the clipboard. The command is added to the context menu of the `TodoOverviewPart` part. A part-specific key binding will make the command also accessible via the keyboard.

Therefore, you will:

- Re-implement the handler class for the previously implemented copy command.
- Create a local copy handler for the *TodoOverviewPart* part
- Add the command to the context menu of the table

Afterward, you add a key binding for the part to the application. For this you:

- Create a new binding context
- Create a binding table for this binding context with a shortcut for the copy command
- Assign this binding context to the *TodoOverviewPart*

130.1. Create a copy command

130.2. Create a handler

In a previous exercise, you were asked to create the following command.

- ID: com.vogella.tasks.ui.command.copy
- Name: Copy

If you have not done so, add this command to your application model, if it already exists; reuse it.

Implement or update the following handler class.

```
package com.vogella.tasks.ui.handlers;

import java.util.List;
import java.util.stream.Collectors;

import jakarta.inject.Named;
```

```
import org.eclipse.e4.core.di.annotations.CanExecute;
import org.eclipse.e4.core.di.annotations.Execute;
import org.eclipse.e4.core.di.annotations.Optional;
import org.eclipse.e4.ui.services.IServiceConstants;
import org.eclipse.jface.dialogs.PlainMessageDialog;
import org.eclipse.jface.util.LocalSelectionTransfer;
import org.eclipse.swt.dnd.Clipboard;
import org.eclipse.swt.dnd.RTFTransfer;
import org.eclipse.swt.dnd.TextTransfer;
import org.eclipse.swt.dnd.Transfer;
import org.eclipse.swt.widgets.Display;
import org.eclipse.swt.widgets.Shell;

import com.vogella.tasks.model.Task;

public class TasksCopyHandler {

    @Execute
    public void execute(Shell shell, @Optional @Named(IServiceConstants.ACTIVE_SELECTION)
List<Task> tasks) {

        Clipboard clipboard = new Clipboard(shell.getDisplay());

        String transferString = tasks.stream().map(task -> task.toString()).collect
(Collectors.joining(", "));

        TextTransfer textTransfer = TextTransfer.getInstance();
        RTFTransfer rtfTransfer = RTFTransfer.getInstance();
        LocalSelectionTransfer localSelectionTransfer = LocalSelectionTransfer
.getTransfer();

        Object[] transferData = new Object[] { transferString, transferString, tasks };
        Transfer[] transfers = new Transfer[] { textTransfer, rtfTransfer,
localSelectionTransfer };

        clipboard.setContents(transferData, transfers);

        clipboard.dispose();

        PlainMessageDialog.getBuilder(shell, "Copied to clipboard").message("Selected
task copied to clipboard. Paste in any editor")
                .buttonLabels(List.of("Close")).build().open();
    }

    @CanExecute
    public boolean canExecute(@Optional @Named(IServiceConstants.ACTIVE_SELECTION) List
<Task> tasks) {
        return tasks != null && !tasks.isEmpty();
```

```
    }
}
```

Find the *Overview* part in your application model and add a new handler for this copy command for this part. This way, the command will only be available if the overview part is selected.

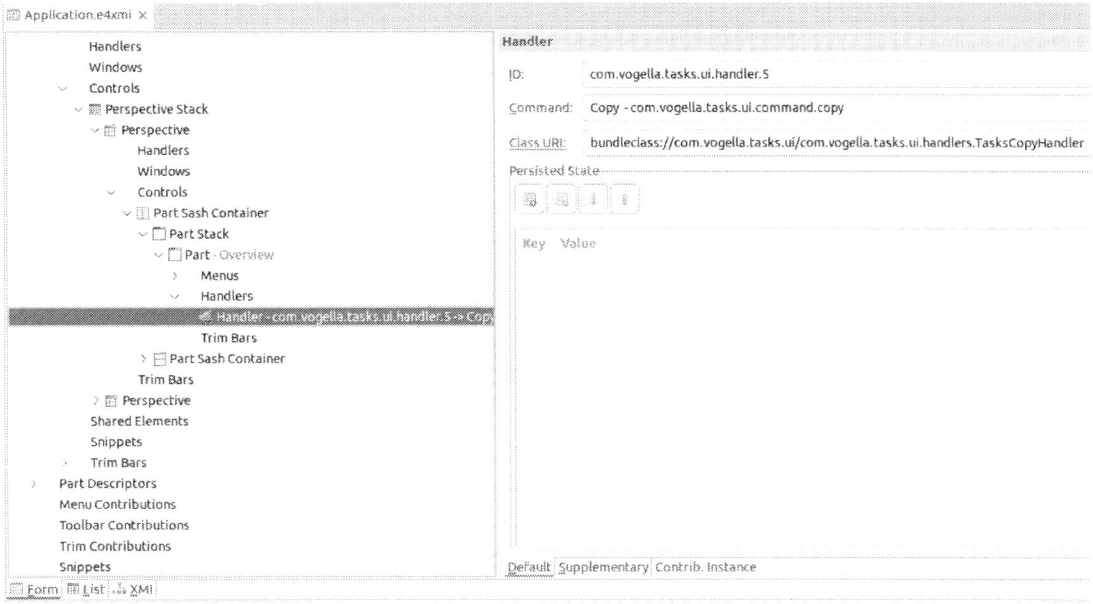

130.3. Add the command to the context menu of the overview part

In an earlier exercise, you defined a context (popup) menu for your table. Add the copy command to this menu via the application model.

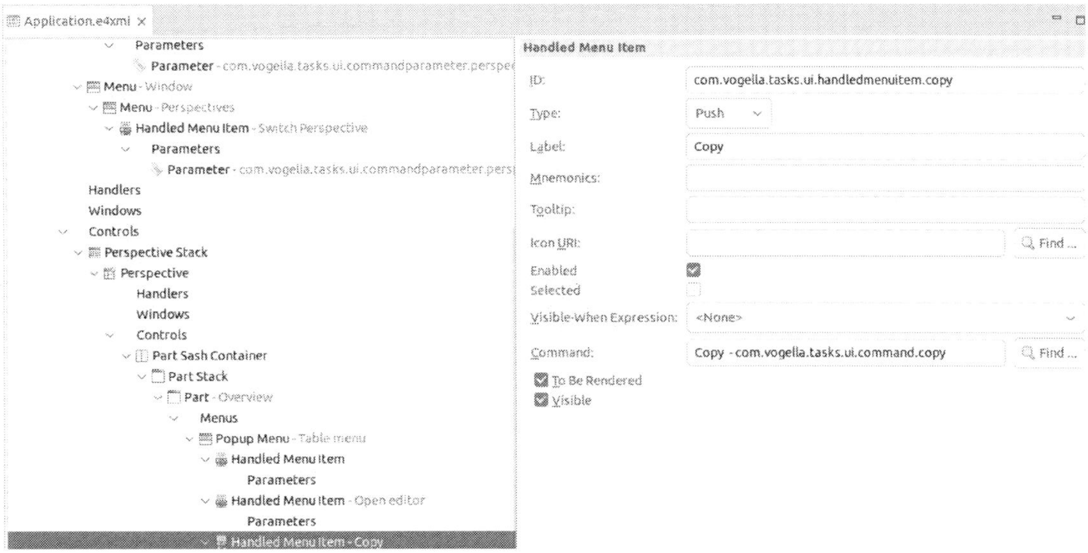

130.4. Validate

Run the application and try to select one or more tasks by selecting the context menu.

Then, open a text editor and paste the contents from the clipboard. If desired, you can, of course, use your own editor.

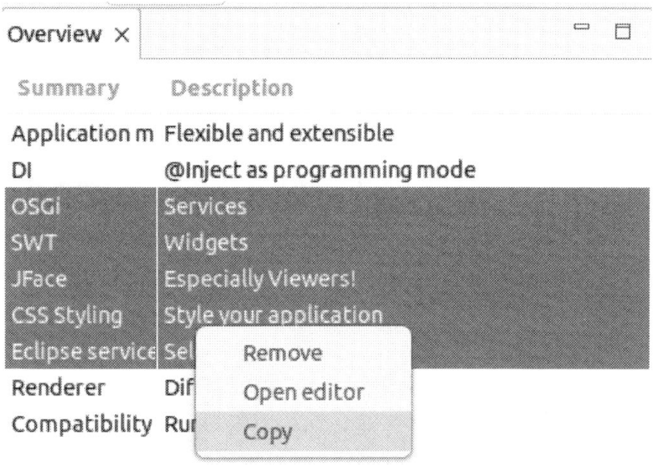

For example, you could paste the copied content into a task description.

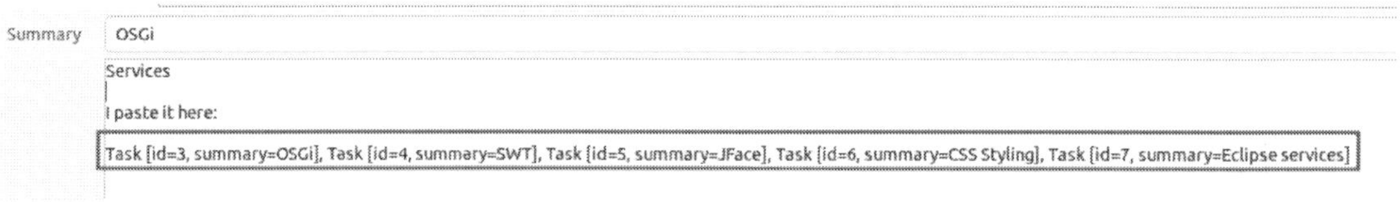

131. Optional exercise: Part-specific key binding

131.1. Creating binding context and binding table

Create a new binding context.

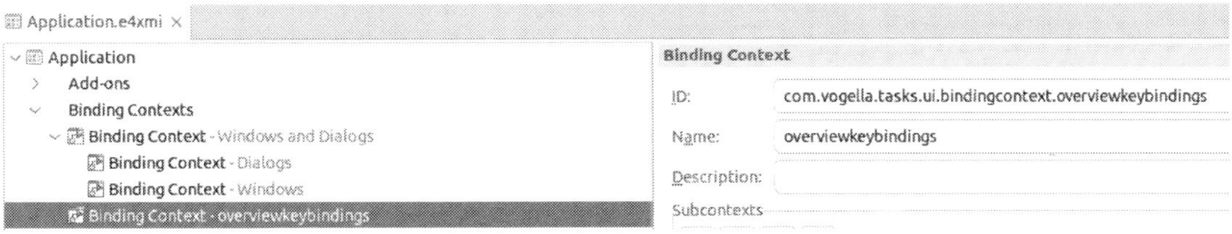

Create a new binding table for this binding context.

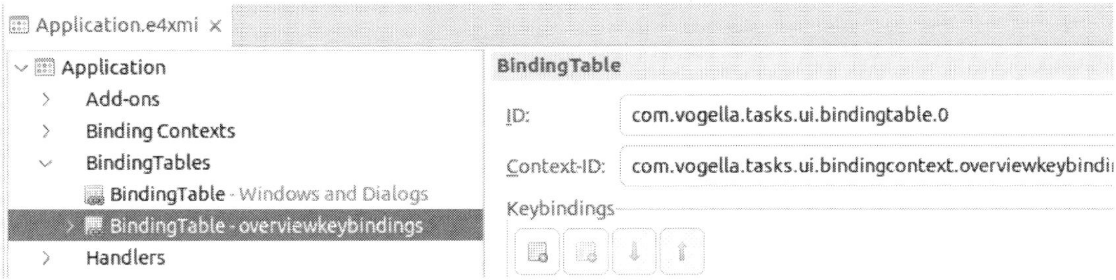

Create a `M1` + `C` key binding for the Copy command.

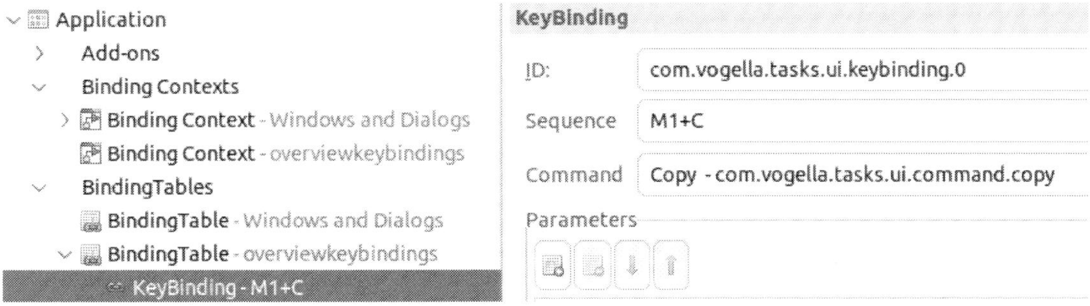

131.2. Assign binding context to the part

If a binding context is assigned to a part, all defined binding tables are available for this part. Therefore, assign the binding context to the part.

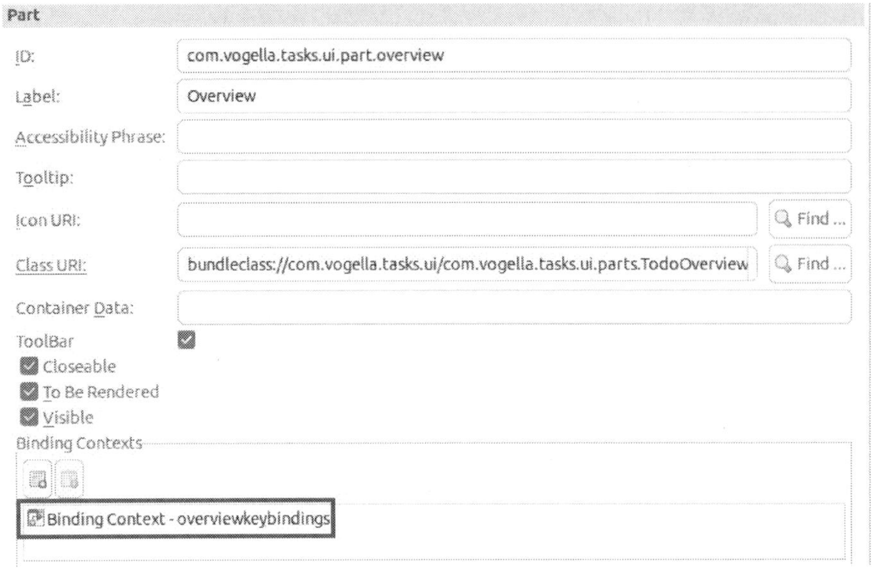

131.3. Validate

Start your application.

The key binding should be listed on the context menu.

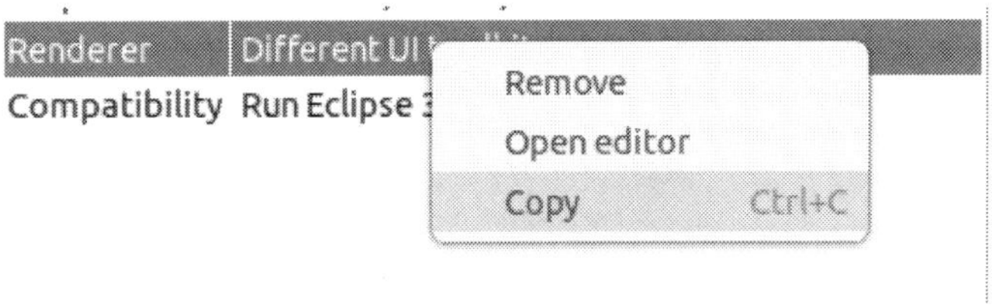

Select a few tasks, and use your shortcut to copy them. Paste into an editor to ensure that the copy worked as expected.

Copy them by pressing `Ctrl` + `C` or on Mac `COMMAND` + `C`.

132. Exercise: Using multiple perspectives

In this exercise, you define two perspectives and implement a menu entry to switch between your perspectives. For this, you will add a perspective stack with two perspectives to your application model.

132.1. Create a perspective stack with two perspectives

If you followed the exercises so far, you should have added your sashes and stacks directly to the window similar to the following screenshot.

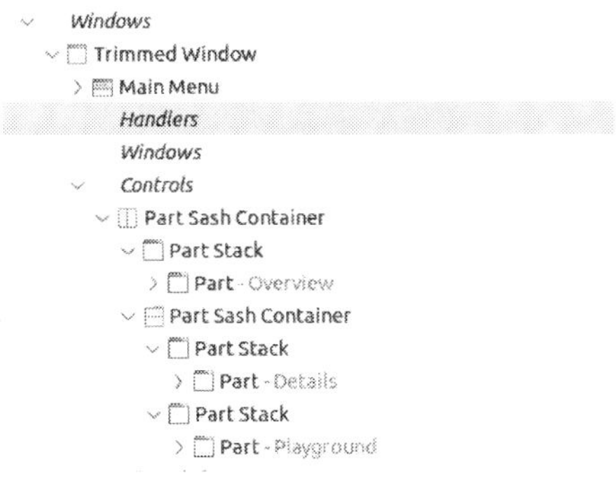

Navigate to your window inside the *Application.e4xmi* file. Select the *Controls* node and right-click on it. Add a *Perspective Stack* via the context menu on the *Controls* entry.

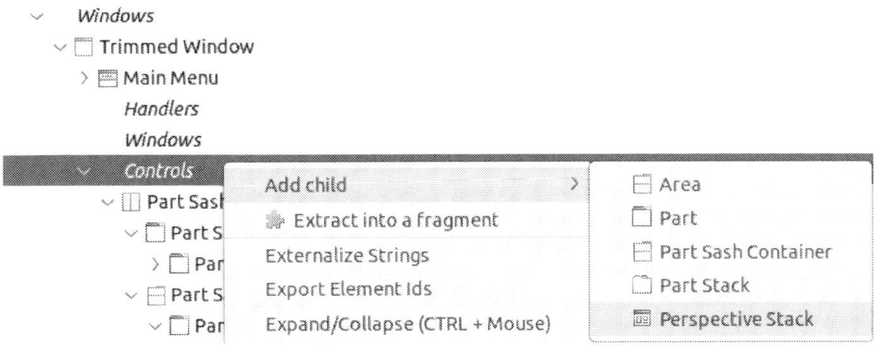

Perform a right-mouse click on your perspective stack and add a perspective to it

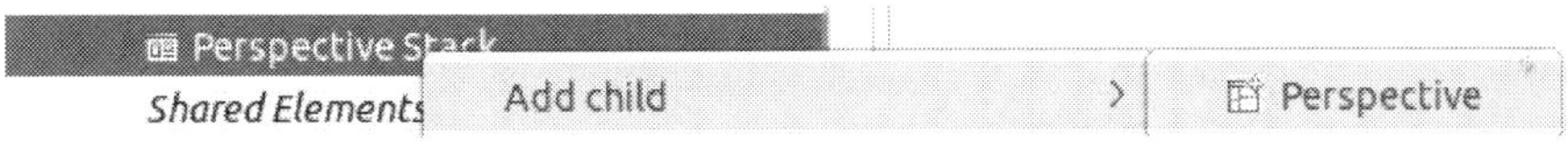

Assign the `com.vogella.tasks.ui.perspective.tasks` ID and the `Tasks` as a label to the new perspective.

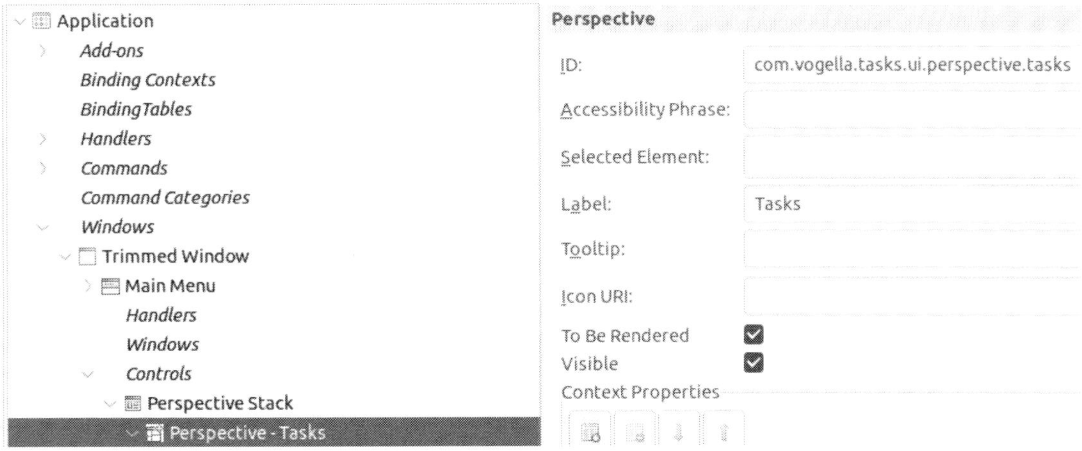

Move the existing elements from your window into the new perspective by dragging the controls there.

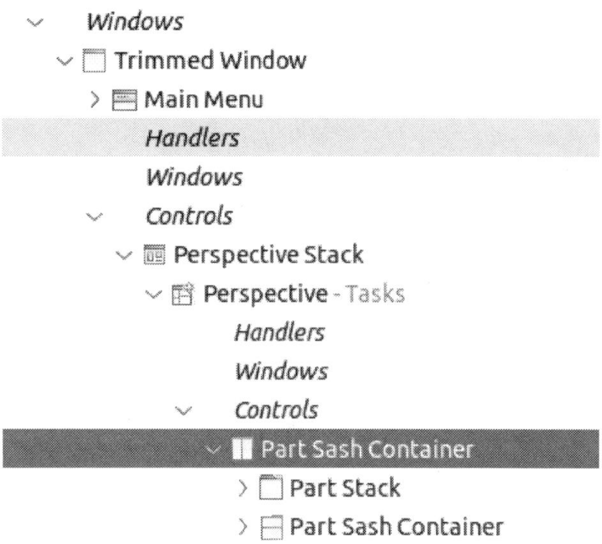

Afterward, define a second perspective with the *Manager* label and the `com.vogella.tasks.ui.perspective.manager` ID to your application.

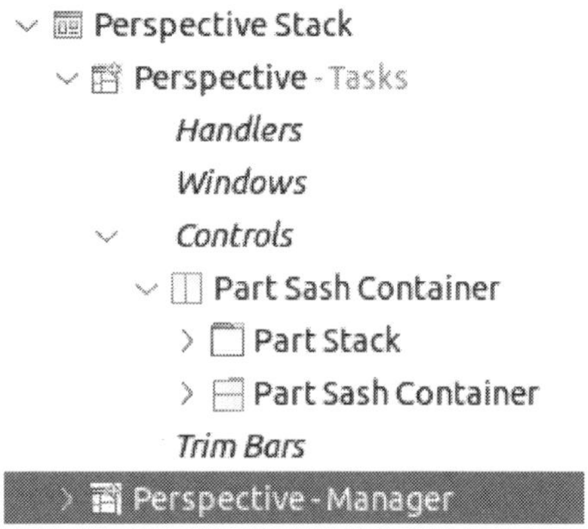

Add at least one part stack and one part (contained in the part stack so that the part label is visible) to this new perspective. Either create a new part implementation class or reuse one of the existing part implementations.

> Ensure that both perspectives are part of the perspective stack and that all parts, part sash, and part stack containers have been assigned to a perspective.

132.2. Create new menu entries

Create a new command and a new handler to switch between perspectives. The handler class for switching perspectives might look like the following.

```
package com.vogella.tasks.ui.handlers;

import java.util.List;

import org.eclipse.e4.core.di.annotations.Execute;
import org.eclipse.e4.ui.model.application.MApplication;
import org.eclipse.e4.ui.model.application.ui.advanced.MPerspective;
import org.eclipse.e4.ui.workbench.modeling.EModelService;
import org.eclipse.e4.ui.workbench.modeling.EPartService;

public class PerspectiveSwitchHandler {
    @Execute
    public void switchPerspective(MPerspective activePerspective,
            MApplication app, EPartService partService,
            EModelService modelService) {
        List<MPerspective> perspectives = modelService.findElements(app, null,
                MPerspective.class, null);
        // assume you have only two perspectives and you always
        // switch between them
        for (MPerspective perspective : perspectives) {
            if (!perspective.equals(activePerspective)) {
                partService.switchPerspective(perspective);
            }
        }
    }
}
```

Create or update a *Windows* menu entry in your menu main with a sub-menu named *Switch Perspective*.

Add a new menu entry in your application model to switch between your perspectives.

Test if you can switch between your perspectives with your new handler.

You could add the perspective switcher command to the toolbar. In a later exercise, you will add a dynamic perspective switcher to the toolbar that automatically shows your available perspectives.

133. Optional exercise: Use command parameters

Currently, your perspective switcher only allows switching between two perspectives. Use parameters in your command and menu entries to specify which perspective you want to open.

Check the Section 83.1 about command parameters to learn how to use parameters. Apply this learning to solve this exercise.

Use the `perspective_parameter` as the ID for the command parameter.

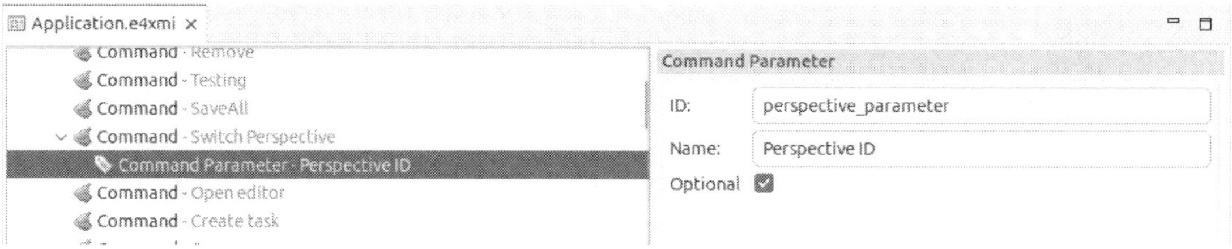

The handler for switching can, for example, look like the following:

```
package com.vogella.tasks.ui.handlers;

import org.eclipse.core.runtime.ILog;
import org.eclipse.e4.core.di.annotations.Execute;
import org.eclipse.e4.core.di.annotations.Optional;
import org.eclipse.e4.ui.workbench.modeling.EPartService;

import jakarta.inject.Named;

public class SwitchPerspectiveHandler {
    @Execute
    public void execute(EPartService partService, @Optional
            @Named("perspective_parameter") String perspectiveID) {
        if (partService == null) {
            ILog.get().error("No perspective ID received");
        }
        partService.switchPerspective(perspectiveID);
    }
}
```

The above implementation assumes that the ID of the command parameter is set to `perspective_parameter`.

134. Optional exercise: Integrating a perspective switcher

It would be great to add a user interface element to the application that allows switching to all available perspectives. If new perspectives are added to the application, this element should automatically retrieve them.

A similar functionality is available in the Eclipse IDE. It is called *perspective switcher*.

The following screenshot shows the Eclipse IDE perspective switcher and the dialog you can open via the first button in this control.

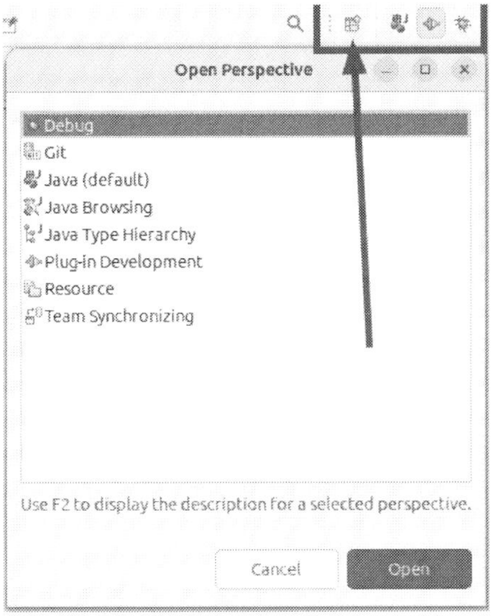

Fortunately, it is not necessary to implement this yourself. You can use the implementation from GitHub repository [https://github.com/vogellacompany/e4-perspective-switcher] that already provides an implementation.

134.1. Check the implementation

Clone the repository or download its content as an archive file. Import the three projects into your workspace. Review the example application, feature, and implementation.

If you check the application model of the example application, you see that it contains a few tool controls. The last tool control points to a class that will create the dynamic perspective switcher.

134.2. Think how you would integrate this into the application

To integrate this functionality into your application, you have to solve two problems.

- Make the implementation available to your application
- Integrate it into your application

134.3. Add the perspective switcher implementation to the application

You can add the perspective switcher implementation to your application using two different ways:

- Copy the plug-in into the same directory as the other plug-ins and import the plug-in into your regular workspace. In case you are using a Tycho build, also add it to your pom.xml as a `module`.
- Build the project with Tycho, as the example project has already a working Tycho build, and add the created update site to your target platform.

134.4. Integrate the perspective switcher into the application

Once the implementation is available, integrate it by adding the appropriate tool control to your application model. To add the dynamic perspective switcher into your application, add `org.eclipse.e4.ui.workbench.perspectiveswitcher` to your feature.

The example application contains a tool control, you also need to add this to your application.

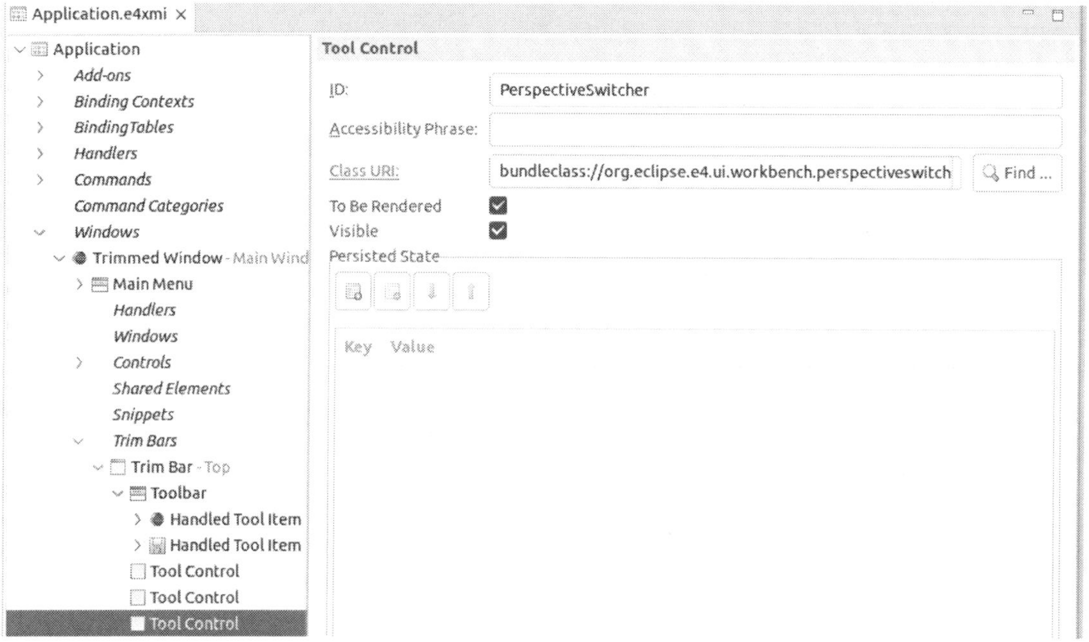

If you want to move your tool control to the right side, add also the additional two tool controls. Ensure you add the same tags on the *Supplementary* tab.

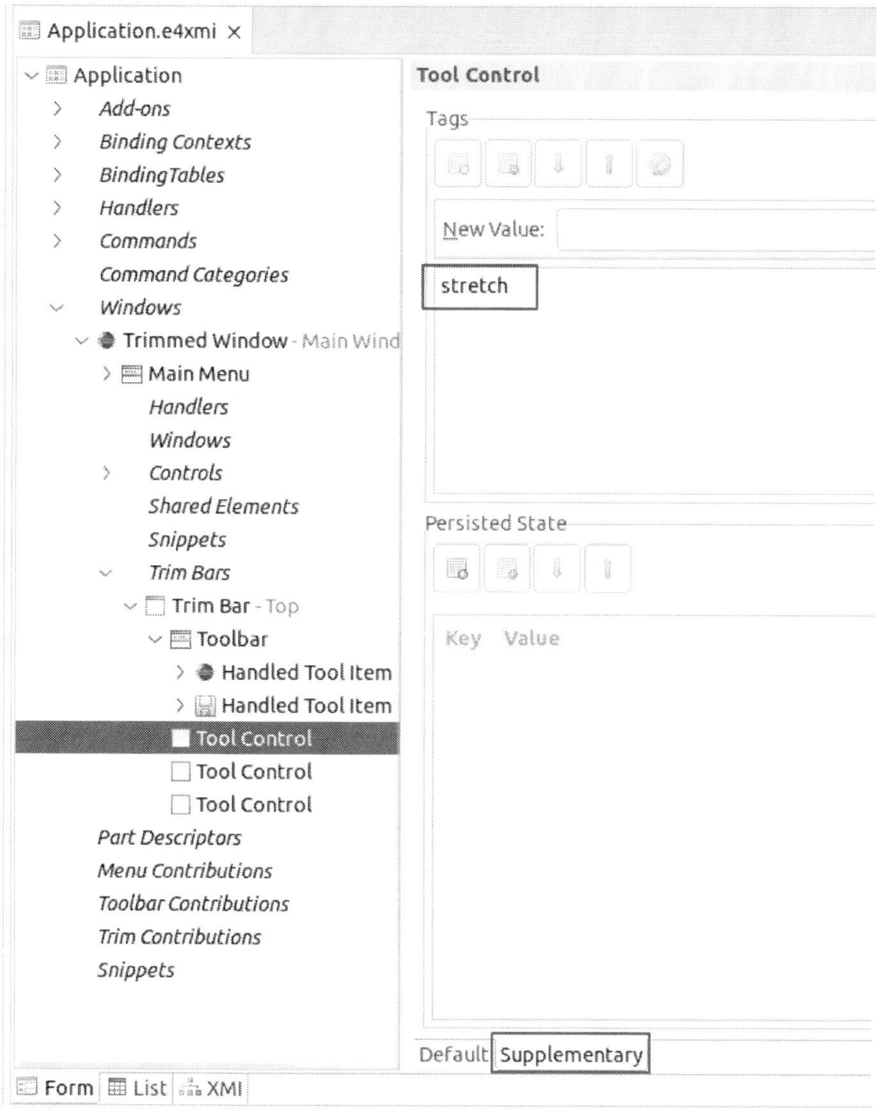

Start via the product to update your runtime configuration.

135. Exercise: Implementing multiple editors

135.1. Prerequisites

This exercise assumes that you have defined a context menu for your table. Alternatively, you can add a new menu entry to your application menu for displaying the details of a task. In this exercise, you create a handler to open a separate editor for the selected task item.

135.2. Adding new menu entries

Create a new command named *Open Editor*, create a new handler for it, pointing to the following new class `OpenEditorHandler`.

```
package com.vogella.tasks.ui.handlers;

import java.util.List;

import jakarta.inject.Named;

import org.eclipse.e4.core.di.annotations.Execute;
import org.eclipse.e4.core.di.annotations.Optional;
import org.eclipse.e4.ui.services.IServiceConstants;

import com.vogella.tasks.model.Task;

public class OpenEditorHandler {
    @Execute
    public void execute(@Optional @Named(IServiceConstants.ACTIVE_SELECTION) List<Task>
tasks) {
        System.out.println("Will open a new editor");
    }
}
```

Add another entry to the context menu of the table, which you created and registered in the `TodoOverviewPart`.

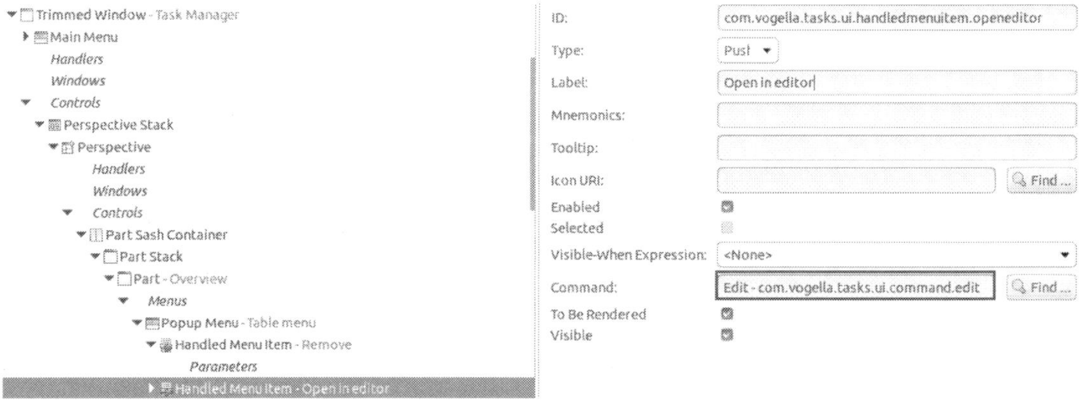

135.3. Validate the ID of the part stack

Verify that the part stack ID in the application model is set to `com.vogella.tasks.ui.partstack.bottom`. This ID will be used later to search for the part stack in your code.

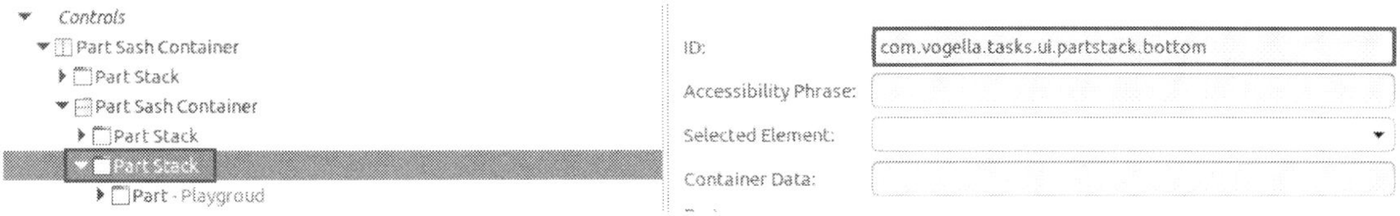

In a later exercise, you will implement that the save handler can only be executed if a dirty editor exists.

135.4. Adding a part implementation

Create a new `TaskEditorPart` class.

You can copy the `TodoDetailsPart` code. In this case, you need to remove the method that listens for the current active selection. You also need to retrieve the ID from the persisted state of the `MPart` object.

▼ *Solution example*

```
package com.vogella.tasks.ui.parts;

import java.util.HashMap;
import java.util.Map;

import jakarta.annotation.PostConstruct;
import jakarta.annotation.PreDestroy;
import jakarta.inject.Inject;

import org.eclipse.core.databinding.Binding;
import org.eclipse.core.databinding.DataBindingContext;
import org.eclipse.core.databinding.beans.typed.BeanProperties;
import org.eclipse.core.databinding.observable.value.IObservableValue;
import org.eclipse.core.databinding.observable.value.WritableValue;
import org.eclipse.e4.ui.di.Focus;
import org.eclipse.e4.ui.di.Persist;
import org.eclipse.e4.ui.model.application.ui.basic.MPart;
import org.eclipse.jface.databinding.swt.typed.WidgetProperties;
import org.eclipse.jface.layout.GridDataFactory;
import org.eclipse.jface.widgets.LabelFactory;
import org.eclipse.jface.widgets.WidgetFactory;
import org.eclipse.swt.SWT;
import org.eclipse.swt.layout.GridLayout;
import org.eclipse.swt.widgets.Button;
import org.eclipse.swt.widgets.Composite;
import org.eclipse.swt.widgets.DateTime;
import org.eclipse.swt.widgets.Text;

import com.vogella.tasks.model.Task;
```

```
import com.vogella.tasks.model.TaskService;

public class TaskEditorPart {
    private Text txtSummary;
    private Text txtDescription;
    private DateTime dateTime;
    private Button btnDone;

    // define a new field
    private java.util.Optional<Task> task = java.util.Optional.ofNullable(null);

    // observable placeholder for a task
    private WritableValue<Task> observableTodo = new WritableValue<>();
    private DataBindingContext dbc;
    @Inject
    private MPart part; ❶

    @Inject
    TaskService taskService;

    // pause dirty listener when new selection is set
    private boolean pauseDirtyListener;

    @PostConstruct
    public void createControls(Composite parent) {
        parent.setLayout(new GridLayout(2, false));
        String string = part.getPersistedState().get(Task.FIELD_ID);

        task = taskService.get(Long.valueOf(string));
        GridDataFactory gdFactory = GridDataFactory.fillDefaults();
        LabelFactory labelFactory = LabelFactory.newLabel(SWT.NONE);

        labelFactory.text("Summary").create(parent);

        txtSummary = WidgetFactory.text(SWT.BORDER).layoutData(gdFactory.grab(true,
false).create())//
                .create(parent);

        labelFactory.text("Description").create(parent);
        txtDescription = WidgetFactory.text(SWT.BORDER | SWT.MULTI | SWT.V_SCROLL)
                .layoutData(gdFactory.align(SWT.FILL, SWT.FILL).grab(true, true).
create()).create(parent);

        labelFactory.text("Due Date").create(parent);

        // Factory planned for 2020-12 release
        // https://bugs.eclipse.org/bugs/show_bug.cgi?id=567110

        dateTime = new DateTime(parent, SWT.BORDER);
```

```
        dateTime.setLayoutData(gdFactory.align(SWT.FILL, SWT.CENTER).grab(false,
false).create());

        labelFactory.text("").create(parent);

        btnDone = WidgetFactory.button(SWT.CHECK).text("Done").create(parent);

        bindData(); ❷
        updateUserInterface(task);
    }

    private void bindData() { ❸
        // this assumes that widget field is named "summary"
        if (txtSummary != null && !txtSummary.isDisposed()) {

            dbc = new DataBindingContext();

            Map<String, IObservableValue<?>> fields = new HashMap<>();
            fields.put(Task.FIELD_SUMMARY, WidgetProperties.text(SWT.Modify).observe
(txtSummary));
            fields.put(Task.FIELD_DESCRIPTION, WidgetProperties.text(SWT.Modify
).observe(txtDescription));
            fields.put(Task.FIELD_DUEDATE, WidgetProperties.localDateSelection
().observe(dateTime));
            fields.put(Task.FIELD_DONE, WidgetProperties.buttonSelection().observe
(btnDone));
            fields.forEach((k, v) -> dbc.bindValue(v, BeanProperties.value(k
).observeDetail(observableTodo)));

            // set a dirty state if one of the bindings is changed
            dbc.getBindings().forEach(item -> {
                Binding binding = item;
                binding.getTarget().addChangeListener(e -> {
                    if (!pauseDirtyListener && part != null) { //
                        part.setDirty(true);
                    }
                });
            });
        }
    }

    // allows you to disable or enable the user interface fields
    // if no task is set
    private void enableUserInterface(boolean enabled) {
        if (txtSummary != null && !txtSummary.isDisposed()) {
            txtSummary.setEnabled(enabled);
            txtDescription.setEnabled(enabled);
            dateTime.setEnabled(enabled);
            btnDone.setEnabled(enabled);
        }
```

```
    }

    private void updateUserInterface(java.util.Optional<Task> task) {
        if (!task.isPresent()) {
            enableUserInterface(false);
            return; // nothing left to do
        }

        enableUserInterface(true);
        // the following check ensures that the user interface is available,
        // it assumes that you have a text widget named "txtSummary"
        if (txtSummary != null && !txtSummary.isDisposed()) {
            pauseDirtyListener = true; //
            this.observableTodo.setValue(task.get());
            pauseDirtyListener = false; //
        }
    }

    @Persist ❹
    public void save(TaskService todoService) {
        task.ifPresent(todoService::update);
        if (part != null) {
            part.setDirty(false);
        }
    }

    @Focus
    public void setFocus() {
        txtSummary.setFocus();
    }

    @PreDestroy
    public void dispose() {
        dbc.dispose();
    }
}
```

Create a part descriptor in the application model, where this `TaskEditorPart` is referenced. Ensure you set the `Multiple` flag.

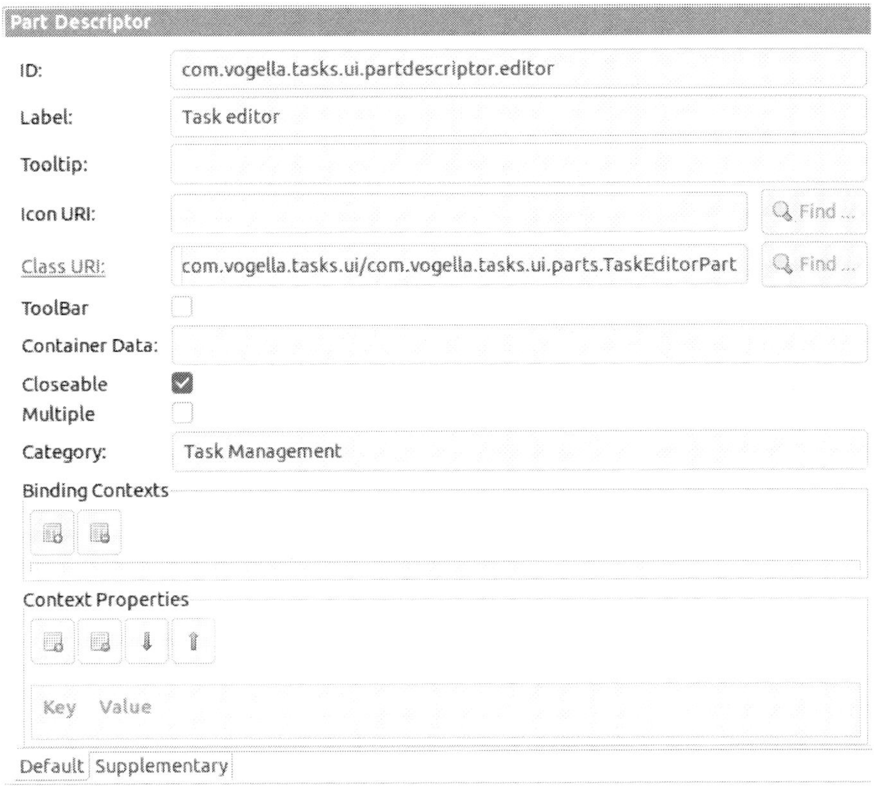
Part Descriptor
ID:
com.vogella.tasks.ui.partdescriptor.editor
Label:
Task editor
Tooltip:
Icon URI:
Find ...
Class URI:
com.vogella.tasks.ui/com.vogella.tasks.ui.parts.TaskEditorPart
Find ...
ToolBar
Container Data:
Closeable
Multiple
Category:
Task Management
Binding Contexts
Context Properties
Key
Value
Default
Supplementary

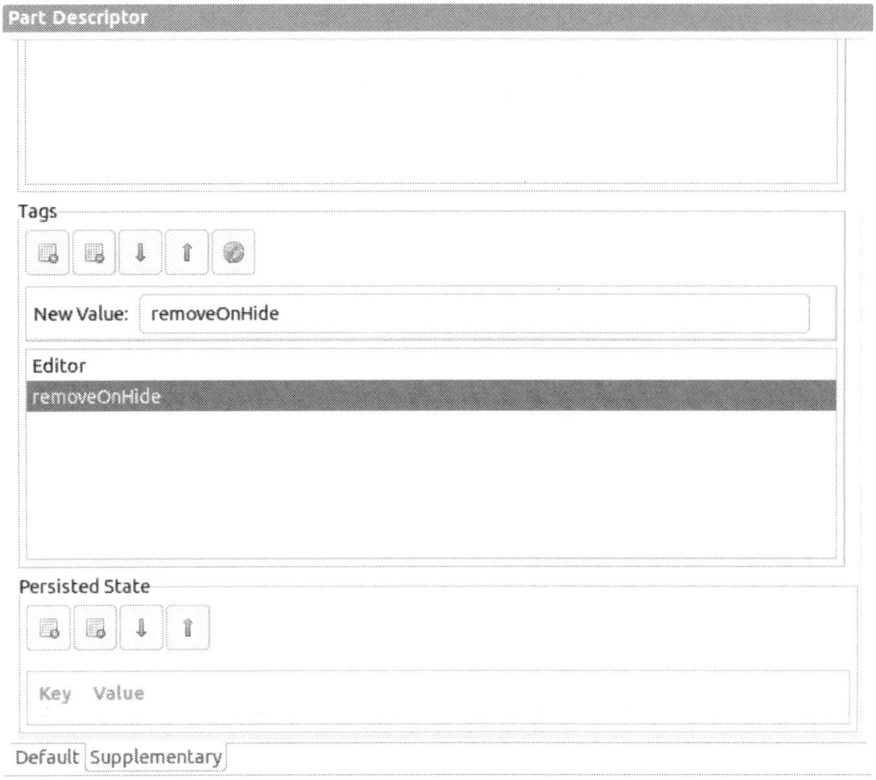

You could also adjust the `TodoDetailsPart` code to handle both use cases. The approach to create a new class for the multiple editors has been chosen in this book to keep your existing implementation as an alternative reference.

This implementation uses the `getPersistedState()` method from the `MPart` class to retrieve the ID of the task for which the editor is responsible.

135.5. Ensure the tag editor is removed from the application model after being closed

Without additional configuration, the framework does not remove the part from the application when it is closed. The model element will only set the `toBeRendered` property and dispose of the underlying object for the part. To remove the part also from the application during close, set the "removeOnHide" tag on the part descriptor. Use the *Supplementary* tab on the model element for that.

Be sure to press the **Add** button after entering the tag.

135.6. Adjusting handler implementation

Change your handler to open a new editor in case a corresponding editor is not already open. If the editor is already open, set the focus to it.

▼ *Solution example*

```
package com.vogella.tasks.ui.handlers;

import java.util.Collection;
import java.util.List;

import jakarta.inject.Named;

import org.eclipse.e4.core.di.annotations.CanExecute;
import org.eclipse.e4.core.di.annotations.Execute;
import org.eclipse.e4.core.di.annotations.Optional;
import org.eclipse.e4.ui.model.application.MApplication;
import org.eclipse.e4.ui.model.application.ui.basic.MPart;
import org.eclipse.e4.ui.model.application.ui.basic.MPartStack;
import org.eclipse.e4.ui.services.IServiceConstants;
import org.eclipse.e4.ui.workbench.modeling.EModelService;
import org.eclipse.e4.ui.workbench.modeling.EPartService;
import org.eclipse.e4.ui.workbench.modeling.EPartService.PartState;

import com.vogella.tasks.model.Task;

public class OpenEditorHandler {

    private static final String EDITOR_ID =
"com.vogella.tasks.ui.partdescriptor.editor";

    @Execute
    public void execute(@Optional @Named(IServiceConstants.ACTIVE_SELECTION) List<Task>
tasks, MApplication application,
            EModelService modelService, EPartService partService) {

        // sanity check
        if (tasks == null || tasks.isEmpty()) {
            return;
        }

        var task = tasks.get(0);

        String id = String.valueOf(task.getId());

        // maybe the editor is already open?
        Collection<MPart> parts = partService.getParts();
```

```
        // if the editor is open show it
        for (MPart part : parts) {
            String currentId = part.getPersistedState().get(Task.FIELD_ID);
            if (currentId != null && currentId.equals(id)) {
                partService.showPart(part, PartState.ACTIVATE);
                return;
            }
        }

        // editor was not open, create it
        MPart part = partService.createPart(EDITOR_ID);

        part.setElementId(id);
        part.getPersistedState().put(Task.FIELD_ID, id);

        // create a nice label for the part header
        String header = "ID:" + id + " " + task.getSummary();
        part.setLabel(header);

        // add it to an existing stack and show it
        MPartStack stack = (MPartStack) modelService.find
("com.vogella.tasks.ui.partstack.bottom", application);
        stack.getChildren().add(part);
        partService.showPart(part, PartState.ACTIVATE);
    }

    @CanExecute
    public boolean canExecute(@Optional @Named(IServiceConstants.ACTIVE_SELECTION)
List<Task> tasks) {
        return tasks != null && !tasks.isEmpty();
    }
}
```

135.7. Validate the implementation

Ensure that you can open multiple instances of your editor with your context menu and that an existing editor gets focused if you reselect it. The expected output is shown in the screenshot below.

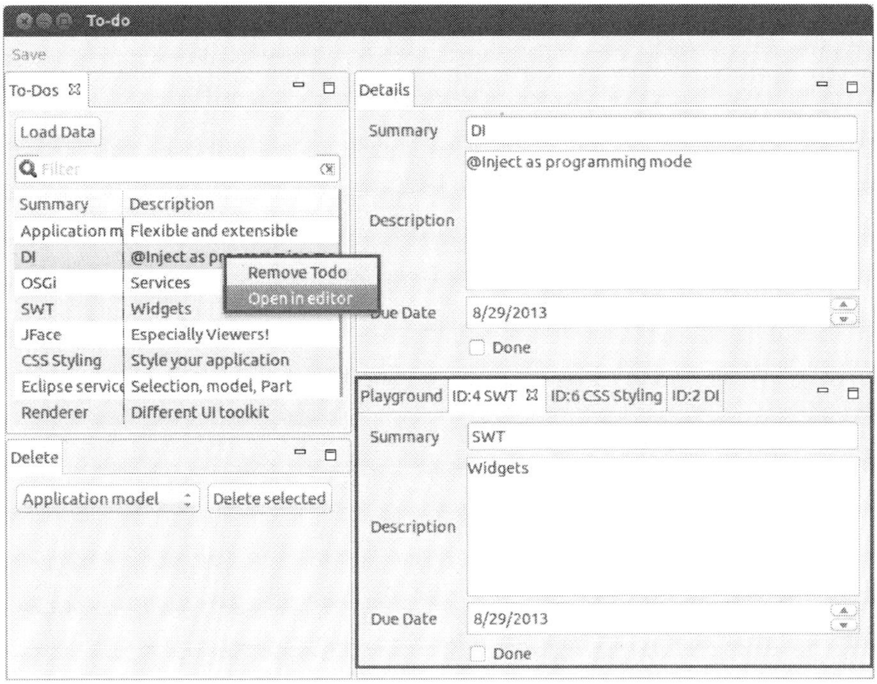

Change a task object in the new editor and save it. Reload the data in your table via your Load Data button and ensure that the data has changed.

136. Optional exercise: Implement a toolbar button to save

Implement a save toolbar button for the active editor. It should only be active if the current active editor is dirty, e.g., needs saving and it should only save the selected editor.

137. Optional exercise: Layout the part arrangement in the sash

In this exercise, you define the initial space for the two elements displayed in the first sash container.

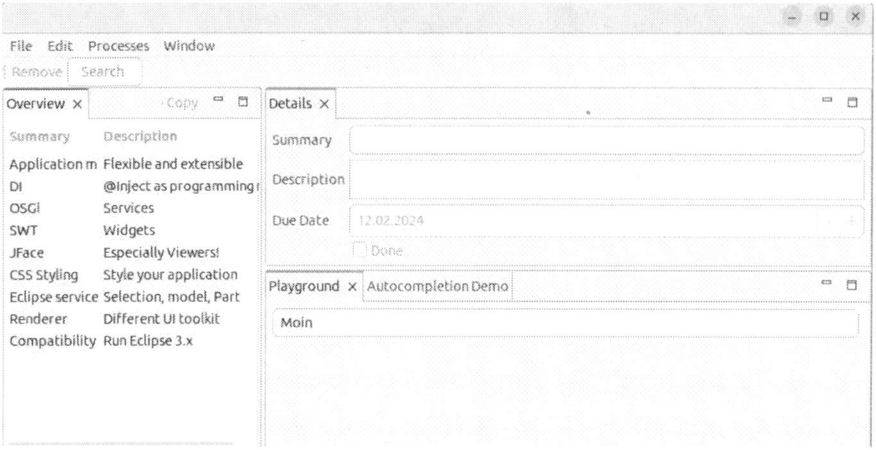

137.1. Allocating space to the stacks at startup

A sash container allows you to define the space allocated to its children via the `container data` attribute.

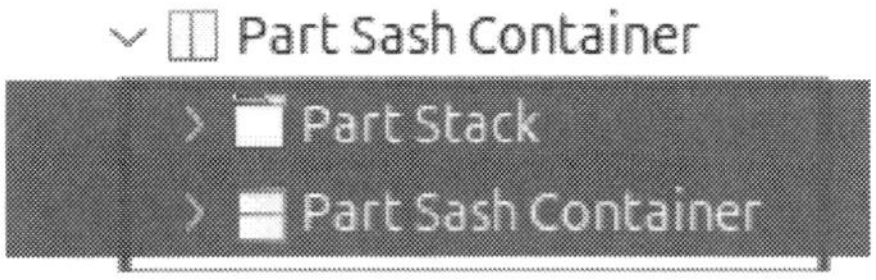

Set 30% of the available space to the first child and 70% to the second by using 3000 and 7000 as values for their `container data` attribute.

You have to set the `container data` attribute correctly for both children (3000 on the first child, 7000 on the second child), otherwise, the layout will not work as expected.

137.2. Allocating space to the stacks during runtime

The user might change the space allocated to the two stacks during runtime by using the separator between the two stacks. In this exercise, you implement the option for the user to change the available space for the two stacks in the main sash. If the menu entry is selected, assign 30% of the available space to the first child and 70% to the second one.

For example, this would be the layout before the resize.

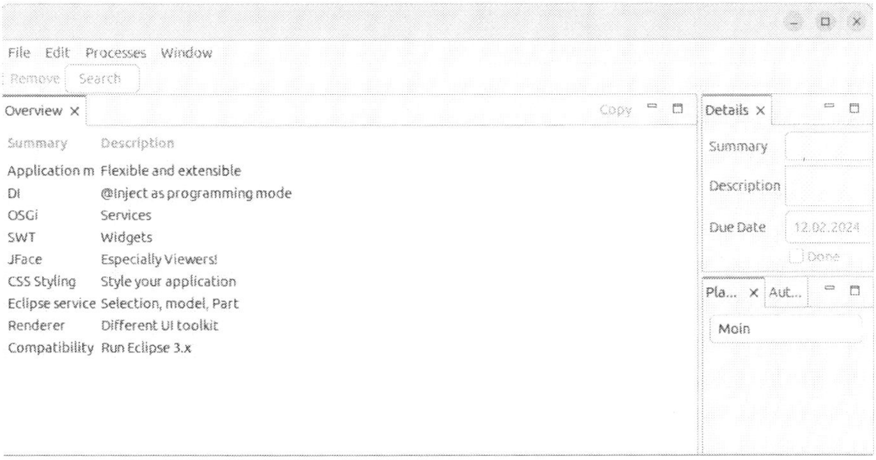

After the resize, the available space should be redistributed as defined in the initial application model.

137.3. Implementing Resize

- create a new `ResizeSashChildren` class
- create a new command named `Resize sash elements`
- create a new handler for the new command, pointing to the `ResizeSashChildren` class.

Use the model service to find the correct part sash container. Afterward, change the `container data` attribute of its children to a suitable integer value.

`SashRenderer` uses the `container data` attribute, review its code to understand how this data is used.

▼ *Solution example*

```
package com.vogella.tasks.ui.handlers;

import org.eclipse.core.runtime.ILog;
import org.eclipse.e4.core.di.annotations.Execute;
import org.eclipse.e4.ui.model.application.ui.MUIElement;
import org.eclipse.e4.ui.model.application.ui.basic.MPartSashContainer;
import org.eclipse.e4.ui.model.application.ui.basic.MWindow;
import org.eclipse.e4.ui.workbench.modeling.EModelService;


public class ResizeSashChildren {
```

```
    @Execute
    public void execute(EModelService modelService, MWindow window) {
        // This code assumes your main sash container uses the
com.vogella.tasks.ui.partsashcontainer.main ID.
        MUIElement muiElement = modelService.find
("com.vogella.tasks.ui.partsashcontainer.main", window);
        if (muiElement == null) {
            ILog.get().error("Could not find the main part sash container, check that
you use the correct ID in your model");
            return;
        }
        if (muiElement instanceof MPartSashContainer container) {
            // we only handle the case in which we have two direct children
            if (container.getChildren().size()==2) {
                container.getChildren().get(0).setContainerData("300");
                container.getChildren().get(1).setContainerData("700");
            }
        }
    }
}
```

138. Optional exercise: Calling commands from the source code

In this exercise, you reuse an existing command in your `EditorPart` and allow the user to save via a button click.

> The handler and command service have not been released as official API.

138.1. Enable the user to save in the EditorPart

```
@Inject
private ECommandService commandService;

@Inject
private EHandlerService handlerService;

@PostConstruct
public void createControls(Composite parent, TaskService todoService) {
    // as before

    // at the end of the creation of the UI
    Button button = new Button(parent, SWT.PUSH);
    button.setText("Save");
    button.addSelectionListener(new SelectionAdapter() {
```

```
        @Override
        public void widgetSelected(SelectionEvent e) {
            ParameterizedCommand command = commandService.createCommand
("org.eclipse.ui.file.saveAll", null);
            handlerService.executeHandler(command);
        }
    });
}
```

You could also specify a parameter for your command with the ID of the todo item should be saved and pass that as a value for the parameter in the handler.

138.2. Use the remove command in the TodoDeletionPart

The following optional exercise uses the `TodoDeletionPart`. This part was created in another optional exercise. If you have not created this part, create a new part and add it to your application in a stack of your liking. Create the `TodoDeletionPart` class and link your part to this class.

Change your `TodoDeletionPart` class so that it uses the `EHandlerService` to trigger the existing deletion handler to delete the selected task from the `ComboViewer`.

Add the following dependencies to your application plug-in:

- `org.eclipse.e4.core.commands`
- `org.eclipse.e4.core.contexts`

Change your `TodoDeletionPart` based on the following example code.

```
package com.vogella.tasks.ui.parts;

import java.util.List;

import jakarta.annotation.PostConstruct;
import jakarta.inject.Inject;

import org.eclipse.core.commands.ParameterizedCommand;
import org.eclipse.e4.core.commands.ECommandService;
import org.eclipse.e4.core.commands.EHandlerService;
import org.eclipse.e4.core.contexts.IEclipseContext;
import org.eclipse.e4.ui.di.Focus;
import org.eclipse.e4.ui.workbench.modeling.ESelectionService;
import org.eclipse.jface.viewers.ArrayContentProvider;
import org.eclipse.jface.viewers.ComboViewer;
import org.eclipse.jface.viewers.IStructuredSelection;
import org.eclipse.jface.viewers.LabelProvider;
import org.eclipse.jface.viewers.StructuredSelection;
```

```java
import org.eclipse.swt.SWT;
import org.eclipse.swt.events.SelectionAdapter;
import org.eclipse.swt.events.SelectionEvent;
import org.eclipse.swt.layout.GridLayout;
import org.eclipse.swt.widgets.Button;
import org.eclipse.swt.widgets.Composite;

import com.vogella.tasks.model.Task;
import com.vogella.tasks.model.TaskService;

public class TodoDeletionPart {

    @Inject
    private TaskService taskService;

    @Inject
    ESelectionService selectionService;

    @Inject
    EHandlerService handlerService;

    @Inject
    ECommandService commandService;

    @Inject
    IEclipseContext ctx;

    private ComboViewer viewer;

    @PostConstruct
    public void createControls(Composite parent) {
        parent.setLayout(new GridLayout(2, false));
        viewer = new ComboViewer(parent, SWT.READ_ONLY | SWT.DROP_DOWN);
        viewer.setLabelProvider(new LabelProvider() {
            @Override
            public String getText(Object element) {
                Task task = (Task) element;
                return task.getSummary();
            }
        });
        viewer.setContentProvider(ArrayContentProvider.getInstance());

        taskService.consume(this::updateViewer);

        Button button = new Button(parent, SWT.PUSH);
        button.addSelectionListener(new SelectionAdapter() {
            @Override
            public void widgetSelected(SelectionEvent e) {
                IStructuredSelection selection = viewer.getStructuredSelection();
```

```
                if (!selection.isEmpty()) {

                    @SuppressWarnings("unchecked")
                    List<Task> selectedElements= selection.toList();
                    // Make a copy and send out only the copy
                    List<Task> copiedElements = selectedElements.stream().map(t -> t.
copy()).collect(Collectors.toList()); ❶
                    selectionService.setSelection(copiedElements);

                    // ensure that "com.vogella.tasks.ui.command.remove" is
                    // the command ID which deletes the task objects
                    ParameterizedCommand cmd = commandService.createCommand
("com.vogella.tasks.ui.command.remove",
                            null);

                    handlerService.executeHandler(cmd, ctx);

                    // update the viewer and remove the selection

                    taskService.consume(TodoDeletionPart.this::updateViewer);
                    selectionService.setSelection(null);
                }
            }
        });
        button.setText("Delete selected");
    }

    private void updateViewer(List<Task> todos) {
        viewer.setInput(todos);
        if (todos.isEmpty()) {
            viewer.setSelection(new StructuredSelection(todos.get(0)));
        }
    }

    @Focus
    public void focus() {
        viewer.getCombo().setFocus();
    }
}
```

Part XV: Background processing

139. Concurrency

139.1. What is Concurrency?

Concurrency refers to the ability to execute multiple programs or parts of a program simultaneously. By performing time-consuming tasks asynchronously or in parallel, concurrency enhances both the throughput and interactivity of applications.

Modern computers typically feature multiple CPUs or cores within a single CPU. Effectively leveraging these multi-core architectures is crucial for building successful high-volume applications.

139.2. Processes vs. Threads

A *process* operates independently and in isolation from other processes. It cannot directly access shared data in different processes. The operating system allocates resources, such as memory and CPU time, to each process.

In contrast, a *thread* is a lightweight process that shares the same memory space with other threads in the same process. Each thread has its own call stack and cache. When a thread accesses shared data, it stores the data in its cache for faster access.

In Java, applications typically run within a single process, but they can utilize multiple threads to achieve parallel processing and asynchronous behavior.

140. Eclipse background processing

140.1. Main thread

An Eclipse RCP application runs in one process. By default, the Eclipse framework uses a single thread to run all the code instructions.

This thread runs the event loop for the application. It is the only thread that is allowed to interact with the user interface (UI). It is called the *main thread*. Sometimes it is called the UI thread, but this is a misnomer because it handles all events, not just UI events.

If another thread tries to update the UI, the Eclipse framework throws an `SWTException` exception.

```
org.eclipse.swt.SWTException: Invalid thread access
```

All events in the user interface are executed one after another. If you perform a long-running operation in the main thread, the application does not respond to user interaction during the execution time of this operation.

Blocking the user interaction is considered a bad practice. Therefore, it is important to perform all long-running operations in a separate thread. Long-running operations are, for example, network or file access.

As only the main thread is allowed to modify the user interface, the Eclipse framework provides ways for a thread to synchronize itself with the main thread. It provides the Eclipse Jobs framework, which allows you to run operations in the background and provides feedback on the job status to the Eclipse platform.

140.2. Using dependency injection and UISynchronize

The `org.eclipse.e4.ui.di` plug-in contains the `UISynchronize` class. An instance of this class can be injected into an Eclipse application via dependency injection.

`UISynchronize` provides the `syncExec()` and `asyncExec()` methods to synchronize with the main thread.

140.3. Eclipse Jobs API

The Eclipse Jobs API provides support for running background processes and providing feedback about the progress of the `Job`.

The important parts of the Job API are:

- IJobManager - schedules jobs
- Job - the individual task to perform
- IProgressMonitor - interface to communicate information about the status of your Job.

The creation and scheduling of a `Job` is demonstrated in the following code snippet.

```
// get UISynchronize injected as a field
@Inject UISynchronize sync;

// more code

Job job = Job.create("Update table", (ICoreRunnable) monitor -> {
    // do something long running
    // ...

    // If you want to update the UI
    sync.asyncExec(() -> {
        // do something in the user interface
        // e.g., set a text field
    });
});

// Start the Job
job.schedule();
```

If you want to update the user interface from a `Job`, you need to synchronize the corresponding action with the user interface similar to the direct usage of threads.

140.4. Priorities of Jobs

You can set the `Job` priority via the `job.setPriority()` method. The `Job` class contains predefined priorities, e.g. `Job.SHORT`, `Job.LONG`, `Job.BUILD` and `Job.DECORATE`.

The Eclipse job scheduler will use these priorities to determine the order in which the `Jobs` are scheduled. For example, jobs with the priority `Job.SHORT` are scheduled before jobs with the `Job.LONG` priority. Check the JavaDoc of the `Job` class for details.

140.5. Blocking the UI and providing feedback

Sometimes you want to change the cursor to give the user the feedback that something is running.

The easiest way to provide feedback is to change the cursor via the `BusyIndicator.showWhile()` method.

```
// Show a busy indicator while the runnable is executed
BusyIndicator.showWhile(display, runnable);
```

If this code is executed, the cursor changes to a busy indicator until the `Runnable` is done.

141. Reporting Progress

141.1. IProgressMonitor and the SubMonitor

An instance of an `IProgressMonitor` is passed to the run method of a `Job` and can be used to monitor the progress of the job. To report feedback on the progress from methods inside the job, pass a child of the `SubMonitor` rather than the parent `SubMonitor`. It is a good practice to convert the `IProgressMonitor` always to a `SubMonitor` before using it. This allows the use of a consistent API for process reporting of child processes and the main process. A `SubMonitor` can be created similar to this: `SubMonitor subMonitor = SubMonitor.convert(monitor, 3);`

```
final List<Task> tasks = taskService.getTasks();
Job job = new Job("My Job") {
    @Override
    protected IStatus run(IProgressMonitor monitor) {
        // convert to SubMonitor and set total number of work units
        SubMonitor subMonitor = SubMonitor.convert(monitor, tasks.size());
        for (Task task : tasks) {
            try {
                // sleep a second
                TimeUnit.SECONDS.sleep(1);

                // set the name of the current work
                subMonitor.setTaskName("I'm working on Task " + task.getSummary());

                // workOnTask is a method in this class which does some work
                // pass a new child with the totalWork of 1 to the method
                workOnTask(task, subMonitor.split(1));

            } catch (InterruptedException e) {
                return Status.CANCEL_STATUS;
            }
        }
        return Status.OK_STATUS;
    }

};
job.schedule();
```

When using a `SubMonitor` it is not necessary to call the `beginTask()` method or the `done()` method, since this is done implicitly by the `SubMonitor` implementation.

141.2. Taking conditions during progress into account

In some cases, the amount of work depends on conditions, which should be reported properly.

This can be done by using the `setWorkRemaining()` method of the `SubMonitor`.

```
protected IStatus run(IProgressMonitor monitor) {
    // convert to SubMonitor and set total number of work units
    SubMonitor subMonitor = SubMonitor.convert(monitor, 100);

    if(taskNeedsPreconfiguration(task)) {
        // Takes 30 % of the work
        preConfigureTask(task, subMonitor.split(30));
    }

    // ensure only 70 % of the work remains
    subMonitor.setWorkRemaining(70);

    // do the rest of the work
    workOnTask(task, subMonitor.split(70));

    return Status.OK_STATUS;
}
```

In case the code in the `taskNeedsPreconfiguration()` if block is run, the `setWorkRemaining()` method does nothing. Only if the code in the `if` block is skipped does it ensure that process monitoring is done properly.

Another use case for using `setWorkRemaining()` is when the actual work is determined later. See `workOnTask` method.

```
protected IStatus run(IProgressMonitor monitor) {
    // convert to SubMonitor and set total number of work units
    SubMonitor subMonitor = SubMonitor.convert(monitor, 100);

    if(taskNeedsPreconfiguration(task)) {
        // Takes 30 % of the work
        preConfigureTask(task, subMonitor.split(30));
    }

    // ensure only 70 % of the work remains
    subMonitor.setWorkRemaining(70);
```

```java
        // do the rest of the work
        workOnTask(task, subMonitor.split(70));


        return Status.OK_STATUS;
    }

    private void preConfigureTask(Task task, IProgressMonitor monitor) {
        SubMonitor subMonitor = SubMonitor.convert(monitor, 100);
        subMonitor.setTaskName("Preconfiguring Task " + task.getSummary());

        // ... do the configuration
    }

    private void workOnTask(Task task, IProgressMonitor monitor) {
        SubMonitor subMonitor = SubMonitor.convert(monitor, 100);
        subMonitor.setTaskName("Work on Task " + task.getSummary());

        SubMonitor loopRelatedTasksMonitor = subMonitor.split(80);

        // get related tasks from a service, which should be preconfigured
        List<Task> relatedTasks = taskService.findRelatedTasks(task);

        // setWorkRemaining can be applied, if the actual work is determined later
        loopRelatedTasksMonitor.setWorkRemaining(relatedTasks.size());

        for (Task relatedTask : relatedTasks) {
            preConfigureTask(relatedTask, loopRelatedTasksMonitor.split(1));
        }

        // ... do work on the actual task with the remaining 20 %
        doWorkOnActualTask(task, subMonitor.split(20));
    }
```

For the loop in the `workOnTask` a new child `SubMonitor`, which is supposed to do 80 % of the work, is created. Later on the actual remaining work for this `SubMonitor` is set by the `setWorkRemaining()`.

141.3. Reporting progress in Eclipse RCP applications

In Eclipse applications you can report progress by implementing the `IProgressMonitor` interface.

You can, for example, add a tool control to a toolbar in your application model. This tool control can implement the `IProgressMonitor` interface to show the progress.

This is demonstrated in the following example.

```java
package com.vogella.tasks.ui.toolcontrols;


import java.util.Objects;

import jakarta.annotation.PostConstruct;
import jakarta.inject.Inject;

import org.eclipse.core.runtime.IProgressMonitor;
import org.eclipse.core.runtime.NullProgressMonitor;
import org.eclipse.core.runtime.jobs.IJobChangeEvent;
import org.eclipse.core.runtime.jobs.Job;
import org.eclipse.core.runtime.jobs.JobChangeAdapter;
import org.eclipse.core.runtime.jobs.ProgressProvider;
import org.eclipse.e4.ui.di.UISynchronize;
import org.eclipse.swt.SWT;
import org.eclipse.swt.widgets.Composite;
import org.eclipse.swt.widgets.ProgressBar;

public class ProgressMonitorControl {

  private final UISynchronize sync;

  private ProgressBar progressBar;
  private GobalProgressMonitor monitor;

  @Inject
  public ProgressMonitorControl(UISynchronize sync) {
    this.sync = Objects.requireNonNull(sync);
  }

  @PostConstruct
  public void createControls(Composite parent){
    progressBar = new ProgressBar(parent, SWT.SMOOTH);
    progressBar.setBounds(100, 10, 200, 20);

    Job.getJobManager().setProgressProvider(new ProgressProvider() {

        @Override
        public IProgressMonitor createMonitor(Job job) {

            StatusUpdateProgressMonitor statusUpdateProgressMonitor = new
StatusUpdateProgressMonitor();
            return statusUpdateProgressMonitor.addJob(job);
        }
    });

    private final class StatusUpdateProgressMonitor extends NullProgressMonitor {
```

```
// thread-Safe via thread confinement of the UI-Thread
// (means access only via UI-Thread)
private long runningTasks = 0L;

@Override
public void beginTask(final String name, final int totalWork) {
  sync.syncExec(new Runnable() {

    @Override
    public void run() {
      if( runningTasks <= 0 ) {
        // --- no task is running at the moment ---
        progressBar.setSelection(0);
        progressBar.setMaximum(totalWork);

      } else {
        // --- other tasks are running ---
        progressBar.setMaximum(progressBar.getMaximum() + totalWork);
      }

      runningTasks++;
      progressBar.setToolTipText("Currently running: " + runningTasks +
              "\nLast task: " + name);
    }
  });
}

@Override
public void worked(final int work) {
  sync.syncExec(new Runnable() {

    @Override
    public void run() {
      progressBar.setSelection(progressBar.getSelection() + work);
    }
  });
}

public IProgressMonitor addJob(Job job){
  if( job != null ){
    job.addJobChangeListener(new JobChangeAdapter() {
      @Override
      public void done(IJobChangeEvent event) {
        sync.syncExec(new Runnable() {

          @Override
          public void run() {
            runningTasks--;
```

```
                if (runningTasks > 0 ){
                  // --- some tasks are still running ---
                  progressBar.setToolTipText("Currently running: " + runningTasks);

                } else {
                  // --- all tasks are done (a reset of selection could be done) ---
                  progressBar.setToolTipText("No background progress running.");
                }
              }
            });

            // clean-up
            event.getJob().removeJobChangeListener(this);
          }
        });
      }
      return this;
    }
  }
}
```

This new element can be accessed via the model service and used as an `IProgressMonitor` for the job.

```
Job job = new Job("My Job") {
    // code as before
};
job.schedule();
```

> A more advanced implementation could, for example, implement a progress monitoring OSGi Service and report progress to the user interface via the event service.

142. Exercise: Asynchronous processing with jobs

142.1. Simulate delayed access

Change your `consume` method in the `TransientTaskServiceImpl` class to the following example code. This code simulates a slow server access with the `TimeUnit` class.

```
private void delay() { ❶
        try {
            TimeUnit.SECONDS.sleep(5);
        } catch (InterruptedException e) {
```

```
            e.printStackTrace();
        }
    }

@Override
public void consume(Consumer<List<Task>> taskConsumer) {
    // Simulate Server access delay
    delay(); ❷
    // always pass a new copy of the data
    taskConsumer.accept(tasks.stream().map(Task::copy).collect(Collectors.toList()));
}

@Override
public List<Task> getAll() {
    delay(); ❸
    return tasks.stream().map(Task::copy).collect(Collectors.toList());
}
```

❶ New method, which simulates a delay in the server response

❷ New code in existing method

❸ New code in existing method

142.2. Validate freeze

Start your application. If you press the Load Data button in the task overview part, your application should freeze. Try to use it directly after the loading of the data to experience the freeze.

142.3. Use asynchronous processing

You have a Load Data button in your `TodoOverviewPart`. Write a custom `Job` implementation to load the data in the background whenever this button is pressed. Once the data is loaded, update the table with the new data. Make sure that this table update happens in the main interface thread.

The following example code can help.

```
// more code....

// you should have this code already to update your table
newButton(SWT.PUSH).text("Load Data").onSelect(e -> update()).create(parent);

// adjust the update method to load the data via a job

private void update() {
    Job job = new Job("loading") {
        @Override
        protected IStatus run(IProgressMonitor monitor) {
```

```
            List<Task> all = taskService.getAll();
            Display.getDefault().asyncExec(() -> updateViewer(all));
            return Status.OK_STATUS;
        }
    };
    job.schedule();
}
```

142.4. Validate

> If you start your application, it takes longer to start if you still read the data somewhere synchronously during startup. For example, if you implemented the `TodoDeletionPart`. If you want to avoid this, you need to perform this reading also asynchronously. We leave this change as an optional exercise to the reader.

Use the wizard to create a new `Task` object. Press the Load Data button to update it. The application should be usable and the table should update after the delay defined in the `TaskService` implementation class.

142.5. Remove delay

After finishing this exercise and validating that everything works correctly, change the delay to one second to prevent long delays in future exercises.

143. Exercise: Asynchronous processing with CompletableFuture

Create the following new part and add it to your application. It allows you to download an image and store it on the file system.

Note that the user interface update checks if the user interface is still present before accessing the user interface via a null and `isDisposed` check Otherwise, if the download takes a long time and the user closes the part before the planned UI update, an `org.eclipse.swt.SWTException: Widget is disposed` exception will occur.

```
package com.vogella.tasks.ui.parts;

import java.io.FileOutputStream;
import java.io.IOException;
import java.net.URI;
import java.net.http.HttpClient;
import java.net.http.HttpRequest;
import java.net.http.HttpResponse;
```

```
import org.eclipse.e4.ui.di.Focus;
import org.eclipse.e4.ui.di.Persist;
import org.eclipse.jface.dialogs.MessageDialog;
import org.eclipse.swt.SWT;
import org.eclipse.swt.layout.GridData;
import org.eclipse.swt.layout.GridLayout;
import org.eclipse.swt.widgets.Button;
import org.eclipse.swt.widgets.Composite;
import org.eclipse.swt.widgets.Display;
import org.eclipse.swt.widgets.FileDialog;
import org.eclipse.swt.widgets.Label;
import org.eclipse.swt.widgets.ProgressBar;
import org.eclipse.swt.widgets.Shell;

import jakarta.annotation.PostConstruct;

public class ImageDownloadPart {

    private Label statusLabel;
    private ProgressBar progressBar;
    private Button downloadButton;
    private Shell shell;

    private final HttpClient httpClient = HttpClient.newHttpClient();

    @PostConstruct
    public void createControls(Composite parent) {
        this.shell = parent.getShell();
        parent.setLayout(new GridLayout(1, false));

        downloadButton = new Button(parent, SWT.PUSH);
        downloadButton.setText("Download and Save Image");

        progressBar = new ProgressBar(parent, SWT.INDETERMINATE | SWT.HORIZONTAL);
        progressBar.setLayoutData(new GridData(SWT.FILL, SWT.CENTER, true, false));
        progressBar.setVisible(false);

        statusLabel = new Label(parent, SWT.NONE);
        statusLabel.setLayoutData(new GridData(SWT.FILL, SWT.CENTER, true, false));
        statusLabel.setText("Status: Idle");

        downloadButton.addListener(SWT.Selection, e -> {
            String imageUrl = "https://www.vogella.com/img/logo/index_logo.png";
            String savePath = promptForSavePath(parent.getShell());
            if (savePath != null) {
                startDownload(imageUrl, savePath);
            }
        });
```

```java
    }

    private String promptForSavePath(Shell shell) {
        FileDialog fileDialog = new FileDialog(shell, SWT.SAVE);
        fileDialog.setText("Save Image As");
        fileDialog.setFilterExtensions(new String[]{"*.png", "*.*"});
        fileDialog.setFileName("downloaded_image.png");
        return fileDialog.open();
    }

    private void startDownload(String imageUrl, String savePath) {
        Display.getDefault().asyncExec(() -> {
            if (downloadButton == null || downloadButton.isDisposed()) {
                return;
            }
            progressBar.setVisible(true);
            statusLabel.setText("Status: Downloading...");
            downloadButton.setEnabled(false);
        });

        HttpRequest request = HttpRequest.newBuilder()
                .uri(URI.create(imageUrl))
                .GET()
                .build();

        httpClient.sendAsync(request, HttpResponse.BodyHandlers.ofByteArray())
                .whenComplete((response, throwable) -> {
                    boolean success = false;
                    String errorMessage = null;

                    // Handle exceptions during HTTP request
                    if (throwable != null) {
                        errorMessage = buildErrorMessage("Network Error",
                            "Failed to connect to server: " + throwable.getMessage(),
                            imageUrl);
                        logError("HTTP request failed", throwable);
                    }
                    // Handle HTTP error status codes
                    else if (response.statusCode() != 200) {
                        errorMessage = buildErrorMessage("HTTP Error",
                            "Server returned status code: " + response.statusCode(),
                            imageUrl);
                        logError("HTTP status error: " + response.statusCode(), null);
                    }
                    // Handle file I/O errors
                    else {
                        try (FileOutputStream fos = new FileOutputStream(savePath)) {
                            fos.write(response.body());
                            success = true;
```

```
                    } catch (IOException e) {
                        errorMessage = buildErrorMessage("File Save Error",
                            "Failed to save file: " + e.getMessage(),
                            savePath);
                        logError("File write failed", e);
                    }
                }

                final boolean finalSuccess = success;
                final String finalErrorMessage = errorMessage;

                Display.getDefault().asyncExec(() -> {
                    if (downloadButton == null || downloadButton.isDisposed()) {
                        return;
                    }

                    progressBar.setVisible(false);
                    downloadButton.setEnabled(true);

                    if (finalSuccess) {
                        statusLabel.setText("Status: Downloaded and saved
successfully");
                    } else {
                        statusLabel.setText("Status: Download failed");
                        // Show error dialog with details
                        showErrorDialog("Download Failed", finalErrorMessage);
                    }
                });
            });
    }

    private String buildErrorMessage(String errorType, String details, String context) {
        StringBuilder sb = new StringBuilder();
        sb.append(errorType).append("\n\n");
        sb.append("Details: ").append(details).append("\n");
        sb.append("Context: ").append(context);
        return sb.toString();
    }

    private void showErrorDialog(String title, String message) {
        if (shell != null && !shell.isDisposed()) {
            MessageDialog.openError(shell, title, message);
        }
    }

    private void logError(String message, Throwable throwable) {
        System.err.println("ImageDownloadPart Error: " + message);
        if (throwable != null) {
            throwable.printStackTrace();
```

```
        }
    }

    @Focus
    public void onFocus() {
        if (downloadButton != null && !downloadButton.isDisposed()) {
            downloadButton.setFocus();
        }
    }

    @Persist
    public void onSave() {
        // Optional save logic
    }
}
```

The part should look similar to the following screenshot

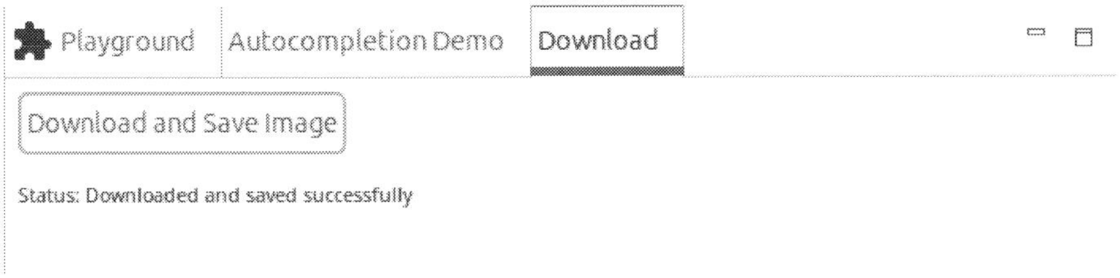

Part XVI: Event service for message communication

144. Communication within the Eclipse application

It is common for parts of your application to need to update other components. Whenever possible, this communication should be decoupled to prevent components from being tightly linked.

This can be achieved using a subscriber/publisher model, implemented as an event system. Software components can register for events, and other components can send events. The event system ensures that all registered components receive the events to which they subscribed.

144.1. The event bus in Eclipse and OSGi

The Eclipse platform and OSGi runtime provide a global, event-based communication system known as the *event bus*.

Any software component with access to the event system can send out arbitrary events, as shown in the following graphic.

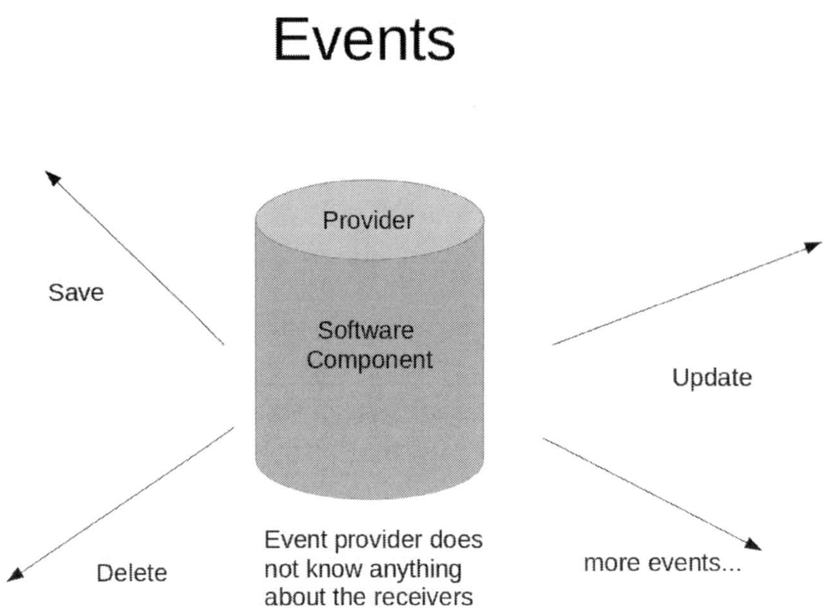

The Eclipse platform ensures that registered components receive the messages. It uses this event system for internal communication.

144.2. Selecting the object type to send

The event system allows for sending and receiving objects of any type. Often, it is enough to send the desired object through an event. However, it is a good practice to use a map-like structure to send events and provide a common interface for them.

145. Event service in Eclipse

The Eclipse framework provides and uses the `IEventBroker` event service for communication. You can use this communication service to allow components within your application to communicate.

The Eclipse event service is based on the OSGi `EventAdmin` service.

145.1. Required plug-ins for using the event service

The following plug-ins are required to use the event service functionality in Eclipse components.

- `org.eclipse.e4.core.services`
- `org.eclipse.osgi.services`

145.2. Sending events in Eclipse

The event service can be injected using dependency injection.

```
@Inject
private IEventBroker eventBroker;
```

In the following examples, assume a class named `TaskEventConstants` contains a `static final` field (constant) that defines a string.

The event service allows notifications to be sent to registered components. This can be done asynchronously or synchronously.

```
@Inject IEventBroker broker;

...
// asynchronously
// sending code is not blocked until the event has been delivered
broker.post(TaskEventConstants.TOPIC_TODO_NEW, todo);

//synchronously sending a todo
//the calling code is blocked until delivery

broker.send(TaskEventConstants.TOPIC_TODO_NEW, newTodo);
```

You can now send arbitrary Java objects or primitives through the event bus.

145.3. Registering to receive events

You can use dependency injection to register and respond to events. In this setup, the Eclipse framework automatically removes all event subscriptions when the model class is disposed.

The `@EventTopic` and `@UIEventTopic` annotations tag methods and fields that should be notified of event changes. The `@UIEventTopic` ensures that event notifications occur in the user interface thread.

```
import java.util.Map;

// TaskEventConstants.TOPIC_TODO_UPDATE is
// a String constant

@Inject
@Optional
private void subscribeTopicTodoUpdated
    (@UIEventTopic(TaskEventConstants.TOPIC_TODO_UPDATE)
```

```
        Task task) {
    if (viewer != null) {
        // this example assumes that you do not use data binding
        todoService.getTodos(viewer::setInput);
    }
}
```

You can register an instance of `org.osgi.service.event.EventHandler` directly using the `IEventBroker.subscribe()` method. To unsubscribe, use the `unsubscribe()` method.

Using dependency injection for subscribing is preferred over direct subscription. This way, the framework manages listener registration and deregistration automatically. However, sometimes it is useful to control when to listen to events, for example, when an event should only be received once.

```
import jakarta.annotation.PostConstruct;
import jakarta.inject.Inject;
import org.eclipse.e4.core.services.events.IEventBroker;
import org.eclipse.e4.ui.model.application.ui.advanced.MPerspective;
import org.osgi.service.event.Event;
import org.osgi.service.event.EventHandler;
public class LazyLoadingAddon implements EventHandler {

    @Inject
    private IEventBroker broker;

    @PostConstruct
    public void lazyLoadInContributorPerspective() {
        broker.subscribe(UIEvents.ElementContainer.TOPIC_SELECTEDELEMENT, this);
    }

    @Override
    public void handleEvent(Event event) {
        Object property = event.getProperty(UIEvents.EventTags.NEW_VALUE);

        if (!(property instanceof MPerspective)) {
            return;
        }

        MPerspective perspective = (MPerspective) property;

        // only load data when this particular perspective is selected
        if ("com.example.speciallazyloaded.perspective".equals(perspective.
getElementId())) {

            // loading data...
```

```
            // unsubscribe afterwards, so that loading is only done once
            broker.unsubscribe(this);
        }
    }
}
```

145.4. Subscribing to sub-topics

You can subscribe to specific topics or use wildcards to subscribe to all sub-events. Sub-events are separated by `/`. The following example defines string constants, including the `TOPIC_TASKS_ALLTOPICS` constant. This constant can be used to register for all sub-events.

```
package com.vogella.tasks.events;
/**
 *
 * @noimplement This interface is not intended to be implemented by clients.
 *
 * Only used for constant definition
 */

public interface TaskEventConstants {

    // topic identifier for all topics
    String TOPIC_TASKS = "TOPIC_TASKS";

    // this key can only be used for event registration; you cannot
    // send out generic events
    String TOPIC_TASKS_ALLTOPICS = "TOPIC_TASKS/*";

    String TOPIC_TASKS_CHANGED = "TOPIC_TASKS/CHANGED";
    String TOPIC_TASKS_NEW = "TOPIC_TASKS/TASKS/NEW";
    String TOPIC_TASKS_DELETE = "TOPIC_TASKS/TASKS/DELETED";
    String TOPIC_TASKS_UPDATE = "TOPIC_TASKS/TASKS/UPDATED";
}
```

Assuming your application starts within 5 seconds and a part containing the following code is visible, you would receive this event via the following code:

```
    @Inject
    public void getFromOSGi(@Optional @EventTopic("YOURKEY") String value) {
        System.out.println(value);
    }
```

145.5. Event system compared to Eclipse context

The `IEventBroker` is a global event bus and is independent of the `IEclipseContext` hierarchy. The `IEventBroker` service supports sending event information without requiring knowledge of the recipient. Interested classes can register for events without needing to know which classes will provide them. This is known as the whiteboard pattern, which promotes loosely coupled application components.

The disadvantage is that it is a global bus with no scoping of events. Publishers must ensure they provide enough information in the topic and sent objects to enable subscribers to determine the relevance of each event.

145.6. Asynchronous processing and the event bus

Your threads can use the `IEventBroker` to send event data. Event listeners are called by the framework. If a method is annotated with the `UIEventTopic` annotation, it is called in the main thread.

```
private static final String UPDATE ="update";

// get the IEventBroker injected
@Inject
IEventBroker broker;

// somewhere in your code you do something
// performance-intensive

button.addSelectionListener(new SelectionAdapter() {
            @Override
            public void widgetSelected(SelectionEvent e) {
                Runnable runnable = new Runnable() {
                    public void run() {
                        for (int i = 0; i < 10; i++) {
                            try {
                                Thread.sleep(500);
                            } catch (InterruptedException e) {
                                e.printStackTrace();
                            }
                            // send out an event to update
                            // the UI
                            broker.send(UPDATE, i);
                        }
                    }
                };
                new Thread(runnable).start();
            }
        });
```

```java
// more code
// ....

// get notified and sync automatically
// with the UI thread

@Inject @Optional
public void  getEvent(@UIEventTopic(UPDATE) int i) {
    // text1 is an SWT Text field
    text1.setText(String.valueOf(i));
    System.out.println(i);
}
```

145.7. Evaluation of the can execute method for handlers

A method annotated with `@CanExecute` is called by the framework if a change occurs in the Eclipse context, such as when selecting a new part. If the method returns `false`, the framework disables any menu and tool items associated with that command.

You can request re-evaluation of the `@CanExecute` methods by sending an event via the event broker.

```java
// evaluate all @CanExecute methods
eventBroker.post(UIEvents.REQUEST_ENABLEMENT_UPDATE_TOPIC, UIEvents.ALL_ELEMENT_ID);

// evaluate a context via a selector
Selector s = (a selector from the application model or an ID);
eventBroker.post(UIEvents.REQUEST_ENABLEMENT_UPDATE_TOPIC, s);
```

145.8. The event bus in OSGi

OSGi provides the `EventAdmin` for handling event-based communication.

145.9. Required packages for using the event admin

The following packages are required to use the OSGi event service functionality:

- `org.eclipse.osgi.services`

You can register an instance of `org.osgi.service.event.EventHandler` directly using the `IEventBroker.subscribe()` method. To unsubscribe, use the `unsubscribe()` method.

145.10. Sending events to the `IEventBroker` via an OSGi service

The `IEventBroker` used in Eclipse applications is based on the OSGi Event Admin service. Thus, you can use the OSGi Event Admin to send events, for example, to send events to your RCP application from another OSGi service.

To make an event relevant for your Eclipse application, add `org.eclipse.e4.data` as a key to the event data you send out. The following is an example of a simple OSGi service that uses the OSGi Event Admin and sends out an event after 5 seconds.

```
package com.vogella.osgi.eventadminuser;

import java.util.HashMap;
import java.util.Map;
import java.util.concurrent.Executors;
import java.util.concurrent.ScheduledExecutorService;
import java.util.concurrent.TimeUnit;

import org.osgi.service.component.annotations.Activate;
import org.osgi.service.component.annotations.Component;
import org.osgi.service.component.annotations.Reference;
import org.osgi.service.event.Event;
import org.osgi.service.event.EventAdmin;

import com.vogella.tasks.model.TaskService;

@Component
public class EventAdminUser {

    @Reference
    EventAdmin admin;

    @Activate
    public void activate() {

        String payload = "OBJECT to BE SEND";

        // When your program starts up
        ScheduledExecutorService executor = Executors.newSingleThreadScheduledExecutor();

        // then, when you want to schedule a task
        Runnable task = new Runnable() {

            @Override
            public void run() {

                Map<String, Object> properties = new HashMap<>();
```

```
                properties.put("org.eclipse.e4.data", payload);
                Event event = new Event("YOURKEY", properties);
                admin.sendEvent(event);

            }
        };
        executor.schedule(task, 5, TimeUnit.SECONDS);

        // and finally, when your program wants to exit
        executor.shutdown();
    }
}
```

Assuming your application starts within 5 seconds and a part containing the following code is visible, you would receive this event via the following code:

```
    @Inject
    public void getFromOSGi(@Optional @EventTopic("YOURKEY") String value) {
        System.out.println(value);
    }
```

145.11. Wrapper for event processing

Since the OSGi Event Admin API is difficult to use, you might wrap it for easier access.

```
import org.osgi.service.event.Event;
import org.osgi.service.event.EventAdmin;

import java.util.HashMap;
import java.util.Map;

public class EventPublisher {
    private final EventAdmin eventAdmin;
    private final Map<String, Object> properties = new HashMap<>();
    private String topic;

    // Constructor
    public EventPublisher(EventAdmin eventAdmin) {
        this.eventAdmin = eventAdmin;
    }

    // Static method to initialize
    public static EventPublisher with(EventAdmin eventAdmin) {
        return new EventPublisher(eventAdmin);
    }
```

```java
    // Set the topic for the event
    public EventPublisher topic(String topic) {
        this.topic = topic;
        return this;
    }

    // Add a property to the event
    public EventPublisher property(String key, Object value) {
        properties.put(key, value);
        return this;
    }

    // Send the event
    public void send() {
        if (topic == null || topic.isEmpty()) {
            throw new IllegalStateException("Event topic cannot be null or empty");
        }
        Event event = new Event(topic, properties);
        eventAdmin.postEvent(event);
    }
}
```

This would simplify the sending of events.

```java
import org.osgi.service.event.EventAdmin;

public class EventSenderExample {
    private final EventAdmin eventAdmin;

    // Constructor where EventAdmin is injected
    public EventSenderExample(EventAdmin eventAdmin) {
        this.eventAdmin = eventAdmin;
    }

    public void sendSwitchEvent(String command) {
        EventPublisher.with(eventAdmin)
                .topic(VogellaEventConstants.TOPIC_SWITCH)
                .property(VogellaEventConstants.PROPERTY_KEY_TARGET, command)
                .send();
    }
}
```

And you could add a static `lookup()` method for retrieving the admin service.

```java
    public static EventAdmin lookup() {
        BundleContext context = FrameworkUtil.getBundle(EventFluentSender.class
```

```
).getBundleContext();
        ServiceReference<EventAdmin> ref = context.getServiceReference(EventAdmin.class);
        EventAdmin eventAdmin = context.getService(ref);

        if (eventAdmin == null) {
            throw new IllegalStateException("EventAdmin service not available");
        }
        return eventAdmin;
    }
```

145.12. Example: Part activation event

A topic that is fired by Eclipse is `UIEvents.UILifeCycle.ACTIVATE`, which is fired every time a part is activated.

```
@Inject
@Optional
public void subscribeTopicPartActivation(@UIEventTopic(UIEvents.UILifeCycle.ACTIVATE)
Event event) {

    Object element = event.getProperty(EventTags.ELEMENT);
    if (!(element instanceof MPart)) {
        return;
    }

    MPart part = (MPart) element;

    System.out.println("Part activated: " + part.getLabel());
}
```

The `Event` class contains properties, such as `EventTags.ELEMENT`, from which you can receive the element associated with this event.

Review the `UIEvents` class and its internal interfaces, such as `UIEvents.EventTags`, to see the other events fired by the Eclipse framework.

145.13. Extracting event information

The `UIEvents.EventTags` interface defines the possible event tags.

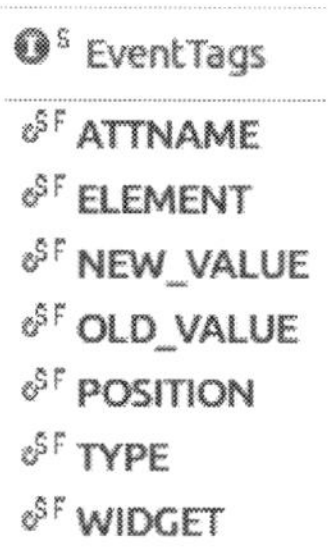

These event tags are explained in the following sections.

145.13.1. ATTNAME event tag

The `ATTNAME` property of the event is the attribute of the model that has been changed.

For instance, if you listen for changes to a model element's label, the `ATTNAME` of the event will be `label`.

```
@Inject
@Optional
public void subscribeTopicLabelChange(@EventTopic(UIEvents.UILabel.TOPIC_LABEL) Event
event) {
    Object element = event.getProperty(EventTags.ATTNAME);

    // will print "label" to the system output
    System.out.println(element);
}
```

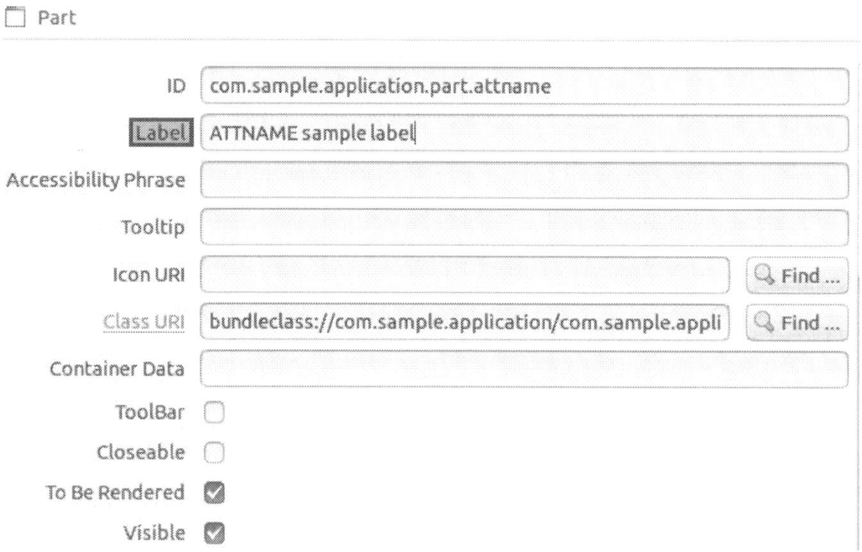

The `label` is an XML attribute and can be found in the source of your *Application.e4xmi* file.

```
<children xsi:type="basic:Part" xmi:id="_9CJOwNgYEeKX2Jv3m0M6IA"
                        elementId="com.sample.application.part.attname"

contributionURI="bundleclass://com.sample.application/yourpackage.attname"
                        label="ATTNAME sample label"/>
```

145.13.2. ELEMENT event tag

The `ELEMENT` event tag generally refers to the model element that is associated with the event.

145.13.3. NEW_VALUE and OLD_VALUE event tags

The `NEW_VALUE` and `OLD_VALUE` properties contain the new and old values of the element's attribute. These tags represent the values before and after the attribute change. For example, use them to detect which value was updated when listening for selection changes in perspectives.

In Eclipse 3.x, you would have registered an `IPerspectiveListener` for the `WorkbenchWindow` and implemented the `perspectiveChanged(…)` method. In Eclipse 4, you think in a DOM (Document Object Model) manner, where `<ELEMENT ATTNAME="NEW_VALUE">` is manipulated and fired within events.

An example of using the values of an attribute in the model is a listener for a perspective change.

```
@Inject
@Optional
public void subscribeTopicSelectedElement(@EventTopic
        (UIEvents.ElementContainer.TOPIC_SELECTEDELEMENT) Event event) {
    Object element = event.getProperty(EventTags.ELEMENT);
    Object newValue = event.getProperty(EventTags.NEW_VALUE);
    // ensure that the selected element of a perspective stack is changed and that this
is a perspective
    if (!(element instanceof MPerspectiveStack) || !(newValue instanceof MPerspective)) {
        return;
    }

    MPerspectiveStack perspectiveStack = (MPerspectiveStack) element;
    MPerspective perspective = (MPerspective) newValue;

    System.out.println("Selected perspective of " + perspectiveStack + " is " +
perspective.getLabel());
```

```
}
```

If you want to listen for an event when the perspective changes, you need to listen for the change of the `selectedElement` attribute of the `MPerspectiveStack`. You can then get the new and old `MPerspective` from the `EventTags.NEW_VALUE` and `EventTags.OLD_VALUE` properties.

You listen for the changed `selectedElement` attribute value of the `MPerspectiveStack`, rather than looking for a "perspective change" event.

It is good to keep the DOM structure of the application model in mind and think about the changes that can occur within the application model.

145.13.4. TYPE event tag

With the `TYPE` event tag, you can determine what action has been performed on the application model.

You can find the various types in the `UIEvents.EventTypes` interface.

With these event types, you can determine whether a model element was added, created, moved, removed, or an attribute was set.

The `UIEvents` class offers convenience methods to check for some types.

- S isADD(Event) : boolean
- S isREMOVE(Event) : boolean
- S isSET(Event) : boolean
- S isCREATE(Event) : boolean

The `isADD(Event)` and `isREMOVE(Event)` methods apply to both single and multiple items (e.g., ADD and ADD_MANY).

145.13.5. POSITION event tag

The `POSITION` event tag contains the new position of model elements. This property is only set if a collection of elements is concerned.

If you move parts in an `MPartStack` or between different `MPartStack` containers, you can listen for changes to the children of an element container like this:

```
@Inject
@Optional
public void subscribeTopicElementContainerChildren(@EventTopic
        (UIEvents.ElementContainer.TOPIC_CHILDREN) Event event) {
    Object element = event.getProperty(EventTags.ELEMENT);
    if (!(element instanceof MPartStack)) {
```

```
            return;
        }

        if (UIEvents.isADD(event)) {
            // check new value, because we check for addition and old value will be null
            Object newValue = event.getProperty(EventTags.NEW_VALUE);
            if (newValue instanceof MPart) {
                MPart part = (MPart) newValue;
                System.out.println("Added " + part.getLabel() + " at position: "
                        + event.getProperty(EventTags.POSITION));
            }
        } else if (UIEvents.isREMOVE(event)) {
            // check old value, because we check for remove and new value will be null
            Object oldValue = event.getProperty(EventTags.OLD_VALUE);
            if (oldValue instanceof MPart) {
                MPart part = (MPart) oldValue;
                System.out.println("Removed " + part.getLabel() + " from position: "
                        + event.getProperty(EventTags.POSITION));
            }
        }
    }
```

If you drag and drop an `MPart` within an `MPartStack`, the `MPart` is removed and then added back to the `MPartStack`.

The details can be seen in the `UIEventPublisher.formatData()` method from the `org.eclipse.e4.ui.internal.workbench` package. The position attribute is only used for the `move`, `add`, or `remove` events.

145.13.6. WIDGET event tag

The `WIDGET` event tag can be used to get the underlying widget, e.g., a `Composite` of the model element that is associated with the event.

You can directly interact with the underlying widget. In most cases, this is not necessary, because the model elements themselves provide most of the methods to interact with the widget, such as `setLabel()` or `setVisible()`.

145.14. Convenience methods for working with events

Besides the convenience methods for the event types, the `UIEvents` class offers two more convenience methods:

- S contains(Event, String, Object) : boolean
- S asIterable(Event, String) : Iterable<?>

145.14.1. The `contains` method

The `contains` method can be used to check whether a certain object is part of an event's property.

Imagine you are listening for changed tags on a certain model element and want to determine if a certain tag is part of the tags of the given model element. In this case, the `contains` method helps you with that task.

An example of this can be found in the `subscribeTopicTagsChanged(Event)` method of the `ToolBarManagerRenderer` class from the Eclipse framework.

```
@Inject
@Optional
private void subscribeTopicTagsChanged(@UIEventTopic
        (UIEvents.ApplicationElement.TOPIC_TAGS) Event event) {

    Object changedObj = event.getProperty(EventTags.ELEMENT);

    // this should only be applied to MToolbar elements
    if (!(changedObj instanceof MToolBar)) {
        return;
    }

    final MUIElement changedElement = (MUIElement) changedObj;

    // In case tags have been added and the new tag list contains the
    // IPresentationEngine.HIDDEN_EXPLICITLY String, the element should be hidden
    if (UIEvents.isADD(event)) {
        if (UIEvents.contains(event, UIEvents.EventTags.NEW_VALUE,
                IPresentationEngine.HIDDEN_EXPLICITLY)) {
            changedElement.setVisible(false);
            changedElement.setToBeRendered(false);
        }
    // If IPresentationEngine.HIDDEN_EXPLICITLY tag was removed, the element should be
visible again
    } else if (UIEvents.isREMOVE(event)) {
        if (UIEvents.contains(event, UIEvents.EventTags.OLD_VALUE,
                IPresentationEngine.HIDDEN_EXPLICITLY)) {
            changedElement.setVisible(true);
            changedElement.setToBeRendered(true);
        }
    }
}
```

This code demonstrates how the existence of a certain tag (`IPresentationEngine.HIDDEN_EXPLICITLY`) is checked with the `contains` method.

145.14.2. The `asIterable` method

The `asIterable` method can be used to get an `Iterable` of an event's property.

Let's take the example where we listened for the `UIEvents.ElementContainer.TOPIC_CHILDREN` event and checked the new position.

This example fails when we add more than one child to the `MPartStack`, which results in the `UIEvents.EventTypes.ADD_MANY` event type. In this case, nothing would be printed to `System.out`, because we have a list in the `EventTags.NEW_VALUE` property rather than an `MPart`.

We need to enhance our `subscribeTopicElementContainerChildren` method like this:

```
@Inject
@Optional
public void subscribeTopicElementContainerChildren(@EventTopic
        (UIEvents.ElementContainer.TOPIC_CHILDREN) Event event) {
    Object element = event.getProperty(EventTags.ELEMENT);
    if (!(element instanceof MPartStack)) {
        return;
    }

    if (UIEvents.isADD(event)) {
        // check new value, because we check for addition and old value will
        // be null
        Iterable<?> asIterable = UIEvents.asIterable(event, EventTags.NEW_VALUE);
        for (Object object : asIterable) {
            if (object instanceof MPart) {
                MPart part = (MPart) object;
                System.out.println("Added " + part.getLabel() + " at position: "
                        + event.getProperty(EventTags.POSITION));
            }
        }
    } else if (UIEvents.isREMOVE(event)) {
        // check old value, because we check for remove and new value will
        // be null
        Iterable<?> asIterable = UIEvents.asIterable(event, EventTags.OLD_VALUE);
        for (Object object : asIterable) {
            if (object instanceof MPart) {
                MPart part = (MPart) object;
                System.out.println("Removed " + part.getLabel() + " from position: "
                        + event.getProperty(EventTags.POSITION));
            }
        }
    }
}
```

146. Exercise: Use the event service for updating the task table

In this exercise, you learn how to update the `TodoOverviewPart` in case new task data is available. You use the event service for this.

146.1. Creating a plug-in for event constants

Create a new simple plug-in named *com.vogella.tasks.events*. See Chapter 36 for more information.

Define the following `TaskEventConstants` interface in this new plug-in. This interface stores the constants for these event topics.

```
package com.vogella.tasks.events;
/**
 *
 * @noimplement This interface is not intended to be implemented by clients.
 *
 * Only used for constant definition
 */

public interface TaskEventConstants {

    // topic identifier for all topics
    String TOPIC_TASKS = "TOPIC_TASKS";

    // this key can only be used for event registration, you cannot
    // send out generic events
    String TOPIC_TASKS_ALLTOPICS = "TOPIC_TASKS/*";

    String TOPIC_TASKS_CHANGED = "TOPIC_TASKS/CHANGED";
    String TOPIC_TASKS_NEW = "TOPIC_TASKS/TASKS/NEW";
    String TOPIC_TASKS_DELETE = "TOPIC_TASKS/TASKS/DELETED";
    String TOPIC_TASKS_UPDATE = "TOPIC_TASKS/TASKS/UPDATED";
}
```

Export the `com.vogella.tasks.events` package in the `MANIFEST.MF` file (via the *Runtime* tab) in your new plug-in.

146.2. Add the new plug-in to the product via the feature

Add the *events* plug-in to your feature so that it is available in your product configuration file.

146.3. Add the dependencies

Add *com.vogella.tasks.events* as a package dependency to your *com.vogella.tasks.ui* plug-in via its `MANIFEST.MF` file.

Start your application to validate that you did everything correctly.

> If the startup fails, ensure that you have added the `com.vogella.tasks.events` plug-in to the feature. Remember to start your application using the product configuration file to update the runtime configuration.

146.4. Send out notifications

Ensure that the following two plug-ins are included as a dependency in your `com.vogella.tasks.ui` plug-in.

- `org.eclipse.e4.core.services`
- `org.eclipse.osgi.services`

Update your `NewTaskHandler` to send out an event to communicate the change in data. The following example code demonstrates that for the `NewTaskHandler` class.

```
package com.vogella.tasks.ui.handlers;

import java.time.LocalDate;
import java.util.Map;

import org.eclipse.e4.core.di.annotations.Execute;
import org.eclipse.e4.core.services.events.IEventBroker;
import org.eclipse.jface.window.Window;
import org.eclipse.jface.wizard.WizardDialog;
import org.eclipse.swt.widgets.Shell;

import com.vogella.tasks.events.TaskEventConstants;
import com.vogella.tasks.model.Task;
import com.vogella.tasks.model.TaskService;
import com.vogella.tasks.ui.wizards.TaskWizard;

public class NewTaskHandler {
    @Execute
    public void execute(Shell shell, TaskService taskService, IEventBroker broker) {
        // use -1 to indicate a not existing id
        Task task = new Task(-1);
        task.setDueDate(LocalDate.now());
        WizardDialog dialog = new WizardDialog(shell, new TaskWizard(task));
```

```
        if (dialog.open() == Window.OK) {
            // call service to save task object
            taskService.update(task);
            // asynchronously
            String todoId = String.valueOf(task.getId());
            broker.post(TaskEventConstants.TOPIC_TASKS_NEW,
                    Map.of(TaskEventConstants.TOPIC_TASKS, TaskEventConstants
.TOPIC_TASKS_NEW, Task.FIELD_ID, todoId));
        }
    }
}
```

146.5. Receive updates in the parts

Register for this event in all relevant parts of your application. If the event is received, update your user interface. The following code demonstrates this for your `TodoOverviewPart` class.

```
import java.util.Map;
// more code

@Inject
@Optional
private void subscribeTopicTaskAllTopics(
        @UIEventTopic(TaskEventConstants.TOPIC_TASKS_ALLTOPICS) Map<String, String>
event) {
    if (viewer != null) {
        writableList.clear();
        updateViewer(taskService.getAll());
    }
}
```

146.6. Validate

Create a new task object via your wizard. The table in `TodoOverviewPart` should get updated automatically, e.g., the new entry should be visible in the table after you finish the wizard.

146.7. Review the implementation

The current implementation is functional but can be improved. Each user interface component that modifies tasks needs to send out events.

It would be preferable if the `TaskService` implementation could send out these events directly.

In a following exercise, we will improve our current solution and move the event sending to the implementation class of the `TaskService` service.

Part XVII: Extending and modifying the Eclipse context

147. Accessing and extending the Eclipse context

147.1. Accessing the context

You can place objects directly in the `IEclipseContext` hierarchy to make them available to other model objects.

To access an existing context, you can use dependency injection if the relevant object is managed by the Eclipse runtime. This is the case for all model objects. The following code demonstrates how to get access to the active `IEclipseContext`, in which the handler is called.

```
package com.vogella.tasks.ui.handlers;

import org.eclipse.e4.core.contexts.IEclipseContext;
import org.eclipse.e4.core.di.annotations.Execute;

public class ShowMapHandler {
    @Execute
    public void execute(IEclipseContext context) {
        // add objects to the active local context injected into
```

```
        // this handler
        // ...
    }
}
```

If a model object implements `MContext`, you can use dependency injection to get the model object injected and call the `getContext()` method to access its context. For example, MPart, MWindow, MApplication, and MPerspective extend MContext.

The following code demonstrates how to get the `MApplication` injected and how to access its `IEclipseContext`.

```
package com.vogella.tasks.ui.parts;

import jakarta.annotation.PostConstruct;
import jakarta.annotation.PreDestroy;

import org.eclipse.e4.core.contexts.IEclipseContext;
import org.eclipse.e4.ui.model.application.ui.basic.MPart;
import org.eclipse.swt.widgets.Composite;

public class TodoDetailsPart {

    @PostConstruct
    public void createControls(Composite parent,
        MApplication application) {

        // getting the IEclipseContext of the application
        // via the MApplication object
        IEclipseContext context = application.getContext();

        // add or access objects to and from the application context
        // ...
    }
}
```

147.2. Objects and context variables

You can add key-value pairs directly to the `IEclipseContext`.

Adding objects to a context can be done via the `set()` method of the `IEclipseContext` interface. The following example creates a new context via the `EclipseContextFactory.create()` factory method call and adds some objects to it. Via the `setParent()` method call, the new context is connected to the context hierarchy.

```java
@Inject
public void addingContext(IEclipseContext context) {

    // create a new IEclipseContext instance
    IEclipseContext myContext = EclipseContextFactory.create();

    // add objects to context
    myContext.set("mykey1", "Hello1");
    myContext.set("mykey2", "Hello2");

    // adding a parent relationship
    myContext.setParent(context);

    // alternatively you can create a new
    // context which has a parent/child
    // relationship via the
    // context.createChild() method call
}
```

Such a context can be used to instantiate an object via the Eclipse framework.

A *context variable* is a key which is declared as *modifiable* via the `declareModifiable(key)` method call.

```java
@Inject
public void addingContext(IEclipseContext context) {
    // putting in some values
    context.set("mykey1", "Hello1");
    context.set("mykey2", "Hello2");

    // declares the named value as modifiable by descendants of this context

    // if the value does not exist in this context,
    // a null value is added for the name
    context.declareModifiable("mykey1");
}
```

Context variables are added to particular levels of the `IEclipseContext` hierarchy and can be modified using the `modify()` method rather than the `set()` method of the `IEclipseContext`. The `modify()` method searches up the chain to find the `IEclipseContext` defining the variable. If no entry is found in the context hierarchy, the value will be set in the `IEclipseContext` in which the call started.

If the key already exists in the context, then `modify()` requires that the key has been declared modifiable with the `declareModifiable()` method, if not, the method will throw an exception.

You can add key-value pairs and *Context variables* at different levels of the context hierarchy to supply different objects in your application.

147.3. Replacing existing objects in the IEclipseContext

Instead of adding new objects to the `IEclipseContext` hierarchy, you can override existing objects by using the same key.

You can change the behavior of your application by overriding certain entries in the context. For example, you can modify the context of the *MWindow* model element. Its `IEclipseContext` is originally created by the `WBWRenderer` class. By default, it puts an instance of the `IWindowCloseHandler` and the `ISaveHandler` interface into the local context of the *MWindow* model element. The `IWindowCloseHandler` object is responsible for the behavior once the *MWindow* model element is closed. The default `IWindowCloseHandler` prompts the user whether they want to save dirty parts (editors with changed content). You can change this default implementation by replacing the object in the context. The following example shows an `@Execute` method in a handler implementation that overrides this class at runtime.

```
@Execute
public void execute(final Shell shell, EModelService service,
    MWindow window) {
    IWindowCloseHandler handler = new IWindowCloseHandler() {
        @Override
        public boolean close(MWindow window) {
            return MessageDialog.openConfirm(shell,
            "Close",
            "You will lose data. Really close?");
        }
    };
window.getContext().set(IWindowCloseHandler.class, handler);
}
```

You could use this example in your lifecycle handler and subscribe to the `UIEvents.UILifeCycle.APP_STARTUP_COMPLETE` event. In the event handler you would replace the `IWindowCloseHandler` in the context.

147.4. Accessing the IEclipseContext hierarchy from OSGi services

OSGi services are not directly part of the `IEclipseContext` hierarchy and are created by the OSGi runtime. The OSGi runtime does not support dependency injection based on the `@Inject` annotation.

The Eclipse framework registers the implementation of the `MApplication` interface as an OSGi service. This allows OSGi services to use the OSGi API to access the `MApplication` and its context via the getContext() method. As the EModelService is part of the MApplication context, you can search for other context elements via it.

147.5. Model add-ons

To participate in dependency injection with your custom Java objects you can add them as model add-ons to the application model. The classes referred to by the model add-ons can access and modify the IEclipseContext or interact with other services, e.g., the event system.

The following screenshot shows a custom model add-on registered in the application model.

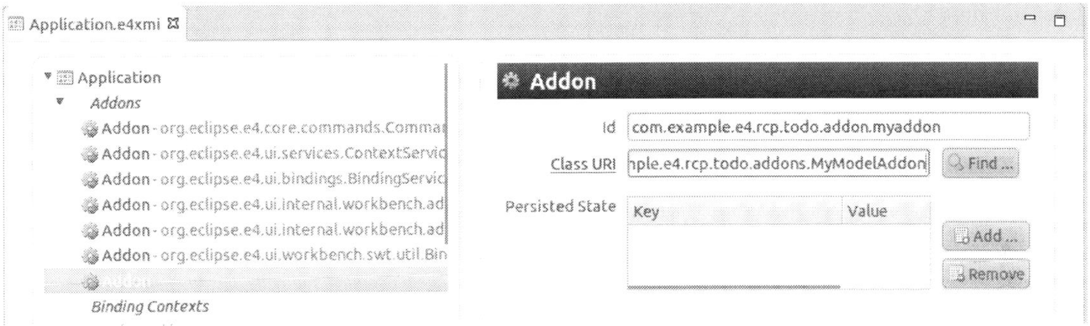

The following code shows an example implementation for the model add-on class. This add-on places an object into the IEclipseContext.

```
package com.vogella.tasks.ui.addons;

import jakarta.annotation.PostConstruct;

import org.eclipse.e4.core.contexts.IEclipseContext;

public class MyModelAddon {
    @PostConstruct
    public void init(IEclipseContext context) {
        // injected IEclipseContext comes from the application
        context.set("test1", "Hello");
    }
}
```

147.6. RunAndTrack

The IEclipseContext allows you via the runAndTrack() method to register a Java object of type RunAndTrack.

A RunAndTrack object is similar to a Runnable but has access to the context.

If the context changes, the `RunAndTrack` is called by the Eclipse framework. The runnable does not need to be explicitly unregistered from this context when it is no longer interested in tracking changes. If the `RunAndTrack` is invoked by the Eclipse platform and it returns `false` from its `RunAndTrack.changed()` method, it is automatically unregistered from change tracking on this context.

Such a `RunAndTrack` object allows a client to keep some external state synchronized with one or more values in this context.

148. Extending the objects available for the dependency injection

148.1. Creating and injecting custom objects

Using dependency injection for your custom objects has two flavors.

- You want to create objects which declare their dependencies with `@Inject` based on an `IEclipseContext` context. See chapter: Using dependency injection to create objects for details.
- You want the Eclipse dependency container to create your custom objects automatically on demand and then get them injected into your model objects.

For more details, see Section 148.3 and Section 148.4.

148.2. Using dependency injection to create objects

Using dependency injection is not limited to the objects created by the Eclipse runtime. You can use the same approach to create an instance of a given class based on a given `IEclipseContext`. The given class can contain `@Inject` annotations. For this you use the `ContextInjectionFactory` class as demonstrated in the following code example.

```
// create instance of class
ContextInjectionFactory.make(MyJavaObject.class, context);
```

The `ContextInjectionFactory.make()` method creates the object. You can put it into the `IEclipseContext` hierarchy after the creation. If you place it into the `IEclipseContext` of the application, the created object is globally available.

For this you can either use an existing `IEclipseContext` or create a new `IEclipseContext`. The new context object can be connected to the context hierarchy. Using a new context might be preferable to avoid collision of keys and to isolate your changes in a local context. Call the `dispose` method on your local context if the object is no longer needed.

The following code demonstrates how to create a new `IEclipseContext` object and to place values into it. This context can be used to create a new object.

```
IEclipseContext context = EclipseContextFactory.create();

// add your Java objects to the context
context.set(MyDataObject.class.getName(), data);
context.set(MoreStuff.class, moreData);

// dispose the context if you are done with it
context.dispose();
```

The next code example demonstrates how you can connect your new `IEclipseContext` object with an existing context hierarchy. The factory searches the hierarchy upwards to find values requested by the class which is instantiated.

```
@Inject
public void createObjectInPart(IEclipseContext ctx) {
    // create a new local_ context
    IEclipseContext localCtx =
                EclipseContextFactory.create();
    localCtx.set(String.class, "Hello");

    // connect new local context with context hierarchy
    localCtx.setParent(ctx);

    // create object of type MyJavaObject via DI
    // uses the localCtx and searches upwards for required objects
    MyJavaObject o = ContextInjectionFactory.make(MyJavaObject.class,
                localCtx);

    //TODO do something with the "o" object
}
```

The `ContextInjectionFactory.inject(Object, IEclipseContext)` method allows you to perform injection on an existing object. For example, if you created the object with the `new()` operator, you can still run dependency injection on it.

148.3. Create the custom objects automatically with @Creatable

If you want the Eclipse framework to create your custom objects for you, annotate them with `@Creatable`. This way you are telling the Eclipse DI container that it should create a new instance of this object if it does not find an instance in the context. The automatically-generated instance is not stored in the context.

If you have a non-default constructor, you must use the `@Inject` annotation on the constructor to indicate that Eclipse should try to run dependency injection on it.

For example, assume that you have the following domain model.

```
package com.vogella.tasks.ui.creatable;

import org.eclipse.e4.core.di.annotations.Creatable;

@Creatable
public class Dependent {
    public Dependent() {
        // placeholder
    }
}
```

```
package com.vogella.tasks.ui.creatable;

import jakarta.inject.Inject;

import org.eclipse.e4.core.di.annotations.Creatable;

import com.vogella.tasks.model.TaskService;

@Creatable
public class YourObject {
    // constructor
    @Inject
    public YourObject(Dependent depend, TaskService service) {
        // placeholder
    }
}
```

As the Eclipse framework is allowed to create instances of the `Dependent` and the `YourObject` class, it can create them if an instance is requested via dependency injection. In this example, the arguments of the constructors can be satisfied. If no fitting constructor is found, the Eclipse framework throws an exception.

Assuming that you have defined the `TaskService` OSGi service in your application, you can get an instance of your `YourObject` class injected into a part. The following example code demonstrates that.

```
// add this for example to your playground part
@Inject
public void setYourObject(YourObject object) {
    System.out.println(object);
}
```

148.4. Automatically create objects in the application context with @Singleton

If the object should be created in the application context, use the `@Singleton` annotation in addition to the `@Creatable` annotation. This ensures that only one instance of the object is created in your application.

```
package com.vogella.tasks.ui.creatable;

import jakarta.inject.Inject;

import org.eclipse.e4.core.di.annotations.Creatable;

import com.vogella.tasks.model.TaskService;

@Creatable
@Singleton
public class YourObject {
    // constructor
    @Inject
    public YourObject(Dependent depend, TaskService service) {
        // placeholder
    }
}
```

149. Context functions

149.1. Definition of a context function

A *context function* is an OSGi service that has access to the `IEclipseContext` of the requester. It allows you to lazily create an object for a given key, if this key is not contained in the relevant `IEclipseContext`.

The context function registers itself for a certain key, for example, a class name. Whenever the Eclipse dependency injection does not find an existing object under this key, it calls the `compute()` method of the context function.

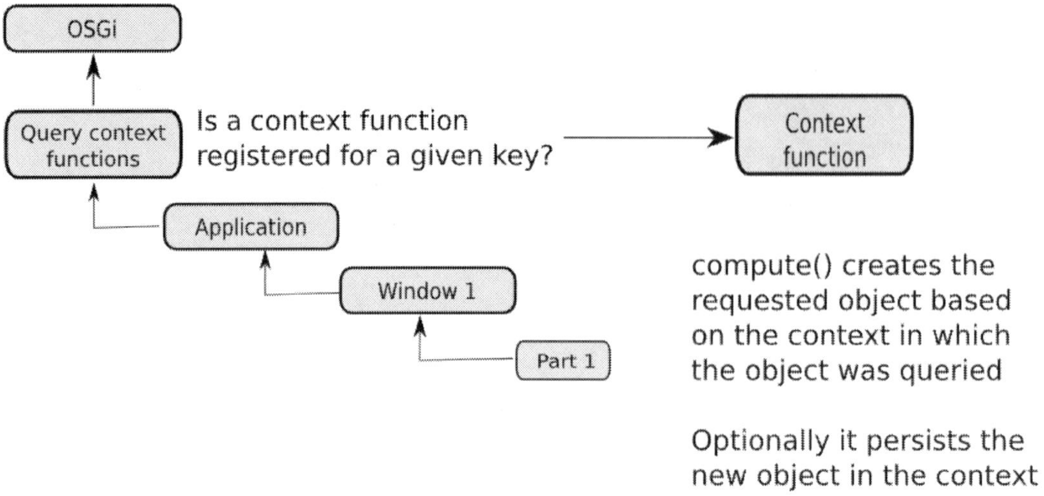

In this `compute()` method the context function can create the requested object. As input you receive the local `IEclipseContext` in which the injection was invoked and the requested key.

It can persist the created object into the context, so that successive calls will return the same generated object.

149.2. Creation of a context function

Context functions can be contributed to the application as OSGi services. They extend the `ContextFunction` class from the `org.eclipse.e4.core.contexts` package. The Eclipse runtime adds context functions by default to the application context.

They register themselves as OSGi service for the `IContextFunction` interface.

> Question: Why should you register your service for the `IContextFunction` interface but extend the `ContextFunction` class?
>
> Answer: If the interface gets extended by a new method your service continues to work, as the abstract class `ContextFunction` can provide a default implementation.

You need to specify the key the context function is responsible for. This is done via the *service.context.key* property in the service definition.

If the key is a class, you have to point to the fully qualified class. This key can be used for dependency injection. If you register a key which is not a class name, a consumer of the injection can use the `@Named` annotation to specify the key.

149.3. Examples for context function registrations

The following example shows the declaration of a context function. This function is available in the application context and responsible for the `vogella` key.

```
<scr:component xmlns:scr="http://www.osgi.org/xmlns/scr/v1.1.0"
    name="com.example.e4.rcp.todo.contextservice.translate">

<implementation class="com.example.e4.rcp.todo.contextservice.Test"/>

 <service>
   <provide interface="org.eclipse.e4.core.contexts.IContextFunction"/>
 </service>

 <property name="service.context.key" type="String"
   value="vogella"/>

</scr:component>
```

This key can be used for dependency injection, as shown in the following example.

```
// field injection
@Inject @Named("vogella") Task task;
```

The following example demonstrates a possible implementation of this context function that uses OSGi DS annotations.

```
package com.vogella.tasks.services.internal;

import org.eclipse.e4.core.contexts.ContextFunction;
import org.eclipse.e4.core.contexts.ContextInjectionFactory;
import org.eclipse.e4.core.contexts.IContextFunction;
import org.eclipse.e4.core.contexts.IEclipseContext;
import org.eclipse.e4.ui.model.application.MApplication;
import org.osgi.service.component.annotations.Component;

import com.vogella.tasks.model.TaskService;

@Component(service = IContextFunction.class, property =
"service.context.key=com.vogella.tasks.model.TaskService")
public class TaskServiceContextFunction extends ContextFunction {
    @Override
    public Object compute(IEclipseContext context, String contextKey) {
        TaskService todoService = ContextInjectionFactory.make(TransientTaskServiceImpl
.class, context);
```

```
        MApplication app = context.get(MApplication.class);
        IEclipseContext appCtx = app.getContext();
        appCtx.set(TaskService.class, todoService);

        return todoService;
    }
}
```

149.4. Use case for context functions

If you compare context functions with OSGi services, you notice the following differences:

- A context function can easily access the `IEclipseContext` hierarchy
- A context function allows you to lazily create objects using values from the context
- A context function can easily create different objects in the Eclipse context hierarchy
- The implementation of context functions is slightly more complex than the implementation of OSGi services

OSGi services are simpler to define; therefore, prefer to use OSGi services over context functions in case the additional functionality from above is not needed.

149.5. Publishing to the OSGi service registry from a context function

OSGi services may need to access the objects created by a context function. In this case, you can publish an OSGi service from a context function.

The following example demonstrates how to publish an implementation into the `IEclipseContext` and to the OSGi service registry.

```
package com.vogella.tasks.services.internal;

import org.eclipse.e4.core.contexts.ContextFunction;
import org.eclipse.e4.core.contexts.ContextInjectionFactory;
import org.eclipse.e4.core.contexts.IEclipseContext;
import org.eclipse.e4.ui.model.application.MApplication;
import org.osgi.framework.Bundle;
import org.osgi.framework.BundleContext;
import org.osgi.framework.FrameworkUtil;

import com.vogella.tasks.model.TaskService;

public class TodoServiceContextFunction extends ContextFunction {
    @Override
    public Object compute(IEclipseContext context, String contextKey) {
```

```
        // create instance of TaskService with dependency injection
        TaskService taskService =
                ContextInjectionFactory.make(TransientTaskServiceImpl.class, context);

        // add instance of TaskService to context so that
        // the next caller gets the same instance
        MApplication app = context.get(MApplication.class);
        IEclipseContext appCtx = app.getContext();
        appCtx.set(TaskService.class, taskService);

        // in case the TaskService is needed in the OSGi layer, e.g.
        // by other OSGi services, register the instance in the OSGi service layer
        Bundle bundle = FrameworkUtil.getBundle(this.getClass());
        BundleContext bundleContext = bundle.getBundleContext();
        bundleContext.registerService(TaskService.class, taskService, null);

        // return model for current invocation
        // next invocation uses object from application context
        return taskService;
    }
}
```

150. Exercise: Create a context function

In this exercise, you create a context function. This allows you to use dependency injection to create an instance of the `TaskService` service using the `IEclipseContext`. During the creation the event service is injected into your service instance; this allows you to send events from this service.

150.1. Add dependencies to the service plug-in

Ensure that the following framework dependencies are present in your `com.vogella.tasks.services` plug-in. Some of them are already part of your manifest file.

- org.eclipse.core.runtime
- org.eclipse.e4.core.services
- org.eclipse.e4.core.contexts
- org.eclipse.e4.core.di
- org.eclipse.e4.ui.model.workbench
- org.eclipse.osgi.services

For this exercise the service plug-in also needs to import the following packages (or plug-ins):

- com.vogella.tasks.model

- com.vogella.tasks.events
- jakarta.inject

The resulting `MANIFEST.MF` file should look similar to the following code (version numbers have been removed).

```
Manifest-Version: 1.0
Bundle-ManifestVersion: 2
Bundle-Name: Services
Bundle-SymbolicName: com.vogella.tasks.services
Bundle-Version: 1.0.0.qualifier
Bundle-Vendor: VOGELLA
Bundle-RequiredExecutionEnvironment: JavaSE-21
Automatic-Module-Name: com.vogella.tasks.services
Import-Package: com.vogella.tasks.events,
 com.vogella.tasks.model,
 jakarta.inject
Require-Bundle: org.eclipse.core.runtime,
 org.eclipse.e4.core.services,
 org.eclipse.e4.core.contexts,
 org.eclipse.e4.core.di,
 org.eclipse.e4.ui.model.workbench,
 org.eclipse.osgi.services
Bundle-ActivationPolicy: lazy
Service-Component: OSGI-
INF/com.vogella.tasks.services.internal.TransientTaskServiceImpl.xml
```

150.2. Create a class for the context function

Create the following new class in your `com.vogella.tasks.services` plug-in.

```
package com.vogella.tasks.services.internal;

import org.eclipse.e4.core.contexts.ContextFunction;
import org.eclipse.e4.core.contexts.ContextInjectionFactory;
import org.eclipse.e4.core.contexts.IContextFunction;
import org.eclipse.e4.core.contexts.IEclipseContext;
import org.eclipse.e4.ui.model.application.MApplication;
import org.osgi.service.component.annotations.Component;

import com.vogella.tasks.model.TaskService;

@Component(service = IContextFunction.class, property =
"service.context.key=com.vogella.tasks.model.TaskService")
public class TaskServiceContextFunction extends ContextFunction {
    @Override
```

```
    public Object compute(IEclipseContext context, String contextKey) {
        TaskService taskService = ContextInjectionFactory.make(TransientTaskServiceImpl
.class, context);

        MApplication app = context.get(MApplication.class);
        IEclipseContext appCtx = app.getContext();
        appCtx.set(TaskService.class, taskService);

        return taskService;
    }
}
```

150.3. Ensure annotation processing and plug-in activation is active

Ensure that OSGi DS functionality is activated via **Window › Preferences+Plug-in Development+DS annotations**.

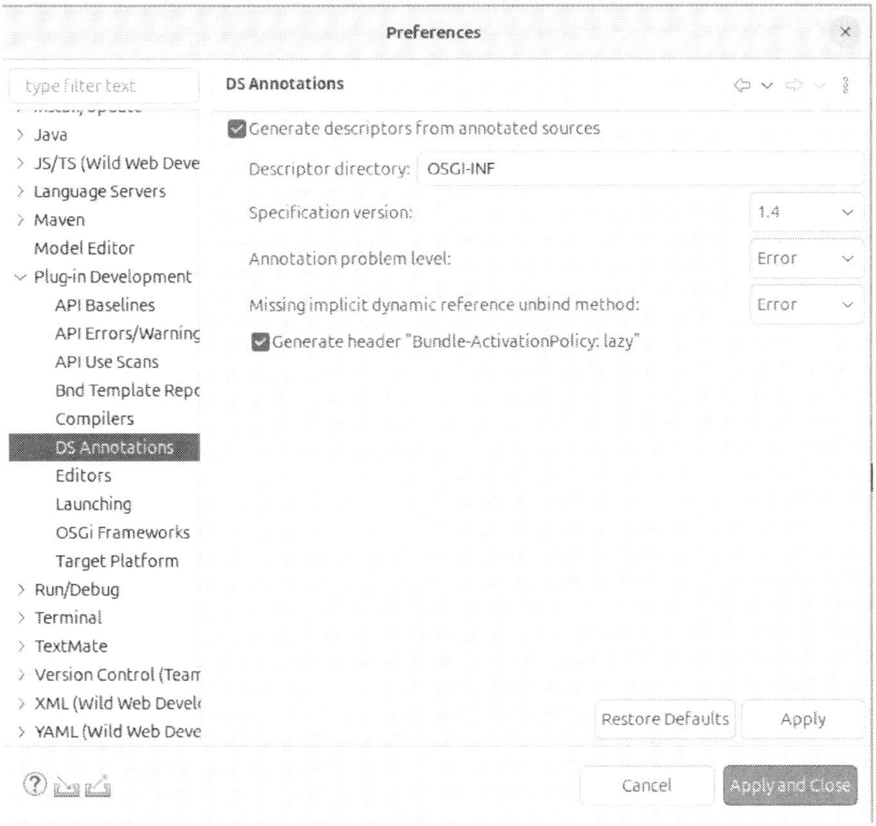

150.4. Deactivate the TaskService OSGi service

Deactivate your OSGi service for the `TaskService` that you have created earlier. For this, delete the `@Component` annotation from the `TransientTaskServiceImpl` class.

> You could leave your OSGi service for the `TaskService` active. Eclipse evaluates context functions before checking for other OSGi services. However, it is a good practice to remove unused elements.

150.5. Notifications from the TaskService

Change the `TransientTaskServiceImpl` class to get the `IEventBroker` injected. Also send out events in case of changes in the data model.

> Dependency injection only works here as we are using the `ContextInjectionFactory` in our context function implementation. OSGi does not natively support the '@Inject' annotation.

```
package com.vogella.tasks.services.internal;

import java.time.LocalDate;
import java.util.ArrayList;
import java.util.List;
import java.util.Map;
import java.util.Optional;
import java.util.concurrent.atomic.AtomicInteger;
import java.util.function.Consumer;
import java.util.stream.Collectors;

import jakarta.inject.Inject;

import org.eclipse.e4.core.services.events.IEventBroker;
import org.osgi.service.component.annotations.Component;

import com.vogella.tasks.events.TaskEventConstants;
import com.vogella.tasks.model.Task;
import com.vogella.tasks.model.TaskService;

public class TransientTaskServiceImpl implements TaskService {

    @Inject ❶
    private IEventBroker broker;

    private static AtomicInteger current = new AtomicInteger(1);
    private List<Task> tasks;

    public TransientTaskServiceImpl() {
        tasks = createTestData();
    }

    @Override
```

```
    public void consume(Consumer<List<Task>> taskConsumer) {
        // always pass a new copy of the data
        taskConsumer.accept(tasks.stream().map(Task::copy).collect(Collectors.toList()));
    }

    // create or update an existing instance of a task object
    @Override
    public synchronized boolean update(Task newTask) {
        // hold the Optional object as a reference to determine if the object is
        // newly created or not
        Optional<Task> taskOptional = findById(newTask.getId());

        // get the actual object or create a new one
        Task task = taskOptional.orElse(new Task(current.getAndIncrement()));
        task.setSummary(newTask.getSummary());
        task.setDescription(newTask.getDescription());
        task.setDone(newTask.isDone());
        task.setDueDate(newTask.getDueDate());

        if (!taskOptional.isPresent()) {
            tasks.add(task);
            broker.post(TaskEventConstants.TOPIC_TASKS_NEW,
                    Map.of(TaskEventConstants.TOPIC_TASKS, TaskEventConstants
.TOPIC_TASKS_NEW, Task.FIELD_ID,
                            task.getId())); ❷
        } else {
            broker.post(TaskEventConstants.TOPIC_TASKS_UPDATE, Map.of(TaskEventConstants
.TOPIC_TASKS,
                    TaskEventConstants.TOPIC_TASKS_UPDATE, Task.FIELD_ID, task.getId()));
❸
        }
        return true;
    }

    @Override
    public Optional<Task> get(long id) {
        return findById(id).map(Task::copy);
    }

    @Override
    public boolean delete(long id) {
        Optional<Task> deletedTask = findById(id);
        deletedTask.ifPresent(t -> {
            tasks.remove(t);
            broker.post(TaskEventConstants.TOPIC_TASKS_DELETE, Map.of(TaskEventConstants
.TOPIC_TASKS,
                    TaskEventConstants.TOPIC_TASKS_DELETE, Task.FIELD_ID, t.getId())); ❹
        });
```

```
        return deletedTask.isPresent();
    }

    // Example data, change if you like
    private List<Task> createTestData() {
        List<Task> list = List.of(create("Application model", "Flexible and extensible"),
                create("DI", "@Inject as programming mode"), create("OSGi", "Services"),
                create("SWT", "Widgets"), create("JFace", "Especially Viewers!"),
                create("CSS Styling", "Style your application"),
                create("Eclipse services", "Selection, model, Part"),
                create("Renderer", "Different UI toolkit"), create("Compatibility Layer",
"Run Eclipse 3.x"));
        return new ArrayList<>(list);
    }

    private Task create(String summary, String description) {
        return new Task(current.getAndIncrement(), summary, description, false,
LocalDate.now());
    }

    private Optional<Task> findById(long id) {
        return tasks.stream().filter(t -> t.getId() == id).findAny();
    }

    @Override
    public List<Task> getAll() {
        return tasks.stream().map(Task::copy).collect(Collectors.toList());
    }
}
```

❶ Use dependency injection to retrieve the event broker

❷ new task event

❸ update task event

❹ delete task event

150.6. Clean up the user interface code

In the previous exercise you sent out events directly from your handler. This is considered bad practice as the user interface would be responsible for sending out updates for data model changes.

Since this logic has been moved to the `TaskService` implementation, you can now remove this code. Thus remove all event notification calls from your plug-in. The following code shows the new `NewTaskHandler` handler implementation.

```java
package com.vogella.tasks.ui.handlers;

import java.util.Date;

import org.eclipse.e4.core.di.annotations.Execute;
import org.eclipse.jface.wizard.WizardDialog;
import org.eclipse.swt.widgets.Shell;

import com.vogella.tasks.model.TaskService;
import com.vogella.tasks.model.Task;
import com.vogella.tasks.ui.wizards.TaskWizard;

public class NewTaskHandler {
    @Execute
    public void execute(Shell shell, TaskService taskService) {
        // use -1 to indicate a not existing id
        Task task = new Task(-1);
        task.setDueDate(LocalDate.now());
        WizardDialog dialog = new WizardDialog(shell, new TaskWizard(task));
        if (dialog.open()== WizardDialog.OK) {
            taskService.update(task);
        }
    }
}
```

150.7. Validate

Validate that the user interface still receives all events for model changes. For example, does the table in the `TodoOverviewPart` class still update when a new task is created by the wizard?

If you delete a task object via your menu, this should also update the table.

150.8. Error analysis in case something does not work

Every service defined by OSGi declarative services must have a unique name.

Start your application. If you encounter an error indicating duplicate names, rename the new service.

If the service still fails, ensure that the service property is correctly entered.

150.9. Review implementation

This implementation is an improvement over using the user interface code for event notifications. It places the responsibility of sending out the relevant events into the corresponding service.

The developer needs only to register for the correct events to update the relevant user interface controls.

150.10. Optional: Publish the TaskServices as OSGi services

If you use the `TaskService` in another OSGi service, such as the OSGi service `TaskConsumer` from the optional exercise, you can also publish it as an OSGi service.

The following code demonstrates this.

```
package com.vogella.tasks.services.internal;

import org.eclipse.e4.core.contexts.ContextFunction;
import org.eclipse.e4.core.contexts.ContextInjectionFactory;
import org.eclipse.e4.core.contexts.IContextFunction;
import org.eclipse.e4.core.contexts.IEclipseContext;
import org.eclipse.e4.ui.model.application.MApplication;
import org.osgi.framework.BundleContext;
import org.osgi.framework.FrameworkUtil;
import org.osgi.service.component.annotations.Component;

import com.vogella.tasks.model.TaskService;

@Component(service = IContextFunction.class, property =
"service.context.key=com.vogella.tasks.model.TaskService")
public class TaskServiceContextFunction extends ContextFunction {
    @Override
    public Object compute(IEclipseContext context, String contextKey) {
        TaskService taskService = ContextInjectionFactory.make(TransientTaskServiceImpl
.class, context);

        MApplication app = context.get(MApplication.class);
        IEclipseContext appCtx = app.getContext();
        appCtx.set(TaskService.class, taskService);

        // also publish task service as an OSGi service
        // so that OSGi services can get it via @Reference
        BundleContext bundleContext = FrameworkUtil.getBundle(getClass
()).getBundleContext();
        bundleContext.registerService(TaskService.class, taskService, null);

        return taskService;
    }
}
```

Part XVIII: Model add-ons and supplementary model data

151. Using model add-ons

151.1. Definition of model add-ons

The application model allows you to create model objects called *add-ons*. These components can enhance the application with additional functionality.

Add-ons add flexibility to the application model. They allow you to extend or change the default Eclipse behavior without having to modify existing Eclipse code. You just have to replace the related model component.

For example, the default drag and drop support of parts in Eclipse is implemented via an add-on. Other examples are the key binding or the command processing. If this functionality is not desired, you can remove the component from the application model. If you want a different behavior, you register your own add-on in your application model.

Add-ons reference Java classes through their Class URI attribute, which follows the `bundleclass://` URI convention.

151.2. Add-ons from the Eclipse framework

Currently the following standard add-ons are useful for Eclipse applications. Their class names give an indication of their provided functionality.

- `CommandServiceAddon`
- `ContextServiceAddon`
- `BindingServiceAddon`
- `HandlerProcessingAddon`
- `CommandProcessingAddon`
- `ContextProcessingAddon`
- `BindingProcessingAddon`

151.3. Additional SWT add-ons

Additional add-ons are available. To support drag and drop for parts you need to add the `org.eclipse.e4.ui.workbench.addons.swt` plug-in to your product configuration file. Then you can use the `DnDAddon` and the `CleanupAddon` classes from this bundle as add-ons in your application model. This plug-in contains the `MinMaxAddon` class that allows adding the functionality to minimize or maximize your application.

The `org.eclipse.e4.ui.workbench.addons.swt` plug-in contributes these add-ons automatically to your application model via a model processor at runtime.

151.4. Relationship to other services

Add-ons are created before the Eclipse rendering framework renders the model and after the event service has been created.

This allows add-ons to alter the user interface that is produced by the rendering engine.

For example, the `MinMaxAddon` add-on changes the tab folders created for the part stacks to have the min/max buttons in the corner.

The Eclipse platform uses events sent via the event service to communicate changes in the application model. For example, if a part is activated, the Eclipse platform sends out an event for this. Add-ons can subscribe to these events from the Eclipse platform and react to them.

152. Persisted model attributes

152.1. Adding additional information on the model elements

The *Supplementary* tab in the model editor allows you to add additional information to model elements. This data can be modified and accessed via Eclipse API.

You have the option to add:

- Tags
- PersistedState

152.2. Tags

All model elements can have multiple *tags* assigned to them. These tags can be used to provide additional information to change or trigger certain functionality.

By default, Eclipse uses some predefined *tags* to determine the state of certain model elements. For example, the following tags can be used on window model elements:

- *shellMaximized* - window will be maximized by the framework
- *shellMinimized* - window will be minimized by the framework

The following screenshot shows how to define the maximization of a *Window* model element.

Tags are automatically persisted by the Eclipse runtime between application restarts. They are represented as a `List` of type `String`.

152.3. Tags as CSS selectors

Tags are available to the CSS Engine as additional class selectors. The currently active part is tagged as *active* by the framework. The CSS engine allows styling such parts with the selector `.MPartStack.active`. If you want to use tags as CSS selectors, do not use whitespace in them. You can define your own tags and define CSS for this.

152.4. Variables

You can define *Variables* in the *Supplementary* tab that can be used as *context variables*. If you use this approach, Eclipse creates keys in the context that are marked as modifiable (by descendants). See the Eclipse RCP tutorial for the concept of dependency injection.

152.5. Persisted state

Model elements can have persisted state key-value pairs assigned to them. If you retrieve the model element, you can get and set this persisted state.

```
String yourKey ="key1";

// modelObject is the model object
// retrieved via dependency injection (e.g., a MPart)

// get the state by the yourKey key
String state = modelObject.getPersistedState().get(yourKey);

// store the state
modelObject.getPersistedState().put(yourKey, state)
```

Persisted data for model elements is automatically restored by the Eclipse application between application restarts and allows to store key-value pairs based on Strings.

Persisted state data can be used by the Eclipse framework to define or change the application behavior.

A useful persisted flag is `persistState` set to `false`. This data tells the Eclipse persistence layer that this model element should not be persisted during shutdown. For example, you can use this tag on a command, handler and menu to ensure that these model elements are only present if the plug-in which contributes them is present.

152.6. Transient data

Each model element can attach transient data to it. This transient data is based on a `<![CDATA[Map<String, Object>]]>` structure and can be accessed on the model object via the `getTransientData()` method.

Transient data is not persisted between application restarts and needs to be generated at runtime.

As transient data is not persisted, it cannot be assigned to model elements via the application model editor. You need to use the `getTransientData()` method.

153. Relevant tags and persisted state keys

The following table lists the most important tags for Eclipse model elements.

Additional tags are defined in the `IPresentationEngine` interface. It is up to the renderer implementation and model add-ons to interpret these tags. Renderers might also define additional tags. For more information, see the Eclipse tags documentation [https://github.com/eclipse-platform/eclipse.platform.ui/blob/master/docs/Tags.md].

Table 30. Relevant tags of application model elements

Tag	Model element	Description
shellMaximized	*Window* or *Trimmed Window*	Specifies that the window is maximized at application startup.
shellMinimized	*Window* or *Trimmed Window*	Specifies that the window is minimized at application startup.
NoAutoCollapse	*PartStack*	Prevents the *PartStack* container from collapsing, even when all parts are removed. This tag is interpreted by the *MinMax* add-on.
FORCE_TEXT	*ToolItem*	Ensures that both text and icon are displayed for a toolbar item.
NoMove	*Part*	Prevents the user from moving the part. This tag is interpreted by the *DnDAddon* class, which manages drag-and-drop behavior in the Eclipse platform.
styleOverride	*MWindow* or *MPartStack*	Allows customizing the SWT style bits of the UI control. For example, to create an SWT shell that cannot be resized, set the style to `SWT.SHELL_TRIM & (~SWT.RESIZE)`, which corresponds to the integer value **1248**. To render *MPartStack* tabs below the parts, use **1024**.

154. Optional exercise: Toolbar visibility dependent on the perspective

In this exercise, you develop a model add-on that allows defining that a toolbar is only visible in a certain perspective. If no tag is set, it is always visible. By default, the toolbar remains visible if no tag is set.

154.1. Create a new class for the model add-on

Create the following new class for the model add-on.

```
package com.vogella.tasks.ui.addons;

import java.util.List;

import jakarta.inject.Inject;

import org.eclipse.e4.core.di.annotations.Optional;
import org.eclipse.e4.core.di.extensions.EventTopic;
import org.eclipse.e4.ui.model.application.ui.advanced.MPerspective;
import org.eclipse.e4.ui.model.application.ui.advanced.MPerspectiveStack;
import org.eclipse.e4.ui.model.application.ui.basic.MWindow;
import org.eclipse.e4.ui.model.application.ui.menu.MToolBar;
import org.eclipse.e4.ui.workbench.UIEvents;
import org.eclipse.e4.ui.workbench.UIEvents.EventTags;
import org.eclipse.e4.ui.workbench.modeling.EModelService;
import org.osgi.service.event.Event;

public class ToolbarsVisiblePerPerspectiveAddon {

    @Inject
    @Optional
    EModelService modelService;

    @Inject
    @Optional
    public void subscribeTopicSelectedElement(@EventTopic
             (UIEvents.ElementContainer.TOPIC_SELECTEDELEMENT) Event event) {
        Object element = event.getProperty(EventTags.ELEMENT);
        Object newValue = event.getProperty(EventTags.NEW_VALUE);
        if (!(element instanceof MPerspectiveStack) || !(newValue instanceof
MPerspective)) {
            return;
        }
        MPerspective perspective = (MPerspective) newValue;
        if(modelService==null) {
            return;
```

```
        }
        MWindow topLevelWindowFor = modelService.getTopLevelWindowFor(perspective);
        List<MToolBar> toolbars = modelService.findElements(topLevelWindowFor, null,
MToolBar.class, null);
        for (MToolBar toolbar : toolbars) {
            // if no tag is there make the toolbar visible
            if (toolbar.getTags().isEmpty()) {
                toolbar.setVisible(true);
                toolbar.setToBeRendered(true);
                return;
            }
            // we assume that toolbars use tags only to define the visibility for a
            // perspective
            if (toolbar.getTags().contains("perspective:"+perspective.getElementId())) {
                toolbar.setVisible(true);
                toolbar.setToBeRendered(true);
            } else {
                toolbar.setVisible(false);
                toolbar.setToBeRendered(false);
            }
        }
    }
}
```

154.2. Registering the add-on with the model

In your application model add a new model add-on with a reference to the new class.

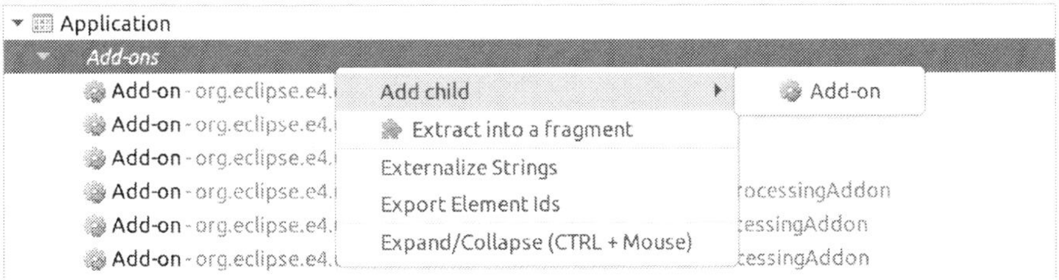

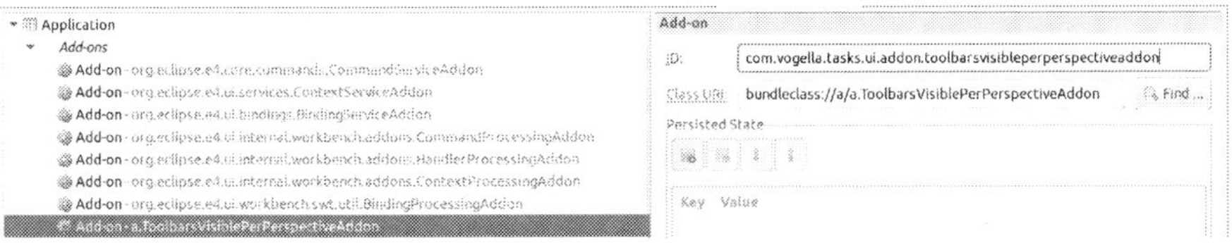

154.3. Tagging a toolbar

In your application model tag at least one of your toolbars with the prefix "perspective:" followed by the ID of one of your perspectives.

154.4. Verifying the model add-on

Start your application. Verify that the toolbar tagged for a certain perspective is only visible if you have selected the corresponding perspective.

155. Optional exercise: Changing the close behavior via an add-on

In this exercise, you ensure that the user is prompted when attempting to leave the application with unsaved changes. This works if the user presses the close button of the application window corner.

155.1. Creating a plug-in

Create a new simple plug-in named `com.vogella.e4.addons`. See Chapter 36 for more information.

Add the following dependencies to your plug-in.

- org.eclipse.core.runtime
- org.eclipse.e4.ui.di
- org.eclipse.e4.ui.model.workbench
- org.eclipse.e4.ui.workbench
- org.eclipse.e4.core.di
- org.eclipse.jface
- org.eclipse.e4.core.contexts
- org.eclipse.osgi.services
- org.eclipse.e4.core.commands

Also, add the package dependency.

- jakarta.inject

155.2. Creating the model add-on

Define the following class.

```
package com.vogella.e4.addons;

import jakarta.inject.Inject;

import org.eclipse.core.commands.ParameterizedCommand;
import org.eclipse.e4.core.commands.ECommandService;
```

```java
import org.eclipse.e4.core.commands.EHandlerService;
import org.eclipse.e4.core.di.annotations.Optional;
import org.eclipse.e4.ui.di.UIEventTopic;
import org.eclipse.e4.ui.model.application.MApplication;
import org.eclipse.e4.ui.model.application.ui.basic.MWindow;
import org.eclipse.e4.ui.workbench.IWorkbench;
import org.eclipse.e4.ui.workbench.UIEvents;
import org.eclipse.e4.ui.workbench.modeling.IWindowCloseHandler;

// @PostConstruct does not work as the workbench gets
// instantiated after the processing of the add-ons
// hence this approach uses method injection

public class WindowCloseListenerAddon {

    @SuppressWarnings("restriction")
    @Inject
    @Optional
    private void adjustWindowCloseHandler(
            @UIEventTopic(UIEvents.UILifeCycle.APP_STARTUP_COMPLETE) MApplication
application,
            IWorkbench workbench, ECommandService commandService, EHandlerService
handlerService) {
        MWindow mainWindow = findMainWindow(application);

        mainWindow.getContext().set(IWindowCloseHandler.class, window -> {
            if (window.getTags().contains("topLevel")) {
                ParameterizedCommand cmd = commandService.createCommand
("org.eclipse.ui.file.exit", null);
                handlerService.executeHandler(cmd, mainWindow.getContext());
                return false;
            }
            return true;
        });
    }

    private static MWindow findMainWindow(MApplication application) {
        // instead of using the index you could also use a tag on the MWindow to
        // mark the main window
        return application.getChildren().get(0);
    }
}
```

155.3. Register new class as add-on

Register this class as an add-on in your application model.

155.4. Update product (via feature)

Add the new plug-in to your feature. Start from your product to update the run configuration.

155.5. Validate

Start your application and close it via the "X" close button of the window. You should get your confirmation dialog.

156. Optional exercise: Window title based on perspective

In this exercise, we will change the window title according to the active perspective.

156.1. Add a new model add-on that listens to perspective switches

Create the following `PerspectiveSwitchAddon` class. This add-on listens for the perspective change event.

```
package com.vogella.tasks.ui.addon;

import jakarta.inject.Inject;

import org.eclipse.e4.core.di.annotations.Optional;
import org.eclipse.e4.core.di.extensions.EventTopic;
import org.eclipse.e4.ui.model.application.ui.advanced.MPerspective;
import org.eclipse.e4.ui.model.application.ui.basic.MWindow;
import org.eclipse.e4.ui.workbench.UIEvents;
import org.eclipse.e4.ui.workbench.UIEvents.EventTags;
import org.eclipse.e4.ui.workbench.modeling.EModelService;
import org.osgi.service.event.Event;

public class PerspectiveSwitchAddon {

    @Inject
    private EModelService modelService;

    @Inject
    @Optional
    public void subscribeTopicSelectedElement(
            @EventTopic(UIEvents.ElementContainer.TOPIC_SELECTEDELEMENT) Event event) {
        Object newValue = event.getProperty(EventTags.NEW_VALUE);

        // only run this if the NEW_VALUE is a MPerspective
        if (!(newValue instanceof MPerspective)) {
            return;
        }
```

```
        MPerspective perspective = (MPerspective) newValue;

        // Get the MWindow, where we want to change the label
        MWindow topLevelWindowOfPerspective = modelService.getTopLevelWindowFor
(perspective);

        topLevelWindowOfPerspective.setLabel(perspective.getLabel() + " Window");

    }
}
```

Now we add a new model add-on via a model fragment.

156.2. Validate

Start your application again. Switch perspectives and observe the window title. It should change to the name of the perspective.

> If the add-on is not visible, try to start your runtime with the `-clearPersistedState` flag to remove persisted model information.

Part XIX: Application model modularity

157. Exercise: Contributing menus via model fragments

In the introduction of the application model you already learned that the application model can be extended. In the following exercise, you will extend the application model with model fragments.

In this exercise, you create a model fragment to contribute a menu entry, a command and a handler to your application model.

157.1. Create a new plug-in

Create a simple plug-in project named *com.vogella.tasks.ui.contribute*. See Chapter 36 for more information. The following description abbreviates the plug-in name to the `contribute` plug-in.

157.2. Add the dependencies

In the `MANIFEST.MF` file, add the following entries as plug-in dependencies to your `contribute` plug-in.

- org.eclipse.core.runtime
- org.eclipse.swt
- org.eclipse.jface
- org.eclipse.e4.core.di

* org.eclipse.e4.ui.workbench
* org.eclipse.e4.ui.di

157.3. Enable activation

Set the *Activate this plug-in when one of its classes is loaded* flag in the MANIFEST. This enables the registration of the fragment via the MANIFEST.MF

157.4. Create a handler class

Create the `com.vogella.tasks.ui.contribute.handlers` package and the following class.

```
package com.vogella.tasks.ui.contribute.handlers;

import org.eclipse.e4.core.di.annotations.Execute;
import org.eclipse.jface.dialogs.MessageDialog;
import org.eclipse.swt.widgets.Shell;

public class OpenMapHandler {

    @Execute
    public void execute(Shell shell) {
        MessageDialog.openInformation(shell, "Test", "Just testing");
    }
}
```

157.5. Create a model fragment

Use the fragment wizard to create a new model fragment via the **File › New › Other... › Eclipse 4 › Model › New Model Fragment** menu entry.

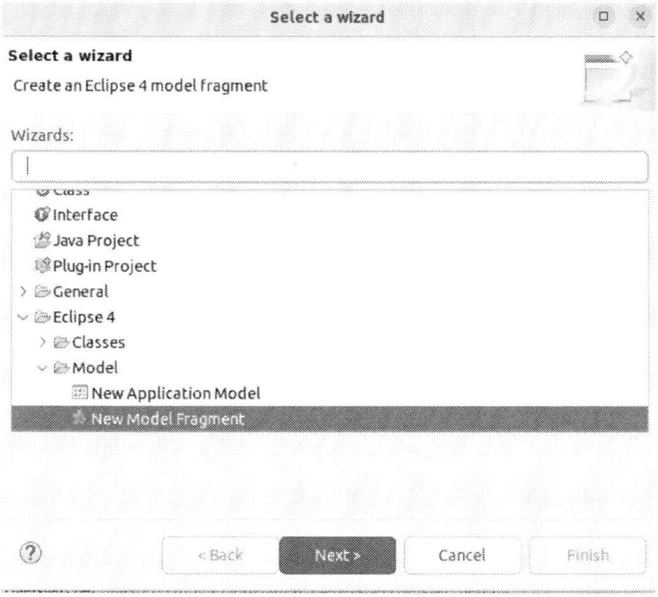

Select the `contribute` plug-in as the container and use *fragment.e4xmi* as the name for the file.

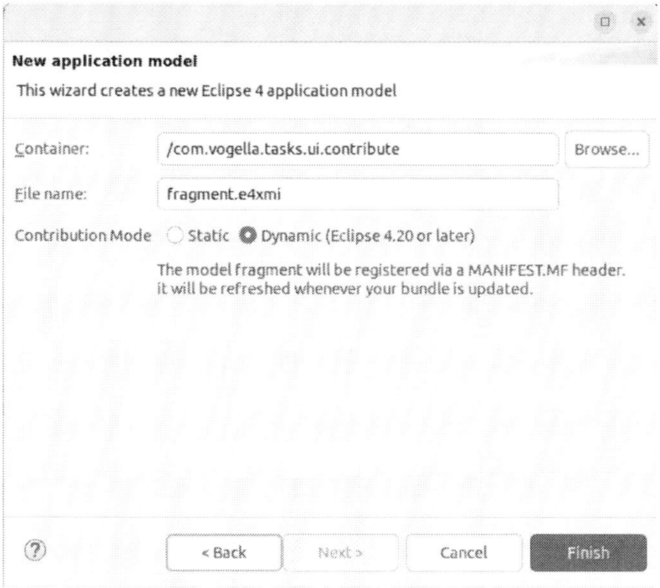

Press the Finish button.

157.6. Validate that the fragment is registered via the MANIFEST.MF

The fragment creation wizard adds the `Model-Fragment` key to your MANIFEST.MF file. To review this, open the `MANIFEST.MF` file and select the *MANIFEST.MF* tab in the editor. The resulting file should look similar to the following code, the versions have been removed in this listing, as the versions you see depend on the release you are using.

```
Manifest-Version: 1.0
Bundle-ManifestVersion: 2
Bundle-Name: Contribute
Bundle-SymbolicName: com.vogella.tasks.ui.contribute
Bundle-Version: 1.0.0.qualifier
Bundle-Vendor: VOGELLA
Require-Bundle: org.eclipse.core.runtime,
 org.eclipse.jface,
 org.eclipse.e4.core.di,
 org.eclipse.e4.ui.workbench,
 org.eclipse.e4.ui.di,
 org.eclipse.e4.ui.model.workbench
Bundle-RequiredExecutionEnvironment: JavaSE-21
Model-Fragment: fragment.e4xmi
Automatic-Module-Name: com.vogella.tasks.ui.contribute
Bundle-ActivationPolicy: lazy
```

157.7. Adding model elements

Open the *fragment.e4xmi* file in its editor. Select the *Model Fragments* node, right-click on it and add one fragment.

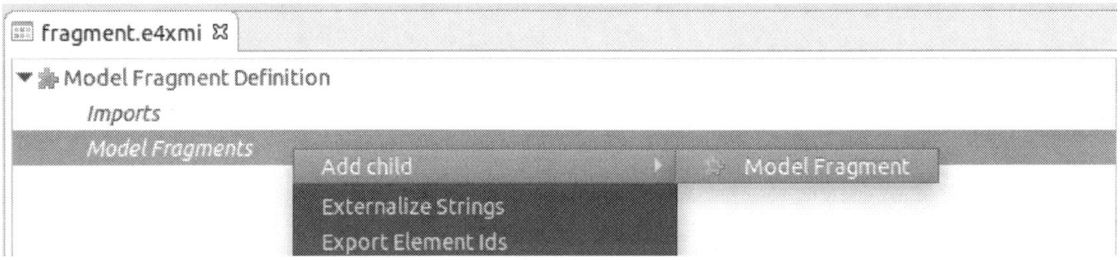

Use `xpath:/` as the *Extended Element ID* to extend any application.

You need to define which feature to add. For *Feature Name*, specify the value *commands*. Make sure you have the *Model Fragment* selected and use the Add... button to add a *Command* to your model fragment.

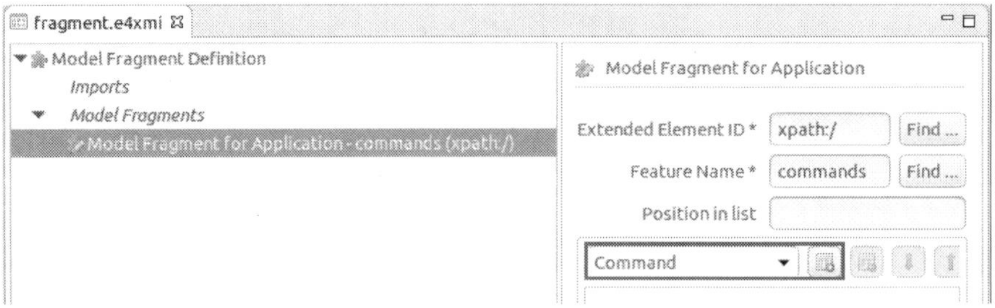

Define an entry similar to the following.

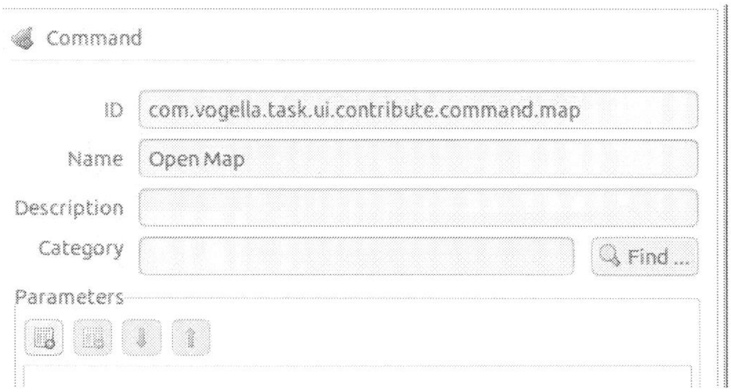

Create a new model fragment for the handler. The *Extended Element ID* is again `xpath:/`, the *Feature Name* is `handlers`.

Add a *Handler* to this model fragment, pointing to your `OpenMapHandler` class.

Use `com.vogella.tasks.ui.contribute.handler.openmap` as the ID for the handler. Point to the *Open Map* command and the `OpenMapHandler` class.

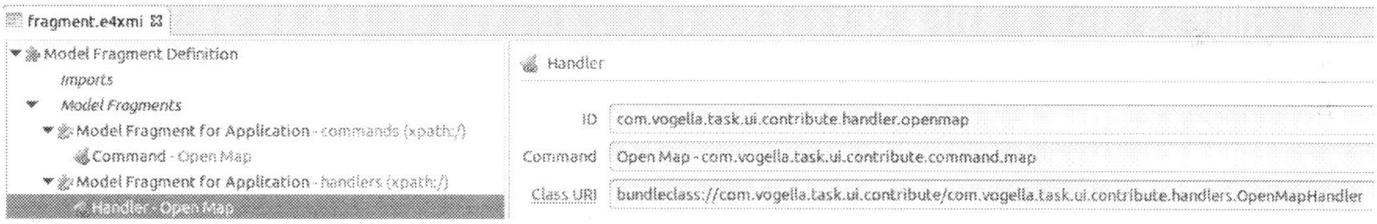

Add another *Model Fragment* and contribute to `menuContributions`.

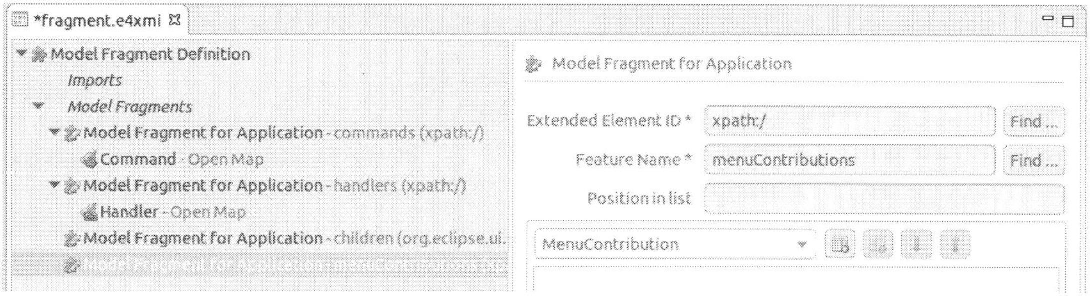

Add a `menuContribution` and use `org.eclipse.ui.main.menu` as parent ID. This assumes that the application you are extending uses this ID, it is the standard ID of the Eclipse IDE.

If your application uses a different ID, you need to use the ID of your main menu.

Now add a menu and a handled menu item to your model with the following attributes:

- ID: *com.vogella.tasks.ui.contribute.menu.map*
- Label: *Map*

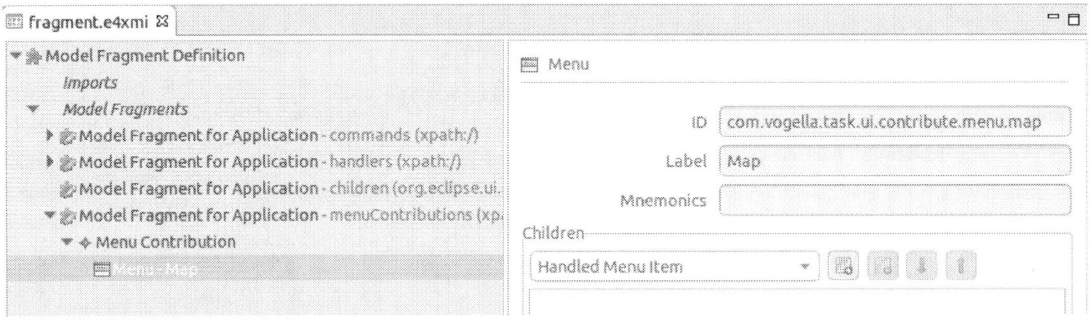

Add a *HandledMenuItem* that points to your new command. The created entry should be similar to the following screenshot.

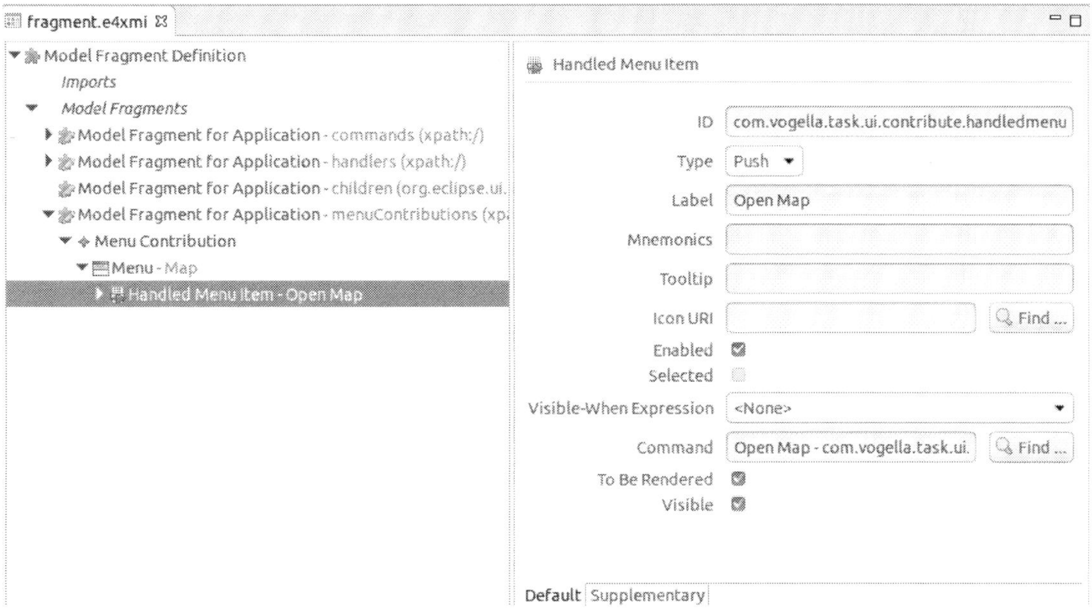

157.8. Update the product configuration (via the feature)

Add the `contribute` plug-in to your feature.

157.9. Validate

Start your application using your product.

> Ensure that this new plug-in is added to your feature and the changes are saved. Remember to start via the product to update the launch configuration.

You should see the new *Map* entry in the application menu. If you select this entry a message dialog opens.

If the menu entry is not displayed, ensure that your IDs are correctly entered. Also ensure that you either use the *clearPersistedState* flag or clear the workspace data in your *Launch configuration*.

158. Exercise: Contributing a part descriptor via model fragments

In this exercise, you create a model fragment to contribute a part descriptor. This extension can be used in the Eclipse IDE or an RCP application.

158.1. Create a new plug-in

Create a simple plug-in project named *com.vogella.contribute.parts*. See Chapter 36 for more information. The following description abbreviates the plug-in name to the `contribute.parts` plug-in.

158.2. Add the dependencies

In the `MANIFEST.MF` file select the *Dependencies* tab.

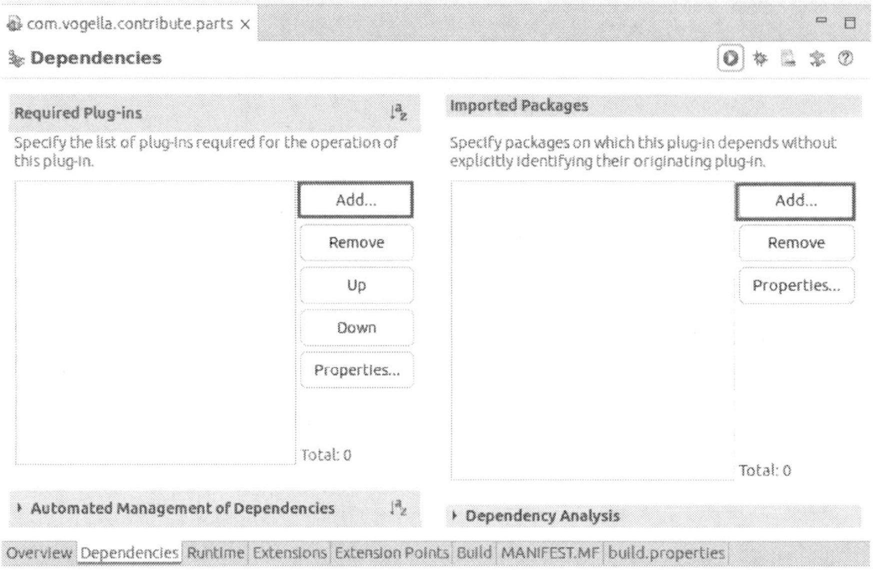

Add the following entries as plug-in dependencies to your `contribute.parts` plug-in.

- org.eclipse.core.runtime
- org.eclipse.jface (that provides org.eclipse.swt)
- org.eclipse.e4.core.di
- org.eclipse.e4.ui.workbench
- org.eclipse.e4.ui.di

Also add the following package dependencies.

- jakarta.annotation

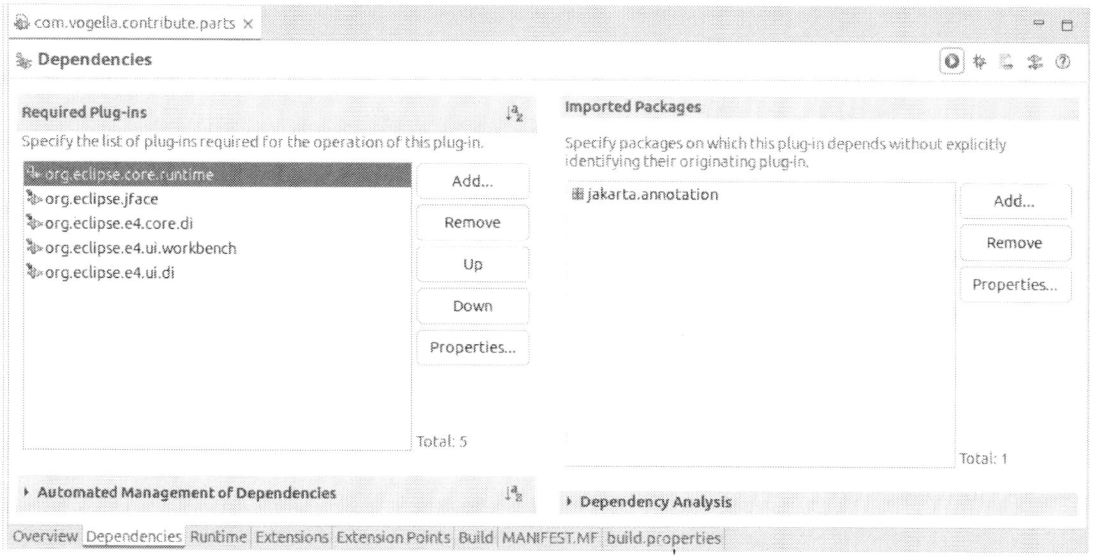

The manifest should look similar to the following listing. Version numbers have been removed as they change frequently.

```
Manifest-Version: 1.0
Bundle-ManifestVersion: 2
Bundle-Name: Parts
Bundle-SymbolicName: com.vogella.contribute.parts
Bundle-Version: 1.0.0.qualifier
Bundle-Vendor: VOGELLA
Automatic-Module-Name: com.vogella.contribute.parts
Bundle-RequiredExecutionEnvironment: JavaSE-21
Require-Bundle: org.eclipse.core.runtime,
 org.eclipse.jface,
 org.eclipse.e4.core.di,
 org.eclipse.e4.ui.workbench,
 org.eclipse.e4.ui.di
Import-Package: jakarta.annotation
```

158.3. Enable activation

Set the *Activate this plug-in when one of its classes is loaded* flag in the MANIFEST. This enables the registration of the fragment via the MANIFEST.MF

158.4. Create a part implementation

Create the following class.

```
package com.vogella.contribute.parts;
```

```
import jakarta.annotation.PostConstruct;

import org.eclipse.jface.widgets.TextFactory;
import org.eclipse.swt.SWT;
import org.eclipse.swt.widgets.Composite;

public class AdditionalInformationPart {
    @PostConstruct
    public void postConstruct(Composite parent) {
        TextFactory.newText(SWT.BORDER |SWT.MULTI).create(parent);
    }
}
```

158.5. Create a model fragment

Create a new model fragment via the **File › New › Other... › Eclipse 4 › Model › New Model Fragment** menu entry.

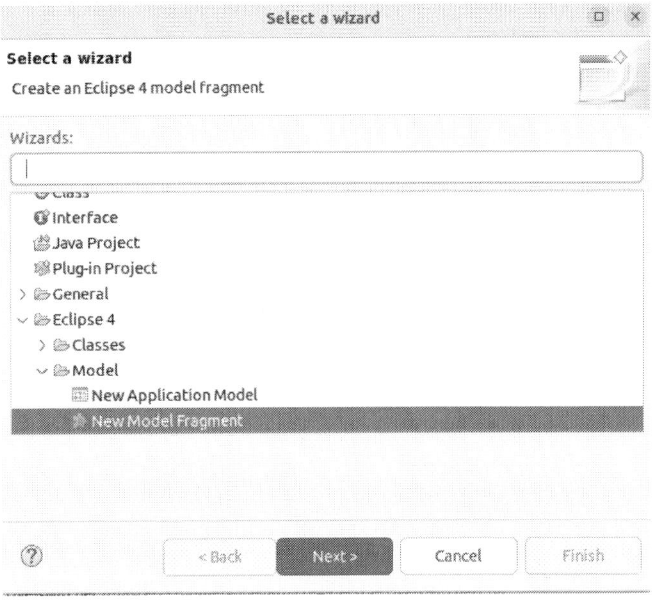

Select the `contribute.parts` plug-in as the container and use *parts.e4xmi* as the name for the file.

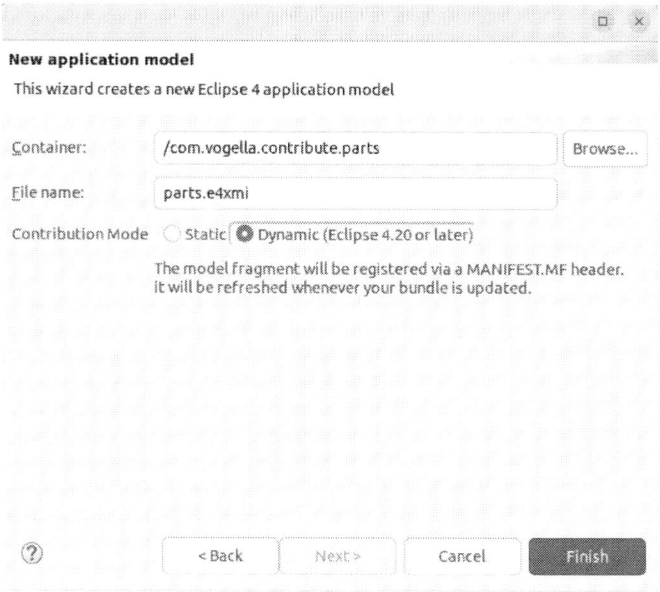

Press the Finish button.

158.6. Validate that the fragment is registered via the MANIFEST.MF

The model fragment creation wizard automatically adds the `Model-Fragment` key to your MANIFEST.MF file for registration. To review this, open the **MANIFEST.MF** file and select the *MANIFEST.MF* tab in the editor. The resulting file should look similar to the following code, the versions have been removed in this listing, as the versions you see depend on the release you are using.

```
Manifest-Version: 1.0
Bundle-ManifestVersion: 2
Bundle-Name: Parts
Bundle-SymbolicName: com.vogella.contribute.parts
Bundle-Version: 1.0.0.qualifier
Bundle-Vendor: VOGELLA
Require-Bundle: org.eclipse.core.runtime,
 org.eclipse.jface,
 org.eclipse.e4.core.di,
 org.eclipse.e4.ui.workbench,
 org.eclipse.e4.ui.di,
 org.eclipse.e4.ui.model.workbench
Bundle-RequiredExecutionEnvironment: JavaSE-21
Automatic-Module-Name: com.vogella.contribute.parts
Model-Fragment: parts.e4xmi
Import-Package: jakarta.annotation
Bundle-ActivationPolicy: lazy
```

158.7. Adding model elements

Open the *parts.e4xmi* file in its editor. Select the *Model Fragments* node and press the Add button.

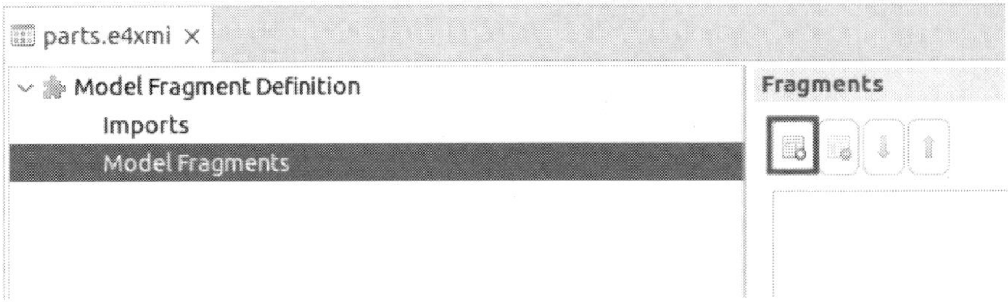

Use `xpath:/` as *extended element id* and `descriptors` as *Feature name*.

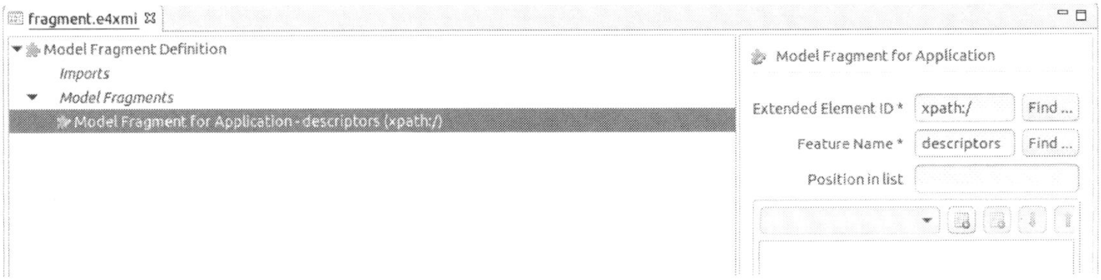

Right-click on this entry and select **Add Child › PartDescriptor**. Select the Part Descriptor and press the Find button for the *Class URI* field. Choose the `AdditionalInformationPart` class.

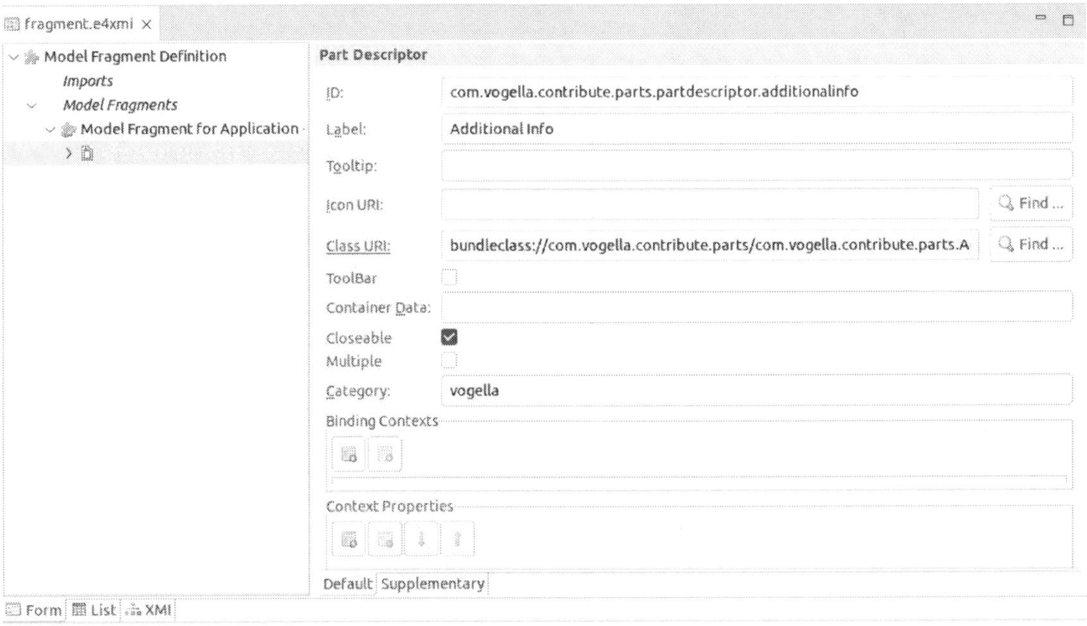

The generated entry should look like the following code:

```
bundleclass://com.vogella.contribute.parts/com.vogella.contribute.parts.AdditionalInforma
tionPart
```

Now switch to the *Supplementary* tab and add the following tag:

- View

To add a tag, enter it and press the *Add* button, after entering the text.

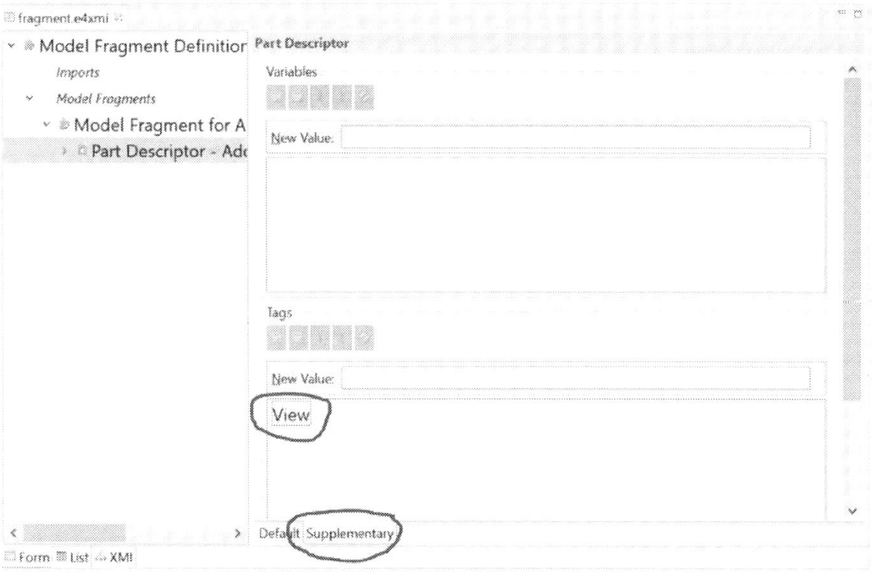

The `View` tag ensures that the Eclipse IDE accepts this part descriptor as a valid view, if you use this plug-in in the Eclipse IDE. For pure e4 RCP applications this flag is not needed.

158.8. Update product

Add the new plug-ins to your feature and start via the product file.

158.9. Validate

As you created a part descriptor, this element will not be visible in the RCP application.

Add the Eclipse model spy to your runtime application and ensure that you see the part descriptor.

Optionally create a new direct menu item via the fragment to open this part descriptor.

159. Exercise: Implementing a model processor

As mentioned in the introduction to the application model, it can be extended. In the following exercise you will change the application model with a model processor.

159.1. Add the dependencies

Continue to use the `com.vogella.tasks.ui.contribute` plug-in for this exercise.

In the `MANIFEST.MF`, add the following entries as plug-in dependencies to your *contribute* plug-in.

- `org.eclipse.e4.ui.services`
- `org.eclipse.e4.core.contexts`
- `org.eclipse.e4.ui.model.workbench`

Also add the following as imported packages:

- `jakarta.inject`

159.2. Verify that you use the correct ID for the file menu

Since the following code assumes that `org.eclipse.ui.file.menu` is used for the ID of the file menu, make sure that this is the case.

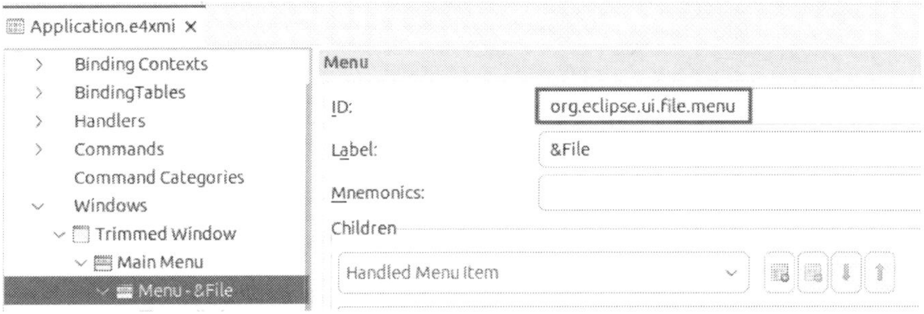

159.3. Create the Java classes

You will now create the close dialog and the logic for opening this dialog. Create the following dialog and handler Java classes.

```
package com.vogella.tasks.ui.contribute.dialogs;

import jakarta.inject.Inject;
import jakarta.inject.Named;

import org.eclipse.e4.ui.services.IServiceConstants;
```

```java
import org.eclipse.jface.dialogs.Dialog;
import org.eclipse.swt.SWT;
import org.eclipse.swt.widgets.Composite;
import org.eclipse.swt.widgets.Control;
import org.eclipse.swt.widgets.Label;
import org.eclipse.swt.widgets.Shell;

public class ExitDialog extends Dialog {
    @Inject
    public ExitDialog(@Named(IServiceConstants.
            ACTIVE_SHELL) Shell shell) {
        super(shell);
    }

    @Override
    protected Control createDialogArea(Composite parent) {
        Label label = new Label(parent, SWT.NONE);
        label.setText("Closing this application may result in data loss. "
                + "Are you sure you want that?");
        return parent;
    }

}
```

```java
package com.vogella.tasks.ui.contribute.handlers;

import org.eclipse.e4.core.contexts.ContextInjectionFactory;
import org.eclipse.e4.core.contexts.IEclipseContext;
import org.eclipse.e4.core.di.annotations.Execute;
import org.eclipse.e4.ui.workbench.IWorkbench;
import org.eclipse.jface.window.Window;

import com.vogella.tasks.ui.contribute.dialogs.ExitDialog;

public class ExitHandlerWithCheck {
    @Execute
    public void execute(IEclipseContext context, IWorkbench workbench) {
        ExitDialog dialog = ContextInjectionFactory.
                make(ExitDialog.class, context);
        if (dialog.open() == Window.OK) {
            workbench.close();
        }
    }
}
```

Create the model processor class. This class removes all menu entries that have "exit" in their ID from the menu with the `org.eclipse.ui.file.menu` ID. It adds a new entry.

```
package com.vogella.tasks.ui.contribute.processors;

import java.util.ArrayList;
import java.util.List;

import jakarta.inject.Inject;
import jakarta.inject.Named;

import org.eclipse.e4.core.di.annotations.Execute;
import org.eclipse.e4.ui.model.application.ui.menu.MDirectMenuItem;
import org.eclipse.e4.ui.model.application.ui.menu.MMenu;
import org.eclipse.e4.ui.model.application.ui.menu.MMenuElement;
import org.eclipse.e4.ui.workbench.modeling.EModelService;

import com.vogella.tasks.ui.contribute.handlers.ExitHandlerWithCheck;

public class MenuProcessor {

    // the menu is injected based on the parameter
    // defined in the extension point
    @Inject
    @Named("org.eclipse.ui.file.menu")
    private MMenu menu;

    @Execute
    public void execute(EModelService modelService) {
        // remove the old exit menu entry
        if (!menu.getChildren().isEmpty()) {
            List<MMenuElement> list = new ArrayList<>();
            for (MMenuElement element : menu.getChildren()) {
                // use ID instead of label as label is later translated
                if (element.getElementId() != null) {
                    if (element.getElementId().contains("exit")) {
                        list.add(element);
                    }
                }
            }
            menu.getChildren().removeAll(list);
        }

        // now add a new menu entry
        MDirectMenuItem menuItem = modelService.createModelElement(MDirectMenuItem.
class);
        menuItem.setLabel("Another Exit");
        menuItem.setContributionURI("bundleclass://"
                + "com.vogella.tasks.ui.contribute/"
                + ExitHandlerWithCheck.class.getName());
        menu.getChildren().add(menuItem);
```

```
    }
}
```

Ensure that your menu entry in the *Application.e4xmi* file labeled with *Exit*, contains `exit` in its ID.

159.4. Register processor via extension

In your `com.vogella.tasks.ui.contribute` plug-in register your `processor` via the `org.eclipse.e4.workbench.model` extension. For this, open the `plugin.xml` file, select the *Extensions* tab and add the *org.eclipse.e4.workbench.model* extension point via the Add... button.

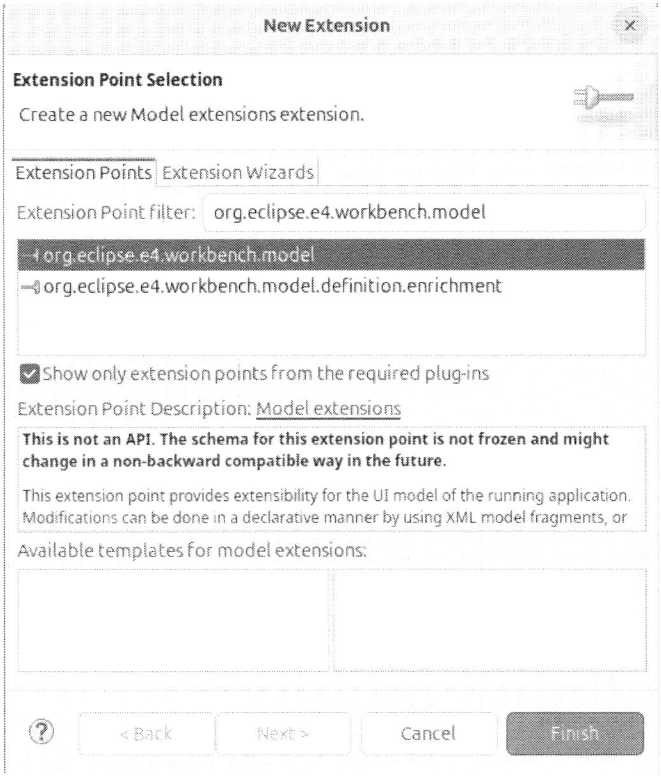

Right-click on the extension point and select **New › processor**. Use your `MenuProcessor` class as the *class* value and run it always and before the fragments are applied.

You need to specify the ID of the model element into which the processor injects model elements. Therefore, right-click on the processor and select **New › element**.

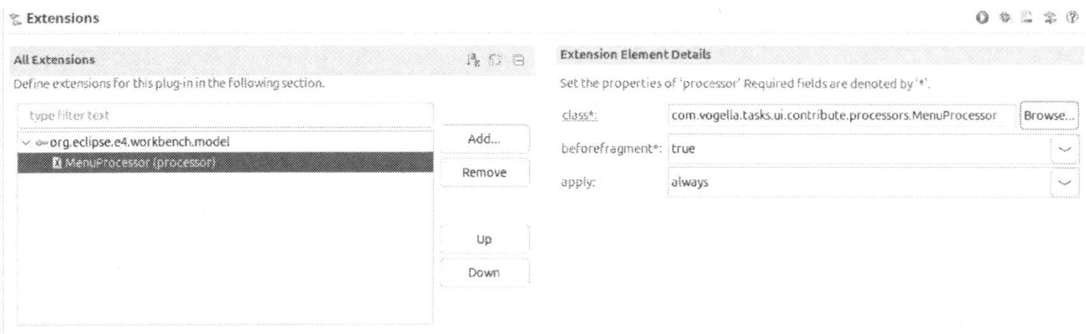

The value of the ID parameter is the ID of the model element injected into your processor class. Use *org.eclipse.ui.file.menu* as the ID parameter.

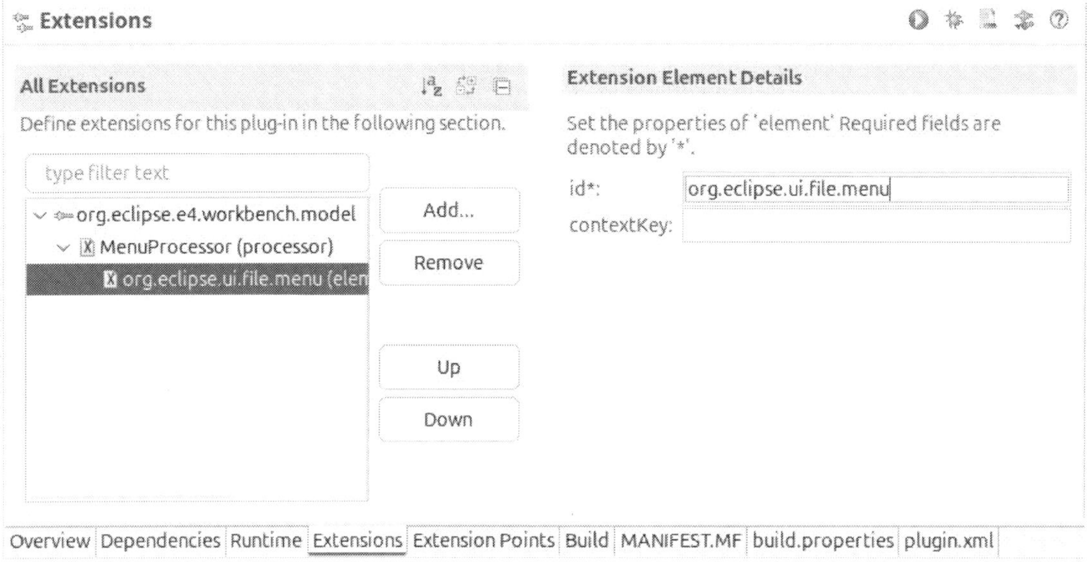

> **Note:** This assumes that you have used *org.eclipse.ui.file.menu* as the ID for your *File* menu in the main application model. The ID of the element defined in the extension point must match the `@Named` value in the processor. If such an element is not found, it is not injected into the processor.

159.5. Validate

Start your application. In the model fragment exercises, the contributing plug-in was already added to your product.

Ensure that the existing *Exit* menu entry is removed and your new menu entry with the *Another Exit* label is added to the file menu.

Part XX: Eclipse application lifecycle

160. Eclipse application lifecycle

160.1. Connecting to the Eclipse application lifecycle

An application may require specific processing during startup or shutdown, such as initialization or cleanup. For example, you may want to start a server connection during startup.

The Eclipse platform allows you to register a class for predefined events in this lifecycle. For example, you can use these lifecycle hooks to create a login screen or an interactive splash screen before the application is started.

160.2. Accessing application startup parameters

The `IApplicationContext` object that can be injected into your lifecycle class contains information about the startup parameters of your application. You can access these parameters via the `getArguments()` method.

This access is demonstrated by the following snippet.

```
// access the command line arguments
String[] args = (String[])
    applicationContext.
        getArguments().
```

```
            get(IApplicationContext.APPLICATION_ARGS);
```

A parameter can be a flag or consist of a name and a value. You can use a method similar to the following to evaluate this.

```
private String getArgValue(String argName, IApplicationContext appContext,
            boolean singleCmdArgValue) {
    // Is it in the arg list ?
    if (argName == null || argName.length() == 0)
        return null;

    if (singleCmdArgValue) {
        for (String arg : args) {
            if (("-" + argName).equals(arg))
                return "true";
        }
        return "false";
    }
    // not a singleCmdArgValue
    for (int i = 0; i < args.length; i++) {
        if (("-" + argName).equals(args[i]) && i + 1 < args.length)
            return args[i + 1];
    }
}
```

160.3. Close static splash screen

If you configured in your product configuration file that a static splash screen should be used, you can call the `applicationRunning()` method on the `IApplicationContext` object. You typically call this method if you want to replace the static splash screen with a dynamic screen developed with SWT.

160.4. How to implement a lifecycle class

The `org.eclipse.core.runtime.product` extension point allows you to define a class as lifecycle callback via a property.

The key for this property is `lifeCycleURI`, and it points to the class via the `bundleclass://` schema.

In the class you can annotate methods with the following annotations. These methods are called by the framework based on the lifecycle stage of your application.

Table 31. Life cycle annotations

Annotation	Description
@PostContextCreate	Is called after the Application's `IEclipseContext` is created, can be used to add objects, services, etc. to the context. This context is created for the `MApplication` class.
@ProcessAdditions	Is called directly before the model is passed to the renderer, it can be used to add additional elements to the model.
@ProcessRemovals	Is the same as @ProcessAdditions but for removals.
@PreSave	Is called before the application model is saved. You can modify the model before it is persisted.

160.5. Example lifecycle implementation

The following example shows how to register a class in your *plugin.xml* file as lifecycle handler. To avoid code wrapping, we use `testing` as BundleSymbolicName and package, you need to replace that with the correct values for your lifecycle class.

```
<plugin>

   <extension
         id="product"
         point="org.eclipse.core.runtime.products">
      <product
        name="testing"
        application="org.eclipse.e4.ui.workbench.swt.E4Application">
         <property
            name="appName"
            value="testing">
         <property
           name="applicationXMI"
           value="testing/Application.e4xmi">
         <property
           name="applicationCSS"
           value="platform:/plugin/testing/css/default.css">
         <property
           name="lifeCycleURI"
           value="bundleclass://testing/testing.LifeCycleManager">
      </product>
   </extension>

</plugin>
```

The following class displays a `Shell` until the startup process of your application has finished. You could extend this example to show a progress bar.

```
package testing;

import org.eclipse.e4.core.services.events.IEventBroker;
import org.eclipse.e4.ui.workbench.UIEvents;
import org.eclipse.e4.ui.workbench.lifecycle.PostContextCreate;
import org.eclipse.equinox.app.IApplicationContext;
import org.eclipse.swt.SWT;
import org.eclipse.swt.widgets.Shell;
import org.osgi.service.event.Event;
import org.osgi.service.event.EventHandler;

// for an extended example see
// https://bugs.eclipse.org/382224

public class LifeCycleManager {
    @PostContextCreate
    void postContextCreate(final IEventBroker eventBroker, IApplicationContext context) {
        final Shell shell = new Shell(SWT.SHELL_TRIM);

        // register for startup completed event and close the shell
        eventBroker.subscribe(UIEvents.UILifeCycle.APP_STARTUP_COMPLETE,
                new EventHandler() {
                    @Override
                    public void handleEvent(Event event) {
                        shell.close();
                        shell.dispose();
                        eventBroker.unsubscribe(this);
                    }
                });
        // close static splash screen
        context.applicationRunning();
        shell.open();
    }
}
```

161. Exercise: Lifecycle hook and a login screen

In this exercise, you create a splash screen that allows the user to enter his or her credentials. This assumes that you have created a `PasswordDialog` class that allows the user to enter a user name and a password.

161.1. Create a new class

The following development is done again in the `com.vogella.tasks.ui` plug-in.

Create the `com.vogella.tasks.ui.lifecycle` package and add the following class.

```
package com.vogella.tasks.ui.lifecycle;

import org.eclipse.e4.ui.workbench.lifecycle.PostContextCreate;
import org.eclipse.equinox.app.IApplicationContext;
import org.eclipse.jface.window.Window;
import org.eclipse.swt.SWT;
import org.eclipse.swt.graphics.Rectangle;
import org.eclipse.swt.widgets.Display;
import org.eclipse.swt.widgets.Monitor;
import org.eclipse.swt.widgets.Shell;

import com.vogella.tasks.ui.dialogs.PasswordDialog;

public class Manager {
    @PostContextCreate
    void postContextCreate(IApplicationContext appContext, Display display) {
        final Shell shell = new Shell(SWT.SHELL_TRIM);
        PasswordDialog dialog = new PasswordDialog(shell);

        // close the static splash screen
        appContext.applicationRunning();

        // position the shell
        setLocation(display, shell);

        if (dialog.open() != Window.OK) {
            // close the application
            System.exit(-1);
        }
    }

    private void setLocation(Display display, Shell shell) {
        Monitor monitor = display.getPrimaryMonitor();
        Rectangle monitorRect = monitor.getBounds();
        Rectangle shellRect = shell.getBounds();
        int x = monitorRect.x + (monitorRect.width - shellRect.width) / 2;
        int y = monitorRect.y + (monitorRect.height - shellRect.height) / 2;
        shell.setLocation(x, y);
    }
}
```

The lifecycle annotations are not yet released as official API.

161.2. Register lifecycle hook

Register the `Manager` class as lifecycle handler in your *plugin.xml* file.

For this, open the *plugin.xml* file of your application plug-in and select the *Extensions* tab.

Open the `org.eclipse.core.runtime.products` extension, right-click on the existing entry and create a new property.

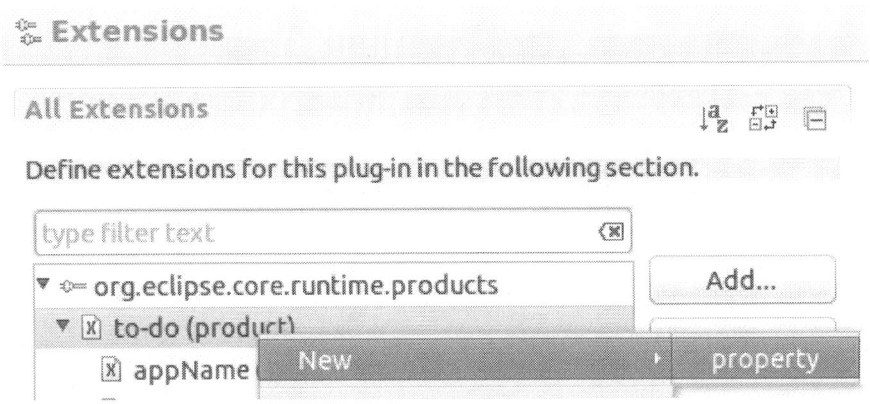

Enter *lifeCycleURI* as the name for the property and use `bundleclass://com.vogella.tasks.ui/com.vogella.tasks.ui.lifecycle.Manager` as the value.

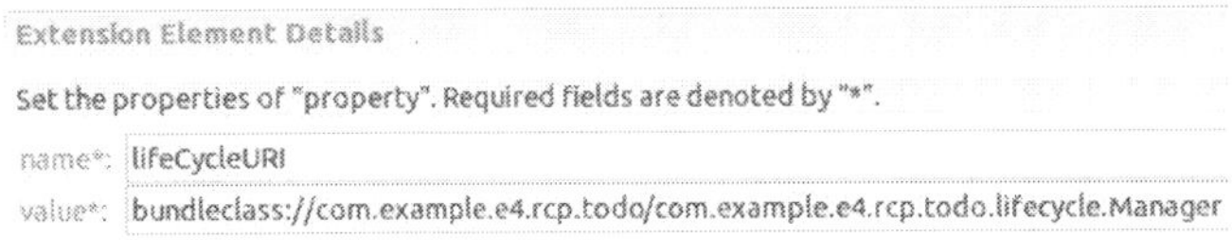

The following snippet shows the resulting plugin.xml file.

```
<plugin>
   <extension
         id="product"
         point="org.eclipse.core.runtime.products">
      <product
        name="to-do"
        application="org.eclipse.e4.ui.workbench.swt.E4Application">
         <property
               name="appName"
               value="to-do">

  <property
     name="lifeCycleURI"
     value=
 "bundleclass://com.example.e4.rcp.todo/com.example.e4.rcp.todo.lifecycle.Manager">
```

```
    <!-- other properties omitted -->
        </product>
    </extension>

</plugin>
```

161.3. Validate

Start your application. The login dialog should be displayed and your application should be started after the user selects the Login button.

162. Optional exercise: Styling the login screen

In this exercise, you will ensure that the widgets created by the lifecycle handler of your application are styled.

162.1. Implement styling

Change your `Manager` class to the following to apply one of your CSS files to the widgets in the login screen.

```
package com.vogella.tasks.ui.lifecycle;

import jakarta.inject.Inject;

import org.eclipse.e4.core.contexts.IEclipseContext;
import org.eclipse.e4.ui.internal.workbench.E4Workbench;
import org.eclipse.e4.ui.internal.workbench.swt.PartRenderingEngine;
import org.eclipse.e4.ui.workbench.IWorkbench;
import org.eclipse.e4.ui.workbench.lifecycle.PostContextCreate;
import org.eclipse.equinox.app.IApplicationContext;
import org.eclipse.jface.window.Window;
import org.eclipse.swt.SWT;
import org.eclipse.swt.graphics.Rectangle;
import org.eclipse.swt.widgets.Display;
import org.eclipse.swt.widgets.Monitor;
import org.eclipse.swt.widgets.Shell;
import org.osgi.service.prefs.BackingStoreException;

import com.vogella.tasks.ui.dialogs.PasswordDialog;

public class Manager {

    private String user;
```

```java
    @PostContextCreate
    public void postContextCreate(IApplicationContext appContext, Display display,
IEclipseContext context) {

        final Shell shell = new Shell(SWT.SHELL_TRIM);
        PasswordDialog dialog = new PasswordDialog(shell);
        if (user != null) {
            dialog.setUser(user);
        }

        // close the static splash screen
        appContext.applicationRunning();

        // position the shell
         setLocation(display, shell);

         String cssURI = "platform:/plugin/com.vogella.eclipse.css/css/rainbow.css";
         context.set(E4Workbench.CSS_URI_ARG, cssURI);
         PartRenderingEngine.initializeStyling(shell.getDisplay(), context);
        // open the dialog
        if (dialog.open() != Window.OK) {
            // close the application
            System.exit(-1);
        } else {
            // get the user from the dialog
            String userValue = dialog.getUser();
        }
    }

    private void setLocation(Display display, Shell shell) {
        Monitor monitor = display.getPrimaryMonitor();
        Rectangle monitorRect = monitor.getBounds();
        Rectangle shellRect = shell.getBounds();
        int x = monitorRect.x + (monitorRect.width - shellRect.width) / 2;
        int y = monitorRect.y + (monitorRect.height - shellRect.height) / 2;
        shell.setLocation(x, y);
    }
}
```

162.2. Validate

Start your application and ensure the splash screen is styled according to your settings.

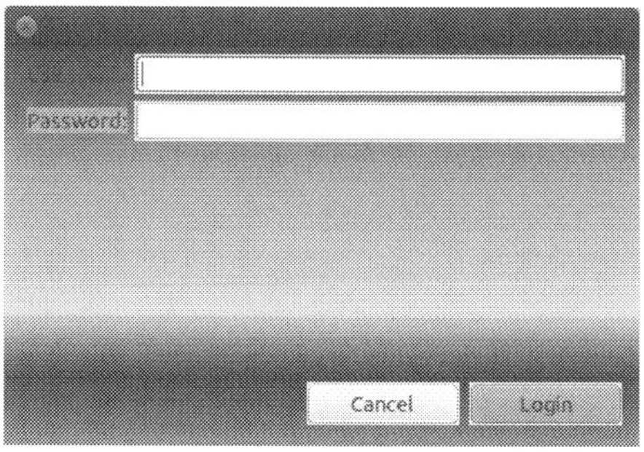

162.3. Optional: Allow setting the workspace location

The workspace location is the place in which the RCP application stores its configuration and its preferences.

Allow the user to select the workspace location and use this to set the `instanceLocationUrl`. The following example code can be used to adjust your lifecycle manager. You also need to enhance your dialog to allow the user to select a directory.

```
import java.io.IOException;
import java.net.URL;

import org.eclipse.core.runtime.Platform;
import org.eclipse.e4.ui.workbench.lifecycle.PostContextCreate;

public class LifeCycleManager {

    @PostContextCreate
    public void postContextCreate() throws IllegalStateException, IOException {
        // Show login dialog to the user
        String userName = "test";

        if (!Platform.getInstanceLocation().isSet()) {
            String defaultPath = System.getProperty("user.home");
            String path = defaultPath + "/" + userName + "/workspace/";
            URL instanceLocationUrl = new URL("file", null, path);
            Platform.getInstanceLocation().set(instanceLocationUrl, false);
        }
    }
}
```

Part XXI: Persisting data with preferences

163. Using preferences to persist data

163.1. Preferences and scopes

Preferences are used to store user settings and data like color preferences, runtime options, etc., between application restarts. Preferences are stored as key-value pairs, where the key is a `String`. The value can be a boolean, String, int, or another primitive type. For example, the *user* key may point to the value *vogella*.

The preference support in Eclipse is based on the `Preferences` class from the `org.osgi.service.prefs` package.

Eclipse preferences are similar to the standard Java preferences API, but support different *scopes*. The scope defines how the preference data is stored and how it is changeable. The Eclipse runtime defines three scopes as explained in the following table.

Table 32. Eclipse Preference scope

Scope	Description
Instance scope	Preferences in this scope are specific to a single Eclipse workspace. If you start an Eclipse application, these settings can be different for each workspace.
Configuration scope	Settings are identical for the same installation. Preferences stored in this scope are shared across all workspaces.
Default scope	Default values cannot be changed. This scope can be used to store default values for all your keys. These preferences are supplied via configuration files in plug-ins and product definitions.
BundleDefaultsScope	Similar to the default scope, these values are not written to disk. They are read from a file, typically named *preferences.ini*.

163.2. Storage of the preferences

Preferences are stored in the workspace of your application under the *.metadata/.plugins/org.eclipse.core.runtime/.settings/* directory as *<nodePath>.prefs* files. By default, the *<nodePath>* corresponds to the Bundle-SymbolicName of the plug-in but can be customized via the preferences API. Typically, the workspace is the directory from which the application is launched.

The storage location for preferences can be adjusted through the "*-data*" launch parameter in Eclipse. For instance, to direct preferences storage to the user's home directory, you can use the *-data @user.home* parameter setting.

163.3. Working with Eclipse Preference API

You can create and manipulate preferences directly via `Singletons` provided by the Eclipse runtime. You have the `InstanceScope`, `ConfigurationScope`, and `DefaultScope` classes, which give access to the corresponding instance via the `INSTANCE` field.

Preference values are read and saved by `get()` and `put()` methods. In the `get()` method, you specify a default value in case the key cannot be found. The `clear()` method removes all preferences, and the `remove()` method allows you to delete a selected preference value. Via the `flush()` method, you persist the preferences to the file system.

```
// We access the instanceScope
Preferences preferences = InstanceScope.INSTANCE.getNode
("com.vogella.eclipse.preferences.test");

Preferences sub1 = preferences.node("node1");
Preferences sub2 = preferences.node("node2");
```

```
sub1.put("h1", "Hello");
sub1.put("h2", "Hello again");
sub2.put("h1", "Hallo"); // German
try {
    // forces the application to save the preferences
    preferences.flush();
    } catch (BackingStoreException e) {
        e.printStackTrace();
    }
}
```

```
// read values from the instance scope
Preferences preferences = InstanceScope.INSTANCE.getNode
("com.vogella.eclipse.preferences.test");
Preferences sub1 = preferences.node("node1");
Preferences sub2 = preferences.node("node2");
sub1.get("h1", "default");
sub1.get("h2", "default");
sub2.get("h1", "default");
```

163.4. Reacting to changes in the preferences

You can register `IPropertyChangeListener` instances to changes in the preference values. These listeners are called by the Eclipse framework if the preference value changes.

```
Preferences preferences = InstanceScope.INSTANCE.getNode
("com.vogella.eclipse.preferences.test");

preferences.addPropertyChangeListener(new IPropertyChangeListener() {
        @Override
        public void propertyChange(PropertyChangeEvent event) {
            if (event.getProperty() == "MySTRING1") {
                String value = event.getNewValue().toString()
                // do something with the new value
            }
        }
    });
```

163.5. Default preference values via plugin_customization.ini

You can use a file to set the default values of preferences. The file that contains these defaults is typically named *plugin_customization.ini*.

Such a file needs to be registered via the *preferenceCustomization* property on the product extension point in the *plugin.xml* file. This is demonstrated in the following screenshot.

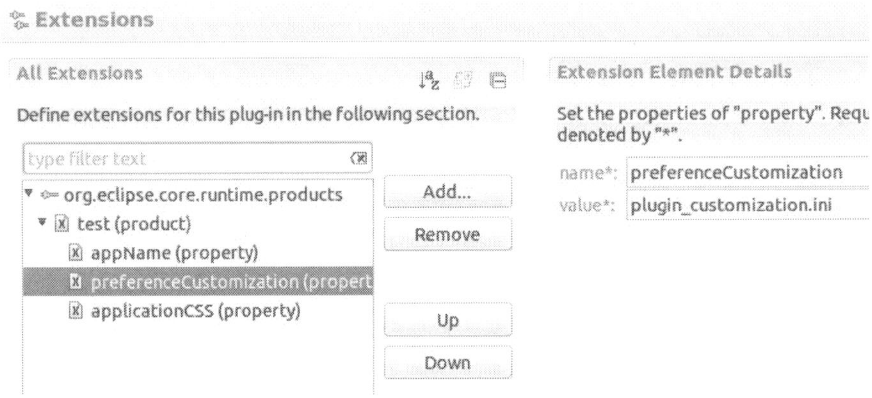

The format to use is `<plug-in id>/<setting>=<value>`, e.g., *com.vogella.tasks.ui/user=vogella*.

164. Workspace Location

An Eclipse-based application requires a place to store its configuration data. This is called the *workspace location*. The default workspace location is the install location of the Eclipse application.

164.1. Using the osgi.instance.area.default property

The `osgi.instance.area.default` property can be used to declaratively define an alternative workspace location.

The property can be specified in the *config.ini* file of the RCP application.

Usually, properties of the *config.ini* file are specified in a product configuration:

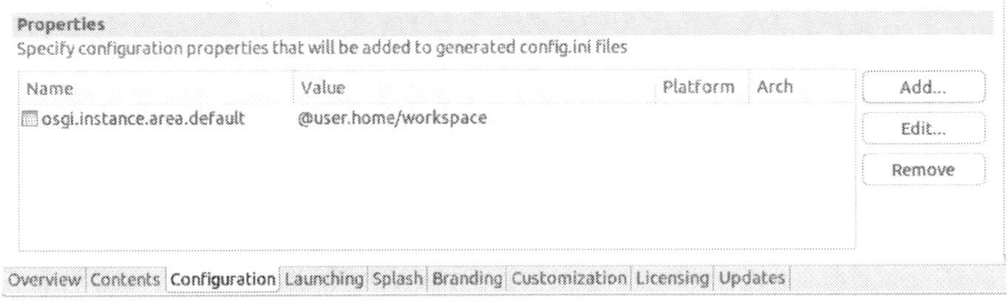

It is possible to use variables like `@user.home` as a value. This is especially useful in environments like Citrix, where multiple users might use the same application but require separate workspaces.

164.2. Setting the workspace location programmatically

Many RCP applications have a login screen at startup and the actual workspace location should be set according to the user being logged in. You typically create a login screen in your lifecycle class in the method annotated with `@PostContextCreate`.

```
import java.io.IOException;
import java.net.MalformedURLException;
import java.net.URL;

import org.eclipse.core.runtime.Platform;
import org.eclipse.e4.ui.workbench.lifecycle.PostContextCreate;

public class LifeCycleManager {

    @PostContextCreate
    public void postContextCreate() throws IllegalStateException, IOException {
        // Show login dialog to the user
        String userName = // get username from login dialog;

        // check if the instance location is already set,
        // otherwise setting another one will throw an IllegalStateException
        if (!Platform.getInstanceLocation().isSet()) {
            String defaultPath = System.getProperty("user.home");

            // build the desired path for the workspace
            String path = defaultPath + "/" + userName + "/workspace/";
            URL instanceLocationUrl = new URL("file", null, path);
            Platform.getInstanceLocation().set(instanceLocationUrl, false);
        }
    }
}
```

The instance location can only be set once! Therefore, the if statement with `if(Platform.getInstanceLocation().isSet())` is used.

When running the RCP application during development from the Eclipse IDE, there usually already is a workspace in the run configuration. To be able to set the location during development, the *Location* field must be empty.

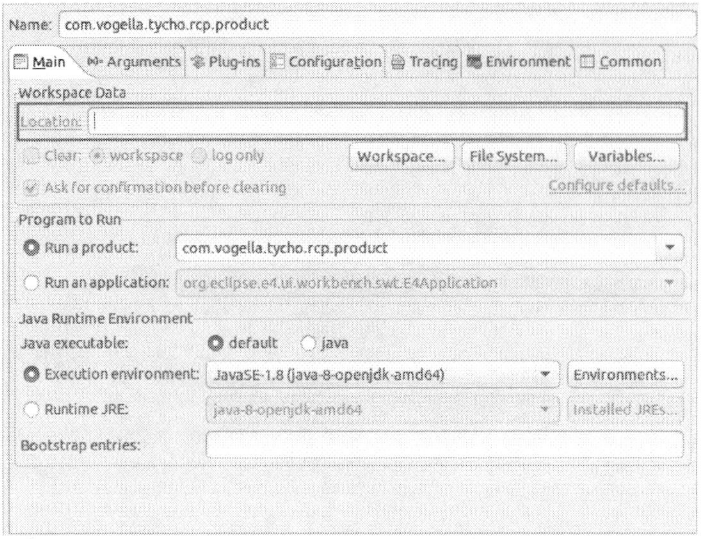

165. Using persistence in Eclipse applications

165.1. Working with preferences via dependency injection

The Eclipse platform allows you to use dependency injection for preferences handling. To access preferences, you use the `@Preference` annotation as qualifier for the dependency injection annotation. This means that `@Preference` must be used together with `@Inject` or with another annotation that implies dependency injection, e.g., the `@Execute` annotation.

The `@Preference` annotation allows you to specify the *nodePath* and the *value* as optional parameters.

The *nodePath* is the file name used to save the preference values to disk. By default, this is the Bundle-SymbolicName of the plug-in. The *value* parameter specifies the preference key for the value that should be injected.

Eclipse can inject the `IEclipsePreference` object. You can use this object for storing values. If you use the *value* parameter, Eclipse injects the value directly. Use the *value* parameter for read access, while for storing or changing values, use the `IEclipsePreference` object.

The following code snippet demonstrates how to put values into the preferences store. Please note that `@Preference` is used in combination with `@Execute`.

```
// get IEclipsePreferences injected to change a value
@Execute
public void execute
    (@Preference(nodePath = "com.example.e4.rcp.todo") IEclipsePreferences prefs) {
    // more stuff...
```

```
        prefs.put("user", "TestUser");
        prefs.put("password", "Password");
        // Persists
        try {
        prefs.flush();
            } catch (BackingStoreException e) {
                e.printStackTrace();
            }
}
```

The next snippet demonstrates the read access of preference values. This time the preference annotation is used as a qualifier for `@Inject`.

```
@Inject
@Optional
public void trackUserSettings
        (
        @Preference(nodePath = "com.example.e4.rcp.todo",
        value = "user")
        String user) {
        System.out.println("New user: " + user);
}

@Inject
@Optional
public void trackPasswordSettings
        (
        @Preference(nodePath = "com.example.e4.rcp.todo",
        value = "password")
        String password) {
        System.out.println("New password: " + password);
}
```

The Eclipse platform automatically tracks the values and re-injects them into fields and methods if they change. Eclipse tracks changes of preferences in the `InstanceScope` scope. Preference values in the `ConfigurationScope` and `DefaultScope` are not tracked.

If you use the injected `IEclipsePreference` to store new preference values, these values are stored in the instance scope.

165.2. Persistence of part state

Eclipse provides the `@PersistState` annotation for parts. This annotation can be applied to a method within a class that is referenced by a part.

Such an annotated method can be used to store the instance state of the part. The Eclipse framework calls such a method whenever the part or the application closes. The stored information can be used in the method annotated with the `@PostConstruct` annotation. A typical use case for such a method would be to store the state of a checkbox.

The usage of this annotation is demonstrated in the following example code.

```
@PostConstruct
public void createControl(MPart part) {
    Map<String, String> state = part.getPersistedState();
    String value = state.get("key");
    ...
}

@PersistState
public void persistState(MPart part) {
    Map<String, String> state = part.getPersistedState();
    state.put("key", "newValue");
    ...
}
```

165.3. Preference pages for e4

See https://www.opcoach.com/en/managing-preference-pages-with-eclipse-4/ for an introduction on how to use preference pages in Eclipse RCP applications.

166. Exercise: Use preferences in the lifecycle class

In this exercise, you store the last logged-in username in the preferences. You continue to use the dialog that you created earlier. In this exercise, you modify your lifecycle handler so that the previously entered user is displayed again in the password dialog.

166.1. Dependency

The `@Preference` annotation is provided by the `org.eclipse.e4.core.di.extensions` plug-in. Ensure you have added a dependency to this plug-in in the `MANIFEST.MF` file of the `com.vogella.tasks.ui` plug-in. If you have followed the previous exercises, this dependency should already be in place.

166.2. Create interface for the preference constants

Create the `com.vogella.tasks.ui.preferences` package and the following interface within this package.

```
package com.vogella.tasks.ui.preferences;
```

```java
public interface PreferenceConstants {
    static final String NODEPATH = "com.vogella.tasks.ui";
    static final String USER_PREF_KEY = "user";
    static final String PASSWORD_PREF_KEY = "password";
}
```

166.3. Using preferences in the lifecycle class

Extend the `Manager` class to get the user preference injected during application startup.

```java
package com.vogella.tasks.ui.lifecycle;

import jakarta.inject.Inject;

import org.eclipse.core.runtime.preferences.IEclipsePreferences;
import org.eclipse.e4.core.di.extensions.Preference;
import org.eclipse.e4.ui.workbench.lifecycle.PostContextCreate;
import org.eclipse.equinox.app.IApplicationContext;
import org.eclipse.jface.window.Window;
import org.eclipse.swt.SWT;
import org.eclipse.swt.graphics.Rectangle;
import org.eclipse.swt.widgets.Display;
import org.eclipse.swt.widgets.Monitor;
import org.eclipse.swt.widgets.Shell;
import org.osgi.service.prefs.BackingStoreException;

import com.vogella.tasks.ui.dialogs.PasswordDialog;
import com.vogella.tasks.ui.preferences.PreferenceConstants;

public class Manager {

    // example uses the optional nodePath parameter
    // allows to move the handler to another plug-in
    @Inject
    @Preference(nodePath = PreferenceConstants.NODEPATH,
                value = PreferenceConstants.USER_PREF_KEY)
    private String user;

    @PostContextCreate
    public void postContextCreate(@Preference IEclipsePreferences prefs,
            IApplicationContext appContext, Display display) {

        final Shell shell = new Shell(SWT.SHELL_TRIM);
        PasswordDialog dialog = new PasswordDialog(shell);
        if (user != null) {
            dialog.setUser(user);
```

```
        }

        // close the static splash screen
        appContext.applicationRunning();

        // position the shell
         setLocation(display, shell);

        // open the dialog
        if (dialog.open() != Window.OK) {
            // close the application
            System.exit(-1);
        } else {
            // get the user from the dialog
            String userValue = dialog.getUser();
            // store the user values in the preferences
            prefs.put(PreferenceConstants.USER_PREF_KEY, userValue );
            try {
                prefs.flush();
            } catch (BackingStoreException e) {
                e.printStackTrace();
            }
        }
    }

    private void setLocation(Display display, Shell shell) {
        Monitor monitor = display.getPrimaryMonitor();
        Rectangle monitorRect = monitor.getBounds();
        Rectangle shellRect = shell.getBounds();
        int x = monitorRect.x + (monitorRect.width - shellRect.width) / 2;
        int y = monitorRect.y + (monitorRect.height - shellRect.height) / 2;
        shell.setLocation(x, y);
    }
}
```

166.4. Validate Lifecycle Handling

Start your application and enter a username. Stop the application and start it again. The login dialog should now display the last entered username.

If persisting the user does not work, you might have an incorrect setting in your launch configuration.

Ensure that the *Clear* flag in the **Project › Run Configurations...** is not enabled. Otherwise, your preference data is deleted during the start of the application.

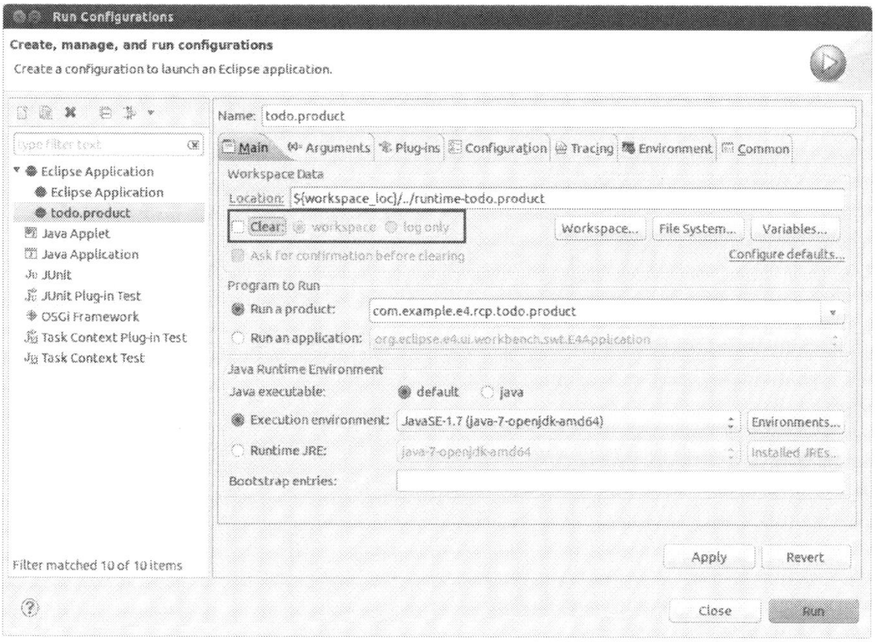

167. Exercise: Use preferences in the handler and the part

In this exercise, you will modify the handler within the application to enter the user and listen to changes in the corresponding preference values in a part.

We do not persist the password in this exercise, because persisting passwords in plain text is a security risk.

167.1. Accessing preferences in the EnterCredentialsHandler

Extend your `EnterCredentialsHandler` handler to get and store the user via the preference values. As `nodePath` is not explicitly set for the `@Execute` method, it uses *com.vogella.tasks.ui*, which is the Bundle-SymbolicName of the plug-in.

```
package com.vogella.tasks.ui.handlers;

import jakarta.inject.Inject;

import org.eclipse.core.runtime.preferences.IEclipsePreferences;
import org.eclipse.e4.core.di.annotations.Execute;
import org.eclipse.e4.core.di.extensions.Preference;
import org.eclipse.jface.window.Window;
import org.eclipse.swt.widgets.Shell;
import org.osgi.service.prefs.BackingStoreException;
```

```java
import com.vogella.tasks.ui.dialogs.PasswordDialog;

public class EnterCredentialsHandler {

    @Inject
    @Preference(nodePath = PreferenceConstants.NODEPATH,
                value = PreferenceConstants.USER_PREF_KEY)
    String userPref;

    @Execute
    public void execute(Shell shell, @Preference IEclipsePreferences prefs) {
        PasswordDialog dialog = new PasswordDialog(shell);

        if (userPref != null) {
            dialog.setUser(userPref);
        }

        // get the new values from the dialog
        if (dialog.open() == Window.OK) {
            prefs.put(PreferenceConstants.USER_PREF_KEY, dialog.getUser());
            try {
                prefs.flush();
            } catch (BackingStoreException e) {
                e.printStackTrace();
            }
        }
    }
}
```

167.2. Receiving preferences updates in the PlaygroundPart

For testing purposes, listen to preference changes in your playground view and print the values to the console.

```java
@Inject
@Optional
public void trackUserSettings(
    @Preference(value = "user") String user) {
    System.out.println("New user: " + user);
}
```

167.3. Validate the implementation

Start your application. Use the menu entry that uses the `EnterCredentialsHandler` handler and enter a user into the dialog. Close the dialog and open it again via the menu. The last entered user should be displayed.

168. Optional exercise: Persist the table column width

In this exercise, you will extend the preferences to store the width of the table columns in the `TodoOverviewPart` view.

168.1. Implementation

Create the following utility class:

```
package com.vogella.tasks.ui.util;

import org.eclipse.core.runtime.preferences.IEclipsePreferences;
import org.eclipse.core.runtime.preferences.InstanceScope;
import org.eclipse.jface.viewers.TableViewer;
import org.eclipse.swt.widgets.TableColumn;
import org.osgi.service.prefs.BackingStoreException;

public class TableColumnPersistenceUtil {
    private static final String PREF_FILE = "tablecolumns.properties";
    private static IEclipsePreferences store = InstanceScope.INSTANCE.getNode(PREF_FILE);

    public static void restoreColumnWidths(TableViewer viewer, Class<?> clazz) {
        TableColumn[] columns = viewer.getTable().getColumns();
        for (int i = 0; i < columns.length; i++) {
            int width = store.getInt(clazz.getName() + "_col" + i, 200);
            if (width > 0) {
                columns[i].setWidth(width);
            }
        }
    }

    public static void saveColumnWidths(TableViewer viewer, Class<?> clazz) {
        TableColumn[] columns = viewer.getTable().getColumns();
        for (int i = 0; i < columns.length; i++) {
            store.putInt(clazz.getName() + "_col" + i, columns[i].getWidth());
        }
        try {
            store.flush();
        } catch (BackingStoreException e) {
            e.printStackTrace();
        }
    }
}
```

Use this utility class in the `TodoOverviewPart` view to save and restore the column widths. To save the width use the `@PersistState` annotation on a method that is called when the part is disposed.

You can call `restoreColumnWidths` in the `createPartControl` method and `saveColumnWidths` in the `dispose` method.

```
@PersistState
    public void saveColumnWidths() {
        if (viewer != null && !viewer.getTable().isDisposed()) {
            TableColumnPersistenceUtil.saveColumnWidths(viewer, TodoOverviewPart.class);
        }
    }
```

In your createPartControl method, you can call the following after you created the columns.

```
// Restore column widths if available
TableColumnPersistenceUtil.restoreColumnWidths(viewer, TodoOverviewPart.class);
```

168.2. Validation

Start your application. Change the column width in your task overview table. Restart the application, the column width should be restored.

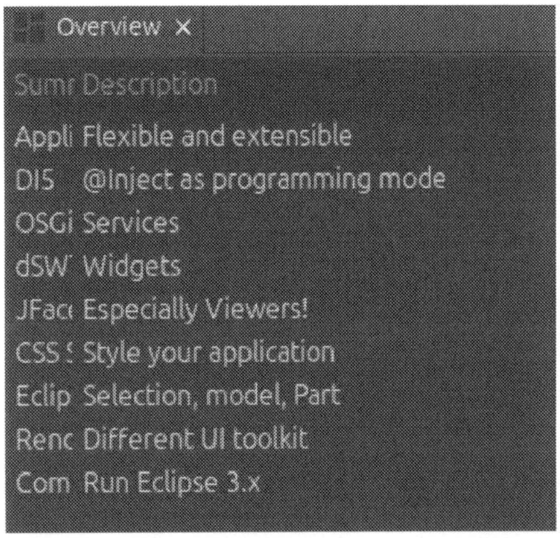

Part XXII: Internationalization

169. Internationalization and localization

169.1. Translation of a Java application

The process of preparing an application for translation into several languages is called *internationalization*. This term is typically abbreviated as *i18n*.

The process of translating the application is called *localization* and is abbreviated as *l10n*.

Java applications are typically translated via *property* files. Such a file contains key-value pairs. The key can be used in your application and is substituted at runtime with the corresponding value. The following listing demonstrates an example content of such a file.

```
# Properties file
part.overview=Overview
part.detail=Details
```

Based on the language of the user, the Java runtime searches for the corresponding resource bundle using language identifiers. If a certain language identifier is not provided, the Java runtime will fall back to the next most general resource bundle.

For example:

- `messages.properties`: default language file, if nothing else is available
- `messages_de.properties`: used for German
- `messages_en.properties`: default for English
- `messages_en_US.properties`: US English file
- `messages_en_UK.properties`: British English file

The Eclipse platform provides functionality to support translations based on properties files, but it allows the usage of alternative approaches.

Resource bundles in Java are always LATIN-1 (ISO 8859-1) encoded. This is defined by the Java specification.

169.2. Relevant files for translation in Eclipse applications

The following table lists the files relevant for localization.

Table 33. Translation-relevant files for Eclipse plug-ins

Entity	Description
Application model, i.e. Application.e4xmi and model fragment files	Describes the application model in Eclipse RCP.
plugin.xml	Primarily important for Eclipse 3.x based plug-ins.
Source Code	The source code contains text, e.g., labels that must be translated.

169.3. Storage location for translation files

Plug-ins can contain their translations. If a translation should be used by several plug-ins, it is a good practice to have one central plug-in that contains the translations. This plug-in contains at least the main language and potentially more.

It is possible to provide translation files via fragment projects. Fragment projects extend their host plug-in at runtime. This approach allows different languages to be maintained in separate plug-ins. This is sometimes easier to handle for the translation team. This approach allows configuring the included languages via the product configuration file.

169.4. Setting the language in the launch configuration

By default, Eclipse uses the language configured in the operating system of the user.

For testing, you can set the language via the launch configuration. On the *Arguments* tab, use the runtime parameter *-nl* for this purpose, e.g., *-nl en*.

169.5. Translation service

Eclipse uses a translation service via the `TranslationService` interface. The default implementation of this class is the `BundleTranslationProvider` that uses property files as input for the translations. You can provide a custom service that uses a different source, e.g., a database, to get the translations.

This service is stored in the application context. You can replace it there, e.g., via a lifecycle hook or via a model add-on that modifies the application context once the application startup is completed.

By storing it in the `IEclipseContext` context hierarchy, you can have different translation services for different local contexts. For example, you can use different translation services for different windows.

169.6. OSGi resource bundles

For the translation of the plugin.xml and application model files, the Eclipse runtime uses by default OSGi resource bundles. These are `.property` files in a specified location. OSGi expects at least one resource bundle in this location.

OSGI-INF/l10n/bundle is the default location and file prefix that the Eclipse translation service is using. Via the *Bundle-Localization* attribute in the manifest file, you can specify an alternative location for the bundle resources. The usage of this attribute is demonstrated in the following listing.

```
Manifest-Version: 1.0
Bundle-ManifestVersion: 2
Bundle-Name: I18n
Bundle-SymbolicName: de.vogella.rcp.i18n; singleton:=true
Bundle-Version: 1.0.0.qualifier
Bundle-Activator: de.vogella.rcp.i18n.Activator
Require-Bundle: org.eclipse.ui,
 org.eclipse.core.runtime
Bundle-ActivationPolicy: lazy
Bundle-RequiredExecutionEnvironment: JavaSE-21
Bundle-Localization: OSGI-INF/anotherlocation/bundle
```

Alternative languages are defined via additional property files. The filename of these files can include a language and optionally a country variant as described in Section 169.1. For example:

- *bundle_en.properties*
- *bundle_en_UK.properties*

169.7. Translating the application model

The translation key can be specified in your application model via the *%key* reference. This usage is demonstrated via the following screenshot of the model data for a part.

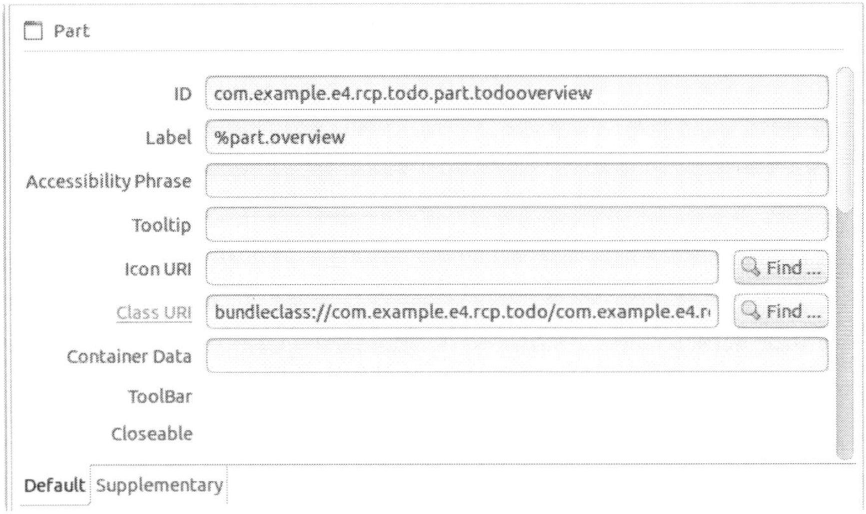

Currently, the application model tooling includes rudimentary support for extracting Strings. Right-click on an empty space in the application model editor and select *Externalize Strings*.

> This action extracts all Strings from the application model. If you want to replace only a set of relevant Strings, you have to do this manually.

169.8. Translating plugin.xml

Similar to the usage of keys in the application model, you can use the key prefixed with % in the *plugin.xml* file. The Eclipse tooling supports extracting existing `String` values from the *plugin.xml* file. Right-click on the *plugin.xml* file and select **Plug-in Tools › Externalize Strings**.

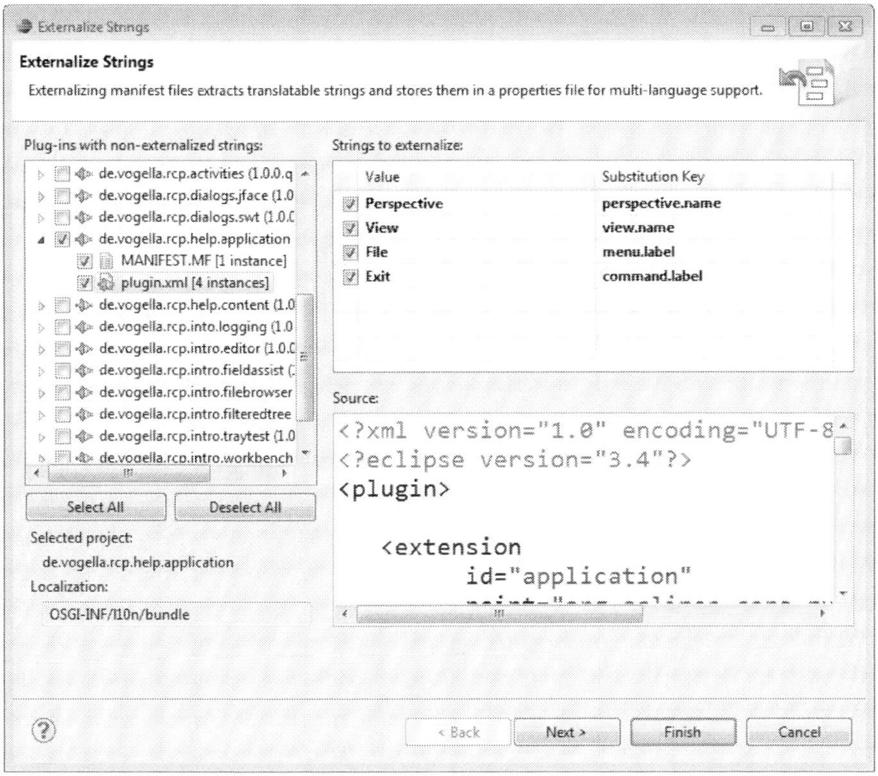

Via **PDE Tools › Internationalize** you can directly create one or several fragments for the result of the internationalization.

169.9. Potential problems with translations

You must include your property files in the *build.properties* file. If not, your translations will be missing in the exported product.

If the translations are not displayed in the application, select *Clear Configuration* in your launch configuration. OSGi may sometimes cache text information.

170. Eclipse internationalization using dependency injection

170.1. Translation with POJOs

To define your translations, you define a Java object with several public fields of type String.

```
public class Messages {
    public String labelSummary;
    public String labelDescription;
```

```
    public String labelDone;
    public String labelDueDate;
    public String labelWithPlaceholder = "{0} says {1}";
}
```

Such fields are initialized when an instance is injected via the `@Translation` annotation. The `org.eclipse.e4.core.services` plug-in contains this annotation.

```
@Inject
@Translation
Messages messages;

// more code
myLabel.setText(messages.label_message);
```

The Eclipse service which handles this annotation searches for property files in the following order:

- Check for a @Message annotation in the `Messages` class. The optional `@Message` annotation can be used to define the location of the resource bundle. It allows you to define how translations should be cached by the Eclipse platform. See the Javadoc of the `@Message` annotation for more information on this topic.
- Check if a property file with a corresponding name is available relative to the `Messages` class.
- Check if a property file is configured via the OSGi-ResourceBundle header in the MANIFEST.MF file.
- Check the OSGI-INF/l10n folder

It is possible to initialize fields via the `@PostConstruct` method in a message object as demonstrated in the following snippet.

```
public class Messages {
    public String labelWithPlaceholder1 = {0} says {1}
    public String labelWithPlaceholder2 = {0} says {1}

    // initialize the first message

    @PostConstruct
    public void format() {
        labelWithPlaceholder2 =
                MessageFormat.
                    format(labelWithPlaceholder2, "Test", "this is
fun.");
    }
}
```

@PostConstruct does not support parameter injection in the context of a message object.

170.2. Dynamic language switch

The currently active locale, e.g., "de" or "en", is represented by an object of type Locale. The Eclipse framework allows you to change the locale dynamically at runtime. This enables your application to update its translated text during execution.

To support a dynamic locale switch, the application must be able to react to locale changes. This requires that the widgets are declared as fields and that a method exists that updates them.

```
public class TranslationExamplePart {
    private Label myLabel;

    @PostConstruct
    public void postConstruct(Composite parent, @Translation Messages messages) {
        // create the UI
        myLabel = new Label(parent, SWT.NONE);
        // as @PostConstruct is executed after field injection, we need to
        // call translate here manually to fill the UI initially
        translate(messages);
    }

    // the method that will perform the dynamic locale changes
    @Inject
    public void translate(@Translation Messages messages) {
        if (myLabel != null && !myLabel.isDisposed())
            myLabel.setText(messages.labelSummary);
    }
}
```

The BaseMessageRegistry described below makes this easier.

To change the locale, use the ILocaleChangeService service. This is demonstrated by the following code, which can be used as part of a tool control.

```
public class SwitchLanguageToolControl {

    Button button;

    @Inject
    ILocaleChangeService lcs;

    @PostConstruct
```

```
    public createPartControls(Composite parent) {

        final Text input = new Text(parent, SWT.BORDER);

        input.addKeyListener(new KeyAdapter() {
            @Override
            public void keyPressed(KeyEvent event) {
                if (event.keyCode == SWT.CR
                        || event.keyCode == SWT.KEYPAD_CR) {
                    lcs.changeApplicationLocale(input.getText());
                }
            }
        });

        button = new Button(parent, SWT.PUSH);
        button.addSelectionListener(new SelectionAdapter() {
            @Override
            public void widgetSelected(SelectionEvent e) {
                lcs.changeApplicationLocale(input.getText());
            };
        });
    }

    @Inject
    public void translate(@Translation Messages messages) {
        // button localization via Eclipse Translation Pattern
        button.setText(messages.button_change_locale);
    }
}
```

To get notified you can use dependency injection.

```
@Inject
@Optional
private void getNotified(@Named(TranslationService.LOCALE) Locale s) {
    System.out.println("Injected via context: " + s);
}

@Inject
@Optional
private void getNotified(@UIEventTopic(ILocaleChangeService.LOCALE_CHANGE) Locale s) {
    System.out.println("Injected via event broker: " + s);
}
```

170.3. Using the BaseMessageRegistry to track language changes

Declaring all user interface components as fields and writing an update method for them, requires a lot of code. To simplify this, you can use the `BaseMessageRegistry`.

The `BaseMessageRegistry<M>` allows you to register controls that are supposed to be translated. Your `BaseMessageRegistry<M>` will be informed about locale changes and then applies the new text to your registered controls.

The `BaseMessageRegistry<M>` itself gets the `Message` object injected.

```
package com.vogella.tasks.ui.i18n;

import jakarta.inject.Inject;

import org.eclipse.e4.core.di.annotations.Creatable;
import org.eclipse.e4.core.services.nls.BaseMessageRegistry;
import org.eclipse.e4.core.services.nls.Translation;

@Creatable ❶
public class MessagesRegistry extends BaseMessageRegistry<Messages> {

    @Inject
    @Override
    public void updateMessages(@Translation Messages messages) {
        // Update the Messages for the BaseMessageRegistry by DI
        super.updateMessages(messages);
    }
}
```

❶ the `MessagesRegistry` class is annotated with `@Creatable`, therefore it is instantiated by the framework

For example, this registry can be used in a part.

```
package com.vogella.tasks.ui.parts;

import jakarta.annotation.PostConstruct;
import jakarta.inject.Inject;

import org.eclipse.e4.core.services.nls.MessageConsumer;
import org.eclipse.e4.core.services.nls.MessageFunction;
import org.eclipse.e4.core.services.nls.Translation;
import org.eclipse.swt.SWT;
import org.eclipse.swt.widgets.Composite;
import org.eclipse.swt.widgets.Label;
```

```
import com.vogella.tasks.ui.i18n.Messages;
import com.vogella.tasks.ui.i18n.MessagesRegistry;

public class MessagesRegistryExamplePartWithJava8 {

    @PostConstruct
    public void postConstruct(Composite parent, MessagesRegistry messagesRegistry) {
        // create the UI
        Label myLabel = new Label(parent, SWT.NONE);
        // Let the MessagesRegistry apply the correct label
        messagesRegistry.register(myLabel::setText, m -> m.labelSummary);
    }
}
```

171. Source code translation with NLS support

171.1. Translating the source code with the NLS approach

> ⚠ This part of the description is included for completeness. It describes the NLS approach for translation. This approach still works, but the Eclipse translation mechanism provides more flexibility, e.g., dynamic switching of languages, less memory consumption, and a translation service that can be exchanged. This superior approach is described in Section 170.1.

It is possible to translate Java source code using two different approaches: based on strings or constants. The approach based on constants is more reliable and should be preferred. To enable this support, you need to configure the `org.eclipse.core.runtime` plug-in as a dependency in your related plug-in.

To translate Strings in the source code, select the file you want to translate and select **Source › Externalize Strings**.

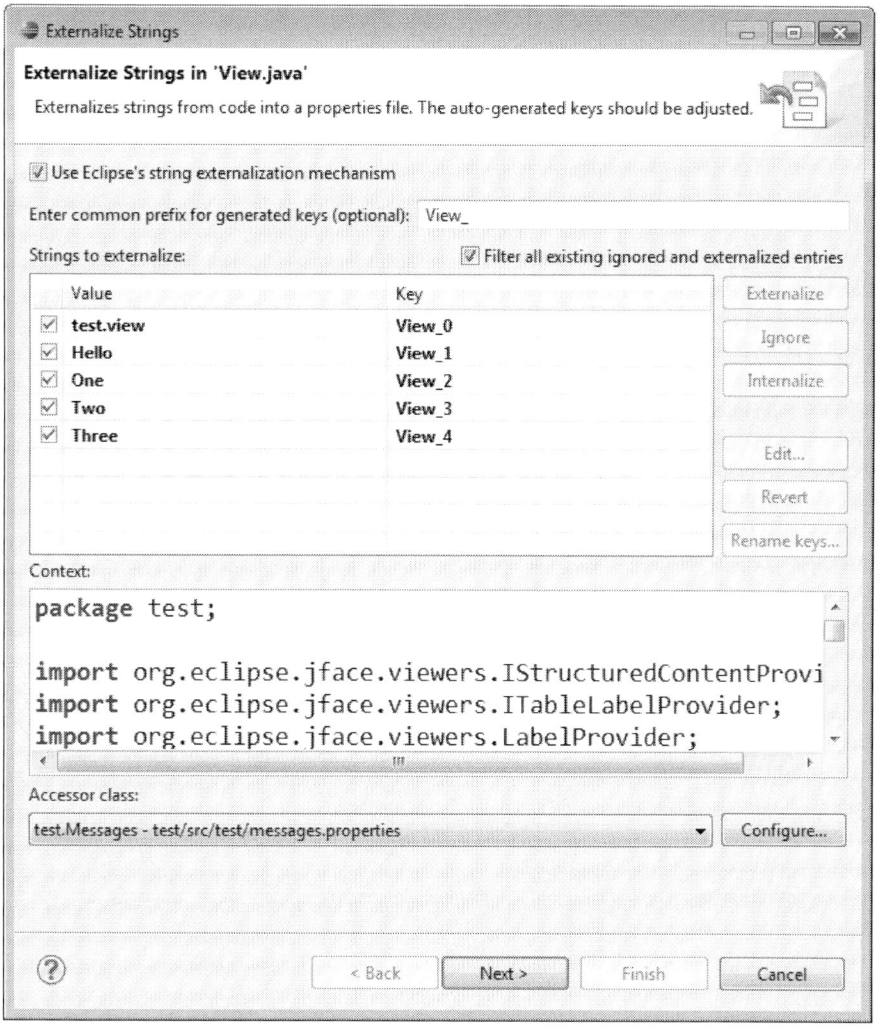

Please note that the *Use Eclipse's string externalization mechanism* option is only visible if you have the `org.eclipse.core.runtime` plug-in configured as a dependency in your plug-in.

In this wizard, you can choose which strings to translate, skip, or mark as non-translatable.

If you select that a string should not be translated, Eclipse marks the occurrence with a `$NON-NLS` comment in the source code.

As a result, a `Messages` class is generated, which serves as an access point for the properties file.

```
package test;

import org.eclipse.osgi.util.NLS;

public class Messages extends NLS {
```

```
    private static final String BUNDLE_NAME
        = "test.messages"; //$NON-NLS-1$
    public static String View_0;
    public static String View_1;
    static {
        // initialize resource bundle
        NLS.initializeMessages(BUNDLE_NAME, Messages.class);
    }

    private Messages() {
    }
}
```

In this example, the `Messages` class uses a constant called `BUNDLE_NAME` to point to the message properties files (e.g., messages.properties, messages_de.properties) in the `test` package. The filename suffix (e.g., `_de` or `_en`) is a placeholder for the locale.

```
View_0=test.view
View_1=Hello
```

In your code, you access the translations via the `Messages` class.

```
label.setText(Messages.View_1);
```

You can use placeholders in the messages and evaluate them with the `NLS.bind()` method.

```
MyMessage = {0} says {1}
```

```
// NLS bind will call the toString method on obj
NLS.bind(Message.MyMessage, obj, obj);
```

If translations should be used over several plug-ins to ensure consistency, it is a good practice to create separate plug-ins or fragments for the translations. All plug-ins that want to use the translations define a dependency on the corresponding plug-in.

Additional languages are typically contributed via Eclipse fragment projects to this message plug-in.

171.2. Translating SWT and JFace code

The SWT and JFace plug-ins include their resource translation files. You can change these default texts and their translations because resource bundles have an override support built in.

If you supply a different file of the SWT or JFace translation bundles in a fragment or plug-in (such as SWTMessage_de.properties), then the bundle matching the current locale is used.

To change the text supplied by SWT and JFace do the following:

- Create two fragment projects that will hold the translations: one with `org.eclipse.jface` and one with `org.eclipse.swt` as Host-Plug-in.
- Create the `org.eclipse.jface` and `org.eclipse.swt.internal` packages in the corresponding fragments.
- Copy the *org/eclipse/jface/message.properties* file from the org.eclipse.jface plug-in and the *org/eclipse/swt/internal/SWTMessage.properties* file from the SWT plug-in to the corresponding packages in your project. See the appendix for the links to their location in the Eclipse Git repository.
- Provide the files with your desired language extensions, e.g., message_de.properties.
- Edit the files to contain your text properties.

> The original *message.properties* in JFace or *SWTMessage.properties* in SWT cannot be overridden by a fragment. Therefore, you can only provide additional **.properties* files for a certain locale like message_de.properties.

You can translate selected properties from the original *message.properties* file.

172. Optional exercise: Application model internationalization

In this exercise, you translate the relevant parts of your application model and use the translation service.

172.1. Create the translations for the application model

Create the `OSGI-INF/l10n` folder in your `com.vogella.tasks.ui` plug-in.

Create the `bundle.properties` file with key-value pairs for the parts in your application model in this folder. The file might look similar to the following.

```
part.overview=Overview
part.details=Details
```

```
command.save=Save
```

Also, create an additional translation file for another language. For example, if English is your default language, create the `bundle_de.properties` file to provide a German translation. Ensure that the translation values are different.

172.2. Adjust the build.properties file

Add the created property files to your `build.properties` file in the `com.vogella.tasks.ui` plug-in to make it available in an exported application.

172.3. Translate the application model

Use the defined keys with the % prefix in your application model. The following screenshot demonstrates that for a part.

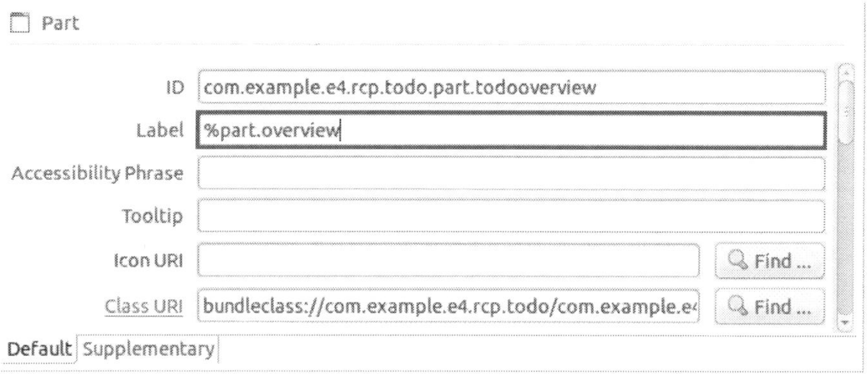

172.4. Test the translation of the application model

Ensure that the application works correctly for the languages you have provided translations for. You can set the language in your launch configuration by using the `-nl` start parameter.

172.5. Application model and translations

By default, it is not possible to define that the translations for the application model are located in another plug-in. If you want this, you have to implement your custom translation service.

173. Optional exercise: Source code internationalization

In this exercise, you translate the relevant parts of your application source code via the Eclipse 4 translation service.

173.1. Creating a plug-in to host the translations

Create a new simple plug-in called *com.vogella.tasks.ui.i18n*. See Chapter 36 for more information.

Add the dependency `org.eclipse.core.runtime` to the new plug-in in its `MANIFEST.MF` file.

173.2. Create a Message class for the source code translations

Create a `Messages` class that contains your translation keys. This might look similar to the following (keys are just examples).

```
package com.vogella.tasks.ui.i18n;

public class Messages {
    public String buttonLoadData;
    public String txtSummary;
    public String txtDescription;
}
```

173.3. Create the translations for the source code

Create the `OSGI-INF/l10n` folder in your `com.vogella.tasks.ui.i18n` plug-in.

> The first letter is a lowercase "L" followed by the number 10. This might be hard to identify as "l" and "1" look similar.

Create a `bundle.properties` file with key-value pairs for the text in your source code. The file might look similar to the following.

```
buttonLoadData=Load Data
txtSummary=Summary
txtDescription=Description
```

> The translation service is capable of matching key names using _ in the properties file to camel-case attributes in the `Messages` class. For example, you could also use `button_load_data` in the `.properties` file to match to `buttonLoadData` as an attribute. This was done to give you more flexibility for defining your keys in the property file.

Also, create an additional translation file for another language, e.g., via a `bundle_de.properties` file. Ensure that the translation values are different.

> The translations for the application model as created in Chapter 172 cannot be

moved to this new plug-in.

173.4. Adjust the build.properties file

Add the created property files to your build.properties file of your new plug-in to make it available in an exported application.

173.5. Export the translations as API

Publish the `com.vogella.tasks.ui.i18n` package as an API via the `MANIFEST.MF` file of the translation plug-in.

173.6. Define dependencies to the translation plug-in

Open the `MANIFEST.MF` file of the `com.vogella.tasks.ui` plug-in. Add a dependency to the `com.vogella.tasks.ui.i18n` plug-in.

173.7. Update the product (via the feature)

Add the `com.vogella.tasks.ui.i18n` plug-in to your feature project. This includes it in your product.

Start your application using the product configuration file and validate that the application still starts and works correctly.

173.8. Using @Translation to get the messages injected

Use dependency injection to inject the translations. Prepare your `TodoOverviewPart` for a dynamic language switch.

```
@PostConstruct
public void createControls(Composite parent,
        EMenuService menuService, @Translation Messages message) {

    // more source code

    // new
    translateTable(message);
}

// more source code

@Inject
public void translateTable(@Translation Messages message){
    if (viewer !=null && !viewer.getTable().isDisposed()) {
        colSummary.getColumn().setText(message.txtSummary);
```

```
        colDescription.getColumn().setText(message.txtDescription);
    }
}
```

173.9. Test the translation

Repeat the test as described in Section 172.4 and ensure that your source code is correctly translated.

Part XXIII: Custom annotations for dependency injection

174. Dependency injection for custom annotations

This dependency injection mechanism of the Eclipse platform is extensible. You can define your own custom qualifiers for `@Inject` and register an extended object supplier for it.

The following code demonstrates how you can define your own custom annotation.

```
package com.vogella.tasks.extendedsupplier;

import java.lang.annotation.Documented;
import java.lang.annotation.ElementType;
import java.lang.annotation.Retention;
import java.lang.annotation.RetentionPolicy;
import java.lang.annotation.Target;

@jakarta.inject.Qualifier
@Documented
@Target({ ElementType.PARAMETER, ElementType.FIELD })
```

```java
@Retention(RetentionPolicy.RUNTIME)
public @interface DirectTask {

    /**
     * An id parameter can be passed to the DirectTask, to inject a
     * java.util.Optional<Task> with a given id.<br/>
     * <br/>
     * Without parameter the injected task is an empty java.util.Optional, because
     * task ids begin with 1 and the default is 0 (see TaskService).
     *
     * @return the id, which is passed to the DirectTask annotation or 0, if no
     *         parameter is passed
     */
    long id() default 0;
}
```

To process a custom annotation, you can register an OSGi service for the `ExtendedObjectSupplier` class. In this registration, you define which annotation the service is responsible for via the `dependency.injection.annotation` property.

The Eclipse dependency injection delegates to this implementation if it encounters the configured annotation.

The following code shows an example of an annotation processor. It returns an instance of the `java.util.Optional<Todo>` class.

```java
package com.vogella.tasks.extendedsupplier.internal;

import java.util.Optional;

import jakarta.inject.Inject;

import org.eclipse.e4.core.di.suppliers.ExtendedObjectSupplier;
import org.eclipse.e4.core.di.suppliers.IObjectDescriptor;
import org.eclipse.e4.core.di.suppliers.IRequestor;
import org.osgi.service.component.annotations.Component;

import com.vogella.tasks.model.Task;
import com.vogella.tasks.model.TaskService;

@Component(service=ExtendedObjectSupplier.class,
property="dependency.injection.annotation=com.vogella.tasks.extendedsupplier.DirectTask")
public class DirectTaskObjectSupplier extends ExtendedObjectSupplier {

    @Inject
    private TaskService taskService;

```

```
    @Override
    public Object get(IObjectDescriptor descriptor, IRequestor requestor, boolean track,
boolean group) {
        // get the DirectTask from the IObjectDescriptor
        DirectTask uniqueTodo = descriptor.getQualifier(DirectTask.class);

        // get the ID from the DirectTask (default is 0)
        long id = uniqueTodo.id();

        // get the task that has the given id or null
        Optional<Task> task = taskService.get(id);

        return task;
    }
}
```

Dependency injection can be used inside an `ExtendedObjectSupplier` implementation, so that services like the `IEventBroker`, `EModelService`, and so on can be injected. Unlike handlers, extended object suppliers do not have access to the `IEclipseContext` for the object that is the target of the injection.

175. Optional exercise: Create custom annotations

The following exercise demonstrates how to create a custom annotation and a processor for it.

The annotation processor is registered for a custom `@DirectTask` annotation, which is a qualifier and therefore has to be used together with `@Inject`. The `@DirectTask` annotation can have an `id` parameter to request a specific task.

175.1. Creating a new plug-in

Create a new simple plug-in project called `com.vogella.tasks.extendedsupplier`. See Chapter 36 for more information.

Add the following entries as plug-in dependencies to your new plug-in.

- `org.eclipse.e4.core.di`
- `com.vogella.tasks.model`
- `org.eclipse.osgi.services`

Also, configure the application to use the jakarta.inject package.

175.2. Define and export annotations

Define the following annotation.

```java
package com.vogella.tasks.extendedsupplier;

import java.lang.annotation.Documented;
import java.lang.annotation.ElementType;
import java.lang.annotation.Retention;
import java.lang.annotation.RetentionPolicy;
import java.lang.annotation.Target;

@jakarta.inject.Qualifier
@Documented
@Target({ ElementType.PARAMETER, ElementType.FIELD })
@Retention(RetentionPolicy.RUNTIME)
public @interface DirectTask {

    /**
     * An id parameter can be passed to the DirectTask, to inject a
     * java.util.Optional<Task> with a given id.<br/>
     * <br/>
     * Without parameter the injected task is an empty java.util.Optional, because
     * task ids begin with 1 and the default is 0 (see TaskService).
     *
     * @return the id, which is passed to the DirectTask annotation or 0, if no
     *         parameter is passed
     */
    long id() default 0;
}
```

Export the `com.vogella.tasks.extendedsupplier` package via your `MANIFEST.MF` file.

175.3. Ensure annotation processing and plug-in activation is active

Ensure that OSGi services can be defined via annotations in the class via **Window › Preferences › Plug-in Development › DS annotations**.

175.4. Create service implementation

Create the `com.vogella.tasks.extendedsupplier.internal` package and the following class. Based on the annotation, this class is registered as a service for the `ExtendedObjectSupplier` abstract class via an OSGi declarative service.

```java
package com.vogella.tasks.extendedsupplier.internal;

import java.util.Optional;

import jakarta.inject.Inject;
```

```
import org.eclipse.e4.core.di.suppliers.ExtendedObjectSupplier;
import org.eclipse.e4.core.di.suppliers.IObjectDescriptor;
import org.eclipse.e4.core.di.suppliers.IRequestor;
import org.osgi.service.component.annotations.Component;

import com.vogella.tasks.model.Task;
import com.vogella.tasks.model.TaskService;

@Component(service=ExtendedObjectSupplier.class,
property="dependency.injection.annotation=com.vogella.tasks.extendedsupplier.DirectTask")
public class DirectTaskObjectSupplier extends ExtendedObjectSupplier {

    @Inject
    private TaskService taskService;

    @Override
    public Object get(IObjectDescriptor descriptor, IRequestor requestor, boolean track,
boolean group) {
        // get the DirectTask from the IObjectDescriptor
        DirectTask uniqueTodo = descriptor.getQualifier(DirectTask.class);

        // get the ID from the DirectTask (default is 0)
        long id = uniqueTodo.id();

        // get the task that has the given id or null
        Optional<Task> task = taskService.get(id);

        return task;
    }
}
```

The `ExtendedObjectSupplier` class has not yet been released as an official API.

175.5. Add the plug-in as a dependency

Add your new plug-in as a dependency to your `com.vogella.tasks.ui` application plug-in via its `MANIFEST.MF` file.

175.6. Update the product configuration (via the features)

Include the new plug-in in your feature to make it available for your product.

175.7. Validate by using the custom annotation

To use your new annotation, add it to a field or method parameter in one of your parts. For example, add the following method to your `PlaygroundPart` class.

```
// more code

// add this to one of your parts
@Inject
public void setTask(@DirectTask(id=1) java.util.Optional<Task> task) {
    // Printing the received t to the console
    task.ifPresent(t-> System.out.println(t.getSummary()));
}
```

Start your application (via the product, as you added a new plug-in). Ensure that you get the task with ID 1 injected based on your `@DirectTask` annotation.

Part XXIV: Using Java libraries in Eclipse applications

176. Using Java libraries in Eclipse plug-ins and OSGi bundles

176.1. Using standard JAR files for Eclipse plug-ins

Java libraries are delivered as JAR files. Eclipse plug-ins and OSGi-based applications require additional metadata in the *META-INF/MANIFEST.MF* file from libraries. If a Java library does not provide the additional metadata, you can convert the JAR file to a plug-in:

- Use the Eclipse Maven M2E extension to add Maven libraries to your target platform
- Manually convert the JAR file to a plug-in by adding the required metadata

The easiest way is to use the Eclipse Maven (M2E) extension to add such libraries to your target platform. This functionality converts non-OSGi Java libraries automatically, if they are part of the target platform. It also allows including dependencies and excluding certain transitive dependencies.

176.2. Adding a dependency to the target file

The following is an example of how to add a library as a dependency, while excluding a certain transitive library.

```
<?xml version="1.0" encoding="UTF-8" standalone="no"?>
<?pde version="3.8"?>
<target name="test" sequenceNumber="170">
        <location includeDependencyDepth="infinite" includeDependencyScopes="compile"
            includeSource="true" label="EclipseLink" missingManifest="generate"
type="Maven">
            <feature id="eclipselink" label="EclipseLink" version="1.0.0.qualifier" />
            <dependencies>
                <dependency>
                    <groupId>org.eclipse.persistence</groupId>
                    <artifactId>org.eclipse.persistence.jpa</artifactId>
                    <version>4.0.0</version>
                    <type>jar</type>
                </dependency>
                <!-- For Lazy Loading
                Warning: Build fails if commented out:
                Missing requirement: org.eclipse.angus.mail 1.0.0 requires 'java.package;
sun.security.util 0.0.0' but it could not be found
                <dependency>
                    <groupId>org.eclipse.persistence</groupId>
                    <artifactId>eclipselink</artifactId>
                    <version>4.0.0</version>
                    <type>jar</type>
                </dependency>
                -->
            </dependencies>
            <exclude>org.apache.ant:ant:1.10.12</exclude>
            <!-- PS: for org.eclipse.persistence:eclipselink the following is needed -->
            <exclude>jakarta.transaction:jakarta.transaction-api:2.0.1</exclude>
        </location>
    </locations>
</target>
```

177. Installation of the M2E-PDE integration

To use the Maven library integration in your target platform, the *M2E PDE Integration* must be installed in your IDE. If that extension is not installed, you can use the following update site to install it via **Help › Install New Software**.

```
https://download.eclipse.org/releases/latest
```

Install *M2E PDE Integration*.

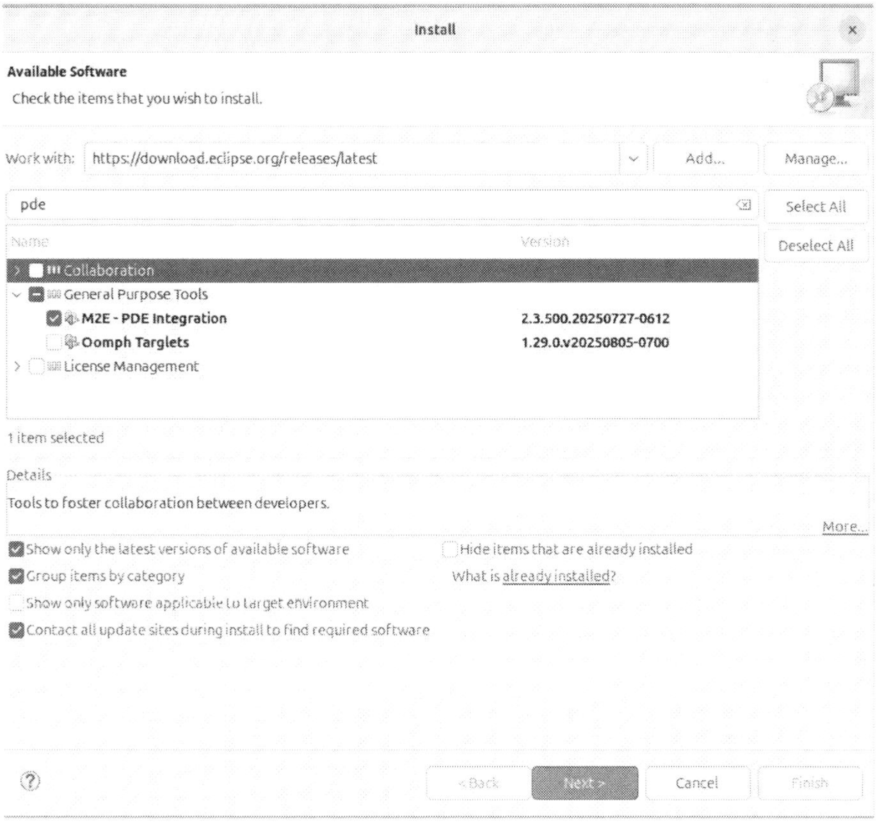

Restart your IDE after the installation.

178. Exercise: Using a Java library via Maven

In this exercise, you add a standard library to your target platform.

178.1. Add Gson library from Maven to the target platform

Open your target platform definition file and press the Add... button on the first tab.

Select Maven in the following dialog.

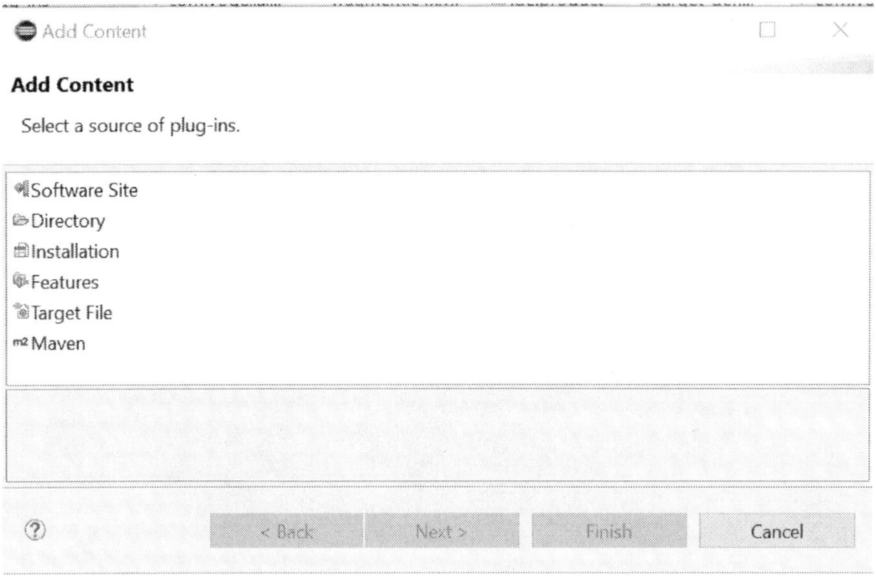

The Gson Maven coordinates that we use are listed below.

```
<dependency>
  <groupId>com.google.code.gson</groupId>
  <artifactId>gson</artifactId>
  <version>2.13.2</version>
</dependency>
```

If you copy a Maven dependency into the clipboard before pressing the add button, the information is used to populate the wizard.

Select to include dependencies. The *Dependencies depth* and *Dependencies scope* define whether dependent artifacts are included or only the master artifact itself. At the time of this writing, the Gson library has no dependencies.

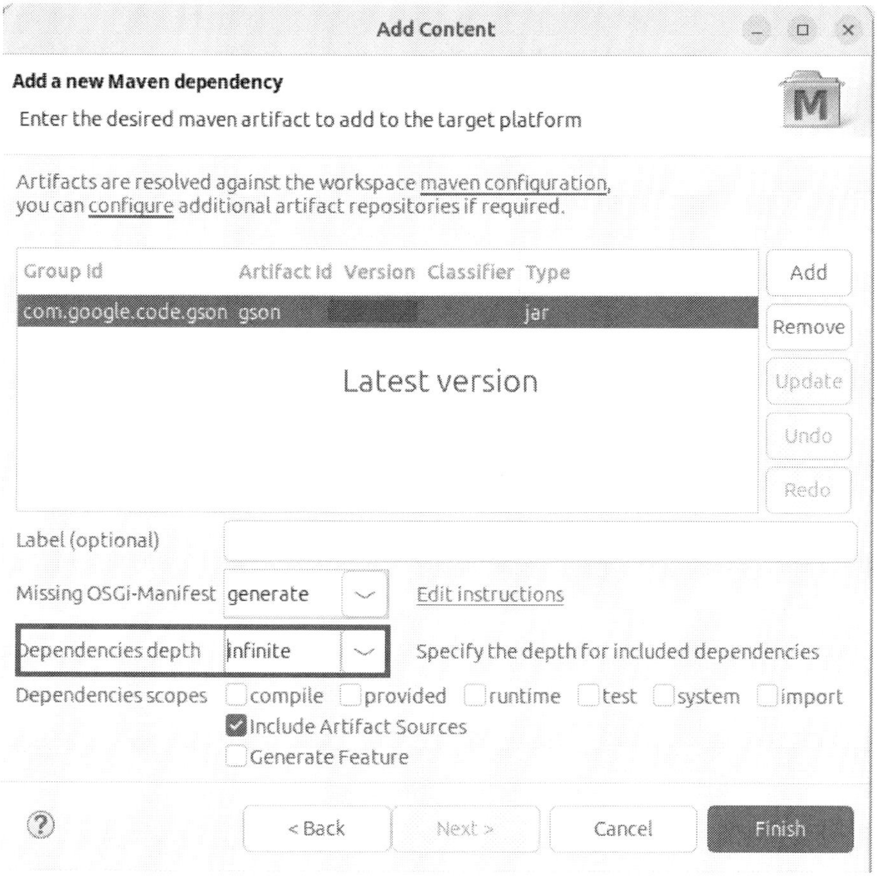

Press Finish. You can now use the library for your plug-in development, even if the original artifact did not contain the OSGi metadata.

178.2. Validate availability of the library

To test if the library is available for you to develop, open one manifest file for an existing plug-in and switch to the dependency tab. Press Add... and ensure that you can add the library as a dependency.

The version in the screenshot has been overdrawn, as this might change over time.

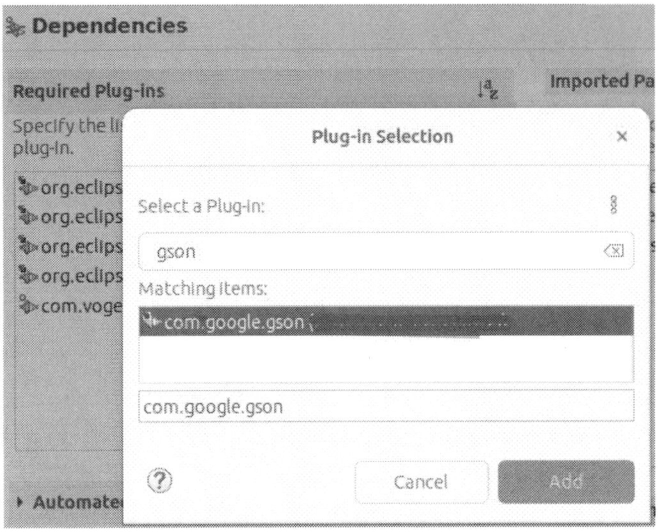

Sometimes you have to restart the IDE to make the update of the target platform available for the MANIFEST.MF editor.

178.3. Add the new plug-in to the product

Add the Gson plug-in to your product via your feature and start your application.

How to exclude a certain dependency if you include the dependencies of a library

You can exclude dependencies of libraries. At the time of this writing, this does not follow the Maven syntax, see https://github.com/eclipse-m2e/m2e-core/issues/286.

```
<?xml version="1.0" encoding="UTF-8" standalone="no"?>
<?pde version="3.8"?>
Bind to grammar/schema...
<target name="target-with-source">
    <locations>
        <location includeDependencyDepth="infinite" includeDependencyScopes="compile" includ
            <dependencies>
                <dependency>
                    <groupId>org.apache.commons</groupId>
                    <artifactId>commons-geometry-euclidean</artifactId>
                    <version>1.0</version>
                    <type>jar</type>
                </dependency>
            </dependencies>
            <exclude>org.apache.commons:commons-numbers-core:1.0</exclude>
        </location>
    </locations>
</target>
```

This is added here for further information but is not required to exclude something for this exercise.

179. Optional exercise: Use Gson to persist the model

179.1. Changes in the data model

`PropertyChangeSupport` and `LocalDate` cannot be serialized (without custom Gson adapter implementations). Therefore, mark these fields as `transient` to ignore them during JSON persistence. Also, add a method to initialize this field after the objects are restored from JSON.

```
public class Task {

private transient PropertyChangeSupport changes = // ❶
// more code
private transient LocalDate dueDate = LocalDate.now();// ❷

// more code

    /**
     * Only needed for JSON serialization and deserialization
     */
    public void restorePropertyChangeListener() { // ❸
        if (Objects.isNull(changes)) {
            changes = new PropertyChangeSupport(this);
        }
    }
```

❶ Skips these fields during JSON serialization and deserialization

❷ Skips the local date field, as the default Gson cannot access this field, which we want to avoid using in this example

❸ New method used during JSON deserialization to recreate the listener

179.2. Add Gson as a dependency

Add `com.google.gson` as a required bundle to your `com.vogella.tasks.services` plug-in via its `MANIFEST.MF` file.

179.3. Add Gson to the feature

Add `com.google.gson` to your `com.vogella.tasks.feature` feature. Start via your product to update the launch configuration.

179.4. Use Gson to persist the data model

Implement the following helper class to handle the JSON persistence. This utility class reads from and writes the task model to the user's home directory using JSON.

```
package com.vogella.tasks.services.internal;

import java.io.File;
import java.io.IOException;
import java.lang.reflect.Type;
import java.nio.file.Files;
import java.nio.file.Paths;
import java.nio.file.StandardOpenOption;
import java.time.LocalDate;
import java.time.format.DateTimeFormatter;
import java.util.ArrayList;
import java.util.Collections;
import java.util.List;
import java.util.stream.Collectors;

import com.google.gson.Gson;
import com.google.gson.GsonBuilder;
import com.google.gson.JsonDeserializationContext;
import com.google.gson.JsonDeserializer;
import com.google.gson.JsonElement;
import com.google.gson.JsonParseException;
import com.google.gson.JsonPrimitive;
import com.google.gson.JsonSerializationContext;
import com.google.gson.JsonSerializer;
import com.google.gson.reflect.TypeToken;
import com.vogella.tasks.model.Task;

public class JSONUtil {

    private JSONUtil() {
        // Prevents instantiation of this utility class.
    }

    private static String fileName = "dataFile";

    public static void saveAsGson(List<Task> tasks) {
        final String dir = System.getProperty("user.dir");

        Gson gson = new GsonBuilder().setPrettyPrinting().registerTypeAdapter(LocalDate
.class, new LocalDateAdapter())
                .create();

        java.lang.reflect.Type type = new TypeToken<List<Task>>() {
        }.getType();
        String json = gson.toJson(tasks, type);

        try {
            Files.write(Paths.get(dir + File.separator + fileName), json.getBytes(),
```

```
StandardOpenOption.CREATE);
        } catch (IOException e) {
            // ignore
        }
    }

    public static List<String> readTextFileByLines(String fileName) {
        final String dir = System.getProperty("user.dir");
        try {
            return Files.readAllLines(Paths.get(dir + File.separator + fileName));
        } catch (IOException e) {
            return Collections.emptyList();
        }
    }

    public static List<Task> retrieveSavedData() {
        List<String> readTextFileByLines = readTextFileByLines(fileName);
        if (readTextFileByLines != null && !readTextFileByLines.isEmpty()) {
            Gson gson = new GsonBuilder().registerTypeAdapter(LocalDate.class, new
LocalDateAdapter()).create();

            var type = new TypeToken<List<Task>>() {
            }.getType();
            String string = readTextFileByLines.stream().collect(Collectors.joining());

            try {
                List<Task> fromJson = gson.fromJson(string, type);
                fromJson.forEach(Task::restorePropertyChangeListener);
                return fromJson;
            } catch (Exception e) {
                System.err.println("Error reading JSON: " + e.getMessage());
                return new ArrayList<>();
            }
        }
        return new ArrayList<>();
    }

    private static class LocalDateAdapter implements JsonSerializer<LocalDate>,
JsonDeserializer<LocalDate> {
        private static final DateTimeFormatter formatter = DateTimeFormatter
.ISO_LOCAL_DATE;

        @Override
        public JsonElement serialize(LocalDate date, Type typeOfSrc,
JsonSerializationContext context) {
            return new JsonPrimitive(date.format(formatter));
        }

        @Override
```

```
        public LocalDate deserialize(JsonElement json, Type typeOfT,
JsonDeserializationContext context)
                throws JsonParseException {
            return LocalDate.parse(json.getAsString(), formatter);
        }
    }
}
```

179.5. Save data in TransientTaskServiceImpl

In your `TransientTaskServiceImpl` implementation, persist your data via Gson. You can, for example, do this every time the user calls the `update` method.

The implementation of saving your content can for example look like the following:

```
    // create or update an existing instance of a task object
    @Override
    public synchronized boolean update(Task newTask) {
        // more code
        JSONUtil.saveAsGson(tasks); // ❶
        // the return statement remains the same
        return true;
    }
```

❶ Add this to the end of the method, it saves the data model

Also save the data model if the user deletes a task.

```
    @Override
    public boolean delete(long id) {
    // more code
        JSONUtil.saveAsGson(tasks);
        return deletedTask.isPresent();
    }
```

You can now read your saved data in the createTestData method. You also have to ensure that the ID counter is set correctly if you load existing data.

```
// Example data, change if you like
private List<Task> createTestData() {
    List<Task> list = JSONUtil.retrieveSavedData();
    if (list.isEmpty()) {
        // Create some initial content
        list = List.of(create("Application model", "Flexible and extensible"),
                create("DI", "@Inject as programming mode"),
```

```
                create("OSGi", "Services"),
                create("SWT", "Widgets"),
                create("JFace", "Especially Viewers!"),
                create("CSS Styling", "Style your application"),
                create("Eclipse services", "Selection, model, Part"),
                create("Renderer", "Different UI toolkit"),
                create("Compatibility Layer", "Run Eclipse 3.x"));
    } else {
        // Find the maximum ID from loaded tasks and set counter to start after it
        long maxId = list.stream()
                .mapToLong(Task::getId)
                .max()
                .orElse(0);
        current.set((int) maxId + 1);
    }
    return new ArrayList<>(list);
}
```

179.6. Validate that the persistence works

Change a few tasks, create a few and delete some. Restart your application and ensure that the data is the same as before the restart.

Use the debugger to identify the path where `JSONUtil` saves your file and check its content.

179.7. Perform the data save asynchronously

Currently the data is saved in the main thread. This might delay the application. Change the saving to asynchronous.

```
// more code in JSONUtil

private static final Object fileWriteLock = new Object();
private static final String fileName = "dataFile"; // Make sure this matches your
existing variable

public static CompletableFuture<Void> saveAsGson(List<Task> tasks) {
    return CompletableFuture.runAsync(() -> {
        final String dir = System.getProperty("user.dir");
        Gson gson = new GsonBuilder().setPrettyPrinting().create();
        java.lang.reflect.Type type = new TypeToken<List<Task>>() {}.getType();
        String json = gson.toJson(tasks, type);

        synchronized (fileWriteLock) {
            try {
                Files.write(Paths.get(dir + File.separator + fileName),
                        json.getBytes(), StandardOpenOption.CREATE, StandardOpenOption
```

```
.TRUNCATE_EXISTING);
            } catch (IOException e) {
                System.err.println("Failed to save JSON: " + e.getMessage());
            }
        }
    });
}

// more code in JSONUtil
```

Test again that the data is saved and correctly shown after a restart.

> Perform I/O operations, such as network or file access, asynchronously whenever possible.

Part XXV: Creating and using custom extension points

180. Extensions and Extension Points

Eclipse provides the concept of **extensions** to contribute functionality to a specific type of API. This type of API is defined by a plug-in through an **extension point**. Extensions can be contributed by one or more plug-ins.

These extensions and extension points are defined in the `plugin.xml` file.

This concept is illustrated in the following graphic, and the terminology is described in the subsequent table.

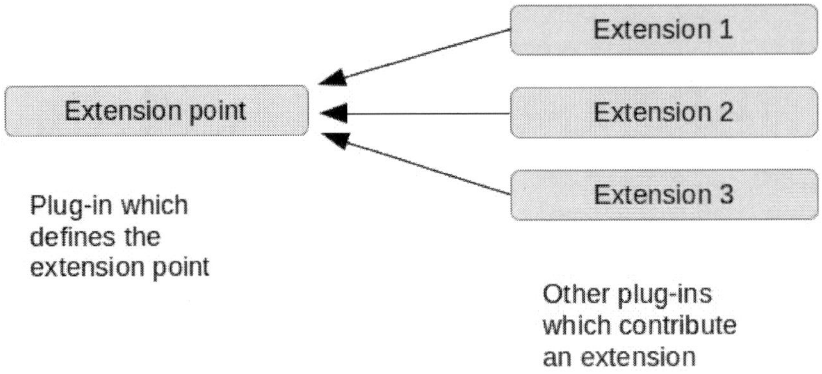

Table 34. Extensions and Extension Points

Term	Description
Plug in defines extension point	The plug in defines a contract (API) by declaring an extension point that allows other plug-ins to add contributions (extensions). The plug-in that defines the extension point is responsible for evaluating the extensions and typically contains the necessary code to do so.
Plug-in provides an extension	This plug-in provides an extension (contribution) based on the contract defined by an existing extension point. Contributions can consist of code or data.

181. Creating an extension point

A plug-in that declares an extension point must declare it in its *plugin.xml* file. You use the *Extension Points* tab for the definition.

Extension points are described via an XML schema file which is referred to in the *plugin.xml* file. This XML schema file defines the details and the contract of the extension point. The following code demonstrates the link to the schema file in the *plugin.xml* file.

```
<?xml version="1.0" encoding="utf-8"?>
<?eclipse version="3.2"?>
<plugin>
    <extension-point id="de.vogella.extensionpoint.greeters"
        name="Greeters"
        schema="schema/de.vogella.extensionpoint.greeters.exsd" />
</plugin>
```

The plug-in typically contains code to evaluate the extensions for this extension point.

182. Adding extensions to extension points

The Eclipse IDE provides an editor for the *plugin.xml* file. It is the same editor that is used for modifying the `MANIFEST.MF` file.

Select the *Extensions* tab in this editor to create new extensions. On the *Extension Points* tab you can define new extension points.

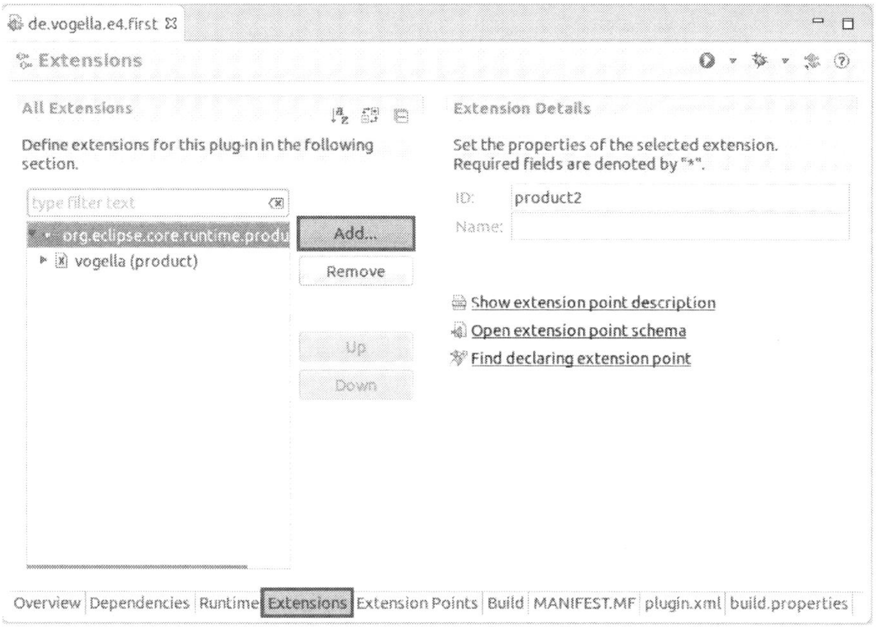

By using the Add... button you can add a new extension. After adding one extension you can right-click on it to add elements or attributes.

183. Accessing extensions

The information about all available extension points and the provided extensions are stored in a class of type `IExtensionRegistry`. The Eclipse platform reads the extension points and provided extensions once the plug-in is in the `RESOLVED` lifecycle status, as defined by the OSGi specification. Via an instance of this interface you can access all extensions in your running application.

To access it, you can use the dependency injection mechanism.

```
@Inject
public void doSomething(IExtensionRegistry registry){
    // do something
```

```
    registry.getConfigurationElementsFor("yourextension");
}
```

For objects not created by dependency injection, you can query a specific extension via the static methods of the `Platform` class. An example is listed in the following code.

```
Platform.getExtensionRegistry().getConfigurationElementsFor("yourextension");
```

184. Extension Factories

If you create your class directly via the `IConfigurationElement` class of the extension you are limited to classes that have a default constructor. To avoid this restriction you can use extension factories.

To use a factory, implement the `IExecutableExtensionFactory` interface and reference it in the `class` attribute of your extension point definition. The factory receives the configuration elements and can construct the required object.

185. Optional exercise: Create and evaluate an extension point

In this exercise, you create two new plug-ins. The first one contains an *extension point*. The second plug-in contributes an extension to the new extension point.

185.1. Creating a plug-in for the extension point definition

Create a new simple plug-in project called *com.vogella.extensionpoint.definition*. See Chapter 36 for more information.

185.2. Create an extension point

Open the `MANIFEST.MF` file or the *plugin.xml* file and select the *Extension Points* tab.

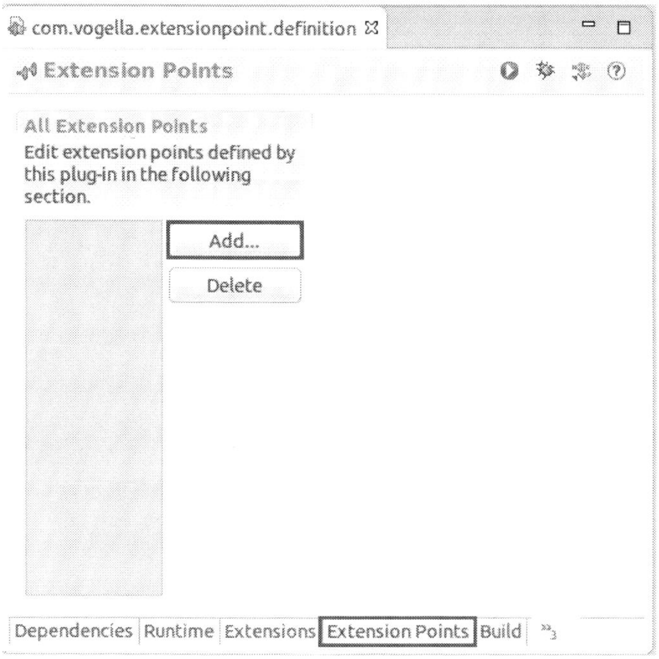

Press the Add... button.

Enter `com.vogella.extensionpoint.definition.greeter` as *Extension Point ID* and `Greeter` as *Extension Point Name* in the dialog. The *Extension Point Schema* field is automatically populated based on your input.

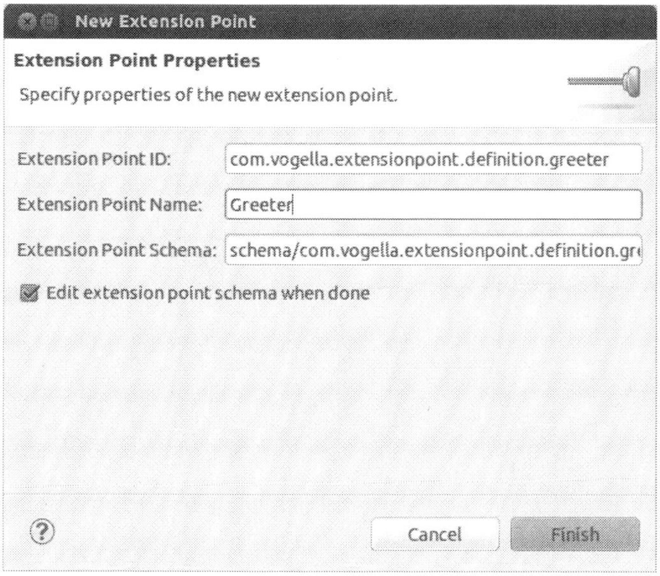

Press the Finish button. The definition of the extension is generated and the schema editor opens. Switch to the *Definition* tab.

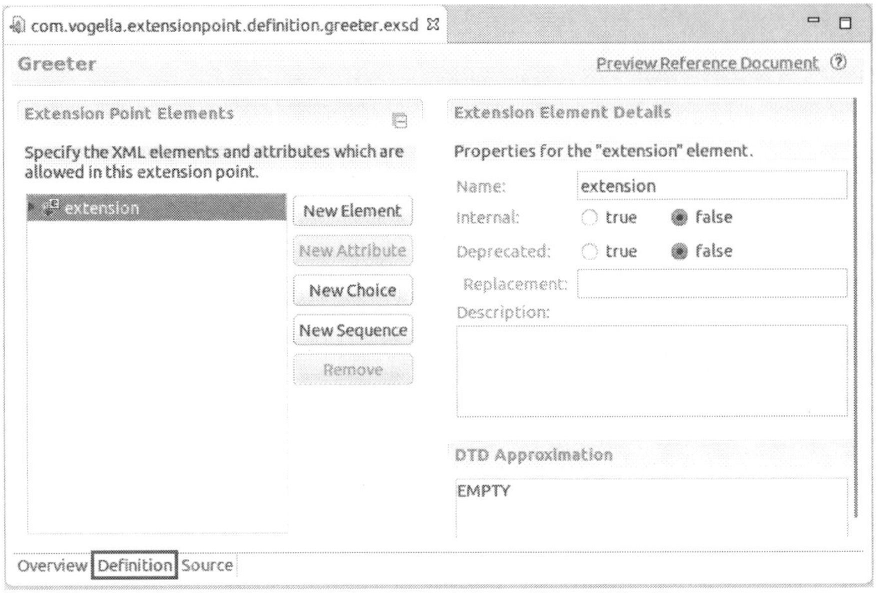

185.3. Add attributes to the extension point

Start by clicking the New Element button. Give the new element the name `client`.

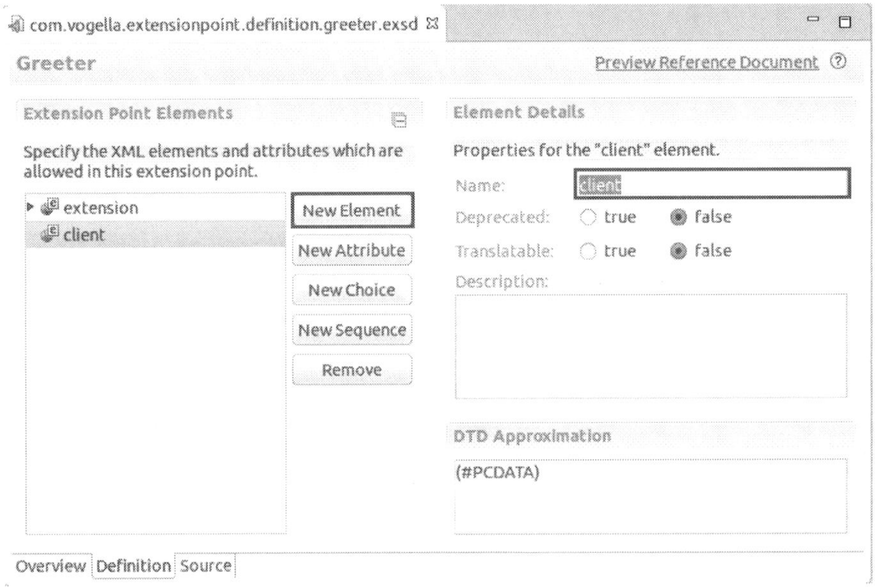

Select the "client" element and press *New Attribute*. Give the new element the name `class` and the type `java`. Enter `com.vogella.extensionpoint.definition.IGreeter` as interface name.

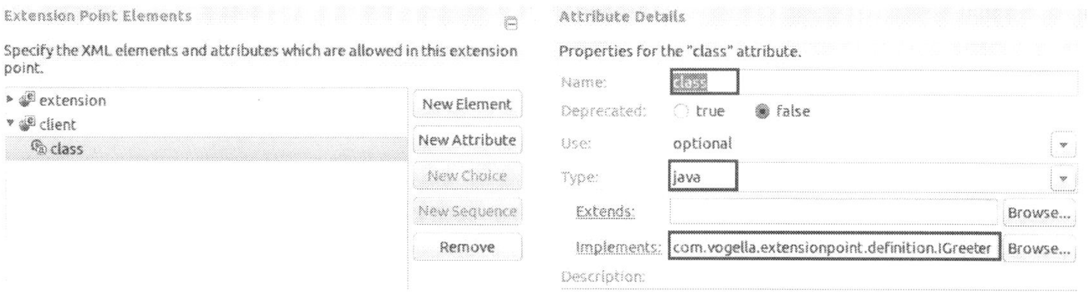

This interface does not exist yet. Press on the hyperlink called *Implements* to create it based on the following code.

```
package com.vogella.extensionpoint.definition;

public interface IGreeter {
    void greet();
}
```

Go back to your extension point definition and add a choice to the extension point. For this select the *extension* entry, right-click on it and select **New › Choice**. This defines how often the extension "client" can be provided by contributing plug-ins. We will set it as unbounded (no restrictions).

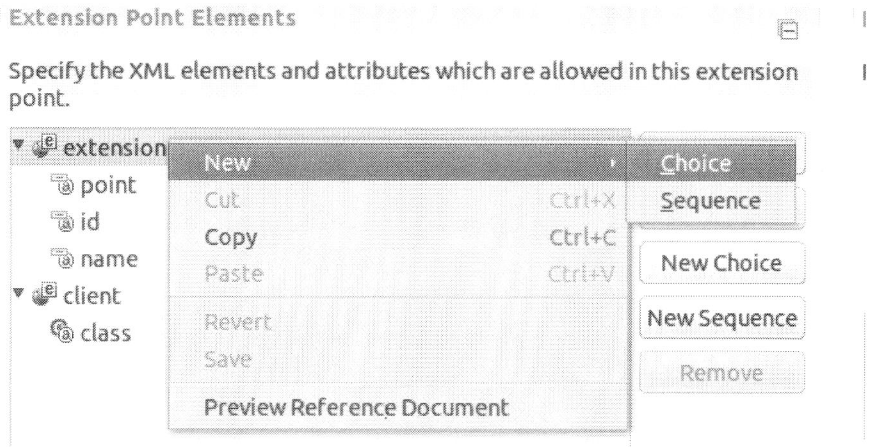

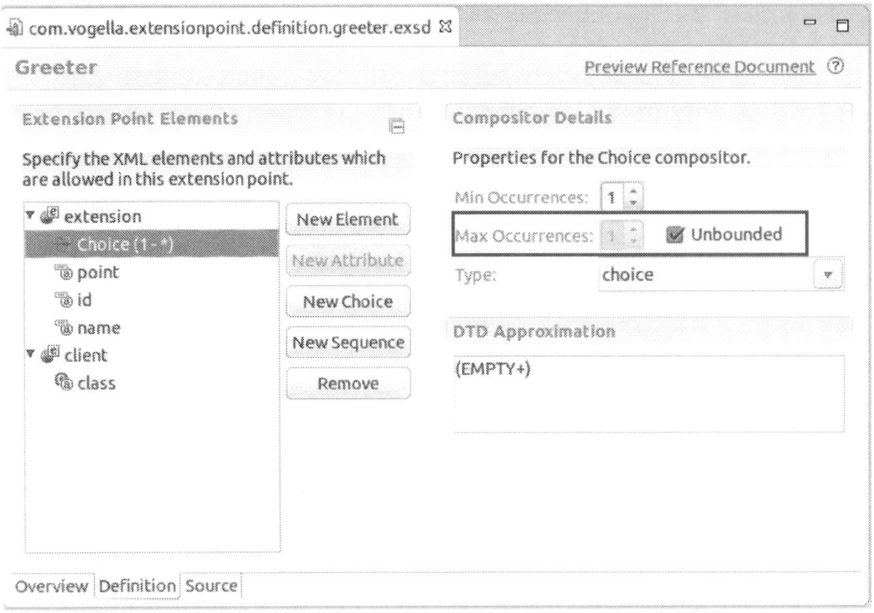

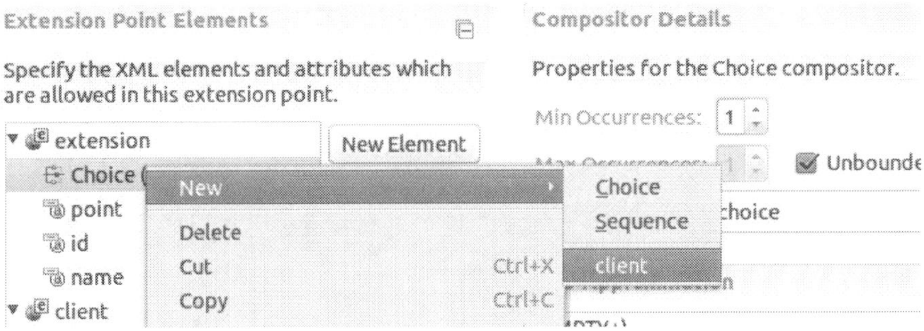

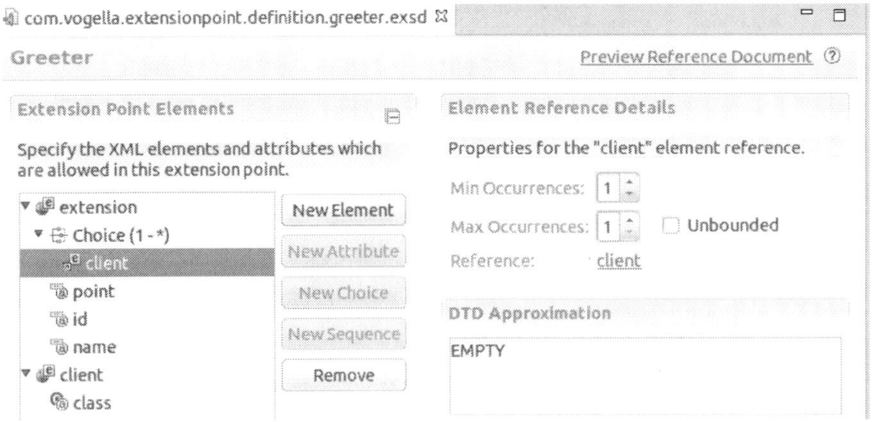

185.4. Export the package

Select the `MANIFEST.MF` file switch to the *Runtime* tab and export the package that contains the `IGreeter` interface.

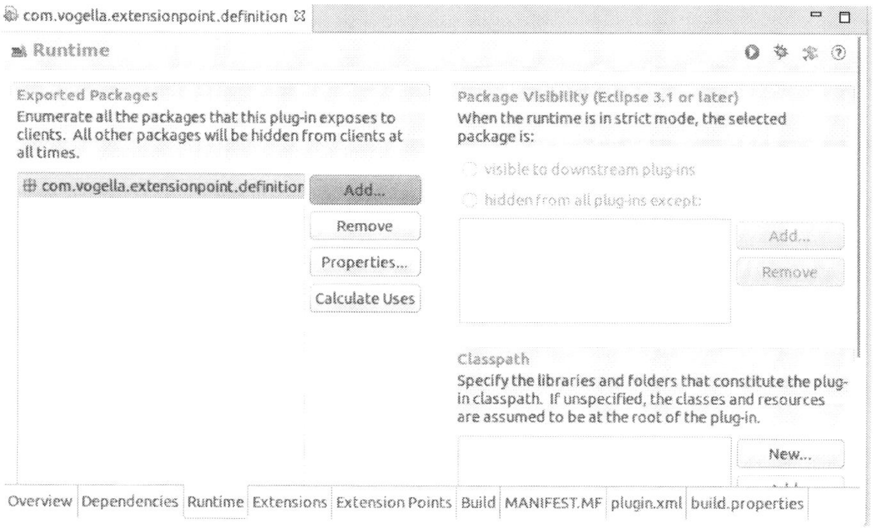

185.5. Add dependencies

Add the following dependencies via the `MANIFEST.MF` file of your new plug-in:

- `org.eclipse.core.runtime`
- `org.eclipse.e4.core.di`

185.6. Evaluating the registered extensions

The defining plug-in evaluates the existing extensions. In the following example, you create a handler class to evaluate the existing extensions.

Create the following class.

```
package com.vogella.extensionpoint.definition;

import org.eclipse.core.runtime.CoreException;
import org.eclipse.core.runtime.IConfigurationElement;
import org.eclipse.core.runtime.IExtensionRegistry;
import org.eclipse.core.runtime.ISafeRunnable;
import org.eclipse.core.runtime.SafeRunner;
import org.eclipse.e4.core.di.annotations.Execute;

public class EvaluateContributionsHandler {
    private static final String IGREETER_ID =
            "com.vogella.extensionpoint.definition.greeter";
    @Execute
    public void execute(IExtensionRegistry registry) {
        IConfigurationElement[] config =
                registry.getConfigurationElementsFor(IGREETER_ID);
```

```
        try {
            for (IConfigurationElement e : config) {
                System.out.println("Evaluating extension");
                final Object o =
                        e.createExecutableExtension("class");
                if (o instanceof IGreeter) {
                    executeExtension(o);
                }
            }
        } catch (CoreException ex) {
            System.out.println(ex.getMessage());
        }
    }

    private void executeExtension(final Object o) {
        ISafeRunnable runnable = new ISafeRunnable() {
            @Override
            public void handleException(Throwable e) {
                System.out.println("Exception in client");
            }

            @Override
            public void run() throws Exception {
                ((IGreeter) o).greet();
            }
        };
        SafeRunner.run(runnable);
    }
}
```

The code above uses the `ISafeRunnable` interface. This interface protects the plug-in that defines the extension point from malfunctioning extensions. If an extension throws an `Exception`, it is caught by `ISafeRunnable` and the remaining extensions are still executed.

Review the *.exsd* schema file and the reference to this file in the *plugin.xml* file.

185.7. Create a menu entry and add it to the product

Add a dependency to the `com.vogella.extensionpoint.definition` plug-in in the `MANIFEST.MF` file of your application plug-in.

Afterwards, create a new menu entry called *Evaluate extensions* and define a command and handler for this menu entry. In the handler, reference the `EvaluateContributionsHandler` class.

> A better approach is to add the menu entry via a model fragment or a model processor; this is left as an additional exercise for the reader.

185.8. Providing an extension

Create a new simple plug-in called *com.vogella.extensionpoint.contribution*. See Chapter 36 for more information.

Open the `MANIFEST.MF` editor of this new plug-in and select the *Dependencies* tab.

Add the `com.vogella.extensionpoint.definition` and `org.eclipse.core.runtime` plug-ins as dependencies. Ensure that the *This plug-in is a singleton* flag is enabled on the *Overview* tab of your `MANIFEST.MF` file.

Switch to the *Extensions* tab and select Add... . Select your custom extension point and press the Finish button.

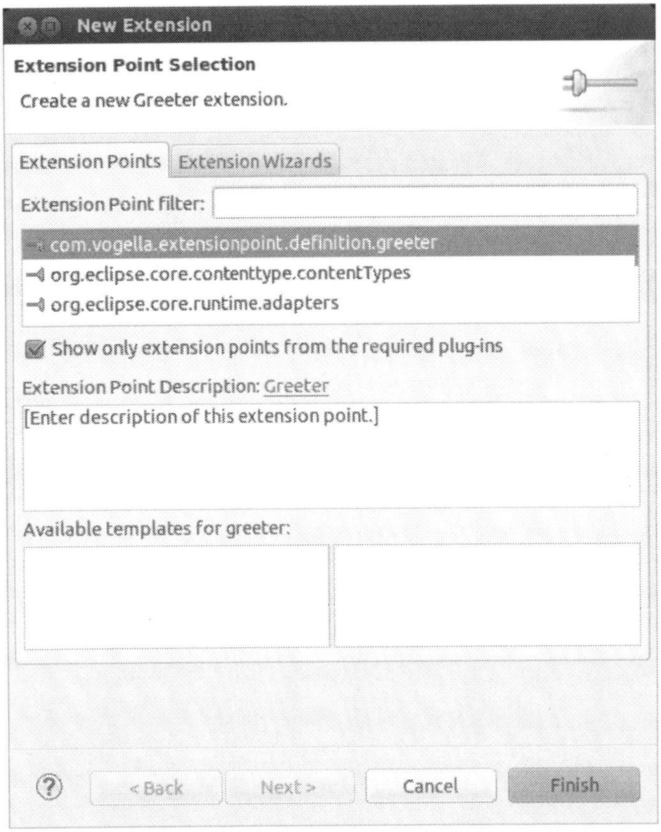

Add a client element to your extension point via right-click.

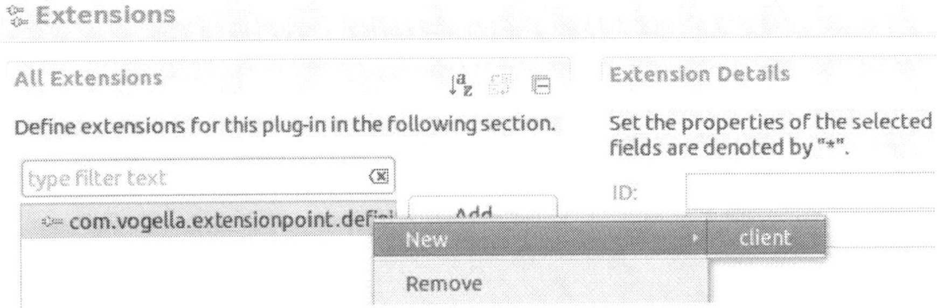

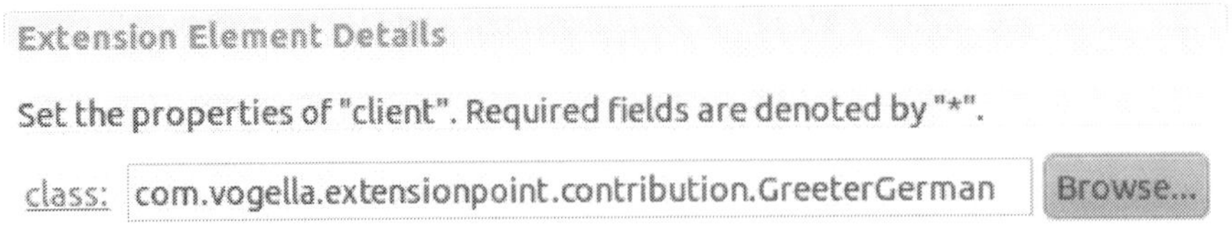

Create the `GreeterGerman` class with the following code.

```
package com.vogella.extensionpoint.contribution;
```

```java
import com.vogella.extensionpoint.definition.IGreeter;

public class GreeterGerman implements IGreeter {

    @Override
    public void greet() {
        System.out.println("Hallo!");
    }
}
```

185.9. Update product

Add the new plug-ins to your product (via your feature configuration).

- `com.vogella.extensionpoint.contribution`
- `com.vogella.extensionpoint.definition`

185.10. Validate

Start your application using the product configuration file. This updates the plug-ins included in the run configuration.

In your running application select your new menu entry. The handler class writes the output of your extensions to the *Console* view of your Eclipse IDE.

Part XXVI: The renderer framework

186. Renderer framework

186.1. Customizing UI rendering

The Eclipse framework supports customizing how model elements are represented and even allows replacing SWT with different UI toolkits. A *renderer factory* within Eclipse assigns each model element a corresponding *renderer object*.

A renderer object is responsible for:

- creating UI objects for model elements
- monitoring and responding to changes in these elements

By default, Eclipse uses the SWT-based `WorkbenchRendererFactory`. The `org.eclipse.e4.ui.workbench.renderers.swt` plug-in provides this default implementation.

186.2. Understanding renderer factories and objects

A renderer factory follows the `IRendererFactory` interface, returning `AbstractPartRenderer` objects through its `getRenderer()` method.

For example, for `MPart` instances, the default Eclipse renderer factory creates

ContributedPartRenderer objects, as shown in the WorkbenchRendererFactory class below.

```
// Other if statements above
else if (uiElement instanceof MPart) {
    if (contributedPartRenderer == null) {
        contributedPartRenderer = new ContributedPartRenderer();
        initRenderer(contributedPartRenderer);
    }
    return contributedPartRenderer;
}
```

186.3. Context management for model objects

Model elements extending MContext have an IEclipseContext object created and populated by their renderer.

For example, ContributedPartRenderer, the default renderer for MPart elements, creates a Composite and injects it into the local context of each part.

186.4. Implementing a custom renderer

The Eclipse platform allows extending or replacing default renderer classes. For instance, you can modify the stack renderer to position tabs at the bottom.

You can implement a renderer for UI toolkits other than SWT, such as JavaFX or Swing. Switching from SWT to another UI technology allows reusing non-UI logic (services, application model, etc.). However, UI components need to be re-implemented. A part written in SWT must be converted to JavaFX to integrate with a JavaFX renderer.

A custom renderer factory is registered via the org.eclipse.core.runtime.products extension point, using the rendererFactoryUri property to specify the custom factory class.

186.5. Customizing renderers for specific model elements

To replace a renderer for a single model element, add the Custom Renderer string from the IPresentationEngine.CUSTOM_RENDERER_KEY constant to the model element's persistentData map. The key's value should be the URI of the desired renderer.

186.6. Tags supported by the default renderer

The IPresentationEngine interface defines constants to customize the application layout and behavior.

Table 35. IPresentationEngine Constants Overview

Constant	Description
STANDALONE	Can be added as *tag* to a `MPartStack` so that only one single part can be shown in that stack.
NO_AUTO_COLLAPSE	Any `MElementContainer<T>` collapses by default when its children are removed. For example, if all parts in a part stack are closed, the stack disappears automatically. To keep the part stack visible even when it is empty, apply the *NO_AUTO_COLLAPSE* tag.
NO_MOVE	When this tag is applied to an `MUIElement`, it cannot be moved anymore, e.g., by drag and drop.
STYLE_OVERRIDE_KEY	This constant can be used as a key in a persisted state of an `MUIElement` to override the SWT style flag that is passed to the widget. One example would be the removal of the trim of a `MWindow's `Shell` by specifying `SWT.NO_TRIM` in the persisted state.
MAXIMIZED / MINIMIZED	When applied to an `MPartStack` as a tag, the stack will be maximized or minimized.

`IPresentationEngine` constants are detailed in their JavaDoc, providing a useful reference.

The active `IPresentationEngine` can be obtained by using dependency injection.

```
@Inject
private IPresentationEngine presentationEngine;
```

Available methods are:

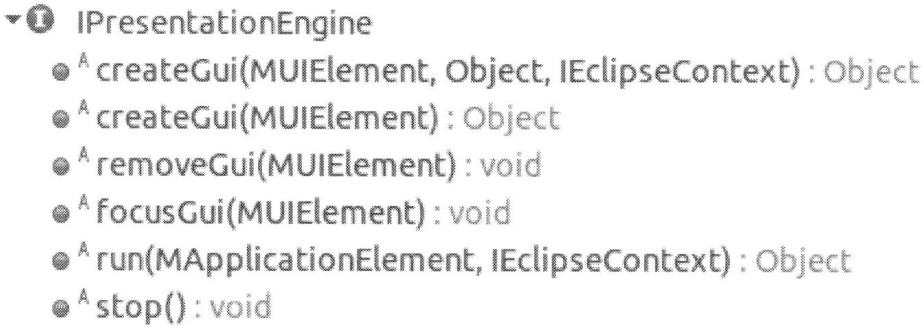

A `Toolbar` widget, assuming the *com.vogella.e4.renderer.toolbar* snippet is an MToolbar, could be populated like this:

```
Composite parent = // ...
MApplication app = // ...
EModelService modelService = // ...
IEclipseContext eclipseContext = // ...

ToolBar toolBar = new ToolBar(parent, SWT.NONE);
MUIElement mtoolbarSnippet = modelService.cloneSnippet(app,
"com.vogella.e4.renderer.toolbar", null);
presentationEngine.createGui(mtoolbarSnippet, toolBar, eclipseContext);
```

186.7. Alternative renderer for SWT

Any user interface technology can be adopted for RCP applications if a corresponding renderer is available. Unfortunately, despite several attempts, no alternative renderer has reached a stable open-source status.

At the time of this writing, SWT evaluates whether a cross-platform framework can be used for the SWT implementation. See https://github.com/swt-initiative31 for details

187. Optional exercise: Define a custom renderer

The following exercise serves as a simple example for creating a custom renderer. It implements a custom stack renderer that uses "**Demo *" instead of** "" to mark an editor as dirty.

187.1. Creating a plug-in

Create a new simple plug-in called *com.example.e4.renderer.swt*. See Chapter 36 for more information. This plug-in is called the `renderer` plug-in in the following description.

187.2. Add the dependencies

Add the following entries as plug-in dependencies to your `renderer` plug-in.

- `org.eclipse.e4.core.contexts`
- `org.eclipse.e4.ui.workbench.renderers.swt`
- `org.eclipse.e4.ui.workbench.swt`
- `org.eclipse.e4.ui.workbench`
- `org.eclipse.e4.core.services`
- `org.eclipse.e4.ui.model.workbench`
- `org.eclipse.swt`

187.3. Create the renderer implementation

In your `renderer` plug-in, create the `com.example.e4.renderer.swt` package and the following classes. The new stack renderer extends the stack renderer from the Eclipse platform.

```
package com.example.e4.renderer.swt;

import org.eclipse.e4.ui.model.application.ui.MDirtyable;
import org.eclipse.e4.ui.model.application.ui.MUILabel;
import org.eclipse.e4.ui.model.application.ui.basic.MPart;
import org.eclipse.e4.ui.workbench.UIEvents;
import org.eclipse.e4.ui.workbench.renderers.swt.StackRenderer;
import org.eclipse.swt.custom.CTabItem;

public class MyStackRenderer extends StackRenderer {

    private String getLabel(MUILabel itemPart, String newName) {
        if (newName == null) {
            newName = ""; //$NON-NLS-1$
        }
        if (itemPart instanceof MDirtyable && ((MDirtyable) itemPart).isDirty()) {
            newName = '*' + newName; //$NON-NLS-1$
        }
        return newName;
    }

    protected void updateTab(CTabItem cti, MPart part, String attName,
            Object newValue) {
        if (UIEvents.UILabel.LABEL.equals(attName)) {
            String newName = (String) newValue;
            cti.setText(getLabel(part, newName));
        } else if (UIEvents.UILabel.ICONURI.equals(attName)) {
            cti.setImage(getImage(part));
        } else if (UIEvents.UILabel.TOOLTIP.equals(attName)) {
            String newTTip = (String) newValue;
            cti.setToolTipText(newTTip);
        } else if (UIEvents.Dirtyable.DIRTY.equals(attName)) {
            Boolean dirtyState = (Boolean) newValue;
            String text = cti.getText();
            boolean hasExclamationMark = text.length() > 0 && text.charAt(0) == '!';
            if (dirtyState.booleanValue()) {
                if (!hasExclamationMark) {
                    cti.setText("* Demo *" + text);
                }
            } else if (hasExclamationMark) {
                cti.setText(text.substring(1));
            }
        }
```

```
    }
}
```

```
package com.example.e4.renderer.swt;

import org.eclipse.e4.ui.internal.workbench.swt.AbstractPartRenderer;
import org.eclipse.e4.ui.model.application.ui.MUIElement;
import org.eclipse.e4.ui.model.application.ui.basic.MPart;
import org.eclipse.e4.ui.model.application.ui.basic.MPartStack;
import org.eclipse.e4.ui.workbench.renderers.swt.WorkbenchRendererFactory;

public class MyRendererFactory extends WorkbenchRendererFactory {
    private MyStackRenderer stackRenderer;

    @Override
    public AbstractPartRenderer getRenderer(MUIElement uiElement, Object parent) {
        if (uiElement instanceof MPartStack) {
            if (stackRenderer == null) {
                stackRenderer = new MyStackRenderer();
                super.initRenderer(stackRenderer);
            }
            return stackRenderer;
        }
        return super.getRenderer(uiElement, parent);
    }
}
```

187.4. Register the renderer

Register your renderer in the *plugin.xml* file of your `com.vogella.tasks.ui` plug-in. For this, create a new property on the extension for your product. Use `rendererFactoryUri` as name and `bundleclass://com.example.e4.renderer.swt/com.example.e4.renderer.swt.MyRendererFactory` as a value. This setting is similar to the `applicationCSS` or `lifeCycleURI` properties; therefore, you should know how to configure it.

```
<?xml version="1.0" encoding="UTF-8"?>
<?eclipse version="3.4"?>
<plugin>

   <extension
         id="product"
         point="org.eclipse.core.runtime.products">
      <product
            name="to-do"
            application="org.eclipse.e4.ui.workbench.swt.E4Application">
         <property
```

```
                name="appName"
                value="to-do">
          </property>
          <property>
                name="cssTheme"
                value="com.vogella.eclipse.css.dark">
          </property>
          <property>
                name="rendererFactoryUri"

value="bundleclass://com.example.e4.renderer.swt/com.example.e4.renderer.swt.MyRendererFa
ctory">
          </property>
       </product>
    </extension>

</plugin>
```

187.5. Validate

Start your application and modify a task in your `TodoDetailsPart`. The dirty indicator should now appear as shown below.

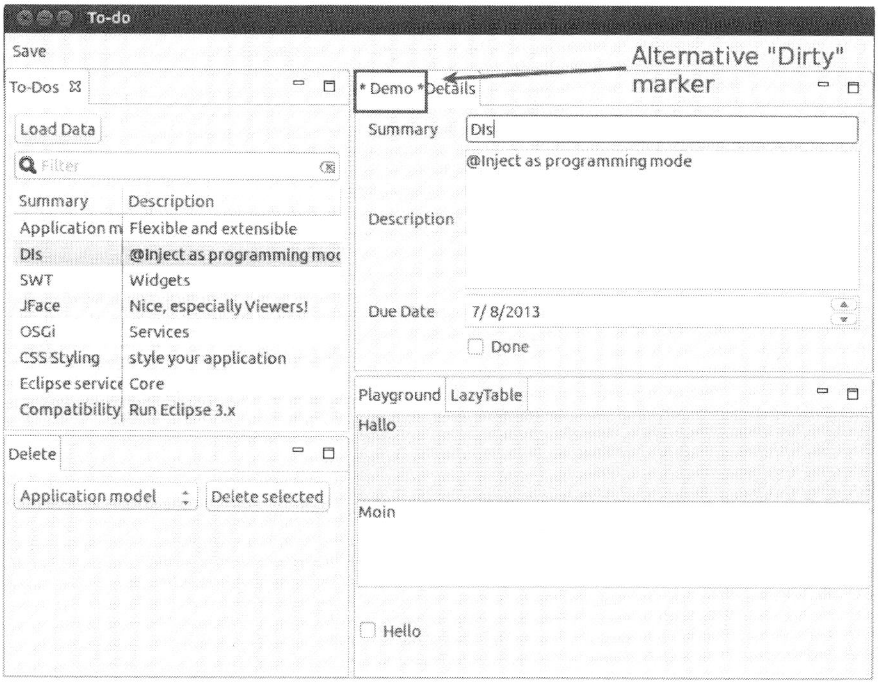

188. Exercise: A custom part renderer

188.1. Optional exercise: Create a custom part renderer

In this exercise, you create a custom part renderer that renders all parts with an SWT browser widget.

> This is just a demonstration of the technology. After you test it, you may want to remove this renderer configuration.

```
package com.example.e4.renderer.swt;

import org.eclipse.e4.ui.model.application.ui.MUIElement;
import org.eclipse.e4.ui.workbench.renderers.swt.SWTPartRenderer;
import org.eclipse.swt.SWT;
import org.eclipse.swt.browser.Browser;
import org.eclipse.swt.layout.GridData;
import org.eclipse.swt.layout.GridLayout;
import org.eclipse.swt.widgets.Composite;

public class MyPartRenderer extends SWTPartRenderer {

    @Override
    public Object createWidget(MUIElement element, Object parent) {
        final Composite mapComposite = new Composite((Composite) parent, SWT.NONE);
        mapComposite.setLayout(new GridLayout(1, false));
        final Browser browser = new Browser(mapComposite, SWT.NONE);
        browser.setUrl("https://www.vogella.com/");
        GridData data = new GridData(SWT.FILL, SWT.FILL, true, true);
        browser.setLayoutData(data);
        return mapComposite;
    }
}
```

Extend the `MyRendererFactory` to the following to use your own part renderer.

```
package com.example.e4.renderer.swt;

import org.eclipse.e4.ui.internal.workbench.swt.AbstractPartRenderer;
import org.eclipse.e4.ui.model.application.ui.MUIElement;
import org.eclipse.e4.ui.model.application.ui.basic.MPart;
import org.eclipse.e4.ui.model.application.ui.basic.MPartStack;
import org.eclipse.e4.ui.workbench.renderers.swt.WorkbenchRendererFactory;

public class MyRendererFactory extends WorkbenchRendererFactory {
```

```
    private MyStackRenderer stackRenderer;
    private MyPartRenderer partRenderer;

    @Override
    public AbstractPartRenderer getRenderer(MUIElement uiElement, Object parent) {

        if (uiElement instanceof MPart) {
            if (partRenderer == null) {
                partRenderer = new MyPartRenderer();
                super.initRenderer(partRenderer);
            }
            return partRenderer;
        } else if (uiElement instanceof MPartStack) {
            if (stackRenderer == null) {
                stackRenderer = new MyStackRenderer();
                super.initRenderer(stackRenderer);
            }
            return stackRenderer;
        }
        return super.getRenderer(uiElement, parent);
    }
}
```

188.2. Verifying the usage of the part renderer

Run your application and verify that every part is now rendered as a browser.

> At present, all parts show the same URL, but you could extend your renderer to access tags in the parts to determine the URLs to be used.

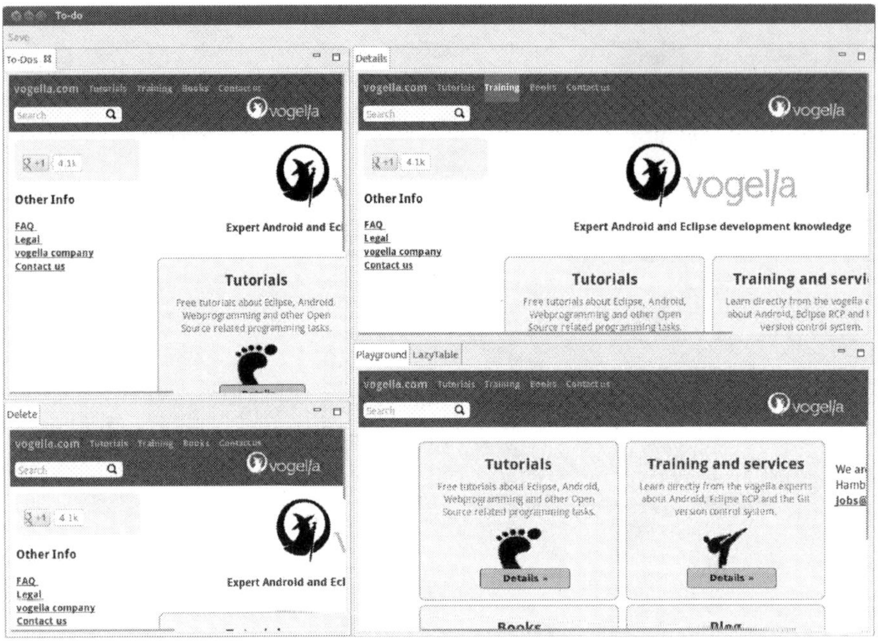

After finishing the test, remove the `rendererFactoryUri` property from the *plugin.xml* file of your application plug-in so that your application works again as before.

188.3. Using the part renderer for a specific part

For testing, configure one of your parts to use the custom renderer via its persisted state model data:

- Key: Custom Renderer
- Value: `bundleclass://com.example.e4.renderer.swt/com.example.e4.renderer.swt.MyPartRenderer`

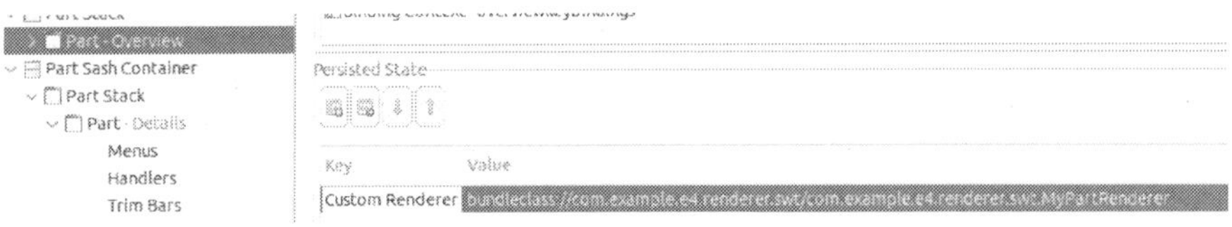

Ensure that the defined part uses the custom renderer. Remove the persisted state afterwards.

Part XXVII: Model persistence

189. Optional exercise: Saving and restoring a perspective

This exercise teaches you how to save and restore the state of a perspective. This exercise assumes that you already know how to:

- create application model entries for menus, handlers, and commands
- link a Java class to a handler in the application model

You can do this exercise in your main application model, one of your existing plug-ins, or in a new plug-in, depending on your personal preference.

189.1. Create application model elements

To add these actions to the application's main menu, you define the required commands, handlers, and menu contributions in the application model, as shown in the screenshot below.

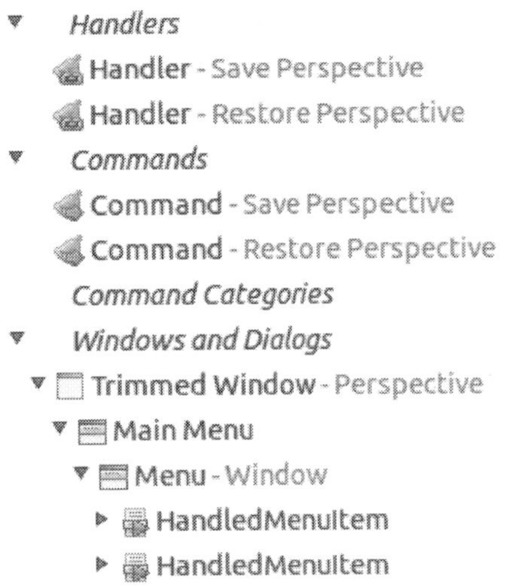

Ensure that the perspective includes movable and closable parts to modify its layout. This allows verification that the previously saved perspective state is restored correctly.

189.2. Dynamically creating and saving new perspectives

The save handler retrieves the active perspective from EModelService and clones it into the window model element. You can add it to the window model element as `MWindow` implements `MSnippetContainer`.

Since `MApplication` implements `MSnippetContainer`, you can save the snippet application-wide by passing `MApplication` as the second parameter to the `cloneElement` method.

```
package com.vogella.tasks.ui.handlers;

import org.eclipse.e4.core.di.annotations.Execute;
import org.eclipse.e4.ui.model.application.ui.advanced.MPerspective;
import org.eclipse.e4.ui.model.application.ui.basic.MWindow;
import org.eclipse.e4.ui.workbench.modeling.EModelService;

public class SavePerspectiveHandler {

    @Execute
    public void execute(EModelService modelService, MWindow window) {
        MPerspective activePerspective = modelService.getActivePerspective(window);

        if (activePerspective == null) {
            return;
        }

        // Clone the perspective
        MPerspective clonedPerspective = (MPerspective) modelService.cloneElement
```

```
(activePerspective, window);

        // Add the cloned perspective to the window
        window.getSnippets().add(clonedPerspective);
    }
}
```

189.3. Implement restoring the state of a perspective

Create the following class as a handler and add a new menu entry to the application model for it.

```
package com.vogella.tasks.ui.handlers;

import java.util.List;

import org.eclipse.e4.core.di.annotations.CanExecute;
import org.eclipse.e4.core.di.annotations.Execute;
import org.eclipse.e4.ui.model.application.ui.MElementContainer;
import org.eclipse.e4.ui.model.application.ui.MUIElement;
import org.eclipse.e4.ui.model.application.ui.advanced.MPerspective;
import org.eclipse.e4.ui.model.application.ui.advanced.MPlaceholder;
import org.eclipse.e4.ui.model.application.ui.basic.MWindow;
import org.eclipse.e4.ui.workbench.modeling.EModelService;
import org.eclipse.e4.ui.workbench.modeling.EPartService;

public class RestorePerspectiveHandler {

    @Execute
    public void execute(EModelService modelService, MWindow window, EPartService
partService) {
        MPerspective activePerspective = modelService.getActivePerspective(window);
        MUIElement findSnippet = modelService.findSnippet(window, activePerspective
.getElementId());

        if (!(findSnippet instanceof MPerspective)) {
            return;
        }

        // Clone the snippet so the original stays intact
        MPerspective restoredPerspective = (MPerspective) modelService.cloneElement
(findSnippet, window);

        MElementContainer<MUIElement> parent = activePerspective.getParent();
        modelService.removePerspectiveModel(activePerspective, window);
        parent.getChildren().add(restoredPerspective);

        // we remove shared placeholders and the shared reference has not been included
in the copy
```

```
        removeInvalidPlaceholders(findSnippet, modelService);

        partService.switchPerspective((MPerspective) findSnippet);
    }

    private void removeInvalidPlaceholders(MUIElement element, EModelService
modelService) {
        List<MPlaceholder> placeholders = modelService.findElements(element, null,
MPlaceholder.class, null);

        for (MPlaceholder placeholder : placeholders) {
            if (placeholder.getRef() == null) {
                MElementContainer<MUIElement> parent = placeholder.getParent();
                if (parent != null) {
                    parent.getChildren().remove(placeholder);
                }
            }
        }
    }

    @CanExecute
    public boolean canExecute(EModelService modelService, MWindow window) {
        MPerspective activePerspective = modelService.getActivePerspective(window);
        return modelService.findSnippet(window, activePerspective.getElementId()) !=
null;
    }
}
```

Create a snippet for a perspective's default in your application model, using the same ID as the perspective to reset.

The `RestorePerspectiveHandler` executes only if a snippet with the same ID as the current perspective exists.

To restore a perspective, the current perspective is removed from the application model, entries from the snippet are added to the perspective stack as a new perspective, and the new perspective is activated.

> After restoring, the snippet is removed and you cannot restore it again.

189.4. Validate perspective saving and modification

Start your application, use the save perspective handler, and alter the perspective by moving or closing parts. Ensure parts can be closed by checking the close attribute in the application model.

Afterward, use the restore perspective handler to restore the state of your perspective.

190. Optional exercise - Using files for perspective persistence

This exercise implements the option to persist your current perspective in an external file. This requires that your application model uses perspectives.

190.1. Add manifest dependencies

Ensure that the following dependencies are entered in the manifest.

- `org.eclipse.emf.ecore`
- `org.eclipse.emf.ecore.xmi`

190.2. Implement a persistence handler

Create a new simple plug-in named `com.vogella.rcp.persistence.handlers`. See Chapter 36 for more information.

The following snippet shows a handler implementation. The handler saves the active perspective's model elements into an XMI file.

```
package com.vogella.rcp.persistence.handlers;

import java.io.File;
import java.io.FileOutputStream;
import java.io.IOException;

import org.eclipse.e4.core.di.annotations.Execute;
import org.eclipse.e4.ui.internal.workbench.E4XMIResourceFactory;
import org.eclipse.e4.ui.model.application.ui.MUIElement;
import org.eclipse.e4.ui.model.application.ui.advanced.MPerspective;
import org.eclipse.e4.ui.model.application.ui.basic.MWindow;
import org.eclipse.e4.ui.workbench.modeling.EModelService;
import org.eclipse.emf.ecore.EObject;
import org.eclipse.emf.ecore.resource.Resource;
import org.eclipse.jface.dialogs.MessageDialog;
import org.eclipse.swt.widgets.Shell;

public class SavePerspectiveHandler {

    @Execute
    public void execute(EModelService modelService, MWindow window, Shell shell) {

        // store model of the active perspective
        MPerspective activePerspective = modelService.getActivePerspective(window);
        if (activePerspective == null) {
```

```
            MessageDialog.openInformation(shell, "No perspective found", "Are you using
perspectives?");
            // no perspective found, return
            return;
        }

        // create a resource, which is able to store e4 model elements
        E4XMIResourceFactory e4xmiResourceFactory = new E4XMIResourceFactory();
        Resource resource = e4xmiResourceFactory.createResource(null);

        // You must clone the perspective as snippet, otherwise the running
        // application would break, because the saving process of the resource
        // removes the element from the running application model
        MUIElement clonedPerspective = modelService.cloneElement(activePerspective,
window);

        // add the cloned model element to the resource so that it may be stored
        resource.getContents().add((EObject) clonedPerspective);

        try (FileOutputStream outputStream = new FileOutputStream
(getFileNameForPersistence())) {
            resource.save(outputStream, null);
            MessageDialog.openInformation(shell, "Persisted perspective", "Persisted as "
+ getFileNameForPersistence());

        } catch (IOException ex) {
            throw new RuntimeException(ex);
        }
    }

    static String getFileNameForPersistence() {
        String currentUsersHomeDir = System.getProperty("user.home");
        return currentUsersHomeDir + File.separator + ".eclipse/perspective.xml";
    }
}
```

190.3. Load stored model elements

The created XMI file can be loaded via the `load` method of the `Resource` class.

The following snippet shows how to apply a stored perspective to an existing application model. In case an existing perspective with the same *elementId* as the one of the loaded perspective is found, it is removed. Afterwards, the code adds and switches to the loaded perspective.

```
package com.vogella.rcp.persistence.handlers;

import java.io.File;
import java.io.FileInputStream;
```

```
import java.io.FileOutputStream;
import java.io.IOException;
import java.util.List;

import org.eclipse.e4.core.di.annotations.Execute;
import org.eclipse.e4.ui.internal.workbench.E4XMIResourceFactory;
import org.eclipse.e4.ui.model.application.ui.MElementContainer;
import org.eclipse.e4.ui.model.application.ui.MUIElement;
import org.eclipse.e4.ui.model.application.ui.advanced.MPerspective;
import org.eclipse.e4.ui.model.application.ui.basic.MWindow;
import org.eclipse.e4.ui.workbench.modeling.EModelService;
import org.eclipse.e4.ui.workbench.modeling.EPartService;
import org.eclipse.emf.ecore.EObject;
import org.eclipse.emf.ecore.resource.Resource;
import org.eclipse.jface.dialogs.MessageDialog;
import org.eclipse.swt.widgets.Shell;

public class ConstructPerspectiveFromExternalSource {

    @Execute
    public void execute(EPartService partService, EModelService modelService, MWindow
window, Shell shell) throws IOException {

        // create a resource, which is able to store e4 model elements
        @SuppressWarnings("restriction")
        E4XMIResourceFactory e4xmiResourceFactory = new E4XMIResourceFactory();
        @SuppressWarnings("restriction")
        Resource resource = e4xmiResourceFactory.createResource(null);

        try (FileInputStream inputStream = new FileInputStream(SavePerspectiveHandler
.getFileNameForPersistence())) {

            // load the stored model element
            resource.load(inputStream, null);

            if (!resource.getContents().isEmpty()) {

                // after the model element is loaded it can be obtained from the
                // contents of the resource
                MPerspective loadedPerspective = (MPerspective) resource.getContents
().get(0);

                // get the parent perspective stack, so that the loaded
                // perspective can be added to it.
                MPerspective activePerspective = modelService.getActivePerspective(
window);
                MElementContainer<MUIElement> perspectiveParent = activePerspective
.getParent();
```

```
                // remove the current perspective, which should be replaced by
                // the loaded one
                List<MPerspective> alreadyPresentPerspective = modelService.findElements
(window,
                        loadedPerspective.getElementId(), MPerspective.class, null);
                for (MPerspective perspective : alreadyPresentPerspective) {
                    modelService.removePerspectiveModel(perspective, window);
                }

                // add the loaded perspective and switch to it
                perspectiveParent.getChildren().add(loadedPerspective);

                partService.switchPerspective(loadedPerspective);
                MessageDialog.openInformation(shell, "Perspective reset", "Reset
perspective");
            }
        }
    }
}
```

190.4. Add a handler, command and menu entry for the new handlers

As of now you should know how to add entries in your menu. Create new commands and handlers and menu entries to call your two new handler implementations.

Part XXVIII: Building Eclipse components with Maven

191. Using Maven Tycho to build Eclipse components

The process of generating an executable application from your source code is called *building your application*. A *headless build* builds your application using the command line or a *build server*, typically without user interaction. The outcome, packaged as a zip file, can then be delivered to end users.

Tycho [https://github.com/eclipse-tycho/tycho] is a collection of Maven plugins dedicated to building Eclipse plug-ins, features, products, and OSGi bundles. A Tycho build is configured via one or multiple *pom.xml* files.

At a minimum, one pom file is necessary to configure the Tycho build process. When building multiple Eclipse components, you typically define an extension named `extensions.xml` in the `.mvn` folder, so that standard Eclipse components do not need their own `pom.xml` file. If the individual modules require special build instructions, you can define separate `pom.xml` files for each module. Or you can set properties via the `build.properties` file, see https://github.com/eclipse-tycho/tycho/wiki/Tycho-Pomless#define-properties.

Example: The following entries in a build.properties file

```
pom.model.property.my-property = a-value
pom.model.property.another.flag = true
```

is equivalent to the following properties-section in the polyglot-pom within the same directory:

```
<properties>
  <my-property>a-value</my-property>
  <another.flag>true</another.flag>
</properties>
```

Optionally, each module can define its own pom file or utilize Tycho's functionality to derive this information from existing metadata.

192. Executing plug-in unit tests with Tycho

For the development of Eclipse components, it is common practice to have a separate test plug-in or fragment project for your tests.

Tycho supports pomless builds for plug-ins that contain tests. Test execution is performed via the Tycho Surefire plug-in, which is aware of plug-in dependencies.

> The runtime behavior of the Maven Tycho Surefire plug-in is slightly different from the Maven Surefire plug-in. Tycho Surefire tests run in the integration-test phase while regular Maven Surefire tests run in the test phase. The integration-test phase occurs between the package and install phases.

If you need to configure the tests, e.g., exclude some tests or specify parameters you can still provide your pom file for the test plug-in.

The Tycho Surefire plug-in supports the execution of non-UI-based and UI-based tests. If you want to run UI tests, you have to enable that explicitly via the `useUIHarness` parameter, as demonstrated by the following listing.

```
<project>
    <modelVersion>4.0.0</modelVersion>

    <!--parent pom... -->

    <artifactId>com.vogella.tycho.rcp.tests</artifactId>
    <version>1.0.0-SNAPSHOT</version>
    <packaging>eclipse-test-plugin</packaging>

    <build>
        <plugins>
```

```
        <plugin>
          <groupId>org.eclipse.tycho</groupId>
          <artifactId>tycho-surefire-plugin</artifactId>
          <version>${tycho.version}</version>
          <configuration>
              <useUIHarness>true</useUIHarness>
          </configuration>
        </plugin>
      </plugins>
    </build>
</project>
```

The tests are executed in a test runtime (based on OSGi), using the dependencies defined in the `MANIFEST.MF` file of the test plug-in. You can include more dependencies in features ("eclipse-feature"), plug-ins or fragments ("eclipse-plugin") or installable units ("p2-installable-unit"). If you define a dependency, you need to include its transitive dependencies in the test runtime, too.

```
<project>
 <modelVersion>4.0.0</modelVersion>

 <!--parent pom... -->

 <artifactId>com.vogella.tycho.rcp.tests</artifactId>
 <version>1.0.0-SNAPSHOT</version>
 <packaging>eclipse-test-plugin</packaging>

 <build>
  <plugins>
   <plugin>
    <groupId>org.eclipse.tycho</groupId>
    <artifactId>tycho-surefire-plugin</artifactId>
    <version>${tycho.version}</version>
    <configuration>
     <useUIHarness>true</useUIHarness>
     <dependencies>
      <dependency>
       <type>eclipse-feature</type>
       <artifactId>com.vogella.feature1</artifactId>
       <!-- This is the minimum required version -->
       <version>1.0.0</version>
      </dependency>
     </dependencies>
    </configuration>
   </plugin>
  </plugins>
 </build>
```

```
</project>
```

192.1. Selection of tests

Similar to the Maven Surefire plug-in, Tycho Surefire executes, by default, all test classes matching the following pattern:

- `**/Test*.java`
- `**/*Test.java`
- `**/*TestCase.java`
- `**/*Tests.java`

These included tests can be configured via the `includes` parameter.

```
<project>
    <modelVersion>4.0.0</modelVersion>

    <!--parent pom... -->

    <artifactId>com.vogella.tycho.rcp.tests</artifactId>
    <version>1.0.0-SNAPSHOT</version>
    <packaging>eclipse-test-plugin</packaging>

    <!-- Define to include all classes in the test run -->
    <build>
     <plugins>
      <plugin>
        <groupId>org.eclipse.tycho</groupId>
        <artifactId>tycho-surefire-plugin</artifactId>
        <version>${tycho.version}</version>
         <configuration>
          <includes>
            <include>**/*.class</include>
          </includes>
         </configuration>
       </plugin>
     </plugins>
    </build>
</project>
```

You can exclude tests from the run.

```
<project>
    <modelVersion>4.0.0</modelVersion>
```

```xml
    <!--parent pom...  -->

    <artifactId>com.vogella.tycho.rcp.tests</artifactId>
    <version>1.0.0-SNAPSHOT</version>
    <packaging>eclipse-test-plugin</packaging>

    <build>
        <plugins>

        <plugin>
         <groupId>org.eclipse.tycho</groupId>
         <artifactId>tycho-surefire-plugin</artifactId>
         <version>${tycho.version}</version>
            <configuration>
                <excludes>
                    <!-- Tests currently fail in the command line build -->
                    <exclude>ThisShouldNotRunViaTychoTests</exclude>
                </excludes>
            </configuration>
        </plugin>
        </plugins>
    </build>
</project>
```

You can specify a specific test or test suite to be executed.

This requires setting the `TestSuite` to the Bundle-Symbolic-Name of the plug-in and the `testClass` parameter to the fully qualified class.

```xml
<build>
 <plugins>
  <plugin>
    <groupId>org.eclipse.tycho</groupId>
     <artifactId>tycho-surefire-plugin</artifactId>
     <version>${tycho.version}</version>
     <configuration>
        <testSuite>org.eclipse.e4.ui.tests.css.swt</testSuite>
        <testClass>org.eclipse.e4.ui.tests.css.swt.CssSwtTestSuite</testClass>
     </configuration>
    </plugin>
 </plugins>
</build>
```

192.2. Using the correct JRE for the test execution

The JDT compiler can be configured to use the compiler source/target level according to MANIFEST.MF settings. It is possible to compile a Java 17 bundle using Java 17, even if the build process was started with a Java 21 JVM.

This does not work for running the tests. By default, the tests run with the build JVM. If your tests require, for example, Java 21, you need to start the build process using a Java 21 runtime.

193. Installing Maven

To run a Maven build from the command line, you need to install the Maven command-line tool. To verify if Maven is already installed, type the following command in your terminal:

```
mvn -version
```

If you see output that includes `Apache Maven`, you already have Maven installed. At the time of this writing, Tycho requires at least Maven 3.9.11. If that is your version you can skip this section.

193.1. Requirements

You need to have a Java SDK installed and set the JAVA_HOME environment variable to point to a valid Java SDK.

▼ *Downloading and installing Maven on Windows and Mac*

For a manual installation you can download Maven from the Maven Download [https://maven.apache.org/download.cgi] page. Extract the downloaded distribution to a selected folder on your computer and add the `M2_HOME` environment variable pointing to this directory. Add `M2_HOME/bin` to your path variable.

See Official Maven installation [https://maven.apache.org/download.html#Installation] for a detailed installation guide.

▼ *Downloading and installing Maven on Linux*

For Linux most distributions include Maven in their main repositories. On Ubuntu you can use the following command on the command line to install it.

```
sudo apt-get install maven
```

193.2. Validate installation

To validate that Maven was correctly installed, open a console and use the following command:

```
mvn -version
```

You should receive output feedback showing the version of Maven installed. It also includes the used Java version.

```
Maven home: /home/vogella/.sdkman/candidates/maven/current
Java version: 21, vendor: Eclipse Adoptium, runtime:
/home/vogella/.sdkman/candidates/java/21-tem
Default locale: en_US, platform encoding: UTF-8
OS name: "linux", version: "6.2.0-36-generic", arch: "amd64", family: "unix"
```

193.3. Optional: Code completion for bash shells

The bash shell is the default shell on Linux.

See https://github.com/juven/maven-bash-completion for a bash shell extension for the command line to have code completion for Maven commands. This should also work with the git bash from Windows.

193.4. Proxy settings

To configure your proxy, add a file named `.m2/settings.xml` to your user home with the proxy settings, similar to the following:

```
<settings>
  <proxies>
   <proxy>
      <id>example-proxy</id>
      <active>true</active>
      <protocol>http</protocol>
      <host>proxy.example.com</host>
      <port>8080</port>
      <username>proxyuser</username>
      <password>somepassword</password>
      <nonProxyHosts>www.google.com|*.example.com</nonProxyHosts>
    </proxy>
  </proxies>
</settings>
```

User and password are only required if your proxy requests basic authentication.

194. Exercise: Setting up a Maven build for an Eclipse application

You'll now learn how to configure a command line build using Maven Tycho for your Eclipse components. The description assumes that all artifacts are placed in the same top-level directory.

194.1. Enable the Tycho build extension

Create a configuration file in the main directory in which all your Eclipse artifacts are stored.

To do this, create a new directory named *.mvn* in the main directory.

To ensure consistent usage of the Tycho version in your build configuration files, create a file named `maven.config` in the `.mvn` directory with the following content.

```
-Dtycho.version=5.0.1
```

This defines the `tycho.version` property for your build. Now you can use this property in the `.mvn/extensions.xml` file and in your `pom.xml` file.

In the *.mvn* folder, create a new file named `extensions.xml` with the following content:

```
<extensions>
  <extension>
    <groupId>org.eclipse.tycho</groupId>
    <artifactId>tycho-build</artifactId>
    <version>${tycho.version}</version>
  </extension>
</extensions>
```

> This is difficult to do from the Eclipse IDE, as the top-level-folder is not inside a project. Use your file explorer and a regular text editor to create this file (this editor must allow saving the content as regular text).

194.2. Create a top-level pom file

Create the following *pom.xml* file in the top-level directory in which your Eclipse artifacts are stored.

> This is difficult to do from the Eclipse IDE, as the top-level-folder is not inside a project. Use your file explorer and a regular text editor to create this file (this editor must allow saving the content as regular text).

The following assumes that all your Eclipse artifacts are stored directly in the top-level directory. For example, the directory structure could look like this:

```
top-level-directory/
├── pom.xml
├── com.vogella.tasks.feature/
├── com.vogella.tasks.model/
├── com.vogella.tasks.services/
├── com.vogella.tasks.events/
├── com.vogella.contribute.parts/
├── com.vogella.tasks.ui.contribute/
├── com.vogella.eclipse.css/
├── com.vogella.tasks.product/
├── com.vogella.swt.widgets/
└── ...
```

The pom file should look like this:

```
<project>
 <modelVersion>4.0.0</modelVersion>
 <groupId>com.vogella.tycho</groupId>
 <artifactId>build</artifactId>
 <version>1.0.0-SNAPSHOT</version>
 <packaging>pom</packaging>

 <properties>
  <project.build.sourceEncoding>UTF-8</project.build.sourceEncoding>
 </properties>

 <build>
   <pluginManagement>
     <plugins>
       <plugin>
         <groupId>org.eclipse.tycho</groupId>
         <artifactId>tycho-p2-director-plugin</artifactId>
         <version>${tycho.version}</version>
       </plugin>
     </plugins>
   </pluginManagement>

  <plugins>
   <plugin>
    <groupId>org.eclipse.tycho</groupId>
    <artifactId>tycho-maven-plugin</artifactId>
    <version>${tycho.version}</version>
    <extensions>true</extensions>
   </plugin>
   <!--Enable the replacement of the SNAPSHOT version in the final product
```

```
configuration-->
   <plugin>
        <groupId>org.eclipse.tycho</groupId>
            <artifactId>tycho-packaging-plugin</artifactId>
             <version>${tycho.version}</version>
             <executions>
              <execution>
                <phase>package</phase>
                <id>package-feature</id>
                    <configuration>

<finalName>${project.artifactId}_${unqualifiedVersion}.${buildQualifier}</finalName>
                    </configuration>
            </execution>
        </executions>
    </plugin>
    <plugin>
    <groupId>org.eclipse.tycho</groupId>
    <artifactId>target-platform-configuration</artifactId>
    <version>${tycho.version}</version>
    <configuration>
     <!-- Optionally, set the Java version you are using-->
      <!--   <executionEnvironment>JavaSE-21</executionEnvironment>-->
     <environments>
      <environment>
       <os>linux</os>
       <ws>gtk</ws>
       <arch>x86_64</arch>
      </environment>
      <environment>
       <os>win32</os>
       <ws>win32</ws>
       <arch>x86_64</arch>
      </environment>
      <environment>
       <os>macosx</os>
       <ws>cocoa</ws>
       <arch>x86_64</arch>
      </environment>
     </environments>
    </configuration>
   </plugin>
  </plugins>
 </build>
  <modules>
   <!-- Fill later-->
 </modules>
</project>
```

The modules with your Eclipse artifacts will be added in the next exercise.

> tycho.version is provided by the maven.config file, you could also set it as property: `<tycho.version>5.0.1</tycho.version>`

194.3. Validate build setup

Run the build via `mvn clean verify`. This build should complete successfully. No build artifact is created. The output should be similar to the following:

```
[INFO] Scanning for projects...
[INFO]
[INFO] ----------------------< com.vogella.tycho:releng >----------------------
[INFO] Building releng 1.0.0-SNAPSHOT
[INFO] --------------------------------[ pom ]---------------------------------
[INFO]
[INFO] --- maven-clean-plugin:2.5:clean (default-clean) @ releng ---
[INFO] ------------------------------------------------------------------------
[INFO] BUILD SUCCESS
[INFO] ------------------------------------------------------------------------
[INFO] Total time:  0.984 s
[INFO] Finished at: 2020-09-07T09:36:03+02:00
[INFO] ------------------------------------------------------------------------
```

195. Exercise: Use a target platform for the build

You can now build Eclipse components that have only dependencies to Java runtime classes. To make additional libraries available, configure the build to use your target definition file. This target definition file specifies the available libraries for the build and should be used for development to ensure you compile against the same libraries.

You can add the target platform project to the build:

- By pointing directly to the target file
- Or by defining a Maven project for the target project

We use the first approach in this exercise, as it is easier.

> See below for a full listing of the top-level pom file.

Adjust the target-platform-configuration to use your target file. This code assumes that you have one project named *target-platform* with your target definition file named *target-platform.target*.

```
<!-- this part already exists.......-->
```

```
<plugin>
    <groupId>org.eclipse.tycho</groupId>
    <artifactId>target-platform-configuration</artifactId>
    <version>${tycho.version}</version>
    <configuration>
<!-- THIS PART IS NEW-->
     <target>
      <file>../target-platform/target-platform.target</file>
    </target>
```

Here is the complete top-level pom file.

```
<project>
 <modelVersion>4.0.0</modelVersion>
 <groupId>com.vogella.tycho</groupId>
 <artifactId>releng</artifactId>
 <version>1.0.0-SNAPSHOT</version>
 <packaging>pom</packaging>

 <properties>
  <project.build.sourceEncoding>UTF-8</project.build.sourceEncoding>
 </properties>

 <build>
  <pluginManagement>
     <plugins>
       <plugin>
         <groupId>org.eclipse.tycho</groupId>
         <artifactId>tycho-p2-director-plugin</artifactId>
         <version>${tycho.version}</version>
       </plugin>
     </plugins>
   </pluginManagement>
  <plugins>
   <plugin>
    <groupId>org.eclipse.tycho</groupId>
    <artifactId>tycho-maven-plugin</artifactId>
    <version>${tycho.version}</version>
    <extensions>true</extensions>
   </plugin>
   <!--Enable the replacement of the SNAPSHOT version in the final product
configuration-->
   <plugin>
        <groupId>org.eclipse.tycho</groupId>
            <artifactId>tycho-packaging-plugin</artifactId>
             <version>${tycho.version}</version>
             <executions>
              <execution>
```

```
                <phase>package</phase>
                <id>package-feature</id>
                    <configuration>

<finalName>${project.artifactId}_${unqualifiedVersion}.${buildQualifier}</finalName>
                    </configuration>
            </execution>
        </executions>
    </plugin>
    <plugin>
    <groupId>org.eclipse.tycho</groupId>
    <artifactId>target-platform-configuration</artifactId>
    <version>${tycho.version}</version>
    <configuration>
     <!-- Optionally, set the Java version you are using-->
    <!--<executionEnvironment>JavaSE-21</executionEnvironment>-->
     <target>
      <file>../target-platform/target-platform.target</file>
    </target>
     <environments>
      <environment>
       <os>linux</os>
       <ws>gtk</ws>
       <arch>x86_64</arch>
      </environment>
      <environment>
       <os>win32</os>
       <ws>win32</ws>
       <arch>x86_64</arch>
      </environment>
      <environment>
       <os>macosx</os>
       <ws>cocoa</ws>
       <arch>x86_64</arch>
      </environment>
     </environments>
    </configuration>
   </plugin>
  </plugins>
 </build>

 <modules>
     <!--<module>your modules will be defined here</module>-->

 </modules>
</project>
```

In the `<artifactId>target-platform-configuration</artifactId>` block you added a reference to the target definition file.

195.1. Validate the build

Re-run your build and ensure that it still runs successfully.

195.2. Potential error resolution with the Java version being used

In the past Tycho used the Java version from the first artifact in the build, if you have mixed Java requirements for your build, you may have to specify the Java version to build against.

In the above build file, the following line is used for that purpose.

```
    <executionEnvironment>JavaSE-21</executionEnvironment>
```

196. Exercise: Configure the modules

To add your Eclipse components to the build, you must add them as modules to the top-level `pom.xml` file. A minimal setup contains only one plug-in that has no dependencies on any other module.

In general, all your plug-ins, features and products should be part of the build. All libraries will be provided by the target platform.

> You may have created more plug-ins than listed below during the optional exercises; ensure that they are part of your build.

196.1. Building the RCP components

```
<project>

<!-- CONTENT AS BEFORE -->

  <modules>
    <module>com.vogella.tasks.ui</module>
    <module>com.vogella.tasks.feature</module>
    <module>com.vogella.tasks.product</module>
    <module>com.vogella.tasks.model</module>
    <module>com.vogella.tasks.services</module>
    <!-- This one is from an optional exercise -->
    <module>com.vogella.imageloader.services</module>
  </modules>
</project>
```

197. Exercise: Validate the build

197.1. Run the build

Run the build from the main directory via the following command:

```
mvn clean verify
```

This should result in a success message, such as the one below.

```
[INFO] Reactor Summary:
[INFO]
[INFO] releng 1.0.0-SNAPSHOT ............................ SUCCESS [  0.114 s]
[INFO] [bundle] First 1.0.0-SNAPSHOT .................... SUCCESS [  0.803 s]
[INFO] [feature] Feature 1.0.0-SNAPSHOT ................. SUCCESS [  0.283 s]
[INFO] [product] Custom IDE 1.0.0 ....................... SUCCESS [  4.311 s]
[INFO] ------------------------------------------------------------------------
[INFO] BUILD SUCCESS
[INFO] ------------------------------------------------------------------------
[INFO] Total time:  17.499 s
[INFO] Finished at: 2020-09-07T16:16:15+02:00
[INFO] ------------------------------------------------------------------------
```

Press F5 in the Eclipse IDE on your feature project to refresh it. You should find a new *target* folder in your project that contains the JAR file for your feature. This JAR file also has the SNAPSHOT suffix. This suffix is replaced with the build timestamp once you build a product or an update site with the `eclipse-repository` packaging type.

197.2. Error resolution

If Tycho cannot find a required plug-in or feature, it gives an error message. The following is an example for a feature that requires a bundle but this bundle is not part of the build.

```
[ERROR] Missing requirement:
 com.vogella.tycho.feature.feature.group 1.0.0.qualifier
 requires 'com.vogella.tycho.plugin1 0.0.0' but it could not be found
```

If an independent build of the feature is required, you need to make the plug-in available via a repository. This can, for example, be done by building and installing the plug-in into the local Maven repository with the `mvn clean install` command.

In this case, you need to either add the required module to the build or, if you are using it in binary form, add it to the target platform.

198. Exercise: Adding a JRE to the application

> The JRE is constantly updated, so this exercise might not work exactly as described here. The Java and Eclipse ecosystems are evolving rapidly.

To bundle a JRE with your product, select the *This product includes a JRE* flag. If you target platform uses the `planner` mode and finds a JustJ JRE in one of your update sites, Tycho adds a fitting JRE to your product.

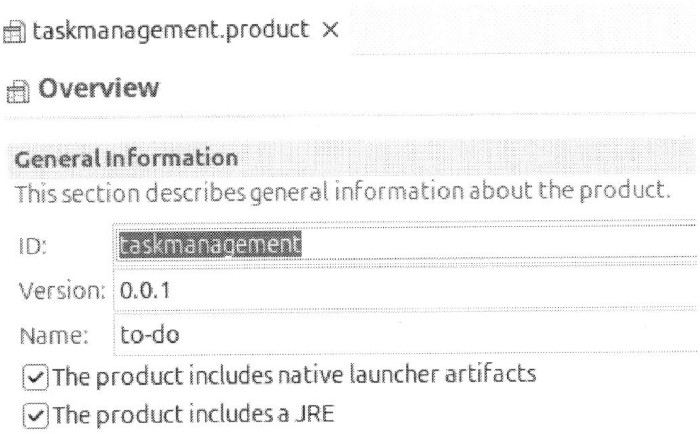

You can find this JRE in your `plugins` folder of your product and also a reference to it in your `.ini` file. For example, your `.ini` file would have a `-vm` argument similar to the following.

```
-startup plugins/org.eclipse.equinox.launcher_1.7.0.v20250519-0528.jar --launcher.library
plugins/org.eclipse.equinox.launcher.gtk.linux.x86_64_1.2.1500.v20250801-0854
-clearPersistedState -nl de -vm
plugins/org.eclipse.justj.openjdk.hotspot.jre.full.linux.x86_64_25.0.1.v20251108-
1451/jre/bin/java
```

199. Exercise: Tycho build for update sites

This exercise demonstrates how to create Eclipse p2 update sites using Maven Tycho.

The Tycho build generates similar content for the product in the `target/repository` folder. The distinction between an update site created from a category file and the `target/repository` folder generated for a product build primarily lies in their intended use cases and content organization.

- An update site created with Tycho based on a category file is specifically designed for distributing Eclipse plug-ins, features, and other components to Eclipse users. The category file (`category.xml`) serves as a manifest that defines how components are organized into categories, making it easier for users to discover and install them through the Eclipse Update Manager.

- The `target/repository` folder generated during a product build with Tycho is part of the build output that contains the assembled product, including all required plug-ins, features, and configuration files. While it can serve as an update site for the product, its primary purpose is to package the product build. It includes similar metadata files that describe the product's contents, allowing it to be used to update or install the product.

199.1. Create a new project

Create a new project named *updatesite* in a project of type general.

199.2. Creating a category definition file

Right-click the project, navigate to New > Other... > Plug-in Development > Category Definition, and name the file *category.xml*. Create a new category by clicking the New Category button with:

- `com.vogella.tasks.update` ID
- `Task management update site` name.

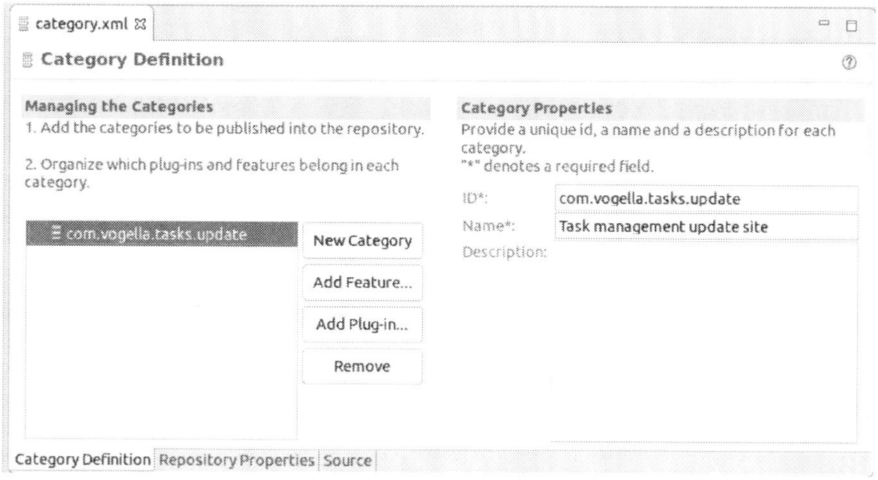

Click Add Feature... to add your feature project to the category.

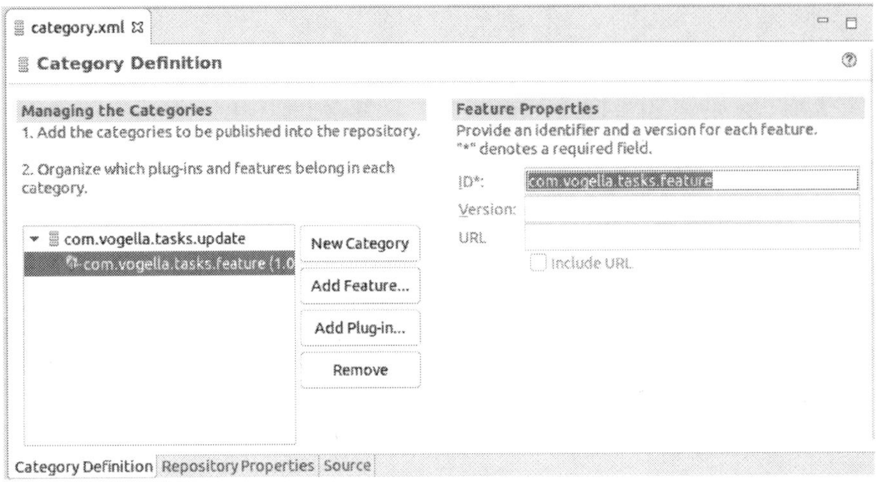

199.3. Updating the root POM

Include the new module in your root pom file.

```
<modules>
   <!-- all modules as before -->
  <module>updatesite</module> ❶
</modules>
```

❶ Adds the updatesite project to the aggregator build

199.4. Running the aggregator build and validating the update site

Execute the build from the main directory, ensuring it successfully completes and builds all components, including the update site.

Refresh your update site project in Eclipse IDE by pressing F5. A new *target* folder containing a *repository* folder, which holds the update site, should appear.

Ensure that the SNAPSHOT suffix in the *repository* directory's JAR files is replaced with the build qualifier.

199.5. Creating a self-contained p2 repository

Most Tycho components have options that can be configured. The following configuration will instruct Tycho to not build a zip file of the update site and to include all dependencies of the JAR files that are packed in the update site.

```
<plugin>
 <groupId>org.eclipse.tycho</groupId>
 <artifactId>tycho-p2-repository-plugin</artifactId>
 <version>${tycho.version}</version>
  <configuration>
    <skipArchive>true</skipArchive>
    <includeAllDependencies>true</includeAllDependencies>
  </configuration>
</plugin>
```

Run the build again and verify that all required libraries are part of the `/target/repository/plugins` folder.

200. Exercise: Tycho build for test plug-ins

The following exercise demonstrates how to run unit tests with Tycho.

> Testing libraries are evolving at a high speed, therefore the required libraries may have changed if you read this.

200.1. Adding the test dependencies

For testing, JUnit is usually used, and you can add additional libraries like Hamcrest and Mockito. Therefore, add the Maven dependencies to Mockito to your target platform.

```
<!-- Add this to an existing Maven in the target file or create a new one -->
<dependency>
    <groupId>org.mockito</groupId>
    <artifactId>mockito-core</artifactId>
    <version>5.20.0</version>
</dependency>
```

For test purposes the new target entry could look like this:

```
<location includeDependencyDepth="infinite" includeDependencyScopes="compile"
includeSource="true" missingManifest="generate" type="Maven">
    <dependencies>
        <dependency>
            <groupId>org.junit.jupiter</groupId>
            <artifactId>junit-jupiter-engine</artifactId>
            <version>5.14.1</version>
            <type>jar</type>
        </dependency>
        <!-- https://mvnrepository.com/artifact/org.junit.platform/junit-platform-suite-
api -->
        <dependency>
            <groupId>org.junit.platform</groupId>
            <artifactId>junit-platform-suite-api</artifactId>
            <version>1.14.1</version>
        </dependency>
        <!-- https://mvnrepository.com/artifact/org.junit.platform/junit-platform-suite-
engine -->
        <dependency>
            <groupId>org.junit.platform</groupId>
            <artifactId>junit-platform-suite-engine</artifactId>
            <version>1.14.1</version>
        </dependency>
        <!-- https://mvnrepository.com/artifact/org.junit.platform/junit-platform-
launcher -->
```

```
        <dependency>
            <groupId>org.junit.platform</groupId>
            <artifactId>junit-platform-launcher</artifactId>
            <version>1.14.1</version>
        </dependency>
        <!-- https://mvnrepository.com/artifact/org.junit.platform/junit-platform-suite-
commons -->
        <dependency>
            <groupId>org.junit.platform</groupId>
            <artifactId>junit-platform-suite-commons</artifactId>
            <version>1.14.1</version>
        </dependency>
        <dependency>
            <groupId>org.mockito</groupId>
            <artifactId>mockito-core</artifactId>
            <version>5.20.0</version>
            <type>jar</type>
        </dependency>
    </dependencies>
</target>
```

200.2. Create a new plug-in for the tests

The tests of the implementation belong into a separate plug-in or fragment project called `com.vogella.tasks.ui.tests`.

Create a new plug-in fragment project named *com.vogella.tasks.ui.tests*.

Define a package dependency on `org.junit.jupiter.api` in its `MANIFEST.MF` file.

```
Manifest-Version: 1.0
Bundle-ManifestVersion: 2
Bundle-Name: Tests
Bundle-SymbolicName: com.vogella.tasks.ui.tests
Bundle-Version: 1.0.0.qualifier
Bundle-Vendor: VOGELLA
Fragment-Host: com.vogella.tasks.ui;bundle-version="1.0.0"
Import-Package: org.junit.jupiter.api;version="5.14.1"
Automatic-Module-Name: com.vogella.tasks.ui.tests
Bundle-RequiredExecutionEnvironment: JavaSE-21
```

The defaults are sufficient for this test plug-in, hence we do not need a separate pom for the test plug-in.

200.3. Create a unit test

Create the following unit test, as an example. Of course, this test does not test anything meaningful. It is only used to demonstrate how Tycho runs the tests.

```
package com.vogella.tasks.ui.tests;

import static org.junit.jupiter.api.Assertions.assertTrue;

import org.junit.jupiter.api.Test;

public class ExampleTest {

    @Test
    public void test() {
        // just an example
        assertTrue(true);
    }
}
```

200.4. Run the build with the tests

Run the build from the main directory. This should work fine.

If you want to skip the test execution use `mvn clean verify -DskipTests=true`

200.5. Create test report

Run the following command to create test reports:

```
mvn clean verify surefire-report:report
```

You find the report in `{basedir}/target/site/surefire-report.html`.

200.6. To debug Maven Tycho tests via Eclipse

To debug Maven Tycho tests, add the `-DdebugPort=8000` parameter to your Maven build command. Maven will then pause during execution and you can create a *Remote Java Application* debug configuration to connect to the test.

Part XXIX: Migrating Eclipse 3.x components and applications

201. Migration options of 3.x based applications to 4.x

You have two options for migration:

- only migrate the runtime to Eclipse 4, minimizing the changes in your code
- or migrate your code to leverage the Eclipse 4 API

201.1. Reasons for migrating to a newer runtime

If you have an existing 3.x Eclipse-based plug-in or RCP application, you should migrate to a newer Eclipse release. Older Eclipse releases:

- do not support newer Java runtime environments
- are slower
- contain less functionality

- contain more bugs
- might contain security vulnerabilities

The good news is that you can run Eclipse 3.x API-based applications on recent releases of the Eclipse platform. The Eclipse 3.x API has been reworked to use the 4.x API underneath. This is sometimes called the *compatibility mode*.

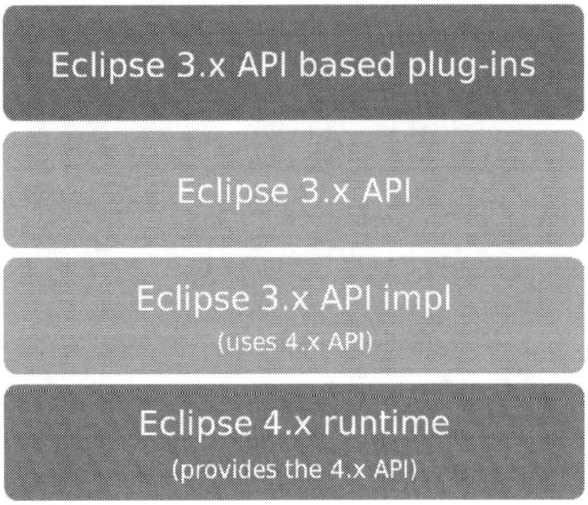

The Eclipse platform team plans to support this layer for an unlimited period of time. Therefore, if you have an existing Eclipse 3.x application, you do not have to migrate to the new API.

202. Using the Eclipse 4.x API

202.1. Reasons for migrating to the API

The Eclipse 3.x API is effectively frozen. Therefore, you should migrate to the latest API to participate in API enhancements.

By migrating, you can use the 4.x API, which is both consistent and well-designed. The explicit concept of the application model and dependency injection makes your application code concise and flexible. Services and the renderer toolkit can be replaced, which adds more flexibility to your implementation.

The event service and the extensible Eclipse context hierarchy provide powerful ways to communicate within your application.

Also, CSS styling allows you to give your application a modern, custom look. It may help you to remove code related to styling.

202.2. Migration steps for moving to the 4.X API

It is possible to migrate only a part of your application to the Eclipse 4 API. You can:

- start using dependency injection in 3.x views
- migrate a 3.x view to be an Eclipse 4 part
- migrate a menu or a toolbar entry to Eclipse 4
- migrate the whole application to Eclipse 4

203. Migration steps for moving to a newer runtime

The migration of an Eclipse 3.x-based plug-in and RCP application should be done in the following steps.

203.1. Preparation steps

Before you start the migration, you should:

- ensure you have a working and valid target definition file
- ensure the code compiles
- ensure the application can be started
- ensure the application works as expected
- improve your code and remove obsolete and redundant code (cleanup)

The cleanup step is optional but helpful when making potential code changes. It ensures that you have code that is easier to update during the migration. During the cleanup phase, focus on standard readability and Java code usage, as the Eclipse API may change later.

203.2. Define and use a new target definition for 4.x

Create a new target definition for your target Eclipse 4.x release.

The following features include the necessary Eclipse platform plug-ins.

- `org.eclipse.e4.rcp`
- `org.eclipse.emf.ecore`
- `org.eclipse.emf.common`

As a general rule, each Eclipse release offers improvements, so targeting the latest Eclipse release is recommended.

Now activate your target definition file for 4.x. This may result in compilation errors that must be fixed in the next step.

Create an additional target platform definition with the 4.x release you want to target.

203.3. Fix compilation errors in the code

If activating the new target platform results in compilation errors in your code, you need to fix them. The internal Eclipse API may have changed, so if your code is using internal 3.x API, you need to rework or remove it.

Sometimes a fast approach to get started is to comment out the code to reach a point where you can start the application. Once the application starts, you can return to the code and update it.

> The Eclipse platform marks almost all packages. Packages that are not considered stable API are marked with the *x-internal* or *x-friends* flag in the `MANIFEST.MF` file. Avoid using packages that contain `internal` in their name, as these classes can be modified at any time.

203.4. Replace org.eclipse.equinox.ds with org.apache.felix.scr

Depending on which Eclipse release you are migrating from, you have to replace `org.eclipse.equinox.ds` with `org.apache.felix.scr`. Equinox changed the declarative service implementation in the 4.11 release.

This requires that you update your features if your product is not based on the default `org.eclipse.e4.rcp` feature and potentially startup settings in your product configuration file. The simplest way to find all required locations is to perform a full-text search for `org.eclipse.equinox.ds`.

203.5. Start the application in the new target environment

This should work if you have the correct platform plug-ins included in the startup. You can use the `org.eclipse.e4.rcp` feature to include a typical set of plug-ins into your product configuration file.

If the above works and your application starts fine, you have successfully migrated your application to the new runtime.

> If a 3.x RCP application runs on a 4.x runtime, the platform translates the information from the relevant `plugin.xml` based extensions into model elements.
>
> See `org.eclipse.ui.internal.registry.ViewRegistry` for an example of how the platform processes 3.x views and translates them into Eclipse 4 model elements. In this example, the extension point information for `org.eclipse.ui.views` is converted at runtime to `part descriptors`.

203.6. Test the application

Once you successfully started your application on the Eclipse 4 runtime, you have successfully migrated the application.

The next step is to update your code base.

204. Using e4 API in 3.x applications

204.1. Using the e4 API-based components in a 3.x application

It is possible to define new e4 API-based components and use them in an application that still uses the Eclipse 3.x API. This allows contributing e4 API-based views, menus and toolbars to such an application. By using this approach, you can convert these 3.x components step by step to the e4 API. How this can be done is shown in the following chapters.

204.2. Extending the Eclipse IDE

The Eclipse IDE uses the same approach as an Eclipse 3.x application on top of an e4 runtime. The e4 API-based extensions described in this chapter can, of course, be used to extend the Eclipse IDE.

In this scenario, you can start to convert certain parts of your application into Eclipse 4.x API based parts. After you have migrated sufficient parts of your application you should switch over completely.

204.3. Migrating an Eclipse 3.x application completely to the e4 API

If you want to migrate your Eclipse 3.x RCP application completely to the e4 API, you cannot directly reuse existing *plugin.xml*-based user interface components. All 3.x API-based views and editors must be reimplemented in e4.

Migrating these components involves:

- Converting existing user interface contributions via extension points to the application model.
- Removing the usage of Singleton objects of the Eclipse platform, e.g., `Platform` or `PlatformUI` and use the dependency injection programming model.

204.4. Reusing platform components in a 4.x RCP application

Most Eclipse IDE components are still based on the Eclipse 3.x API. The Eclipse platform plans to migrate more and more existing components to the e4 API in future releases. This means that certain components that could be reused in Eclipse 3.x RCP applications are not available by default.

Currently, most IDE components are based on the Eclipse 3.x API and therefore cannot be used without modifications in an e4 API-based application. This includes, for example, the IDE perspective switcher, the view switcher, the *Progress* view, and the new project wizard.

204.5. Existing replacements for 3.x components for e4 API-based applications

The vogella GmbH [https://www.vogella.com/company/index.html] provides an open-source project for an e4 API-based perspective switcher [https://github.com/vogellacompany/e4-perspective-switcher].

205. Exercise - Runtime migration of an Eclipse 3.x application

205.1. Create 3.x RCP application

Use the plug-in wizard to create a new Eclipse RCP application called `com.vogella.eclipse3x.rcp` based on the *RCP 3.x application with a view* template.

205.2. Run application based on latest Eclipse platform

Right-click on the project and select **Run As › Eclipse application**.

Your 3.x application should start without problems.

You finished a simple 3.x to 4.x migration as an application using 3.x API runs without modification on top of the latest Eclipse platform.

206. Exercise - API migration of an Eclipse 3.x application

This exercise is based on the generated Eclipse 3.x RCP application from the last exercise called `com.vogella.eclipse3x.rcp`.

206.1. Review the view code

Open the generated `View.java` file that represents your view. Notice that you can use `@Inject` in your view.

To enable dependency injection for 3.x-based views, you need to set the `inject` field for this view to `true` in the plugin.xml.

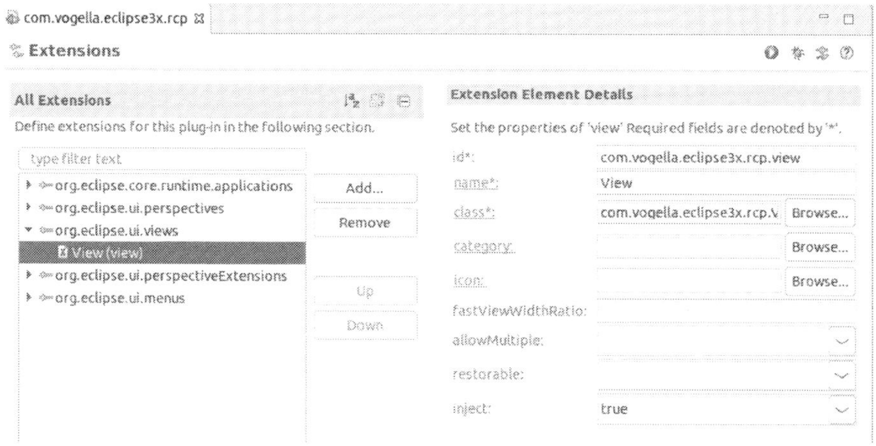

This allows you to start using dependency injection in your 3.x views. This is an ideal first step for the migration.

As a first step of migration, check whether you can use dependency injection for your view. Doing so reduces the need to access platform singletons.

206.2. Migrate the view to be a pure e4 part

The next step is to migrate the full view to be an Eclipse 4 part. As a first step, we add the following plug-ins as a dependency to the `MANIFEST.MF` file.

- jakarta.annotation
- org.eclipse.e4.ui.di

Now migrate your view to e4. For this, we remove the inheritance from `ViewPart` and replace the `@Override` methods with the correct annotation.

Old code:

```
package com.vogella.eclipse3x.rcp;

import java.util.Arrays;
import java.util.List;

import jakarta.inject.Inject;

import org.eclipse.jface.viewers.ArrayContentProvider;
import org.eclipse.jface.viewers.ColumnLabelProvider;
import org.eclipse.jface.viewers.TableViewer;
import org.eclipse.jface.viewers.TableViewerColumn;
import org.eclipse.swt.SWT;
import org.eclipse.swt.graphics.Image;
```

```
import org.eclipse.swt.widgets.Composite;
import org.eclipse.ui.ISharedImages;
import org.eclipse.ui.IWorkbench;
import org.eclipse.ui.part.ViewPart;

public class View extends ViewPart {
    public static final String ID = "com.vogella.eclipse3x.rcp.view";

    @Inject IWorkbench workbench;

    private TableViewer viewer;

    private class StringLabelProvider extends ColumnLabelProvider {

        // getText is used from super class ColumnLabelProvider

        @Override
        public Image getImage(Object obj) {
            return workbench.getSharedImages().getImage(ISharedImages.IMG_OBJ_ELEMENT);
        }
    }

    @Override
    public void createPartControl(Composite parent) {
        viewer = new TableViewer(parent, SWT.MULTI | SWT.H_SCROLL | SWT.V_SCROLL);
        viewer.setUseHashlookup(true); // use a faster hash lookup of data model

        viewer.getTable().setLinesVisible(true);
        TableViewerColumn column = new TableViewerColumn(viewer, SWT.NONE);
        column.setLabelProvider(new StringLabelProvider());
        viewer.getTable().getColumn(0).setWidth(200);
        viewer.setContentProvider(ArrayContentProvider.getInstance());
        viewer.setInput(createInitialDataModel());
    }

    @Override
    public void setFocus() {
        viewer.getControl().setFocus();
    }

    private List<String> createInitialDataModel() {
        return Arrays.asList("One", "Two", "Three");
    }
}
```

New code:

```
package com.vogella.eclipse3x.rcp;
```

```java
import java.util.Arrays;
import java.util.List;

import jakarta.annotation.PostConstruct;

import org.eclipse.e4.ui.di.Focus;
import org.eclipse.jface.viewers.ArrayContentProvider;
import org.eclipse.jface.viewers.ColumnLabelProvider;
import org.eclipse.jface.viewers.TableViewer;
import org.eclipse.jface.viewers.TableViewerColumn;
import org.eclipse.swt.SWT;
import org.eclipse.swt.graphics.Image;
import org.eclipse.swt.widgets.Composite;

public class View {
    public static final String ID = "com.vogella.eclipse3x.rcp.view";

    private TableViewer viewer;

    private class StringLabelProvider extends ColumnLabelProvider {

        // getText is used from super class ColumnLabelProvider

        @Override
        public Image getImage(Object obj) {
            // In pure e4 you cannot use sharedImages.
            // If images are still required, you have to provide your own copy.
            return null;
        }
    }

    @PostConstruct
    public void createPartControl(Composite parent) {
        viewer = new TableViewer(parent, SWT.MULTI | SWT.H_SCROLL | SWT.V_SCROLL);
        viewer.setUseHashlookup(true); // use a faster hash lookup of data model

        viewer.getTable().setLinesVisible(true);
        TableViewerColumn column = new TableViewerColumn(viewer, SWT.NONE);
        column.setLabelProvider(new StringLabelProvider());
        viewer.getTable().getColumn(0).setWidth(200);
        viewer.setContentProvider(ArrayContentProvider.getInstance());
        viewer.setInput(createInitialDataModel());
    }

    @Focus
    public void setFocus() {
        viewer.getControl().setFocus();
    }
```

```java
    private List<String> createInitialDataModel() {
        return Arrays.asList("One", "Two", "Three");
    }
}
```

> Please note that the access to the shared images was removed, as e4 does not provide shared images. This was always a bad idea. Why should you ship lots of shared images in your application if you do not need them? If your code should still support this image, you have to include a copy in your plug-in and load it directly.

As the last step, you have to change the `plugin.xml` file to contribute an e4view instead of a view.

```xml
<?xml version="1.0" encoding="UTF-8"?>
<?eclipse version="3.4"?>
<plugin>

   <extension
         id="application"
         point="org.eclipse.core.runtime.applications">
      <application>
         <run
               class="com.vogella.eclipse3x.rcp.Application">
         </run>
      </application>
   </extension>
   <extension
         point="org.eclipse.ui.perspectives">
      <perspective
            class="com.vogella.eclipse3x.rcp.Perspective"
            name="Perspective"
            id="com.vogella.eclipse3x.rcp.perspective">
      </perspective>
   </extension>
   <extension
         point="org.eclipse.ui.views">
      <e4view
            class="com.vogella.eclipse3x.rcp.View"
            id="com.vogella.eclipse3x.rcp.view"
            name="View"
            restorable="true">
      </e4view>
      <view
            inject="true"
            name="View">
      </view>
```

```
    </extension>
    <extension
          point="org.eclipse.ui.perspectiveExtensions">
       <perspectiveExtension
             targetID="*">
          <view
                id="com.vogella.eclipse3x.rcp.view"
                minimized="false"
                relationship="left"
                standalone="true"
                relative="org.eclipse.ui.editorss">
          </view>
       </perspectiveExtension>
    </extension>
    <extension
          point="org.eclipse.ui.menus">
       <menuContribution
             locationURI="menu:org.eclipse.ui.main.menu">
          <menu
                label="File">
             <command
                   commandId="org.eclipse.ui.file.exit"
                   label="Exit">
             </command>
          </menu>
       </menuContribution>
    </extension>
</plugin>
```

206.3. Validate

Start your RCP application and ensure that the view is still displayed.

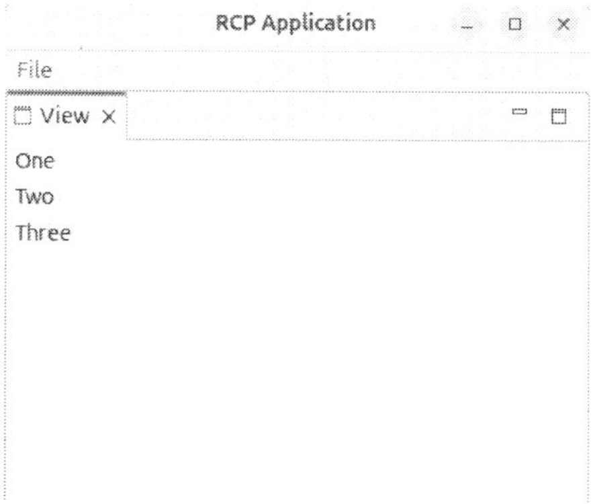

206.4. Migrating to model fragments

As a next step you could migrate the view to be contributed via a model fragment. Eclipse provides a `View contribution using 4.x API` template for a new plug-in to demonstrate this.

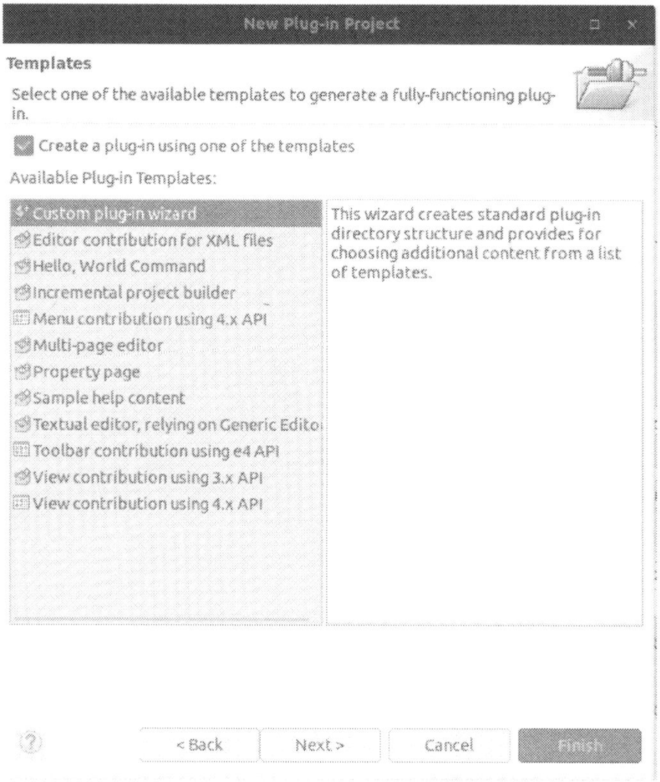

206.5. Migrating menus and toolbars

Similar to the above step, you can contribute e4 toolbars and menus via model fragments to your 3.x application.

Eclipse provides a `Toolbar contribution using 4.x API` template for a new plug-in to demonstrate this.

206.6. Complete migration

Once all views, menus, and toolbars have been migrated, you can replace the base plug-in with your custom application model.

Part XXX: Where to go from here

207. Outlook for the Eclipse framework

You have finished this script and should now be well-equipped to implement and maintain Eclipse RCP applications. What lies ahead for the Eclipse framework? Is this a framework you want to use for your company or a personal application?

The Eclipse framework continues to evolve as a cornerstone of the developer ecosystem, offering a modern and innovative toolset for building robust applications. The team behind Eclipse remains committed to aligning with cutting-edge technologies and improving the developer experience. By updating the codebase to support the latest Java versions, Eclipse provides developers access to new language features, enhanced performance, and improved security. This compatibility ensures that the Eclipse framework remains an ideal choice for modern Java development.

Recognizing the central role of Maven in Java development, the Eclipse team has streamlined its integration. Developers can now easily manage Maven dependencies within Eclipse, reducing friction in accessing and updating external libraries. Improvements in the Maven integration ensure faster dependency resolution and better compatibility with complex project structures, empowering developers to focus on their core tasks.

This is a general trend in platform development. The framework is steadily moving toward adopting widely accepted standard technologies. This transition simplifies development workflows, improves compatibility with external tools, and lowers the learning curve for new developers joining the Eclipse ecosystem.

The Eclipse team places a high priority on simplifying and optimizing the codebase. By refactoring legacy components and deprecating outdated APIs, the framework has become leaner, easier to maintain, and less prone to bugs. These efforts result in a cleaner architecture, enabling contributors to navigate and enhance the framework with confidence. On the flip side, this sometimes requires Eclipse RCP clients to update their code during release updates. However, they benefit from faster performance, simpler APIs, and fewer framework bugs.

The team has also made significant strides in optimizing the framework's performance and reducing its memory footprint. Leveraging profiling tools and community feedback, they have addressed bottlenecks and enhanced the responsiveness of the Eclipse framework.

The introduction of automated workflows, including build validation for pull requests, has transformed the team's development process. Continuous Integration pipelines now rigorously test every contribution, ensuring high-quality code merges. This automation accelerates development cycles, reduces manual overhead, and enhances collaboration among contributors, creating a seamless and efficient development environment.

Its future-focused development and vibrant community ensure that Eclipse will remain a top choice for building modern Java applications. With ongoing improvements in compatibility, performance, and usability, coupled with a vibrant and active community, Eclipse continues to set the benchmark for open-source development environments. The framework's commitment to embracing modern technologies and practices underscores a bright and sustainable future for developers and users alike.

208. Contributing to the Eclipse IDE and the Eclipse framework

The Eclipse IDE is an open-source project in which companies and individuals advance the code. Everyone has read access to the code repositories. You can clone the source code, modify it and provide the change back to the project. Most Eclipse projects use a code review process based on *GitHub* pull requests. Some use *Gitlab*, which offers a similar workflow.

Contributing to an Eclipse project allows developers and organizations to fix bugs which affect them and to drive the project in a desired direction.

Especially Eclipse plug-in and Eclipse RCP developers have the advantage that they already know the technology to change the framework. As the Eclipse framework is developed using a workflow which is common, it is increasingly simple to contribute to the framework.

Every pull request is automatically verified via GitHub build actions and Jenkins build server, in most cases on multiple platforms and with multiple Java versions. The huge test suite of the Eclipse framework will automatically run against every change before it is merged and provide a green or red light to the contributor.

Currently the project uses a Jenkins build server and Github actions to validate changes on multiple operating systems. This makes it easier for contributors to spot potential issues in their contributions and allows committers to review only the critical part of the code.

209. Eclipse bug reports and feature requests

If you encounter a problem with the Eclipse framework or the IDE or think about a potential improvement for it, you should report this to the Eclipse project. The Eclipse project uses GitHub issues as the primary issue tracker for its projects. To participate actively, you need to have a GitHub account.

These issues are specific for the GitHub repository. Here you can search for existing issues and review them.

Here is a list of the Eclipse projects that use GitHub issues:

- Eclipse Platform (Main repo)
  - GitHub: https://github.com/eclipse-platform/eclipse.platform
  - Issues: https://github.com/eclipse-platform/eclipse.platform/issues
- Eclipse Platform UI
  - GitHub: https://github.com/eclipse-platform/eclipse.platform.ui
  - Issues: https://github.com/eclipse-platform/eclipse.platform.ui/issues
- Eclipse Platform SWT (Standard Widget Toolkit)
  - GitHub: https://github.com/eclipse-platform/eclipse.platform.swt
  - Issues: https://github.com/eclipse-platform/eclipse.platform.swt/issues

Other repositories can be found at https://github.com/eclipse-equinox, https://github.com/eclipse-pde and https://github.com/eclipse-jdt.

Part XXXI: Appendix

A. Solutions for the exercises

A.1. Getting the example implementation

The solutions can be found on https://github.com/vogellacompany/eclipse_rcp_example in the `main` branch.

If a next edition of this training is published, the main branch will point to the latest solution. This repository is also frequently updated with updated solutions.

If you have the Git tooling for Eclipse installed, you can clone the repository via **File › Import › Git › Projects from Git**. Select *URI* in the next wizard page and press the Next button. In the following wizard page enter git@github.com:vogellacompany/eclipse_rcp_example.git or https://github.com/vogellacompany/eclipse_rcp_example.git in the first line of the dialog.

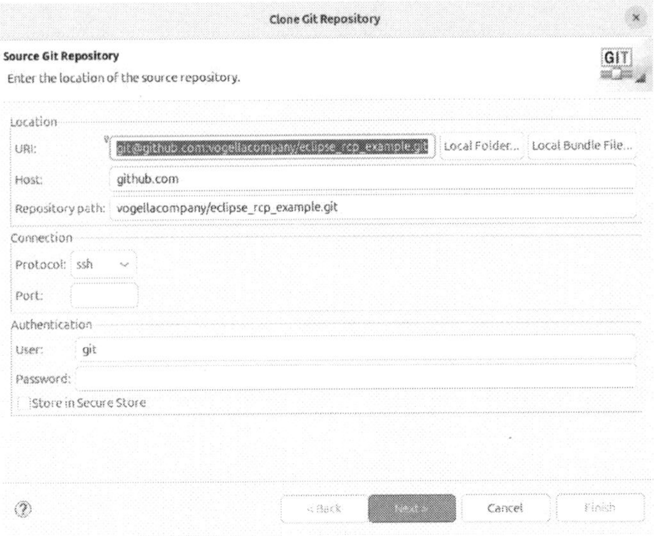

Select all the branches you are interested in to get example solutions to the exercises of this training. The *main* branch contains the finished state of the exercises in its latest version.

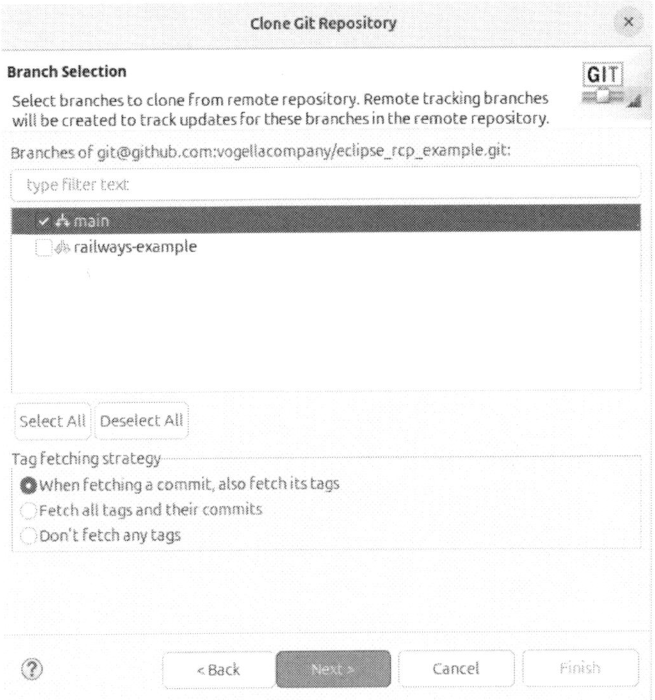

Continue the wizard and select the option to import existing projects.

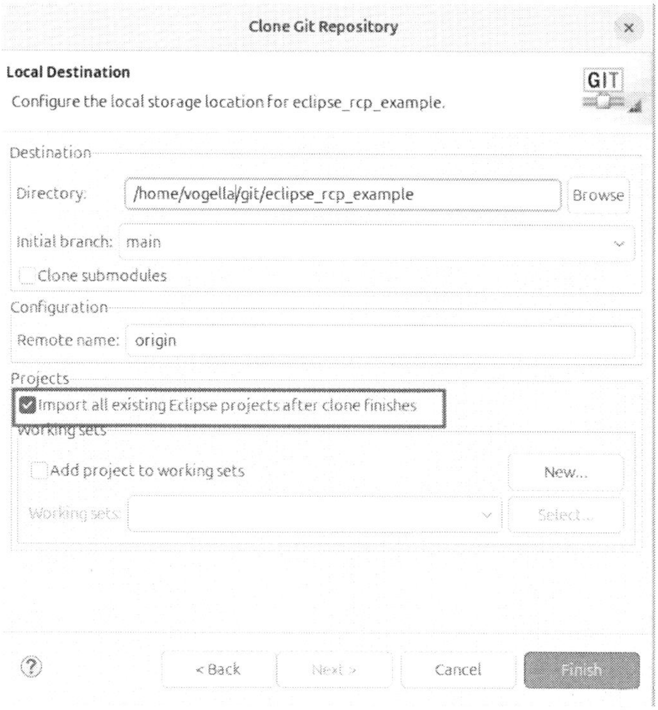

Afterwards, finish the wizard to import the projects into your workspace. Active the target platform located in the `target-platform` project to ensure that all dependencies are resolved.

A.2. More information about Git and Eclipse

See Eclipse Git tutorial [https://www.vogella.com/tutorials/EclipseGit/article.html] to learn more about the usage of the Eclipse Git tooling.

B. Standard annotations in Eclipse

The following table lists the default annotations of Eclipse and contains a link to the chapter that covers this annotation. This list is sorted by importance of the annotations, please see the index for an alphanumeric sorting.

Table 36. Annotations for dependency injection

Annotation	Link Description
`@jakarta.inject.Inject`	See Section 24.2.
`@jakarta.inject.Named`	See Section 24.2.
`@Optional`	See Section 24.2.

Annotation	Link Description
`@jakarta.annotation.PostConstruct`	See Section 26.3.
`@jakarta.annotation.PreDestroy`	See Section 26.3.
`@Focus`	See Section 26.3.
`@Persist`	See Section 123.2 and Section 26.3.
`@Execute`	See Section 80.3.
`@CanExecute`	See Section 80.3.
`@AboutToShow`	See Section 81.3.
`@AboutToHide`	See Section 81.3.
`@UIEventTopic`	See Section 145.3.
`@EventTopic`	See Section 145.3.
`@Preference`	See Chapter 165.
`@PersistState`	See Section 165.2.
`@PostContextCreate`	See Section 160.4.
`@PreSave`	See Section 160.4.
`@ProcessAdditions`	See Section 160.4.
`@ProcessRemovals`	See Section 160.4.
`@Creatable`	See Section 148.3.
`@Singleton`	See Section 148.3.
`@GroupUpdates`	See Section 24.2.
`@Active`	See Section 24.2.

C. Additional links

C.1. General Eclipse RCP development resources

Eclipse platform documentation root folder [https://eclipse.dev/eclipse/markdown/?file=eclipse-platform/eclipse.platform/master/docs]

Eclipse platform UI documentation root folder [https://eclipse.dev/eclipse/markdown/?file=eclipse-platform/eclipse.platform.ui/master/docs]

Eclipse RCP FAQ [https://github.com/eclipse-platform/eclipse.platform.ui/blob/master/docs/Rich_Client_Platform/Rich_Client_Platform_FAQ.md]

Official Eclipse FAQ [https://github.com/eclipse-platform/eclipse.platform/blob/master/docs/FAQ/The_Official_Eclipse_FAQs.md]

vogella Eclipse Tutorials [https://www.vogella.com/eclipse.html]

Eclipse dependency injection documentation [https://github.com/eclipse-platform/eclipse.platform.ui/blob/master/docs/Eclipse4_RCP_Dependency_Injection.md]

Eclipse documentation for application model tags [https://github.com/eclipse-platform/eclipse.platform.ui/blob/master/docs/Tags.md]

C.2. Eclipse plug-in development resources

Eclipse Plug-in Development FAQ [https://github.com/eclipse-platform/eclipse.platform.ui/blob/master/docs/EclipsePluginDevelopmentFAQ.md]

Adapters in Eclipse [https://www.eclipse.org/articles/article.php?file=Article-Adapters/index.html]

Eclipse resource deltas tutorial [https://www.eclipse.org/articles/Article-Resource-deltas/resource-deltas.html]

Using markers, annotations, and decorators in Eclipse (IBM) [https://web.archive.org/web/20160709033540/https://www.ibm.com/developerworks/opensource/tutorials/os-eclipse-plugin-guide/]

C.3. Eclipse product and export resources

How to create .ico files automatically [https://tomsondev.bestsolution.at/2007/06/26/branding-for-windows-how-to-create-ico-files-automatically/]

C.4. OSGi Resources

OSGi homepage [https://www.osgi.org]

Equinox homepage [https://www.eclipse.org/equinox]

Gogo shell commands [https://enroute.osgi.org/FAQ/500-gogo.html]

Tracking multiple services [https://enroute.osgi.org/FAQ/300-declarative-services.html]

Access OSGi services via web interface [https://blog.vogella.com/2017/04/20/access-osgi-services-via-web-interface/]

Equinox documentation [https://equinox.eclipseprojects.io/]

OSGi blueprint services [https://www.ibm.com/developerworks/xml/library/os-osgiblueprint/index.html]

OSGi runtime properties [https://help.eclipse.org/latest/topic/org.eclipse.platform.doc.isv/reference/misc/runtime-options.html]

C.5. OSGi services resources

OSGi remote service tutorial with ECF [https://www.eclipse.org/community/eclipse_newsletter/2013/july/article3.php]

OSGi Blueprint services [https://www.ibm.com/developerworks/xml/library/os-osgiblueprint/index.html]

Bnd build tools [https://bndtools.org/]

Bndtools tutorial [https://bndtools.org/tutorial.html]

C.6. SWT resources

SWT Widgets [https://eclipse.dev/eclipse/swt/] - Webpage showing all SWT widgets with links to examples and Javadoc

SWT Snippets [https://github.com/eclipse-platform/eclipse.platform.swt/blob/master/examples/org.eclipse.swt.snippets/Snippets.md] - Short examples demonstrating the usage of the SWT API

HDPI support on Windows [https://github.com/eclipse-platform/eclipse.platform.swt/blob/master/docs/hidpi-support-for-windows-dev-guide.md]

SWT effect implementation examples [https://github.com/lcaron/SWT-OldSchoolEffect]

Understanding Layout in SWT by Wayne Beaton [https://www.eclipse.org/articles/article.php?file=Article-Understanding-Layouts/index.html]

SWT design [https://www.eclipse.org/articles/swt-design-2/swt-design-2.html]

Eclipse Nebula Project with additional SWT widgets [https://eclipse.org/nebula/]

SWT Graphics [https://www.eclipse.org/articles/Article-SWT-graphics/SWT_graphics.html]

SWT Development Tools [https://eclipse.dev/eclipse/swt/] - Tools include Sleak (analyze memory leaks in SWT graphics resources) and the SWT Spy plug-in, which prints out information about the SWT widget under the cursor.

C.7. JFace resources

JFace snippets, e.g., small code examples [https://github.com/eclipse-platform/eclipse.platform.ui/blob/

master/docs/JFaceSnippets.md]

NatTable for flexible table or data grid [https://eclipse.org/nattable/]

Eclipse SWT Tutorial [https://www.vogella.com/tutorials/SWT/article.html]

Eclipse JFace Table [https://www.vogella.com/tutorials/EclipseJFaceTable/article.html]

Eclipse JFace Tree [https://www.vogella.com/tutorials/EclipseJFaceTree/article.html]

Eclipse JFace Data Binding [https://www.vogella.com/tutorials/EclipseDataBinding/article.html]

Eclipse JFace Dialogs [https://www.vogella.com/tutorials/EclipseDialogs/article.html]

Eclipse JFace Wizards [https://www.vogella.com/tutorials/EclipseWizards/article.html]

Preferences and Preference pages [https://www.vogella.com/tutorials/EclipsePreferences/article.html]

C.8. Eclipse Data Binding resources

JFace data binding project information [https://github.com/eclipse-platform/eclipse.platform.ui/blob/master/docs/JFaceDataBinding.md]

C.9. Eclipse Jobs resources

Java Concurrency Tutorial [https://www.vogella.com/tutorials/JavaConcurrency/article.html]

SWT Tutorial [https://www.vogella.com/tutorials/SWT/article.html]

Eclipse Jobs API [https://www.eclipse.org/articles/Article-Concurrency/jobs-api.html]

C.10. Eclipse i18n resources

Internationalization with the WindowBuilder [https://code.google.com/javadevtools/wbpro/features/internationalization.html]

How to Internationalize your Eclipse Plug-in [https://www.eclipse.org/articles/Article-Internationalization/how2I18n.html]

Bug concerning overriding SWT and JFace resource bundles [https://bugs.eclipse.org/bugs/show_bug.cgi?id=46595]

Git location of the JFace message properties file [https://github.com/eclipse-platform/eclipse.platform.swt/tree/master/bundles/org.eclipse.swt/Eclipse%20SWT/common/org/eclipse/swt/internal]

Default SWT Language Packs [https://www.eclipse.org/swt/language.php]

C.11. CSS styling resources

Eclipse Wiki for CSS attributes [https://github.com/eclipse-platform/eclipse.platform.ui/blob/master/docs/CSS.md]

Paul Webster's CSS presentation [https://paulweb515.github.io/eclipseExamples/eclipseCon2014/org.eclipse.e4.examples.css.presentation/index.html]

Part XXXII: Index

D

E

F

L

M

Q

R

S

T

U

V

W

X

Made in United States
Orlando, FL
05 November 2026

90243290R00398